Art and Education in Contemporary Culture

IRVING KAUFMAN

Art and Education in Contemporary Culture

THE MACMILLAN COMPANY • New York
COLLIER-MACMILLAN LIMITED • London

135424

Library of Congress catalog card number 66–22531

The Macmillan Company, New York
Collier-Macmillan Canada, Ltd., Toronto, Ontario

PRINTED IN THE UNITED STATES OF AMERICA

To My Wife Mabel

Preface

A BOOK about art and the teaching of art skirts pretentiousness for, in a very basic sense, art communicates on its own level while the successful teaching of art remains a very personal affair. The arts are felt directly through the individual senses, emotions, and perceptions. They are created in unique and complex ways, while teaching is largely a sequence of particular interpersonal relationships achieving its most desirable condition during the subjective I-thou dialogue of which Martin Buber wrote. To reduce these emotional and sensual characteristics to words is to do them a disservice, unless it is through poetry, for they tend to become adulterated. Yet arbitrary convention and academic propriety often veil the directness of art and the methods of its teaching. This, at the very least, suggests that it is important to lift the veil wherever possible and to point to some of the external conditions and attributes when these can be recognized.

This process cannot always be a simple or a straightforward one; the elements involved are frequently intangible and just as often inconsistent. To speak of sensitivity and awareness, both basic to the making, appreciating, or teaching of art is to grapple with amorphous shadowy attributes of human nature that dangerously approach meaninglessness because of their generality and tendency toward cliché presentation. These qualities, however, are much more important as objects of examination than all the skills and techniques of art and education. They deserve an emphasis just as the aesthetic factors of art education are to be stressed over and above the description of appearances and procedures. Imaginative and intrinsically significant qualities make art and good art teaching meaningful. These are often devious in their development and uncovering them may also lack a logical directness. Intuition more nearly comes to the heart of the process.

Consequently, there is much that is implied in the book and little that is objectively explicable. The lack of precision in some of the writing mirrors some of the contingency and openness that are inherent aspects of art and teaching. Furthermore, the book may itself suffer from occasional inconsistencies, if not even paradoxes that remain somewhat unresolved. There will be repetitions and perhaps important omissions, though the latter are inadvertent. The repetitions, however, are deliberate, but have been hopefully put into varying contexts, each time to stress the author's belief in the significance of a certain idea. For instance, the reference to the individual and subjective nature of understanding or the triviality of aesthetic concerns in a technological society are frequently mentioned. These among several others are the underlying concepts the author presents as inescapable philosophical propositions that any teacher, either a specialist or an elementary classroom teacher, is obliged to give some consideration.

The book, therefore, is not within the style or tradition of most texts. It does not pretend to cover the entire area of art education, but it does deal with major philosophical concepts derived from contemporary living. At times the relevance of these concepts to art education is demonstrated, at other times there are allusions to them in looser terms, and the pertinency of the relationship is left for the reader to determine. This reflects the inherent condition of art and its teaching in that the creative processes characteristic of both are open and continuing, finding resolution only in the symbolic behavior and critical merit of an individual, and then only for a period of time, rather than forever.

It is hoped the book will raise more questions than it answers, its content should act as the provoking gadfly impelling one to action, its reading a kind of "jumping off" point for the individual reader to seek his own answers. A further hope is that the book will serve as a means of relating prospective and student teachers to the more ineffable contributions an art education methods class or instructor provides. The latter should act as the necessary link between the teasing, puzzling, perhaps vague realization of some idea in the book and its resolution through discussion or personal involvement with art materials and classroom pupils.

A text in art education cannot hope to offer definitive guides nor should it, given the nature of art education. *The primary responsibility for the development of an efficacious and positive philosophy of art teaching lies with the student.* The instructor can only point up relationships, demonstrate various approaches, stimulate uncertain interest, and otherwise act as benevolent guide. In the final analysis, however, the student discovers his or her own understanding and values, creating subsequent contexts within which unique teaching methods unfold. These are fundamentally the product of a direct and committed involvement with the form of art and its materials, and with an enthusiastic search for insight, most often accompanied with a sense of passion.

I would like to make the following acknowledgments: to Dr. Jerome Hausman of Ohio State University, for his invaluable comments on reading the initial manuscript; similarly, to Dr. Kenneth Beittel of Pennsylvania State University, and Seymour Schneid, Curriculum Coordinator of the New Canaan, Connecticut Public Schools. Especially helpful as sources for illustrations were the University of Michigan Museum of Art and the University of Michigan News Service. I wish also to thank the following individuals and institutions for a wide variety of assistance in preparing the manuscript: Mr. Lloyd Chilton, Macmillan college editor, for his keen editorial judgment and good-natured patience; the University of Michigan, for the initial context within which the manuscript was nurtured, the City College of the City University of New York, for a continuing support; Mrs. Margo Flower, Mrs. Hope Irvine, and Miss Olive Riley, Director of Art, Board of Education, New York City, for providing a number of illustrations; Miss Kitty Goldfarb and Mrs. Jean Martin, for grappling with the seemingly unending typing and retyping; and my wife, Mabel Kaufman, who withstood the exigencies and annoyances of authorship with good spirit and constant assistance.

I. K.

Contents

xi

The General Responsibilities of Art Teaching

Educate or abdicate.

JOHN FOWLES

TEACHERS and teaching have always been lively topics for wits, savants, and for fools as well. Like the weather and taxes, they draw observations from those professionally involved and from every other imaginable source. They are lauded and condemned in a wide variety of guises; the prospective teacher has literally volumes of advice and comment from all and sundry from which to accept insight, develop understanding, and establish an individual direction. In the past G. B. Shaw wagged a finger in their faces when he wrote that, "He who can, does. He who cannot, teaches." The provoking critic of American life, H. L. Mencken was sarcastically caustic in his barbs, "The average schoolmaster is and always must be essentially an ass, for how can one imagine an intelligent man engaging in so puerile an avocation?" He does not even grant teaching the status of a vocation! Yet Henry Adams, the prophetic late nineteenth century writer was moved to say, "A teacher affects eternity; he can never tell where his influence stops." In a more contemporary setting, the importance of teaching and the dedicated merits of teachers are daily voiced in increasing acclaim through many communication sources. The remarks may be sober or hilarious, entertaining and enlightening, but they do little, unfortunately, to assist a teacher in the necessary, day-to-day happenings in a classroom.

The concerns of any and all teachers span a wide range; the elements on the list of their responsibilities are numerous in addition to being diverse. There is primarily, the subject to be taught—a body of knowledge or a series of processes in specific areas with all of the attendant emphases on currently pertinent content and method. There is the recognition of individual needs of particular students, necessitating an understanding of psychology and the human developmental apparatus as well as a sensitivity to the general requirements of class or ethnic groups, presuming a sociological insight. There are the shared aspects of school policy that have to be considered along with the larger commitment to community and national welfare. The physical responsibility for the classroom, the equipment and the supplies may not appear excessive at first glance, but when seen against the mounting spread, the proportions of the job may become individually harassing. Add to this the development of communication skills, the requirements of patience, integrity, good will, and an indefinite number of supplementary yet indispensable teaching attributes and the list takes on almost an omniscient quality.

The pressures from both inside and outside the school make themselves felt. Society, on one hand, insists upon its own reflection and expression in education through the transmittal and conservation of the accumulated store of traditional knowledge. This is somewhat complicated when a new "takeover generation," as *Life* magazine characterizes it, arrives periodically on the scene, assessing the old in terms of the new, asking fresh questions, posing novel problems and expecting answers and resolutions that may differ radically from preceding understanding. On the other hand, individual pupils may evidence considerable deviation from normal and common behavioral patterns, throwing out of focus the pragmatically acceptable methods that are successful with groups. The strong influences of unique differences may be of such a compelling nature that even when collective approaches are refined and sophisticated through the efforts of group dynamics, the individual needs may not be fully met. In addition, ineffectual learning, the large dropout rate, the delinquency of many adolescents, and similar conditions attest to this as a continuing state of affairs. Then, the explicit pressures of content must be implemented in the everyday lessons of the classroom. This concentration on the subject bedrock of teaching is being fostered while the larger and more implicit means and ends of learning hover about alternately, like benign or annoying disturbances depending upon the cast of a teacher's attitudes. Someone has called the elementary teacher the last of the encyclopedists, while those on the higher levels must figuratively match wits with a Picasso and an Einstein in their daily lessons. Teachers obviously have a rather heavy accounting—to the subject or subjects they teach, to the students, to the school, to the community, and not least, to themselves as well.

THE NEED FOR EVALUATION OF TEACHER TRAINING

To create an image of the ideal teacher may be a worthwhile and inspirational assignment, but it is a frightening one as well. The "hero image" may be as tentative and as misleading as the most dogmatic and negatively drawn portrait of an incompetent or bad teacher. The merits, in either instance, are essentially relative, the good and the bad depending upon the particular perspective of the one who is judging.

Yet, even when they are agreed upon generally, the qualities of good teaching, let alone ideal teaching, do not coincide consistently with what actually does occur in the classroom. Some of this may be due to the changing emphases of the environment, a reorientation in thinking that has become apparent over the past couple of decades though its dynamics have always been present. The sometimes unavoidable time lag between advanced theory and implementation in the schools and colleges eventually closes; though in past history, education has suffered from a wide time gap that was not bridged for long periods. The teaching deficiencies accumulate, in some instances to an appalling degree. The education resources may also have been stretched past their limits in an ever increasing attempt to provide good teaching for a never ending stream of pupils. The store of good teachers may have been depleted beyond an earlier proportion, pointing up a weakness in the educational system on all levels. This requires a fresh and continuing examination which should result in positive measures.

Despite the sense of commitment and the serious concerns of our colleges and training institutions, the needed qualities of background, broad understanding, and developed sensibilities are not always adequately provided for either in a formal or an informal sense. Some of the faulty and misdirected teaching probably stems from partial training that bungles along with picayune and unsuitable interests. The development of the prospective teacher takes on a tangential quality. There is either an insufficient involvement with the fundamental aspects of the area that is to be taught or an inordinate stress is put upon relatively inappropriate and trivial aspects of educational method. Not enough attention is paid to the kind of person that would be most adept at teaching or educationally supporting that person with the necessary academic, humanistic, and professional substance. It is true that there is no common consensus that delineates the necessary characteristics of the good teacher. This does not excuse the attempts of some colleges to train individuals by local fiat and pious philosophizing, sanctioning the procedure through a prescriptive proliferation of broadly generalized methods courses that paradoxically invite a tight structuring. J. D. Salinger, in his novel, *Franny and Zooey* says, "Scratch an incompetent school teacher—for that matter, college professor—and half the time you find a displaced first-class automobile mechanic. . . ." The teaching of method is not sufficient nor is the rote recital of abstract aims. It is not only the old idea of putting a square peg in a round hole, but the more current one of determining if, indeed, the hole is round or the peg is square. Knowledge in understanding the mechanics of teaching and learning is not too definitively formed but this need not stop experienced instructors, at least intuitively from assessing the attributes and potential worth of a prospective teacher and acting upon these insights; in fact, students themselves have to be encouraged in this kind of honest self appraisal. The resultant thinking may lead to the kind of evaluative guidelines by which education as a profession can greatly benefit.

In the final analysis, there is probably no substitute for the individual responsibility of each student who has to assess the worth of the education he or she is being exposed to, not only in objective terms, but in the more fundamental and subjective ones and through the realization of actual educational experience. This may not be more true in art education than any other area. But the eager and enthusiastic promise of students in teacher training, despite sincere and often conscientious instruction for the most part, founders on the uncertainties and insecurities as well as the challenges of actual art teaching. Herbert Gold, the novelist, in writing about his own teaching experience comments, ". . . it happens that most misty exaltation of the blessed vocation of the teacher issues from the offices of deans, editors, and college presidents. The encounter with classroom reality has caused many teachers, like Abelard meeting the relatives of Eloise, to lose their bearings." [1] Nevertheless, an art teacher much like a producing artist must do something, creating concrete learning situations as the artist fashions concrete forms in particular media. This something has to be done every day, as long as the teacher is in a classroom with students, again like the painter in front of an empty canvas or a sculptor eyeing a bin full of unformed clay. Though learning may be superficially intangible, its actual process in the classroom is real enough. Procrastination and negligence rarely can be accepted for any length of time, either by the pupil or the teacher (or the artist for that matter). If there is to be teaching or an expression through a work of art, there has to be interaction between the artist and material or the teacher and pupils. In a rather profound sense then, an art teacher has a responsibility that cannot easily be evaded, that of concretely influencing a student, hopefully in a creative manner. Perhaps each teacher requires her own ideal image, a model to emulate, to achieve this positive awarenes and to channel art teaching in imaginative and successful ways, but there can be no utopian concept that suffices for everyone. Students, at least in retrospect, are unconsciously aware of the tentativeness, the demands, and the uncertainties of teaching in any subject. William B. Yeates knowingly captures this attitude in his short poem, "Gratitude to the Unknown Instructors": [2]

> What they undertook to do
> They brought to pass,
> All things hang like a drop of dew
> Upon a blade of grass.

The Flexible Image of the Art Teacher

The inherent demands and responsibilities of teaching art run parallel with the other areas of a school curriculum on one general level. On another level the particular qualities of art insist upon unique understanding which cannot always be gleaned from the broad educational picture. There is a network of interrelating factors in art teaching which must be accounted for, either deliberately in the way the teacher approaches both the subject and the class, or more indirectly, in the way the teacher experiences the world. The personality of any art teacher is bound up with both the more objective educational implements of art and creative method as

[1] Herbert Gold, "A Dog in Brooklyn, A Girl in Detroit," *Encounter*, January 1963, p. 20.

[2] William B. Yeats, *Collected Poems* (New York: Macmillan, 1936), p. 249.

well as inherent subjective elements. The former have their own distinctive characteristics which are basically understood best in their own particular terms, while the latter are involved with broad psychological insights.

Yet teaching in a general sense is a means of translation. This is a common philosophical point underlying all educational speculation as it is in the specific instance of art teaching. Insight into the particular concerns of an individual area may be gained from informed and pertinent though general examination. The initial point that could be made is that the teacher is the prism through which the student views some segment of knowledge and existence. The viewing is significantly determined in as yet little understood ways by the figurative prism of the teacher. There are infinite modifications, distortions, and surfaces to the prism, each finally existing as a unique interpretive device.

The teacher becomes a ready channel toward significant experience, her personality focused for educational purposes or intensified in interpersonal terms of student growth. If there is more than usual clarity or depth of intensity, the student is fortunate in his teacher. Perhaps an intangible intrigue of character, a unique and unusual disposition, can provide worth to the prism, provoking stimulation in the student as well as the more acceptable image of the confident and normal teaching personality. However, if the uniqueness of the image is blunted by an assembly-line conformity, a rigidity based on doctrinaire assumptions, a timid projection of personal dynamics, or any other of a large list of congenital or imposed defects, then the student is faced with a confused vision and may not have the level of educational experience he deserves. The teacher then, is one of the key factors in developing a positive educational climate. This is perhaps even more true in the teaching of art to children than in the teaching of other subjects due to the symbolic, emotional, and otherwise intangible characteristics of art. The lack of conceptual structure in art and the exceedingly personal nature of its activity stress the psychology of behavior, the interpersonal relationship, and the uniqueness of the aesthetic experience.

The Subject as Focus

However, there are some who argue that the prism, the channel toward creative understanding, is not the teacher, but is rather the subject. This is a valid idea and as easily justifiable in argument as the above approach. No matter who the teacher is, the argument insists, it is through art or history or mathematics, through the discipline of a particular subject, that the student is coming to grips with knowledge and its consequences in living. It is through the particular attributes and characteristic qualities of art or of any other subject area that the sudent grows and becomes aware of the world, preparing his response to it and for his place in it, creating finally a personal and authentic sense of existence. Obviously, this must also be accepted as a genuine philosophical tenet. The two ideas are not really antithetical to one another, though at different times and in different places, the stress is either upon one or the other.

*The teacher's
awareness and
understanding of art
is largely based upon
direct, personal
experience with the
materials and
processes of visual
symbol making.
These are primary
influences in the
development of a
creative teaching
method.*

In art education, for instance, prior to this century and well into its early decades, art in the schools emphasized rigid exercise techniques, neatly pinning down the manner in which the student was to be led to a mastery of the subject. The teacher provided the drill and lessons. After the turn of the century under the influence of the art for art's sake movement and the later support of progressive education, the actual creative process itself was stressed as a psychological means of inducing desired growth in students. The teacher became more important as a beneficent guide and interpreter. However, when a relatively undisciplined self-expression became the dominant note in art education, the art teacher became little more than a dispenser of materials. Though this is grossly oversimplified and offered without value judgment, it demonstrates the swings in educational fashion which frequently overstate a position and do not arrive at a balance or a synthesis of contributing educational factors.

The pupil-teacher relationship resolves itself essentially as translation, interpretation, interaction, exposure, and mutual learning; the teacher and the subject area both contributing to the educational process the student is experiencing. The subject area is the core that informs, excites and enriches the student, providing for the creative growth of the individual both in imaginative and in rational terms. The teacher facilitates

this process, offering motivation, stimulation, and value judgments, serving as a resource person in the best sense without finality or absolute authority. Both the objective study of course content and the factor of individual teaching idiosyncracies form the prism through which the individual student apprehends the conditions of his environment and his own nature. In this manner, the student achieves knowledge and perhaps insight and is given the means with which to act, perhaps creatively.

Individual Emphasis of Method

It appears to follow that there is no abstractly correct way of teaching, just as there is no really ideal type of teacher or objectively unchanging course of study. At least, in the teaching of art, it would be difficult, if not educationally disastrous, to narrowly define classroom methods. However, there may be suggested procedures, the interchange of various individual teaching insights that lend themselves to a common formulation and a list of desirable attributes which hopefully would help produce a successful teacher. There is a range of information and a projected insight into process that assists in sensitizing the basic characteristics of teaching. Yet, to deliberately predetermine the main body of these characteristics of method and personality in art education may also do violence to the essentially fluid structure of art and its encompassing qualities.

This may seem a paradox, or a contradiction, perhaps even an evasion of responsibility. After all a text book in art education, designed to assist teachers in the teaching of art, may be expected to offer not only the "whys" of teaching art, but its "hows" as well. Yet, because of the unique nature of art, its novel and constantly forming structure, and because of the open-ended character of the creative process which feeds on the rebellious, obstreperous, and unconventional as well as on accepted rational and ordered understanding, the "how" aspect cannot be closely defined and categorically offered as a contained body of information.

Each teacher develops his or her own skills of communication and interaction. This coupled with a mature yet unique set of attitudes offers the most natural and salutary means of reaching children. Enriched in the subject area by participation, exposure, and learning as well as through the intrinsic and differing factors of personality, the teacher need not resort to a doctrinaire "how to" manipulation of materials, nor depend upon the shallow and self-defeating "bag of tricks" with which to entice students, ostensibly providing creative experiences, but in reality, merely conforming to the expected, the unadventurous, and the essentially uncreative. Each prospective art teacher has too much positive and exciting internal resources to have to turn to narrowly, preformed notions as the basis of their teaching method and content. These have been arbitrarily organized by others who cannot have the faintest inkling of the conditions, the understanding and the attitudes to be found in even one other classroom that may be hundreds of miles away physically, or more important, psychologically removed from the premises of the predetermined experience.

*Students on all
levels discover
meanings and
satisfying personal
experiences through
direct involvement
with art.* [*Toledo
Public Schools;*
PHOTO: *Tom
O'Reilly*]

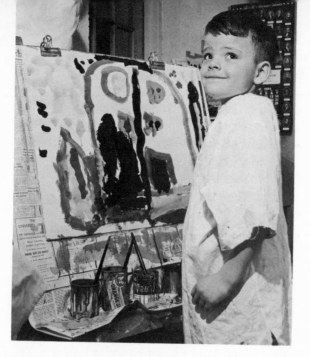

What is required, if any honest and pertinent meaning is to be achieved in the teaching of art, is a bringing together of the varying factors—the subject of art itself, an understanding of and an active involvement in the creative process, a comprehension of the underlying educational philosophy as well as of the methods currently employed or those proposed for the future, all synthesized in a mature development of individual personality. This has to be further seen in context, against the backdrop of a liberal examination of twentieth century life, its minus qualities as well as its positive attributes. Though artistic understanding and creativeness are basically the consequence of subjective qualities, objective factors cannot be ignored. The art teacher, perhaps even more than the artist, has to be overtly aware of the surrounding culture and its influences in education. A personal philosophy is called for, not arrived at by default or puerile mimicry, but through the alert realization of individual characteristics that implicitly shape attitudes as well as the explicit elements of culture that may direct them. This can lead to abstract and often controversial philosophical concerns. It may, at first, appear remote to discuss such considerations; yet how we teach is either the conscious or unconscious result of the personal philosophy to which we are heir. The very way we conduct ourselves in the classroom, the actual teaching quality that is acted out rather than just thought about, are attempts in a personalized manner to gratify existing philosophical viewpoints, whether they are narrowly biased or openly speculative. If we deliberately ignore the theoretical supports of art and education and the attendant personal influences of emotional and intuitive forces for the more immediately practical and objective methods, the consequences may be the manipulation of students rather than the teaching of individuals.

The teaching of art, to reiterate, is part of the broad stream of an educational heritage and procedure which share common problems requiring common resolutions. Yet, it is also a rather special and even extraordinary happening because of its highly unique nature and its stress upon singular creative expressiveness. The subject matter is innately exciting. It is frequently intangible in its psychological impact, consistently reaching the emotions; it is provocative and pleasing, ambiguous yet concrete in form, spanning the objectively intellectual and the subjectively feeling components of experience. An art teacher has to encompass not only these qualities of art, but relate to the rest of the curriculum and the individual student as well. The necessity for a continuing and open kind of resolution speaks for itself.

It is not intended that a strictly dichotomous choice be presented to the prospective teachers between predetermined, rigid structure on one end and a free, creative process on the other. This in itself predetermines a situation which requires individual and sensitive appraisal. At some points, a structured determination may be quite necessary to an art lesson or the development of a student's understanding. However, unless the art teacher approaches the teaching act with a spontaneity that characterizes an act of discovery, the preformed concepts degenerate into unexamined and meaningless forms, safe and secure, but without the verve and elan that creative expression insists upon.

In this sense, unless the open quality of creative expression and aesthetic resolution are genuinely operating, there is an imposition of values either as

The free exploratory and playful expressiveness of the early elementary child is a natural condition that should be encouraged in the classroom. [Toledo Public Schools; PHOTO: *Tom O'Reilly]*

tiresome exhortation or a doctrinaire methodology, which even if it advocates a free approach, denies it the natural immediacy of its character.

The Necessary Personal Attributes in Art Teaching

The art teacher's personal image should be a mature and profound one though spiced with the humor that makes for positive relationships. It should also reflect those broad and open qualities which make teaching a socially constructive and personally creative vocation. Without engaging in a homily that could be both tedious and moralistic, these qualities may be briefly summed up in the following manner by expanding upon four basic personality attributes: awareness, inspiration, empathy, and knowledge.

1. *Art teachers must be persons of awareness if they are to alert students to their own capabilities and potential.* Too many people in contemporary culture live in a climate of indifference and vagueness, responding most often only to the necessary or automatic inner drives and the most insistently compelling and conforming pressures from the outside. Self motivation leading to a quality of intellectual alertness and aesthetic sensitivity is not readily evidenced in large quantity in "the common man" without the prodding and stimulation of the processes of education. This is particularly true in a mass culture that emphasizes technological and other generally passive though specialized procedures. The process of awakening and growth toward maturity may be a painful one; it is more immediately satisfying to accept "what comes naturally." The average response makes little demand on an individual and since it is easier to accept the relatively painless orientation of the mediocre, too many students do so without being challenged or motivated sufficiently by teachers who themselves unwittingly accept mediocrity.

Art continues as a serious mode of personal expression throughout adolescence and after, in response to sensitive teaching. [Toledo Public Schools; PHOTO: Tom O'Reilly]

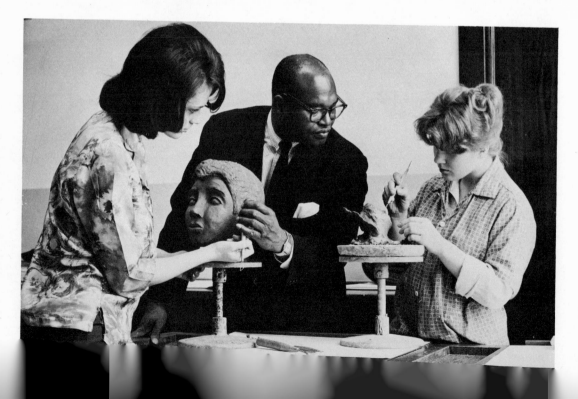

The qualities of art, if they are to be experienced in any degree of fullness, richness, or satisfaction, make demands and insist upon efforts that are beyond the gray confines of this prevailing mediocrity. In realizing this, teachers should also appreciate what may be initially insecure and almost distressing reactions for the individual. Mature understanding implies not only insecurity, but the ability to live with it, a recognition that ordinary standards or even so called lawful conclusions may be fallible, that change is a natural condition of life. Therefore, awareness is a primary factor in a teacher's personality, particularly if the subject is art. Art is predisposed to an adventuresome attitude and a searching outlook. It combines a breadth of experience with intensity of vision based upon alert sense perceptions leading to aesthetic consciousness—an enriched way of seeing.

2. *Art teachers have to create the appropriate climate in which students may respond, learn, and create.* Another way of saying this is that teachers have to be inspirational. This is an old fashioned word that has been suspiciously regarded as a high level verbal abstraction that has no real teaching meaning behind it. As it is generally understood, this is probably justified. However, the connotations of the word ring true, despite the meaningless manner in which it has been bandied about. To inspire is to influence, and there is nothing negative in that meaning. To be an influence is one of the basic and abiding responsibilities of the art teacher. Perhaps if we slough off the supernatural or romantically immature semantic meanings it would be easier to accept the idea of teachers being inspiring without conjuring up visions of halos and sentimental dedication.

Thomas Edison in a characteristically practical though mundane quote said, "Genius is one percent inspiration and ninety-nine percent perspiration." Both genius and inspiration are often connected to art or the creative process. But even in the impractical area of art, there is a good deal of perspiration. This is not activated in the students, however, unless inspiration releases the trigger of work, no matter what the mathematics of the equation are. An individual teacher may not feel equal to the task of inspiration, pleading inadequacy or modesty. But neither one of these factors has a place in good teaching. Just as no one is great who does not think of himself as great (humility being only a cultural inversion of this), no teacher can inspire unless he feels himself capable of doing so. Obviously, teachers who do not reach out, who do not project some inner quality that students may come into easy contact with, concurrently cannot create the classroom climate in which the student may then experience art honestly, openly, and creatively on its own merits. In art education when there is an inspiring teaching quality there is, as a result, a gratifying sense of appreciation and a fulfilling sense of doing—expressing the sense of one's self in a creative form as well as communicating its unique quality to others. The teacher as a generative source not only provides external excitement and stimulation but may awaken in the student those very qualities of self motivation that grow from internal springs of inspiration.

3. *Art teachers need also to sense a relationship to other people.* Though there is growing belief, despite the spread of science, that the world is

mirrored in our own ego and that the subjective self is the necessarily fundamental judge of understanding, this does not rule out the existence or the consideration of fellow men. The self exists on a parallel plane with the sentience of others, the teachers' along side of their students. Where there is active tension or attracton in the interchange, there is a touching of personalities and a relationship is formed. This may suggest a feeling of transcendence that need not violate the sufficiency of the individual in his own ego.

Albert Camus, in accepting the Nobel Prize for literature cited this idea in a broad relationship to art:

I cannot live as a person without my art. And yet I have never set that art above everything else. It is essential to me, on the contrary, because it excludes no one and allows me to live, just as I am, on a footing with all. To me art is not a solitary delight. It is a means of stirring the greatest number of men by providing them with a privileged image of our common joys and woes. Hence it forces the artist not to isolate himself; it subjects him to the humblest and most universal truth. And the man who, as often happens, chose the path of art because he was aware of his difference soon learns that he can nourish his art, and his difference, solely by admitting his resemblance to all. The artist fashions himself in that ceaseless oscillation from himself to others, midway between the beauty he cannot do without and the community from which he cannot tear himself. This is why true artists scorn nothing. . . .[3]

In order to "stir the greatest number of men" teachers have to practice a balance, finding the midpoint that does not negate the sense of self, that is a "beautiful" and intrinsically necessary human condition, yet that finds and encourages an interchange with the others, to which the self is just as necessarily related. The analogy of teaching with art has many positive insights to be appreciated. The relationship established in either instance has to be open and mutual. Teaching methods should never be frozen into codified means, impersonally implemented. At times the teacher may even assume the role of student, the relationship increasing the dimensions of understanding and expression of all the participants. In all, it is necessary in the teaching of art to be cognizant of and sympathetic to the social qualities of art.

4. *Art teachers should possess pertinent knowledge and broad understanding leading to a development of insight.* Though all teachers, in any area need a command of concepts, facts, and structure of that area, this usually implies an abstract understanding. For instance, a teacher presenting the basic ideas of algebra need not be a practicing mathematician in order to teach properly. However, though all teachers who provide art lessons for their classes need not be practicing artists in the full sense of commitment, they most certainly have to attempt some serious creative expression themselves. This is a necessity in understanding the processes of artistic appreciation and creativity and in providing an appropriate atmosphere in which expressive understanding may be achieved by students.

[3] Albert Camus, "Camus at Stockholm: The Acceptance of the Nobel Prize," *Atlantic Monthly*, May 1958, pp. 33–34.

Real awareness and a resulting comprehension are developed from personal involvement. This leads to a naturally positive climate in the classroom within which students can then undergo a meaningful creative process themselves based upon sympathetic and insightful guidance. Personal expression and mature understanding that become educational insights for a teacher are no ideal goals; they are the actual stock in trade for educators.

However, in art as it is in any area, this is generated and developed through effort, through personal crisis, and an immediate involvement with creative and expressive processes—an intent teaching for qualities that may not be easily apprehended or accepted with facility. Very often, the interest in an area may be the result of this effort, rather than the cause of it. In any case, without expending effort or committing himself to active participation the individual remains superficially informed: a mere dilettante. For the teacher, this is evasion of responsibility; for the creative aims of art education this may spell failure. Understanding art must take into consideration unique experience of the world outside and its creative transformation through active personal expression.

To stress these broad and encompassing personal attributes as general and fundamental conditions for successful art teaching does not rule out the desired development of unique characteristics. There are many paths that may be cut and traveled in the teaching landscape, though the essential physiognomy of the landscape is discernible. In recognizing the underlying pattern, a teacher instinctively accepts what may be the most valid and positive basis for meaningful education. In any case, the conditions stressed lay a groundwork for the kind of dialogue between teacher and student which stems from a broad and vital realization of the many actual as well as potential facets of human nature. On such a foundation the teaching of art may provide genuine personal, aesthetic, and creative experiences for everyone involved.

The listing of these attributes may be without the hard core and tangible substance that educational training frequently and properly implies. However, as long as teaching remains fundamentally an art rather than a science, particularly in the area of creativity and aesthetics, there will be no foundation for systematic listing of tangible and isolated teaching characteristics. The most that can be expected is a reiteration of what may appear to be platitudes at times, but are necessary assumptions all the same.

THE ENERGIES OF CHANGE

Of course, the educated individual would want to subject these assumptions to proper examination; teachers in addition have an obligation to do so, for they directly affect many people through subsequent action. Yet, because of its unfixed nature, some of the assumptions underlying art are difficult to dissect with any analytical nicety or controlled evaluation. This spills over into the teaching of art, forming an intuitive reservoir of understanding that presumes certain conditions. An additional one that has a large bearing in all education is that change is a constant phenomena.

Change occurs in children's art forms through developmental yet individually paced sequences.

[TOP LEFT] *"Going for a Ride," First Grade Drawing: Exuberant and direct expressiveness.* [PHOTO: *S. Martin Friedman*]

[BOTTOM LEFT] *"My Classroom," Fourth Grade Drawing: A characteristic attempt to render representational surroundings.* [PHOTO: *Stuart Klipper*]

[RIGHT] *"Portrait," Eighth Grade Tissue Paper Collage: Deliberate aesthetic control and an emerging unity of feeling and form.* [*Ann Arbor Public Schools;* PHOTO: *Stephen C. Sumner*]

The context as well as the particular implications of society and culture, the "outside" world and its pressures as they relate to the teaching of art are frequently ignored if they do not conform to commonly accepted patterns or are related in an esoteric way. This happens despite their inherent influence and their moulding of the actual forms and essential cultural meaning of art, and by extension, the content of and the manner in which teachers present the subject (or unconsciously ignore or distort it). Consequently, change is one of the most important external conditions that has a significance in art teaching. It is part of a necessary understanding in the development of any successful teaching program and in a realization of an art content that reflects and expresses its times as well as influencing the values and tastes of students.

Change is a predominant feature in any observation of the contemporary scene. It is of increasing force in an already highly complex environment, the pull and tug of vigorous and often opposing ideas, the premium of the new, the floundering of old shibboleths and the rush of exciting discoveries. The solid supports of yesterday become the rubble of today. The sureness of tradition is shaken by the defiance of the novel and unfamiliar. At the very least, a mechanical determinism inherited from the nineteenth century is no longer regarded in the twentieth century as the effective measure while any doctrinaire philosophy has long given up being the rule whereby an intelligent observer confidently defines the world.

Many of the older values which until recently have been regarded as eternal, or at least not easily subject to change, have succumbed to the prodigious onslaught of radically new ideas and the consequent beliefs stemming from them. The solid virtues of an agrarian outlook have given way to the raw thrust of industrialism; a personal craftsmanship has become an impersonal technology. The mechanistic universe of Newton with its perfection of functioning parts has been disrupted by the disturbing theories of Einstein and later physicists. These in turn, have become the jumping-off point for a remarkable leap into new frontiers of knowledge which scientists are exploring in an ever ascending spiral of new understanding of the universe. The voyages of discovery no longer are confined to the mundane stretches of earth but avidly prove the reaches of space.

The religious ethic that bound entire societies into tightly knit groups has become a thinly maintained faith in the face of a rampant materialism and a philosophical skepticism. Politics hops, skips, and jumps around the globe with daily happenings of momentous note. All this change has infiltrated every level of living and is as much reflected in the arts, as in science and social structure. Literature expands into new dimensions with the provoking styles of a Joyce, Faulkner, or Beckett, defying accepted stylistic techniques and normal grammatical syntax; music creates novel realms of sound with revolutionary tones of Schoenberg, Cage, and other composers utilizing electronic instruments grating on the ears of the uninitiated; while the developed rules of perspective and pictorial composition become in Picasso or Pollock the impertinent abstractions of an aesthetic visual order which, unfortunately, is more like disorder to most people.

Though the variety of our altered world may animate us, it also dispossesses our security. The old search for the good, the true, and the beautiful is now an anxious grasping for identity. The way to spiritual fulfillment has been lost by the average man; the road to happiness is a devious one and the expected, desired satisfactions are not always realized. The current turmoil in education is but one manifestation of this vast cultural metamorphosis.

We may regret the loss of permanence and stubbornly cling to supposedly solid footings of absolute values. Yet even a cursory glance at our environment would suffice to demonstate the inexorable force of change. However, it is not only in the readily observable objective conditions of environment that change is seen. It pervades a much more fundamental strata of existence; in fact, it appears to be a universal and basic phenomenon of all matter, both organic and inorganic.

Awareness of Change

More pertinent to the understanding of a teacher is the shifting manner in which people relate to others and to the environment, the flexible and continuously emerging orientation of the individual to the world. Since most comprehension seems to derive from the way we subjectively connect the various strands of our attitudes—the image we have of ourselves against and in relationship to the conditions, pressures, and possibilities of external surroundings—the resulting vacillation and lack of permanence create basic problems of identification and meaning. It is not sufficient to express verbally and accept casually the inevitability and presence of change; an attempt has to be made to incorporate the concept of change as an intrinsic part of our mental and emotional makeup; we are compelled to live with it and to fashion our attitudes in accordance with the realities of on going process. At the same time we cannot ignore the concrete products of the environment and the traditions they engender. Nevertheless, the very security we seek is more likely to be found in the kaleidoscopic variety and force of change than in the so-called stable and frozen aspects of an unchanging surrounding.

Obviously, if the world about us were an immobile one of fixed ideas and of permanence, the initially fixed reactions in the form of accepted symbols and assumptions would suffice for understanding and necessary action. Even the concept of permanence has now come to mean merely the rather slow moving aspect of change in some matter, that cannot be readily observed, but is there nevertheless such as the movement of land masses. Change is the rule and an understanding of its constancy a requirement in achieving a deep sense of realization appropriate to a particular time and place. The realization of change is a response to experience that is not dragging its heels, stagnating in the mistaken acceptance of relatively absolute and hidebound beliefs. Since knowledge, understanding, and process is subject to the force of change, education which attempts to teach within the framework of these factors must necessarily take it into account, stressing a liberal approach to its constituting elements.

The infinitely variegated structure of contemporary art, for instance, is based upon the uniquely qualitative and varying understanding of the creating individual. Though there may be large areas of common forms and processes that are generally agreed upon by groups, it is the singularly personal insight of an artist or a creative student in a classroom that achieves the realization of expression or the recreation of appreciation of another's work. The stream of art has developed out of this individual expression that, matured within a cultural context, possesses a dynamic quality of change. Similarly, educators have to be profoundly aware of

*Changes in the
forms and styles of
art occur because of
differences in time,
place, materials, and
cultural viewpoints.*

*The United Nations
Building.* [PHOTO:
United Nations]

the warp of the environment, the crossing woof of experience and the
unique patterns of understanding they create when figuratively woven by
the individual. The art teacher has also to be aware of the tentativeness
of his own understanding, the need to keep it open and receptive, if art
education is to help develop the intrinsic qualities and the innate learning
potential of pupils, not as conglomerates but as individual people adapting
creatively to change.

Restrictive Reactions

However, the continuous flow of new information and a parallel surge
of novel activity create an unnerving flux for many individuals. Because
of this, the complexity of contemporary life and the multiplicity of pressures, a reaction sets in. A ridiculous example has been the advocacy of a
small group of parents and educational critics in the early 1960's to return
to McGuffy's readers for elementary schools. There is a restrictive reaching
out for a base that grants a feeling of solidity and relief, despite its illusory
nature. A quality of permanence is sought after as a foothold on meaning
that does not have to be questioned. This may be understandable, but it

is a limiting desire, nevertheless. It deliberately colors ideas, circumscribes attitudes and predetermines the cast of our actions, disregarding those forces which may require new and differing means of control. The assumptions and beliefs that are held by individuals and groups tend to be continuously validated by them and preserved for as long as they serve their intended function. Any evaluation that occurs tends to be selective, filtering out new and provocative experiences, screening out those contradictions which tend to upset the traditional assumptions and the "permanent" beliefs. The process is generally below the conscious level; only extraordinary or genuinely upsetting occurrences tend to disturb the neutrality of most commonly and conservatively held opinions. Consequently, there is a quality of resistance to change. The introduction of the sciences into the curriculum experienced unprecedented hostility for a long period of time toward the second half of the last century, just as the arts today, though generally tolerated are not genuinely accepted as a necessity in the schools. Science itself was only given the recent impetus and broad support it has because of the Russian challenge.

Translated in terms of teaching methods in art, even at this late date, there are many holdovers from earlier days in the classroom. An example is the mimeographed or otherwise duplicated picture that the teacher herself has copied that is given to children to "color in." There is the continuing insistence of primarily utilizing art lessons to serve a purpose beyond itself, such as in illustrating a social studies lesson or in expressing the cliche of a holiday, or on the other end of the spectrum, a persistent dwelling upon complete self expression with no deliberate control by the teacher. There is the unconsciously selective presentation of material and projects that have filtered out the provocative and tradition destroying

Architectural Fragments from Different Historical Periods, College of Architecture and Design. [University of Michigan News Service]

qualities of contemporary art and new explorations in form. Since art rarely becomes an important enough activity for the average individual (teachers included) to experience extraordinary response, there is little opportunity for a genuine realization of the need of change. Felt more keenly in art because its values and practices are suspect anyway, the cautious bias of many educators spreads a timid and restrained attitude throughout a good part of the curriculum. This creates the impasse and the inadequacies of tight teaching, forcing a quality of educational planning that is laid down as a hard and fast doctrine, as good tomorrow as it was yesterday. Thus is underscored the stubborn commitment that so many educators have to the formulated curricula of their schools, in the conservative cast of most teachers who resist change. Fred Hechinger, in writing about teaching innovations in the *New York Times*, noted: "The startling fact— as one looks over the list of innovations . . . is that few, if any, of the experiments were begun by public school educators or, having been started, welcomed by the rank and file."

*The formal elements
and the content
of art changes
though there may
be a continuity
of expressive
intensity.*

*"Trellis-Sunlight,"
Albert Mullen.
[Courtesy of the
artist; PHOTO: O. E.
Nelson]*

"Temptation of Christ"—Duccio di Buoninsegna. [Copyright The Frick Collection, New York]

Education Suffers a Time Lag

Education should yield to the demands of change as readily as other areas of living. New knowledge, in our contemporary setting, however, is often suspect if it does not wear the armor of a glamourized science or the mantle of solid practically diverting entertainment. Challenging the earlier, traditional footholds creates continuing tension around education and an anxiety about its methods and goals. Yet school can no longer be regarded as the place where there is a simple transfer of the three R's from teacher to pupil. The ideas of the little red schoolhouse have long ago passed into what is for some a fond memory and for others a hopelessly antiquated concept of learning. The rise of democracy, the surge of new artistic expression, the development of science and modern technological industry over the past century have caused a major and continuing upheaval in the structure of society, in the conduct of life, in the means of knowledge and in the individual's self image. Acting upon the institutions of society, these pressures have caused a ferment of change in educational philosophy. The announced aim of providing a full education for all children, acting upon the democratic base of contemporary western life calls for a broad and enriching curriculum attuned to the particular conditions of today and providing a flexible base for the desired qualities of tomorrow. This makes urgent the need for a curriculum that favors more than the recital of facts, the acquisition of practical skills, and a stress on narrowly intellectual factors or one that on the other end preaches "adjustment to life" in overly simple terms that gloss over the demands of the intellect and the creative imagination.

However, there is the seemingly intrinsic gap of time between the forces of a growing society, the pertinent utterances of philosophers, and the oftentime grudging implementation of change in the schools.

Though the ideas of the little red schoolhouse are generally considered an anachronism in the twentieth century, there are those critics who would have the schools revert to their fundamentalist concerns, in part if not totally. The general concept that supplanted the rigidly limited intellectual syllabus of the nineteenth century and its reliance on drill and rote was formulated before 1900. The ideas of John Dewey and the instrumentalists, of those that desired to liberate and expand teaching in the classrooms have been given a hard, critical examination only since the end of World War II. The assumption that a child-centered and socially oriented curriculum has had universal acceptance since Dewey first appeared merely indicates the lack of information and understanding the critics of progressive education have had. At best, Dewey's contribution was as ideal philosophy and a goal. It was not incorporated basically into the actual practices of a great majority of teachers, though the progressive influence did act as a catalyst for many basic changes in educational philosophy, teacher training, and school policy. This merely points up the gap that so dishearteningly appears in education. In reality, it was not until the critics of progressive education began to voice their judgment and censure that the practices in the classroom began realistically and significantly to reflect Dewey's ideas.

Change in Education: A Foregone Conclusion

Education for the third quarter of the twentieth century will be undergoing a massive state of transition. There are a variety of contending forces urging their biases on the schools. Education, in midcentury and after, seems caught up in a contest in which learning is narrowly acknowledged by some as a tool, in which partisan social and political consideration frequently determine the ways and means of education. Others, just as sincerely conscious of the external situation, insist upon the need to maintain an openness and a freedom of unencumbered learning. Many educators themselves are divided and uncertain about the issues and the most appropriate manner in which to respond to them. Whatever the viewpoint, the forces for change are apparent.

However, the call for a diligent serious attitude in education, though it is a justifiable request on broad philosophical terms by any school of thought, is not really too appropriate in the suggested implementation of its specifics. The scientists themselves do not insist upon a narrow, rigorously exclusive education, but are more generally committed to a broad liberal education. They deplore the unintelligent stress on technical studies without the leavening quality of the humanities. In this they are joined by most educators and lay people who have a regard for the total picture of the individual relating to his environment through education. Actually, what is at issue, is not so much our ability to produce appropriate numbers of technical people (we have always risen to the occasion of national needs in a practical way), rather, the concern is with the national attitude toward learning as a part of culture. This does invite change of current thinking. One of the central considerations is the most intelligent manner in which to introduce a broadly disseminated knowledge about the arts as a part of the humanities which in turn is a central concern of culture. The multiple roles of art education cast it as a proselyting cultural tastemaker, a personal and symbolic channel for expressive communication, as well as a viable agent for dynamic insights into shifting contemporary viewpoints.

Art is a direct channel for self-awareness. "Self-Portrait," First Grade. [Ann Arbor Public Schools; PHOTO: David Churches.]

INDIVIDUAL RESPONSIBILITY

In the face of this, it becomes a necessity to divest oneself of the timeless dictates of an unchanging educational tradition. This may not be as unfortunate as it appears on the surface, disturbing the metaphoric yet arrested sleep of the contented. We obviously cannot escape the world in which we live, and we should not even attempt it. The challenge, for teachers particularly, is a stimulating one. Not only do they acquire and disseminate facts and attitudes about things and translate them into learning situations, confronting the student with the necessary awareness of his own existence, but they are called upon to practice the Socratic injunction, "know thyself," against the exciting panorama of contemporary life.

The teaching of art on any level is profoundly bound up with this attitude. Change, introspective insight, and uniquely oriented formative qualities, though they may be difficult to structure in practice or to codify in pedagogical theory are, nevertheless, the essential conditions that form the context of the making of art and any method by which it is successfully taught. The impinging factor of society, its promulgations and pressures, only intensifies and colors the act of teaching art; it cannot mechanically shape it without a resulting chaos or emptiness of concept and product. Yet the environment is all around and does not permit itself to be ignored. Somewhere between the opposing, or perhaps complementary factors, a knowing and sensitive teacher can provide what is at best a tentative but sincere insight that honestly assesses and responds to pertinent pressures, but is an effective base for educational action, nevertheless. However, this positive note may be achieved only as the consequence of an individual's own self-realization and sense of educational responsibility. This, in turn, is subject to the flow of conditions, forces, and changing pressures that become the open-ended and changing material of living that each individual has to digest figuratively and transform into new symbolic forms.

A note of caution may point up the distinctions between an artificial obsolescence and an actual quality of change. Despite the hold traditional attitudes have on the average mind, the fast-paced conditions of contemporary society and its own internal forces, economic as well as cultural, build up a superficial quality of change. Fad, fashion, and deliberately built-in material elements of obsolescence lead the popular mind a merry chase after the constantly altered image of what is correct today, of short lived novelty and of artificially primed styles. The fundamental patterns of understanding are not displaced, however, in this constellation of cursory variations; the old appetites and the ingrained habits of attitude are merely reinforced, being titillated by the sycophantic and childishly flattering nature of an ingenious novelty. Art education should plumb below these surface manifestations of change, not wooing obsolescence for its own sake but expressing the vital nature of flux and flow characterizing all forms of living.

The general responsibilities of teaching art cover a rather wide span, becoming, finally, individual responsibilities. They involve the subjective state of the individual consciousness, the objective conditions of an environment that impinge upon that consciousness, and the symbolic attributes of art, as well as a passion and commitment to its natural values. These factors require a unique insight growing out of an active participation in both the sensory and critical elements of the art processes and the ways by which students as individuals become engaged in creative expression. A personal, independent relationship with the unfolding elements of education, the substance of art, creative learning methods, together with insight into, and sympathetic regard for, cultural forces—all are necessary to meet the responsibilities of teaching. They complement the more structured offerings of teacher training.

It is the latter that teachers have to guard against, for teachers are natural academicians, and institutions reinforce, even if in an involuntary manner, a search for rules, regulations and standardized procedures. The art teachers have to give rein to more visionary and imaginative personal fancies. They have to naturally commit themselves to the playful and searching aspects of art as well as its disciplined qualities, acting the "Pied Piper" to students, as Allan Kaprow refers to the inspirational role of art teachers, radiating the creative verve of art.

2

The Aims of Art
in Education

> The relation of art to life is of the first importance,
> especially in a skeptical age since, in the absence of
> a belief in God, the mind turns to its own creations
> and examines them, not alone from the aesthetic
> point of view, but for what they reveal, for what
> they validate and invalidate, for the support they
> give.
>
> WALLACE STEVENS

W HY include art in the curriculum? In what way does art function to
answer the needs of a student in contemporary culture? The answer
probably lies in a more general query as to the significant worth of art in
the active outside world as well as for its value for the child in the classroom. If a teacher can develop a personally significant understanding of
this question, then he or she is in a position to translate the understanding
into effective teaching situations on whatever level is necessary in intrinsic
terms of art, rather than of trivial or extraneous qualities.

In responding to the above questions, it would be improper to refer
only to the visual arts (the area generally the concern of art education).
What is true of painting, sculpture, and design is also true, in most instances, of literature, drama, dance, music and the other arts.

THE FUNCTIONS OF ART

There is an obvious and lengthy list of responses to the question of the
function and uses of the arts in modern times. They provide pleasure and
diversion, commitment and fulfillment, answering the fundamental compulsion of humans to express ideas and feelings symbolically or to simply
while away in amusement and satisfaction what are regarded as leisure
hours. The arts afford opportunities for a large range of experiences; vicarious, immediate, projected, removed, intimate, emotional, sensual, spiritual,
intellectual, and aesthetic. They permit us to engage in wish fulfillment
through fantasy, precise delineation and recording of knowledge through
representational images, or communication through a wide variety of

forms, exciting our senses, provoking our emotions, deepening our perceptual understanding, and providing a vital source of meaning. They may be
a form of escapism permitting us to supersede a distateful or hostile present
or they may act as the outlet for the many psychological promptings in
human nature to ensure a more pleasant present. They may be a vehicle
for social comment, embodying the virtues and the defects of society, a
collective symbol of a society, or they may be an individual avenue of
expression, embodying a sensual and symbolic transformation of ideals
and visions as well as physical states of being. They tickle and titillate an
audience or move it to tears, rage, or ecstacy. They serve as emblems of
the past, as precursors of the future, and as the actual and vivid, yet spiritual projection of the present. They, the arts, become the joy of creation
for the artist and a vital source of personal meaning for everyone. They
can do all of these things and more, because they elicit countless responses
and are themselves the symbolic reflection of an innumerable array of
human interests and needs. They are, as a general concept, an idealized
version of experience which includes the outer world of things and appearances as well as the inner one of impulse, intuition, and emotion in a
limitless variety of forms. A painting by Albers or one by Sloan elicits differing responses. The harmonious and sensuous painting by Mullen serves
quite another need as does the still different sculpture of Rodin. The
intriguing rhythms of a modern building arouse yet other qualities of response and answer changing needs from those of historical architectural
forms.

There is an unending list of possibilities that enriches artistic function.
Obviously, they are also related in basic individual ways to the needs of
the observer as well as to what the particular artist has wanted to express,
embody, or communicate. This is one of the central concerns of art in the
school curriculum: defining, expanding, enriching, and responding to the
sometimes unknown but always felt needs for expression of experience.
This seeks a symbolic fulfillment in form or in appreciation of another's
vision that is characteristic of human nature, and has been at all times.
What is most required at this time is that the need for expression and
appreciation and fulfillment be given a dynamic individual as well as
mass or imposed cultural direction that is vital and of some significant
purpose.

The goals of art education have to encompass all the feeling and thinking attributes of people. The teaching of art has to be a contagiously enthusiastic and qualitative engagement with living experience.

The Problem of Individual Identification and Social Purpose

The development of an appropriate direction in education and teaching
method runs parallel to the larger vision in society of what constitutes an
adequate and rewarding way of life. The "Age of Anxiety," as the twentieth century has often been dubbed because of its continuing sense of
crisis, its violence, and its uncertainties, has not permitted any simple or
stable understanding or translation of what the vision of "the good life"

*The visual forms
that are experienced
in works of art are
unique, embodying
an innumerable array
of differing insights,
viewpoints, and
purposes.*

"Welded Steel,"
Joseph Goto. [Allan
Frumkin Gallery,
New York; PHOTO:
Nathan Rabin]

may be. The vacillating beliefs and shifting values have not had a shared point around which to cluster, and it is this focus of attitude, this concentration of a core understanding that is required to render the beliefs and values most effective. Modern man no longer has the commitments of earlier rituals or the devotional attitude of unquestioned world views. The particular sentiments that colored and impelled the earlier processes of meaning and their consequent sense of identification are no longer valid, though the structural process of a relationship between man and his world remains a necessity. Yet the sense of identification, of meaningful purpose has withered away in the upheavals of the past century; modern man stands shorn of his old supports, but more important, he is, as well, bereft of an ability to erect new ones, deprived of authoritative guides by which to steer his way.

This basic condition is also reflected as well in the psychological bewilderment that besets many students in a seemingly anchorless society. It is sensed in the lack of inner realization that confounds the modern temperament and is further reflected in an uncertain educational atmosphere. It is also seen in the glib and facile identification that is made with superficial values or with those that a mature mind would regard with skepticism—the stress on material goods, on surface appearances, on conformity and on "success" usually with small attention paid to how it is achieved.

Change is not a vital agent in this viewpoint but only an opportunistic point of departure from an unexamined fear and apathy.

Education, despite its efficacy in spreading knowledge and developing values, suffers almost as much from this shallowness as does the larger sphere of living. To offset this there is need of a vital personal vision coupled with a sincere but sophisticated orientation toward the positive goals of society. There has to be a belief in the efficacy and the guidance of an education that permits mature yet individual loyalties. A moral authority may result that is attractive because it stems from the natural propensities and aspirations of men. These latter need not be the chaotic or negative qualities that are sometimes ascribed to them, despite the

"The Young Mother," Auguste Rodin. [Collection The University of Michigan Museum of Art]

modern sense of despair and material aggrandizement. Cultivated through an experience of values that are of vital spiritual and aesthetic concerns, as well as practical and self-aggrandizing ones, the guiding principles may be socially beneficial and individually rewarding. They are certainly necessary to "the good life."

This rather profound aim of qualitative purpose would be difficult to attain at any time, given the errant penchants and impulsive desires that men do possess. In a time of radical transition and disaffection with prevailing values, it becomes even more a poet's idealization rather than a condition in living that may be eventually fulfilled. However, even if qualitative purpose exists primarily as an ideal, it serves a most vital function in that it infuses the aspirations of the human community with a laudable and a genuinely desired goal. This creates the need to shape life as a form that can be lived in accordance with pertinent and meaningful principles in its fullest aesthetic sense as well as the intellectual and the material; education could not want any more appropriate definition of its function and aim. Though there may be an element of sermonizing in this attitude and a too easily accepted virtue of outlook, there is at the same time, the need of education honestly and realistically, rather than abstractly or with mere lip service and sloganizing, to involve itself with a vision of an adequate and influential contemporary ideal.

No matter what the ideal, in order for both the individual and his society to sense its quality and its impetus toward action, a response from both individual and group has to develop. Sheer response, however, is rather mindless; it has to be enriched with an awareness of the conditions of life and it has to reflect, or better yet—express, a real meaning and authentic purpose. It is on this rather fundamental level that the arts offer education a means of activity and engagement which can bring about a quality and a meaning that is necessary to a full realization of experience.

This is not meant to suggest that the arts themselves constitute the prime meaning of existence that is desired, nor that they are the only source in its development. It would be almost absurd to suggest that the fulfillment of the aesthetic urge is the single important purpose, no matter how central it is to human nature. There are other moral, physical and intellectual qualities that are easily as important in man's make-up. Nor is art the only source of meaning. Abstract thought, religion, and physical satisfaction among others just as readily provide sources of meaning and guide the purposes of individuals and groups. Each of these provides the basic factors of understanding that go beyond simple perception, permitting an individual a quality of realization of ideas, emotions, or objects that then guides response into some channel of action, hopefully of a genuinely felt nature.

Qualitative Realization of Experience

Realization of one's experience in a qualitative way implies that a vital confrontation has occurred between the individual—his perceptions and

*"White Front,"
Joseph Albers.
[Collection The
University of
Michigan Museum
of Art]*

*Abstract as well as
representational
images offer
aesthetic means
of realizing human
experience*

*"Dust Storm, Fifth
Avenue," John Sloan.
[The Metropolitan
Museum of Art,
George A. Hearn
Fund, 1921]*

understanding and what his senses communicate to him. It suggests that there is more than a passive transfer of the data of living, that somehow the individual poseses the experience more acutely than in the mechanical or motor reflex stage. In order to realize, for instance, a positive atmosphere in a classroom, a student has to do more than learn a lesson by rote; he has to be aware of more than an orderly arrangement of furniture, a well lighted room or a willingness of effort and discipline, he has to "catch on," be alerted to the entire range and nuance of meaning that the situation provides. Similarly, a teacher has to "go" beyond adequate preparation and lesson planning, "do" more than pleasantly smile or efficiently present the necessary material in order to realize her own teaching role. She has to "dwell" in the situation, engrossed in its possibilities, possessed by its qualities, establishing a personal identity.

The arts, in any case, offer a ready means of achieving this sense of search that is more than momentarily satisfying or abstractly correct. They embody values which enrich not only an individual sense of existence but qualitatively pervade a culture. Education cannot hope to achieve its positive potential of individual and group development without an intimate relationship between the aesthetic elements of consciousness and the overall activities of a curriculum. The little first grader who unselfconsciously wields a brush dripping with color and texture delight is as much engaged in a necessary process of education as when he is laboriously putting letters together in an effort to make words. The high school student who is intensely forming an image in clay is as much on the pedagogical road to development of his potential as when he is referring to logarithms. In all of the instances, there is a confrontation with experience. More than likely, the more vivid encounter is through art (though not necessarily more important) and the student is afforded a level of personal realization that colors, consciously or otherwise, his subsequent actions.

In teaching art, the level of realization will be determined by what Hans Hofmann, the great teacher of art, calls "the search for the real." He indicates this perhaps cryptically, yet with an intensity of awareness when he says (the words in parentheses belong to the author), ". . . quality, a pure, human value, results from the faculty of empathy, the gift of discerning the mystery of each thing through its own intrinsic life. In this life, an intuitive artist (or teacher) discovers the emotive and vital (and educational) substance which makes a work of art (or a learning experience). In the passage of time, the outward message of a work (or an individual lesson) may lose its initial meaning; the communicative power of its emotive and vital (and educational) substance, however, will stay alive as long as the work (or the student expression) is in existence. The life-giving zeal in a work of art is deeply imbedded in its qualitative substance." [1] The "measurement" in art education may be intangible and implied, but it is nontheless present. It may be unconsciously pertinent, yet the qualitative aspects are intensely felt in art activities, set against presumed if not actual goals.

[1] Hans Hofmann, "Search for the Real," (Andover, Mass.: Addison Gallery of American Art, 1948), p. 54.

The goals of art education may be summarized in one sentence. Art education seeks to develop sensitive, imaginative, creative, and artistically literate individuals who may grow aesthetically, emotionally, and intellectually through active expression or reflective appreciation in the arts. In the process a qualitative personal vision is formed. On the other hand, the goals may be exhaustively treated in general classifications and in specific categories, delineating all of the pertinent factors. The latter course would be a tedious one to do in a single outline and no doubt would fall short of including each of the goals that may touch upon artistic activity both in school and in the outside world. Actually, the aims of teaching art are implied in most of what follows throughout the entire text.

The Individualizing of Personality

Art education puts a premium on what is singularly particular to each person. It stresses the unique and the personal, permitting each student to listen to himself and to discover his own sources, inclinations, possibilities, and limitations. The processes of art may be therapeutic, offering a catharsis of personal problems, allowing for a "staged" enactment of hostilities, inhibitions, and other behavioral disorders that then acts as a psychic cleansing agent. However, even more basic, the teaching of art aims for the development of a healthy individual, accepting the differences that naturally distinguish people, utilizing these subjective distinctions as personal channels of self realization. It becomes a means of real and meaning-

A typically spontaneous expression, transforming childhood sentience into visual symbols. "A Bright Day," First Grade. [New York Public Schools; PHOTO: S. Martin Friedman]

ful identification with experience, and despite the initial chaos, structuring the experience for personal ends.

Art helps develop a gratifying sense of personal identity and a feeling of natural integrity. These needs are perhaps most basic in our age. The imposition and acceptance of mass, undifferentiated values in the general public has led to what many observers have referred to as a loss of personal identity. The standardized code of the group has supplanted the "inner gyroscope" that more clearly offered preceding times a choice of identification. Work and other basic undertakings in contemporary culture often does not provide satisfaction for the individual. It categorizes him in groups, his cues for belief and action generated by outside factors and conditions—the mores of his culture and the satisfactions that stem from "keeping up with the Joneses" rather than listening to the inner propensities of one's own self. Yet the need for individual identity remains in an integrity of achievement. Since so many of the normal conditions of living seem to conspire against this, the individual has to find some form of expression which permits an unhampered search for self. The arts, in a wide range of possibilities not only provide this opportunity, they become concrete symbols of personal identity the individual himself has created. The integrity of his purpose is circumscribed only by his own sense of honesty which need not be compromised by any social or group demands.

Art in education can develop a sense of personal and unique worthwhileness. Paul Goodman has referred to the prevalent lack of self-respect evident in the students today in his book, *Growing Up Absurd*. With so many of the fundamental values that inspire man to positive action and belief removed from sight or fractured into mechanized and oftentimes insensitive components, it is difficult for young people to feel what they are doing as being worthwhile. A job is no longer basically regarded as an honest means of contribution of labor in order to gain the wherewithal to sustain life, but is thought of as a status symbol or as a disagreeable task that offers no intrinsic reward. The arts in themselves cannot offset this social malaise; it is much too deeply rooted in a pervasive relationship of the individual in society to the characteristic means of production. It is economic and political in nature and art cannot hope to counter these influences in any obvious way. Yet the arts offer in themselves a quality of intrinsic personal value that permits an individual sense of achievement and expression. They become a means of counteracting cultural deterioration by insisting on the worth of the individual, by respecting his personality idiosyncrasies, and by appealing to his unique being through the directness of the senses and the satisfactions of the imagination.

The Heightening of Sensibility

Art education aims particularly to expand the individual's response to the aesthetic and emotional qualities of experience. The teaching of art is intimately and fundamentally involved with the senses. It hopes to educate them so that the imaginative and perceptual responses will be of some consequence. Tasting, hearing, touching, smelling, seeing, and the wide

Art offers a creative means of personal expression and realization of experience, particularly through active participation with the materials of art. [New York Public Schools]

range of sense response to heat, cold, pressure, movement and such, all are bound up with qualitative experience and require development through educational processes. An innate and beneficially symbolic form of "play" is involved in art that also permits experience to be formed into imaginatively satisfying and perceptually exciting ways. The heightened interrelationship between the sense receptors, perceptual understanding, and imaginative transformation lead to an enriched sensibility of feeling. This leads further to the "expansion of ones personal horizon"—an enlargement of the sense of self in both space and time. This is one of the most characteristic offerings of the arts, its innate ability to transcend the limits of ordinary happenings, permitting the individual an extension of his experience into a realm of vivid and dramatic realization that always possesses a larger potential. The student who charges his own senses with the visual excitement of painting and sculpture, the pure tonalities of music, the expressive movement of the dance, or with the mind's eye imagery of poetry is going far beyond the normal bounds of experience. He is in a very practical as well as a symbolic sense enlarging the territory of his knowledge and his capacity for more experience.

The Intensification of Learning and Meaning

Art education provides channels of communication through image formation and symbolic meaning that are definite necessities in the general learning process. It deals with concrete qualities and creative procedures that involve instances of transformation and substantial interpretation of raw experience. Art may provide forms of creative insight and orient thinking in characteristic and significant ways that result in productive learning as well as emotional or aesthetic satisfaction. It not only stimulates spontaneous and intuitive insights, it insists as well upon elements of analysis and evaluation making for real decisions that affect and direct both intellectual and aesthetic understanding. It aims to integrate the various elements of the cognitive process, the rational ordering of parts with the imaginative, intuitive, and nonrational traits of human understanding. A high order of learning is involved in art, the central and various attendant processes affording the student fertile opportunities for discovery and comprehensive insight into the various orders of existence so that personal meaning may be established.

This leads to a sense of personal development. The more immediate sense of active involvement in one's continuing sense of development is sometimes difficult to know. The arts in their sensual and unique qualities of expression and form, offer this immediacy of participation that may be vital to a worthwhile development of purpose for the individual. However, growth as an end in itself is a rather uncritically accepted abstraction, especially among the progressive educators. Growth alone is an inadequate goal; it must be leavened with an affirmation and a realization of experience that has some moral authority internally sensed as well as measured against objective standards of excellence. The existential plight of all individuals, the contingency of events and action, if genuinely made aware to the individual particularly through the arts, provides for a more intense development of insight and commitment to qualities that may be regarded as positive. There is a sense of discrimination as to what constitutes learning, what is of intrinsic worth. The artist is often a model of commitment, pursuing an ideal or a goal with a fervor that sets him apart and frequently makes him the envy of other men. It is only in an "engagement" with the creative forces of one's own psyche that the errant and often absurd conditions of existence are, at least for the moment, overwhelmed.

The Enrichment of Culture

Art education is an important access for the student through which he becomes acquainted with past or foreign cultures as well as his own present pattern of living and social attitudes. Participation in the arts and their appreciation aims not only to accommodate the student to the prevalent features of his surroundings, but to assess them in both objectively critical and subjectively feeling ways. It provides a basis of evaluation that may lead to admiration for past accomplishments, rapport with present ones or an attempt to modify and otherwise change, by addition to or rejection of cultural viewpoints, when it is deemed necessary to do so. The goal of art education in this respect is to establish a rapport between student and culture so that a vital dialogue can ensue between the two, intensifying a sense of community. At first it may appear that the arts cannot offer a sense of community, for the independent, personal idiom has been largely stressed. Nevertheless, in a very real way the arts permit the individual to sense the drama of creation as shared by others. They are the most concrete symbols and communicative devices that man possesses whereby the deepest feelings and emotions, the most personal and subjective experiences of other human beings are made concrete and available. There is in

A *study group at the University of Michigan Museum of Art. Art also offers personal satisfactions through the recreative experiences of appreciation.* [University of Michigan Museum of Art]

this attribute of art a form of that profound I and Thou experience that Martin Buber writes of—a sharing of oneself with the sentience and being of other people. Art may provide the basis of a joining of moral and aesthetic community interests, for a common good.

THE VITAL RESPONSE TO EXPERIENCE

The response to these goals of art education is a value-laden one that a "realized" quality of education will determine through the immediacy of classroom experience. The student in the classroom will be stimulated by the atmosphere, or he may feel a contrary reaction. Other values that have been internalized may intrude to color his attitude, depending upon the effects of past experiences and present inclinations. Or he may weigh the stimulation in the classroom against the beckoning day outside and find learning at the moment undesirable, no matter how intensely motivated. However, if the realization is strong enough, the response is likely to be in accord with its intensity. Similarly, a teacher could feel zestful and enthusiastic, thinking up ways of sustaining a creative atmosphere or she may feel tired and depleted, having given too much of herself, anxious to modify the mood. Each individual colors his responses in unique ways, and each response need not be exact, predictable, or similar, though each may be reacting abstractly to the same experiential stimulus. What is of importance though is that individuals respond to the realized element in ways that are meaningful to themselves leading to some kind of action response that is either contemplative or actual but imbued with feeling and vision.

Experience is obviously the core of existence, its realization subject to the degree of intensity with which we grasp its significance. Subsequent actions and attitudes are the individual ways we respond to the realization of experience. The characteristic response of a person determines whether the vision of existence that is heeded "passes muster." In this manner, democracy, public education, commitment to cultivation of taste, or any other pattern of living is tested.

In what way do the arts contribute to the enrichment of experience? As the philosopher Irwin Edman indicated, "they intensify, clarify and interpret experience," [2] permitting a realization of greater than average depth. This is achieved in the particularly characteristic manner of the arts, by imaginatively expressing in symbolic form the experience otherwise felt or thought of in a prosaic and routine manner or it remains as a locked agitation in the confines of the dim unconscious. The imaginative symbolic forms evoke a quality of individual experience that is vital, immediately stimulating, "intensifying, clarifying, and interpreting," that experience in a way no other approach is capable of achieving. The arts open up the spiritual and aesthetic values, permitting a degree of realization of self and environment that could inform, support, and shape the vision each person creates. The arts become among the most fertile sources for orientation with a creative resonance of quality, providing natural opportunities to define and achieve intrinsically satisfying purpose. It is the central distinguishing attribute of imagination that functions to establish art in this role.

The Significance of Imagination

Brewster Ghiselin has broadly defined imagination "as the realization of life in form." [3] He continues . . .

only the first and third items of this statement, realization and form, can be defined satisfactorily. By the central term life I mean the mysterious substance of our being; but that statement is not offered as a definition. I would understand realization to mean both an actualization, as opposed to ideal or fancied subsistence, and a coming into possession. And, therefore, by the whole phrase "realization of life," I would imply the actual, concrete flourishing of our being. By form I mean aesthetic and intellectual structure, not such structure as is thought of abstractly, but rather as it lives through serving in an act of apprehension, in that use which is its only mode of life and which identifies it with the energies of our being. Form is intrinsically the play of energies of our inner life composing themselves in the configurations of some medium, paint or stone, musical tones, words, mathematical symbols, or the life, whether the material

[OPPOSITE] *The creative process, particularly in art, is usually marked by an intensity of endeavor and commitment to personal expression, stressing an imaginative focus of activity.*
[PHOTO: © *Roy Stevens*]

[2] Irwin Edman, *Arts and the Man*, (New York: Mentor Books, 1949), p. 30.
[3] Brewster Ghiselin, *Education and the Imagination*, (Irving Kaufman, ed.) (Published jointly by The University of Michigan and The Museum of Modern Art, N.Y., 1958), p. 18.

of the medium is present to the senses as when clay curves before the eyes and feels firm to the hands, or whether the configuration is envisaged only subjectively, as when the terms of a mathematical theorem are assembled in thought without being written down.[4]

Ghiselin reiterates the most important function in life as "realization" of its experiences. He expands the idea that this can only happen in a relatively complete or fulfilling way through the structuring of form and that this requires the uses of imagination. The aesthetic uses of imagination find their forms through the various media of art. Experience is transformed through the agency of art into meaning, corresponding in its forms to the innumerable but inherently underlying patterns of human nature. In this manner there is a meaningful realization of individual experience that also fits into the purposes of human vision and existence. It is the function of art education to implement this understanding in the school by stimulating and deepening individual imagination.

It may be helpful if we very briefly examine some actual examples of art in this respect. In Roualt's "Christ on the Cross with Disciples," the painting has a rough but clear representation of human figures. The content is obviously religious in nature, the image of Christ and the cross being universally recognized. Is it that the artist wants simply to record an important event in human history, to represent one of the most significant episodes in the Christian theology? No one can deny these as being present, but it is just as obvious that the artist has gone beyond the mere visual representation of an important event. He has expressed very directly his perceptual and intellectual comprehension of the event, but more profoundly, he has symbolically created a form that is full of emotion and feeling. He has brought into play his intuitions and inner attitudes, *realizing* in an art medium a blend both of his subjective and objective attitudes. He has evoked an imaginative experience (for he was not present at the crucifixion) intensifying his understanding, expressing it in a sensuous symbol of color, shape and light value—all visually plastic elements. The audience feels an empathy with the agony of Christ, the devotion and grief of the disciples and may comprehend the religious compulsions that inspired the painting even if the belief is not shared.

Roualt has gone beyond simple recording and has imaginatively expressed the intense quality of his insight and vision, which the onlooker may share. He has also created a bold and sensuous visual composition, structuring the elements of art: color, mass, light values, texture, and line which excite the eye and reward the aesthetic sense. This may be appreciated abstractly in terms of itself: the intensity of its color, the vigor of its line, the dynamics of its patterns, the measure of its rhythms and proportions. The content may also be seen separately, pointing up a moral, attempting to edify and improve character and belief because of the lofty theme. However, the morality is then merely a repeated one like a rote catechism and the art form a particularly apt tool that is dependent upon other than its intrinsic properties to provide it with real meaning.

[4] Brewster Ghiselin, *ibid.*, p. 19.

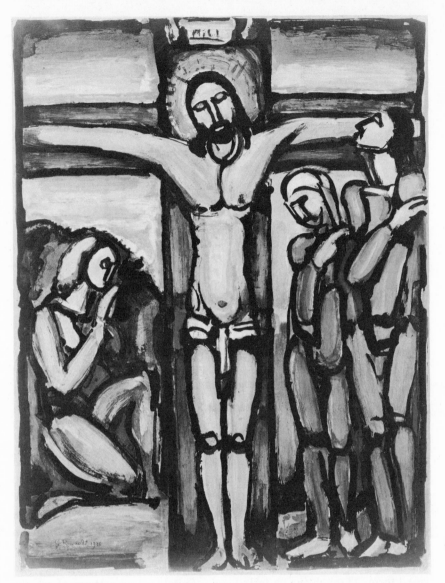

*"Christ on the
Cross," Georges
Roualt. [Collection
The University of
Michigan Museum
of Art]*

Actually, Roualt has sensitively and passionately interwoven the two
aspects of form and content, organically united them into a new configuration that is more than the simple blend of parts. A new vision has resulted
that creates an intensity of realization that goes beyond the average connotations of morality and beauty. It is an *imaginative* symbol that possesses
its *own* moral authority, providing a *direct* means of recognition of spirit
for both the artist and his audience. As such it is a fundamental "realization of life in form."

Similarly, in Mondrian's "Composition with Yellow and Red," the art
symbol is an imaginative construction of human experience. However,
the more characteristic twentieth-century style of abstraction is employed.
Mondrian has written that it took him a long time to "discover that the
peculiarities of form and natural color evoke subjective states of feeling,

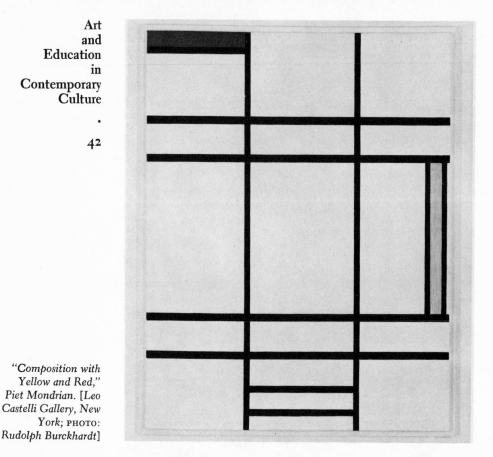

"*Composition with
Yellow and Red,*"
Piet Mondrian. [*Leo
Castelli Gallery, New
York;* PHOTO:
Rudolph Burckhardt]

which obscure pure reality. The appearance of natural forms changes but
reality remains constant. To create pure reality plastically, it is necessary to
reduce natural forms to the constant elements of form and natural color
to primary color. The aim is not to create other particular forms and
colors with all their limitations, but to work toward abolishing them in
the interests of a larger unity." [5] This larger unity included the spiritual and
harmonious relationships, as well as the basic elements of plastic and
visual form. Through the perfected and infinitely varied patterns of art, the
visual forms should demonstrate to man a symbolic means of achieving
harmonious living and spiritual grace in his life. This is as obviously an
intense realization of experience and certainly an imaginative one as is a
more representational or "realistic" method, though it may require a cultivation of understanding and sensibility to share the artist's attitudes or
to simulate personal ones on a parallel plane of serious purpose.

The delightful drawing of a first grader (page 33) shares in the more
mature artist's quality of realization of experience, though the level of
conscious creativity may be quite different. The spontaneously painted
image of the self in rather droll relationship to the flowered surroundings
is also symbolically expressive of a larger and personally felt sense of
existence that somehow extends on into an infinite universe. Yet the

[5] Piet Mondrian, "Plastic Art and Pure Plastic Art," *Documents of Modern Art,*
(New York: Wittenborn and Company, 1945), Vol. 2, p. 10.

child has made her encounter with the mysterious but wonderful experience of sentience, into a concrete form. She has transformed the searching yet ineffable qualities of her young life into a visual symbol. She has perceived her own state of being, realized it with an intensity that led to an artistic response. In the process she has learned something; she has had a vivid moment; she has perhaps allayed a fear and affirmed a feeling; she has structured an idea and embodied an emotion. All of this could not have occurred without a freely functioning imagination.

ART, AN IMAGINATIVE SYMBOL OF EXPERIENCE

The various art forms then imaginatively structure life's experiences so that they may be more fully realized. It is always a personal kind of experience because it is involved with the subjective conditions of living: emotions and values, as well as the objective ones: sense data, physical manipulation, and reason. It brings the two levels of experience together and shapes them into a new whole. This is in keeping with the individual artist's vision and results in a unique symbolic configuration. Yet, the artist's realization of his experience, while it develops and enhances his own sentience also provides a bridge between himself and other people. Art is a channel through which experience is shared in an essential and felt manner. It infuses the individual with a vitality that is different, more sensitive and forceful than ordinary existence, enriching the consciousness beyond its otherwise limited capacities. At the same time it invites a participation in the visions of great men and in the myriad attitudes of countless others. The implications for education are obvious.

However, art is no perfect quality or the complete panacea for the evil, ignorance, insensitivity, triviality, and apathy in society. Like the other modes of man's expression, it has its congenital limitations; its participants do not possess an infallible judgment simply because they are engaged in making or appreciating "beauty" or expressive form. Because of the unique and personal aspect so central to art, the intrinsically "moral" authority of its forms may escape general recognition or acceptance, given the wide diversity of individual temperament and background. Despite the symbolic unity of form and content that the best of art possesses, man tends to analyze and fragment his experience. The relations among the artistic elements, the intellectual awareness, the emotional subject, the aesthetic values, even where they are implied or abstract, are always in a kind of tentative balance that may either ignore or contradict one or another of the parts or vacillate between them. The precision and clarity of execution, the purity of line, color and value in Mondrian's painting may be considered as valid aesthetic experiences. At the same time, the vision of harmonious living may be regarded as a fanciful and foolish dream of a very impractical artist, his concept of the balance and purity of forms as a reflection of "the good life" no more than a static and esoteric belief with no real significance for the mass of men. Similarly, the subject-form plastic tensions in the Roualt may be regarded as arbitrary visual rhythms caused by crude unrefined daubs. Many persons may feel a positive and sublime identification with the disembodied symbol of Christian faith, but find the forms of the painting crude and inappropriate. The girl's painting may be seen as a mere doodle, the nonsensical untutored fancies of the very young that signify nothing. There is no guarantee that art may not imagine a so-called false object or event as well as a true one, call up visions of erroneous understanding or nonexistent chimeras rather than those that may be of material substance and logically affirmed.

What art does provide though, is the variety of media through which experience may be symbolically yet vividly perceived and intensely realized. It is this attribute that commends it as a necessary means in education. The values that are inherent in its fluid structure will be felt by the students as they participate in the experience. These are fundamental, geared to a responsive chord in human nature. Yet they are not complete, they do not preempt the source from which individuals draw their understanding of right and wrong, good and bad, and other moral, ethical, intellectual, and emotional imperatives. This encompasses all of living, not only a part of it.

The Role of Art in Education

Art as a part of the school curriculum may be regarded as the imaginative device by which students may learn and grow through aesthetic expression. It offers a particularly apt and natural channel in addition to the intellectual one that brings about an awarenes of intuitive knowledge as well as a reasoned logical kind. It supports the individual propensities of students at the same time that it opens up the range of other possible responses to experience. It is an open invitation to transform emotion into communicable form.

A student who paints a picture, sings a song, dances a step, or fashions a verse is involved with a direct means of experience. They are not only learning in the very real sense of that word, but they are stimulating their powers of imagination so that all of their experiences, unconscious as well as those that have perceptual clearance, will be intensified and presented in a more vigorous light. They are further, permitting an avenue of expression, that is not only rewarding in its own sense of creative formation, but is basic to the full maturation of the individual as a knowing and alertly responsive person.

This does not insist that each student prepare himself to be an artist. That aim is a rather special affair. Though at the moment of his art experience there is no reason why the school child cannot think and act as an artist in the play of his imagination and his need to express it in some sensuous form. Art is not only the solemn or dedicated involvement of the totally committed individual; it is, as well, broadly engendered and developed in the imaginative potential of experience and transformation that everyone possesses, from the sensuous data of seeing, hearing, and touching and from the emotional sources that feel, are empathetic, and compelling in the wide variety of human ways. All experience is fit for art, its only requirement being its genuineness and its need of realization. Art education should have as its most important aim the opening up of this quality in all students, stimulating and provoking the imagination in a creative way, making the conditions of art, its forms and methods viable, permissable, and expressive for the student.

Appreciation and Participation

This stress in art education therefore has to be twofold—one, that art is an external realization of experience that someone else has created and, two, despite this, that art is also an internal quality, resident in some imaginative degree in all individuals and capable of expression. The first leads to an awareness of the life about, of imaginings perhaps congruent to one's own but still equally separate experiences of appreciation of the world's wonders, delights, and despairs as others have symbolized and formed them through art. It provides a sensitive and empathetic base to sharing experiences, to escaping, if even only as an illusion, from the confines of the self and entering the precincts of other personalities. The appreciative experience may be vicarious at points but it is also a fundamental one. The second affords a direct involvement that shapes a very individual and creative realization of personal experience, offering not only the satisfactions and growth inherent in individual expression, but activating an engagement with the very sources that give meaning to existence.

As an educational device then, art functions as a means of expression which other areas cannot readily fulfill. It is almost impossible for anyone to directly communicate his subjective and singularly colored view of the world. Words tend to generalize the uniqueness of the experience so that what is being discursively expressed is more the universal condition that man shares in the world rather than the particular reception of personal experience in that world. The commonplace characteristics dominate, falsifying or adulterating an honest or more adequate and vivid realization of an individual occurence or thought. The experience is more likely to communicate on a sympathetic or felt level if it is transformed into a sensuous medium when it becomes a picture or a song. It is when this is openly expressed that a vital and an authentic experience may be said to have occurred beyond the ordered exposition of intellectual logic.

Social Relationships

Beyond this, the arts are the reflections of a social order in a very discerning manner. They are the outward manifestations of all of the inner happenings of culture. As such they are the symbolic touchstones of the values of that culture. Though even the artist himself does not always understand the significance of his forms, the art itself, if it is a felt realization of experience, will embody important meanings of any particular period as well as casting light on past times and indicate the shape of things to come. It is a sensitive instrument attuned to the innermost qualities of man.

The values of the contemporary world find their ways into the diverse styles and forms of today's art. However, they are most clearly seen in the apparent divisions between the serious or fine art forms and those of the popular variety. The latter appear to satisfy the average tastes, despite the fact that their mass production and standardization render the critical faculties and the basic "hunger for beauty" futile. The indolent responses so ubiquitously reflected in the comics, in mail order catalogs, in most of the Hollywood movies or television programs, in the greater mass of advertising and public illustration, not only manifest the lack of artistic merit of the forms but they support the notion that average, commonplace needs will accept an environment devoid of any real commitment to values beyond the practical and the distracting. Yet, it cannot be said that there is any real lack of opportunity to experience the fine arts; there are more numerous avenues of access than ever before. There simply is no great yearning or groundswell of genuine sentiment in that direction. This bespeaks, not only a personal deficiency on the part of the countless individuals who exist in a state, relative to the arts, as one of torpor and apathy, but a lack in the educational patterns of the schools, which seeks practical or intellectual excellence yet accepts aesthetic sloth. If education does have responsibilities, they are toward the full development of students and an influence on the social milieu. Just as the individual student has to act himself out, attempting to achieve an authentic self, so a culture strives to epitomize its worth in its art as well as in the other areas of human endeavor. In both situations, the single and the group, there is an encumbent responsibility in education to present the most vital realization of the experience of existence in more than a vouchsafed manner.

Students tend to express cultural values in their art work. "Folk Dance," Sixth Grade Drawing. [New York Public Schools; PHOTO: *S. Martin Friedman]*

This necessitates the conditions of fine art which cannot lend themselves to abridgment or adulteration, but have to be fully affirmed in a passionate way. This is summed up very adequately by August Heckscher:

. . . But the real reason for the fosterng of art is, I suggest, that art is important in the life of the people, and that without it the political community falls short of its ideal potentialities.

"It is through the forms of art, I have been arguing, that the inherent tendencies of a civilization are made visible and potent. And it is through the enjoyment of art . . . that the public happiness is ultimately attained. The beginning of the long separation of art and politics saw the withdrawal of painting and sculpture from public places, from the churches and squares and buildings of the city, to become the adornment of the homes of private citizens. The typical museum was at its start a closed collection, and only gradually became a place for people to visit. The tradition of private ownership of art has persisted, no doubt greatly enriching individual lives. It has led, in the age of mass democracy, to the tendency for art to be adulterated, commercialized, consumed. What we need to restore is not so much the love of art—that has never vanished—but the tradition of art as a source of common enjoyment, a focus for the pleasures and delights of the citizenry.[6]

These beliefs may then blossom into the personal visions that art generates, creating one area of moral authority in means and ends that clearly finds its source in a natural and particularly characteristic human activity.

THE CONDITIONS OF ART

The aims of art in education can only be realized if there is an understanding of the conditions of art. Admittedly, these conditions do not lend themselves to simple categories or precise definition. Nevertheless, there are a sufficient number of general characteristics that provide a necessary theoretical and educational direction.

Art possesses a dynamic quality, a moving, living force that permits it to mesh with the vital energies of human activity. Similarly, art education when it is of positive value in the schools reflects a dynamic interaction between the student and his experiences resulting in the creative process and a shaping of forms. These forms and processes synthesize the many strands of human activity, the emotional and the reasoned, the abstract nature of ordered design and the concrete presence of sensory response, the need for expression and the search for understanding, bringing together the frequently disparate elements into a realizable unit.

This realized unit of expressed experience possesses the additional benefit of being concrete. It has tangible properties, though it may have transformed intangible feelings. As such, it is somewhat unique as an educational device because it provides an immediate and relatively complete means of giving shape to a learning experience in other than the more normal pedagogical abstraction that is also usually a fragment of a larger understanding.

This shaping process is a natural one for students of all ages, but most

[6] August Heckscher, *The Public Happiness* (New York: Atheneum, 1962), p. 282.

particularly of the elementary years. The elan and spontaneity with which young children approach their art work is an indication of the direct means that art and its creative possibilities offer as an educational channel in the schools. This creative joy and expressive fulfillment answer some basic human needs; its natural charm and emotional attraction are another of its characteristic elements.

Parallel to the natural creative quality that art provides for students is the aesthetic factor which is another basic condition of art. The ease with which a young child will accept the pleasure of drawing, the thrill of a brush stroke, the marvel of colors combining, the feeling of mass in a clay project, or of texture in a construction, reflects the completeness of the artistic experience, the fact that its doing or appreciation is an end in itself. The experience of making or appreciating art is thus self-sufficient and largely given over to the aesthetic. It provides an area of student realization that does not have to be useful or instrumental towards other ends. The aesthetic experience is both a condition of art education and one of its goals leading to personal satisfaction that does not depend upon complex, extraordinary, or devious combinations of endeavor and under-standing. Yet because it is complete in itself, it is of invaluable assistance in the general learning atmosphere, helping the student to integrate what might otherwise remain as diverse fragments of knowledge and under-standing.

Invention, improvisation, imaginative imagery, and discovery are also attendant conditions of art in education, because they are fundamental to the process of making artistic forms. These have become desired character-istics in the education process, so that they may well be of broad conse-quence when they are motivated during the art lesson. A sure hallmark of successful art teaching lies in the presence of these qualities and they are indispensible to individual development.

Some other conditions that merit mention (and which will be referred at greater length elsewhere) are the intensity and fullness of observation, the rich associations, the originality of insight, the enhanced perceptions and the developed sense of discrimination of parts and qualities. These are all a part of the experience of art education.

In summary, in order to determine and achieve any of the goals of art education, it is essential that the conditions that make for art or art appreciation be appropriately understood. Though no predetermined list-ing is possible, certain large groupings of attributes stand out, such as the aesthetic, the interrelatedness of various human faculties, the direct spontaneity of approach, the inventiveness leading to discovery, and the sense of creative joy even when the experience is frustrating or difficult.

Art can be considered as one of the guides towards a more meaningful response to experience and a more intense realization of that experience, providing a unique yet genuine insight into living. As an educational channel it fits naturally into the curriculum. It offers a means of learning and growing experience that other areas cannot provide easily. It aims at no less than the full exploitation of each student's potential.

Finally, art education aims to unify through its activities the many faceted attributes, potentialities, and understandings of any, one, and of all students. It brings together the emotions and the intellect, intuition and logic, fusing imaginative play with concrete technique, personal identification with cultural mores, expressing the general values of a society or a time or a place, while it stresses the uniqueness and separateness of the aesthetic element. As a synthesized aim, it may be said that the teaching of art creates opportunities for a fuller quality of living, at once more speculative and intrinsically rewarding, more personally inventive and adventuresome, and individually pertinent in that it invokes the unique wellsprings of creatively expressive and aesthetic play that each person possesses.

These goals are implicit in any successful teaching of art. They may be properly implemented if the teaching designed to elicit them is artistic itself. The art classroom has to be a workshop—a workshop of forms and fancies, of visions and techniques, of symbols and expression and of play and problem resolution. It should embody all of the romantic but serious atmosphere of an artist's studio coupled with the alertness and vivacity of an inspired classroom. Then, the most natural aims of achieving self-realization have an opportunity to succeed, as well as the parallel aims of mastery of environment and positive sense of community.

3

Contending Ideas in the Teaching of Art

> Humane learning, it seems to me, has as its principal aim the education of what we quaintly call the human predicament, that is, the eternal conflict between the aspirations and frustrations of man. Its subjects, or rather its companions in this enterprise, are philosophy and art in the widest sense of these two great words. The object of learning is coterminous with the object of philosophy, and the object of art is to seek that stay against confusion, which is joy.
>
> HOWARD MUMFORD JONES

NOT only is there the bewildering multiplicity of contemporary visual impressions mentioned in another chapter, there is a parallel profusion of concepts and influences that dog the heels of education. The variegated contrasts of contending ideas may stimulate the enthusiastic mind but it can also burden the teacher who is seeking a salutary philosophy; it usually bewilders the student who is attempting to discover the most appropriate methods to take into an art teaching career, or in implementing the aims of art education.

THE PITFALLS OF EDUCATIONAL FASHION

Art education has a particularly wide variety of viewpoints which in one sense may be an indication of its vitality. However, on another level, it is rife with attitudes and prescriptions that frequently conflict with one another. Even when there is no opposition between differing ideas, unless the relationships are clearly pointed up, there is a dubious complementing of various concepts. This is somewhat compounded in that art reflects durable concerns with continuing art values which have extended through all the expressive centuries of man's consciousness of his aesthetic self. This contrasts sharply with the great velocity of intellectual and social change predicated characteristically on values of commercial, scientific, and technological progress. The teaching of art has to bridge this gap, while the individual teacher is faced with developing a personal synthesis out of the divergent and multiple viewpoints.

The last few generations have been schooled to think of methodological fashion, disguised often as valid change, as inherently progressive. Fashion becomes a key attitude not only in the latest dress style, automobile grill, or book-of-the-month, but in ideas, in educational and even institutional values. Though an open and flexible mind is essential to teaching, there are dangers in the constant treadmill of innovation or even periodic improvisations that are forever supposed to be progressive, but are in reality an unexamined commitment to novelty.

Though change, as stated earlier, is a necessary and indeed an organic factor in all existence and an open attitude toward it is essential to creative and maturing processes, both social and individual, its being equated with the arbitrary fashion of the day makes for superficially determined viewpoints, shallow behavior, and thin education. Too often the fashionable change is slavishly accepted and it then degenerates into fad more readily than we are prone to admit. The deeper and more abiding sense of individual purpose and social goals are then lost sight of and eventually mangled. Many of the public and private symbols vacillate in their meaning, developing a cloud of obfuscation for the teacher who would interpret them for his students. The symbols of fashion rarely offer stable teaching connotations or understanding of more than superficial merit. The subsequent confusion does not permit any more than the rudiments of important human values to emerge from the classroom. The process of personal growth—the existential idea of becoming—remains a tentative or circumscribed one. The collectively held attitudes sporadically break through one's consciousness as momentary instances of great immediacy, but are little more than a succession of narrowly topical concerns.

In art education, for example, we see this sporadically coming to the surface with such teaching enthusiasms as finger painting more than a generation ago or chip-knife carving farther back in time or the sudden interest in the twenties in Greek and Egyptian design motifs that children had to copy laboriously. More recently, such interests as copper enameling or mosaic tablemaking have found their way in the upper levels while the idea of junk art and infinite experimentation with literally hundreds of materials permeates the whole range of school. It is not only materials and processes but philosophical attitudes that are arbitrarily altered as well.

Yet paradoxically, the diversity, the rapid tempo, and the stress on a changing fashion is peculiarly counterbalanced by the national tendency to excessive conformity. This rather odd note, may be an attempt to fix certain values so that they do not disappear into the limbo of yesterday's newspaper, demonstrating the difficulty of accepting true change. Or perhaps the profound changes that stem from the dynamics of our society are felt, at a great distance from the center, by the average individual through the easily acceptable artifice of fashion which, at the same time, insists upon a firm conformity that guards against the disintegrating nature of rapid change. Whatever the underlying factors, the prospective teacher has to come to grips with them in his or her own manner. This can only be done if they are broadly cognizant of the past and structurally pertinent ideas in their area as well as the contending current ones. Openly and honestly examined the forces that nurtured structure and change can be more readily understood and creatively converted into the qualities of a salubrious teaching experience.

There is a great variety of individual teaching methods in art education. Most of the approaches can be successful if there is a classroom enthusiasm and an adherence to the natural qualities of art. [Elementary School; University of Michigan News Service]

THEORETICAL RANGE OF ART EDUCATION

The teacher of art has a seemingly prodigal choice of avenues of approach to teaching; there is a proliferation of theory and an embarrassment of riches in the sources that in one way or another relate to art. He may concentrate on the "whole" child, considering the inherent qualities of the aesthetic and creative experience as one among other important factors that develop the ideal individual. He may focus on what is sensory and immediately "meaningful" in the art experience for the individual, building on this for the student an awareness of his own creative endeavors as well as the art work of others. The teacher may study the developmental stages of children, carefully plotting the maturation process, then deliberately design art activities that are commensurate with each stage of growth. He may utilize the environmental concept that suggests the most rewarding art experience for children is to be found in the patterns and objects of his own everyday living in a kind of aesthetic functionalism and responsible citizenship. Or he may insist upon the inculcation of perceptual or manipulatory skills that supposedly derive from the creative and/or craftsmanlike process.

On the other hand, there may be stress on the analytical and appreciative traits to be engendered as a base for the necessary empathies and insights of a mature relationship with art. The teacher may stimulate self expression for its own sake as an appropriately desirable emotional characteristic or point to the remedial and therapeutic nature of creative work. He may give prominence to the notion of artistic criteria and standards that emerge from a work of art rather than from the so-called student's needs or he may bring together the art work with other subject areas integrating it as a visualization and expression of interdisciplinary values. Then too, the art class may concentrate on providing a playful dabbling that may become a satisfying personal agility with art to fill the otherwise "empty and wasteful" leisure hours that the greater majority of Americans, workers and white collar alike, may look forward to as against the art teacher who may have a vision of school art as a fulfilling and continuing experience of aesthetic quality that will cut across all the hours of a person's life, providing an expressive and creative base for individual satisfaction.

There are numerous other attitudes, each exerting an influence, commanding a following, and overlapping one another. But whether we generalize in a product-process, a child-subject, or individual-society manner, the oppositions or better the polarities, become a confusing array of pedagogies. Though the antagonisms may be artificially imposed and the polarities really ends of a continuum, there is no doubt that some of the attitudes mentioned do conflict with one another when they are dogmatically utilized as desirable methods in a classroom. Of course, all of the factors that have a bearing on the development of children and of consequent teaching attitudes are important; it is the points of stress and the multiple paralleling of concepts which cause the concern for the teacher seeking an amenable philosophy.

In addition, to reiterate, the teacher of art must face up to the opposing ideas of what is to be prized in contemporary life. Though there is a burgeoning of art activity and a corresponding acceptance of a creative involvement, there is also the common supposition that the values of art are peripheral in the dynamics of current society. The acceptance of creative behavior cannot be generally assumed; where it is evidenced, it tends to be tentative, hesitant, and suspicious, always with one eye on the stock market, the productive machinery, or on the button that may send ballistic missiles flying across oceans. In this atmosphere that is further thickened with the lightly held beliefs but overwhelming prejudices of popular culture, it may be somewhat difficult for the teacher of art to disentangle the myriad and confusing values.

Early Development

The teaching of art in the schools has had a history that only infrequently touched that of the history of art itself. In the United States it has been closely allied to the development of public education and popular culture. The spread and shape of public education evidences the social, political, and psychological pressures of the society that was forming it and often mirrors the interests of mass culture.

In a like manner art education has reflected many of the theoretical suppositions, practical applications, and inherent pressures of general education. This has tended to shape the teaching of art, as it has other subject areas, more often in response to external considerations than in terms of the internal structure of a given subject area. The essentially significant qualities of art as it is created within the context of an artist's understanding have played only an incidental role in the development of art education, while the adjunctive considerations of vocation, social adjustment, psychological development, citizenship, leisure planning, and well rounded personality among a host of others have had a changing but extremely influential effect on the direction of the teaching of art in the public schools. This is more apparent in elementary education than secondary, but exists on both levels.

Though drawing instruction existed in the schools prior to the Civil War, it was not until after 1870 that a deliberate and organized attempt was made to include art in the school curriculum. In the early decades of the nineteenth century, as the birth pangs of public education subsided and the attendant prescriptive attitudes deepened into a severely restricted intellectual emphasis, the pattern of the three R's emerged: reading, 'riting and 'rithmetic. Little room was permitted for the fancies—the later "frills and fads" of the art experience. The frontier pushing society that moved ever westward and the growing industrial revolution made its own demands that permitted little if any intimacy with an aesthetic culture, particularly for the sake of what was generally regarded as a vain and wasteful use of time. The practical considerations of the surroundings, the business of wresting a livelihood from the land, the exigencies of factory labor could not countenance an intent concern for art.

Yet it was the requirements of the industrial revolution itself that prompted the systematic introduction of drawing in the schools, thus formalizing the inclusion of art in the curriculum. Farnum, in a brief historical essay writes, "In the middle of the nineteenth century . . . a group of industrialists in Massachusetts came to the conclusion that skill in drawing and a knowledge of historic forms of ornament were essential to their manufacture, and later, in 1870, an act of the state legislature was passed permitting drawing ("industrial and mechanical") to be "freely" taught in any city and town, and making "free" instruction compulsory in cities and towns of over 10,000 inhabitants." [1]

Horace Mann, whose influence in early American education was both profound and salubrious, was particularly wedded to an extension of the curriculum to include more than the three R's. "Drawing is a form of writing and should be taught with it." [2] Fred Logan, in commenting on Mann's inclusion of drawing as an appropriate experience for school children rightly interprets this dictum as ". . . the copying of forms." [3] Though there was a vague hope of fostering some kind of "artistic" experience there was no real sense of the aesthetic needs of children, of expressive quality or of creative capacity that entered into the beginning ideas

[1] R. B. Farnum, "The Early History of Art Education," *Fortieth Yearbook NSSE, Art in American Life and Education* (Bloomington, Ill.: Public School Publishing Co., 1941), p. 446.
[2] Frederick Logan (quoting Mann), *Growth of Art in American Schools* (New York: Harper and Bros., 1955), p. 21.
[3] *Ibid.*, p. 21.

of art education, or the appreciation of art for its own sake, for that matter. The drawing slate was to be taken away if the children "played" with it. Rather, "Horace Mann admired drawing . . . because (it) . . . might answer the criticism that the schools did little for the future mechanic or industrial worker. Manual skill, accurate judgment of line and proportion, ought to be good background for a shipwright, a book-keeper, a weaver, a carpenter, indeed all tradesman." [4]

It was this strong vocational interest, the desire to educate adequately trained personnel for the manufacture of general consumer needs and to staff a blossoming technology that prompted the inclusion of art in the schools. It was to be a pedagogical device in its simplest and most utilitarian manner, not complementing the three R's but supplementing them in a much lower form. This is a far cry from the revolutionary new thinking, for instance, of one of the finest American designers of the later nineteenth century, the architect Louis H. Sullivan. He was developing the visual symbols and intellectual concepts among which was the fertile idea that "form follows function" which laid the groundwork for Frank Lloyd Wright and a later modern design that was not confined to architecture alone. He wrote in his *Kindergarten Chats*:

When the mind is actively and vitally at work, for its own creative uses, it has no time for word building: words are too clumsy: you have no time to select and group them. Hence you must think in terms of images, of pictures, of states of feeling, of rhythm. The well trained, well organized and well-disciplined mind works with remarkable rapidity and with luminous intensity; it will body forth combinations, in mass, so complex, so far-reaching that you could not write them down in years. Writing is but the slow, snail-like creeping of words, climbing laboriously, over a little structure that resembles the thought: meanwhile the mind has gone on and on, here and yonder and back and out and back again.[5]

However, this kind of thinking broadly supporting the idea of art education as expression was several decades in the future in implementation, indicating the depressing lag of genuine change that exists so often between our most developed thinkers and the practices in our educational institutions.

Method and Substance

Early drawing experience was tightly controlled, rigidly prescribed, and periodically progressive in nature, even though there was participation by the student directly with "art." Exacting and craftsmanlike exercises were considered appropriate activities for young children as well as for the teachers in training indicating the stress on method rather than substance that so tenaciously dominates the strictly pedagogical mind. Though we now know that these were too exacting a performance to demand of young children both from a psychological and aesthetic viewpoint, the lingering security of predetermined method is still a potent crutch for many

[4] *Ibid.*, p. 23.
[5] Louis Sullivan, *Kindergarten Chats* (New York: Whittenborn, 1950), p. 50.

teachers. For instance, though art educators have waged a kind of holy war against mimeographed "turkeys for Thanksgiving" and the mass of patterns available to teachers on the elementary level, they are still very much evident in many classrooms. On all levels of art teaching we still find remnants of the ideas of Walter Smith, who became Director of Art Education for Massachusetts in 1872. In his introduction to a teachers' manual, he writes: ". . . thus, sharp points to pencils, and clean hands and rubber, and a book neither dog-eared, defiled, nor crumpled, should be absolutely insisted on; and incorrigibles should be made to draw upon slates only until they can be trusted in contact with white paper without defiling it." [6] The broader admonitions to achieve neatness in art work is redolently reminiscent of this atmosphere. It is most noticeable, however, in crafts, shop and mechanical drawing classes where it, no doubt, is quite necessary though often at the expense of creative design.

Of course the discipline that is supposedly inherent in deliberately controlling the work of the student may be a desirable quality in one aspect of art education. There has been a current and growing emphasis in this direction, of developing visual problems which have defined and more exact aims of learning the elements of art as a basis for their knowing manipulation, providing a visual vocabulary. The stress of a more or less exact experience in art certainly has its value, especially if it induces an experience in depth and particularly when it is set next to the arbitrary and totally undisciplined activity that does occur in a good number of classrooms today. Nevertheless, the stress on procedure and method, the preoccupation with supposed norms of visual understanding is in contrast to the skeptical attitude that most artists have concerning strict formulation in either artistic creation or appreciation. There are no recipes in art other than in the chemical constituents of the materials employed. The realization of form is uniquely arrived at. It may be limited or completely negated if an intrusive methodology impresses and obscures the art itself, if the prescriptions from an earlier time are too deeply ingrained, forming arbitrarily correct patterns of method and substance.

The Arbitrary Synthesis of Practical and Aesthetic Qualities

The vocational stress of art education had an interesting corollary at the time that reflects one of the major controversies in contemporary art education. This revolves about the separation of fine art from industrial art or crafts, the distinctions that are sometimes made between drawing and design, and is important in forming the values that art education tends to support.

During the beginning stages of formal art education there were apparently no distinctions: drawing and crafts training were related and often taught as one. For the child in the nineteenth-century classroom there was no divorce between the utilitarianism of design and the aesthetic significance of drawing (or art in its larger connotations as some art educators

[6] Walter Smith, *Teachers' Manual of Freehand Drawing and Designing* (Boston: 1873).

are wont to imply). The training that prospective teachers received under Smith, if they completed the full course, which was not mandatory, included painting, water color, and sculpture as well as the more vocationally oriented projects such as architectural elevations, diagramatic rendering, and related activities. This "cafeteria" style curriculum has set the pattern, though in a modified manner, for the training of art teachers ever since. What is of importance in this approach is what it led to in the schools. As Logan notes, "The entire curriculum of the first quarter of a century (after the initiation of formal art education) obviously considered drawing and art education generally, and the beginnings of what we now call manual training and shop work, as basically a united study." [7] However, the stress on the mechanical and manipulatory aspects of drawing, the tight idea of one craftsmanship of artistic process, the lean products that lacked general artistic merit as well as expressive power are only a few of the reasons that the unity did not remain. Art went off in a direction that was more promising for its purposes, splitting away from the unoriginal technique emphasis that exists in shop training.

Logan obviously deplores the fact that this separation has occurred and has become a growing practice over the last half century, ascribing this in part to the "growing division of subject-matter fields" that took possession of the schools. He feels there is an artificial separation of art and craft and advocates, "Every trend in industrial and furniture design, in professional art education, in educational philosophy, indicates a reunion of the teaching of the arts and shop crafts in our school systems." (He goes on to emphasize his point.) "Here is an area where the Massachusetts Normal Art School was doing a better job for its time than we are doing today." [8]

However, though we cannot question the unity that probably did exist in the earlier schools, we can look askance at its quality and its appropriateness for the individual child. The very fact that many of the methods that were employed in the late eighteen hundreds are regarded by contemporary art educators as destructive of creative development and niggardly dogmatic in aesthetic insight in itself contradicts the efficacy of the "unified" approach, at least, of that time. Even more damaging, to reiterate, is the quality of the "art" that was produced which with our admittedly hindsight understanding, we refer to as dull, banal, restricted, sentimental, and academic, when it was not garishly flamboyant in its applied design or heavy with pretentiousness. The child was rarely treated as an individual and his art never was regarded as expression. He was merely to train and sharpen one of the faculties which would be socially and economically useful in keeping with the primitive psychological ideas of the day. Though this was to be remedied, if not overly counterbalanced with progressive thought later, and could be blamed on the pressures and prejudices of the times, the implied concept is that the unification of fine art and crafts was and still is a desirable goal, that exists outside of time.

[7] Frederick Logan, *Growth of Art in American Schools* (New York: Harper and Bros., 1955), p. 72.
[8] Frederick Logan, *ibid.*, p. 73.

Actually, what did happen was that the child became a vessel into which was indiscriminately poured the supposed accumulation of artistic technique and a limited aesthetic lore that arbitrarily cut across all of the hierarchies of creative endeavor. And even this is questionable, for what in reality was created did fit into the framework of shoemaking, weaving, carpentry, and tool making, but hardly into the aesthetic framework of art. It was the economic and productive needs of a rapidly accelerating society that dictated the inclusion of art education in the curriculum, not any legitimate ideas of aesthetics or personal expression.

THE SEPARATION OF FINE AND APPLIED ARTS

It was only as the art educators grew in sophistication and understanding, evolving an intrinsically appropriate philosophy that the separation of visual disciplines became not only inevitable, but desirably so. Though there were many surface similiarities between fine art and crafts, there was the emerging recognition of fundamental differences that led to an "art-for-art's-sake" movement, swinging the pendulum far over to another extreme. This was not simply due to the prevailing trend toward a division of labor of a stress on specialization. It was more basically an awareness of philosophical distinctions that insisted upon, in a practical sense, differing educational factors and methods to suit differing ends.

The fine arts are essentially involved with unique, expressive forms that communicate such intangibles as emotion, meaning, and "beauty" for their own sake with no real "use" other than the gratification of aesthetic sensitivity, if one discounts the popular idea of uplifting the mind through "culture." They are concerned with genuine values on a comparatively abstract and conceptual plane but capable of being felt through a sensuous realization and as such create the most intense symbols of meaning a society can produce. While there is an important factor of value in the crafts as well, they usually are utilitarian in outlook. Many of the factors in craft design are given ones, largely predetermined either in terms of tradition, shape, size, or in material and in application, while these design factors are never as binding, if at all, for the fine arts. There are other distinctions which are dealt with elsewhere. It is sufficient to say that a responsible and justifiable argument can be marshalled to support the differences, even when there is an idealistic desire not to do so. This understanding, either consciously or not, led to the separation that may have occurred simply because it had to, just as the development of creative expression in the fine arts was gradually divorced from the work of artisans or others engaged in utilitarian production of a visual nature.

Historical Perspectives

There are many historical and cultural reasons for this perhaps unfortunate but necesary dichotomy, though they are amply documented in many other books and would, in this space require much too lengthy a dissertation. Only the main points can be briefly mentioned. The simpler and

more cohesive productive schemes of primitive societies permitted, indeed encouraged, the integration of the symbolic, the purely decorative—the aesthetic aspects of a piece of work with its utilitarian values. The early artist-craftsman had an artistic Eden in which to create that was not complicated by the intricacies of an overly complex and multileveled culture. In the relative innocent simplicity of his cave or hut he fashioned objects and forms which naturally blended the aesthetic and utilitarian into masterful works of art. However, when the complexity of a developing society did come into play and the productive systems assumed an instrumental as well as a class intricacy, the pristine relationship was shattered. As Dewey notes, "The divorce of useful and fine art signifies even more than does the departure of science from the traditions of the past. The difference was not instituted in modern times. It goes as far back as the Greeks when the useful arts were carried on by slaves, and 'base mechanics' and shared in 'the low esteem' in which the latter were held. Architects, builders, sculptors, painters, musical performers were artisans. Only those who worked in the medium of words were esteemed artists, since their activities did not involve the use of hands, tools and physical materials." [9] This changed little during the Middle Ages and through the

[9] John Dewey, *Art as Experience* (New York: Minton, Balch, 1934), p. 341.

beginnings of the Renaissance when art was still regarded as common to all of the processes of manufacture. Art was considered an essential part of the artisan's training in the master-pupil and guild atmosphere, a necessary condition of his performance as a workman. A knowing understanding of the elements of art, of color, of drawing, of composition were as necessary as computation, tool handling, and crafts techniques. Artisans were not visual philosophers, pursuers of dreams, or symbolic creators though in fact their work often reached these heights. Though his efforts upheld a sacred doctrine, the artisan was not always regarded as one of the elite. This was changing, however, as the patterns of the Renaissance became bolder and more clear. It is only during the high Renaissance that the artist achieves the pinnacle described by Battista Alberti in 1436, "Painting contains . . . this virtue that any master painter who sees his work adored will feel himself considered another god." [10] But painting and sculpture had by this time been divorced from the more utilitarian concerns that controlled it in the preceding centuries. Though the content was religious, the utilization of art in a didactic function had changed so drastically from the Byzantine times that one can paradoxically claim that Renaissance art despite its subject matter was a celebration of man's secular nature, and that the artist was a divine being who "makes the dead seem alive." The symbolic and the aesthetic factors are the most important here, while the crass functions of utility have been left far behind.

Though the Renaissance artist still combined in his image the qualities of an artisan and designer (he planned buildings, laid out gardens, formulated mathematical theorems, and built objects that were not painting and sculpture), he actually was creating monuments, the "practical" utility of which was only a secondary concern. A Michelangelo or a Leonardo was very much different in kind from the artisans that had preceded them and their own contemporary journeymen craftsmen. They ushered in on one level, and a revolutionary one, the division between the fine arts and the useful that is a part of the modern consciousness and was heightened later by such solitary giants as Rembrandt, Goya, Van Gogh, and Picasso. However, the divinity of the artist has become a more likely modern counterpart, the "genius" of the artist. Painting and sculpture may not be the only forms of creative expression today that have a fundamentally indivisible quality of aesthetics, nor the artist the only and relatively "pure" creative spirit. However, they are still largely regarded, not only by the critics, but by the lay public as well as the essential core of the fine arts, exploring its fundamental intrinsic nature as well as its spiritual relevance to man.

Internal Pressures of Technology

It was not until the advent of the Industrial Revolution that this became a clear and recognized demarcation—the distinction between artist and artisan. The increasing complexity of production could not allow for the

[10] Leon Battista Alberti, *On Painting*, trans. John R. Spencer, (New Haven: Yale University Press, 1956), p. 63.

conditions that nurtured the earlier workers; it could not tolerate the spread of time, the lacks of specialization of labor and the essentially wasteful behavior, in productive terms, of the aesthetically inclined artisan. As is obvious in our surroundings, the machine has come to dominate our means of production and in its first century of development, it almost totally ignored the aesthetic quality of its products. As a parallel development, popular culture has pursued the aim of democratic profit, catering to the least common denominator of taste. This created a situation in which the artistic forms were severed from their traditional places in the scheme of production. New architecture, painting, sculpture, and other high graphic means came to be associated with the studio and artist, and all other products were relegated to the workshop and the craftsman. Educationally, this led to the independent art school that was meant for the professional and the establishment of official academies that presumed to regulate the tastes of the artists and their patrons. The common man was left with his labors and his mechanical operations that were devoid of most aesthetic qualities. The manufacturing processes themselves were predicated on efficiency, utility, and economy, profit being the prime motivation. The idea of beauty of form, of grace, of design, of aesthetic delight, or of spiritual expression disappeared or was aborted in vulgar terms when related to products of manufacture. If any art was to be a part of the manufacturing process, it was something that was added to the essentially mechanical means of production, rather than integrated with it. This led to the appalling taste and unmitigated ugliness of the general products that flooded the early consumer and industrial markets. The international exhibitions of art and manufactured goods such as the one in London in 1851

The craftsman who combines technical skill with the traditional cultivation of sensitive and artistic forms is a disappearing element in contemporary society. [Corning Glass Works]

or the Centennial Exposition in Philadelphia in 1876 literally showed acres of tasteless and "horrendous" design. The spirit of the times aesthetically is summed up by Oliver Larkin as, ". . . whether it took the form of a picture or a chair, a statue or a stove, it must be a prevarication, a torturing of materials up to their limits of endurance." [11]

Accommodations and Reactions

Obviously, the fruitful relationship that had earlier existed between the normal daily experiences of mankind and the more timeless aspects of art had ceased to function as a serious force. In the nineteenth century, if the two were bound together, not only was the utilitarian object made a travesty of taste, but art itself became trite, spurious, and shallowly academic. It has been indicated that it was largely the economics of production which brought about this separation. This is more profoundly supported by the American philosopher of the times, Henry Adams, who said the break occurred when the Virgin ceased to be a power and became merely a picture—when the Dynamo became the new symbol of veneration. Thorsten Veblen, the economist-philosopher, pointed out that conspicuous consumption became an index of great wealth, art being one of the conspicuously consumed "commodities"; therefore, it could not be bound up with the ordinary or the currently created popular styles. Whatever the reason, the educated individual turned to the forms of the past to satisfy his aesthetic needs while the creative artist pursued his own images. This is one of the reasons that in architecture, for instance, we saw a neoclassicism arise, with many buildings aping the façades of Greek and Roman temples. The artist who catered to this backward looking, painted and sculpted in a manner reminiscent of past glories and his "kitsch" or popular counterpart in a soft sentimental glow that applauded uncritical taste and gave rise to what is commonly called "calendar art," the darling and criterion of popular taste.

There was a reaction as well in the actual philosophy of the means of production. William Morris and John Ruskin in England were passionate advocates of a return to handwork, to the satisfactions of personal creation before the mechanical age that served mankind's needs. Morris advocated a guild system, in a kind of medievalistic fervor, wherein the workman still had control of manufacture of an object from beginning to end in an atmosphere which affirmed the values of wholeness and craftsmanship. He insisted that the industrial processes pauperized man's spiritual and aesthetic nature as well as making poor robots out of the workmen. His views were influential and flowed into the thinking of American art educators, supplementing the ideas of "art for art's sake" with an emphasis on the joys of "handwork." However, the concept was foredoomed to failure, for the machine was not to be denied; a return to the guild system was like turning the clock back, denying hundreds of years of history. Ignoring the economic and political implications of Morris' ideas, the translation of the

[11] Oliver Larkin, *Art and Life in America* (New York: Rinehart, 1949), p. 240.

primacy of handwork into American art class practices had only a thin veneer and an inescapable flavor of watered down dilletantism, without the supporting social structure.

THE EMERGING SIGNIFICANCE OF MODERN FINE ART

Of much more significance was the modern spirit that became evident in the new artists, which necessarily paralleled an alienation from the moral and artistic ugliness of the industrial age. This encompassed the rehabilitation of the artist both as a spokesman-creator of his times and as a maker of symbolic forms. In the former case, the artist was to claim a new spirit of artistic and personal freedom which would unhinge his dependence on older visual and empty aesthetic conventions, while in the making of forms he was to be provocative, experimental, and insistent upon a vital aesthetic integrity that was sufficient unto itself, not requiring the plaudits of the mass of people or the representation of an academic reality. He generated private myths in new forms which later became the conscience of his culture. The artist could then be restored to a sense of values appropriate to his reason for being. He and his work had no neeed to be justified in the marketplace. This resulted in an unfortunate but necessary estrangement from the public and provided little ground for mutual understanding. Yet the artist was then unencumbered, permitting a free play of his emotions, intellect and spirit and his sympathies for the visual material with which he was concerned. Artists such as Cezanne, Van Gogh, Rodin, and later, Picasso, Mondrian, Miro, and countless others in a variety of visual disciplines thus ushered in and intensified the modern spirit in art which has developed in a lusty and unabashed manner over the last century. This new spirit of the artist, either as a "hero" image of integrity, as a uniquely committed being, as a romantic rebel and visionary, or as a freewheeling speculator, producing an art that was justifiable both in its own terms and as an aesthetic measure of man, has never really found its way into public art education. Though the forms that he has created have had a very undisputed influence, it is more because they seeped into the thinking of the art teacher almost by osmosis rather than enthusiastic or deliberate acceptance.

The separation between the fine and the so-called applied arts was an accomplished fact. Nevertheless, the desire to re-engage the two elements in a fruitful unity has never really disappeared from the thinking, not only of art educators, but of social critics and many designers themselves. The stress on the integrated social needs of aesthetics and utility, of the dynamo and the palette, underlies much of contemporary philosophy in the teaching of all of the humanities as well as in art education. John Dewey put the idea succinctly, "As long as art is the beauty parlor of civilization, neither art nor civilization is secure." [12] This sentiment colored the thinking of much theory in art education during the first half of this century.

[12] John Dewey, *Art as Experience* (New York: Minton, Balch, 1934), p. 344.

THE IDEAL OF PRAGMATIC AIMS IN ART EDUCATION

The very decades that see art developing as a symbolic form that is deliberately detached from the consciousness of everyday living, give birth to a parallel exhortation on the part of philosophers and educators to bring the two together. This may be a deliberate response to the undesirability of a fragmented situation, but it does not always take into consideration the very factors that produce the insecure and disconnected yet necessarily divided parts of our society. Education should be encouraged to teach toward ideal goals, but with a clear recognition of the obstacles and dangers that lie in the path and the real goals that are actually achieved. The commitment to a broad and democratic base in education cannot permit any statement of aims other than the best and most exhaustive kind of curriculum, geared as much to the individual as it is to society. Obviously this would include the productive means of our current technology, the consumer goods it supplies, the everyday environment that it creates and the development on the part of the student of a personal and discriminating sensibility, so that the environment and the objects in it will be collectively pleasing as well as aesthetically and individually rewarding.

There have been many scholars and other interested observers who have given their attention and thinking to this attitude, attempting to set up an interrelatedness between the various arts and the current technology of society. The aesthetic ideas are similar to those that were so much in evidence at the Bauhaus and articuated by such artist teachers as Albers, Kandinsky, Bayer, and Gyorgy Kepes who transposed some of the ideas to the United States along with Moholy-Nagy. Others such as Herbert Read, Lewis Mumford, Sigfried Gideon, and John Kouwenhoven are only among the better known advocates of establishing lines across the qualities of art and those of a machine culture. There are many who would favor the integration of art and industry, seeing or implying the necessity as well as the desirability of a designed world. In art education, Fred Logan is one of the most sincere, convincing, and articulate of these advocates, suggesting that the designer is the appropriate and more necessary image for art education to emulate, rather than the esoteric, aloof, obscure, and somewhat exotic fine artist. They point to the actual conditions that set mass aesthetic patterns: the houses that people live in and the prevailing concepts of interior design, the buildings that are otherwise serving productive functions and the booming ideas of architecture, the commercial advertising, illustration, and typography that underlay so much of normal daily vision, the expanding fields of industrial design, photography, and the various other applied areas through which art considerations are provided for everyone. These, it is argued, are the very stuff out of which the average consciousness of art is developed; consequently, they must be a central thesis in the spread of artistic knowledge and sensibility. This leads to the belief that art may ethically redirect the energies of mankind into the development of newer, more positive, functionally proper, and aesthetically pleasant environment.

*The blend of fine
and applied arts was
a natural condition
in less complex and
primitive cultures.
This Mexican
Funeral Urn is a
typical example of
the daily products
combining aesthetic
design and craft
created in pretechno-
logical societies.
[Collection, IBM]*

Art Education and "Vernacular" Design

Kouwenhoven's thesis of the "vernacular" sources of design, for example, can easily serve as one of the theoretical structures for an art education which aims at sensitizing the student to the need and quality of good design based upon vital, meaningful experience encountered in normal existence. The supposedly characteristic democratic yet functional responses to the problems of a surrounding technology and a mass culture can serve as the aesthetic base of form.

The intricacies and involvements of the design process and the approaches of the designer would become the fundamental basis for the development of experience in art education. Though this would not always, or even frequently, rely upon the specifics of commercial designing, the philosophical considerations of craft, social living, self expression, and contemporary attitudes toward technology and its popular visual manifestations would blend into a supporting presence, even if they were not always actively referred to.

With this in mind, many of the current experiences in art education have at least an indirect goal of fashioning a kind of functional sensibility. On the one hand this takes the method of extolling the "well" designed factors in technology, valuing the contributions of the commercial, industrial, and interior designers, building an appreciation of pragmatic everyday visual objects that are not intrinsically objectionable. On the other hand, in a complementary way, there are many craft techniques that are taught from mosaic to enamelling, from pottery to wood carving, from plastics to metal forming. These acquaint the student with "problems" similar to the ones that designers have to "solve." Though the activities overlap in the junior high and high schools, the processes are shared by the shop teacher as well as the art teacher though rarely with any communication between the two. On the elementary level they are normally in the domain of the art specialist or the self-contained classroom teacher who feels competent enough to teach the techniques. The unfortunate aspect is that all too often, and usually unknowingly, the intrinsic art values are either sloughed off in a frenzy of handwork for its own sake, distorted as a tool that makes an otherwise bland utilitarian object "pretty," or thinned out to a picayune concern with effects. Educators in an attempt to counteract this reflect a very prevalent attitude that art for the child cannot be thought of in the same way as art for the artist. They state there would be less general misunderstanding if another term, such as creative thinking or creative process replaced the term art for the works of children.

This is fundamentally an unfortunate attitude, because it does not really reflect the positive aim so widely held that "Every craft should help the aesthetic growth of the child and bring about a greater awareness of the art and beauty in the world about him" [13] Surely this is a simplification, though still a truth that can be said exists between art and artist as well. The fact remains though, that there are differences, not only in nomenclature, but in kind, that put as much value on a trivial, momentary, and easily satisfied desire such as in collectively making a "Christmas gift for Mom," as it does upon a quest for symbolic expression in a personally demanding form of art with its insistence upon aesthetic and spiritual considerations. Just as important is the dependence upon a kind of "creative thinking"—which for the most part has not really been clearly defined to anyone's satisfaction, yet skirts the true mystery of creativity. The feeling, empathetic, and ambiguously imaginative yet functionally present considerations, that are a part of the creative process as it relates to making art, shaping forms, rather than making objects is denied its central significance. As important, is the condition in the art class, that does not question many of the values that are a part of the designing process today. Perhaps an art class is no place to seriously examine sociological, ethical, or other adjunctive considerations, but where one should primarily be involved with

[13] Edward Mattil, *Meaning in Crafts*, (Englewood Cliffs, N.J.: Prentice Hall, 1959), p. 133.

*New conceptual
explorations into the
relationships of
design, function, and
engineering develop
novel visual forms
from vernacular
sources. The Army's
Solar Furnace.*
[PHOTO: *U.S. Dept.
of Defense*]

resolving artistic problems and creating form. Yet, it is, perhaps, impossible to divorce the value aspects of both the processes and products of art and their significance to the individual as not only individual expression but as social taste making. The advocates of design oriented art education support this contention. What is questionable is the emphasis given to the problem solving technique that is employed, to the utopian presentations that generally refuse to take stock of the real state of the "designed" environment and to the instrumental values of art that are supposedly the road to developed personalities. Art, indeed, becomes a quality which in its intangible, intense, and mystifying ways may be dispensed with, its remaining "methods" of insight and creation, not as self transcendant factors, but as almost practical tools with which to get on with the world's work.

THE NEED FOR VALUE APPRAISAL OF TECHNOLOGICAL DESIGN IN ART EDUCATION

It certainly is, at the very least, somewhat confusing to remove the term art from art education. This is much more disastrous when it leads to an involvement with the marginal values of a consumer society that merely requires entertainment in its art rather than expression, practical value rather than a difficult wisdom, social adjustment rather than individual commitment, fun in its creative processes rather than fulfillment, and hobby, do-it-yourself, by-the-numbers "merriment" rather than significant creation of form. Certainly, most art educators, support the more profound aims of art education, upholding the intrinsic values of the aesthetic experience. Nevertheless, an unsophisticated stress is often put on the momentary satisfactions and the instrumental qualities of what is essentially an aesthetically unanchored creative experience in the classroom. This may antagonize or confuse those very values of sensibility and of the value of art as an end rather than a means that everyone seemingly agrees should be engendered in all children.

In emphasizing the process alone, concentrating primarily upon "adjusted" growth and arbitrary pressures to develop a sensitivity and a yearn-

The prospective art teacher is expected to learn the skills of a variety of crafts, such as ceramics, to supplement the basic knowledge of art principles underlying all visual creativeness.

Aluminum foil wall
covering and heating
unit by Ilonka
Karasz. A projection
into the future of
the combining of
the fine and applied
arts into an inte-
grated production
unit of aesthetic and
utilitarian elements.
[Photo Courtesy
Aluminum Company
of America]

ing conducive "to creative living," there is a thinking that is somewhat
askew. The environment which is made up of things, products, and objects
(as well as intangible tastes, attitudes, and ideas) loses none of its import
in a material sense, though the evaluation of its "things" is set off in some
limbo of uncertainty. The longer range of social and asethetic meaning
is confined to an immediacy of reaction that need not find justification or
support in any tangible or external manner in the concrete forms of art or
even in the commodities of the day. The student is set adrift just as much
as are the larger aesthetic concerns in a technological matrix that generally
prizes utility, wealth, and diversion above most other values. A pleasant
and ideal instrumental situation is evolved that has only the loosest connections to the intrinsic concerns of art.

The chief fault in this entire attitude of integrating the arts and uses of
technology, lies in this idea that sees art chiefly as a means, almost as an
adjusting technique, essentially denying it its own sense of being. It pre-

sents art as a "way," whereby the values of life in a machine dominated and technically productive, efficiently coordinated and architecturally planned environment could be programmed for the common good. In this instance, this means the elevation of taste and the building toward a new, bright future that has not ruled out collective aesthetic applications in daily functions. But a corollary would seem to insist upon the existence of an almost definitive body of knowledge, that art is a process that merely requires practice, that sensitivity is the result of efficiently establishing the correct connections between varying social points and cultural relationships.

Art in this sense becomes an engineered understanding, amenable to the manipulations of programmed methodologies. Simply cover a sufficient number of variables with an input of correct knowledge and learning in art would occur. The presumption is that "learning" in art is fundamentally a progressive affair, with the necessity of having to uncover the "correct" understanding and association of variables in order to achieve proper design. The designer, for instance, has a backlog of prototypes to study, the assistance of the motivational researcher, the specifications of the engineer or the sales manager, the system of the color wheel and other art "aids" and the whole gamut of behavioral responses that the psychologists are providing, the imagery of the camera, the pantograph and an extensive array of other mechanical gadgets as well as still additional identifiable factors. Cleverly and professionally juggling the component qualities, the good designer supposedly comes up with correct and pleasing forms as well as profitable ones. The thought may be somewhat facetious, yet, in essence, the instrumental approach to art education would almost have to insist upon similar considerations. The philosophy of an integrated art program would have to develop certain correct rather than felt responses to presented problems, logically arising out of the search for a related design. This supports a consideration of "correct" ways of creating art, and it is this factor which weakens the entire viewpoint. For if there is any one idea that most artists would concur in, and that all art history points to, it is that there is no one right way to create art. There are instead many and innumerable ways of practicing art; that in the final analysis, the development of artistic form is very much the product of inner vision, combining the unique perceptions and emotions of the individual with the sensuous and symbolic possibilities of the art material within a cultural context.

INDIVIDUAL AND CREATIVE FREEDOM IN ART EDUCATION

This latter point does not necessarily deny the relative worth of an integrated art program, but it certainly would not permit it to be accepted as a central thesis in the development of any intrinsically meaningful understanding of art education. The inherent limitations seem somewhat evident, upon closer examination, of this hopeful but frequently misguided approach to the teaching of art. It would severely circumscribe any open-ended and rebelliously creative tendencies in the student, aiming for a tasteful but careful awareness, a proper yet circumscribed sensitivity, and a liberally developed adjustment to the given problems and conditions of society, ruling out, for the most part, the sorrowful discontent or disenchantment that poetry often points to as a part of the human condition. Essentially, there is a rejecting of true independence and a deflecting of originality that may not conform to social expectancies, that may, at first, and perhaps forever, be shocking and more often than not housed in the introspective sentience and intense symbolically transforming and mysterious aspects of the individual involved creatively with art. The individual in reaching out for authentic and felt experiences through art may sometimes evidence an obstreperous creativity and an insightful imagination that could hurdle over the imposed patterned and designed technology of the moment, wanting to divest himself of its images and practices rather than strengthening them. It may be difficult, if not impossible, to sense spiritual and significantly aesthetic qualities in a mass produced object or in collective design wrought by committee procedure. Or if these qualities are sensed or otherwise hoped for, the individual emotions and intense personal symbol making that has always been a part of art may atrophy for want of honest concern and unmitigated involvement. Some new condition of a collective nature would supplant it, reflecting the "other directed" vision of a corporately designed world.

The current synthesis of the fine and applied arts blends into a utopian thinking that has little real reference to expressiveness through art and a minimum insight into existing productive conditions and their relationships to art. It presupposes that the productive factors in democratic culture are

The genuinely expressive act in art on all levels is a unique one, growing out of sensory exploration and symbolic inventiveness, whatever the theoretical educational context.

geared, at least in some measure, to altruistic and aesthetic concerns or to creating a new enjoyable environment and tasteful, egalitarian and collective visual patterning that transcends profit taking and other business concerns. It opts for a reconstruction of the social order, though it, paradoxically, at the same time, imposes the mechanics of production as an almost fixed factor that has to be contended with. Though the emphasis is put upon the sensibility of the child, centering the methodology around stimulating individual growth, a duality (which it had hoped would be overcome) is in reality intensified, that of child vs. society or the individual vs. culture. The optimism of the outlook, ground in reverent consideration of the social good, by educating the individual through progressive exposure that builds an awareness "of the art and beauty in the world about him" nevertheless, circumscribes the conditions of art and provides prescriptions dangerously approaching the mechanical and impeding the truly creative.

The obvious stress on the aesthetic that genuine art experiences require need not rule out the democratic ends and social harmony that is an indigenous philosophic tenet of American education. Yet, it would be superficial to link art with democracy, or art education with social and environmental engineering simply because of the desire to see the elements in a positive relationship. The qualities of art possess their own characteristics, their development often an individually expressive affair that has only tentative or cursory relationships to group or social goals.

The teaching of art, if it is to have effective and significant influence upon students, requires a creative freedom. It must be free from any deliberately impinging attitudes, its growth the directly felt, expressively conceived and sensuously executed creation of aesthetic forms individually organized by the creator. This is often an intangible process, subject to internal idiosyncracies and unconscious motivations. It appears to provide the most original, satisfying, and individual results if it is spontaneously generated and related to already existing works of art, to a tradition of seeking original insights and new forms.

The technological landscape and the forms of popular culture cannot be considered by most observers as artistic, or their purposes overly aesthetic. The intention to make them so is not sufficient to ward off their negative influences. The value aspects have a way of directing the shaping of forms which cannot be overcome by slogans. Similarly, art education has to guard itself against the other extreme; the esthetes, the professionally obscure avant-garde, the insistent purveyors of the latest art fads for their own fashionable sake. These have little of lasting educational value to offer.

Art education has to remain an openended process, subject to controversy, and contending ideas, but always committed to the underlying concepts of individual sovereignty, aesthetic merit, and creative expression.

Further Backgrounds of Art Education

> Art teaching has a meaning for America, and should be more general and significant. The problem of civilizing this enormous country is not finished. The teaching of art must be directed toward the enrichment of the student's life. The teacher must be a guiding personality for the student, and develop his sensibility and his power for "feeling into" animate, or inanimate things, with sympathy.
>
> HANS HOFMANN

THE child centered curriculum, the reconstruction of society through education, the concern for practical synthesis, the stress on methodology, on objective measurement, on creativity, the idea of natural activity as against intellectual rigor in the classroom, and the classroom as a microcosm of life itself are but a few of the ideas that have theoretically prevailed in educational thinking during the twentieth century. All of these have had an influence on art education.

PROGRESSIVE INFLUENCES

Many of the ideals that have oriented the thinking of education over the past half century and provided the basis for healthy controversy have grown out of the philosophical ideas of John Dewey and the many resultant theoretical strands of the Progressivists. These have had a direct bearing on art education, as well as a general orientation. It would be unfortunate to underestimate the ideal influence that Dewey has had on all of education and the various redirections it has been exposed to since World War I. At the same time it would be folly to conclude that progressive education has had any other than a diffused effect in the truly revolutionary direction that was implied by Dewey's educational philosophy in other than as an ideally stimulating force. A compromised and adulterated philosophy actually was developed, a pastiche from a variety of sources and pressures that had been uncovered or felt, arbitrarily synthesized and frequently distorted under Progressivism's banner, in art education as in more general fields.

73

fervent belief in the individual proceeded from the democratic and

ralizing influences, though the underlying base of thinking has often

been patronizing or even faulty. For instance, Dewey at a late date deplored the intense emphasis on methodology, even though he stressed teaching method in early doctrine, pointing to teachers being taught the right things in the wrong ways and the confusion of means and ends. Nevertheless, an immense literature became broadly evident extolling the new virtues of experimentalism; the concept and all of its ramifications were strongly advocated in the schools, engendering many changes in educational structure and procedure. The individual was generally placed in the context of society and the teaching idea became one of adjustment to individual and social conditions, any reconstruction of society being implicitly presented rather than explicitly planned for. A frequently fragmented scientific method became a central article of faith stressing empirical "doing." The statement became the object of a lush social curriculum that included an intensification of art teaching.

The resulting growth supposedly developed along individually paced methods that offered subject areas of education in terms of meeting the needs of the student, both as a unique personality and as a member of society. It is because of these aims that the arts fit into the curriculum. Art was regarded as one of the necessities of student expression and culture. At its best, a lexicon of significant pedagogical properties has resulted, designed not as an absolute dictionary of teaching, but among the more perceptive schoolmen, as a continuing examination of student, environment, and their interaction, the subject acting as a communicating device, the individual student, the seeker after and activator of experience, and the teacher as beneficent guide.

In a very positive sense, the progressive movement shook the schools free from a deadening attitude that ignored the worth of the individual and concentrated on outmoded scholastic values. All of the subject areas were appraised and new important ones added to the curriculum. Most thoughtful critics have accepted this reorganization and believe it would be, not only reactionary but disastrous, to return to the hard and fast curriculum and teaching methods of the turn of the century variety. On the other hand, the indiscriminate mass approach obviously has been dissatisfying and relatively unsuccessful in a variety of areas and frequently referred to as anti-intellectual as well as failing as a properly serious tastemaker or cultural uplifter. The early vital and educationally revolutionary spirit of progressivism is to be courted, in the opinion of many liberal thinkers, though its direction requires mature understanding and serious but critical commitment and a reassessment of methods in all areas.

Art education owes whatever continuing foothold it has in the schools to the preceding educational change. The humanities themselves in a fuller range assumed a more vital aspect. The student was recognized and expectantly treated as an individual with inherent worth and dignity possessing a creative potential that could be realized theoretically in art, even if only as a means of self realization that circumvented aesthetic

*Even the simplest
involvement with art
in school should
reflect an aesthetic
and personally valued
quality of expression.*
[PHOTO: *Stephen C.
Sumner*]

standards. The schools were seen as viable operating institutions in which there could reside a dream of achieving the greater good of democratic living, through the hopefully not finite potential of each person, "scientifically" and harmoniously resolving the inherent tensions of new experience. Education became a way of life for many rather than enhancement of living for the fortunate few.

A Way of Life

A characteristic example of this idea is to be found in the four axioms Italo L. De Francesco [1] states form the basis of American education: (1) We believe in education. (2) We believe in the worth of the individual. (3) We believe in a democratic society. (4) We believe in freedom.

[1] Italo L. De Francesco, *Art Education, Its Means and Ends* (New York: Harper and Bros., 1958), pp. 30–34.

These he paraphrases in relationship to art education as follows: (1) We believe in education for all, therefore art education is for all the children of all the people. (2) We believe in the worth of the individual, therefore, one of the major tasks of art education is to develop individual potentialities and unique personal expression. (3) We believe in a democratic society, therefore, art education must foster a wholesome relationship and a feeling of responsibility to the social group. (4) We believe in freedom, therefore, one of the tasks of art education is to foster freedom of expression.

Despite the positive aims the fact that an uncritical freedom of expression may on occasion be at odds with the social good, may perhaps be antagonistic to the majority attitude and even their welfare is not given any credence. More important, the self sufficiency of the art experience is not given any appropriate base of support; it is only grudgingly noted, almost as an aside, but the social, community, national, and abstractly defined individual growth considerations are enthusiastically sloganized. The genuinely aesthetic demanding aspects of art are rather restricted in tone—the province of artists, perhaps—and not to be confused with developmental needs of children.

The stress is on harmony and balance—on the associational life. The well being of society is implied as the greatest good and it is believed that this may be best achieved by emphasizing the unique potential in each person. Paradoxically, however, though individuality is recognized as a basic human condition, it is the total welfare of the group that is of the greatest concern. Correspondingly, the instrumental value of the art experience as a basic learning process is implied to be its most positive attribute, while the intrinsic qualities of symbolic expression and aesthetic evaluation are sensed primarily as pragmatic influences. The wonder, joy, mystery, and pain inherent in art take on a "Cinderella syndrome."

The stress thus has been in most of contemporary ideal mass education on developing an intelligence and a personal sensitivity that is essentially useful in nature. "As for methods, the prime need of every person at present is capacity to think, the power to see problems, to relate facts to them, to use and enjoy ideas." [2] No one would really argue with Dewey on this point. He pinpointed a need that is always present in education and a rewarding guide for teachers to have. Learning is seen as a creative undertaking, yet it is also attuned to the characteristic American pragmatism that values the use of ideas and things as well as their elegance.

It is difficult and probably a negative gesture to criticize what are on the surface wholesome and positive educational objectives. Not only superficially, but in a more profound sense the progressive influences in art education have consistently and hopefully aimed for decent, liberal, democratic, and aesthetically worthwhile conditions and inherently satisfying as well as edifying experiences for students. This may have a more attuned and adaptive significance in the area of social studies, but it interjects unreal, or at the very least, extraneous considerations in the art area. By solemnly

[2] John Dewey, *Problems of Men* (New York: Philosophical Library, 1946), p. 44.

providing the aesthetic experience in education with attendant patriotic and soicological values to be realized, the actual core of artistic meaningfulness may be bypassed. By deliberately emphasizing functional interrelations of an almost self evident nature, the humanistic morality of the art experience becomes moralistic rather than an intrinsically natural, unfolding process. The responsibilities of the individual to art are rarely mentioned, the reverse being the general tenor. The need for personal integrity, for honest exploration, for free form making, for symbolic search to face pain and frustration as well as joy and achievement in the process, to gain insight, all of which makes for frequent outsize demands on individual attention and commitment, is reorganized into ordered and circumscribed sallies into the "domain of the imagination." There are the attendant pleasures, supposedly gratifying instruction and, moulded, well roundedness of students which superficially may occur. But the deep, abiding, and intrinsically significant considerations of real aesthetic experience are unwittingly sloughed off as troublesome, not amenable to structure or organization or just simply ignored, if even recognized a good part of the time.

DEWEY'S IDEAS ON AESTHETICS

This may have come about from a misreading of Dewey. In his thinking, he elevated aesthetics to one of the highest, if not the highest experience. Dewey says that "esthetic experience is experience in its integrity. Had not the term 'pure' been so often abused in philosophic literature . . . to denote something beyond experience, we might say that aesthetic experience is pure experience. For it is experience freed from the forces that impede and confuse its development as experience; freed that is from factors that subordinate an experience as it directly had to be something beyond itself. To aesthetic experience, then the philosopher must go to understand what experience is." [3] This Dewey did do in his study of *Art As Experience* and the implication is that teachers should do likewise in setting up educational method. His greatest contribution, perhaps, lies in the importance he attached to aesthetics as a real experience rather than as a shadowy quality existing only in the realm of thought or as a beautiful but mindless impression on the senses. It is his approach to the very question of the analysis and uses of the symbol in artistic ways that is a parallel and equally valid contribution and the one that has most influentially oriented the direction of art education, when it has not been deflected in the course of misunderstood enthusiasm.

Dewey maintains that the arts provide opportunities to engage the whole man, that great art elicits the most vital responses and provides man with the fullest measure of experience. Experience is most realized when the emotional and sensual as well as the intellectual elements of the individual are integrated in an imaginative symbol. In its highest form this is art and as such infuses experience with meaning and vitality. We have already

[3] John Dewey, *Art As Experience* (New York: Minton, Balch, 1934), p. 274.

examined this idea as an aim in art education. However, Dewey also maintains that the aesthetic experience is inherent on all levels of relationship, its definition essentially reducing itself to one of empirical validation to suit the purposes and needs of the individual. The worth of the experience lies in the working relationships the individual establishes with the aesthetic object and is not either a subjective or an objective understanding other than that it happens to be either unique at the moment, or the actual stimulation for creative transformation. Consequently, the work eliciting aesthetic response, the medium of artistic transaction, is an experience in which the objective and subjective elements are integrated into a *new* object with aesthetic significance.

This varies from one experience to the next and is based upon prior learnings the individual has amassed and his own inherited propensities and special manner of vision. The meaning is established *as* it is experienced and thus art creates a satisfying condition that uniquely colors experience. This provides a quality of realization in art that permits the individual to assess his role, creating insights, catharses, and gratifications that are positive and inherently rewarding. In distinction to life's experiences which are primary and permit no relief, existing as acts beyond the control of man, art is identifiable as a human symbol which offers existence more than the exposure to the random acts of nature. Admittedly, this oversimplified and brief examination of one of Dewey's most important ideas leaves much to be desired. Too many of Dewey's adherents have misread the intent of these concepts, visualizing an empirical objectivication of the aesthetic experience.

EMPIRICAL OBJECTIFICATION

This objectification is shared with contemporary psychology; most particularly, the common acceptance with the Gestalt psychologists of the fundamental human movement, in all situations, to an underlying perceptual and experiential structure of order. The tensions that are organically a part of any confrontation with experience that an individual faces are the perceptual stimulations and dissonances that must be resolved. The harmony with which this is achieved supposedly determines the specific perceptual quality as well as the extent of the growth in the individual (the new information received and its relative significance, the elegance of the reorganized configuration, the sense of propriety and rightness that results from merging the varying elements of the experience, and so on). If the utilitarian, practical considerations have outweighed other considerations, then there probably can be no aesthetic realization in the individual experience and there are only pragmatic qualities. But if there are intangible, yet intrinsic qualities of order that remain in an experience, above, beyond, or in addition to the practical, then the aesthetic element comes into play. Consequently, a farmer who enjoys the fall of rain because of the patterns it creates in the puddles is having an aesthetic experience as against the one who sees the rain primarily as a necessity for the growth of his crops. A member of the audience at a play, if caught up directly and empathetically with the action even as illusion, is involved in an aesthetic experience, while we may question the aesthetic nature of the experience of his neighbor who has come to "improve his mind" or to be solely entertained as a condition of mass understanding.

There is a relative factor in operation and it largely revolves upon the unique responses of the individual. Dewey was very much aware of this and he argued that the various art forms were vehicles through which the singular nature of individual personality may be realized. There was, as well, an acceptance of the largely intuitive base of the aesthetic experience, the complex and psychological nature of the striving in each instance of experience that created a sense of harmony or artistic order that was far removed from simple mechanistic considerations. Yet there was also a broadening of the base as to what constitutes valid aesthetic experience, wherein the philosophical and psychological objectification of the experience could be considered a broad justification for its existence and reason enough for gratification, for aesthetic satisfaction. Thus subjective and objective elements are uncritically merged.

Instrumental Values of Art

It was not only when Johnny stood in front of an easel that he was capable of having aesthetic experiences; actually, every experience during the day provided him with an opportunity for potential aesthetic satisfaction. The levelling, egalitarian concept entered the heretofore sacred and admittedly often sanctimonious citadel of what constituted art. No hierarchy of value was broadly accepted, simply the sense of the individual intensity of the experience determining whether it was, in fact, of a true artistic nature, or more broadly an aesthetic experience. The realization flowed from the objective and almost measurable quantity as well as quality of the experience. Despite the understanding of the uniquely individual nature of the perceptual act, the instrumental factors, supposedly determining the possibility of personality growth in the abstract, were made to be of basic importance. It was this factor that many art educators were to seize upon in expanding the role of art education. The essential mystery of the act of creative expression or appreciative realization was largely denied, the intangible symbolic transformation was pressed into neat little holes of growth patterns, or ignored when it overflowed its pedagogical containers.

Nevertheless, Dewey recognized that art is not a simple affair, that it does not lie superficially available to any who would partake of it. Simple experience is not sufficient to know art, though aesthetic reaction exists for the human being only through the experiences that he undergoes in relationship to the works of art in Dewey's understanding. The experience also has to be of a knowing kind based upon instruction, evaluation, and synthesized thinking, of a cultivation of taste. One of the roles of education is to provide the necessary backgrounds and understandings with which to have these sensitive, mature, and valid aesthetic experiences. In this sense, the teacher becomes a critic, guiding his students through the maze of experiential anarchy as well as through the prism of his own personality or especially that of "scientific" methodology. Personal predilection may be dangerous in this sense, distorting or limiting the experience the teacher is presenting or guiding, but on the other hand, the dogmatic or unexamined factors of a shared and "responsible" outlook may lead to similar and even more deadening results. Yet the objectification of the art experience may lead to just such a situation. Dewey himself, despite his warnings to the contrary, tends to construct a particular and personal vision and to confuse this with a normative condition. The biases and idiosyncratic distinctions that color and complete an individual personality thus confound and bewilder a mass belief that has been imposed or grafted onto its understanding. The supreme rationality and stress on empirical values that in the final analysis bend to personal vision limits Dewey's ideas on art in education and more so his uncritical followers. His commitment to vital experience, germinal and radical as it was, was spread too thinly in suggesting all of life's experiences as containing a potential aesthetic base at the same time that he narrowly defined the good and bad styles in art. Though he himself regarded art as the highest means of providing meaningful experience, he was at the same time committed to what his followers referred to as a "scientific humanism." Dewey's profound understanding could bridge the paradoxes and disturbing elements of implied contradiction, transcending the trivialities of a position by suggesting radical innovations and insisting upon new and experimental departures of meaning. As a result, there is a genuine statement of ideals that are hopeful and seemingly informed in outlook. However, the very empirical quality with its built-in aspects of evaluation is distressingly accepted on its most unstructured level as containing the educational implementation of Dewey's idea of art as experience.

It must be recognized though because of Dewey and the growth of progressive ideas, art education has experienced a great expansion. Despite the futility of some of its conditions, the groundwork has been laid for the attempt to actualize the easily verbalized ideals. Opportunities abound for cultural and creative involvement, even if the scene is not a clear one. Though this may have degenerated at times into an empty form of self expression (a concept that Dewey himself did not favor) the importance and the validity of the arts in education have remained a generally recognized need, though sadly or haphazardly catered to and understood in a confusing manner.

From the middle thirties on there has been a burgeoning of art expression and a spread of art education in the schools. In the wake of the vitality that the early progressive educators stimulated and in response to Dewey's philosophical pronouncements, there has been a continuing and growing amount of theorizing and implementing activity that has carried art education into most schools and conferred upon it a legitimacy in educational councils as well as providing a serious base to its own internal development.

Progressive Humanism

The influential educators who helped to shape the progressive concepts in art education were vitally concerned with meaningful values. They wholeheartedly accepted the concept that education should be centered around the natural uninhibited qualities of childhood or the intense if bewildering character of adolescence experience. School was to be a real experience, not merely an avenue to adulthood. They rightfully insisted that the art experience is a vital and organically present one during the preadult years, that education somehow has to cater appropriately to this situation by informed and sensitive means that at the same time does not lose sight of the large aims of education.

The importance of relating the child to the environment was regarded as a fundamental educational responsibility though not, through any formalistic or intellectually rigorous training that everyone arbitrarily had to undergo, but by noting individual difference and tailoring the classroom climate and procedures to collate with the personal growth patterns of children. There was to be a natural unfolding of capacities, utilizing a scientific methodology. Subsequently, the processes of the creative periods were intensified and respected as a legitimate means of aesthetic and creative growth, while the product was held to be only a concrete reflection of the more vital experience of creative process. This latter factor supposedly had some generalized power of transference, so that the various situations that an individual would probably encounter during his lifetime might conceivably benefit from the problem solving, or supposedly transforming and hence creative experiences, that art education offered. And in a burst of liberal yearning, with all manner of cooperative and elevated social connotations, the belief was prevalent that a new society was being fashioned, formulated on rational and aesthetic grounds, wherein the cross fertilization between educated personalities and among enlightened and sensitized groups or the positive interrelationships between men and institutions, desires and capacities, would somehow surmount the dark forces of evil, ignorance, and vulgarity.

Though there was a similar realization of the importance of relating appreciation of art to active expression, it was of a relatively narrow nature. The reaction against art appreciation was felt in the thirties when it was almost completely cut out of the teaching curriculum, in favor of a virile, immediate self-expressive experience with materials without the need of an intellectual sense of order for the individual student to worry about. Lately, there has been some reconsideration of this attitude; but what is being discussed is a broad and generalized version of appreciation. This more current thinking would build upon the familiar daily, local "art" experiences.

These ideas have a reference to the work of such educators as Edwin Ziegfield of Columbia University in the Owatonna project and the book *Art Today*, which he co-authored. They have been relatively quiescent for several decades, yet exerting obviously a strong undercurrent of influence.

The environment within which students create art is considered by many theorists a product of differing cultural and social forces.

[ABOVE] a painting class in the Toledo Public Schools. [PHOTO: Tom O'Reilly]

[BELOW] Abandoned children of Mrs. Mehta's school in Bombay, India, drawing with colored chalks. [UNESCO/ Alaine Peskine]

[TOP RIGHT] A drawing lesson in a Russian classroom located in Moscow. [UNESCO/Y. Katsenbargas]

[BOTTOM RIGHT] A painting class at Woodberry Down Secondary School in London. [UNESCO/ A. Tessore]

This influence stresses the familiar visual objects, and the aesthetic experience as it is encountered in normal, average living, on the assumption that these are the realizable, active sources of value formation and it is upon such first hand factors that comparison, awareness, and growing sensitivity to art may be stimulated and developed. This attitude is very congruent to the electric flow of thinking in progressive education.

Distinctions of Artistic Commitment

A humanistic and aesthetic injection into education, however, cannot really suffice or follow its own inner logic if it is subjected to an adjustment that is essentially foreign to itself. For instance, to speak of the nature of art again: It has its own rather fluid structure; if a generalized idea of structure may even be permitted; an imposed or an implied utilitarianism distorts its form and its meaning. Unless there is an organic craftsmanship involved, as in pottery or jewelry making, there is likely to be a confusion and adulteration of values in the aesthetic experience. In art education practice though craftsmanship underlies all art teaching, there is yet a distinction between a student—a boy of fifteen, for instance, making a piece of enameled jewelry for his classmate Mary to wear (someone he likes) and a committed artist seriously working in his studio transforming his experience into profound symbolic forms. Though the student is engaged in a perfectly legitimate process, he should not be encouraged to believe that it is on the level of really serious or profound art creation. As shattering to democratic ideals as it may sound, there is an innate hierarchy of aesthetic values and a cultivation of taste requiring time and effort in art that has to be recognized if any real art experience is to be hoped for. A growing student sensitivity is fed on this reaching for more profound aesthetic meaning and personal vision as contrasted to the mere acquisition of skills or the "fun" of the process. Art education, as it has developed under the aegis of progressive thought has often leveled the distinctions, seeking and encouraging an essentially noncritical experience as an end in itself where local or arbitrary examples are the prime comparative criteria even where the aesthetic content is dubious.

Deliberate and comparatively closed research has addressed itself to evoking the experience, rarely attempting to furnish aesthetically significant criteria for the substance of the experience. The cut-and-parse procedures of an almost inviolable scientific method introduced an alien grammar into the "language of vision." The emphasis was subtly, and probably unknowingly, moved from the individual communing with himself and expressive symbolic values through creative form to one that elevated the personal and socially therapeutic qualities of the artistic process with the consequent devaluing of the worth of the object produced and a diffusion of the symbolic meaning of the creative process itself. As in the larger sphere of social and political action, egalitarianism insisted on the equality of worth and effort; the teaching process being justified in eliciting mass "creative" response. Though the individual supposedly develops a social sense of successful involvement under this gross experiential method, in reality, there is also an atrophying of true artistic consciousness, of critical sensitivity and searching creative exploration. The norms of a practical society where artistic endeavor is ill favored seep in, especially in the absence of a teaching method that does not insist upon artistic integrity and intrinsic aesthetic values that derive their quality from the worth of the object produced as well as in the making of the object, and from profound spiritual and symbolic concerns rather than relying upon the exigent nature of much of the local visual scene. The process itself is left, dragging its anchor through all of the debris and clutter of an emerging personality, finally rusting during adolescence.

Some of the failure may be laid to Dewey himself, in his faith in scientific method as the panacea of our times. Though his own belief was not the dogmatic scientism of his followers, it provided the source that later flowered into an etiolated but enveloping plant that had excluded the vital light of basic educational substance. Yet it was the disciples of Dewey who basically skewed the thinking: experimentalism became almost an end in itself, negating the original purpose that gave it impetus—the needs of the individual child and the development of a mature freedom of understanding and responsibility in the individual in terms of authentic values. Based upon a late nineteenth-century belief in progress and in active experience as the source of meaning, empirically understood through the efficacy of science, the followers and popularizers of Dewey elevated an analytical and pragmatic intelligence as the desired individual product in education ignoring many implicit aesthetic values which Dewey later made more concrete. However, when this occurred in the 1930's progressive education had already established its own academic outlook. This intelligence, based upon the experiences it encountered, would then engage in problem solving, providing solutions that meet individual needs, but prescribed insofar as those needs reflected a social good. The philosophy was and remains enlightened and democratic in the characteristic American tradition of a free individual existing in harmony with the community *summum bonum*, for its greatest welfare. However, the essentially naive belief in scientific method was already a dated one that led to a comparatively simple but one-dimensional instrumentalism particularly in the popular but anti-intellectual ideas prevalent among many educators who resisted a real involvement with the aesthetic sense as well. The physics of Einstein and Planck and the esoteric mathematics of the twentieth century have shattered the simple pragmatic experience of a predetermined scientific method. It is no longer sufficient to assess experience in terms of simple problem solving; there are the perplexing tangents of comprehension and the seemingly random actions of physical nature that poke holes in any easily imposed fabric of meaning. There is a counterpart to this in the symbolic approach to human behavior. The relative nature of things precludes any absolute or specifically deterministic understanding. Not that Dewey was narrow in his philosophy; he always believed in viable knowledge as well as in the intrinsic and aesthetic worth of experience in addition to its utilitarianism. He advocated an exceptionally liberal approach that accepted the humanities as well as science. Not the least has been the intimate relationship between culture and education that has followed on the practices of progressive education, the bringing together of art and curricular development, of the creative process and the child, in what could be fruitful learning and individual realization.

Several other individuals and groups have been prominent in this development of art education and each has had a pertinent influence in directing the aims and the methods of the area.

THE WORK OF THOMAS MUNRO

One of the most important of these individuals who went far beyond his role as curator of education of the Cleveland museum was Thomas Munro. As a quiet presence that exerted strong and fundamental pressures, Munro has examined all of the important considerations and problems in art education, pinpointing many of the channels of investigation that art education was to explore, and he has posed inherent problem considerations that have not been resolved as yet.

Munro appears to have assessed many of the implications of progressive educational thought. In posing many of the problems art educators must address themselves to, he has broadly structured the field with a Deweyan emphasis. Roughly, he points up the basic concerns such as: What is the nature of art, its forms and interrelationships? What constitutes a proper teaching method of translating artistic qualities in the classroom? How do individuals develop aesthetic sensibilities and how can art education stimulate these through creative and appreciative experiences that are translated through teaching methods? He says: "Not all the issues in art education arise from issues in the outside world of art production and consumption. Some are more indigenous to the educational realm itself. Education in youth is not now regarded merely as preparation for later life, but as a period of life that has its own intrinsic values. Deciding on the right sort of art education is not, therefore, merely a matter of deciding what sort of mature artists or art appreciators we wish to produce. Even if we knew that none of our students would become artists, and none would have access to art, there would still be reason—so much the more reason—for letting them enjoy and practice the arts in the schools. Art is coming to be recognized, in other words, as a necessary part of general education for all persons, on all age levels—necessary to the full exercise and development of personality, especially in its sensory, emotional, and imaginative aspects, and in muscular coordination." [4]

Emphasis on Rational and Psychological Research

Munro, however, is far too sophisticated and knowledgeable in art to consider the teaching of art as some life adjustment condition that could

[4] Thomas Munro, "Introduction," *Art in American Life and Education*, 40th Yearbook National Society for the Study of Education (Bloomington, Ill.: Public School Publishing Co., 1941), p. 18.

be simply generated in the laboratory of the school art room. Yet, in his rational and sensible attitude he does objectify the art experience in an extremely attractive manner. This has encouraged idealist yearnings in art education and has set one of the significant tones for art education theory since the beginning of World War II. Its balanced blend of critical examination of eclectic teaching and that of sympathetic belief in the broadly humane and personally rewarding experiences of art which are then correlated with the psychology of child development has created almost a corps of evangelical enthusiasts among art teachers. This is particularly true since the psychological studies Munro called for were forthcoming in the decades of the Forties and the Fifties and continue to do so in the Sixties. These see a sophisticated, culturally based psychology being employed in conjunction with the freedom and growth potential of artistic and creative behavior to bring art, to the individual and his society, to their mutual benefit. Munro aptly orients this outlook, for example, writing: "Art especially is a warmly personal subject, though not always so presented in schools and colleges. It is concerned directly and constantly with human individuals and groups, rather than with impersonal facts or logical abstractions. It deals with concrete experiences and their objects; with emotive sense images, aspirations, loves, and hates. The forms and activities of art can be fully understood only in the light of the motives that inspired them and the experiences they arouse. Psychology should and will illuminate these for us . . ." [5]

Munro called for a liberal though essentially presumptive psychological understanding. This was to chart the creative process and provide research guides for the teaching-learning relationships in art understood in terms of enriching the individual's personality and the recognition of methods most attuned to successful developing of "valuable mental and bodily abilities." He felt that an organically integrated understanding could be worked out, given time, patience, and research that brought together the intrinsic nature of art, the natural unfolding of the creative process and the comprehension of personality growth and child development as it is related to art. The subsequent responsibility and capacity of education (and art being one of its basic components) would be to create balanced individuals who could better cope with the repressive forces of society.

CREATIVE AND MENTAL GROWTH

One of the most developed and organized responses to the impetus of progressive ideas coupled with psychological research was that of Viktor Lowenfeld. He organized a very structured body of knowledge centered around scholarly information regarding children's art work and its relationship to individual personality growth. What is significant may be summed up in the following paragraph from Lowenfeld:

Growth is on an everchanging continuum. Aesthetic growth appears to be the component of growth responsible for the changes from a chaos on the lower

[5] Thomas Munro, *ibid.*, p. 249.

The individual pupil should be the focal point of any philosophy of art education. [Pittsburgh Public Schools; PHOTO: Martin Herrmann]

end of the continuum to the most complete harmonious organization on the upper end. This striving for higher forms of organization does not necessarily refer to the elements of art; it may also refer to a more intense and greater integration of thinking, feeling, and perceiving and thus be responsible for our greater sensibilities in life. Indeed, one of the distinctions between the basic philosophies in art education and those in the fine arts may be a difference in emphasis regarding harmonious organizations. Art education primarily deals with the effect which art processes have on the individual, while the so-called fine arts are more concerned with the resulting products. It is then quite logical to say that art education is more interested in the *effect* of a greater and more harmonious organization of the elements of art on the individual and his development, while aesthetic growth in the fine arts generally refers to the harmonious organization of the elements of art themselves.[6]

[6] Viktor Lowenfeld, *Creative and Mental Growth* (New York: The Macmillan Company, 1956), p. 393.

This clearly separates the process from the product in art education, the former seemingly becoming the means of personality growth while the latter becomes insignificantly anticlimactic for the purposes of art education. The student's work of art is regarded as merely the concrete proof that a process has occurred. It is the process that educators have to concentrate upon. This Lowenfeld does, though paradoxically, by consistently referring to the work examples that permit him to make his analytic researches. This stress on process and growth has strong ties to the progressive ideas that value the involvement of self in action. In addition, Lowenfeld contributes an important emphasis upon the transforming nature of the creative process, wherein, the central consideration of interpreting one's own experiences in some kind of form is underscored. This he considered as basic to the role of art education and the resulting psychological structuring by age groups and by haptic or visual types he regarded as a helpful and necessary means of knowledge for the teacher that assisted in channeling and guiding proper personality development. Utilizing this developmental information on methodologies could be enacted by individual teachers that figuratively, if not literally, would ignore the aesthetics of the finished product, thus in a sense excusing the teacher from a fundamental understanding of art, if the logic is carried even not to too extreme a point. The concentration appeared to be progressively an almost clinical or case history approach with overtones of an unsophisticated "mental health" attitude. This became evident despite the sincerity and the scholarly research. As in Dewey's case there was also an adulteration of a valuable understanding by disciples.

Fallacies in Method

In separating the process from the product, particularly in their aesthetic interrelationships, Lowenfeld unwittingly created an attitude that easily valued so-called psychological insights. This made for relatively uninformed teaching analysis in art on the part of a vast horde of psychologically but superficially directed teachers who really did not comprehend the subtleties of his position. The teachers generally did not possess the necessary training to make proper classroom judgments dependent upon psychological theorems. The values of art could too easily be buried and were virtually extinguished in some instances under the guise of a methodology that relied upon pseudopsychology and what finally became for the most part, trivial experiments in therapy through art.

Despite the evident awareness of Lowenfeld to value, judgment, individual perception, and the stress on self realization, there was no accompanying intensification of the critical eye and significant aesthetic values. The outside environment, the jumble of superficial and only momentarily rewarding but actually insignificant forms may have been deplored. But there was no attempt to examine critically the culture and its frequently insidious and unconscious effect upon the individual and his tastes in and understanding of art. There was a strong reliance on the instrumentality of the art processes. "If the senses have been refined and cultivated it will be revealed in the aesthetic product." This may well be the case. What is at issue here is how are the senses refined and cultivated. It would seem an approach that relies heavily on psychological guidelines to the complexities of aesthetic creating and appreciating rather than aesthetic ones would only be successful in a very limited fashion and with secondary goals at that. At least, in the better part of a generation that has passed since many of these ideas have been employed methodologically there does not seem to be a significant upsurge in the general creativity of the average person. Despite the superficial indications of taste which really breaks down under the pressures of novelty and mass communication, there has been no noticeable "upgrading" of the public's "harmonious organization of aesthetic elements." And one may wonder if there has been any corresponding personality growth beyond the natural one of normal maturation in the mass of individuals.

Yet Lowenfeld was an extremely telling and widespread influence and deservedly so. In a sense, he most clearly epitomized the progressive search in art education for a system of psychological behavioral research stemming from developmental sequences as mirrored in the art work of students, for which Munro called. This, it was hoped would serve as a vehicle of method by which teachers could systematically conceptualize the underlying factors present in problems of art teaching and efficiently put into practice the most successfully structured approach. In this sense, Lowenfeld almost succeeded in setting up the bases for an art education discipline. Though these are waning in their influence, the intensity and seriousness of the endeavor has made art education a term of respect among many educators. Yet, efficiency cannot be considered an important element in relationship to art, nor will the systematized codifications of developmental states provide more than a tangential rudiment of aesthetic understanding, even for the purposes of teaching.

CREATIVE TEACHING IN ART

A parallel influence to Lowenfeld in time and in goal, though basically not in approach of method, was Victor D'Amico's ideas. Though D'Amico shares with Lowenfeld a concern for the child's individual growth in developmental stages through art experiences and also agrees that the experience is far more precious in the teacher-learning act than is the art work produced, he believes the aims of art education can be best achieved by stressing the innate design factors and creative understanding of the art experience in a free, open teaching situation that parallels, though in a simplified fashion, the attitudes and processes of the professional artist.

D'Amico claims "the child is the true artist." In the early version of his book he wrote, "The concept of the child as artist implies that every child is a potential creator endowed with those sensibilities that characterize the artist." [7] The art lesson should provide the individual student with experi-

[7] Victor D'Amico, *Creative Teaching in Art* (Scranton, Pa.: International Textbook, 1942), p. 1.

ences that are honestly artistic and reflect an integrity and concern with aesthetic involvement that "transcends the idea of art as a performance or a product and looks upon art as a way of living. . . ." To achieve this, the art curriculum has to concentrate on genuine art experiences, not upon arbitrary inventions, stereotyped projects, or cute ideas that are cribbed from teacher magazines. These experiences D'Amico lists under the traditional headings of Painting—Easel and Mural, Sculpture, Pottery, Graphics, Stage Design, and General Craft Designer. He later adds a section on Creative Invention that deals with collage and construction. This listing and insistence upon "professional" areas in art is not designed to make the average child an artist, but is designed to provide him with meaningful experiences in the only proper visual areas of design with which art is honestly involved.

D'Amico further insists upon an independent expression on the part of the child that arises only from a beneficently stimulated but otherwise unencumbered use of the materials of the artist. Perhaps this is why there was a later stress on the relatively fresh experiences of collage and construction. D'Amico believes these possess a great advantage for the child in working directly with a design medium that is supposedly suited to his nature. He believes techniques of design and material handling that may be necessary to realize a form should be offered for individual children as they come upon the problem in their own creative search for expression. This organically oriented teaching method is a positive and appropriate understanding of the creative process and its needs (sensing the negativism of formalized, arbitrarily timed mass demonstrations). Yet, no one has worked out neatly the practicalities of this individual approach in a mass education situation. Nor is there always the realization of the innumerable problems of a formal or technique nature that do annoyingly arise in great and conflicting number during an art lesson. Nor do the schools have as yet teachers in adequate numbers, especially on the elementary level, who have a command of the art techniques, let alone a realization of their significance in achieving an artistic vision and aesthetic forms and can sensitively, and adequately assist students when the need arises. This obviously leads to a militant demand that art specialists, well trained, as well as eager and enthusiastic about both art and the education of children be employed in large numbers. This, D'Amico has advocated for a long time.

D'Amico also gives cognizance to the developmental aspects of child growth and the unique relationships this possesses for art education. However, unlike Lowenfeld, he eschews the doctrinal aspects of psychology. His approach to the developmental sequence is looser and generally more intuitive, based upon the practical experiences of teaching.

Child-Artist Relationship

Because his earlier thinking may have been somewhat misconstrued in theory as well as in practice, D'Amico in his revised book begins,

In recent years there has been too great a tendency to compare the child and

*For children as well
as for artists
the art experience
is more a search for
personal and
aesthetic values than
an instrument for
social development.*

"Self-Portrait"
*[New York Public
Schools;* PHOTO: *S.
Martin Friedman]*

the artist, thus implying that they are alike . . . the distinctions between the creative child and the professional artist should be clearly drawn. If the child is like the artist, the similarity is in his awareness of design for its own sake and his ability to subordinate subject matter and the story element to the elements of form, line, and color. Another interesting similarity is that the child, like the artist, integrates the elements and responds to them emotionally. But these reactions on the part of the child are usually unconscious. He does not call design by name, but merely responds to it with the enthusiasm with which he reacts to anything that he enjoys or that is dear to him. Unless the distinction has been made for him he does not distinguish between a subject matter picture and an abstraction.[8]

This is a true and valuable insight, though it seems to stop short at an early school age. What may be considered the "golden age" of child art, the unconscious, uninhibited, symbolically natural and wonderful years of

[8] Victor D'Amico, *ibid.,* (1953 edition) p. 1.

the first two or three grades reflect D'Amico's discriminating viewpoint. However, after that period there is a progressive decline for the mass of students, average and otherwise, until the early adolescent years have become barren of individual symbolic vision and generally devoid of creative expression. Perhaps what is required is that the image of the committed professional artist be introduced as an ideal if not as an immediately workable example of achievement, just as the mathematician, physicist or the biologist, their attitudes, concepts and methods, are regarded as goals in elementary science training. At the very least, like the mature artist, the growing child has to learn that he cannot escape the burden of consciousness that accompany his creative acts. Perhaps if this developing awareness is honestly sensed by the preadolescent, the pains, frustrations, demands as well as the delights, the emptiness of the adolescent and later years in regard to creative expression may not have to occur. It would seem that the artist as a mature, sensitive, capable, searching individual who expresses inner visions by a command of techniques and skills should be regarded as an integral element, certainly as a desirable goal in the theoretical concerns of art education as well as in the practical implementation. Otherwise, it appears that students must engage in what passes for creative self realization but is in reality unanchored experiences in a limbo of well meaning but progressively empty acts. This is fun and play in an aesthetic sand box, rewarding for the moment and even beyond, but without significantly last-

"Self-Portrait"
[*New York Public Schools*; PHOTO: *S. Martin Friedman*]

ing values that have real reference to mature personality growth or meaningful creative experience.

D'Amico's stress on the dignity and integrity of the artistic experience and the child's response to it has been an important guidepost. His blend of progressive ideas with practical studio techniques has engendered an aesthetically worthwhile and otherwise personally rewarding experience with art, where it has been integrated with the mature personal vision of sensitive teachers. Though there is a stress on the instrumental values as much as on the intrinsic ones of the art experience for the student, there is a corresponding insistence upon an art education that is based upon art values, rather than upon those that may be foreign to aesthetic understanding. If there has not been a wholesale acceptance of this significant approach, the fault lies more in the overall pressures of a culture that overwhelms the teacher's sense of responsibility to values of integrity and substance than in the merit of the position.

Children's Art as a Separate Discipline

Many of the newer and progressive ideas in art education have suffered from a sapping of strength that impinges from the outside. But there are internal weaknesses as well. Perhaps one of the pitfalls is the insistence that child art is always a separate and different activity, essentially divorced from the more mature models of adult professional work and creativity. There appear to be a number of considerations that support this idea of separateness, among them, the natural enthusiasm of the child for artistic expression that progressively wanes with growing older, the schematic patterns of various age groups, the inherent "playfulness" and imaginative projection of the child, the innately creative reaching for understanding of the world during the early years that acts as a spur to self motivated activity particularly in the need to make experience and knowledge concrete through visual symbols. These considerations have prompted many art educators to set up what they regard as a discipline centered around the unique elements that supposedly are found in children's art work. For fear of contamination, unnecessary complexity or confusion, they have systematically and continuously excluded the influence and the immediate presence or example of the professional artist. Perhaps, this has been as well an unconscious criticism directed at the values that most mature artists subscribe to. These tend to be markedly different from the ordinary and more commonly accepted ones. It may have been, as well, a tacit recognition that the middle class virtues and popular mores that overwhelmingly infuse the philosophical attitude of school boards, administrators, and teachers alike would reject the more virile, questioning, and disturbing value systems of artists, thus alienating the large group of educators who must pass on the propriety of art in the schools.

The aesthetic condition is manipulated through circumscribed educational methodology, rather than permitting it its errant, rather mysterious, and unpredictable course in ordinary existence. A relatively closed approach to art is formulated and imposed upon the teacher's consciousness, claiming a number of distinguishing attributes that supposedly elevates the making of children's art and its teaching into a conceptualized and separately justifiable discipline. The child's activity in art is regarded as an almost venerable condition, with nevertheless, more or less recognizable bounds that are responsive to the external pedagogical methods that various examinations of the discipline uncover. This basically externalizes and collectivizes the existential relationship that children have with aesthetic awareness and artistic shaping of experience despite almost doctrinaire assertions that artistic creativity is an individual affair.

As a result, though there may be a divergence of approach in method, as for instance, between behavioristically research oriented art teachers and those who are closer to the more practical and artistic guidelines, there is in the final analysis, a sharing of concepts. There is a strong belief in the efficacy of art to promote personal growth and in the understanding that children's art possesses inherent and recognizable limitations that education can scientifically, practically, or even intuitively examine. The complexities of mature art are ruled out; the example of the professional artist looked upon as essentially a disruptive force that could and does upset the neat arrangements characterizing the examination of children's relationships to art, the categorizing of their work disturbing the relatively ordered ideas of art teaching that stem from a self contained art education discipline.

Subsequently, though there are a remarkable number of wonderful artistic experiences available to children and excellent examples of their work demonstrating a verve and a genuine transformation of their experiences into aesthetic symbols, there is an overall mediocrity of art education in the schools and disappointingly little evidence of a mass taste and appreciation of art that is beyond the level of immediate novelty or diversion. Whatever is genuine in the children's art is more due to the natural resiliency of childhood and the factor of innate expressive needs being realized despite imposed methodologies rather than because of them.

Questioning Elements

This may indicate that art education as a discipline may not be as contained as its supporters claim it to be. It may further indicate that art education will have to sense the living continuum between child and artist and recognize that the values as well as the methods of the latter are the natural goals and insights of aesthetic development. This is especially true if the development and maintainence of a creative outlook is to grow beyond the early years rather than atrophy and if the general taste level is to exist substantially higher than that which our culture has demonstrated so far.

Several additional elements appear to mitigate against the close structuring of a child art. There is, for instance, the persistence or reappearance of childlike schemas in adult art work when the adult has been uninvolved with creative expression for many years. Any college instructor who has taught a methods course in elementary art to prospective teachers is well aware of the infantile forms that otherwise intelligent twenty-year-old college students can turn out. This is experienced again and again in extension classes with teachers who have had many years of experience in the classroom. Their artistic efforts are little removed from the fourth or fifth grade level, though some few in a regressive, belated but charming innocence would give a first grader competition in expressing naive forms. Then too, the mentally disturbed individual or those who have suffered a variety of other than normal pressures socially or psychologically give evidence in their art of child-like schemas. There does not seem to be any hard and fast development of form that is uniquely and only part of childhood. Rather it may be said that artistic form, from an educational viewpoint, may be broken down between the untutored and that which results from specific training, between the innocent, naive, primitive directness, and frequent awkwardness of expression and that of an intensified, sensitive and complex vision. Age or other temporally developed considerations appear to have little or unimoprtant bearing on the matter of artistic form other than as a prelude to individual maturity.

This is not meant to totally depreciate the educational values of many otherwise legitimate studies of behavior. Rudolph Arnheim and his researches in the psychology of perception is an example of the substantive work going on in the field. Arnheim theorizes that there are distinctions between adult and child perception, that there are a variety of factors that will influence the way each group will perceive objects and translate them into expressive symbols. Elements such as prior readiness, subcultural influences, perceptual development, hand-eye coordination, and other similarly deterministic factors operating within the Gestalt framework all have direct bearings upon the particular responses an individual makes, probably as much by age as by differences in background and training. Though these may prove helpful to teachers, they cannot be but adjunctive considerations that have no vital bearing on the total place of aesthetic values in culture. In the latter sense, an adult who has figuratively been narcotized by the mass media, by hypocritical standards, by material pressures and such, is spiritually a child while the child who may as yet be free of these forces has the potentiality of mature adulthood.

There are other elements that may not be too profitable to elaborate upon here for they are somewhat obvious in recognition and implication; for example, the waning of creative activity in the preadolescent as a culturally accepted condition. Yet some few individual students do not lose their aesthetic and creative orientation, they even intensify it and later become the artists, writers, composers, and poets. If it was the efficacy of a method of teaching that pulled these fortunate few through, based upon a concept of creativity that had special childish connotations or restrictions, why so small a number. Certainly if the method was successful in a small number of instances, it should have been more widely diffused in its influence if indeed it was the cause. It could not have been that selective a process, especially not when the announced aim is for mass creativity.

[OPPOSITE] *All methods of teaching art find their source in the full professional preparation of teachers as artists as well as educators.*

Conceivably, the will toward, and the congenital attributes for, creativity may be of a limited nature, touching only a relative few. But then the high minded aspirations and sanguine theories have built in contradictions and operate in an unrecognized atmosphere of futility. However, this is the ultimate heresy, to consider that there may be a strong inequality of creative potential. Yet, if this were so, no amount of theorizing about the enclosed area of children's creativity could mitigate the condition, while the processes of creativity went their own merry way, playing havoc with the carefully structured balances of nature and, unfolding in its own mysterious manner. Properly, art education cannot accept this extreme viewpoint, it has an inherent obligation in the other direction. Yet to posit this responsibility in terms of wishful thinking that projects cleverly conceived though unsubstantiated beliefs that too easily pass muster as philosophical fundamentals is to engage in an act of self deception or at the very least violates the integrity and meaning of art as a creative, positive, and profound interpretation of life.

PERCEPTION—DELINEATION

One of the more recent theories is that of June McFee, elaborated in her book *Preparation for Art*. It broadly attempts an eclectic merging of many of the more dominant trends in art education of the past half century and in the behavioral sciences that have such current educational ramifications. The theory ties the theoretical package together with insights from cultural anthropology and psychology. McFee labels the total concept as Perception-Delineation Theory.

The diagram [9] graphically illustrates the neat manner in which McFee presents a relatively complete analysis and ready formulation of the creative art experience of the individual child. The process is, of course, centered in the individual child. It specifically starts at Point I, "Readiness." McFee identifies the following factors that differentiate the degree of readiness that a child may possess in relating to a stimulus that could generate an art experience: (a) flexibility-rigidity patterns that vary greatly in individuals, (b) orientation to space, a tendency that grows out of child rearing habits, (c) the learned aspects of the perceptual, information-handling process that result from the broadly accepted values of a culture, (d) the perceptual "constancies" that induce a variation in dealing with size, shape, and color due to what one "knows" about them rather than responding to the "actual" visual image, (e) subcultures, the local variances from the larger units that will determine attitudes and responses and finally, (f) prior learnings that produce mind "sets" toward experience. Because of these individualized and differentiating factors the implications for practice are that the art program need "to be flexible and varied to provide for differences in readiness in children." These differences are broadly categorized into three classifications: art learning periods, self-directed activities, and integrated art activities. All of this may lead to the desirable

[9] June McFee, *Preparation for Art* (Sacramento: Wadsworth, 1963).

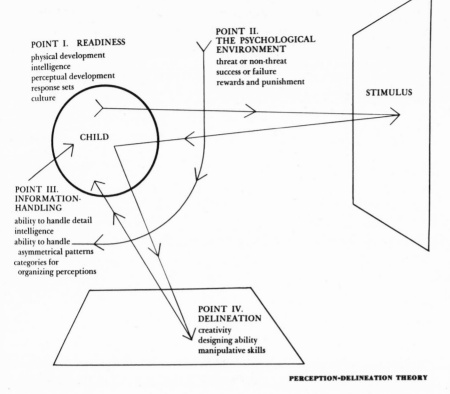

POINT I. READINESS
physical development
intelligence
perceptual development
response sets
culture

CHILD

POINT II.
THE PSYCHOLOGICAL
ENVIRONMENT
threat or non-threat
success or failure
rewards and punishment

STIMULUS

POINT III.
INFORMATION-
HANDLING
ability to handle detail
intelligence
ability to handle
asymmetrical patterns
categories for
organizing perceptions

POINT IV.
DELINEATION
creativity
designing ability
manipulative skills

PERCEPTION-DELINEATION THEORY

Charts of Perception Delineation Theory. [From Preparation for Art *by June King McFee. © 1961 by Wadsworth Publishing Company, Inc., Belmont, California. Reproduced by permission of the publisher.]*

condition in education wherein one recognizes that the "critical analysis of one's perceptions is as important to critical thinking as analysis of one's ideas." Consequently, the training in art could sensitize perceptual awareness "dealing with the elements of art—form, line, color, texture, space—and then interactions, then aesthetic judgment will develop as well." The mechanics that make for realization seem readily discernible and perhaps too simply so, toward the goal of creative realization.

Point II takes cognizance of the psychological environment, making note of the fact that the various personal drives and forces that result in anxieties, threatening situations or calmly adaptive one, and the whole gamut of unconscious as well as conscious motivations that modern psychology has managed to unearth have a decided effect upon the perceptual processes of individuals and in the individual's manner of response. The implications for practice in art education indicate the need for the teacher to have psychological insights into setting up varying systems of reward in the classroom, in stressing the relative factors of support or acceptance necessary for different children. Similar comprehensions of broadly patterned personality development through psychological workings and anthropological propositions are necessary teaching tools. The various groupings of art experiences should then range across a gamut of possibilities and qualities which the knowledgeable teacher would present along the lines most appropriate to the psychological and cultural conditioning of the students in the class.

Art
and
Education
in
Contemporary
Culture

.

100

Point III deals with information handling. This is largely dependent upon the analytical and statistical examination of various groups to determine the distinctions in handling information that occur with age, physical condition, social background, and such. These all will influence the manner and depth of perception and the point is made that the teacher has to be acquainted with these factors so that the classroom practices may conform with the innate possibilities of the individuals that are present. This is important not only because of general psychological sets but because of the particular distinctions in understanding that become ingrained in individual and group understanding due to prior learning and identification with particular social elements. The learning then that accompanies the differing methods of observation and organization permits the visual material to be presented, perceived, manipulated, and expressively transformed in its most skillful and individually most appropriately meaningful manner.

Point IV of the P.D. process is the synthesis of the above mentioned factors. "It is the point at which the three other teaching functions, assessing and improving readiness, developing a good working atmosphere, and helping children use the visual information, produce 'art'." The implications for art teaching in realizing the need for this synthesis are generally but also explicitly spelled out. They strongly urge the teacher to be professionally aware of the various studies that attempt to delineate the causitive or otherwise influential elements of creative and expressive behavior. They further underscore the continuing need for the teacher's own logical analysis of particular situations in order to most directly and successfully provide stimulation and nurture for children's attempts to express themselves in art and engage in creative behavior. The teacher not only has the responsibility of expanding the child's possibilities for experimentation and handling materials in art, but has the further responsibility of fitting the experience to the child and vice versa, in response to the supposedly ever progressively informative, and helpfully delineating findings of psychology, anthropology and so on. This body of "professional" teaching knowledge is then related to the elements and principles of design that intrinsically are a part of art: the factors of color, shape, texture, light values, space, time and the visual concepts organized under such groupings as unity, proportion, rhythm, balance, and the other formal principles. McFee does caution teachers that the experiences the teachers set up have to allow for "playfulness," expressiveness and experimentation. But the emphasis is upon art as a communicative, educational tool by which the child's personality is enriched and sensitized to better develop his individual potential of creative growth that has to fit into the complexities of modern civilization. This understanding is charted in another of McFee's graphic summaries that is illustrated.

The Integrating of Elements of Art Education

This latest influence in art education has attempted a full integration of the varied and disconcertingly divisive approaches to the discipline that

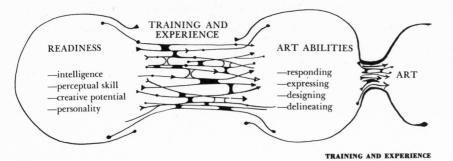

TRAINING AND EXPERIENCE

Charts of Perception Delineation Theory. [*From* Preparation for Art *by June King McFee.* © *1961 by Wadsworth Publishing Company, Inc., Belmont, California. Reproduced by permission of the publisher.*]

have been inherited from the past. At the same time, it is pertinently conscious of the large array of research that has been concentrated upon individual behavior, patterns of learning, cultural analysis and how all of these have in one way or another related to and impinged upon education. McFee sorts out those studies which supposedly have a more or less direct bearing upon creative and expressive behavior, winnowing out the elements that seem to specifically deal with visual education.

McFee, like her predecessors has opened up a variety of avenues to art education as well as offering a serious level of content to the field. The viewpoint seems to falter at one point on the belief that the teacher has to develop as a behavioral technician, despite the realization that the ultimate worth of art education is in its humanizing and aesthetic influence. The theory, like so many other contemporary educational concepts that stress systematized understanding and scientifically experimental structuring does not admit to a contradiction between means and ends. There is no value judgment of the means of an educational technology, that though it may efficiently convey masses of information and so-called individual experiential opportunities to masses of students may be in conflict with its own major objectives. At the very least, there is little attention paid, not only in McFee's approach, but in many of the art education concepts of the past three decades, to the individual and cultural moral qualities inherent in the art process rather than its reverse. These qualities of moral integrity that are inherently a concern of creative endeavor are subject to the manner in which they are to be realized and cannot be presented merely as educational tools in the guise of a particular subject matter.

Students drawing with a crayon in the first grade or attempting a difficult watercolor technique in high school have to sense, intrinsically in their value systems, not only that their "personalities are growing," not only that there is satisfaction in creative expression and that some important learning is occurring, but also, and more important, that the art process is ultimately one of the few really human acts that offers an individual a true sense of existence, transcending the merely physical, material, and utilitarian demands. The experience has to be founded on a relationship that hews closely to the intrinsic values of art, rather than its instrumental ones. These values include the expressive needs of the individual, his emotional involvement, and his psychological manipulation of the art

Art
and
Education
in
Contemporary
Culture

·

102

elements. These obviously are basic, but so is the inherent appropriateness and self-sufficiency of the sensual art qualities, the structural "morality" and propriety of the combination of elements, the natural satisfactions of symbolic composition, in short, the creation of aesthetic relationships.

ART EDUCATION REQUIRES INDIVIDUAL APPRAISAL

It is probably appropriate at this point to caution against a naive and unstudied acceptance of so-called psychological principles on the part of the teacher in the light of recommending personal philosophies of art education. It is too easy to fall into the trap of acting decisively on too little information that has been erroneously blown out of proportion by an eager but unsophisticated or untrained teacher. Obviously, long and rigorous study is necessary in psychology or any of the other behavioral sciences in order to understand them and even more so in applying the findings. This is not possessed by the average teacher. Then, it is only since the middle 1950's that the social sciences have begun to be interested in any depth in creativity and those areas of artistic perception which may have relevance to art education. The results so far have been meager and far from reliable, though, certain psychological insights have become evident, several of which are mentioned elsewhere. Teachers have an obligation to study these areas in a liberal way and to examine intelligently their own ideas and behavior in the light of contemporary findings. But they have a concomitant responsibility to be wary of how they personally interpret and utilize these findings as well as in accepting the entire procedural paraphernalia of social and behavioral research.

The behavioral sciences are self limiting in relationship to creative education. They cannot honestly, at least at this point of their development and perhaps always, provide teachers with specifically appropriate and operationally fool-proof data. The whole area of creativity, image formation, aesthetic perception, the differentiations of cognition, the relationship between sense and meaning as they develop in our objective and subjective states, as well as many other pertinent psychological factors have not been adequately explored. The concept of feeling is just beginning to be examined as a global hypothesis in psychology and this is very much relevant to art education. The qualitative rather than the quantitative aspects of creativity are beginning to be looked at, not as fractured components of a larger pattern of behavior, but as the expressive sum of many combining human characteristics.

The more sophisticated and sensitive investigators are being professionally provocative in that they are pursuing new and unfamiliar paths of examination. They are permitting their studies to be shaped by the intrinsic and individual life forces of the subject and action being observed, discarding the highly sophisticated tools of a more academically accepted psychology which relies upon certain preconceived techniques. However, since most studies in the social sciences have been established within the shadow of the natural sciences, there will be an implicit orientation in all the "scientific" investigations, which cannot stray too far from the empirical base which relies on observation, analysis, logical evaluation, and verification. The aesthetic values may be so differently structured that the essentially pragmatic approaches of a regularized scientific attitude may not be able to reach them, let alone knowingly examine them. The aesthetic experience or the work of art is not the starting point in the typical psychological study, rather some abstract hypothesis of human behavior is. Consequently, the works of art and the kinds of response they elicit in people are tailored usually to fit an idea imposed from the outside while the creative process becomes merely one more means of adapting to the environment.

Too often, the behavioristic and sociologically oriented researcher (and most cannot escape these colorations, even in art education) is bound by an empiricism that frequently becomes intemperate. The data and the findings of research suffer from a chronic irrelevance, a triviality of concern if not an outright flatulence. Values are generally considered outside the domain of material, scientific, or empirical analysis. There is a tendency to isolate art and the humanities, to distort them even as they are being examined.

Therefore educators would be well advised to congenitally look askance in a larger professional sense, at the elaborate research structure with which they have surrounded themselves. Its validity and uses are probably genuine and helpful, but the factor of values or ideals does interject itself in a philosophical manner. These are more likely to determine a direction than the raw data that comes from investigators or computers. For instance, if we accept efficiency and quantity as the imperatives of mass education (even though we always have something to say about quality), then the growing field of programmed, taped, and machine learning will appear as a necessary and desirable education innovation. However, if the values of individual growth and liberal learning are the basic guiding values no matter what the cost, then the mechanical aspects of "the little black teaching box" may be regarded with great reservations, if not rejected outright and the considerations of personal interchange and the intrinsic struggle with knowledge and creativity retained.

Perhaps the most damaging aspect of scientific generalization in relationship to artistic behavior or process is that the investigator usually has only minimal or relatively thin personal art experiences. This cannot create the fundamentally essential and subjective involvement with art that is an inherent condition of its comprehension. It is not sufficient to formulate theoretical constructions of a supposedly objective nature concerning artistic performance and appreciation and hope to arrive at any vital intensity of aesthetic understanding, let alone the problem of virtual significance. There is the necessity of individual involvement with the materials of art. Parallel to this is a subjective struggle to find form or otherwise create it from the stubborn and often intractable qualities of the elements of art, and an indispensable personal confrontation between the willing protagonist and his experiences that insist upon expression through direct symbolic transformation. The would be scientific investigator by the very nature of

Art
and
Education
in
Contemporary
Culture

·

104

his work is rarely involved with aesthetic and artistic problems on this level. An art teacher who permits his understanding to be developed chiefly in terms of the theoretical assertions that nonart persons make consequently permits himself to minimize his own necessary artistic growth. In almost all instances there has to be an active interrelationship between theorizing, no matter how logical or facile, and personal involvement in art otherwise the result may be suspect in its authenticity.

Art as a Primary Source for Art Teaching

Art education, if it is to have a quality of individual but responsible expression and sensible recreation, if it is to encourage creativity and a sensitization of individual understanding of values and their presentation through the forms of art, cannot permit itself to depend fundamentally on foreign, ambiguous, or unrelated interests and knowledge and understanding. Though the teaching of art may be assisted and guided by the adjunctive information of the social and behavioral sciences and general educational theory, the very first source of understanding for the art teacher, and the most fertile, lies in art itself and in the larger body of the humanities. A teacher who is steeped in the knowledge of music, literature, the visual arts as well as in other areas of the humanities is putting his or her best foot forward. It is this teacher who is likely to teach with a grace and an affirmation, a pedagogical wisdom and an inherent inspiration that could not be comparably induced, artificially or otherwise, by any battery of tests, experiments, or abstract hypotheses that are *about* art rather than *of* it.

In stressing the appropriateness of the primary sources of the arts as determining their own inherently pertinent content and processes, the teacher of art is certain of the reliability of the source at the very least. However, there are also the factors of the fitness of the information and the feeling of natural belonging that requires no rationalizing or other forms of justification. In addition, personal aesthetic awareness grows apace of the educational understanding, and this can only have positive repercussions; very often the two are quite interdependent.

Importance of the Artist as Guide

Just as the arts themselves are to be utilized as the basic sources for content in the area of art education, so should the artist and his working habits serve as examples of the suitable nature of particular teaching methods as well as an essential source of relevant values. This does not imply that each school child will be trained as an artist, but it does suggest that if any worth is to be derived from a program of the arts in the schools, it will stem from a real and direct involvement with the various arts. The partial, ersatz, or pseudoart that is often the level of creative involvement in the schools shapes itself as a blind educational image. It achieves this dubious state by ignoring the very person who creates its content—the mature artist, either by referring to him only as someone who lived in the past or by consistently bypassing him when seeking assistance in structuring school art programs. Yet if we set for ourselves the problem of providing the most worthwhile experiences in art for children, it would seem proper to go to the artist for guidance in determining just what might constitute this experience. The science programs in the schools have wisely begun to avail themselves of the help of eminent practitioners in the various fields. In physics, in biology, in mathematics and in other currently popular subject areas, there has been a revitalization of the curriculum due to the studies of interested scientists, who are not themselves educators on the public school level. As a result, teaching method in these areas has come in for a salubrious and refreshing overhauling that will have lasting influences in science teaching.

If a similar drive is to characterize the teaching of the arts in the school, it would seem that the artist is one potent and necessary source that will generate forceful understanding and intrinsically suitable direction. Because he is always involved with problems similar to those the students are experiencing, albeit in a much more profound manner, the artist may offer the insight required for personal growth and aesthetic resolution. The teacher of art in paralleling this insight can then more honestly, and with a natural grace, lead, guide, or assist school children in a growing awareness of the world about them. They can enhance their growing appreciation of its wonders, beauties, and sensations, enriching their growing ability

The art lesson should invite dramatic experiences that lend themselves to interpretive visual and manipulatory activities. Making Hand Puppets. [Detroit Public Schools]

Art
and
Education
in
Contemporary
Culture

.

106

to communicate the special meaning the world may have for them, communing with its qualities and changing states of being. Finally, they can intensify an expression that sentiently explores the inner and outer worlds with pencil, crayon, paint and brush, clay, string, metal, or any other of the vast array of media that the children's own fancies and the conditions of art offers, which then reveals and shapes the images, feelings, and emotions of each child.

The environment for education has become a complex one. For art education it also has become an eclectic accumulation of concepts, sometimes in harmony, more often as contending and confusing demands that could well bewilder a young teacher. The continuing exploration in the visual arts and the extremely numerous array of aesthetic attitudes and artistic styles offer an overwhelming source from which to accept guidance.

The environment is a rich and abundant one, the times exciting, the ideas stimulating, the potential almost without limits. Each practicing teacher and prospective teacher has a wealth of choice. The responsibility is an individual one, to make the kind of commitment which will most honestly assist in establishing an effective and felt method of teaching.

Value Relationships in Art, Education, and Society

> One of my problems is to find the Self, which has
> only one form and is immortal—to find it in animals
> and men, in the heaven and in the hell which
> together form the world in which we live.
>
> MAX BECKMANN

TEACHING has to be concerned with aspects beyond the verifiable and formally intellectual ones. It is not sufficient to consider pupils as passive receptacles that are to be stuffed with objective truths, tangible techniques, and programmed procedures. Their education is developed primarily through their own varying experiences and perceptions and the manner in which they either deliberately or unconsciously interpret these experiences. This suggests that teaching is as much involved with the factors of attitude and value as it is with subject content, especially so in art.

For instance: One of the aims of an art education program in the schools is the awakening and growth of appreciation of the "beautiful and tasteful" things in life, a development of the individual aesthetic sensibility. Children should learn to love the arts, to develop personal perception, to express themselves in fulfilling ways and creative forms, to fashion a pleasant and satisfying environment, as well as intensely and joyfully to appreciate the work of the great artists in their own and other times. This is not fully achieved by the techniques and artifacts of the arts themselves, through exposure to and analysis of paintings, architecture, music, dance, and literature alone. There is no basically significant learning in these subjects, in any meaningful way, or in that of science or history for that matter, without the appropriate attitudes on the part of the pupils. It is only when the individual student accepts the presence of generally worthwhile or specifically rewarding values, that serious involvement with educational substance and processes occur, opening the way for "true" learning. The individual not only "knows" and "does" but believes in what he "knows" and "does."

Art
and
Education
in
Contemporary
Culture

•

108

VALUE AS A FACTOR IN THE CLASSROOM

Hadley Cantril [1] sums up the need of values giving them a very important place in the scheme of things. He points out the outstanding characteristic of man as being his capacity to participate in the creation of emergent value attributes which enrich the quality of his experience. He explains that this characteristic of man is the one which makes him "human," and is common to all members of humanity, no matter how varied their individuality. Finally, it is because of this characteristic that both the individual and the species appear to follow an ever ascending path. This suggests an incumbent responsibility on the part of teachers, that of sponsoring and stimulating values. These values cannot be limited to the simple translation of those that the teacher accepts and believes to be important, though it is impossible and probably undesirable to escape completely the internal compulsion to stress one's own beliefs. Teachers cannot easily circumvent their inherently evangelical and indoctrinating role, even if they may want to. Yet their first responsibility is to motivate and then refine the values which pupils individually possess as the result of their own unique experiences. The student then may become sensitive to the choices of action as he confronts his own emerging personality and the environment outside through vivid and compelling realizations of experience. These are made meaningful and concrete in a natural way through the processes and inherent forms of a creative involvement with art.

Some observers claim that the development of values and consequent teaching methods are largely deterministic, that is, based on many factors outside the immediate control of the teacher: the student's background, the larger school environment, the unconscious drive of the teacher's innate personality, and the prevailing forces of society, in short, the culture in which one lives. Others suggest that teachers have a large measure of control, of individual will, which can be particularly and effectively utilized in the classroom for the teacher's purposes. Whatever the source, where an effective and salutary teaching climate exists, it is palpably recognized and felt despite the intangibles that have created or influenced it. Perhaps one aspect which may be common to these successfully felt situations in an art class is the emphasis given to honest and spontaneous values that are naturally developing as the result of genuine aesthetic and interpretive experiences. In these situations the teacher, in his or her own way, is aware of the importance of values in providing a depth and meaning to creating and learning. This need not be a consistently deliberate direction on the part of the teacher, but it is obviously an underlying condition of enthusiasm and educational honesty that manifests itself within the very methods of teaching employed and in the resulting student responses that occur over a long-range period. Prospective teachers of art, even in personally experiencing examples of successful teaching and aware of the necessity of value orientation in education, must for themselves, assess each situation with which they are to be faced. In the final

[1] Hadley Cantril, *The Psychology of Social Movement* (New York: John Wiley, 1941).

Value
Relationships
in
Art,
Education,
and
Society

.

109

The critical
evaluation of art
work by students
should be sensitively
guided into legiti-
mately aesthetic
value judgments and
a consciousness of
the need of such
values. [Pittsburgh
Public Schools;
PHOTO: Martin
Herrmann]

analysis, they are confronted with problems of communication of subject
matter, of creative process, and with the internal teaching dilemma of how
best to establish rapport with children, clearly, convincingly, and effectively guiding them. This has to be achieved without strongly interposing
the ambiguity of overly contending ideas, contrasting personalities, and
the resulting inhibiting confusions yet at the same time, not abjuring
healthy controversy and a stress on individual propensities.

The teaching of art is closely dependent upon these considerations of
value. Sincerity of outlook and sympathy of insight are necessary but not
always sufficient for the teacher. A professionally critical eye, a felt commitment to a personal value system, and a teaching enthusiasm also enter
the teaching situation, as does a clear understanding of cultural influences.

The competently detailed and expertly panoramic drawing (p. 110) of a
city by a fifth grade boy indicates a number of value factors that a teacher
may investigate. Obviously, the youngster enjoys his art work and has
developed proficiencies of technique and handling of material well
beyond his peers. The delineation of the various vehicles and buildings
is precise, the rendering of the scene visually proportionate for the most
part, with the slight exaggeration of parts controlled more for effect than
because of an inability to handle perspective. There is a sureness of execution that is distinctly well developed above the hesitant and awkward
drawing usually found in upper elementary attempts. This could be cause
for satisfaction. Yet an examination beyond the superficial elicits some
further understanding. The vehicles, particularly the airplanes, are the
stereotyped diagrams found in popular technical illustrations. The overall
drawing techniques conform to the insipidly factual and conventionalized

Art
and
Education
in
Contemporary
Culture
.
110

pictures found in so many school textbooks. The symbolic quality of the scene refers more to the imposed mass imagery of the Sunday supplement than the direct or even fanciful imagination of a fifth grade experience. The art experience, as the drawing expresses it, is more a derived one rather than a personal one bound up with the many form complexities yet one-dimensional values of a technological society. The boy's artistic talents, in this instance at least, have been skewed away from a more intensely aesthetic experience, and reflect in the derived forms a bland acceptance of popular values. A teacher would have to make some important pedagogical judgments along value lines in evaluating the work and in discussing it with the student.

The Difficulty of Communicating Values

However, even when the intrinsically aesthetic values of the arts are accepted, there has to be an awareness of the continuing problems that would be encountered. A variety of classroom situations develop that are difficult to disentangle. The values, techniques, pressures, and levels of understanding are unfortunately confused, or otherwise obscure, particularly when the teachers themselves are uncertain of their own aims or are committed to arbitrary or superficial daily routines that are no more than an unthinking acceptance of what is purported to be "good" education.

Imposed and highly derivative images frequently find their way into children's art work, despite a talent for precise rendering as is evident in this example. "Cityscape," Fifth Grade Drawing. [Ann Arbor Public Schools; PHOTO: David Churches]

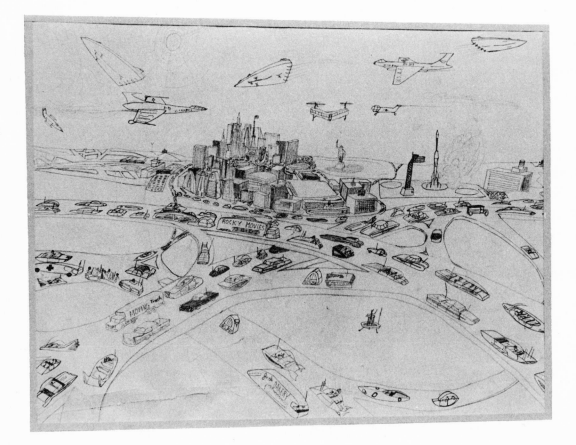

For instance, there is the impasse between the elementary school teacher who values art as an expression of "cuteness" and the child's intense attempts at making forms that have a meaning and may be crude rather than cute. He or she may have no range of acceptance for the uninhibited youngster who adamantly explores the possibilities of form and color for his own sake, consistently destroying the results because they have not satisfied some inner vision (that is also far from cute), or find sufficient satisfaction in the exploratory act itself—in the immediate, imaginative and vivid realization of sensuous relationships without bothering about the extraneous desires of the teacher. Or conversely, a teacher of sensibility may despair of the trite and repetitious forms that her students insist upon because of the pressures of the popular environment, or the conforming transactions aimed at security; her efforts to awaken freedom and individual discovery met with the readily manufactured visual delineations of comics, television, and stereotyped images. A tenth or eleventh grader may narrowly, though justifiably, value art because it provides an opportunity to draw and perhaps create clothing fashions or car designs when the teacher is hopefully, and subtly but most often unsuccessfully, attempting to expand the individual artistic horizon to include more challenging material. Or on any level, students in an art class may become frustrated and reject art because at particular times they require the knowledge of specific techniques, which the art teacher refuses to demonstrate or otherwise teach because he is committed to "unencumbered free expression."

Value
Relationships
in
Art,
Education,
and
Society

.

111

The appreciation of modern art cannot be taught in some instances because it is believed to be "radical" by some, while the old masters are shunned by others because they are not of today. These are only a few of the many varieties of misunderstandings in art education due to conflict in values. Since it is the personal understanding of art that essentially influences the values in art that any teacher will disseminate, the procedure is necessarily a unique one. This parallels the contingent aspects of art, but there is a corresponding educational need to provide relatively organized and knowledgeable insights from which contingent procedures may develop in positive and creative ways. Art education cannot serve only as a catalytic channel, but must become, for the individual, the cultivated base of personality, the internally satisfying search for significant expression and sensitive awareness.

There are inherent difficulties in evolving positive teaching methods stressing these vital values. It is not an easy matter to achieve. David Riesman, a leading writer of social interpretation can write, "I believe that the processes of communication are inherently ambiguous, since we understand other people's symbols in terms of our own character and the experience it has let us have." [2] Educators have to be aware of the equivocal, shifting interrelationships resulting from experience that confound the easy formulation of profound social values which deserve a common hearing in the classroom. Yet a teacher is compelled to accept the troublesome and

[2] David Riesman, *Individualism Reconsidered* (Garden City, N.Y.: Doubleday Anchor Books, 1955), p. 10.

Art
and
Education
in
Contemporary
Culture

•

112

puzzling nature of communication, the continuing dynamic evolution of values in the individual *vis à vis* the group as well as the problems and the challenges these create for teaching.

In accepting the educational sponsorship of values, a teacher must also accept the responsibility of making judgments of value about subject areas, methods of teaching, the learning attributes of pupils and their symbolic behavior all against the looming presence of society "outside." The intricacies of the interrelationships may be difficult to discern in all instances. It requires not only persistency, but an open responsiveness and educational sensitivity to both the abstractly general and specifically pertinent factors involved. Of course, no matter how the teacher acts, some kind of decision, consciously or not, has been made; the necessity is that the action represents an informed, sensitive, concerned, and educationally sound understanding that transcends a narrow doctrinaire prejudice.

This is particularly true in art education, for communication in art, though vital, direct, and concrete in a sensory way, is at the same time intangible, ambiguous, and not really reducible to the logic of verbal discourse. The teacher may excite a class about the sparkling vigor of a wintry scene for instance: its brilliant whiteness, pristine purity of surface, its quality of strong contrasts of light and masses, shaping a cold isolation that blankets a pending anticipation of rejuvenation underneath. The intensity of the teacher's feeling may be personally rewarding, a felt response and realization to a poetic experience; it may even enthrall the class, touching them in its appreciation of quality and perhaps even imparting a momentary and direct sense of being. However, further communication, of a more lasting and methodological kind has to occur. The communication has to transcend the raw data, the merely sensuous; it has to generate a value transformation into individual symbolic expression or perceptive appreciation.

DETACHMENT AND COMMITMENT

Perhaps a measure of interested detachment on a teacher's part is indicated without a corresponding loss of involvement. This may be a paradox in attitude, but it seems probable that a teacher can be detached without the connotation of being isolated for purposes of developing understanding. This is a dynamic and frequently elusive quality and many observers are suspicious of the average teacher's ability to accomplish it. The detachment is not a simple examination of the factors present in teaching situations, but reflects a much more profound ability to comprehend the movement of rather intangible forces. This has to be an almost unconscious capacity based not only on the growth of individual understanding but on the recognition of the specific confines of individuality which though they are personal innate characteristics are also ambiguously subject to the universal force of human culture. The relationship leads to a corresponding need to assess social values as they influence the unique personality not in the strict formulations of hard and fast equations that are statistical and analytical, but in the more indigenously fluid balance that does exist very often not on a superficially discernible level but on a more obscure yet profound and intuitive one.

But David Riesman implies that teachers perhaps should not attempt a critical examination of values, for they tend to engulf them in shallow sentiment and trite solemnity of acceptance. In commenting upon the ideas of progressive education, "via the patronage networks of various teachers' colleges, (when it) was installed in many ill-equipped school-houses throughout the country," Riesman rather forcefully remarks, "I am not attracted by the picture of a crusade to implant self-consciousness of values in all the pious and platitudinous teachers of America. I would rather have them teach languages and algebra and biochemistry." [3] However, though one may rightfully be suspicious of the instrumentalist ideas as teachers have generally implemented them, nevertheless, observers still cannot insist upon a mechanical-like teaching of factual information alone or the rote transference of ideology and aesthetics. Education cannot be stripped that bare and still exist as education. It is most inappropriate to hope to teach art techniques or stylized appreciation bereft of the vitalizing cultural climate that impinges upon the learning experience and tends to mould it, whether we want it to or not. Of course, the danger of platitude and piousness is frequently present. Teachers, unfortunately, tend to develop pragmatic programs, oversimplifying the complexities of relationships in their need to develop foolproof teaching methods, turning philosophy into dogma.

For instance, the old proverb "Cleanliness is next to godliness" has been operationally accepted as not only a practical but a basic value in life and in education. American society stresses the need to be clean, not only as a health precaution and an element in personal attractiveness, but as a cardinal virtue of morality. It almost seems as if we can wash our sins away merely by being clean. Europeans frequently make comments such as, "The Americans will go down in history as master plumbers." The implication is double edged; not only humorous but suggestive that there will be little else to remember of the clean American civilization but its technology. This is grossly exaggerated; yet consider the factor of a strong emphasis on cleanliness as it affects the mess, clutter, and unavoidable "dirtiness" of a creative art experience. There may be an opposition of values which both pupils and teacher may find personally rather uncomfortable to overcome at the very least. Though the problem of cleanliness has unfortunately annoying value connotations and is very pertinent, many other more profound value considerations remain in a state of bewilderment, antagonism, and frustration. But this does not stem from the values themselves; rather it is the result of an immature and narrow interpretation of them, of a myopic utilization of the values, good and bad, merely as abstract sources for efficient classrooms. Propriety and abstract order become themselves overwhelming value elements, rather than successful instruction.

[3] David Riesman, *ibid.*, pp. 10–11.

Value
Relationships
in
Art,
Education,
and
Society

.

113

Art
and
Education
in
Contemporary
Culture

·

114

*The art teacher
requires a sense of
detachment in order
to offer guidance and
helpful criticism at
the same time that
she feels a passion
for and commitment
to art and to the
education of
youngsters.* [PHOTO:
Stephen C. Sumner]

Teaching Assessment as Related to Creative Art Processes

The confusion may be due to the lack of detachment—a quality of mature and balanced examination—a successful teacher should possess. The detachment does not connote a lack of commitment or rule out a passionate avowal of particular values. It merely provides a perspective by which a teacher, avoiding cant, can more honestly introduce values into the classroom without distorting them or freezing them into inflexible attitudes. This detachment most probably comes with a developing individual wisdom, based upon an expansive scope of experience, experiment and judgment.

The quality of detachment suggested is not the classical aloofness of the "schoolmaster" or the clinical withdrawal of the scientist, but is more akin to the act of "getting out of oneself" so as to understand better what is going on. Artists constantly take advantage of this psychological possibility when they create, psychically moving from an intense preoccupation with the actual elements they are shaping to a condition of contemplation and evaluation that is more than a simple physical stepping back from the canvas. The artist is attempting to sense the relevancies of the elements he has ordered and the appropriateness of these elements to his feelings and ideas. Similarly, the teacher "steps back" from the class and the lesson, assessing the innate factors in each, sensing the relationships, feeling the interactions, and generally appraising the overall situation.

Another analogy may be made between the estimation of values in a classroom by teachers and the perception of values in an art form. Similar to the "stepping back" process that occurs during the creative act, there is the state of aesthetic "distance" that onlookers experience when they are responding to art work that already has been formed. In good drama or cinema, for instance, though the audience is caught up in the happenings on the stage or screen, there is also present an awareness of being removed from the action, of looking on from a "distance" despite the feeling of being identified with the protagonists. While there is empathy, the imaginative projection of one's own consciousness into the stage characters, there is also a realization of not being actually a part of the dramatic action. Critics call this "aesthetic distance." It provides the individual, without personal fear of directly suffering the consequences of the events enacted, an ability to perceive the dramatic experience. The onlooker conveniently and comfortably bridges the gap between identification with values and the need to respond spontaneously to them in an active manner.

Teachers may sometimes regard their classes in this way, from a "distance" with the consequent opportunity of assessing the values, discriminating between those being observed and generally developing a sensitive attitude toward their own opinions, habits, and prejudices as well as those of the pupils. The analogy may be slightly forced, for the teacher *is* faced with a live situation, not an imaginative one. Yet there can be valuable insights gained, for a dramatic relationship does exist, even if it is tenuous at points.

The Mechanistic Fallacy

The "stepping back" process and establishing aesthetic "distance," however, are rational acts in part and perhaps mechanical as well. That is, they are deliberately invoked during teaching as a means of understanding the various elements and conditions present in a classroom and to assist in developing a possible channel of effective communication—a climate for creativity. Even if the teacher intuitively engages in the process, we may liken the inner workings to an instrument. The teacher's perceptions are like pointers on a dial. These are activated by the condition of the elements present (the kind of students, the nature of the lesson, and the like). The dial is the teacher's own attitudes and understanding set into the total person, which constitutes the instrument itself (the teacher). Like all dials set into machines, information is recorded. Then action which is deemed appropriate is taken; this is largely automatic in the human organization of response. This human "instrument" already has a built-in awareness of the values that are to be accepted or encouraged. Teachers have a large inventory of assumptions against which the incoming perceptual sensations are measured. The resulting action is one of acceptance, modification, or rejection, depending upon the intake of data and the resulting inferences.

However, there is another part of the process which exerts influence—the emotional, feeling reaction of the teacher that figuratively may throw a "monkey wrench" into the mechanical evaluation described thus far. The artist is in a similar predicament, for if he is well trained in technique,

Art
and
Education
in
Contemporary
Culture

•

116

knowledgeable in content, he should be able to follow the resultant internal advice of the evaluation process and consistently paint successful pictures, if not masterpieces. But the emotions, of which he may despair but which create his humanity nonetheless, plague and confound easy or mechanical resolutions. And it is this that forms the art that is expressed in the work that he produces. In a like manner, teachers have to contend with the feeling aspects of any perception and realization of a teaching situation. The values that are being expressed are most likely to be buried in the unconscious or preconscious element of personality, the detached image of the teacher in judging and stimulating them in the classroom metaphorically understood like the well known picture of the iceberg that has only a very small part of its bulk above the surface. Yet teachers, despite the subliminal nature of the process, have to make deliberate choices in teaching, providing the necessary relevancies for themselves as well as for students, recognizing the pertinent influences that are at work in all instances. This, like the making of art, is an open "feeling out" process requiring a fluidity and flexibility of manner as well as frequent originality.

The insights that art teachers apply to the classroom situation have their subsequent figurative reverberations in the individual attitudes of the children they influence and in the expressive quality of their work. Art teachers do not only objectively impart information, guide technique, suggest avenues of approach, and correct mistakes, but in the fullest sense of the relationship, they act as exemplars. They become sounding boards bouncing back for the edification and stimulation of the student representing a way of seeing things, a manner of transforming them, a means of evaluating them.

The natural spontaneity of a student's act of expression cannot but help being patterned, after a time, by the teacher's own acts of commission or omission. There is a strong affinity between the questioning curiosity of the child and his or her actual artistic endeavors. The affinity expands beyond the child in a compelling way to the teacher's presence. The consequences are reflected in not one work but the whole range of a student's endeavors over the school year. However, this exists hand in hand with the unique emotions that play around any specific art experience and are of great influence. It may be seen that the art teacher has to ride the paradox of detachment and subjectivity in his or her role as "the head of the class."

THE UNCONSCIOUS FORMATION OF MANY VALUES

It seems probable to many observers, particularly psychologists, that man has few behavioral reactions that are not conditioned in one way or another. That is, outside of the very basic and automatic physiological processes that are required to maintain life, most of the behavior in response to man's needs are learned, the result of experiences within a particular environment. The cultivated aspects of a social environment generally form the base of its culture. Though this concept may deny or overwhelm the existence of individual will, it deserves the attention of teachers. The art teacher has a particular realization to make in light of the fluid and psychically hidden nature of the creative and artistic processes.

The subsequent values are then inculcated in the individual through a conditioning process that is particularly effective in the infant all the more so because it is unconscious. In the classic stimulus-response manner an infant unconsciously learns the standards of behavior that will be expected of him. Certain actions on his part will elicit "good" or positive responses, others will bring "bad" or negative reactions. The "good" are rewarded, the "bad" are punished. The child learns a whole series of behavior patterns that his environment demands of him, normal and otherwise, sensed in terms of "good" and "bad." These generally oversimplified judgments are rarely justified or explained to the child; they seem to exist arbitrarily as almost indisputable elements of "right" and "wrong." "Isn't it nice to be on time"; "You must not knock down your sister's blocks"; "That's it! Fight for your rights. You can punch Johnny if he hits you first"; "Oh! the picture is a beautiful copy"; "Don't play in the dirt—" are but a few of the judgments that youngsters are constantly subjected to, and it is doubtful if parents or teachers could always rationally explain the need for the behavior even if the child could understand. In this way, many cultural values are introduced into the individual's personality and passed from one generation to the next, without the reasonable presentation of pertinent or supporting criteria.

The consequence of this unexamined conditioning is the development of later value judgments that are primarily feeling responses. Adolescents and adults too, then respond emotionally to the suggestion of value changes, because they have been unconsciously tuned to an earlier "good" and "bad" reaction that required no immediate justification. Even when an individual has a mature and controlled outlook, he may not be aware of the disparity between his overt actions and his inner feelings. If he is aware, he may be puzzled or frustrated, not always understanding his own behavior. This makes for many unseen difficulties and complexities in teaching and is often an unexamined determinant of artistic form and expression.

The realization of this inner influence upon a person's thought and actions stems from the Freudian concept of the unconscious. In a very simple statement, this concept recognizes that a person may be motivated by forces of which he is not consciously aware. Because of this, the individual may lack an insight into the nature and origin of many acts and impulses failing to recognize that early experiences have colored his emotions and that the force of this emotion compels the manner of his behavior. G. W. Allport says, "Thanks to Freud, even the man in the street now knows that we act for reasons that we do not understand, and that we harbor unconscious sentiments that would surprise us if we knew we had them . . . of the whole of our natures, we are never directly aware nor of any large portion of the whole. At any given moment the range of consciousness is remarkably slight. It seems to be a restless pencil point of

Value
Relationships
in
Art,
Education,
and
Society

.

117

Art
and
Education
in
Contemporary
Culture
·

118

Emotional qualities underlie many expressive works. West German Student's Art. [Exhibition Circulated by the Smithsonian Institution. Reproduced by Permission of the Smithsonian Institution]

light darting here and there within the large edifice of personality, focused now within, now without." [4] This force that is beneath the threshold of our consciousness is as important in creating and understanding art as it is in personality development.

Unconscious Classroom Determinants

Therefore, people rarely recognize the extent to which their value judgments, the supposedly conscious estimates of what is or is not worthwhile, are due to standards of which they are not conscious at all. Consequently, old and unconscious values, usually negative, inhibiting or cautious exert strong pressures when new ideas are proposed or new behavior is suggested. An example of a particular instance of unconscious pupil reaction in a classroom during an art period may be traced to punctuality. If there has

[4] Gordon Allport, *Pattern and Growth in Personality* (New York: Holt, Rinehart and Winston, 1961), p. 145.

been an earlier stress on "being on time," of exposure to a strict schedule that valued being at an appointed place at an appointed time, then the child is likely to feel inhibited in his artistic explorations. Since the art experience is a flexible one, sometimes dependent on mood, it cannot be subjected to strict time limitations; there may be a feeling of frustration and inadequacy if time limits are introduced. Certainly, if teachers insist that every pupil in their class finish art projects within prescribed periods, as is usually the case in school schedules, there will probably be a curtailment of genuine creative behavior. The unconscious values of punctuality will dominate an experience that requires a freedom of activity divorced from the tyranny of the clock. Teachers have to recognize such unconscious attitudes and plan to neutralize or alleviate them if they will interfere with the learning and creative process in art.

Another practice in art teaching may further indicate how these unconscious frames of reference are influential. Much has been made of the possibilities of integration of art with other subject matter. In the elementary school, on the middle levels particularly, art is considered a good tool in teaching social studies. With the mind set that what is being learned is essentially historical or geographical in nature, the teacher will suggest that students make murals, charts, copies of textbook illustrations, and a host of other visualizations of their social studies topic. Because the pupils as well as the teacher are aware of the need for precise, accurate, and informative work, the attempts by the pupils usually reflect this concern. The drawing or painting is unfortunately tight and restricted, contrary to what the pupils are generally encouraged to do in the art room. There is a concern for objectively verifiable visualization which probably was internalized much earlier than the fourth grade in our technologically oriented society with its stress on the utility of the elements in any situation. The looser, more exploratory factors in a creative art situation with the emphasis on the handling of elements for an aesthetic end is regarded as inappropriate for the integrated experience. Yet the actual "making" experience is primarily artistic in nature, even if the content has a discursive validity. That is, the making of a picture or a piece of sculpture is essentially concerned with ordering the concrete elements of line, mass, color, values, and other art elements. The process is a pictorial or sculptural one. The concerns are aesthetic, involving harmony, balance, relationships of color or light and dark intensities as well as many other design factors that are initially artistic rather than narrative. Though communication of ideas is important, for the artist it is subject to the sensitivity with which he forms and manipulates the visual parts of the creative experience. The form should reflect the content which is more a *reaction to* ideas than the ideas themselves. The aesthetic experience is violated and adulterated if the content (the literary, representational image) is the only concern. Therefore, we often find the situation where an art teacher must counter the generally unconsciously formed pseudo-creative attitude of an arbitrary but predetermined "accuracy" in drawing, painting, and modelling. The contrary is too often true of the classroom

Art
and
Education
in
Contemporary
Culture

•

120

teacher. The bewildered children have to learn to adapt to differing frames of reference. They develop a pigeonholing technique in art that attempts to answer similar problems differently depending upon current circumstances. Their own unconscious frames of reference are thus too rigidly formulated or exist in a vacillating fog of uncertainty, neither attitude assisting in the realization of the various teaching goals or of their own selves. Obviously, the teaching and the subsequent making of art have to be approached in a free and exploratory manner.

THE IDENTIFICATION OF SELF WITH VALUES

The fact that many values are unconsciously present in the individual and operate within a unique frame of reference, which in itself is subject to change, creates problems for the teacher of recognition and response. Another impinging factor that teachers have to be aware of and allow for is the self-identification that the individual experiences through the internalized social values with the happenings and objects of the outside world. Every student's ego is involved, indicating the individual's internalized consciousness of his own self and is an important psychologically interpretive element in the censoring of his reactions, thinking, feeling, and judgments. Ralph Linton, an anthropologist, sums up the working of the ego in this way:

Classrooms frequently, even if unconsciously, instill values of mass conformity in art and learning experiences.

The functional importance of value-attitude systems derives primarily from their emotional content. Behavior which is not in accord with the individual's system elicits responses of fear, anger or, at the very least, disapproval. This holds equally whether the behavior is his own or that of others. Thus, an indi-

Value
Relationships
in
Art,
Education,
and
Society

•

121

vidual who performs an act contrary to one of his own established value-attitude systems will experience considerable emotional disturbances both before and after. In most cases, he will have a reaction even though he knows the act will not entail punishment. This disturbance will diminish with repetitions of the act, but will reappear with each new situation involving the particular system. Similarly, other people's acts which are contrary to one of these systems will elicit emotional responses even when they do not threaten the individual in any way.[5]

This may perturb the teacher as well as the student as the following anecdote indicates. A friend of the author's, a young middle class fledgling teacher, accepted a temporary assignment as a substitute art teacher in a lower working class, urban school that had a reputation of being "rough." However, he regarded it potentially as a good experience, one that would deepen his own teaching personality even if the experience would be a trying one. On the first day of class, coming rather unprepared (substitutes rarely have an opportunity to write lesson plans), the young man asked an eighth grade class of pupils, both boys and girls, to draw something they like to do. He thought this would provide him with an insight for later art lessons. To his horror and dismay when he looked at the results, he found that a majority of the drawings were of a sexual content with the individuals depicted in very compromising positions. The teacher reacted to the work and the smirks of the pupils by running out of the room. He found the principal and announced that he could no longer teach in the school. Fortunately, the principal understood and took over the class himself. The young man left and did not attempt to teach again for a long period of time. He obviously felt threatened, or terribly disturbed by the values the students had expressed and he reacted in a personal way.

Teachers have to be aware of these extremely pertinent personal value influences, in many cases differing markedly from their own attitudes. The recognition has to be not only as an abstract consideration, but as having a direct bearing on individual expression and learning in the classroom. The detachment mentioned earlier would serve a purpose here, permitting a critically transient disengagement from the teacher's self image for teaching effectiveness. At the same time, the student has to be encouraged to pursue a vital image of himself and assisted in shaping it through art forms of his own creation.

THE MATRIX OF CULTURE

Unfortunately, the creative fervor and understanding that a truly contemporary teaching spirit would want to instill in the classroom and in each individual student runs counter to many of the group ideas and to conforming educational beliefs and practices. Jules Henry points out that, "As he acquires new knowledge, modern man becomes perplexed by the

[5] Ralph Linton, *The Cultural Background of Personality* (New York: Appleton-Century-Crofts, 1945), p. 112.

The exploratory art work of children, no matter what the background, is usually delightfully expressive, possessing a naive charm as well as an inherent realization of aethetic relationship.

"New York Skyline." [*New York Public Schools*]

fact that old ideas and preoccupations bind; that in the process of teaching his children he acts in ancient ways, fettering mind and spirit. But while acknowledging that this hampers the capacity to move, man is yet afraid that unchaining the young intellect will cause overthrow and chaos." [6] Consequently, the transmitted, stable factors in culture assume an "obsessive" power, throwing reins of contained learning upon the disturbances that new ideas or experiences may bring. The attendant anxieties, Henry indicates, tend to obscure the very positive and creative core of education. Even when contemporary education deliberately undertakes change, it does so not so much in attempting to achieve an ideal directly, but in "destroying a nightmare" that has been inherited from earlier times. These are very real, if diffused factors, that an art teacher comes up against.

Culture is a continuing and omnipresent force. Responding to external stimuli of which man-made culture is a good part, human beings naturally act out their biological natures within a sociological context. The large environment consisting of complicated and diverse parts: physical geography, political development, economic patterns, social mores, and traditional beliefs all have a voice in particularizing the influences that impinge

[6] Jules Henry, *Culture Against Man* (New York: Random House, 1963), p. 320.

upon personal understanding and behavior. It would seem that the art work of children as well as their teacher's emphasis in method could not escape certain deliberate culturally predetermining tendencies as a result, in addition to unconscious factors.

These tendencies are derived from the accumulation of tradition, the accepted understandings, the approved responses of the social group the individual was born into and continues to live with deliberately fostered as well as unconsciously internalized. The individual possesses a *Weltanschauung*, a world view that has a particular quality of interpretation. The art work of a student in Africa, Germany, or Bali is likely to be different in many ways from one another just as all will be different from American examples even when there is a shared childish outlook. However, within a large, sprawling society such as the American one there are a great number of subgroups which possess local cultural inflections that also give a particular and differing flavor to the work produced. A Negro child's drawing from the tenement district of Harlem would not coincide in cultural derivation with a white, midwestern, suburban child's interpretation of even a similar subject. At the same time though, the homogenizing disposition of a mass society is standardizing the cultural influences to a point where they overcome the weaker force of local distinctions making for a broad conformity of forms.

It is obvious then that education is not limited to the formal procedures of the classroom. For the child, the home, his friends, the mass media of communication such as television and a host of other factors have already

Value
Relationships
in
Art,
Education,
and
Society
.
123

Paintings by Young Africans. [Exhibition Circulated by the Smithsonian Institution. Reproduced by Permission of the Smithsonian Institution]

Art
and
Education
in
Contemporary
Culture

.

124

been at work in the educative process long before he enters school. These factors consistently pace the efforts of teachers once the child is in school. In a sense, school can be called a continuing re-education and a synthesizing of cultural influences. In fact, it is not until the individual's perception is dominated and enriched by a system of values free from pretense, that are both subject to a maturing conviction and yet open to change, that it can honestly be asserted that real learning, artistic or intellectual, has taken place. This is difficult to achieve even at adult levels, so teachers are compelled to grapple with very gross aspects of cultural prescriptions. These potently install themselves as primary attitudes in the developing personality. Since the personality is also self-oriented and motivated by self-esteem (except in the perverse and infrequent inversion of self hate) these cultural attitudes are organically accepted as the proper projection of one's self without too much questioning. Subsequently, the student engaged in expressive behavior will reflect all of the ingrained values that have been derived from a particular environmental condition good and bad and perhaps more so than normal in art because of the emotional directness with which art is implemented. In a later chapter this will be more specifically examined. Generally we can say life in the form of a characteristic culture largely coerces the nature of student response and expression.

A young girl will draw symptomatic forms that cast back her sexual role in society (relatively delicate, pretty, herself as a ballet dancer, nurse, and so on, without any harsh overtones of clash and conflict) while a young boy will not inordinately create his own masculine but culturally derived images (sharper, bolder, active, and concerned with "manly" content). These deterministic factors are easily observed, though there may be some question as to whether they are cause or effect in a freely uncommitted and intelligently critical analysis. The element of individual consciousness, of unique personal sentience, is too easily neglected by a deterministic approach, the restlessness, uncertainty and solitary nature of the human condition glossed over by repetitious, positivistic logic. Perhaps, if there were truly an atmosphere of real teaching stimulation, the child would search out his own expressive resolutions to experience more readily than those that culture, with such grim persistence, passively provides for him. Yet the latter are so pervasive the art teacher must take cognizance of them in very fundamental ways.

Group Conformity

The stress of cultural values tends to cluster into an average and standardized acceptance of what the group considers proper or adequate. At least, the supposedly less creative individuals demonstrate this tendency. The individual, despite his unique faculties and background of experience, is made to emphasize those elements of his background that conform to group understanding. If his ability to resist group pressure is low, there is a parallel lack of independent thought and creative action. This raises as well the question of identity. Can the individual really assume an identity

Value
Relationships
in
Art,
Education,
and
Society

.

125

*Whether the creative
impulse is direct or
circumspect, sym-
pathetic or critical,
the uniquely inter-
preted forms of
contemporary artists
express the basic
values of the society
they live in.*

*"Still Life #28 with
Live TV,"* Tom
Wesselmann. [*The
Green Gallery, New
York;* PHOTO:
Rudolph Burckhardt]

divorced from a social group or, conversely, is identity continuously compromised and "alien" if it is subject to group assent? An experience with art
in a direct and uncompromised fashion may begin to answer this for the
individual.

The urge to conformity, though, has its positive as well as negative elements in the art experience. On any level of development, an individual
student may learn by studying the works of those that are about him. The
attempts of his peers stimulate a need of his own to follow suit. If the
dependency is not too deep, not only is an interest awakened in trying to
express himself, but certain realizations of material handling, technique, and
image formation will be provided in a simple direct way. This most
teachers could not hope to stimulate in their more sophisticated or collective methods. Group activity that must involve a good measure of individual restraint (or positive conformity if you will) also provides for a
seemingly healthy interaction among students and between the participating individual and the large purpose of creative involvement. A respect
is developed for the necessary disciplines so that an overall unity is achieved.
Without some degree of conformity man could not live in communities
and share even the symbolic yet solitary efforts of artistic expression
through a process of communion or communication. The symbolism invokes some basic common denominators of comprehension.

The core understanding and the tried methods of response to experience
are thus transmitted to succeeding generations. It follows that the cultural
pressures within a context of conformity could be put to positive use on one
level. The procedures of the educational enrichment programs are predicated on this kind of understanding. Expose the underprivileged child to

Art
and
Education
in
Contemporary
Culture

·

126

the so-called privileges: attendance in theatres, trips to concert halls, visits to museums, sympathetic, stimulating and first-hand experiences in the arts and these will exert their own attractions, fomenting a conformity to values different and "higher" than those previously held. Of course, here too, there are many holes and bewilderments for the student, setting up internal antagonisms in response to the contradictions that he is subjected to in school and at home. Nevertheless, teaching method in this instance recognizes the efficacy of conformity.

Finally, there is the natural desire on the part of all young people to be influenced by that which is great, important, beautiful, stirring, and otherwise exciting. Almost all great artists undergo periods of submitting themselves to someone else's vision that they admire. In doing this, they enrich and expand their own capacities and possibilities. However, the values that are conformed to are selective in this instance. That, too, is a cue for all teachers of art. It is desirable and necessary that students be exposed to any influence by a genuine interchange with high levels of art.

There are also additional negative elements of cultural conformity to consider as they affect art education. These have been broadly discussed in a variety of contexts throughout the book. We will touch only upon the most pertinent dangers as they relate to the art work of students and the creative climate in which they have to operate.

Group art experience develops social values. This may be all to the good yet aesthetic experience requires an emphasizing of solitary expression and unique understanding as well. [PHOTO: *Stephen C. Sumner*]

The making of art is, essentially and most honestly, a solitary affair in its creative phase. The values in it for the individual student stem from this realization. Painting a picture or carving a model insists upon an interior dialogue, a plumbing of inner emotional states and to the extent that it is subjected to externally allotted conditions of creative expression, it is an adulterated, and partially realized experience. Unless each student is permitted the groping attempts of his own expression, no matter how awkward or culturally displaced, there is no corresponding genuine individual growth and value development in the aesthetic and expressive area of personality. Though a child may receive certain social and perhaps even general learning benefits from working on a mural, for instance, with classmates, these benefits may be more than offset by the inhibited personal experience in art. The art experience in a shared endeavor too frequently becomes divorced from the aesthetic concerns and becomes an instrument for values other than those that are a natural part of art. The several children painting the spots on the giraffe mural may be having a good time, collectively developing a learning experience. It is doubtful though, if in the measure of conformity to the group idea and in the subsequent diminution of self realization there is a real artistic process involved, incorporating an aesthetic and personally emotional base, though there is positive social interaction.

The lute-playing woman by a fifth grade girl and the falling soldier by a sixth grade boy (p. 128) are typical examples of the distinctions in form and content that are determined by the roles each sex is expected to maintain in American culture. The girl's drawing is relatively soft, poetically evocative, romantic and rhythmically contained, with a charming content distinctly feminine in its imagery. The boy's drawing is harsher, its lines sometimes discontinuous; it is direct and adventurous, mirroring all of the gory and gallant war stories with which boys feel compelled to be acquainted. In each instance the work derives primarily from cultural contexts that relate to sexual roles.

The picture of the oriental looking man (p. 129) created by a student in Hawaii is not a typical American image, despite the fact that Hawaii is now one of the states of the union. The strong cultural emphasis of oriental forms makes itself felt in the kinds of shapes and the nature of the content of the children's art work, because of the spread of these ethnic factors in Hawaii.

There are cultural influences that affect color, shape various relationships, delineations of form and choice of materials and techniques dependent upon social, economic, racial, and various other traditional sources of cultural values. They would be too numerous to illustrate individually. In each instance, the student thinking he is asserting his own self, projecting his ego images, is in reality the unknowing pipeline through which culture is demonstrating its predominant influence. Until quite recently, women have believed that they could never become important artists, that they were congenitally unfit for such a role. With the newly won social freedom, contemporary women have demonstrated an intrinsic artistic competence on a par with male quality.

Value
Relationships
in
Art,
Education,
and
Society

.

127

Art
and
Education
in
Contemporary
Culture

·

128

*The drawing reflects
feminine interests
and identification.
"Lady with a Lute,"
Fifth Grade
Drawing. [Ann Arbor
Public Schools;
PHOTO: Stuart
Klipper]*

*Typically popular
masculine character-
istics often motivate
boyish responses in
art. "War Picture,"
Sixth Grade
Drawing. [Ann Arbor
Public Schools;
PHOTO: Stuart
Klipper]*

Value
Relationships
in
Art,
Education,
and
Society

•

129

Hawaiian Children's Art. [Exhibition Circulated by the Smithsonian Institution. Reproduced by permission of the Smithsonian Institution]

The Example of Modern Art

We may consider the common attitude generally displayed by the average teacher in regard to the ideas and forms of modern art as an example of the need for sensitive and generally continuing value changes because of encroaching cultural inhibitions. More likely than not, the average teacher's experience with modern art either in a personal or a professional classroom sense has been of a limited nature, if it exists at all. There is apt to be an open dislike and an evident out of hand rejection or, at the very least, a great sense of bewilderment. The puzzling content of the newer painting or sculpture and their improvisation of form so typical of contemporary works of art, have no ready reference in earlier and more familiar pictorial experiences. They trespass the accepted bounds of representational

Art
and
Education
in
Contemporary
Culture

·

130

images. The artist has departed from a photographic naturalism and a sentimentalized academism that had achieved a sacrosanct respect heretofore. There is also the continuing indoctrination of a relatively conservative nature that still is a strong trend in many of the higher art schools and which broadly filters down into teacher education. As a recent President characterized new art form, for many teachers, and pupils too, it is a "ham and eggs" art.

In the classroom, this may be more true where specialized art teachers are not available in a particular building or are completely lacking. This attitude persists, sometimes despite the supposedly sympathetic and specialized knowledge presumed of an art teacher when she does visit classrooms periodically. Generally, the average exposure to modern art and its philosophical implications is insufficient. Though the Sunday supplements and popular periodicals which teachers are exposed to occasionally have articles and reproductions of modern works, these usually are most superficial and hardly lend themselves to a necessary, very time consuming

An artist's interpretive understanding of cultural conditioning expressed through the content of popular boyish play. "The Defenders," Richard Wilt. [Courtesy of the artist; Collection The University of Michigan Museum of Art]

Value
Relationships
in
Art,
Education,
and
Society

•

131

The cultural context
strongly influences
the art forms of
children as in this
symbolic representa-
tion of folk song and
the Beatles. "The
Beatle Song," Sixth
Grade Drawing.
[Ann Arbor Public
Schools; PHOTO:
Stuart Klipper.]

understanding. The infrequent visits to museums that feature modern
works may be helpful, but too often they are more like picnics or other
popular outings with "fun" as an undisguised element in the visit. The
art objects are experienced through a haze of popular prejudice, ridicule,
apathy, or timid misdirected questioning. There is little significant opportunity to build up the kind of affirmative and intensive experiences that
most of the contemporary art forms require if they are to be sincerely seen
and aesthetically understood on more than a superficial level.

Therefore, in many of the situations, the experience aspect of value
formation in contemporary art is shallow. It is bound by trivial concerns
and lack of genuinely meaningful opportunities in which to enjoy and
come to grips with a modern work of art. This has its antecedents in a cultural stress on practical values, a technological civilization and the conforming qualities of mass standardized living as well. Commercial and advertising art, though they make use of the bold powerful design of modern
art, utilize the lowest common denominator of illustrative art to sell its
products. From infancy on the individual is unconsciously subjected to the
tastes of his surroundings. These become an attitude based on internalized
values which develop mass assumptions later determining the responses
of so many people. Society is left with a general lack of comprehension of
the philosophy of modern art, a relative emptiness of real aesthetic experience and a backwash of intellectual tradition that denies the potent improvisations, searching creativeness and powerful symbolism of modern art.

Art
and
Education
in
Contemporary
Culture

•

132

As suggested earlier, the school itself is not the only agency that fosters values; obviously its role in this regard is complicated by the forces outside that influence teacher and pupil alike. A teacher, in examining the values he is sponsoring in a classroom, during an art lesson in this instance, should face the possibility that his own values and that of his pupils may be impoverished in the very area he is attempting to enrich. This could be overcome in part in examining one's own understanding critically. The older traditions in art may be enjoyed but of necessity challenged, recognizing the change that is inherent in all phenomena.

The teacher's probing of the symbolic art structure that is presented by contemporary art work, is encouraged by the "stepping back" process. However, this is limited by the nature of the formal experience and other kinds of personal experience the teacher has had in art and by the amount of welcome he is willing to give to the swirl of personal involvement with what may be, at first and perhaps always, provoking and challenging issues. Even when these are not barriers, the answers that teachers find for themselves may only be beginnings that pose new questions. There are influential thinkers today, as an example, who believe that the large public may intuitively understand the symbolic nature of contemporary art, but dislikes it because of its rather negative implications.[7] That is, the artist is showing us a rather untidy and chaotic world of which there are many elements that a rational and a benign individual (the image of the well rounded product of democratic schools) should be ashamed. If this can be granted, then the educational endeavor becomes even more difficult, particularly if an understanding is to be effected between the individual in a mass society and the aesthetic and implied moral insights of art. In any case, a more sensible response to the aesthetic qualities of modern art is required, as well as a wider acceptance of its content.

Despite the generally negative mass response to modern ideas in art, there has been a growing influence of these ideas in the visual context of the environment. Industry and commerce have incorporated many of the new forms into their design and products outside of a popular profit motive, while important architecture has blossomed into a style that is novel and dependent, stylistically at least, upon the aesthetics of modern art though there is frequently more adulteration than creative improvisation. Children, as well as their adult mentors, are subjected to a changing surrounding. Though the earlier visual forms have thus been modified, sometimes very drastically since World War II, drawing upon the work of contemporary artists, there is still a very potent barrier between the average individual and the acceptance of the newer ideas in art. Too often, the common experience in this area is thin, facetious, and rather unreliable. Earlier values that are currently in operation both on a conscious and internalized level are not easily discarded and form an effective block against change. The whole area of popular culture and the values it fosters will be more fully examined in a later chapter.

[7] An example is found in Walter Abell's, *The Collective Dream in Art* (Cambridge, Mass.: Harvard University Press, 1957).

But surely, in "stepping back," teachers assume responsibilities that, if they are to be significant and influential have to be passionately pursued, oriented around individual insight but conducive to collective understanding as well. These responsibilities are tied to current and controversial exploration of forms as much as to familiar and older ones. Here the feeling aspect enters. It is bound to be buffeted about by internal pressures and the exposure to the flux and flow of the conditions that exist today as well as the traditions of yesterday. But if teachers exercise a maturing sense of discrimination, they can recognize the emotional ferment that underlies individual perception and other subconscious determining factors. Incorporating and orienting these feelings they can perhaps more appropriately then provide, for themselves as well as for pupils, the necessary and positive experiences with which to enlarge and sensitize value judgments. The example of modern art may consequently have fair, meaningful and honestly felt presentation.

The cultivated and generalized classroom response to the provoking images and ideas of contemporary art forms need not be, "It is nutty," "That artist is crazy," "Anybody can do that; it does not mean a thing!" The child in concert with the aware and unprejudiced guidance of an art teacher may have an opportunity to relate not only to the imposed cultural dictates, but to an individually created dialogue with his art experiences. The new creative images and happenings of the world could then reflect a pertinent and contemporary feeling.

A Contemporary Emphasis

The twentieth century, however, is not easily categorized in its art forms for there have been an immense range of varying styles. Parallel to the popular and traditional forms, are many new explorations in expression, employing new materials, expressing a changing content and attempting orginal techniques. These may be strange and shocking at times, novel and provocative in their approaches, abstract and frequently esoteric in their philosophy, yet they generally seek the fitting images and expressive symbols that will capture the vast cultural metamorphosis that is occurring. Perhaps even the art forms that have evolved over the past century are only a prelude to a newer and currently emerging synthesis of style. The emphasis since the end of World War II has been upon an ideational art, upon an abstraction of cultural concepts and movements, which set up an antithesis between the individual and society. The individual is paired with a sensate, personal approach whereas society, through its technological and philosophical changes, is artistically experienced as geometric, collective, functioning in elegant order outside the transitory impulses of single individuals. Both approaches stress the formative nature of human ideas and imagination, though one emphasizes the sensual as the avenue to expressive understanding and the other utilizes the impulses that emanate from the newer scientific, political and social forces. The latter may well be the harbinger of the future. Art education, in any instance, is to be held accountable for presenting the substance of these newer and

Art
and
Education
in
Contemporary
Culture

.

134

pertinent artistic expressions, whether in exasperation or aspiration, for these are the emerging qualities of tomorrow's manner of living.

The concept of change infuses the very creative functions of the contemporary artist and provides an ideological basis for formal improvisations, experiments in media and content and also achieves novelty in rediscovering and altering older art styles. Improvisation and experimentation become fundamental ways of seeing that should find a counterpart in the art classroom. However, for teachers and students, as it is for artists, the emphasis cannot be on novelty for its own sake, but rather upon searching out the original and appropriate manner for a contemporary mode of expression. The implied break with the past, even if it is only a partial one, indicates that the sureness of traditional forms can no longer be counted upon and that the future of artistic expression for society, as well as for the individual, student and artist alike, is one of uncertainty. This may provide as much a feeling of adventure as it does a difficulty to overcome because of strangeness. Certainly such values are fundamental to a contemporary climate in the classroom.

The teacher of art has to recognize that the twentieth century is one of movement, of transition, of radical alteration, and that these facets of civilization have primary impacts upon art. Similarly, the means of adjusting to new images and to differing evaluations of process and product deserve an unprejudiced assessment that has divested itself of outmoded or limited frames of reference. The art that should be stimulated in the classroom requires an understanding reflecting the remaking of the environment and an alteration of the inner vision that is so characteristic of most contemporary creative ventures. On one level, these artistic improvisations, attuned to the flux and flow of the environment, are no more than a reflection of one important societal facet that is undergoing change; but on another level, they can be the primary means whereby the student's personality may achieve a rapport with his emerging culture and a way of becoming a dynamic part of it.

Influence and Individuality in the Child

Children react in innocent and spontaneous ways, at first, to the bolder and more ambiguous works of modern art. There is a natural affinity in their own art work to the direct statements and improvisational creativeness of the twentieth century artist. The vigorous use of color, the strong rhythms of line and masses, the sharply or simply delineated shapes, the intensive symbol content share a parallel development, though on differing levels of personal expression and artistic consciousness. As the various binding cultural pressures make themselves felt, however, the early confidence becomes weaker, and the art work less sure. Somewhere in the middle grades there starts the faltering attempts to more "realistically" copy the popular conventional heritage of the Renaissance of correct proportion and perspective to pinpoint one element. Since there are relatively few knowing influences at this point to adequately shape an artistic discipline of skills and techniques, the personal work and the identification with art generally deteriorates and eventually disappears, almost by default of education.

There is no saving virtue in appreciation, except in the most cursory and generally uninformed manner. Since the growth of awareness is unusually dependent upon the teacher's projection of values and understanding, the artistic literacy of the great mass of students remains undeveloped, reflecting the teacher's own inadequacy in this area as well as the larger cultural inroads that limit personal vision.

Where there is personal and authentic involvement by the teacher with art, modern as well as the preceding periods, there could be a corresponding aesthetic blossoming on the part of students. The work produced might bear an easier relationship with the vital outside artistic currents. The students would then experience an unfolding of aesthetic insights that could permit them to develop the necessary personal values with which to respond independently, positively, and sensitively to culture and hopefully adapt to its patterns, without pretense or philistine attitudes. Though ideally stated, any art teacher cannot aim for less. The aim becomes one of accenting individual and honest self-realization, in a qualitative, existential way, not ignoring culture, but not being circumscribed by it either; establishing a vital coexistence, so to speak.

The generalized theorizing on this note, however, has little actual value for the individual in a particular creative sense and in the actual nature of his specific expressive patterns and artistic understanding. Art work varies greatly from one student to another. This is so much true, that despite the similarities of forms and outlooks at various age levels, in shared geographical backgrounds and social surroundings, each child, for the most part, produces unique works. For the discerning teacher there is a great range of distinction in the individual examples of art work created by children. The values that are expressed demonstrate these singularly developed and existential lines of direction as well as broader patterns of conforming to group attitudes. These existentially individual patterns are innumerable and almost infinite by definition. Yet a teacher's insight into them may be more acutely sympathetic and understanding if the larger cultural patterns that also play a part are recognized.

CULTURAL INFLUENCES IN ART

The broad patterns do provide helpful insights that could assist the teacher in understanding, not only the works of art that are a part of culture but the influences that in many ways shape the individual's own work and comprehension in art, and have recognizable, observable features.

All art is dependent not only upon the cultural envelope it is created in but its form and content are also drawn from interpretations of the past. The particular styles that different countries and different times evolve and the fact they may be distinguished one from the other is evidence of this.

New styles reflect new cultural stresses, embodying the changing conditions, habits, value formulations, social ideas and ideals that the artist

Art
and
Education
in
Contemporary
Culture

.

136

incorporates in his work alongside the personal factors of expression. The forms that are employed, despite the fact that they may have universal qualities and timeless significance are paradoxically also of a time, a place. The painting, "Historical Monument of the American Republic" (p. 138), is definitely not a great painting, clearly demonstrates nineteenth-century American cultural values, ideally in the notions of progress, grand scale, monumental solidity, and thick fantasy concept. At the same time, it reflects the neoclassical revival, a current taste for big, turgid, spatial volumes and is circumscribed by a traditional attitude and a balanced, relatively practical sense of order and unimaginatively logical relationships that unfortunately do not buckle under the heavy, encumbered vulgarity of taste.

Jasper Johns' "Three Flags" (p. 138), however, eschews an easy patriotism, evidencing a twentieth-century condition that emphasizes a searching experimentalism, an artistic quest that questions easy symbolic understanding, attempting to delve beyond the simple appearance or common understanding of things. It is bold yet ambiguous, beautifully brushed yet simple in form. It presents a challenge to the audience, much as does contemporary living, giving no recognized world view but requests a committed response, nevertheless—a cultural idea that has widespread acceptance among artists if not the general public.

Piero della Francesca's Christ (p. 139) is a Renaissance concept. It is highly rational, structured within the visual comprehension of the senses, bending its intense religiosity into an outward looking quality. This is in keeping with the Renaissance attitudes that were emerging, of a mass centered world accepting the hegemony of Christian theology but curious as well about the physical world, its nature and the scientific manner of its operation. It discards the mysticism and other worldliness of the earlier Middle Ages and the painting forms reveal the reasoned Renaissance mind. The artist has transformed into concrete symbols some of the most important cultural conditions of the time.

Paul Burlin's painting, "Jazz in Heaven" (p. 139), is easily experienced as a twentieth-century image. Its distortions of form, its intense color, and its irreverent subject matter have drawn from the vast cultural changes that have metamorphosized the world since the Renaissance. The decline of religion and a return to subjectivity are only two obvious factors. It could not have been painted at the same time as Piero della Francesca's work for any number of other reasons, mostly stemming from the very different cultural conditions that prevailed. Despite a universal quality of the works, they speak of different times. Each artist has succeeded in embodying some aspect of a contemporary cultural influence. There is also the role of the artist as he is regarded in society, rather than his work, which culturally influences students' art responses.

AN ANTAGONISM OF CULTURAL VALUES

The artist has enjoyed a peripheral position in the unfolding American scene at best, where he has not been rejected outright or treated with overt hostility. Too often disdain or ridicule have been the reactions to the artists' attitudes and to their creations. Even today when there is some relief from the formerly broad unrelenting suspicion of artistic endeavor as a serious activity, especially when it is utilized commercially as in advertising or in some popular form of entertainment such as comic strips or magazine covers, the artist is regarded as someone not quite on a par with other professionals. The fine artist still exists, for most people, on some peculiar and generally distasteful or esoteric plane, well without the pale of average acceptance. His values, particularly, are often contrary or tangential to the commonly held values derived from mass understanding. These values stress emotion along with reason; individual integrity of purpose along with action, aesthetic and introspective concerns as basic to exisence. Expression, for the artist is a primary human function with the intensification of individual perception and sensitivity as a biologically inherent aim rather than as an abstractly ideal one, stressing a real cultural enrichment.

Value
Relationships
in
Art,
Education,
and
Society

.

137

Though it may be presumptuous to categorize in any real and significant way the shared attitudes, the so-called core values of the larger American culture (and a parallel emerging Western European culture), there is sufficient empirical and historical evidence to do so in a broad sense. The historian, Henry S. Commager, succinctly characterizes some aspects of the mind of the mid-twentieth century American and his culture in the following way:

His culture was still predominantly material, his thinking quantitative, his genius inventive, experimental and practical . . . He cherished individualism but was less sure of the virtue of nonconformity . . . The persistence of fundamental philosophical beliefs and assumptions was as tenacious as that of practices, habits, and attitudes. Puritanism lingered on, not so much as a search for individual salvation or as a celebration of the virtues of thrift and industry but as a recognition of the dignity of the individual and of his duty to achieve both spiritual and material prosperity . . . For the most part, Americans still believed that such words as honor, virtue, courage, and purity had meaning, and if science had injected some doubts, their standards were confused rather than their conduct.[8]

Commager goes on to cite the use of technology and the relative leisure that developed, yet notes that Americans still work harder than other national groups and seek security as an overwhelming aim. In the decade that has passed since the midfifties, there has been little change in attitude even though fundamental changes have occurred in science and international politics. Despite the stress on the individual in ideal terms, most social actions are the result of group thinking. Pragmatic planning with "down to earth" reason or readily recognizable justification bolstering it is still considered the most advanced social aim, though the "smart operator," the shrewd business man and the successful self seeker are in actual fact also accepted as practical models of behavior. The earlier anti-intellectualism has lifted somewhat to create new and naïve hero images of the scientist, though

[8] Henry S. Commager, The American Mind (New Haven: Yale University Press, 1952), p. 416.

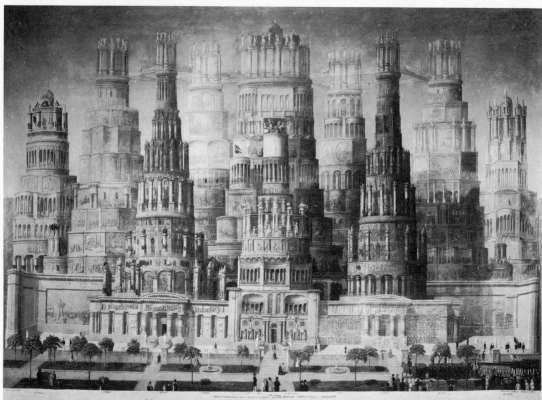

HISTORICAL MONUMENT OF THE AMERICAN REPUBLIC.

Value
Relationships
in
Art,
Education,
and
Society

.

139

[LEFT, TOP] *"Historical Monument
of the American
Republic,"* Erastus
Salisbury Field.
[*Courtesy of the
Morgan Wesson
Memorial Collection,
Museum of Fine
Arts, Springfield,
Mass.*]

[LEFT, BOTTOM]
"Three Flags,"
Jasper Johns. [*Leo
Castelli Gallery;*
PHOTO: *Michael
Katz*]

[RIGHT, TOP] *"Resurrection of Christ,"*
Piero Della
Francesca. [*Istituto
Italiano di Cultura,
New York*]

[RIGHT, BOTTOM]
"Jazz in Heaven,"
Paul Burlin. [*Collection, IBM*]

Art
and
Education
in
Contemporary
Culture

.

140

it is the technician rather than the speculative thinker who is admired. As for intellectual interests, it is usually left to the professors, writers, or artists to pursue them. Though the typical American hungers for culture, he is willing to satisfy his appetite for the most part, by being a passive spectator through television, record playing, reading the popular periodicals, or making pilgrimages to highly advertised special shows at local museums among other mass attractions in entertainment. He is a consumer of culture, rather than a maker or appreciator of it and the schools reflect this.

In brief, on the surface and in some other more profound ways, there are some antagonisms or, at the very least, contradictory influences between the core values of the large mass of Americans and those that mature artists subscribe to. An average individual student, feeling pressures being exerted on his ego, unconsciously makes the kind of identifications that will encourage or inhibit his judgments and consequent behavior in keeping with the large environmental patterns.

The frame of reference that is influencing the emerging values of an average student as he moves from early elementary to upper elementary, then to junior and senior high undergoes subtle but accumulative changes. The early joy of the primary grades in frequent art work is transformed into one of evasiveness and the necessity of overcoming impediments for the pre-adolescent. The sporadic opportunities during the middle years taper off to a complete divorce from art experience for an overwhelming majority of adolescent high school students. This is further abetted by a secondary counseling pattern that discourages good students from electing art.

The seemingly universal change that occurs around puberty from a natural enjoyment of, and easy identification with, artistic behavior to one of inhibition and lack of satisfaction in experiencing and creating art is not too well understood. There may be deep seated psychological and physiological influences at work which have not been fully probed as yet. However, it is probably justifiable to blame in part the emerging values that students are reacting to as a source of limiting aesthetic and creative activity. Particularly in the case of boys, the vague but insistent fear of being considered a "sissy" does not permit a smooth identification with artistic values. In the mass sense, it is the women who are concerned with aesthetic matters, either in the home or socially in the community, despite the fact, as was mentioned earlier, that until recently women were not regarded as capable professional artists. Girls generally accept the activities of the art class more openly and produce results more readily, though the work itself is not any more advanced or skillful than that which boys produce in good situations. Art is not normally considered a masculine undertaking in American culture. From another viewpoint, the young pupil absorbing the currently accepted values that stress practicality, utility, and groupness cannot make the necessary adjustment in their maturing personalities (particularly after the period of childhood—the first ten years of life are over) to artistic values that are nonutilitarian and stress a desirable uniqueness. More important, even if the choice and adjustments were conscious, as we have seen they largely are not, the student would not recognize a need to identify with values other than those commonly accepted because of the earlier unconscious internalization that has occurred.

Value
Relationships
in
Art,
Education,
and
Society

.

141

A deeply imbedded anti-intellectualism, that is documented by Richard Hofstader,[9] an outgrowth of earlier and similar attitudes runs parallel to the general lack of artistic sensibility. It is only since the orbiting of Sputnik that there has been any great attention paid to the intellect in the mass consciousness, and this as a practical answer to the threat of political competition. This may be an opportune base upon which to build a mature educational philosophy, yet we are left with the following doubts when the intellectual pursuits invite a humane supplement of culture: If art stresses personal integrity above convenience and security, this is seen as an alien or foolish attitude when the latter is so ubiquitously present in popularly accepted attitudes. If a group idea is regarded as a means of democratic process in preference to the ostensibly "snobbish" individualism of the artist, then why should anyone want to defend an elite group, even if the standards of art can be upheld in no other way at this point. If artistic expression is felt to be a form of play that is not concerned with the supposedly more serious business of accumulating facts and preparing for a vocation, to identify with the former is to defy common sense needlessly. If reason in a material and deterministic way is regarded as man's highest state as some present day scientists and educators insist is the mature legacy of tradition, why revert to the relative savagery of emotion? However, if emotion is congenitally a human attribute despite the ordering of our senses and our mind, why squander it on the frills of art? There are many other more useful or worthwhile purposes it can serve, particularly through personal relations and social entertainment.

These attitudes may be rather exaggerated and the questions naive, but they are unconsciously part of the process of value formation that each person in our society undergoes. There are many other aspects of a similar nature that do not permit pupils in our school systems to identify easily with aesthetic values.

Even when there is a recognition of the need for artistic activities, there is a grudging holding back of a genuine and wholehearted experience in most cases. The massive and powerful pragmatic influences still pervade the unconscious mind relegating art to a minor role in education. It is much simpler for the teacher and the pupils to suspend an attitude that goes against the grain. However, in doing so, a vital and intensely rewarding experience is renounced, and a natural process of human growth is aborted.

Youngsters, during their first learning experiences, both before formal school and for the first three and four grades seem to evidence characteristically free and creative attitudes, naturally and enthusiastically experimenting with expressing and enjoying art. As a matter of fact it would be practically impossible to teach the early grades without art. There is a positive acceptance of creative invention and an eager relationship with art. This may be due to the lack of adult pressures on this educational level; the

[9] Richard Hofstader, *Anti Intellectualism in American Life* (New York: Alfred Knopf, 1963).

Art
and
Education
in
Contemporary
Culture

·

142

"serious" business of training is still in the future. However, as soon as the large social values make themselves felt—the realization of adult "responsibility," there is the alienation from art mentioned earlier, that progresses until the normal separation between adolescent and art is an accomplished fact.

This in itself may not be a negative or detrimental condition in the eyes of many adults, including a disheartening percentage of teachers. However, the real loss is not confined to a narrow artistry or special aestheticism. Educationally, the individual student also renounces a fundamentally creative attitude, a willingness to explore and improvise in an open and expressive way as well as in achieving a sense of self identity. This does have direct education significance.

Government Support of The Arts

Despite the patterns outlined above, the changes inherent in a technologically expanding and materially affluent society have made themselves felt. Easier means of production, the utilization of cybernetics and automation, the lessening of the hours of work, the availability of money, the speed and convenience of travel and communication, have whetted a latent mass appetite for the arts. The performing arts, the visual arts and the popular scholarship and journalism that surround them have enjoyed a growing and continuing appeal reflected only fitfully in the schools and, for the most part, cynically exploited in the mass media. Some of this may be due to an understandable unfamiliarity with aesthetic values and the context of art. More likely, it results from looking upon art as an entertainment and a commodity that the democratically common man may now enjoy as well as the culturally elite.

In any case, even government, as well as private foundations, has assumed what may be considered fundamental responsibilities in arts education and the encouragement of artistic creativeness. Beginning just before the middle 1960s, Congress has voted respectable sums of money directly related to both the improvement and expansion of education in the arts, and of support and dissemination of art to the general public. Grants are offered a wide range of institutions and even to individuals for artistic purposes. These may be very important steps in counteracting the crass and philistine nature of much of American culture and of enriching education through better and enlarged arts programs. If the monies provided can be freely used in genuinely artistic and creative endeavors and, more important, if they can be administered without bureaucratic timidity and the interference of mediocrities, then a truly heroic and revolutionary cultural growth may occur. However, even a fledgling observer should note the remarkable turnabout and intensification of educational effort that must take place before any widely legitimate and honestly uncompromised aesthetic and artistic literacy can flourish.

An emphasis has to be established that does not simply bring the arts to the audience, but, without adulteration, lifts the audience to the best of art. The expansion of "culture" should not be merely an explosion of the old, the safely traditional, the accumulated storehouse of an earlier cultivated taste. This may degenerate into expensively subsidized forms of entertainment, mocking the worth of a Vivaldi sonata, a Shakespearian tragedy or the tremulous sensitivity of a Turner landscape. Just as vital as an appreciation of an arts heritage are the uses of the past to shed light on the present and future, to awaken an enthusiasm for current creativity.

The new support of the arts by government, on the other hand, cannot be regarded as akin to a Roman circus even if the potential for such is evident. Creative and concerned people, artists and critics alike, should seize this opportunity as a means of achieving the very goals they aspire to personally and to elaborate on them for the whole of society. A larger responsibility remains with arts educators to honestly appraise the new programs, to insist only on the highest and genuine artistic values, to abjure the gilted, the shallow and the still prevailing mediocrities. An enthusiasm and a willingness for personal and cultural satisfactions through art of high quality must be evidenced. Only in this sense can a vitally functioning community arise that embraces the ineffable, the mysterious and the aesthetic, as well as the delights of the moment, the creature comforts and the entertaining.

Value
Relationships
in
Art,
Education,
and
Society

•

143

Bridging the Gap in Value Attitudes

Obviously, teachers are in a position to be aware of the clash of values that is current and to influence the kinds of relationships that students establish as a result, yet they should also realize that it is not necessary to reject many of the central values in American living to reach a happy involvement with art. Though there is frequent contradiction and antagonism on even fundamental factors between the common social attitudes and those accepted by artists, there is good reason to believe that a mutually beneficial understanding may be reached through education.

For instance, an artist enjoys his work (and work sociologists tell us is not something most Americans enjoy); unfortunately it is generally regarded only as a necessary means that has to be accepted in order to earn a livelihood or gain status. Work is good in the Puritan sense in that it is morally uplifting but it is not a source of intrinsic gratification. It may be an end in itself but to confuse it with joy is to adulterate it in the popular mind. This may create a suspicion in the mass mind where there are potent traces of Puritanism, for how can enjoyable work be productive? Perhaps enjoyable is too easy a term to use here and not exactly correct. For often the artist literally suffers when he is working. But of significance is the sense of commitment the artist has in his work, the deliberate and affirmative manner in which the choice to do what he does do is made. Yet in doing this the artist on this simplified breakdown of relationships is no different from many other workers, for though he may feel positive about his work and experience, though it is fulfilling when it may be compulsive, he also works very hard at it. The serious artist is rarely the happy-go-lucky "beat-

Art
and
Education
in
Contemporary
Culture

·

144

nik" of popular legend; he is more often the disciplined and conscientious worker who in knowing he has a particular "job" to do, does it with great élan. In explaining this, an art teacher can appeal to some of those same core values that are being developed in the average student's mind, though with a somewhat different emphasis. There maybe a danger of sophistry or even fraudulent thinking in the analogy, though a sensitive teacher could present the analogy in a meaningful manner without surrendering to sloppy or thin thinking.

Another example of bridging the gap in the differing set of values may be seen in the idea of individual expression as a necessary and desirable "growth" goal in education or in art as an end in itself. Yet both aspects have worth and significance. The teacher can point out that the artists serve a larger, figurative, and more fundamentally "utilitarian" end when they stress aesthetic creation in that they are answering the intrinsically present (and probably biological) needs of being human. Since art is a basic human activity, it would appear quite "impractical" from a psychological viewpoint to starve certain innate hungers for expression and form making. However, there is the danger of confusing this with our national acceptance of expediency and technological insistence upon efficiency. To put an inordinate value on the concept of art as educational instrumentality is to fall into a trap of self seduction with the practical, seeing all education as narrowly meeting needs in a mechanical fashion rather than as a genuine and open avenue of individual development in a dynamic and organic sense. Real art experiences are never expedient, though they are spontaneous, and to "sell" them in any way that might suggest they are is to misrepresent their educational values. Yet the teacher has an incumbent responsibility of somehow offering the values of creative behavior and of artistic endeavor as worthwhile and rewarding within the context of a material philosophy and a utilitarian ethic. This must be accomplished with an honesty and integrity, otherwise there is a confusion of understanding and a bastardization of values. Perhaps the only workable method is one that involves the teacher as exemplar and guide, not in one or two easily formulated situations, but over an extensive period of time, and through a continuing accrual of perceptive and stimulating experiences.

Time, Work, and Leisure

However, no method, despite its apparent efficacy will possess any real significance if the values of the teaching circumstance or the proposed creative act are not possessed of intrinsic worth. Much of the body of commonly held values which currently serve as the value system of American culture and which invade the atmosphere of the classroom and the spirit of the student require not only a full examination, but probably a stimulus toward change. The attitudes toward work, toward time (both free and accounted for) and toward leisure that impel contemporary behavior and thought are a relic of the past, not consonant with the emerging potential of an educated society. Sebastian de Grazia in a provoking and brilliant study has divested many of the traditional concepts of work, time and

Value
Relationships
in
Art,
Education,
and
Society

.

145

*The questions of
work, leisure, and
play as they inter-
relate in the life of
the individual are
necessary value
considerations of art
education. The
contemporary artist
expresses some
aspects of these
elements as they are
evidenced in ordinary
living.*

*"Sun Bather,"
Raymond Mintz.
[Rehn Gallery,
New York;* PHOTO:
*Oliver Baker
Associates]*

leisure of their outmoded and inaccurate qualities, and has cut to the truth
the beliefs concerning the questionable uses of "free" time, the illusion of
efficiency in production, the intrinsic substance of work and of the nature
of leisure. He upsets many of the accepted notions concerning the ethic
surrounding work and the commitment to creative understanding that
characterizes true leisure. He almost advocates a fabulous land of leisure
and luxury, of untidiness and solitary habits not for their own sake, but
as the most appropriate means of the worthwhile leisurely life in the good
society. Leisure is regarded as the means by which man creates himself and
a desirable end product of educational training, productive capacity and
political freedom. However, leisure is not simply free time, it is time uncluttered by tedious obligation and devoted to a search for meaning. Since
leisure time can well be afforded even the average individual in the coming
technological society, even more so than at present, the necessary value
systems will have to be developed and attitudes established so that leisure
will be the "felicity, happiness, and blessedness" de Grazia pictures it as.
"Certainly," he says, "the life of leisure is the life for thinkers, artists, and
musicians." [10] Their values make it worthwhile and education should aim
in a corresponding direction so that, at least, some part of the frequently
transcendental, and always significant values may be offered to the as yet
unfinished promise of students. The arts suggest themselves as ideal conditions of such development, but only if they are presented in terms of
their own values and with an abiding enthusiasm and integrity.

[10] Sebastian de Grazia, *Of Time, Work, and Leisure* (Garden City, N.Y.: Doubleday, 1964), p. 415.

6

Psychological Assessment in Art Education

> I would prefer my madness to the rest of the world's sanity.
>
> VINCENT VAN GOGH

TEACHING art is intimately bound up with the behavior of the student. No doubt the subject taught, whether it is art or any other academic area, may be the substance of any learning situation and rightfully its central concern. The nature of the student's response, nevertheless, as has been indicated in another chapter, is justifiably an important element in the total educational process. The individual psychology that underlies student attitudes and reactions in the classroom has a direct bearing on the quality and direction of both the teaching methods that are to be stressed and on the creative process-product of art education.

THE CREATION OF DEFENSE MECHANISMS

An individual does not passively stop at failing to learn or avoiding involvement with any subject or classroom condition if it tends to confuse his perceptions and undermine his value systems. If his ego is involved there will be a counter attack, a way of fighting back that usually takes the shape of what psychologists refer to as defense mechanisms, a technical term that may be broadly but literally translated as self-deception. A more altruistic attitude may regard the various defense mechanisms as means of protecting the self, but the protection is usually bought at the price of rejecting some part of maturity and avoiding the confrontation of new and what may be disturbing but still intense learning experiences. Everyone is subject to the development of these defensive responses, teachers and pupils alike. They are also intimately associated with making of art.

The understanding of these factors stem principally from psychoanalytical interpretation. We may assume that in response to the innate pride that is universal in humans, there are behavioral patterns that tend to support a self love when it is threatened from the outside by unfamiliar or personally distressing pressures. The most important of these behavioral mechanisms are repression, rationalization, and projection. There are several others we can write about together as they may affect the teaching of art. These are defensive and psychological measures primarily when the individual finds it difficult to cope with the factors present in any given situation. That is, the deliberate and conscious ability to order one's experience and act in accordance is frequently denied because there are threatening actions present that are unconscious as well as ones open to conscious consideration. In not knowing how to cope or act appropriately in his own good interests, the individual engages in a defensive attitude because of pressures below the level of consciousness, unamenable to reasonable examination, or damaging to a self image. Examples in children's art may be an excessive repetition of forms, a reliance upon teacher or peer examples, a denial of an ability to draw, and so on.

Teachers, in recognizing these behavior patterns provided they have a clear understanding of their relevance and a "light" touch, may bring certain hidden protective psychological devices to the surface. This is probably best done indirectly, functioning as an attractive possibility for the student to sense; hopefully changing a defensive attitude to one of coping, of personal and imaginative exploration. Rather than running away from or ignoring a challenging and developmental experience a student may meet it and integrate it into his own emerging personality if the insights and methods of the teacher have been sensitive and competent. Experience in the arts is for the most part coping with the environment rather than circumventing it. However, this engagement with psychological factors takes great teaching skill and a fund of experience, besides a sympathetic understanding, a feeling of empathy and a quality of inspiration particularly if the deceptions are well laid. For the inexperienced teacher it may be necessarily prudent to excite his own perceptions and enrich his own sensibilities at first, without deliberate attempts to undo dramatically the defense mechanisms of others with one fell swoop. The danger is that much greater harm may be done if the attempt is unsuccessful. Further, it may be that some of the defense mechanisms function as sources for creative expression. These have to be carefully modified in order not to destroy an imaginative balance of creative forces in the individual.

Repression

The most basic of the psychological defense mechanisms is repression. As is indicated by a respected practitioner, "Everything contradictory to the ruling tendencies of the conscious personality, to its wishes, longings and ideals, and everything which would disturb the good opinion one likes to have of oneself is apt to be repressed." [1] The examples of this psychological truism are countless and there are many such repressions evident in the teaching of art and in student responses to experience. We have seen some of these at work when adolescents will "forget" their childhood freedom of artistic activity, acting as though they have always been hard

[1] F. Alexander, *The Medical Value of Psychoanalysis* (New York: Norton, 1932), p. 79.

Art
and
Education
in
Contemporary
Culture

·

148

headed and "sensible" within the confines of their peer culture, not soft, "gushy" and interested in "pretty" things. The image of the physically active and operationally useful self may be damaged by the emotional concerns of art, so the earlier acceptance is buried deep in the unconsciousness. Or, on another level, an example of a boy who would draw only female figures indicating the unconscious repression on the part of the boy of knowledge of the male figure. This may be due to a variety of reasons, but the most obvious is the classic one of the Oedipus complex. Very briefly, this Freudian concept indicates a strong attachment and sexual attraction to the mother and a corresponding unconscious hate and disavowal of the father on the part of the boy. Even though such ideas may be open to strong criticism, there are indications of their workings in the art of children. Another example of an ordinary yet a severe repression is indicated by the classroom teachers who will not have their classes engage in any art experiences which they consider extraneous or disorganized, despite their training in this direction in college. They repress or forget their own emotional experiences and professional knowledge in their conscious emphasis on intellectual skills or in their need to prepare their students in the accepted image of the very practical world outside. Some school administrators and members of boards of education are even more guilty of this than teachers. In all, most everyone, teachers and students alike, engages in personal repression which has direct influences in his art work.

Rationalization

The concept of repression is a very broad one and it spills over into rationalization. This may be defined as giving "good" reasons for behavior rather than real ones. Teachers, for instance, may defend a very academic and trite way of drawing, or coloring within the adult predrawn lines of a workbook by saying, "that this is the way children learn the facts of proportion and the discipline of graphic representation." This attitude is defensively rationalized though there is no real evidence to support it, or that children will not have a better and more basically informative art experience through an approach that is less narrowly structured. In this manner, a range of fictions from the simple to the elaborate may underlie a particular attitude. In a further instance, in children's art we may find at any given period of time a reflection of outside fads.

When the Disney movie of Davy Crockett was popular years ago, there was an overwhelming amount of drawing and painting of that fabulous and largely mythical figure that had been imposed on young minds. Children said they "liked" to draw him because he was adventurous and a figure stimulating their own colorful world. Perhaps so, but actually they were artificially motivated by the mass spread of publicity the movie enjoyed. Similarly, boys will draw grandiose scenes of battle, bombings, air duels, and pyrotechnical rockets, all because they are exciting and stimulating; and girls will spend hours delineating the symbolic physiognomics of imagined beauties, movie stars, dancers, horses and other feminine prototypes because they are "nice," "beautiful" and very "artistic." In both instances, the children always, and too often the teachers, do not recognize the imposing of social compulsions and cultural values that are determining the art experience, rationalizing the experience in "good" rather than real terms.

Projection

Projection is another psychological technique that is rather widespread in teaching, both among teachers and pupils. It is actually a kind of rationalization that assigns to others the motives and behavior that one disguises in one's own self. Using the subject of discipline in the teaching of art, it is easy to envision a very flexible and permissive teacher being accused of "letting the children run wild, doing as they please, talking and acting up all over the place while *she* sits by placidly letting it happen." Though this may be the secret wish of the more authoritarian teacher seeking relief of pressures, she remains the disciplinarian who feels strongly about "attention and covering the material" in spite of the youngsters' resistance, projecting a quality of blame.

Actually, what happens is that we absolve ourselves of any fault or the pain of wrong doing or "bad" thinking if we can pin the blame on someone else. To use the example of physical order in the classroom again, it is quite simple to blame the art experience for mess, for needless disarray, for extra work even when the individual making the accusations would love to express herself in a free and unencumbered way, disregarding totally the surface appearances that she feels should be maintained.

Children, of course, are involved with projection a good part of the time, expressing the fault and blame of others in their art work. The menacing figure in black that is sometimes seen in the work of a timid child is a kind

Children express more frequently what is felt rather than what is perceived visually. "Friends," First Grade Drawing. [New York Public Schools; PHOTO: S. Martin Friedman]

Art
and
Education
in
Contemporary
Culture

·

150

of complementary projection in which distress is clothed. The child who will vindictively tear up his own work in a rage or smash his modelling is undergoing a quality of projection, while the fawning upon and flattering of the good "drawer" by other pupils in the class is another form of projection. Projection is also a more positive and broadly based art source.

Wish Fulfillment

Closely allied to projection is the psychological function of wish fulfillment. Through this device the child will gratify his desires in his imagination, a kind of fantasy and day dreaming that all of us practice at one time or another. The child who paints a pony even though she does not possess one when asked to portray her pets is a good example. Though in a more profound sense, the first grader's ebullient painting of a bright, smiling yellow sun, benignly warming the happy, complete gingerbread-like home, next to the sprightly lollypop tree that is shading the gloriously exuberant daisies, is an image of the lost innocence and wishful consummation of the adult's most treasured though unguarded moments. The danger in wish fulfillment through any medium is that it may tend to replace the actualities of living too smoothly, affording a pleasant and emotionally rewarding interlude that makes the rude factors of reality all the more shocking.

Compensation

There are a variety of other factors that psychologically influence a response in behavior that has defensive undertones, which in terms of art teaching denies to the individual an open, full, and expressive experience in the classroom. Compensation is a means whereby feelings of inferiority are counteracted by strong emphasis in an opposite direction. It is not too uncommon to meet a student, who, because he or she has not met academic requirements, turns with a kind of resignation or desperation to art (though the general choice is more often sports or a more socially approved non-academic area).

Conversely, a student who has more than average talent in art may make a fetish of sports to offset the negative attitudes of artistic behavior that friends may voice, despite the attraction to expressive artistic experience. Of course, there may be some confusion here between compensation as a defensive factor and acts that are positive instances of coping with an environment. Glenn Cunningham, the great track star, developed his running abilities despite the fact that his legs were badly burned as a child. The almost mythological image of the sickly young Theodore Roosevelt who later became the Rough Rider and eventually President is another positive instance, though the line of demarcation is ambiguous. Marcel Proust, the dramatically introspective novelist retired to a long neurasthenic seclusion during which he wrote his famous *Remembrance of Things Past* after a very socially full and personally gay earlier life. It would be difficult to determine the propriety of any compensatory act in this instance; what was important though was the creation of a great work of literature. The art teacher has to sense when a student is compensating in a negative sense, or attempting to meet certain challenges. There are no clear guidelines other than a teacher's own intuitive understanding of each situation.

Sublimation

Quite close to compensation is the process of sublimation. In this the person who has inhibiting conditions to contend with resolves his need for action by substitute means. The classic example of this is the sadistic urges of an individual being sublimated as the socially beneficial practices of a surgeon. Many great artists are supposed to have sublimated potently erratic desires that are unacceptable in a civilized culture as great works of art. Freud analyzes Leonardo's painting of St. Anne as the work of a man with an unresolved Oedipus Complex. The child who chews his pencil is substituting that for his mother's breast while the ever present irrational cruelties of an undeveloped child's mind may find expression in macabre drawings. This process of substitution may occur with deeply buried drives existing in all of us, but the teacher again should exercise caution before ascribing expressive acts to sublimated desires. On the other hand, with children particularly, the awareness of sublimation may provide insights which may otherwise be provoking behavior that is extremely difficult to comprehend. Teaching sensitivity is again the key concept.

Fixation and Denial

Children also develop fixations or regress to earlier patterns of behavior. Because it may be difficult to face up to more mature responsibilities, some boys and girls revert to infantile acts or to behavior of a much younger age. This is relatively simple to do and offers a haven of security for there isn't much that may be expected from very young people. The fourth or fifth grader who draws like a kindergartner, attempting representations no more complicated than stick figures is a good example. If the pattern is insistent, the teacher has good cause for further inquiry into the child's background and motivations.

Finally, there is the psychological device of denial, where children may purge their minds of a threat, or the existence of any disturbing element. Victor Lowenfeld writes of such a case and his method of overcoming it in the following excerpt.

There is the example of the youngster who says, "I cannot draw." The boy was completely incapable of (or better, inhibited from) producing any kind of picture. He did not want to draw a line. Under no circumstances could he be brought to use visual percepts. The child made a very nervous and unfree impression. His mother told me that he usually came from school without speaking or telling anything of his experiences. He was very inhibited in his bodily movements. He had no friends at all . . .

I investigated this case more closely and found that this child, the child of a teacher, had been influenced repeatedly to copy nature, to draw 'beautifully' in correct proportions. Such an influence, which came in this case from the father, who wanted to see "good" and "nice" pictures and not the drawings of a child, had stifled the imagination of the child and diverted it into visual,

Art
and
Education
in
Contemporary
Culture

•

152

rather than personal experiences. As the child learned that he could not draw as his father required, . . . he lost confidence in his creations and stopped his work. This loss of confidence inhibited the child as a whole.[2]

The result was a denial of his ability to draw, a defense against unreasonable and upsetting values. Lowenfeld had an intense psychological insight and his positive response based on that insight was able to free the boy. In a more general way he was able to offer an imperative maxim to art teachers, "Do not impose your images on a child."

However, some doubt may be expressed about the general efficiency of the psychologically oriented Lowenfeld approach and the startling therapeutic claims he advanced in the name of art education. Yet, the expressive nature of students' art work does offer a significant channel through which teachers may gain understanding not only of the artistic endeavors of the individual student, but the psychological conditions which may have prompted the art work.

PAINTING AND PERSONALITY

Alschuler and Hattwick have written a rather detailed and convincing two volumes which trace the relationships between the child's overt social behavior, the inner psychological dynamics and their expression in drawing and painting experiences. "As we began to analyze their earliest drawings and paintings, we note that the very features which we first regarded as meaningless errors—the exaggerations in size or number; the omissions; the unrealistic sometimes persistent, use of one or another color, and the seemingly strange, meaningless forms—become the most revealing aspects of each child's products. Those features of the drawing or painting that are most highly individual and are peculiar to any given child's work become our clues to understanding the child's inner life and the dynamics of his behavior." [3] The investigators limited their age group from two to five feeling that most direct psychological responses and spontaneous expression in art occurs at an early age. The older children become the more likely they are to attempt "realistic" literal delineation rather than uninhibited emotional expression. It was also found that the abstract pictures were more revealing than the more literal ones. Pure improvisation of art elements: color, mass, line, rhythmic movement, and so on evidently invites a more unrestrained personal confession during the expressive act. The limitations of age and form were as much dictated by the experimental situation as they merely pointed up the strongest areas of observable emotional expression in art. There is little doubt that all art work, whether in the classroom or studio, captures some individual quality of the creator, that the form has locked in its essence some residue of the psychological nature that shaped it.

[2] Viktor Lowenfeld, *Creative and Mental Growth* (New York: The Macmillan Company, 1956), pp. 13–14.

[3] Rose Alschuler and Le Berta Weiss Hattwick, *Painting and Personality* (Chicago: University of Chicago Press, 1947), I, p. 10.

The high school art students are as acutely engrossed emotionally and personally in their art activities as are the kindergarten children, if they are seriously expressing themselves. Though the external pressures of peer values, a tendency to objective perception and a need to present a "finished, knowledgeable" product may strongly motivate junior high students, they also leave telltale and necessary traces of their personalities and all its turbulent unfolding in their works of art. Similarly, the upper elementary student—it takes the discerning and trained eyes of a teacher, attuned in his or her sensibilities to expressed relationships however, to "read" the signs. More important, the stress has to be on the aesthetic rather than the psychological and therapeutic values. The latter may well divert the course of art education into undesirable directions, demanding of both teachers and students an esoteric understanding that requires very strenuous and specialized training. Then too, uncovering emotional disturbance or psychological aberration through art may be an unnecessarily involved process when simple interview techniques may provide answers more directly. Sometimes, a plain question can elicit, more clearly, the kind of information the teacher is seeking. Yet the workings of the human psyche are devious and indirect, often unconscious and hard to understand, not always capable of being put into words; at such times the art work of students may more keenly manifest the inner person, offering a natural way of expression.

The Limitations of Psychological Assessment in Art

In addition to the defense mechanisms it may be helpful to scan a list of psychological processes that Allport has presented which indicates those individual characteristics that intrinsically make for a "normal" or "abnormal" personality. It assumes a value orientation of theoretical psychology which desires the healthy personality to function as a warm, secure, perceptual, interrelating human being.

Making for Abnormality	*Making for Normality*
Escapism (fantasy)	Confrontation (reality testing)
Ineffective repression (with troublesome after effect)	Effective repression (total exclusion of unwanted impulses and thoughts)
Self-deception	
Disintegration (dissociation)	Self-insight
Narrowing thinking to concrete adjustments	Integration (progressive orientation)
Uncontrolled impulsivity	Abstraction (ability to think about things)
Fixation at juvenile level	
	Frustration tolerance
	Autonomy appropriate to age and experience

Though Professor Allport qualifies the list [4] because there may be philo-

[4] Gordon Allport, *Pattern and Growth In Personality* (New York: Holt, Rinehart, and Winston, 1961), p. 154.

Art
and
Education
in
Contemporary
Culture

·

154

sophical disputes between the appropriateness of the right or the left columns, he generally presents the list as a fair summation of normal (or desirable characteristics) as against abnormal (or undesirable characteristics). The normal list produces "a continuous flexible development within the personality," while the abnormal "taken by themselves, lead to a rigid and closed mode of existence, and to an arrest in the process of individuation and becoming." These are extremely valuable guidelines, the result of mature and capable research and thought "in the pattern and growth of personality," by a deservedly eminent and respected psychologist. Their aptness in general for teaching is on a high level especially by sophisticated teachers. Yet there is a danger in applying them too confidently to the specifics of art education.

Again we are probably faced here with a question of values, of ultimate desirable goals. These lists that the behavioral sciences offer are as much subject to being the result of culturally biased models rather than of any absolute truths. Psychologists have developed profound, logical and cleverly formed ideas that are valid within their own (and even in their case sometimes unconsciously) projected models. Though the mature psychologist is probably more aware of this than most people, those who respond to the models, the novice teacher or interested layman, do not always possess such an insight. As Bruner suggests in commenting upon the psychological research into creativity that has been apparent since the end of World War II, "We, as psychologists, are asked to explicate the process, to lay bare the essence of the creative. Make no mistake about it: it is simply not as technicians that we are being called, but as adjutants to the moralist." [5] Similarly in providing lists of behavioral characteristics, the psychologist is not only providing us with objective lists of characteristics, but with moral designations of good and bad as well, even if unwittingly. And this, of course, tends to reflect the dominant aspects of a culture which in innumerable ways designates the acceptable and unacceptable behavior patterns and instructs in those terms. These are not always amenable to a natural acceptance of art and art education, to the searching, questioning and subjectivity required in creative processes.

The list provided by Allport may be given only a cursory examination in this space, against the values that an artist may possess. Though art education theory may not always be based directly on genuinely artistic models as they exist in a culture, or as an individual construction, certainly its greatest impulse should be derived from such sources. Otherwise the art may be safely dropped from the education for some other pedagogy is being perpetrated. The comparison may have some relationship to developing the most appropriate climate for an intelligent art education that has its roots in art itself, rather than primarily in the abstract developmental sequences of a psychologically oriented understanding without negating the value of the latter. The case of the Lowenfeld approach quoted above is a good example of art education being geared to a belief in psychology

[5] Jerome Bruner, On Knowing (Cambridge, Mass.: Harvard University Press, 1962), p. 18.

guiding child growth as almost an exclusive basis for art education. The more current attitude emerging sees art education as a fundamental involvement of art and child, the developmental aspects then following naturally. The stress is on the intrinsic properties of art. However, a strong emphasis on psychology has marked art education. There was always the idea of art education acting as a surrogate or a channel for a personality interest or utilized as a therapeutic device. Similarly, any teaching comprehension that supports itself largely in psychological terms, no matter what the individual psychological orientation, is in danger of adulterating or vitiating the subject matter to conform to behavioral statistics.

Fantasy and Reality

If we take the first items: escapism or fantasy as against confrontation or reality testing we are immediately beset by what appears to be a paradox. In the average vocabulary of comprehension art is an escape; one often hears of the artist retreating into fantasy, while in early elementary art education the child is frequently encouraged to make those same flights of fantasy in his painting. The art teacher is quite sorry when the pupil loses this ability as he progresses through school. And the plethora of amateur and Sunday painters rue the day they buried their fancies under the necessities of "normal" living, of facing "reality." In any event, the popular following in art is somewhat predicated on the idea of escaping from the everyday cases; in gerontology, of offsetting the reality of the advancing years and retreating from boredom. Just as frequently one hears that a serious artist does not face reality in his work, that he will not confront the so-called important factors of life. As Howard M. Jones says, "We are, we believe a practical-minded nation; and albeit philosophy and the arts and the languages are all very good things in their way, we say those who advocate their study never meet a payroll and those who practice them never seem to make much money in the stock market." [6]

At the first inspection then, pursuing art may appear to be "abnormal"; it superficially seems to be on that side of this list. If we stopped here, then the danger of "a little knowledge" in psychology may be apparent, for we would advocate the exclusion of the arts in education. This attitude is amply voiced by those who regard art as a "frilly" quality, a flippant juvenile escape from the more pressing factors of reality as symbolized by the need to learn a vocation required by society, that then contributes to it skills and productive capacities, and is rewarded with material gain.

However, the psychologist may be employing the concept of fantasy as an extreme measure of flight from responding to real situations that incapacitates the person involved in such a way as to deny him normal expression and resolution of underlying tensions. The uncertainties and tribulations of a neurotic personality can never be an approved aim in life, though the blind acceptance of blatant injustice, overtly criminal behavior, questionable commercial ethics as business necessities or smug selfishness and philistin-

[6] Howard Mumford Jones, *Reflections on Learning* (New Brunswick, N.J.: Rutgers University Press, 1958), p. 15.

Art searches for the imaginative forces that lie behind the appearance of things. "Earth Storm," Gerome Kamrowski. [Courtesy of the artist]

ism is not a healthy normality either. The world has too much of these negative features for a mature, sensitive and healthy personality to accept without a great deal of damage to the psyche. But if confrontation is regarded in a sophisticated and mature way, the artist may be seen as challenging himself with the most profound problems of determining "what is real." In this sense, there is no escaping, but a reaching towards something beyond the ordinary.

The work of a Rembrandt, a Van Gogh, a Pound, a Faulkner or a Beethoven, no matter what their misanthropic or idiosyncratic ways were, may be said to exist on this level. To a much lesser degree, but not as a difference in kind, the child in an art class may be seeking similar confrontations. However, it is not a simple semantic problem that is posed here, but one of establishing an appropriate level and avenue of understanding. For the average person, a paradox would probably exist: how could the pinching of clay or the spattering on paper be accepted as a means of reality testing when in common sense terms, they are looked upon, at best, as pleasant escapes from the daily routine. Even on a more profound level the art teacher is faced with certain ambiguities. If the artists themselves are to serve as models of behavior, their strangeness and eccentricity (in popular images) require far reaching explanations. If, on the other hand, only their commitment to and the quality of their work is to be the model put before pupils—the image of their creativity, then some of the basic psychological concepts of the relationship between personality and behavior go begging. Actually, there is no easy answer here and certain ambiguities remain.

These have to be resolved in some positive way by art education theorists and by the individual teacher as well in the specifics of an art experience.

Nevertheless, fantasy, daydreams and highly imaginary experiences exist for school children full blown and are often lavishly elaborate in their expression. From the very earliest grades where the condition of fantasy is most natural and expected, right on through all of the educational levels students engage in fanciful thoughts and their symbolic expression. These gradually lose their force and intensity as the child grows older and a concern for facts intrudes, redirecting the earlier overflowing whimsy and even capricious imaginings into the stultifying materialist positions associated with normal, commonplace living.

The early fancies may be unsophisticated, and probably inappropriate for coping with the dry daily concerns, but they do assert the sense of self and an intensity of realization of experience. The mature artist retains this imaginative outlook with, of course, an adult consciousness. The seething and fervent imagery of fantasy is openly utilized by such painters as Chagall, Kamrowski and Spencer. Chagall disregards the logical basis of the actual world, utilizing it mainly as a setting, like a theatrical backdrop against which the more vividly real projections of the imagination act themselves out. Kamrowski's fantasy is more organic in that it is invested in the very forms themselves, the writhing dynamic convolutions of "Earth Storm" suggestive, in the contortions of rhythmic masses, and dramatic light and dark

The visions of fantasy are shaped by the forms of art. "Over Vitebsk," Marc Chagall. [Collection, The Museum of Modern Art, New York. Lillie P. Bliss Bequest; PHOTO: *The Museum of Modern Art]*

Art
and
Education
in
Contemporary
Culture

·

158

*The artist evokes a
disturbing image of
the child's world.
"The Nursery,"
Stanley Spencer.
[Collection, The
Museum of Modern
Art, New York. Gift
of the Contemporary
Art Society, London;
*PHOTO: *The
Museum of Modern
Art]*

composition, of some monstrous upheaval of forces paralleling the frenzies of an erratic mind. Spencer, in a surrealistic manner, captures the disordered and displaced senuous and psychological formations of the very young child's encounter with the forces about him. Each employs fantasy as a means of communication and uncovering of experience that possesses a heightened understanding of the individual's encounter with the world.

The first-grade drawing of prehistoric animals has a cast of fantasy through which a personally emotional impact is made. The unreal and invented shapes of the animals are not only the result of an unskilled comprehension of anatomy (for a seven year old they are actually remarkably well formed). They are an imaginative invention set conveniently in the long ago (and removed from the immediacy of dangerous contact) that symbolically (and safely) expressed vague apprehensions and fearful states. Note that the prehistoric animals are eating what appear to be people. But fantasy may be pleasant such as in the third-grade drawing in which the girl sees herself as a bareback circus rider performing in the ring for everyone's pleasure and her own satisfaction. The transformation in either case is not labored or hesitant but clear and strikingly alive, reflecting a genuine engagement with feelings and thoughts. This vigorous and useful fantasy

*The prehistoric
setting and the
improvised animals
are typical examples
of childhood fantasy.
"Prehistoric Times,"
First Grade Drawing.
[Ann Arbor Public
Schools;* PHOTO:
Stuart Klipper]

need not dissipate into the hidden, inhibited uneasiness of puberty and
adolescence. The remarkably adept painting of the princesses and the evil
witch is a fantasy laden expression by a junior high girl. The talent is well
above average, though the process of acting out through expressive forms
is within every student's capacity. The work was freely improvised and not
an illustration for a story. As such it retains a fertile and natural involvement with fantasy that is of benefit to the student though it is not too
readily evident in peer activities. (See illustration, p. 160.)

The student communicates metaphorically expressing a resemblance to
actual states, but deliberately not in a literal fashion. The transposing of
the suggestive and the unusual with the known and prosaic is not necessarily
an escape from the real but a characteristically human means of testing
that reality, investing it with feeling and heightened meaning.

Of course, fantasy covers an immense range of possibility. Some fancies
may be idle, injurious of healthy adaptation to circumstances and debilitating in a psychological sense. These a teacher has to be on guard against
for they may not only fail to contribute to any educational purpose, they
may actually disrupt personal and classroom relationships. However, it is
extremely difficult to discriminate between beneficial and harmful fantasy.
The teacher's own intuition as well as the particular existing conditions
around the student have to serve loosely as guides.

Human history has indicated a profound range of fantasy as a means of
expression and communication. Almost all of art by definition partakes of
imaginary thinking and feeling, simply because what is created did not,
in actuality, exist previous to the creative invention. More intense though
have been such areas as myth, religious revelation, and fairy tales which
bent language to imaginative ends as well as the sensuous art forms such
as tribal dancing, ritual music, and enactment of dramatic fiction. Each

Art
and
Education
in
Contemporary
Culture

•

160

A sophisticated
elaboration of an
imaginative theme
by a talented early
adolescent. "The
Witch and the
Princess," Junior
High School
Painting. [Courtesy
of Robin Wilt;
PHOTO: Stuart
Klipper]

has flowed from the artist's ability to freely associate the images and dreams of his inner life and to relate them to the more ordinary external environment. They usually have been directed or controlled by a purpose beyond themselves though they are primarily self sufficient in the aesthetic elements. Imaginative flights have rarely become handicaps, except when purpose has been totally absent in a decent social sense or when the standarts of morality have succumbed to anti-human levels. This parallels the individual's enactments and expressions of fantasy. For better or worse, however, art education is fundamentally bound up with fanciful imagery because it is a basic attribute of creative seeing and doing—the substance of the preconscious mind and the matrix of the artistic form.

Effective and Ineffective Repression

In dealing with effective vs. ineffective repression, the psychologist is telling us that it would be literally impossible to live in any organized way if we could not discriminate between the welter of impressions, stimulants, and other perceptual elements that we are constantly being subjected to without repressing (consciously suppressing or unconsciously forgetting) a majority of them. This, coincides with the "selective eye" and discriminating perceptive sense that all creative people display and most particularly the artist. But whereas the artist bases his selectivity and consequent repression of unwanted material on aesthetic and reasonable grounds that have been subjected to the flush of emotion and the convictions of morality, the average person will more likely repress the very qualities the artist is seeking, looking for an objective rationalism, an entertaining diversion, or a practical utilitarianism. This level of meaning cannot always deny emotion, but rarely enhances it with more than a cathartic quality. However, the line marking the effectiveness as against ineffectiveness of these

Disturbing images often provide a basis for psychologically symbolic expression in children's work. "The Fight," Sixth Grade Painting. [Ann Arbor Public Schools; PHOTO: Stuart Klipper]

processes is not an easily fixed one. Again, it may be individually determined by the sense of values that is brought to bear on the subject.

The experience of art may ask of a pupil, at certain points, to dredge up disturbing memories, so as to infuse a depth and added dimension to his expressive forms, which otherwise may be bland or cliché-ridden images. This may have some troublesome after effects, but it may also give worth to a piece of art work.

The frightening narrative details that occur on the roof top of the sixth-grade painting of the violence, plunging bodies and fearsome birds upend a repressive instinct as does the high school painting (see p. 228), which is dreamlike, fraught with accusation, remorse and solitary, psychologically painful suffering. The student has dug deep to live up to a situation of disturbance.

Certainly the great artists do this all the time, where a romantic notion sometimes has an artist deliberately courting suffering, living in a garret and buying paint instead of food. Though most artists would not claim this

Art
and
Education
in
Contemporary
Culture

•

162

as an essential condition for creating there is a basis for the "romanticism" as Claude Monet's letter indicates, "I am literally penniless here, obliged to petition people, almost to beg for my keep, not having a penny (even) to buy canvas and paint . . ." [7] The artist was certainly ineffective in repressing those factors which led to his passion for painting; he did not give up painting for ordinary work so he would have material means, yet he was creating a revolutionary art form—Impressionism—that had immense influence for later artists.

Not only in the visual arts, but in literature, music, the dance, and in other art forms there are innumerable examples of what may be regarded as the artist not exercising "normal" effective repression which, nevertheless, was probably essential in producing great art. However, we may again say the list is correct for artists if by "total exclusion of unwanted impulses and thoughts" we assume this means repressing those qualities which would inhibit creative work. Yet these qualities are generally in conflict with those values of adjustment our society deems proper for the normal individual. The art teacher has to exercise a remarkable sensitivity that mediates between the necessary conditions for a creative climate, which may require a probing of unsavory and tumultuous elements of inner existence, and those conditions considered psychologically sound in a society that values continuous fun, ease, comfort, and urges adjustment of peculiarities of disposition to fit shared norms of behavior and value. Otherwise the art work or appreciative interest are trivial and spurious geared to dilletantish concerns.

Self-Deception and Self-Insight

Self-deception and self-insight may appear as self-explanatory items in the list but they cannot be too readily dismissed. No doubt, psychologists would agree with most mature and creative individuals that the greater majority of mankind live in some comfortable, yet pernicious miasma of illusion. To the extent that an individual can objectify himself and gain an understanding of his own nature, to that extent the illusion is pierced and a relative normality of insight into reality is achieved. Yet, our literature and art in many ways inform us that we normally desire to live within a set of illusions. We even court it when necessary as Thomas Gray writes:

> Where ignorance is bliss,
> 'Tis folly to be wise.

It is not certain if it is proper to equate ignorance with self-deception or illusion but in a pragmatic culture that values convenience and security this seems appropriate even though there is the objectivity of science to consider. Therefore, at a certain point we can say that it is normal to deceive oneself. Certainly, in many of the daily commercial and personal interchanges as well as in the larger sphere of diplomacy and politics this occurs and is accepted as necessary whether in the interest of oneself, business or national survival. It may be facetious logic but it is easy to demonstrate.

[7] Richard Friedenthal, ed., *Letters of Great Artists* (New York: Random House, 1963).

*Girls delight in
drawing horses,
making a very
common kind of
identification. "My
Horse," Fourth
Grade Drawing.
[Ann Arbor Public
Schools;* PHOTO: *
Stuart Klipper]*

However, what is of significance is the comparative lack of self-deception that characterizes the serious artists, poets, writers, and musicians. There are countless instances wherein these creative individuals held on to an integrity, sacrificing the material and other coveted rewards of normal living, because they insisted upon a self-insight that threw its light of understanding on the activities of their average contemporaries as well as themselves.

In terms of the values that are often voiced in education this would seem to be a very desirable attitude to aim for as a consequence of learning. On the one hand to pursue truth dispassionately, on the other, to insist upon its dissemination and acceptance.

Perhaps a semantic difficulty again interferes, but what also does occur is that normal is equated with average. In actual practice this most often becomes an acceptance of mediocrity, with all of the self-justification and arbitrary finger pointing that follows. Certainly the Allport list does not have this as its one criterion. It suggests that the healthy individual rises above the mediocre in achieving a self insight. Nevertheless, the experiences that most customarily inform and influence normal actions support the contention that self-deception is a wide spread phenomenon. In accepting the subjective nature of one's being this can only be expected. The essential worth that education has at this point is to demonstrate that self insight, difficult though it is, may be achieved through creative and expressive acts on the part of individuals. The arts are among the most fruitful in this area, with the visual arts among the most natural and direct ways of expressing self insight.

The self portrait by Rembrandt (p. 165) is a model of the understanding that an artist can turn upon himself. The artist at one and the same time is very much himself, a singularly unique human entity having no exact

Art
and
Education
in
Contemporary
Culture

·

164

The introspective elements and sensitive forms emerge from the student's turning inward for understanding. "Self-Portrait," High School Painting. [Ann Arbor Public Schools; PHOTO: David Churches]

like anywhere or anytime, his being plastically impaled on his own probing artistic scalpel with no false modesty and sparing details and is also the image of everyman poignantly aware of the human condition. The self portrait of the high school junior is also a sensitive inward looking symbolic representation of his own being, providing the creator with a means of personal identity and self awareness that transcends an easy stereotyping and is devoid of the small ordinary deceptions so commonly practiced. Yet, like Picasso says, "I lie in order to tell the truth," each of these pictures is an artistic contrivance that is only aesthetically and spiritually uttering its truth; representationally it is a distorted visual paradigm, an epigram of line, light and color.

Dissociation and Progressive Organization

In its basic psychological meaning disintegration or dissociation on the part of an individual may lead to serious difficulties, a break with former

A masterful example
of self-understanding
by one of the
great artists.
"Self-Portrait,"
Rembrandt. [Copy-
right The Frick
Collection, New
York]

personal safeguards and a flight into disturbed and psychotic states. There
the person could not function in any meaningful manner. Conversely, to
integrate all of life's important experiences is to organize a progressive succession of acts into a synthesizing whole that provides productive thinking,
learning, meaning, and mature satisfaction. Obviously, the aims of art education lie in the latter direction. The hope is that creative participation
and an affirmative and emerging sense of appreciation for the "good things
in life" can be one of the synthesizing agents. Educational theory presupposes that the total curriculum stimulates the personality in such a direction, and for the most part it does exactly that with differing levels of
success in the case of differing individuals.

Here too, art education has a slightly different emphasis, if not a contrasting one. As we will see elsewhere in the text, the artist over the last
century or more has had to disaffiliate himself from certain aspects of the
prevailing culture in order to pursue his own ends. Though this is not the

Art
and
Education
in
Contemporary
Culture

.

166

personal disintegration that Allport refers to, it is somewhat related super-ficially in that artists, writers and other creative individuals have deliberately sought to disassociate themselves from the large body of men. This was done, not because they necessarily felt superior to any other individual, though in truth they did feel above the cultural climate itself; but pre-cisely because they did value the uniqueness and inherent dignity and worth of each person, they were compelled to divorce themselves from the easy self satisfactions of the common run of attitude. This separation be-came the necessary prelude to an honest and productive association with experience and meaning. Their integrative drives were in bringing together their unencumbered perceptions, their developed sensibilities, their imagi-native free associations, their symbolic understanding, and skills of trans-formation and craftsmanship, all bearing on the creation of a work of art which then satisfied their own personal hungers for expression and signifi-cant experience. The integrative process could not be an innocuous blend into the conforming or acquisitive general tendencies of a mass attitude, nor is this what the alert behavioral scientist desires. Yet the affective quality of a great deal of educational effort is exactly in that direction.

Art education, in being the evocative stimulation of unique understand-ing, is not easily placed into a superficial operative relationship with other educational channels. To blithely consider the teaching of art just another device, either in developing skills or in fostering personal growth is to deny it the force of its own character. Not that it is more important than other subject areas but it is necessary to recognize that it is different from them in many respects, even when it shares certain common attitudes. Art edu-cation is one of the few areas of the curriculum that asks a pupil to actively and personally contribute from the very first to the experience at hand, rather than passively receiving information which must then be logically reasoned and related in prescribed manners. There is no real contained body of knowledge in art education as there is in many of the other aca-demic areas.

There are many complications in this concept, but it is sufficient for our purposes here to say that creative understanding, particularly in artistic expression is dependent upon the singular "truth" of each individual. Though there is a grammar of the arts that should be learned, what is of significance for art education is the inherent expressive power of each person. For the art teacher, this sometimes suggests a necessity to disasso-ciate from the more binding and formal aspects of methods of teaching in other subjects. In this sense, the normal and abnormal understanding is vague, though its relevance as a guide in the broader aspects of personality formation would be foolish to deny. However, for art education the inte-grative process and progressive organization of material may be quite outside the generally accepted channels.

Narrow Thinking vs. Abstraction

In the implied psychological model that specifies tendencies toward normality, abstraction may be one element that does not fit too easily into the popular version of the successful personality. In the American society, it is the man of affairs, the specialist and expert who is valued, and this value stems from the expert's ability to respond concretely to a problem in his particular area, to fix or explain or remedy a situation. The stock broker, the auto mechanic, the doctor and the lawyer are examples of this professionalized expertise. The psychologist who is himself a specialist in many instances, believes that a mature personality should be able to generalize— to develop an "ability to think about things," rather than simply to respond to them as momentary adjustments or as an immediate answer to tensions, and as an alleviation of real or imagined disorders in the environment or in subjective states.

Our inherent human tendency to inhibit reaction so that judgment and reasonable choices of action may follow underlies this understanding, as well as the outlook that a high and healthy state is attained by those who can "philosophize" about life. This is probably a justifiable attitude, for the personality that is capable of absorbing all of the perceptions it is subjected to, repressing the unwanted and unnecessary ones, examining the remaining sense impulses through a heightened screen of meaning, then creating a sense of order within the confines of healthy emotion and sharpened reason is a mature one, to say the least.

Art education has no hesitancy in listing these desirable attributes as long range goals of the daily lesson plans. Yet the entire assumption, positive and civilized as it is bears some further thinking; at least the method of achievement of the goals merits examination. In the art process particularly, a distinction has to be made between two complementary attitudes of understanding which are sometimes confused with one another. The distinction lies in the difference between thinking *about* something and thinking *of* something. Perhaps if we substitute the word knowledge for thinking, the dual aspect of learning (and this is what abstraction vs. concretion is about) may come through more clearly.

If we have knowledge about art we are collecting information, engaging in scholarly research, making objective analysis and bringing together known associations concerning either the artist, his work or his method of creating. If we have knowledge of art we are empathetically involved with art, feeling and sensing its qualities, either as our own in original creation or experiencing the works of others through recreation. Art education attempts to involve the pupil in both efforts. Actually, the division is not as neatly drawn as we have made it, for the two learning processes actually overlap and are often dependent upon one another. Nevertheless, we may sense the damage that can be done to the growth of aesthetic and personal sensibilities when an inordinate stress is put on one or another of these approaches to learning in art.

To all these teachers art is an imaginative visual language in which the organization of space, shape, color, and line to communicate ideas and feelings is the essence of aesthetic form. The beauty of a work of art is in the unity and order that has been created. These are among the reasons why all the teachers

Art
and
Education
in
Contemporary
Culture

.

168

emphasized the quality of the artistic expressions by encouraging their children to recognize such characteristics as the beautiful colors, the combinations of textures, and the relationships among the forms. Their goal was to encourage their children to improve their judgment through increasing sensitivity to the nature of organic unity in works of art. This was good teaching of art because it was true to the nature of aesthetic form.[8]

The knowledge *of* and about art both come into play in the good art lesson. The child, at one and the same time, marshalled his past learning in the area and his recognition of the immediate materials and content that have to be combined with the open, creative and feeling attempts in the actual expressive act.

The fifth-grade drawing of a basketball game is an illustration of the need of the various integrative learning conditions. It falls short of utilizing both specialized art knowledge and abstract thinking of a general nature, bringing together the formulations of perspective, the conceptualization of bodies in space, yet concerned with the verve and freedom of aesthetically perceived and expressed movement, play content, and narrative relationships. Its awkwardly expressed motions, its arbitrary grouping, its lack of sensuous life are typical of the limited work of upper elementary drawing.

It may also reflect the common lack of understanding of artistic insight and process of a contemporary nature—a lack that may be traced to the average teacher's unawareness of modern viewpoints in art. These latter viewpoints stress an *idea* basic to artistic interpretation, an abstraction from experience that relegates craft and technique to secondary conditions and devalues the need for imitation in artistic expression. Individual and artistic self-consciousness take over, offering a symbolic richness and a continuing sense of improvisation. The concrete and "narrowed" forms are only the visually sensory paradigms of ideas and feelings that would otherwise be inaccessible to communication, and as art symbols continue to be open-ended.

It is assumed in art education that both tendencies, the narrowing of thinking to concrete adjustments as well as the ability to abstract ideas and feelings, are essential to the processes of art itself. They have a significant interdependence in teaching method. The particular adjustments that are necessary in order to decide upon a color, make a thin or thick line, choose the symbols to communicate what is being felt and the countless other concrete decisions inherent in the making of a work of art or in its recreative interpretation are the very essence of the art experience. Yet they would be trivial and abortive if the broad quality of abstraction, the ability to associate and objectify were not provided as a necessarily human dimension in the making and understanding of art. Teachers of art may find themselves leaning toward one extreme or engaged in a bewildering vacillation between the two. The normality of the situation is not to be found in any projected list of normal tendencies, but in the unique conditions of art itself.

[8] Manuel Barkan, *Through Art to Creativity* (Boston: Allyn and Bacon, 1960), p. 349.

Typical awkwardness of upper elementary attempts at representational expression. "Basketball," Fifth Grade Drawing. [Ann Arbor Public Schools; PHOTO: Stuart Klipper]

Impulsiveness and Tolerance

The popular image of the artist includes that of regarding him as a creature of impulse. Van Gogh cutting off his ear in a fit of rage and self pity, Picasso engaged in whimsical pranks and sudden eccentricities of dress or behavior are only typical examples of the impulsive character of many artistic natures. Art itself has becomes as a part of its diversity over the past half century a mingling of the spontaneous, momentarily inspired, the accidental and the automatic such as a painting by Yunkers or an abstraction by Hofmann (pp. 432–433). This too stems from impulsive factors in the creative process, which only recently have made themselves felt.

However, set against this we may cite the example of Cézanne (p. 460), a deliberate, ordered artist, or Mondrian (p. 42), who was exceedingly exact in the planning of his work. Again we find that in certain psychological areas, artists and their work are subject to opposing aspects, occasionally at the very same time. Certainly, the precise canvases of Mondrian reflect a tolerance of frustration, in that he had to paint his canvases slowly and with exceeding care, planning and adjusting rather than instantaneously producing his artistic vision.

Critics of art recognize these two tendencies, generally classifying them as the Romantic and the Classical. As with all academic designations, these categories are sometimes arbitrary and too thin to really encompass all of the variables encountered. However, it does provide some context within which to classify and appreciate the disparate styles in art. The Romantic category would include those artists who valued intuition and emotion, generally making the actual form of their work subject to the intensity or spontaneity of what was being communicated, the compulsions of their inner visions. Byron in poetry, Brahms in music, and Van Gogh in painting

Art
and
Education
in
Contemporary
Culture

•

170

are good examples of this tendency. The classical artist, on the other hand, values his rational powers and imposes a deliberate sense of order on his work, sometimes subjecting his content to the all important development of the form of his work. The poetry of T. S. Eliot, the music of Mozart and the paintings of Cézanne fall into this category.

These separate tendencies have a relevant interest for art education. Viktor Lowenfeld developed the theory that there are two creative types of students, the visual and the haptic. "We can now clearly distinguish two types of art expression both by the end product and by the attitude toward experience. When we investigate the artistic products of these two types in their pure forms we find that the visual type starts from his environment, that he feels as a spectator, and that his intermediaries for experience are mainly the eyes. The other which we shall call the haptic type (derived from the Greek word haptikos meaning 'able to lay hold of'), is primarily concerned with his own body sensations and the subjective experiences in which he feels emotionally involved." [9] If these two types do actually exist, teachers would have to tailor their understanding and methods in accordance. But the existence is not that "clearly distinguishable" and Lowenfeld readily says that "most people fall between these two types." These designations merely serve as general theoretical understanding rather than specific indicators of differing attitudes.

To return to the idea of impulsivity that Allport deals with. Actually he labels *uncontrolled* impulsivity as the abnormal end of his scale while a *tolerance* for frustration indicates normality. Yet, because of the differing characteristics of people, it seems difficult to abstractly pinpoint the line that would put one type, in terms of art at least, on one or the other ends. The haptic type would tend to be impulsive and he would not be normal if he exercised great restraint, while the visual type of student who gave vent to momentary compulsions would destroy his own sense of correctness of method that is deduced from experience and imposed with care on the proprieties of form. Then too, each person is subject to both aspects depending upon the exigencies of a particular time, place, and problem to be solved. The forceful, direct quality of Hofmann's approach may be uncontrolled disaster for the carefully plotted art of Wyeth (see p. 432) with its painstaking technique. The careful, detailed and ordered drawing of a reserved little girl may be an intolerable burden for the uninhibited, and emotional torrent that impels a brash young boy in the same class.

If we consider the total aspect of art education in comparison to other subject areas, we are also justified in commenting that it cannot be happily and successfully pursued under the same burden of frustration tolerance that has to be exercised in mathematics or science. Art in its open free qualities invites impulses, while the theorems of mathematics or the controlled methodology of science insist upon an objectivity that demands a high frustration tolerance. Our natural propensities simply must be checked in the latter areas, while they are encouraged in the former. This does not

[9] Viktor Lowenfeld, *Creative and Mental Growth* (New York: The Macmillan Company, 1956), p. 259.

place a good or bad lable on either, it simply points out the differences that do exist.

Juvenile Fixation and Mature Autonomy

One of the elements of art education is its apparent lack of a progression as a body of learning. The experiences during the school art period are not too often the piecemeal segments of education that are encountered in many other areas characteristically accumulative and interdependent. Though there is a loose accrual of knowledge, an inherent development of sensitivity, and a deepening of skill that is dependent upon various art lessons given over a period of time, the distinguishing aspect of most genuinely aesthetic and creative experiences is that they are complete ends in themselves during the very time they are evolving or being appreciated. This does not deny a long range set of goals to art education or preclude the need for appropriate planning. However, it does suggest that the early and generating conditions that a child undergoes in making or appreciating an art object are as rewarding as any developing and consequently inherently retrospective feeling. The immediate aspects in art, the process as well as the product are their own rewards, as the intent, absorbed, and satisfying atmosphere during any successful art lesson will demonstrate. Because of their natural and unprodded motivation, the art experiences of young children are among the most successful of their school career.

This does not dispute the critical idea that the beginnings of any experience need necessarily determine its final form and ultimate understanding. However, in even superficially looking at art history it becomes noticeable that the most vital, characteristic, and exciting time of any style seems frequently to be at its beginnings, when the artist is in the first flush of inspiration, fresh and inventive as he dominates the shaping of his material. R. G. Collingwood, an important philosopher of art, documents this.

In science and philosophy successive workers in the same field produce, if they work ordinarily well, an advance; and a retrograde movement implies some breach of continuity. But in art, a school once established normally deteriorates as it goes on. It achieves perfection in its kind with a startling burst of energy, a gesture too quick for the historian's eye to follow . . . But once it is achieved, there is the melancholy certainty of a decline. The grasped perfection does not educate and purify the taste of posterity, it debauches it.[10]

It seems then that the early levels in art education, as it is during the evolution of a style in art history, may be the closest to its "golden age," so to speak. In this sense the "juvenile" level of understanding is of significance for the teaching of art. Many important artists of the twentieth century, particularly in painting, have pursued a stylistic attitude that attempts to retain the direct and naive wonder of early childhood. The artist is not arbitrarily putting himself in the child's place nor is he innocently naive

[10] R. G. Collingwood, *The Map of Knowledge* (Oxford, Eng.: The Clarendon Press, 1924), p. 82.

Art
and
Education
in
Contemporary
Culture

·

172

Many artists have
deliberately sought
the directness,
spontaneity and
naive outlook of
childlike creation of
form.

"Personages
Oiseau Etoile," Jean
Miro. [Leo Castilli
Gallery, New York;
PHOTO: Rudolph
Burckhardt]

"Snack for Two,"
Jean DuBuffet.
[Collection, The
Museum of Modern
Art, New York. Gift
of Mrs. Sadie A.
May; PHOTO: The
Museum of Modern
Art]

"Icebox #3," Peter
Saul. [A. Frumkin
Gallery, New York,
Collection of Albert
Bedford; PHOTO:
Nathan Rabin]

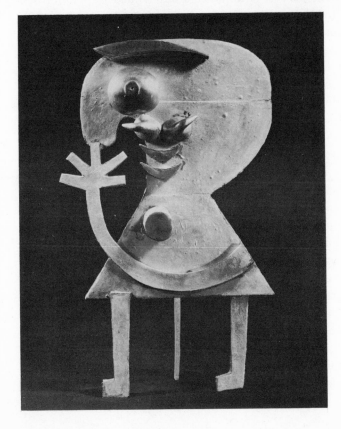

"Scratching His
Nose," Pierre Caille.
[Galerie Chalette,
New York; PHOTO:
O. E. Nelson]

Art
and
Education
in
Contemporary
Culture

·

174

in his artistry. However, the children's emotional honesty, their unburdened curiosity and untrammeled form, that permit a free and alert expression fascinates the artist who is searching for styles that are aptly reflective of our times. Frequently in going back to the child and to the primitive arts (seen as the childhood of the human race), the contemporary artist believes he can develop once more a powerful form of expression to counteract the exhaused styles of five hundred years of Renaissance influence.

The teachers of art could excite their own curiosity and imagination as they sharpen their pedagogical insights by studying the work of such artists as Picasso, Dubuffet, Klee, Miro, Saul, and Caille among many others. These painters and sculptors have developed their own tradition, known to some artists and critics as *"l'art brut,"* liberally translated as rough or unpolished art. In a studied reflection of the unself-conscious artistry of young children and primitive people, these modern innovators in the arts have discarded many of the artistic imperatives of an earlier time and have created a forceful art. They are playful, shocking, raw, whimsical, and tender, as the mood dictates, but always with a disarming and open perception similar to the free expressions of young children or the mythical forms of the primitive.

In recognizing the expressive validity of children's work, the forthright forms, the intense color and the instinctive sensitivity of composition, the teacher accepts the child's own consciousness and level of awareness. This may not be finished, may in fact require a great deal of instruction and refinement, but not at the cost of imposing arbitrary models of correctness on the child or a tightly predetermined progressive structure.

It would be indefensible to suggest that art teachers attempt to fix their growing pupils' ideas at a charming but inappropriately juvenile level. However, it would be justifiable to suggest that in the processes of maturation the early relationships to art can be used as guides to the kinds of attitudes that should be maintained between the child and his art. The developing sense of knowledge and the experiences that may be appropriate to advancing ages need not appreciably diminish the feelings of control and the joy of spontaneous involvement that do beset the pre-adolescent and adolescent child as they falter in their approaches to art. The tendency to normality would be to change, to divest oneself of childish or juvenile concerns. The involvement with detail, for instance, is probably a necessary artistic challenge for the upper elementary pupil. The child should attempt to resolve the problems of drawing and material manipulation; they are indigenous to a deepening of artistic production and understanding. Yet, it is disheartening to see this change occur at the expense of a real aesthetic experience. Perhaps, if the earlier eagerness and enthusiasm can be retained without the fixation at or regression to kindergarten form the autonomous development of the personality in accord with age and experience may be realized in a fuller manner.

The psychological assessment of behavior in relationship to art education contains the paradox of providing genuine but limited understanding at some points; yet it also confuses the natural elements with wrong scents, straying signs, and circuitous, if not erring, leads at other points. An art teacher requires a keen sense of artistic comprehension and as much an intuitive and informed insight into human behavior, but either in a separate condition may end up in unsuccessful or purposeless teaching. The two elements require a fusing and an animated, inspiring teaching implementation that is highly susceptible to authentic and qualitative art experience.

7

Perception and Experience

The young people everywhere must learn the forgotten art of seeing life with their own eyes.
OSCAR KOKOSCHKA

O BVIOUSLY, as man assesses himself and his relationship to his
environment, he does discover certain regularities of behavior and
repeated patterns of interaction with the environment. These provide a
measure of understanding and may act as a guide within the context both
of the inner territory of the psyche and the outer reaches of physical and
social surroundings. The teaching of art may benefit from such guidance.

One of these human behavioral areas that has been investigated in depth
is perception. There is a basic pertinency in the study of perception to all
of art education. How and what we see, the ways of transference of raw
sensory data into recognition of objects, and the various facets of interpretation of the presented data are the very subject materials that serve as underlying constituent parts of art activity. If these elements may be more
clearly structured without imposing a mechanistic understanding or violating the transforming nature of the creative and symbolic processes, they
may be of assistance to teachers of art.

PERCEPTION AS AWARENESS

Though man alone appears to be able to know and control his environment to any marked degree, it is probable that most living things have
some measure of awareness of their surroundings. However, in man this
capacity reaches its fullest development, with a sensitivity and a refinement
that raises man well above his closest living cousin on the evolutionary scale
permitting him not only to successfully adapt to his environment, but to
greatly modify it or create it anew as well.

This awareness of the environment, feeling the force of its dynamic
pressures and the quality of its physical and operating components is made
available to humans through his senses, which in turn activate the processes
of perception. It is this perceptive base that permits man to establish a
relationship with his environment that transcends the simple state of mere
existence, providing a base for his sentience, communicative needs, and

significant expression. Human perception is the particularly characteristic means whereby man places himself in his environment, knows it and acts upon the incoming information after he has "coded" it for himself and given it a meaning. It is a basic and beginning ingredient of the artistic and creative processes.

The maturing of the processes of perception bring the infant from its earliest stages which William James called a "big, growing, buzzing confusion" through its formative childhood years of dependence upon first home, then school with its attendant sense of wonder and newness, to the ultimate state of adult reflection and mature, responsible evaluation and understanding. In short, perception influences learning of all kinds in a profound way, and the quality of art is intimately dependent upon its personal functioning.

Visual perception is a unique, dynamic act, originative and productive in its mode of operation. Gyorgy Kepes captures this quality of visual functioning when he says, "To perceive an image is to participate in a forming process; it is a creative act. From the simplest form of orientation to the most embracing plastic unity of a work of art, there is a common significant basis: the following up of the sensory qualities of the visual field and the organizing of them. Independent of what one 'sees,' every experiencing of a visual image is a forming; a dynamic process of integration, a 'plastic' experience." [1] Perception at its optimum level is a living, forceful act that actively seeks out an equilibrium. In this process it is a vital experience that achieves resolution by establishing meaning for the individual.

The degree of sensitivity and intensity of awareness during the perceptual processes have a direct bearing upon the art work of students on all levels of schooling. The sensuous realization of objects becomes in art not simply recognition of form, texture, mass, and light values, but a jumping-off-point for the imaginative transformation of even ordinary experience. The coffee pot, that the boy is using as a model in the illustration (p. 178), serves as a perceptual stimulus for a real aesthetic experience in color improvisation and compositional invention. The typical first-grade drawing (on p. 192) of houses, street, sky and clouds was the result of the child doing more than just looking at his surroundings. He perceived the things, not only recognizing their shapes and sizes but infused them with a quality of meaning that added up to personal "objective" knowledge and significant understanding of structure and relationship. The houses have mass and weight as well as characteristic contours. The cobblestones provide a feeling of texture, a sense of detail that enriches the aesthetic element as well as communicating a road to be travelled, anchoring the houses above. The clouds are puffy and full, while the smoke from the house chimneys is thin and relatively wispy. The various elements have been perceived in a felt way dynamically integrated, becoming the basis for an expressive experience that transposed the mind's knowledge into concrete visual symbols, transforming the data of vision into meaning.

[1] Gyorgy Kepes, *Language of Vision* (Chicago: Paul Theobald, 1944), p. 15.

Art
and
Education
in
Contemporary
Culture

•

178

The Complexity of Perception

Physiologically, the receptive system that provides perception with raw data is based in the nervous system. This system has a developed network of receptors, such as the eyes, nose, tongue, ears, and several other sensitive organic antennae that gather information from the environment. They are sensitive to the array of stimuli in human surroundings: pressures, light and sound waves, movement, odors, and the other rich and infinite amount of sensuous material of the world. This information is then conducted through the nervous system to the brain, where interpretation takes place and meaning is bestowed, leading to some kind of reaction, either passive or active, intellectual, aesthetic, or emotional that is symbolically sensed or projected. This is based on a profoundly complex combination of such factors as various inherited qualities, the broad external conditions, the so-called objective state of the perceived object, the memory of past experiences, the force and richness of preconscious imagery and the intrinsic needs of the personality at a particular moment of time.

The process of perception then is an extremely complex one, dependent upon a large number of variables. It would be superficial to indicate, for instance, that in looking at another human being the perceiving organism is merely acting as a receptor, that the perception through the visual sense is coming from the reality of the person "out there," the one that is being observed. As teachers well know, students will respond to the image they have of the person (the teacher) who is sitting in the front of their room

The perceived object becomes a "jumping off" point for a creatively aesthetic experience.
[PHOTO: *Pearl Greenberg*]

*The graphic
expression of young
children's perceptions
rely more on motor
stimulation than
visual cognition.
"Jonathon's
Painting," [Courtesy
of Harris Rosenstein;
PHOTO: S. Martin
Friedman]*

in markedly variable ways ranging from experiencing an authority figure
to the image of a friend and many states in between.

PERCEPTION IS A UNIQUE PROCESS

A picture or any other art object that is being looked at is not really
identical other than superficially with the perceived image of the receiver;
the latter establishes patterns of meaning which are unique to their own
memory and experience. What is actually being perceived is not a mental
copy or visual imitation of the object in the external world, but a singularly
individual interpretation of it. To illustrate this point, the example is often
given of sending out a dozen well trained artists to paint the very same
landscape. Invariably, there will be twelve differing interpretations of the
same scene. This has an important bearing on the teaching of art, operating
constantly on the school level.

The "real" object that started the perceptual sequence exists without a
doubt, but not in any categorical or inviolate manner of understanding,
nor is it independent of the manner in which it is being interpreted for
each individual. The student's work of art becomes the concrete symbol
and expressive means of the singularly felt experience of interpretation.

In dealing with visual factors of perception we can say that all objects exist
within an encompassing flood of light qualities. From this chaos of stimuli
and confusion of images, a student may select particular patterns that then
become entities of meaning for him. Actually he is involved in a real cre-

Art
and
Education
in
Contemporary
Culture

·

180

ative process as Kepes indicates when he is visually perceiving, for he is forming in a basically organic and dynamic manner the image that is being experienced. Though the light reflected from the object outside that is being observed registers as values and colors on the retina in a physical manner, the perceptual process is only just beginning. The visual message is then carried through the nervous system to the brain and only then, after an organizational patterning and forming of the sense data does the student really "see" anything.

The actual experience of what we see is a form image that has resulted from the intrinsic organizational functioning of the brain. As such it has a creative "plastic" quality; that is, it acts like a living organism, being viable and open to change and modification depending upon the circumstances that attend its formation. It actually exists through forces that are an interaction with one another, the forces themselves being conditioned by the living situation they find themselves in.

For instance, the internal and external growing forces determine particular leaf pattern of a plant: the amount of sun, the soil and water condition, the inherited tendency to a particular shape. In turn, we see the plant selectively, as a particularly lovely example in a field of other plants, as an isolated and forlorn shape that may exist after a fire has swept the surrounding area, as a flickering mass of light and color when it is lost amidst its fellows in a sun drenched meadow or as a graceful decorative arabesque of line, rhythm and internal movement when we set it against the wall in a house. There is the interaction of unique forces that create a particular unity, a spatial, temporal, and organic perception. In each instance, the perception is a whole one, the recognition and understanding of which is not determined by that of its individual components, but where conversely, the parts are themselves determined by the intrinsic and immediately apprehended nature of the whole. Actually, this makes each perception a closed one, in the sense that the unity of the experience is determined by the aesthetically related and harmonious integration of its parts, by the pattern and "correctness" of what is being perceived as it is balanced against the internal factors and the brain shaping the sensory experience. The perceiver does not visually sense the various parts of what he is looking at in a specifically fractured way. Each part is given a meaning and related to the overall imagery, the "total configuration" of forces present. What is seen first is the whole which then provides a function for the component parts. However, perception itself in a larger philosophical sense remains an open and malleable activity in addition to being a very personal one.

GESTALT UNDERSTANDING

This understanding of perception is based upon the work of the Gestalt psychologists. They have made intriguing studies in the psychology of perception which have rather interesting implications for art education. However, the field deserves a thorough study if any teacher would hope to utilize the many findings. It is complex and, as yet, not without certain contradictions. At best it is only a guide that should enrich the teacher's understanding and not direct it. Its most important contribution lies in pointing up the relationships between physical functioning, emotional feeling, and intellectual ordering. Rudolf Arnheim is one of the leading practitioners in the Gestalt study of perception as it relates to art education. He is quoted: ". . . any description of form in static terms of sheer geometry, quantity, or location will fatally impoverish the facts. Only if one realizes that all visual form is constantly endowed with striving and yielding, contraction and expansion, contrast and adaptation, attack and retreat can one understand the elementary impact of a painting, statue or building and its capacity to symbolize the action of life by means of physically motionless objects." [2]

Though this is written in relationship to artistically developed form, it is a fair estimate of the general manner by which all humans may respond with intensity to the external world about them. The experiencing of probably all images is the result of the forces mentioned, of the relationships that are actively established between the uniquely formulated internal forces of the individual and the mass of external physical forces: the latter forces as we have said, mechanically act on the eye, producing changes on the retina and exciting the nervous system. The internal forces react in a dynamic fashion after the disturbance from the outside, attempting to restore a stable balance, so that the organism is then permitted to be at rest after a new excitation or a repeated meaning has been experienced. The process is an enriched and exceptionally vivid one in art.

Mind and Feeling in Artistic Perception

However, art experiences are based on much more than simply physical visualization. The aesthetic or artistic act of perception involves a range of human functioning that is peculiar to the species and sets it apart from the other orders of living animals. It involves not only a state of awareness but an ordering aspect that gives the awareness a quality of meaning, structuring it in ways that are different from the happenstance performances of nature. A characteristic blend of intellect and emotion, of reason and feeling provide the aesthetic perceptual framework, making for art. The intrinsic unity is a particularly human one. Though it might ultimately derive from sources in nature, on the immediate and sensuous level as well as on the reflective and creative one, perception in art calls for an added factor of symbolic understanding, separating the artificial or humanly produced functioning of form in art from that which occurs naturally by chance, offering a characteristic interpretation of experience in school or studio.

The drawing (p. 182) of the children swimming is an excellent elementary expression of the organization of visual dynamics of movement, position in space and proportion. The child's Gestalt of the activity leads to the necessary symbolic patterning of line and shapes in relationship. The children on the right approaching the lake are "folded over" but appear correct

[2] Rudolf Arnheim, "Gestalt Psychology and Artistic Form," *Aspects of Form*, Lancelot L. Whyte, ed. (New York: Pellegrini and Cudahy, 1951), p. 199.

Art
and
Education
in
Contemporary
Culture

•

182

A good elementary
school example of the
organization of
visual dynamics of
movement and
position in space,
indicating an alert
perception.
"Swimming," Second
Grade Drawing.
[Ann Arbor Public
Schools; PHOTO:
David Churches]

in movement (if not in actual perspective) leading to the central theme of bodies in the water swimming, breaking water and generally having a jolly time sporting with the fish in their own habitat. There is a particular *conceptual* construction as well as a recording of sensory data.

The picture of flying objects (below), both airplanes and birds, is a delightful illustration of motor mimicry the child has devised; movement or kinaesthetic elements of expression are reflected in the usual forms. The initial vision may not have been a secondary state mechanically stemming from a perceptual experience. It possesses a quality of empathy, of an entering into the sense and spirit of another thing, of not only congruent but mentally shared states of comprehension and feeling. In this regard, perception has led to a felt artistic expression. As the symbols are formed they become the perception in metaphor.

The child meta-
phorically expresses
a feeling of motor
mimicry, of empathy
with flight. "Birds
and Airplanes,"
First Grade Draw-
ing. [Ann Arbor
Public Schools;
PHOTO: Stuart
Klipper]

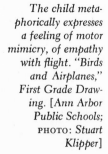

These in turn are not mechanical or static, but are rather creative instruments that engender a personal vision permeated with strong individual as well as commonly held meaning. They are the indispensable and underlying elements of any creative learning situation and especially so in artistic undertakings. In the very first stages they may be regarded as filtering out processes after the eyes have scanned the surroundings to determine if danger threatens or satisfaction is to be gained. However, this is a simple animal response and humans have evolved much beyond this in that they do not regularly rely on short range and direct responses for their information and the significance it presents. Human beings have a tremendous store of symbols, words, images, and fragmentary mental offerings which have an innate meaning, but no clearly distinguishable identity. These are manipulated preconsciously and otherwise brought into play in the perceptual process and may be developed independent of the immediate sensory impressions. At a higher and more refined level, in relationships between perception and action, such independent shaping of meaning is frequently present as symbolic activity in the form of planning and prediction, reflection and speculation, imaginative creativity in the arts or in imposing orderly relationships in science or law and most effectively in formulating new interpretations of life's experiences. There is this intellectual element in artistic perception as well as the more fundamental sensory attributes and emotional interpretation.

Perception then is not a simple stimulus-response phenomenon. It is a rich and fertile means that humans have at their disposal, biologically and psychologically, with which to experience the world, not as if they were cameras registering a scene, for instance, when the shutter of their eyes is open. The perceiver has a greater responsibility and correspondingly a greater reward in being able to make his own world in a most creative manner, symbolically transforming the raw experiences into human meaning, the shifting imagery into concrete artistic forms.

The Structuring of Images

The structure of the images that are objectively present are dependent upon the forces that are internally and externally shaping them as was previously mentioned. The size, shape, and color of a cloud for instance, is determined by the amount of water vapor it holds, the air pressure around it, the strength and direction of the winds in the surroundings, and the balance between the temperatures inside and outside of the cloud. The shape of a giraffe's neck has largely been determined by his evolutionary need to find food in comparatively high places. Soft rocks are rapidly worn by the elements into characteristic shapes while hard rocks resist erosion for longer periods of time, thus being shaped differently. A tree or a flower grows as it does because of the genetic forces motivating it, its patterns that are perceived the result of this inherent quality as well as the conditions that surround it at any given period of time. However, when man creates any objects himself, particularly in a work of art such as a painting, there are no real internal forces. All of them have been imposed by the artist.

Art
and
Education
in
Contemporary
Culture

·

184

This X-ray drawing
illustrates the intel-
lectual awareness that
parallels an artistic
activity. Even though
the boat is under-
stood to have solid
opaque sides, the
child expressed what
he knew to be in the
boat. "Noah's Ark,"
Second Grade
Drawing. [Ann Arbor
Public Schools;
PHOTO: David
Churches]

In this sense man regards himself as a creator similar to nature for he induces whatever internal forces exist in his handiwork. He draws from his
own will the means of manipulating the elements of what he is creating.
Whether natural or artificial, the visual impressions received by the observer are the same. Physiologically there is the excitation of the retina with
light waves, detailed in the fovea, the center of the eye lens and only
peripherally and broadly stimulated on the sides, while the rods and cones
register color, but the meaning is subject to a vast range of individual
possibilities, as we have seen, even though there may be general agreement
on the gross visual characteristics.

The student in an art class is being organically creative, "making himself
his own God" when he is engaged in forming his own and new images. The
experience is a qualitative one, uniquely ordered and individually felt. The
drawing of the two girls (p. 149) is not only the result of a physiological act
of perception. It is a felt and innately ordered structuring of visual elements
that have been placed in some kind of relationship to human values. This
occurs not only on representational levels, but on more abstract ones as the
junior high example of geometric design demonstrates (see p. 188). It is
this element of aesthetic structuring that one can accept as a core learning
element central to all experiences in art education. The Gestalt psychologists correspondingly have proceeded beyond just the simple point of recognition of structure in perception. They also present a theoretical analysis
of the functioning interrelationships.

The Formative Element

It is not the mere physiological registering of sensory fragments that permits us to recognize what is in our field of vision. What is at work is a

principle known in Gestalt as similarity. This process groups visual units that resemble each other into a spatial pattern that has relevance for the observer. Those units having a semblance with each other will be grouped together in terms of size, shape, direction, color, brightness, and location. In addition, this principle organizes the elements stimulating our senses into temporal sequences, so that perception may be regarded as a continuing process that is periodically punctuated by sensory stimuli. Therefore, in viewing an object at a particular moment, the observer is in reality responding to that object, not only in terms of the immediate sensation, but as well with the "memory traces" that have preceded this particular experience. John Dewey in his *Art as Experience* notes that any person in looking at a work of art is bringing his whole past life's experiences to bear upon the apprehension of the art work and what has gone before in the individual's experience is an integral element in perceiving the work. There is a particularly individual anticipation of the form to be perceived that colors the actual act of perception.

The eye does not stop simply in recognizing similarities, but is actively engaged in forming a satisfying pattern, one that utilizes the regularities of the sensory experience to provide an order that tends towards its simplest condition. In accepting this factor of basic shape as motivating the formative aspects of perception, the Gestalt psychologists are relying on certain fundamental physical laws such as the one the physicists assume when they postulate that the world tends to pass from less probable to more probable

Children's art work may draw upon a wide range of actual or imaginative experience. "The Pirate," Second Grade Drawing. [Courtesy of Margo Flower; PHOTO: Stuart Klipper]

Art
and
Education
in
Contemporary
Culture

·

186

configurations or states. It was Cézanne who said that everything we see could be reduced to the cylinder, the sphere and the cone. Though oversimplified this led to a truly ordered structuring through symbolic forms in art based on visual dynamics.

The tendency in all of these viewpoints is to provide extrinsic elements by which an act of perception is developed; the various external factors becoming clues to the realization (the recognition and meaning) of what is being perceived. A basis of comparison is thus a necessary factor in Gestalt perception, a contextual standard without which communication in art, for instance, probably could not occur. Not only for the audience who is passively perceiving another's works of art, but for the creating artist himself, this is a required process.

The Gestalt principles as they relate to the sensory data that physically form the context may be summed up in the following categories: (a) The person who is perceiving sees relationships between things that share similarities such as color, size, texture, shape or any other condition of pattern. (b) The closer the similarities are to one another the stronger will the relationships be. Consequently, the farther apart that objects or patterns are, the more difficult it is to assess similarities. (c) The person who is per-

The teacher acts as a guide in the student's "seeing" process, intensifying the perceptions, enhancing a feeling of empathy, sensitizing a response to experience. [PHOTO: Stephen C. Sumner]

ceiving responds to what may be called a continuity of pattern. This quality
can also be regarded as closure, suggesting that the perceiver tends to group
patterns into some kind of structured order indicating direction, repetition,
and the like. (d) The perceiver also tends to group in terms of dominant
and subordinate patterns.

These principles also suggest that an organizing quality is rather important if perception is to have even rudimentary significance and if the memory of former images is to carry over structurally in the recognition of new
sense data. The further suggestion is that certain cognitive factors are at
work, imbuing not only perception but any consequent scope of learning
with an intellectual cast. Meaning is the result of the mind's activity. That
is, some of the basic perceptual patterns may be learned qualities rather
than instinctual ones. As such, this has a great significance in education
and may have a fundamental bearing in certain phases of art education if
the theoretical concepts are provable in all instances.

Intuition and Intellect

No doubt the experiments of the Gestalt psychologists have uncovered
a wealth of information that can inform the processes of artistic creation
and appreciation. Their relationship to art education is a fruitful one and
possesses a large potential for further knowledge and conceivably, implementation of principles. An additional contribution was the implicit recognition of intuition as one of the basic cognitive functions that permits
humans to attempt to find order and regularity in an otherwise chaotic
world. It is this faculty that permits the recognition of a Gestalt configuration most frequently. Intuition allows an individual to aptly consider a vast
range of possibilities that impinge upon his senses, gleaning out the relevant, making connections and generally aiming for a closure, a satisfying
unity of perception. This faculty works in all areas of human realization,
but it is most often found in the arts, or at least so tradition has it. Its
presence is almost taken for granted in the art room and it is a faculty the
teacher imaginatively stimulates in all students.

Notwithstanding this reliance upon an element that appears somewhat
elusive in analysis and ill suited for experimental control, there have been a
number of theoretical assumptions derived from the primary relationships
of the sensory elements of Gestalt process. They tend very often to
mechanistic or purely reasoned understanding. The emphasis is put strongly
on the intellectual interaction and reasonably logical nature of perception.
There is a consequent stress upon procedures that can be abstractly transferred in learning situations, in art as well as in other areas. The extrinsic
clues that form perception are emphasized as those most likely to implement a development in the student and are most amenable to educational
structuring. There may be some partial truth in these assertions, but they
fall short of encompassing the full art experience that educational method
in perception should lead to. Arnheim, as well as many other psychologists,
are fully aware of this, leading to a recognition of selectivity and subjective
influence in perceptual studies.

Art
and
Education
in
Contemporary
Culture

·

188

*Abstract design may
start a chain of
creative development
that could lead to an
abstract expression of
a pupil's "inner
vision." "Abstract
Design," Junior
High School Collage.
[Ann Arbor Public
Schools;* PHOTO:
Stephen C. Sumner]

SELECTIVITY IN PERCEPTION

We can readily accept the fact that a natural object itself may be quite differently perceived by different people depending on their background, their occupation and the inherently varying needs each will possess. In looking at a tree, a forest ranger may see one thing, a timber merchant another. An Eskimo who had been living on the barren wastes of the Aleutians may marvel at the vertical trunk and its dark foliage while some woodsman lost in his travels may not see the tree at all for the forest that is haunting him. Omar Khayam would sit under the tree to enjoy his jug of wine perceiving it as a symbol of stability while someone else may consider the tree an excellent one to cut for the Christmas season. Culture exerts a strong influence, in perception, as much as in other areas of human functioning.

Though it may not always appear to be the case, no object or event is merely perceived in idle curiosity; it has an underlying reason for being noticed. Those things that are uninteresting for an individual are usually not even perceived. How often does one take a walk along a familiar path and if asked to enumerate the things seen will neglect to mention quite often that which someone else will note, simply because they were not consciously perceived. This is the selective factor at work, taking note of those elements in the environment that have a pertinence and passing over those that are irrelevant to the individual. If the latter filtering out process did not happen everyone would be beset by an avalanche of stimuli, all of which would be vying for attention, creating a maddening confusion.

All teachers should be aware of this perceptive selectivity that operates in human beings. They as well as their students are exercising the oftentime unconscious prerogatives of their value systems, as well as the conscious attention to what is considered personally interesting and rewarding. This selective device is originally biological in nature, stemming from primeval days when man existed closely tied to an actively hostile environment so that danger could be readily identified through movement or change in external conditions. It is also probable though that the higher faculties that have evolved stress the interpretive nature of the perceptual experience based upon the personal experience and memory of each individual—upon a human need to infuse personal meaning into experience. A teacher, then, who attempts to orient or stimulate perceptual behavior within what he considers desirable directions may be free to do so. There is no jungle or other dangerously external environment that requires a keenly alert perceptual power to assist the individual in coping with the unknown. However, there are the internal sets and the outside social pressures that help to determine values. In this regard teachers have to be sensitive to the dangers of imposing inhospitable images or insisting upon fundamental classroom practices that follow narrowly formal lines. The perceptions that may result may be mere shadows or distortions of what they were intended to be. The act of "seeing" and the resulting creative and formative expression of what is being experienced are not mechanical ones. Its positive learning aspects and growth potential lie in the ability of the student to perceive within a meaningful, independent and *personal* framework. He has to undergo his own process of transformation in art, albeit with teacher guidance.

Perception in its natural, creative state is internally influenced in the nature of the experience it will have. It oftentime finds in the environment that which had been personally and psychologically anticipated rather than presenting the mind as the blank—the tabula rasa that the surroundings may impress an image on. The needs, desires, exigencies, and cultural pressures that insinuate their way into the act of perception, stay and help to determine its outcome. The percept becomes a projection of inner feelings as much as visual recognition. This is even more true in the artistic process than it is of any other formative or conceptualized experience man undergoes. In the examples of art work depicting the human figure (pp. 198, 199), the degree of skill is not the only factor determining the final form

Art
and
Education
in
Contemporary
Culture

190

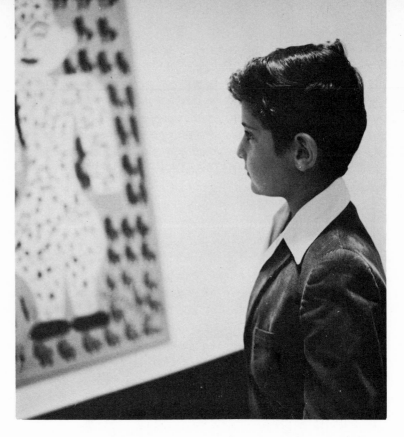

Art appreciation involves a complex set of perceptions in children as well as adults. [PHOTO: *Sara Schwartz*]

(and essential meaning) of the art work. The individualized personal reactions to experiences with human form also influenced the artists' perceptions and their artistic transformation.

Perception Reflects Learning

Children's art works are excellent examples of fundamental expressions of an individual's direct but emotional perception of his environment. The example of the scribbling picture (see page 232), done by very young children, indicate what appears to an average adult's eyes as meaningless scrawls. However, the children are responding to their senses and are making concrete, through visual form, their perceptions either as a simple translation of kinesthetic feelings, but more often with mental rather than purely visual concepts of a particular form in mind. Given the undeveloped faculties of a young child, their strong reliance on an anticipated understanding of the appearances of things and the influential emotional charge that each stimulus has for the young mind that has not as yet stored up a large memory bank of images, the pictures of disproportionate figures, exceedingly simplified or partial images can be understood for what they are. The young child has not yet learned to abstract his responses, inhibit his judgment or to seek a refinement of association; his perceptions are pure and relatively untrammeled, his expression of them direct and unsophisticated.

However, in the very act of making his images concrete, the child is learning to control not only his reasonable depiction, but the unique quality they have for him as they exist in the environment. His perceptions become richer, more detailed, and cognizant of the relationships of relevant factors that may be examined as associations or contradictions become evident. He is learning in the very best sense of the word. This is of an intellectual nature as well as an emotional one. The gratification of learning how to manipulate one's own body, as children's drawings demonstrate, is expressed in a direct perceptual manner by the youngsters through visual form. The ability to order this form has a rational base as well as an emotional one, for the symbolizing process presumes the ability not only in recognizing semblances of form, but in establishing associations and in determining relationship. These relationships of size, position, direction, proportion, and other intrinsically visual elements are means whereby the child creates an organization of meaning that makes the environment understandable to him and upon which he may develop a structure of reason.

INTERNAL FEELINGS INFLUENCE PERCEPTION

Similarly, all human beings integrate their personal histories, inherited dispositions, social mores, and the current image that is being presented in his surroundings to form the unique perception that is their own. Creative behavior, in part, is an intensification and refinement of this process to begin with, based primarily in the visual arts, for instance, on the spon-

Intensified observation and critical analysis of art works assist in establishing independent aesthetic insights. [New York City Public Schools]

Art
and
Education
in
Contemporary
Culture

·

192

taneous and immediate evidence the created form suggests. This is usually tied to direct sensory experience, almost providing a tactile and kinesthetic experience as well as a visual one. However, if this was all that good art required, then an incisively analytical investigator could isolate the various elements and prescribe them like a doctor prescribes certain activities to maintain a healthy body or as an engineer diagrams a blueprint for a particular building function. Obviously, this is not the case and we are compelled to recognize still other factors that operate in both the creating and understanding of art. These factors could only be the so called ineffable ones of emotion, feeling, and for some, spiritual qualities. Since these cannot be reduced to words except in a very crude way, they operate beyond the boundaries of refined and categorized understanding.

To put a label on an object, or a happening, or a feeling for that matter, often convinces an individual that he understands what he is labeling, that

Visual symbols may transform the raw sensory data and individual perceptions of experience into an artistic order. "Landscape," First Grade Drawing. [Ann Arbor Public Schools; PHOTO: *David Churches]*

he has "perceived" it fully. In the beginning was the word, and there is almost a magical connotation of possessing whatever one names. Yet in calling an emotion love, or grief, or joy we are only giving that emotion an arbitrary designation. We can speak of fraternal love, mother love, selfless love, sexual love, of intense love, and false love, but in no instance does the word actually give us the defining quality of the emotion. It does not provide us with an actual understanding as a differentiation of the infinite range of emotion that love is. The words are really abstract symbols that we have crudely paired with certain inner states of being. Actually the emotions cannot be explored in depth through discursive means. It is only in action and through the non-verbal qualities of art or the extra verbal elements of poetry that emotions are experienced directly in the first instance, and extrinsically symbolized by the actual forms created. There is an existential base of understanding that organically integrates feeling and action.

The emotional factor then is the added aspect by which human perception may become more than a mechanical response to the stimuli of living, transcending the diagrammatic blueprint of simple cause and effect, infusing a quality of meaning to life which may be transformed into significant artistic symbols. Since there is probably as variable an approach to this creative endeavor as there are people in the world, it seems that no hypothetically devised method would encompass it.

Nevertheless, there are many common aspects which will be examined elsewhere. These act as a funded source of perceptual sharing. Very often, the measure of a good work of art seems to be the degree to which an artist can utilize the common understandings without violating the integrity of his own individuality. Hopefully, this process is encouraged, perhaps in its best form, as "free development." However, the very existence of an organized school and an ordered approach to learning and experience compels

Artistic perceptions emphasize the unique interpretive vision of the artist rather than the simple recording of sense data. Student Model. [New York Public Schools; PHOTO: The New York Times]

the development of perception along predetermined lines or within particular confining structures. This is especially true in the case of young children who have no means of challenging the presumed authority of the adult teacher even if they could reach the state of abstractly recognizing the need for such a dialectical situation. Everyone exists within some kind of context, though youngsters have almost no voice in the choice of their surroundings. Of course, they are incapable of establishing a proper context even in a relative sense. This merely underscores the responsibility that education and its practitioners must be aware of when learning is as organized as it must be in a school situation.

Education Helps To Order Emotional Experience

Teachers either deliberately mould the experiences of children or achieve similar conditions by default or carelessness. This is inherent in the shared

Art
and
Education
in
Contemporary
Culture

·

194

educational process; the danger lies not in its existence, but in its arbitrary or narrow minded practice. It is the innate process of perception itself that is the rightful concern of a teacher. In art education, for obvious reasons, it is harmful to direct the experience in any doctrinaire way, spelling out canons of correctness and generally channelizing the understanding of any child within the already frozen or insistent images of adults, though in later adolescent experiences it may be beneficial to encourage an outside influence as long as the individual student's emerging and independent sense of self has not atrophied or been distorted along prejudiced lines.

The individual requires a healthy, challenging, yet permissive atmosphere within which to develop the conditions which will form his perceptions. This kind of an educational atmosphere requires specific translation into stimulating and efficacious teaching methods that go beyond clichés and shallow lip service. In art education, this cannot be a concentration merely of the fantasies or undeveloped personal visions that an immature or unknowing mind can express. Nor is art education to be involved primarily with a stress on skills and proficiencies which may create an ordered form, but one that is unfortunately either devoid of real emotion, relying upon the pseudoemotion of sentimentality or divorced from the messy pressures of living experiences. Art education has to integrate the various and disparate strands of human thinking and feeling into an educational and creative unity.

Individual personality is thus an important influence on the learning and teaching of both student and teacher. Just as there are those who say that you can tell a man by the books he reads, there are many who believe that an individual's perceptions that have been translated into some concrete form are a key to that individual's personality. There is probably no doubt that in any mark, figurative and literal, an individual makes, any manner in which he disturbs the stability of what is around him—acting upon it, he is leaving some trace of himself, and a clue for educational guidance.

SOME PSYCHOANALYTIC INTERPRETATIONS

The psychoanalytic school stemming from Freud proposes that the quality of experience during infant sexuality may be the determining characteristic of one's behavior in life. Obviously, this is closely related to perceptual understanding. They hold that these early life experiences that all infants have with their mothers, and later their family, send out tentacles of influence through time, thereby coloring the perceptions of the individual. All persons are then reliving the infantile experience in symbolic and displaced ways, constantly seeking gratification, the redressing of early wrongs, the amelioration of frustration because of former deprivation and generally searching out in its most intense form a way of returning to the security, warmth and satisfactions symbolized by the mother's womb and the first dependent months of living. The various mental illnesses and neuroses, the everyday revelations of trivial incidents such as words that slip or are exchanged, the banter and play between parents and children, between men and women or others of the same sex, and dream symbolism, as well as the creation of art are among some of the manifestations of each person's attempts to resolve the tensions of his infancy or to regain its relatively pure state.

There are a variety of approaches that have been modified since Freud's original presentation, but he still reflects the basic beliefs of the whole school of psychoanalysis. In writing of the artist particularly, despite the fact that he despaired of really arriving at any verifiable information, Freud sums up the artistic vision and its formation by suggesting that the artist is generally more sensitive to psychic stimuli, that in increasing or avoiding the responses to that stimuli, which would tend to be neurotic, he utilizes the means of artistic creation. When a psychic disturbance builds up to a point that threatens to destroy the unconscious restraints that hold it, the artist channels the energy into a creative act, transforming the anxiety into an expressive quality, rather than in some other way. The level of pressure subsists until the perceptual processes acting in response to external and internal stimuli builds up again to creative expression.

Actually, in this manner the really creative artist can shape the stuff of his daydreams, fantasies, and such into expressive and satisfying symbols of the underlying psychic drama. In a like manner, anyone who engages in creative forming experiences may be able to dispel certain repressions, balancing off the level of internal dissension. However, it is only the true artist who does this with skill and with a constancy that develops a body of work revealing a unique personality.

In essence, the psychoanalysts suggest that an individual who engages in art work is attempting to recapture a real or an imagined loss, that often perceptions are such to stimulate a symbolic search for the images and feelings of the infantile past.

In modified guises there are many theories that accept some form of unconscious motivation as the reason for the particular kind of vision and symbol formation that characterize a personal creative activity. This may appear somewhat logical in that it offers an explanation for the seriousness of purpose that usually underlies children's play activities, whether it is in games, art, or in response to parental pressures. The child clings with a fierceness to his own modes and reveals a profound commitment to the inspiration of the moment. Similarly, the adult creator is often inextricably bound up with the nature of what he is doing, frequently ascribing esoteric or private meanings to his work which are not superficially apparent to any observers. Yet this approach not only does not designate a good or bad value to the forms that are being created, it seems to insist that the only valid reason for much of human experience is therapeutic in nature. It does not provide any clear means by which man can divest himself of his past in a positive sense. As Freud has commented, Man always drags his feet in the mud.

Obviously, the clinical and therapeutic needs of human behavior are present. All one has to do is to look about at the confused and absurd happenings that are the daily lot of each person to understand such a need.

Art
and
Education
in
Contemporary
Culture

·

196

However, to suggest that the entire pattern of existence is predetermined by an inescapable biological and psychological relationship may be ignoring the many other open attributes and potentialities inherent in human behavior. Though education has never significantly accepted, even in a small part, many of the ideas of psychoanalysis, the insights of the field have made themselves felt, particularly in art education. These are vital and explain a great number of classroom happenings and products, but offer no necessary value judgments of an aesthetic nature.

The art work of children has been considered fair game for many interpretive theories. There is great merit in some of them, but also present is the danger of utilizing the art period as a therapeutic session rather than as a free and creative time during which students may enrich their transforming and symbolic powers, as a gratifying end in itself, rather than as a key to a psychological mystery. There are correlations between the forms that are created through art and the psychic life of the student, but the variables are great and the contending hypotheses are uncertain and subject to change. It is only in truly clinical situations that such correlation may be helpful in diagnosing a disturbance. In a classroom they are intriguing, but harmful if too specifically accepted as a base for understanding.

ART EDUCATION AND PERCEPTION

Perception is a central factor in learning and in the realization of experience for the individual. It is the essential core as well in the art process, for creative involvement does not terminate with internal comprehension. It proceeds to a concrete manifestation in media and form. All varying factors that impinge upon that process may be reviewed again. Without genuine insights into this area, an art teacher cannot hope to provide the purposeful and individually enlightening experiences that creative behavior during an art lesson should engender.

First, there must be the recognition of each person as an individual, a living, uniquely functioning and inherently extraordinary clustering of beliefs, attitudes, cultivated, and inherited characteristics. It is this singularly organized concentration of attributes that constitutes the individual student. If there is to be an affirmation of those qualities and a genuine expression of their nature, there also has to be the acceptance of the "indivisible individual." It is this existential personality who experiences internally and in an interpretive way the perceptions that are pressed upon him by his environment. He "abstracts" or selects those forms and relationships which have significance for him and these provide the basis of knowledge and meaning. Artistic expression acts as a mediating agency by which the assumption and purposes of the individual gain concrete form. This in turn corroborates and further enhances the initial and other formative perceptions.

In a more general sense, the so called facts of perception are always given in concrete terms. That is, there is an external environment of particular properties to excite the sense organs of the perceiver. These are given to the organism through excitation and stimulation, light, sound, and the various other physiological impingements making themselves felt by the observer, setting up a condition of awareness. This "outside" world is constructed by the individual and presumed to exist even without his physical presence. This construction provides the student with the visual sources of his form, though there has to be a comprehension of the forces that produce particular shapes, light values, colors, or other forms.

However, though the "outside world" may be said to exist independent of the individual, his sense of it is generated only through his consciousness, through the awareness of the "I" quality. Consequently, there is a recognition of the self, of the "I" as different from the external conditions, though related to them in order to stabilize, and establish meaning. It is this relationship that is so variable, requiring a sensitivity of teaching.

This is the consequence of unconscious factors such as fears and aspirations, values and attitudes that have emotional and infinitely individual psychic configurations. Past experiences, internalized pressures, and a host of variegated purposes that provide an abundance and often a confusion of cues, therefore, create grossly divergent perceptions on the part of individuals and provide a range of teaching possibilities for art teachers.

The act of perception is never really an absolute one, dependent as it is upon the changing and variegated promptings and considerations that influence an individual at any given moment. Yet for purposes of consummating the desire for action, for concrete expression and transformation of experience into form, the individual has to accept particular perceptions as correct or at least concrete despite their somewhat relative nature. This is only one paradox that exists alongside many others in the human make-up.

Obviously, if there is to be any authentic closing with experience, particularly in the artistic process, there has to be an intensity of awareness and an evaluative judgment that is in keeping with the purposes and values that impel the individual. Education itself is largely made up of the qualitatively perceptual judgments that teachers and students both develop and act upon and the process is particularly dynamic in the teaching of art.

Art education seeks to enrich the "seeing" aspects of perception primarily, though it is also involved with the total receptivity of the individual. This ability to "see" in a workable and intense way is not a particularly ingrained ability that only a few possess. Though there are the special talents that only great artists seem to be born with that permit them to see deeply and create masterpieces, the average individual is capable of a wide and profound range of visual sensitivity and an intensification of insight.

It is this sensitivity that art education trains for in the classroom. Its development is not acquired without effort. The experience during art lessons have to go beyond the simple act of looking. Looking is sometimes a problem in itself to get children to be actively engaged in as many teachers know. However, looking if it is to be the beginning factor in cultivating perceptual sensitivity in art education requires its own manner of study. It is not sufficient, for instance, to have a child look at a tree. The image has to be examined, its rough texture noted, its sporadically distributed light

Art
and
Education
in
Contemporary
Culture

·

198

Each artist expresses
a personal vision,
despite a similarity
of subject.

"Woman, I,"
Willem de Kooning.
[Collection, The
Museum of Modern
Art]

"Female Figure,"
Sherman Drexler.
[Courtesy of the
artist]

"Unstable Woman,"
Stanley W. Hayter.

"Roman Slave Mar-
ket," Jean León
Gérôme. [Courtesy
of The Walters Art
Galley, Baltimore]

Art
and
Education
in
Contemporary
Culture

·

200

patterns acknowledged, its thrust upwards from the ground, the joining of the branches to the trunk, the spreading cover of foliage related to the underlying structure, the cylindrical mass fanning out into intricate linear patterns observed, and the whole organic interrelationship of parts heeded. Once the eyes have expanded and detailed the configuration and the elements of what is "out there" then the important process of thinking and feeling comes into play involving the uniqueness of a sentient self. Consequently, the perceptive act may be enriched, forming the generative basis for a felt and sensitively formed artistic experience. This building up of visual experience, of continually and qualitatively replenished association has to exist through all the levels of schooling. It has to be cultivated in the appreciating of art as well as in its making. Further, the experience must be a personal, individual, and independent one for the student. There is no lasting or valuable learning or development in art achieved for the student if his experience is primarily a vicarious one, by way of the teacher's remarks and demonstrated insights. Though teachers are an indispensable element in the learning process, they serve their purpose primarily in bringing the child to the threshold of his own mind and spirit and not in invading that mind or coercing that spirit.

Finally, the perceptual base of art education should be attuned to the shifting cultural currents, to the changes in the physical and philosophical landscape. The twentieth century has proven to be one of drastic transitions, of vast alterations, of fundamental redirections in most aspects of existence. The new society that is emerging may evoke differing ways of "seeing" new cultural stresses and aims that require pertinent and mature educational attitudes reflecting technological orientations, changes in how the individual is related to his environment, indeed, perhaps alterations in the very nature of the physical world. The values born out of this new world may change the forms of art and of aesthetic realization. Art education has to accept the implied invitation to grow with the times.

Developmental Differences in Art

Let childhood ripen in children.
ROUSSEAU

MANY interested observers have attempted to explain the basis of children's art work. The reasons have ranged in scope. There has been and continues to be a sincere desire to uncover the modus operandi of students' creative efforts so as to more effectively assist in individual educational development. Some few esoteric investigators have approached the field in a "pure" spirit, simply desiring to further knowledge in the particular area of children's art. The largest number have had a psychological orientation hoping to derive formulations of process in the creative and expressive area that would fit into larger theoretical schemes of explaining human personality patterns and behavioral interaction. The line least pursued has been the aesthetic one, the one derived from art itself.

DEVELOPMENT DIFFERENCES IN ART

Basically, the individual student on all levels and at any age must be regarded as an artist. The degree of skill, the profundity of insight, the imaginativeness of vision span a great range, making the ends almost different kinds of activities. Nevertheless, the child is as much engaged in creating a work of art in his own understanding as is the artist in a mature way in his studio. For the most part this is an individual endeavor and the literal (or figurative) solitary commitment and the uniqueness of the experience should be understood and respected as such. Only with this comprehension as a base of guidance can the teacher of art inculcate values and creative procedures that are inherently artistic. To disregard this approach, to set a formalized procedure and structure, is to develop learning situations that are inhospitable to valid art experiences and that too easily categorize the work of children into arbitrary groupings.

However, children's art work and the gross though orderly pattern of similarity it displays offers some objective evidence of the intrinsic symbolic workings of human expression. The drawings of children at various age

Art
and
Education
in
Contemporary
Culture

•

202

Early, direct attempt
to depict human
form through
painting. "Two
Girls," Kindergarten
Painting. [Ann Arbor
Schools; PHOTO:
Stuart Klipper]

levels are general indicators of the natural unfolding of the kind of non-discursive thinking that has been mentioned. Some loose groupings appear to congregate that can assist teachers by informing them of the developmental context within which school art unfolds. To repeat this can only be useful if it is tempered by aesthetic values and a respect for the single distinctiveness that should naturally underlie students' endeavors in the arts, and lead to spontaneous and interpretive experiences.

For a long time investigators imposed a preestablished formula in explaining the developmental aspect of children's art work, and the tendency still remains, if not ardently conscious in many interested observers; at least the thought is strong enough to influence the way teachers generally regard art activities in the classroom. The formula insisted that the child was attempting to copy a thought or a mind's image or a physically perceived object when he set about his drawing activity. This reflects the philosophical attitude that all basic thought processes are rational ones, logically leading to an intellectual mastery. First comes contemplation as the basic process of understanding. Then as the rational faculties are educated and the perceptions tamed through naturalism, judgment and abstract understanding ensue. Eventually, the student could explain any phenomena he studied, and the auxiliary experience of art was one leading to a representative rendering that followed an objective reality. Art could then only be regarded as a secondary means of understanding, one that was dependent upon the emerging abstract thought processes and the growing precision of a student's intellectual ability.

Two Hypotheses

Herbert Read more logically suggests two additional hypotheses that may explain the initial, natural, and spontaneous art work of all children and its eventual development during the elementary years of school.

*The preschematic
search for expressive
form. "Drawing,"
Five-Year-Olds.
[Courtesy, Margo
Flower;* PHOTO:
Stuart Klipper]

The first hypothesis suggests that a child develops symbols to make associative relationships between the felt or experienced image and the schema that stands in its stead because he cannot create adequate graphic or plastic representation. The schema is the configuration of marks and scribblings in the early stages and the outline drawings that appear somewhat later with visual thrift including all of the necessary parts of an image, though without a literal correctness. However, this idea is not too far removed from the first and does not permit the art activity the independence it deserves. Children very often retain the use of schematic drawing well after they are able to draw with some imitative ability. The

*"Two Figures" by
three-year-old
Jonathon. [Courtesy
Harris Rosenstein;*
PHOTO: *S. Martin
Friedman]*

Art
and
Education
in
Contemporary
Culture

·

204

development of schema seems rather to be a visual method of symbolizing the states of being that the child possesses. It serves as the graphic creation of expressive form by which the child is communicating his feelings and emotions, existing as independent symbolic shapes. They possess their own meaning, not at all dependent upon the urge to comply with imposed naturalistic representations of objects, though they do serve as visual signs or signals at certain times.

This leads us to the other hypothesis that Read advocates. "The child is seeking to escape from the vividness of his eidetic (photographically real) images, from an omnipresent realism. He wants to create something relatively fixed and personal . . . something which is 'his own'. . . . He has a feeling . . . which is independent of his conceptual thought . . . and of his perceptual images." [1] Living and experiencing potent feelings, the child's conceptual machinery simply has not developed the sophistication for adequate social expression. He is "charged" with these rich emotions and he must somehow shape them expressively. "He therefore creates— and it is here if anywhere the use of this word is justified—a visual symbol, a cipher in this language of line, which will express his feelings, communicate its quality to others, fit it in the shifting world of appearances." [2] The child finds that he has a sensuous language at his disposal that does not require the slow progressive development of discursive thought, yet is as significant in achieving, shaping and communicating meaning. The art experience becomes the private and enchanted expression whereby the child can listen to himself as well as inform the world of his being.

Read has very aptly captured the spirit of the symbolic transformation. He indicates that the other language, the one of feelings so radically different from the intellectualized aspect of logical discourse has its own character and structure and is a complete way of knowing in itself. The child, through the symbolic process, achieves a vital and a natural purpose, exercising through art a function of shaping the dynamics of subjective experience, making concrete in a sensuous and felt way the personal conditions of sentience, reflecting a vitality that has an unknown connection with the innate and active emotions and feelings. The child engages in metaphoric understanding which is not only a boon to his psyche but underlies the development of rational thought itself. The imagination is activated and the fertile train of associative and connotative thought is stimulated. Though it may not be precise or objectively contained within a logical order, it has its own very important personal and educational reasons for being, establishing a groundwork for personal meaning and individual gratification that is an end product for art education.

THE DEVELOPMENTAL SEQUENCE

A more complete understanding may be offered if the various stages of development are briefly outlined. Viktor Lowenfeld has provided art educa-

[1] Herbert Read, *Education Through Art* (New York: Pantheon Books, 1945), p. 130.
[2] *Ibid.*, p. 131.

tion with a developmental scale that has limited and general validity.[3] Though the various stages have become too narrowly defined, the categorizations tightly fixed in age spans and the affective qualities of the structure too psychologically oriented, the groupings may still offer a convenient guide into the artistically symbolic growth of children.

Scribbling

The first stage is the scribbling one. It almost explains itself; it is kinesthetic in intent. That is, the scribbling is an active graphic reflection of the motor activity that all very young children possess in great quantity, but have little control over. Lowenfeld puts this group between two and four years of age. At that age the child probably does not recognize his pencil or crayon as an instrument for symbolizing activity, but merely as a tool for physically making marks on surfaces. The muscular coordination is not sufficient to control these marks and there is probably little relationship between the marks (see drawing, p. 232) and representative images at first.

Initially the scribbling involves a good part of the upper body, the scribbles themselves being rather simple strokes and disordered in nature. As the child continues and motor coordination becomes finer, the strokes become differentiated, some of the rambling lines become shorter, more numerous and relatively controlled. This develops into longitudinal motion with straight lines, then into circular and on into spiral combinations.

At this point the child is on the threshold of fine symbolic activity. In his scribblings the spontaneous accidents of form may begin to suggest outside ideas or objects. The child begins to find "things" in his work and he starts on a process of elaboration and visual formulation. He may name his subjects if asked or in other ways prompted, but they seem satisfactory as experiences in themselves as well. The motor activity combines with a beginning ability in visual organization to lead to the next stage, the pre-schematic.

PRE-SCHEMATIC STAGE

The pre-schematic stage usually extends from four to seven years of age. It is very much a formative time. Frequently, the art work of the young child entering school is fragmentary in nature. That is, the work lacks a quality of unity, which is fundamental to any artistic activity. The child has a paucity of experience to draw from and an ineptness of handling to contend with. Though some of the activity may appear purposeless at times, the making of lines, dabbing of paint, mixing of colors, and general material manipulation leads to discovery. This bears artistic fruit in the elaboration mentioned above (see drawings, pp. 202, 203, and 236).

Valid objective guides for teachers, at this stage, are almost nonexistent; the methods have to particularly focus on the understanding of the individual child. The sometimes meaningless relationship of parts, the overexu-

[3] Viktor Lowenfeld, *Creative and Mental Growth* (New York: The Macmillan Company, 1956), pp. 504–508.

Art
and
Education
in
Contemporary
Culture

•

206

The torn paper of
the background has
acted as an imagina-
tive "jumping off"
point for the
exploration of form.
"The Fox," Fourth
Grade Drawing.
[Ann Arbor Public
Schools; PHOTO:
Stuart Klipper]

berant working of too many ideas in one artistic attempt, or the inadequacy
of the expressive forms are indicators of specific inabilities. The child has
only rudimentary insights into experience, limited control of motor abilities
and a lack of discriminating selectivity in perceptual responses. These form
obstacles to successful visually symbolic realization. In taking this inexperienced personality into account the teacher can more readily guide the
artistic efforts of the young child.

As the child exerts a growing mastery over the form making process
there is an accompanying development of symbolic understanding. The
conceptualization of the familiar elements of the environment takes on
more clarity and has a greater sense of organization. Similarly, the inner
promptings, internalized values, and other unconscious forces make themselves increasingly felt, providing the fledgling student with a vast storehouse
of symbol making material. There is an increasing complexity of interplay
between broad experience, sensory stimuli, conceptualization, and material
handling. This is a dynamic interaction that feeds on the appropriate and
direct kind of educational stimulation and guidance. For teachers to "over-
explain" an art activity at this point is almost a pedagogical crime, as it is
during most of the early elementary years. The child bridles at the procedural bit, wanting to figuratively run the course of expression without
having to wait for the formality of a starting gun. Fantasy, imagination,

conceptualization and sensory excitement combine with motor activity to lead to enthusiastic form making.

Sensory Interrelationship

During this time the child becomes aware that he can engage in "real" art activities and for him this becomes a way of thinking and feeling—of relating his experiences with the reality of the world. He can "capture" an object and shape it to his will. A circular motion of the crayon becomes a head and simple straight lines become the bodily extensions. These bodily elements the child is first aware of, probably not in any emerging realization of representational form, but simply because the emotional and thinking seat of the bodily functions is located in the brain which is in the head and contains most of the senses. The arms and legs are also soon given expressive form because they provide the locomotive means, the motion that the young are so charged with. This is a somewhat oversimplified reference to kinesthetic sensations, the movement of muscles and their relationship to children's artistic activity. The rhythmic patterns of movements appear to have some formative counterparts in the kind of symbolic conceptualiza-

"The Baseball Game," Fourth Grade Painting. [Ann Arbor Public Schools; PHOTO: Stuart Klipper]

Art
and
Education
in
Contemporary
Culture

•

208

tions that will be created. The muscular forces and the patterns they trace in space produce characteristic gestures, which influence the shapes and processes of art activities during this time.

The relationship between kinesthesia and art forming points up the larger and rather complex interactions that occur among the senses and their integral workings in the visually creative process. The act of perception we have examined elsewhere as an intricate, emotionally and culturally tinted sensory condition that is intimately bound up with conceptualization and expression. At the early levels of children's art, the preschematic and the schematic, the sensory workings are of a relatively crude but vivid nature. The degree of receptivity from the external world is highly imaginative and given to close identification with inner states of being. There are strong sensorimotor connections as well. These strong physiological drives are directly and vigorously felt by the elementary age child with a freshness and a vitality. There is a corresponding intensity of psychological quality inter-woven in these ingenious responses. The child's perceptions and sensory acceptances are of a candidness in their unfolding that is largely divested of the deceits, corrupting or deliberately determining influences, which will later inhibit the art expression. With the awareness that the expressive drive can be channeled into drawing and painting, the beginning restraints of the preschool age are dropped; the attempt to communicate—to convey thought and feeling is expanded beyond the element of speech. This is confirmed by Jean Piaget's explorations in child psychology, ". . . he (the child) is not satisfied with speaking, he must needs 'play out' what he thinks and symbolize his ideas by means of gestures and objects, and repre-sent things by imitation, drawing, and construction." [4]

The child overcomes the initial barriers of incompetence, exuberantly committing himself or herself to paint, crayon and clay. The delightfully alive dog or children going to a party (opposite page) attest to this capacity of children's art to invest symbols with manipulative reactions to the kin-esthetic sense, making for a bold and assertive imagery. Jerome Kamrowski's painting "Earth Storm" (see p. 156) is an example of how the mature artist may utilize this interaction of motion, gesture and manipulative handling of materials to create a dynamic work of art.

The expressive combination of these various physiological and aesthetic elements lend themselves to loose developmental sequences in the child. The connection between various muscular, motor, or sensory states and the conception of a visual symbol continues on into adult expression. The obvious and naive relationships are changed into subtle and sophisticated interaction. The physical and sensory states may even be internalized in the preconscious mind, coming into play as the formative aspects of symbol making are activated on any occasion. The body and its functioning, in that sense, play an important role in artistic expression.

[4] Jean Piaget, *The Psychology of Intelligence* (New York: Harcourt, Brace, 1950), p. 159.

*The motor vitality
of children's work
reveals a kinesthetic
source of art form.*

*"Our Dog," First
Grade Painting.
[Ann Arbor Public
Schools;* PHOTO:
Stuart Klipper]

*"Going to a Party,"
First Grade Drawing.
[Courtesy, Hope
Irvine;* PHOTO:
S. Martin Friedman]

Emactional elements
blend with
manipulatory
techniques during a
child's art activities.
"Finger Painting."
[New York Public
Schools]

The Mental and Feeling Context

The ability to separate the world from the self does not normally occur during this early period. The young child is congenitally egocentric. The environment and the inner compulsions are integrated into this sense of self so that it is virtually impossible for the youngster to hold or express any views that only appear to exist. To think or feel a thing or to engage in an expression of its qualities is to make it exist, per se. There are no discriminating niceties for the child separating inner imaginative fancies from the cold "fact" of outer "reality." The egocentric identification and lack of psychological and intellectual distance do not permit any refinements of distinction. The child reacts globally, and expresses his thoughts and feelings in the same manner.

Consequently, there are many logical distortions, disjointed and discontinuous symbols created that conform to the child's sense of order rather than to that of visual or conceptual reality or adult understanding. The illusions may be considered even as delusions, though they are redeemed in two ways. They are striking, effective metaphors, with an intensity of imaginativeness and an economy of statement. There is also the latent potential of achieving individual selfhood which gradually unfolds after years of bewilderment, search, discovery, and the encountering and observation of the conditions of existence.

Due to this context and to the compelling force of strong sensory stimuli the child can block out any extraneous stimuli for the moment, concentrating upon the particular intentional aspects in view. The intermingling of self and experience is itself felt in this regard by the inability of the child to place his symbols within any appropriate context. The drawing and painting have a helter-skelter quality, though each symbol image has a sympathetic convincing aspect due to the inability of the child to engage in visual or expressive extrapolation. The range of possibility is always narrowed down to the affective considerations; the interaction with things and events is spontaneously sympathetic. Some bond that is colored by an intense ego-centricity permits the child to absorb into his primitive sensibilities the "thereness" of experience, incorporating the drama of existence into the bounds of his undifferentiating self.

Relationships to the Primitive

The child is involved in his own mythical world, and like the primitive mentality, the child's activity is one of spontaneous thinking. This mental activity is not usually of conscious nature, of a logical cause and effect, but generally derives from the unconscious. Its symbolic representation has an almost direct line to those psychic human attributes that are below the threshold of ego understanding. The conscious mind of the young child, again like the primitive individual, has an undeveloped scope and makes little differentiation between the higher mental activities of abstract thinking, personal will, imaginative insight and imagery. The world may have its delights and joys but it is also a menacing place that abounds in unknown forces and ambiguous fears.

Some manner of immediate adjustment has to be made and the mythical properties of imaginative symbolizing appear to suffice. In some magical way, the primitive mind finds spiritual succor and emotional security in the magic, myth, and ritual of his culture. The myths become his entrance into existence permitting him to come to terms with both the symbolic and original revelation of his preconscious mind and the constant presence of an otherwise hostile environment; they become his experiences of life that transcend mere invention. There is an empathetic peering and symbolic entry into the conditions and objects of existence. Similarly, the young child in his drawing creates the civilized counterpart in visual form, groping about in what may alternately be a carefree abandon or a desperate need. The preschematic attempts are basically inchoate, just loose forms struggling to emerge. The process itself is, no doubt, a satisfying and a necessary one even if it is a trying one at points. However, the child does not achieve the true counterpart of a personal myth until he has developed what Lowenfeld refers to as the achievement of a form concept.

The psychological context of early childhood does not permit the student to utilize any skilled conventions of artistic vision: perspective, gradation of tone, textural discrimination, and the various other techniques of visual expression and representation. Even when they occur accidentally, they are not recognized by the child. The child simply does not recognize alternatives and cannot shuttle back and forth between experience and a removed contemplation of that experience.

The teacher then must be sensitive to the various conditions, sensory, emotional, intellectual and such, that exert influence and controls over the work of rather young children. Since growth rates are so individual and inexactly standardized, this insight into the evolution of expression cannot

Art
and
Education
in
Contemporary
Culture

•

212

The sensuous inter-play of forms, colors, visual rhythms and direct expressiveness evoke imaginative and lyrically poetic responses from both the child and the mature artist. This symbolic joining of child and mature artist exists outside any developmental patterns. Expressive spontaneity is common to all ages.

"Via Aurelia," Helen Frankenthaler. [Courtesy: André Emmerich Gallery, New York; PHOTO: Eric Pollitzer]

be too safely confined to just this very early grouping. There has to be a knowing and intuitively attuned organization of activities that lead to an expanding realization on the part of the child. The enlargement of possibilities has to keep apace of the inherent capacities of the individual child, though a reaching for new and important experiences should be excited in the child. There has to be a continuing and individually progressive acceleration based upon manipulative activities, suggestive motivations, and new first hand experiences. In this sense, the child is led naturally through a process of individuation and an enrichment of sensibilities. To comment on the relationship to primitive ideas sums up this highly formative stage.

The child continues a search for symbolic concepts with which to express his sentience. The forms become more detailed, less naively dependent upon bodily movement and more conceptually controlled, more the conscious creation of form. However, the representations are fluid and exploratory, constantly searching out a spontaneous but visually conceived relationship of parts. This will eventually lead to a particular and fixed schema for representing particular objects, though this occurs, in the author's experience, somewhat before Lowenfeld suggests that it does. At this stage the child is perhaps at the freest time of his beginning school career; nursery, kindergarten or the first year of primary school. All the wonder, excitement, bewilderment, anxiety, and intensity of becoming an independent human entity make their first serious appearance. The child can give this exhilarating but frightening awareness some concrete shape through his art. In this manner he engages in a symbolic activity that has intrinsic worth not only as a psychological alleviation of fear and resolution of expressive tensions but as a process of learning—learning that is imaginative and intuitive as well as logically certain.

SCHEMATIC STAGE

The schematic stage, generally running from seven through nine, is probably the most distinctive period of child art, the one that typically decorates the school corridors and that parents gush over, hoping too often underneath though, that Mary or Johnny will be able to outgrow the childishness. Even at the earliest stages of art work, the creative process is an expression of the individual. It achieves its highest point of childish realization during this period of schematic art when a definite symbol is evolved to uniformly stand for everything that is to be represented.

Like the making of myth wherein the component parts each represent a

*"Improvisation,"
Sixth Grade Water-
color Painting.
[Ann Arbor Public
Schools;* PHOTO:
Stuart Klipper]

Art
and
Education
in
Contemporary
Culture

•

214

particular of the environment or the conditions of life, the child's drawing will symbolically fix a human quality or an environmental factor of his experience within a particular form. Though myths have a range of forms they do not possess the uniquely individualized scope that children's drawings do. The myth usually is commonly shared by a tribe or any other social group while the child's drawing is particular and his alone. This probably accounts for the discrepancy in forms, though children's art and myth-making seem to share a very similar creatively symbolic urge. The child creates his own myth in his drawing, apprehending the quality of living through the sensuous medium of line, color, shape and mass. Play activities, early musical explorations, dancing and rhythmic movement and connotative verbal inventions are among some of the other symbolic modes that achieve the same purposes. All of these activities have a common core in being creative manifestations of underlying needs that find expression in some sensuous form and then have a ritual established about the invoking of the form.

Archetypes of Form

Once the child has drawn his schema he tends to repeat it again and again for a period as a ritual pattern, just as in the repetitive satisfactions of a dance step or a game of blind man's bluff or the rereading of a favorite story. This is the mythical point of purest form and the one at the time that offers the greatest security and gratification if it is not disturbed by various external pressures. Carl Jung, a brilliant and innovating psychologist who broke away from the classical Freudian concept, suggests that the human race is subject to the foreboding pressures of prehistoric and primal images that he calls archetypes. These archetypes are instinctual urges, the preformation of basic ideas or dormant representations that are a heritage from the distant past. We tend to experience them in a "collective unconscious." Primitive man is much closer to these archetypes than is civilized man and Jung indicates the latter excludes from his consciousness ". . . the laws and roots of his being. This means, on the one hand, the possibility of human freedom, but on the other it is a source of endless transgressions against one's instincts. Accordingly, primitive man, being closer to his instincts, like the animal, is characterized by fear of novelty and adherence to tradition. To our way of thinking, he is painfully backward, whereas we exalt progress. But our progressiveness, though it may result in a great many delightful wish-fulfillments, piles up an equally gigantic Promethean debt which has to be paid off from time to time in the form of hideous catastrophes." [5] The schemata that children develop during this classical period of form consciousness may be likened to the archetypes that Jung refers to, each child drawing from the "collective unconscious" a unique variation of the much earlier dominant forms.

This is, as noted above, ritually repeated as long as there is no drastic change in the individual situation of the child, the representations for

[5] Carl C. Jung, *Psyche and Symbol* (Garden City, N.Y.: Doubleday Anchor Books, 1957), p. 126.

humans, houses, trees, and all space in fact falling within general categories. The human generally has head, body and limbs—a circle or a square and various sizes of cylinders. Trees have a trunk and an elliptically shaped upper form, space is either a blue line drawn above denoting sky or a base line drawn below denoting ground. The relationships in three dimensions are portrayed without factual reference to reality, but are symbolically abstract either in touching or in folding over, the depiction of three dimensions on a two dimensional surface proving too advanced and rational a concept. If learning stopped at this point there would be a visual lexicon of forms which would not deviate and everyone could refer to. Though the actual symbol would be individually realized it would, however, be based upon certain common underlying forms. But as Jung seems to sorrowfully note, "progress" occurs.

Idiosyncratic Nature of Schematic Forms

Nevertheless the schemata of characteristic child art are bound up with some very fundamental sources of form as well as with the individual self. As for the latter, the personal idiosyncratic attributes of an individual child find expression in his art; and any malformation or physical or even mental handicap is likely to find itself symbolized in the drawing, painting, or sculpture. The blind, the crippled or the emotionally disturbed child will graphically act out his condition, very often unconsciously on a piece of paper. The assertive child may have a bold quality to his work where the anxious youngster is given to a thin uncertainty in his drawing. One way or another the child reveals himself in his work and this is an important point to recognize for it parallels the unconscious instinct or the sublimating process of the artist. Though it may be overgeneralized to say that basically all artistic creativity stems from broad dispositions or universal emotional attitudes the idea may not be far off the mark. Certainly, the

A typical Elementary painting with schematic forms. "Circus," Third Grade Painting. [Ann Arbor Public Schools; PHOTO: Stuart Klipper]

Art
and
Education
in
Contemporary
Culture

.

216

state of being of the artist, child or adult, and a degree of intensity, however varying, with which emotions are felt seem to be consistently present in the creative process, at least insofar as the making of art is concerned.

Therefore in arriving at the schematic stage the child achieves a natural state of symbolic satisfaction. Though there may be no skillful correlation between the objects portrayed and their counterpart in objective reality and only a potentially evolving yet slight visual connection, the child has nevertheless achieved a workable symbolic and creative solution. He is not really trying to draw the objects as he is looking at them, but rather as he "sees" and "knows" them internally—actually as he *feels* them. The child may be said to be diagramming feelings as he is spontaneously creating art forms. This factor deserves further emphasis for it underlies not only child art, but much of adult art as is to be repeated throughout the text. Mere imitation has never really been the artistic criterion and from its first appearance as an impulse in man the making of art has had symbolic and emotional connotations. The forms are symbolic rather than imitative and tap a far more fundamental root than that of rendering *la belle* nature.

Many observers hold that children's early artistic development may be separate in many ways from the child's growing awareness of objective reality. The individual schemata that are devised are, as we have seen, unique plastic symbols that have very little to do with any visual acuity. Lowenfeld is particularly adamant on this point. All of the senses are brought into play during art activities and the resulting perceptions are rich and fertile sources for form, but these are transformed in the young mind into that imaginative, symbolic, and mythic "waking dream" that in the young is often the envy of the old. The forms that a child invents, the entire gamut of graphic schemata are the bringing together of a host of sensory, social, and psychological experiences with the individual personality inextricably woven into the development of the synthesized form.

The middle grader begins to take more cognizance of the environment in his drawing, referring closely to objective observation. "Building a Log Cabin," Third Grade Drawing. [Ann Arbor Public Schools; PHOTO: *Stuart Klipper]*

*Intentional
experience may be
expressively
dramatized for
children through art
work. "The
Skyscraper," Fourth
Grade Painting.
[New York Public
Schools; PHOTO:
S. Martin Friedman]*

Intentional Experience

This spontaneous childhood activity and its attendant forms appears to cut across national and racial lines, for the children of all countries are reported essentially to have a similar kind of development. The visually artistic symbolizing process is an omnipresent and characteristic factor in child growth. During this time there is a passion and a positive attitude on the part of young children toward their art activities that is a very pleasant experience and one that all educators who teach the early elementary levels are aware of. However, when the pressures of social conformity begin to be felt, when there is a gangling consciousness of self to contend with that is fed by a growing accumulation of factual material, a change occurs.

Lowenfeld indicates that the schemata undergo change, become deviant from their original form when there is an "intentional experience." That is whenever basic learning takes place, whenever the child is subjected to some new awareness about his body, his environment or their relationships then a new schema will be attempted to meet the new conditions. However, this is not necessarily only the result of a growing intellectual awareness. There is also the expanding sense of capacity for symbolic creativity so that the child may naturally wish and be compelled to dramatize through his imagination as well as push back the frontiers of his rational mind. Both are of prime importance.

Art
and
Education
in
Contemporary
Culture

·

218

The child emerges from the egocentric cocoon during this schematic period. The world takes on a separateness and the child achieves a widening cognizance of the things about him. There is an intensification in the correlation among physical, psychological, social, and symbolic awareness; the child ranges in the possibilities of interaction with the external surroundings.

Representation of familiar objects and living things takes on more precise and detailed form than was present earlier in response to a beginning descriptive urge. These configurations, however, do not conform to the purely visual; their supposed imitativeness perhaps is confined by the lack of real manipulative and expressive skills of developmental inadequacies. The metaphoric urge is still urgent in that the child has not yet completely divested himself of his earlier "waking dream" state and may be loath to do so.

However, there is an exciting, naive and exploratory interest in a host of possibilities and things. The child is willing to tackle almost any subject fearlessly with the expressive lance of his brush, crayon, or pencil. He or she feels compelled to give a visual recital of whatever claims a somewhat volatile interest. If it were possible children would imaginatively account for whatever befalls them. This immense store of experience awaiting realization in some expressive form inundates children at a period when they are spiritually, intellectually, and emotionally eager to incorporate its essence into their understanding. But the skills, insights, and developmental comprehension can only carry a part of the load. The schematic art forms are devised, becoming in a sense, symbolic shortcuts to embody the compelling expressive needs.

The wave of expansion, however, backs up, perhaps appalled at the limitless nature of what is in the outside world. Referred to above as a ritual pattern, certain favorite subjects come to the forefront, influenced by peers, culture, or particular psychological conditions and propensities. The schemata are pushed to the end possibilities of their symbolic nature. During these years children devise a symbolic visual language of characteristic and vivid representations. There is more tendency to naturalistic delineation, perhaps, though certain stiffly formal conventions of human or animal figures are adhered to. Other elements of the artificial landscape or not familiarly known objects are ingeniously reinvented in form by the child. Certain additional broad usages of visual symbols are stylized into shared expressions such as, for instance, the importance of an object or a figure determining its size rather than actual proportion, the fanciful play of color, the silhouetting and profiling of forms, and the use of the base lines to denote spatial conditions or the ground and sky lines so ubiquitously employed by first and second graders particularly. The slightly older children may not depart too far from many of these stylizations, though they do tend to elaborate on the naturalistic factors. Nevertheless, during this "golden age" of expression, there are no real logical obstacles that deter the child.

Rational and Nonrational Qualities

The child is impelled by a strong, creatively expressive urge that surmounts any inconsistency of vision and circumvents difficulties that are otherwise perceptually obvious to them. At this point of his development the child experiences his closest spiritual kinship with the more mature artist. Both are primarily bound up with the act of expression. They do not necessarily want to explain things in any precisely logical manner. Rather,

"Circus Rider," Third Grade Painting. [Pittsburgh Public Schools; PHOTO: Samuel A. Musgrave]

Art
and
Education
in
Contemporary
Culture

•

220

they want to interpret what is happening to them, to transform those impinging outer pressures and compelling inner forces into a felt, concrete symbol. If common sense, or coherence of imposed ideas of form proves to be a hindrance to expression, then they either question its compatibility, defy its sense or just simply ignore it. They rely upon the magic of the created symbol and the inventiveness of their own conglomeration of feelings, ideas and sensory manipulation to carry them through.

This has a ready reference to the nonrational core that invests man with a restlessness and an awareness, a reaching out for meaning that may figuratively remain a dynamic potentiality rather than a finished actuality. The child is operating at the frontiers of his imagination and at an optimum level of intensity and receptiveness to experience. This also parallels the condition in mature artists. It is probably not inappropriate to refer to this kind of activity and creative symbolizing as nonrational, but it is a typically human mastery of experience as well. Trees may not be blue, sky and ground do meet prosaically in the normality of vision, facial expressions are more subtle than the wide grimaces or button-eyed physiognomies of children's making. Yet the significance that children and artists invest in their distortions often tells a greater truth and offers a richer realization of experience. The supposed contradictions and uncertain juxtapositions in much of children's work do not create nearly the amount of confusion or rejection that would be expected if the channels for receiving the images are open and sympathetic.

The child and the artist both juggle rational and nonrational conceptions concurrently without any hesitation or uncertainty. These are the symbolic residue of emotional qualities, and there may be in the case of the child the beginning insight into aesthetic concerns. Despite the apparent contradictions or lack of logically developed relationships the child, as with the artist, does not suffer any more than the normal confusions of perception and behavior in daily undertakings. The expressive works simply conform to a different logic, to an aesthetic and individual structuring that has its own manner of organization. The logic of aesthetic understanding is based on imaginative, freely associative, even on exaggerated and deliberately displaced elements rather than on reasonably sequential or primarily an intellectual determination of parts.

As a result, it would appear to be incorrect to consider this emotional symbolization and aesthetic forming as subject to irrational limitations or aberrations. This would suggest that the intensity of immediate genuine artistic behavior is less than a later more developed intellectual understanding or practical cast of perceived experience. The artistic mode for the child and for the artist is at least on the same functional level, paralleling reason and utility as a way of insight into existence and providing pertinent means of coping with it.

The particular value laden pressures from the outside tend in many ways to make teachers, as well as the students themselves, see their art experiences in another light. Rather than sensing the strong urge to a controlled, highly conscious structuring of form as a reduction of artistic and imaginative capabilities, it is felt to be a progression toward a more ordered thinking and skilled visual rendering. The innocent but striking emotional schemata assume an undesirable naivete. This, in most instances, the teacher convinces children they have to leave behind.

The well intentioned teacher may even recognize that the so called irrationalities of the seven- or eight-year-old do not appear as such to the child. Consequently, they look into the early work with the children, hopefully on their own level. The sympathetic understanding, it is felt, offers children the security and reassurance they require to develop onto further levels. The irrationalities are merely considered to be the prominence of emotional drives at this level. Though the forms produced may not be considered as representative of what is being expressed, the experienced and understanding teacher recognizes them as emblems of feeling, perhaps even as profoundly fertile symbols of the child's inner life.

The whole process is considered a necessary one, but one that is transient, a way station on the road to a later more rational expression on the part of the child. The abundant and almost vehement visions of the young child, though they may possess charm and vigor are not too frequently appreciated simply in terms of their innate imaginative quality. The largely natural aesthetic elements are regarded as extraneous. The works themselves are believed to reflect the undeveloped perceptions and unskilled techniques of the children, who have yet to experience a more apt depth of expression. It is not felt that children create pictures for an aesthetic or self contained satisfaction, but always a kind of learning experience.

Natural Symbolic Integration

All of this may well be true, but the understanding is based upon a value orientation, not on any absolute factual structure. Certainly, the young child lacks in the perceptual and technical proficiencies. There is no doubt that what is individually and symbolically experienced is contained within the limited store of competence and understanding afforded a first or second grader. But what is of significance is the eager and gratifying process the child is reaching for, the undaunted and naturally felt kinship with expression, the original, expansive and rich visions that excite the senses, body, and mind, the readily available imaginative and direct transformation of experience. In these ways, the children in their real, creative, and spontaneous involvement with symbolic realization have already attained an enviable state of confident and emphatic humanity.

The qualities of children's art work may be primitive, innocent, untutored, technically blasphemous, and painfully lacking in reserve or order, but they are unmistakably felt. Consequently, at this time, art education enjoys a natural bringing together of means and ends; the child's open means of creativity meeting the educational aim of investing experience with meaning. It is this symbolic forming that has to be encouraged, that the children have to be persuaded to continue in an uninhibited manner. The well trained, sincere, and comprehending teacher is of most use at this point. Frequently, it is the sensitivity and knowingness of the methods

employed that can determine much of the subsequent art attitudes and desire for participation so that the procedure has a bearing on students throughout their lives. We have already recognized that the world is made known to the individual not in any direct fashion, but through the mediation of conceptions and feelings formed by the symbolic process. It would be desirable to retain the verve and enthusiasm of this early artistic stage on into the development of adolescence and adulthood. Of course there would need to be subsequent modifications, objectively oriented examinations and a willingness to adjust and adapt to the conditions that are encountered in more mature experience. Yet, the retention of the ingenuous and creative desire for form making that is characteristic of even the average young child cultivates a more consistently flowing interplay between feeling, thinking, and symbolizing. This assists in developing that balanced and integrated personality that can be more than one of the mythical aims of education.

However, the various and sundry cultural attitudes and intellectual educational prescriptions become quite evident at an early age. Factors other than the intensity of expression make themselves felt and begin to influence the children's art work and their attitudes toward symbolic meaning. This is undoubtedly necessary to the process of learning development, to individual and social maturing. The golden period of a personalized and symbolically magical art is gradually preempted by the acculturation process.

REALISM

The next stage, that of the dawning realism, is the gang age of between nine and eleven. Not only has the child become physically and psychologically independent in the growing awareness of his self, he has become concurrently conscious of his social position. Though there is a maturing factor

[OPPOSITE, TOP]
The later elementary child frequently retains traces of earlier schematic characteristics at the same time that an attempt is made for more "realistic" depiction. "Card Game," Fifth Grade Painting. [Ann Arbor Public Schools; PHOTO: Stuart Klipper]

[OPPOSITE, LOWER LEFT]
A characteristic ineptness is typical of the upper grader's fumbling attempts to portray representational images. "Figure Drawings," Fifth Grade. [Ann Arbor Public Schools; PHOTO: Stuart Klipper]

[OPPOSITE, LOWER RIGHT]
Upper graders love to candidly comment on the social environment if given an opportunity to express the comment through art. "The Beatnik," Sixth Grade Painting. [Ann Arbor Public Schools; PHOTO: Stuart Klipper]

Designing shapes that swing and flutter. [New York Public Schools]

Art
and
Education
in
Contemporary
Culture

·

224

that permits the child at this time to consider himself independent of his family in many significant ways, he exchanges the earlier ties to home for those of his peers in society at large and that of the teacher in the environment of the schools. The ties may not always be positive or emulative ones, they may also be those of rebellion. Generally the upper elementary student begins to be actively aware of the acculturation process. Therefore, he looks around and sees how other children draw, how adults create visual representations and how the "real" world "really" looks. He recognizes that his earlier schematic generalization has been inadequate and he makes his fumbling attempts at representational imagery.

Perhaps even more important with the growing ability to abstractly conceptualize, and to put these conceptualizations into a relatively sophisticated verbal form that almost everyone else appears to accept and praise him for, the eleven-year-old becomes disinterested in art work. When he does attempt any visual expression he normally abjures the "creative" aspect wanting a formula and a technique on how to do it "correctly." His myth-making has been subjected to the hard impinging practicalities of growing up. They do not entirely atrophy, for in being human the preadolescent still relates to the world in a symbolic manner. The generalized and utilitarian factors are stressed, while the rational faculty is elevated beyond the imaginative. Expression becomes social and group oriented and there is left only a vicarious or fitful relationship to creative expression. The highly institutionalized forms of popular culture take over and the earlier instinctual comprehension that Jung speaks of degenerates into the catastrophe of mass man.

Popular culture makes deep inroads into the time, attention, and understanding of this age group. The comic strip still is a potent force that exerts a sway over the youthful mind. The images of the movies and television are influential to a much larger degree while those of commercial design and illustration are ubiquitously experienced. These all provide the homogeneous images of standard illusion that youngsters indiscriminately accept as desirable and necessary models of visual symbols. Most often they do not possess the necessary skills to imitate images with cultural facility so they are forced back to their own childish modes. These become distasteful and the whole idea of art may be rejected or just dropped with a lack of concern. The "realism" of the environment makes itself symbolically felt in many consequent ways that do not always do credit to mature and sensitive development.

The intermediate grades of elementary school see the preadolescent groping for what Lowenfeld called a sense of form. The symbolic schemata of the preceding years are considered inadequate and infantile, though the expressive qualities of the early grades are not too easily sloughed off in a number of ways. The middle grader may not be the dependent individual he was earlier but he still has strong ties to the secure and familiar artifacts and conditions of his life. His ability to control his movements may be more fluent and sophisticated, but this is offset by the beginning inhibitions in his psychological approach to expressive behavior. Though the art work, at this time, retains many fresh characteristics, there is the encroaching evidence of a halting and hesitant grappling with the spatial realities of form and the need to delineate the shapes of things in a socially accepted and artistically approved manner. The latter becomes constrained by the traditional values that are largely operating while the welter of representational data from the outside creates acute problems of technique, material handling, and form making.

These factors continue on into late elementary and junior high ages. There is an intensified interest in the factual material, in an objectified evaluation of things and events. The more rational attributes of thought and meaning begin to be stressed. Consequently, the art work, if it is undertaken voluntarily is an attempt to render an objective reality. The largely flat, two dimensional nature of schematic modes is looked upon as unsatisfactory and is not too frequently referred to, except in disdain.

Other factors impinge upon the student's consciousness and affect the creative process in the arts. The preadolescent begins to lead a much more complex life. A great number of external demands make themselves felt. These influence the art work of this period, unfortunately leading to ineffectual conditions for its development. The peer culture looms as one of the

Industrial arts
during the
junior-high age
can be one of
ebullient artistic exploration. [Scarsdale
Public Schools;
PHOTO: John Gass]

Art
and
Education
in
Contemporary
Culture

•

226

most important here, the tendency to form into gangs of one kind or another strongly impelling the attitudes and actions of children from about nine well on into early adolescence. The sexual mores and psychological reflections act to demand a separateness of boy from girl, fostering a contentiousness of attitude. The various gang groupings seem to be predicated on a competitive spirit, both within its own circle and between rival coteries. This may well develop into a self sufficiency of age and temperament for the period that resists adult authority and shuns any viewpoints that are not indigenous to the age and gang. A more complete break occurs with the home and the security of dependency. There is an ardent desire for approval and recognition by the peer group that is not deplorable in itself but leads to strange and sometimes lamentably grotesque behavior and attitudes. There is a containment of what would normally be exploratory behavior because the taboos of the group have to be respected. This sets the basis for the later prevailing conformity and largely colors the attitudes toward art which are more derived from group concensus than individual understanding.

The Constriction of Artistic Activity

These factors have direct bearing on the art work of later periods. They infiltrate the perceptual screen of the individual and too often stultify the symbolic process. At a time when there should be a consolidation of the manipulative skills that come into evidence during the primary grades, the dexterity that may emerge is shunted into narrow and fragmented concerns. The imaginative creativity of the eight-year-old becomes the embarrassed constrictions of the twelve-year-old. The earlier egocentric eagerness is turned into a self conscious awkwardness of approach. The art work of the primary grades may be stereotyped in that it is made into schematic sym-

The early adolescent can evidence a sense of sophisticated organization. "House Geometry," Eighth Grade Painting. [Ann Arbor Public Schools; PHOTO: David Churches]

bols, yet these are invested with either latent significance, direct intention, or vitality of purpose. The later elementary expressive attempts veer into visual clichés. These are formed because either the intention is not met by the symbolic action and the child resorts to the preceding, tested methods, or the influences from outside sources limit the type of imagery to be utilized.

At the very time that the outside world makes itself so forcefully felt, the preadolescent is also awakening to a mature sense of self. The egocentricity of the six-year-old was not the kind of sentience that characterizes maturity, though that of the emerging adolescent may well be. This realization of individual existence runs counter to the sense of group belonging. Though it is a fundamental search for identity, this awareness of the self as a unique personality is too frequently submerged. It may reveal itself only in group approved activities, but finally bursts forth in late adolescence with an intense and painful romanticism (see painting, p. 228).

Emphasis on Expanded Art Teaching Procedures

It is this individualizing characteristic that the art teacher has to woo and skillfully assist in surfacing through symbolic expression. Because of the evolving sense of order and logic of this stage the art lesson has to offer explanation and demonstration as well as stimulation. Motivation has to possess more structural elements of why, where, and how than heretofore. The observable and the intellectually related aspects of art have to be emphasized so that the student may feel more naturally involved. This in turn may lead to the more genuinely artistic modes despite the efforts that may be required for an honest and rich engagement with expression.

This age level is the most opportune time to start vital, critical and mature efforts at appreciation. The different styles and varying ways of expression of other times and places as well as the current serious art styles are accepted by later elementary students provided that sincere efforts are made to explicate the material in a way that does not offend or bore them.

Observation should be effectively encouraged, perceptions carefully considered and the inherent character of forms in nature and art studied. Otherwise, the cliché images of the surrounding culture impress themselves not only as superficial signs of the times, but as vulgarized value symbols of the good things in life: face, fun and fortune as they are popularly, bluntly and coarsely conceived. The individual sensitivity and the responsiveness to art go by default if the youngsters of this age are permitted to follow their own propensities without at least a minimum of art instruction.

Yet certain psychological and internal changes do occur at this early adolescent stage that are extremely significant from an educational and art teaching viewpoint and have a direct bearing on the individual development of the student. They influence not only the attitude towards art, but towards all of cognition. Not only is the early and easy rapport with a natural state that has its roots in mythical thinking changed, the child actually discovers logical thought. This is a profoundly basic condition of maturation that leads to a fulfillment of man's capacities as a being who at

Art
and
Education
in
Contemporary
Culture

·

228

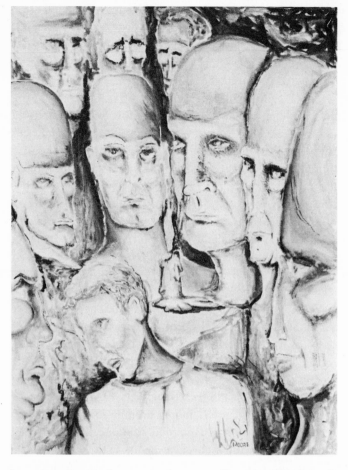

The adolescent is attracted to dramatic content and subjective states. "Candle Thoughts," High School Drawing. [Ann Arbor Public Schools; PHOTO: David Churches]

least in part, is of a rational nature. However, Herbert Read clearly puts the case for art education in the following paragraph.

. . . At about the age of eleven . . . admittedly a profound change of a psychological nature does take place. . . . The child acquires the power of breaking up, or dissociating, his first unitary perceptions, and logical thought begins with this capacity to isolate and compare component details.

No doubt this condition inaugurates a series of psychological changes that would have a radical effect on the manner of a child's expression. His symbolic screen, his relationship with the approach to achieving meaning undergoes a metamorphosis.

But to assume that visual or plastic . . . modes of expression are thereby eliminated is to be the question. They *may* show a tendency to disappear; but it is perhaps this very tendency which our educational methods should oppose, preserving not only the function of imagination, but even more necessarily the essential unity of perception: not only the continuously vitalizing interchange of mind and the concrete events of the natural world, but also the continuous nourishment of the individual psyche from the deeper levels of the mind. . . . The art of the child declines after the age of eleven because it is attacked from every direction—not merely squeezed out of the curriculum, but squeezed out of the mind by the logical activities which we call arithmetic and geometry, physics and chemistry, history and geography, and even literature as it is taught. The price we pay for this distortion of the adolescent mind is mounting up: a civilization of hideous objects and misshapen human beings, of sick minds and unhappy households, of divided societies and a world seized with destructive madness. We feed these processes of dissolution with our knowledge and our science, with our inventions and our discoveries, and our educational system tries to keep pace with the holocaust; but the creative activities which could heal the mind and make beautiful our environment, unite men with nature and nation with nation—these we dismiss as idle, irrelevant and inane.[6]

Art teachers can draw a long list of specific implications from all of the various levels of development. It is not only each child that has unique expressive problems. Each age level shares broad collective variations of capacity and stages of growth. Further, there is a probable relationship between intelligence levels and expressive ability just as there is a tie between cultural influences and the forms they evoke in children. There is a great amount of developmental overlapping with age groups below and above each particular stage, so that the sequence does not respond to simple time lines or easily classified categories of variables. The artistic growth of each child, dependent as it may be upon a number of external determinations, is still largely an individualized affair. The various uncertain "determining" influences should be known to art teachers and the resulting methods must make allowances for them in the actual teaching. In the final analysis though, the art teacher may be best guided by an

[6] Herbert Read, *Education Through Art* (New York: Pantheon Books, 1945), p. 166.

The secondary student is capable of creating skilled, expressive works of art. "Wood Sculpture," High School. [Pittsburgh Public Schools; PHOTO: Samuel A. Musgrave]

Art
and
Education
in
Contemporary
Culture

·

230

adherence to those qualities of creativeness, of aesthetic expressiveness, and symbolic form that the body of art suggests as the most pertinent. These in concert with the insight into personality qualities and the intensity of classroom experience that an individual child is involved with at any given time should serve as the most relevant source of teaching comprehension and method.

The Scope of Learning

> For my part I have the strange and dangerous habit,
> in every subject, of wanting to begin at the begin-
> ning (that is, at my own beginning), which entails
> beginning again, going back over the whole road,
> just as though many others had not already mapped
> and traveled it.
>
> PAUL VALÉRY

GOETHE's Faust after having diligently and widely learned of many things is moved to say, "And here, poor fool, with all my lore, I stand no wiser than before." Knowledge and wisdom may not always be synonymous, and the act of learning a kind of illusion that mitigates the despair and the compulsion of the moment and the vastness of the external world. Yet, disregarding the important element of metaphysics at this point, learning does occur almost every waking moment of everyone's day, and if we are to believe some psychologists, even when we are asleep. Actually, the range of learning an individual is involved with is almost endless; whether through science, language or art, there is a staggering and imposing series of different kinds of knowledge and understanding.

There is the learning that is involved with bodily functions, the early walking, eating and other muscle manipulation that is later expanded into the graceful motion of dance or the coordinated skills in sports. There is the intellectual learning that permits us first to haltingly read, spell, do arithmetical sums and make simple associations of qualities that later becomes the ability to abstractly and operationally engage in the symbolic ideas of literature, the combinatory intricacies of mathematics or the theoretical complexities of science. There is the initial identification with particular biases and so called correct ways of doing things which in time become the moral and value laden basis for our attitudes, prejudices, and interests in general. There are the innocent and natural beginnings of expression and play so intensely occupying the young child that develop in a positive sense into participation and appreciative acknowledgment of the arts and aesthetic sensitivity. This later area is too often aborted or ignored during the school career, suffering a diminution of satisfying experience leading to apathy and a loss of interest.

Art
and
Education
in
Contemporary
Culture

·

232

There are any number of other learnings: memorization, insights, analytical appraisals and intuitive awarenesses, the recognition of signs and
cues, the avoidance of fearful or unrewarding conditions or the reinforcement of pleasant ones. All of them are a part of the complex and overwhelming amount of learning that any one individual undergoes during his
lifetime. The scope of learning is so complicated and so diffusely disseminated throughout a myriad array of variables that no simple theory that
reduces its elements to easy classifications suffices for proper understanding.

The leap that has to be taken in attempting to understand creativity,
into original or otherwise productive learning is even more difficult. While
the basic conditions of learning are subject to various conceptions depending upon the philosophy of the investigator, the complexities are increased
when the learning behavior is untypical or otherwise outside of the normal or
average kind as is characteristic of creative production. However, certain
structural models have been helpful in providing insights in both learning
and creativity. Certainly, teaching of the arts could benefit from a more
comprehensive and synthesized view of the learning process as long as there
is no resulting imposition of a supposedly single correct method. For despite
the rather large amount of research that is going into learning theory, the
findings are at the most tentative and crude. More important is the realization that any theoretical proposition is subject to the philosophical
orientation of the person who is to utilize it and necessarily an adjunct to
implementing values and aims. Programmed, teaching-machine education
conceivably may lead to automated, collectivized student responses while
an emphasis on the creative arts may help in developing independent individuals. Both patterns can find theoretical support.

The theoretically simplest principles of learning tend to be the most mechanical. These revolve around a stimulus-response psychology, but do not normally deal with any progression toward goals which frequently mark learning behavior. They are also free of any real concern with consciously intellectual and aesthetic qualities that utilize choice and symbolic meaning beyond simple intentional considerations.

These relatively primitive learning qualities stem from three biological conditions that are considered basic in a living organism: drive, tension-reduction, and biological inertia. Drive may be regarded as the inherent hungers or appetites that living things possess, such as need of food, to breathe air, bodily elimination, sexual gratification, etc. The drive manifests itself in the nervous activity that is set up when there is a "tissue change" in the organism that upsets the normal and comfortable equilibrium. Tension-reduction is the process whereby the drives are satisfied, restoring the body and its autonomic system to a balanced state. This is most often accomplished through some kind of learning, wherein the individual seeks out some external means of adaptability to offset the pressures of the drives. In this mechanistic fashion a person who is learning how to be an artist may be working to reduce the primary tension of his drives that are sexual or fatigue inducing, just as a stress on vocational learning is assuring the individual of the ability to provide himself with goods to offset the hunger drive. The student in the art class may also be considered from this viewpoint to be engaged in biologically necessary behavior when he or she is painting or sculpting, so that an innate necessity to symbolize experience in some form is responded to. This basically underscores the early and generative tendencies toward learning in the arts. Finally, the factor of inertia (which is biological security or "homeostasis"), forces the individual into learning that will keep the diverse strands of his being in some kind of desirable balance just as we have seen that perceptive acts seek

The child has to order a variety of intellectual processes so as to delineate visual forms in a communicative way. "Drawing," First Grade. [Courtesy, Margo Flower; PHOTO: Stuart Klipper]

Art
and
Education
in
Contemporary
Culture

·

234

closure. This parallels the tension-reduction concept though it presupposes a step beyond the automatic and takes into account the rudiments of purpose, maintaining of a pleasurable bodily status quo. This may have a fundamental relationship to aesthetic development, on a sensory level.

The Mechanistic Learning Concepts

The most celebrated of the learning concepts that derives from this mechanistic [1] level is the one of conditioning. Conditioning is formulated as a drive in an individual which causes him to respond to a stimulus that activates the senses and consequently, the nerve tissue. This results in a motor outlet response. Any additional or secondary stimulus that is present at the same time will tend to acquire the same motor outlet. After sufficient repetition (which varies greatly with the stimulus and the motor outlet) the secondary stimulus will result in the same motor outlet or mechanical learning that was originally activated in response to the original stimulus. Pavlov's famous experiment with the dogs is a classic example of this concept. In its simplest explanation, the dogs attempted to reduce the tension developed by the hunger drive obviously by eating food. Everytime this occurred Pavlov rang a bell. After sufficient repetitions he was able to get the dog to salivate simply by ringing the bell, without any food present. This conditioned learning, some psychologists suggest, underlies much of the acquisition and individual cast of knowledge. For instance, again in a simplified manner, the preference for certain shapes and colors can be traced back theoretically to the secondary qualities present in an immediate environment when the individual student as an infant was responding to his basic drives. As an example, a mother's red blouse during feeding may have set up an unconscious preference for the color. Sophisti-

[1] Gordon Allport, *Pattern and Growth in Personality* (New York: Holt, Rinehart and Winston, 1961), pp. 89–109. The basic material for this section has been suggested by the above cited reference source.

Creating a visual and an artistic sense of space is a learning experience for students. "Horses," Fourth Grade Drawing. [Ann Arbor Public Schools; PHOTO: *Stuart Klipper]*

*Intellectual and
emotional, intuitive
and logical elements
all enter into the
learning that may
occur through art
experience.* [PHOTO:
Stephen C. Sumner]

cated development of this idea indicates that a small part of some earlier
original experience may be reactivated by the remnant of memory imprint
that is occurring in the present which could be then developed into a new
whole. The relevancies to art teaching are obvious.

There are two additional learning principles that merit mentioning in
the quasimechanical category: sensory generalization and reinforcement.
The first simply states that many differing objects are treated alike when
there is a generalized response to a stimulus. The learning is undifferentiated, such as when an infant refers to all movement that recedes from
him as "bye-bye" or calls all present males his "da-da." Similarly, there is
sensory generalization when all artists are referred to as "beatniks" or as
when all female teachers used to be regarded as spinsters. This kind of
learning lumps together in broad and crude classifications all phenomena
or things that share some superficial characteristic. For the young child,
many archetypal shapes or large generalized "first forms" serve multiple
purposes in expression and understanding. The example of the box and
table in the four-year-old's drawing, alike in shape, being differentiated only

Art
and
Education
in
Contemporary
Culture

·

236

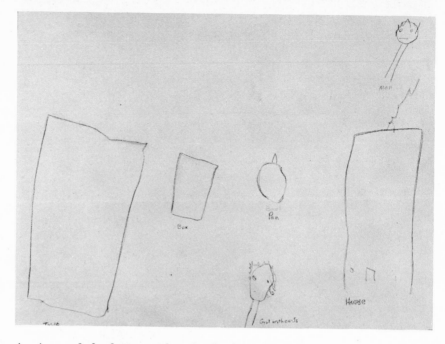

Drawing of a four-year-old reflecting the sensory generalization of form concept and expression. [Courtesy, Margo Flower; PHOTO: Stuart Klipper]

in size, and the house with only the barest addition of a chimney, door and window. The development of visual schemata belongs on this level.

Finally, there is the reinforcement concept. This is a very pertinent factor in education today, because many of the learning ideas supporting the use of teaching machines are based upon it. Briefly, this concept informs us that learning is success and reward oriented. That is, the individual will tend to accept and be impelled by those facts, processes and acts which avoid pain and failure and are "stamped in" with success and pleasure. This is simply provided on the infant level and undergoes modification and change as maturation and different stimuli appear; the learning that occurs is directed to successfully reducing tension: Any learning situation that tends to reinforce this condition should have positive results as a consequence. The attempts, for instance, on the part of middle graders usually to draw in a literal sense has a relationship to this quality of learning reinforcement. For the few successful ones, art continues to be a pleasurable activity; for the mass who experience failure, continued learning and development in art is coming to an end. The shaping of forms limit their possibilities to a reinforcement of only familiar factors of expression. Without a sophisticated understanding the concept of reinforcement may often exert negative influences in art education.

Everyone has experienced all of the preceding learning conditions and can attest to their presence throughout all ages and levels of schooling. They have significant influence in many classroom situations and operate while learning occurs in most of the subject areas, including art. Further illustrations demonstrate that sensory generalization is decidedly present when a child begins to concretely shape his ideas through color, mass and line such as the egg shape referring invariably to a human head, or a cylinder topped by a sphere symbolizing a tree, the familiar lollipop. Similarly, conditioning operates frequently when children will consistently paint with one or two limited colors, the grass always green, the sun always yellow, the sky always blue. Many of the sensory-symbolic meanings that students develop through the arts may be superficially traced to a stimulus-response condition on a simple level.

The learning principles discussed so far appear to be basic; however, they also leave a lot that still has to be answered. Though they may shed some light on learning they do so primarily on those automatic responses in the nervous system that are not too amenable to control. The quasimechanical concepts acquaint us with the nether world of learning, but they do not enlighten the higher faculties of choice, conscious intentional learning, the deliberate risking of novelty, discovery, creative forming, intellectual abstractive structuring, or the uniquely individualized expressive and aesthetic inclinations that parallel them. They neglect the quality of sentience, imagination, and feeling in the human who advances beyond infancy in his thought and behavior, of his compelling self image that can intensify learning sometimes in contradiction of the automatic and reflex responses, symbolically developing learning habits that culminate in the creative arts, sciences and in the area of speculative considerations such as in philosophy and religion. Consequently, the psychological investigations into learning that center about animal behavior and infantile human understanding may be limited, providing insight into how a rat runs a maze or how an infant progresses from sucking to grasping but not giving a clear realization of the higher modes of knowing. They serve only as a prelude to the more developed and complex learning that characterizes human understanding and creative productiveness.

HIGHER LEVELS OF KNOWING

Though learning through art is perhaps the most elusive and most diverse of the learning situations, different in kind as well as in purpose frequently, from that of intellectual development, they both share a common locus. Both are housed within the human organization and are obviously interdependent. This relationship has not been explored in any depth until very recently, though cognitive understanding in its intellectual form has been widely investigated in the twentieth century. Some transference of concepts or parallel understanding in the different areas may be provided if attention is paid to some of the more pertinent findings. It should be noted here that the concept of human meaning as a symbolization process, a very pertinent one for art educators, is fully examined in Chapter 11. As a higher mode of knowing, it synthesizes many theoretical parts.

Jerome Bruner has suggested that knowledge perhaps is best developed through the structural considerations of any particular subject area.[2] That is, teaching can best achieve its ends through transfer of principles and attitudes, the unspecified organization of a discipline to be stressed as a

[2] Jerome Bruner, *The Process of Education* (Cambridge, Mass.: Harvard University Press, 1961), p. 17.

Art
and
Education
in
Contemporary
Culture

•

238

structure rather than unrelated specific topics and skills. It is somewhat easier to propose in the sciences and mathematics than it is in the arts, whatever its merit. The former are by definition intellectual structures while the latter—the arts—frequently defy any imposition or underpinning of logical or standardized structure. Nevertheless, there is a positive method in this attitude that may have a great deal of significance for art education, leading to the presentation of an aesthetic understanding of a general nature, which could then be utilized in personal ways by individual students. We shall return to its consideration at another point.

Bruner indicates that the act of individual discovery is perhaps the most appropriate, successful and rewarding one in cognitive learning.[3] Before structure can be comprehended, the student has to be able to discover for himself its existence, to know that its intrinsic functions in his own personal terms. The cognitive process is different from the earlier quasi-mechanical learning principles in that it is a funded way of knowing that consciously makes choices. It is deliberate in its organization and infused with purpose that goes beyond the mere reduction of tension. In fact, coupled with imagination it seems to do the opposite, to invite tensions so that there may be resolutions that otherwise could not occur. This could be regarded as a basic factor in productive learning and artistic creativity.

Three Levels of Intellectual Development

In his tracing of the what appear to be three levels of intellectual development in the child, Bruner refers to the work of the Geneva school. He singles out the ideas of Jean Piaget,[4] the Swiss psychologist who has done a remarkable amount of germinal study in the area of child development. These may have a generalized pertinence to understanding artistic and creative development as well.

1. The earliest stage of development corresponds to the first five or six years of age. During this period the child engages in a rather unrefined trial and error manipulation of external reality. The manipulation is intuitive in nature and does not really involve any examined comprehension of the outside world, or his internal one for that matter, that may be translated into operational symbolic terms that can be abstracted through the intellect. Understanding is most often directly manifested through action, though the resulting qualities of the unconsciously symbolic production does not make a distinct separation between what is "out there" in the so-called real objective world and the feelings and promptings of internal motivation. Sensory generalization is predominant as is a kind of undifferentiated identification of the self with external phenomena. Ends and means are confused in one wondrous whole that innocently responds with the totality of the self as a subjective world concept.

The kinesthetic scribbles and seemingly random manipulation of color

---

[3] Jerome Bruner *On Knowing* (Cambridge, Mass.: Harvard University Press, 1962), pp. 81–96.

[4] Jerome Bruner, *The Process of Education* (Cambridge, Mass.: Harvard University Press, 1961), pp. 34–40.

and shapes with a brush that are the art evidence of this period are more than chance accidents for the child. They are the direct and sensuous means of identification he makes with his own bodily activities, the end result of kinesthetic elements. His learning as yet does not have the objective "distance" or the recognition of the separateness of concrete qualities from his own all encompassing psyche. The world exists to do him homage and whatever knowledge is available is mostly immediate and direct, immersed in the spirit of myth and the primacy of direct invocation of responses from the outside world that is shared with many primitive peoples. This is a wondrously naive state that adults or civilized individuals often wish for again in the complexity and perversity of their advanced understanding.

However, as can be obviously seen, the intellect, no matter how full of charm it is at that state of development, remains arrested and subject to strict limitations. Once a happening occurs, at this stage, there is no intellectual turning back for the child. There is no "reversibility." As Bruner indicates, it is virtually impossible for the very young child to grasp the idea that once a bar of Plasticine is shaped in a particular way that it may be undone and returned to its original state. Action and consequently, at this point, intellectual understanding and mature aesthetic insight are constrained with the security of the obvious consequences of a motor response. This is a severely limiting factor and one that permits little intellectual or truly symbolic teaching to be done that will progress into immediate enriched and elaborated expression. Reason, analysis, comparison, a range of awareness and sensitivity must wait for the processes of maturation which lead to sophisticated development and deeper experiences.

2. The next step is called the stage of concrete operations. This lasts for most of the elementary school years and is largely involved with intellectually operational factors. Though these are related to the earlier response, they not only can be directly involved with the objects and conditions of the environment but they can be internally constituted by relating to symbols. Actually, at this stage, we find the basic mental factor of transfer motion, wherein the individual can order the information received, sense it as a symbolic construction if need be and choose those aspects which will solve the problem at hand. Learning is occurring, wherein the phenomena that is at hand may be examined and to some extent analyzed. The individual child is capable of going progressively forward in his thought and in returning to earlier states of recognition and understanding if the need arises. This obviously occurs in the academic areas in its purest sense. But its sometimes halting and frequently constrained development is also demonstrated in the visual arts.

The state of transitional development focuses on the internalized learning that a child is undergoing. The mental and symbolic structures that the child is developing permits him to handle and understand his environment in a much more sophisticated manner than that available to him during his preschool days. However, the individual is inherently limited in his intellect at this stage by not being able to easily abstract ideas or create hypothetical propositions. Though the six- to twelve-year-old (which very

Art
and
Education
in
Contemporary
Culture

.

240

roughly corresponds in age to the intellectual capacities of this stage) can anticipate different possibilities from those that are concretely present or otherwise directly available as information, he is largely limited in his systematic ordering to that which is in his immediate environment. He responds to that which is given to him. The mental jump to different potentials and variables appears too difficult at this point. Yet the transforming possibilities that have enriched his mind and his sensual development provide the creative base of artistic endeavor. The immediate and almost one to one relationship of the child to his experience activates a natural generation of symbolic understanding, permitting the environment to become a rich store of experience and the individual personality a vehicle for unique expressive qualities that enhance creative learning. The possibilities for art education are broadly based and full of potential. Though the range of experiences that may be provided the youngster during this period of development are extremely diverse, creative and challenging, they are incomplete in reasoning power.

3. It is not until the third stage that it may be said that an individual truly brings to fruition his mental inheritance and activates a mature intellectual operation. In arriving at the point where he can logically and with fertile association conceptualize necessary methods of understanding, of abstract and freely probing thought, the individual stands on the brink of maturity ready to engage in developed and reasoned thinking and behavior. Previous experience and present data can be formalized. The formal considerations could then act as the intellectual and organizational scaffolding upon which may be erected the necessary structures of a discipline. It is this ability to recognize and utilize the formal structure of a discipline that marks the mature intellect. Combined with the earlier development of transformation of experience. the total potential of a student is ready for a wide range of problem solving and consciously controlled expression in as much as that is personally possible.

The large distinction between the second and third stages of development is the ability of the older child to sense the abstract structure of a discipline and to verbalize or otherwise express its qualities, utilizing the abstracted understanding to resolve intellectual issues and creative problems that occur. The elementary child is generally incapable of this activity and the presentation of learning material has to take this factor into consideration. For instance, in social studies a teacher may present to middle elementary school children the idea of political and social freedom—that civil liberties is not only a means toward freedom, but a desirable end in itself. If the concept is couched in the mature language of the Bill of Rights or other governmental formalizations, there is likely to be a lack of understanding and meaningful response on the part of the children, just as a third or fourth grader could not begin to comprehend the formal language of a geometrical theorem though he would be able to solve practical problems in geometry. However, if presented in terms of concrete situations or in a way through which the child himself could personally handle the materials through individual episodes, audiovisual aids, local functioning examples, or other such concrete manifestations, then some valid learning may occur. Similarly, in art, if elementary children are insensitively exposed to the great ages of art through abstracted and highly verbalized means, no matter how engagingly related, there will be a lack of acceptance and comprehension of the material. A parallel of this abstracted approach in the actual doing of art would be the formalized demonstration of a technique such as water color painting or providing the so-called elements of the color wheel or "laws" of proportion or spatial perspective without relating to the specifics that an individual student may be concerned with at the time of his creative attempts. The young child will ignore or forget, for the most part, the formalized knowledge, concentrating on the direct need to solve the very concrete artistic problem that his need for expression may develop at any one point.

If the three stages of development actually do reflect the various levels of learning readiness, then the high school years may see a change in teaching method as is actually the case in practice. However, Bruner's point is that provided the proper understanding and judgment on the part of the teacher any part of any subject may be taught at any level in various degrees of depth as long as the structure is honestly and adequately presented to children in terms of their capacities to comprehend.

Discrepancies Between Artistic and Intellectual Development

The foregoing simplified structure of intellectual development has many potentialities to offer teachers. However, there appear to be some discrepancies when the concept is applied to progress in art. Actually at about the time that abstract reasoning appears as a mode of thought for the typical American student there is a parallel decline in his active artistic sensitivity, in creative aesthetic production. Intellectual capabilities grow, while artistic concerns become self conscious, and eventually atrophy for the majority of students. On the surface it appears that it is during the second stage of intellectual development that art is experienced as a "golden" or naturally proper time for individual artistic expression. The eager, enthusiastic, intuitive and expressively adequate art work of the six- to ten-year-old corresponds to that time when intellectual development is centered around relating to concrete, immediate situations that require symbolizing. Artistic expression certainly deals with the immediate and the individually felt. In that sense it becomes a positive ally in the child's development during the second stage.

Is it that intellectual progress subsequently supersedes the need to express oneself in concrete and artistic symbols? There are too many educators who hold this concept, if only latently, not recognizing an obvious fallacy. The fallacy concerns the tying of the I.Q. kind of intellectualism to a general concept of intelligence. There is a rather arbitrary limitation placed upon the development of the intellect, confining the properties of its structure to logical, discursive, and abstractly reasoning ones.

Piaget, however, recognizes the distinctions that exist between artistic and other mental functions. He suggests that it is more difficult to structure

Art
and
Education
in
Contemporary
Culture

•

242

any regular stages of artistic development than it is to establish the levels of intellectual progression. Consequently, the seeming retrogression of aesthetic qualities that appears in the early adolescent in contrast to the steady growth of intellectual and social attributes,

lead to one obvious conclusion, that the young child spontaneously externalizes his personality and his interindividual experiences thanks to the various means of expression at his command, such as drawing, modelling, symbolic games, singing, theatrical representation (which develops imperceptibly out of collective symbolic play), but that without an appropriate art education which will succeed in cultivating these means of expression and in encouraging these first manifestations of aesthetic creation, the actions of adults and the restraints of school and family life have the effect in most cases of checking or thwarting such tendencies instead of enriching them. On the one hand, there is the material or social reality to which the child must adapt himself and which imposes upon him its laws, its rules and its means of expression; that reality determines the child's social and moral sentiments, his conceptual or socialized thought, with the collective means of expression constituted by language and so on. On the other hand, there is the life lived by the ego with its conflicts, its conscious or unconscious desires, its interests, joys and anxieties; these form individual realities, often unadapted and always incapable of being expressed solely by the collective instruments of communication, for they require a particular means of expression.[5]

Implicit in this comment is the understanding that learning is involved with more than the rational acquisition of facts and possesses dimensions beyond the recognition of logical relationships. Piaget indicates that the early art creations of children are the attempts to reconcile the pressure from society, the collective, adaptive understanding, the "submission to reality" with the characteristically symbolic and uniquely individual wishful considerations, the pressures from the subjective self. However, the obstacle to growth occurs, to reiterate Piaget's ideas, when we fail, "to reintroduce into the framework of teaching that aesthetic life which the very logic of an education based upon intellectual authority tends to eliminate or, at least, to weaken." [6]

ADDITIONAL ELEMENTS OF LEARNING

Learning theory is still at the brink of fundamental discovery, for its findings up to this point have tended to stem from restricted or parochial interests. There appears to be more than one kind of learning that constitutes the development of man's intelligence, just as even the structure and systematic development of the intellect has many variables and impinging factors that intrude upon its functioning.

Psychologists as well as lay people in the area often refer to intuitive thought, hunches, insights, learnings, sets and other considerations that deviate in one way or another from classic logical thought and intellectual

---

[5] Edwin Ziegfeld, (ed.) *Education and Art*, Jean Piaget, "Art Education and Child Psychology" (Paris: UNESCO, 1953), p. 22.
[6] *Ibid.*, p. 23.

analysis. If we are to accept man's intelligence as possessing more than an ordered system based on reasoned postulates, then these diverse factors assume a good deal of importance. The arts are obviously dependent upon sensory, nonrational modes of knowing, their inherent character appears to stress intuition, and natural or subjective insights frequently unconscious in process. However, cognitive learning itself is not beyond certain determining qualities that are not logically explainable as yet, or objectively understood.

There are, in all likelihood, a variety of considerations which may influence the development of the intellect, yet have no logical or objective control factor. Though they are within the understanding of an organization of relevant elements for the individual in his intellectual growth, in terms of his general intelligence they are so individually variable and different in genesis and effect that it would be virtually impossible to systematize them. These factors include insight and intuition, learning sets and

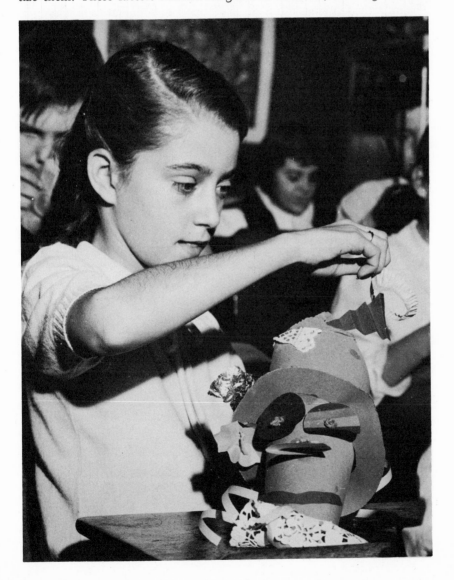

The individual student, in order to develop aesthetically, has to blend feelings and thoughts into a unified artistic insight. [New York Public Schools]

Art
and
Education
in
Contemporary
Culture

•

244

emotional identification. These elements, among others, seem to affect intellectual development as well as determining the cast of a person's total intelligence. They are the elements that also characterize the artistic mode of thinking.

Insight and Intuition

Obviously not all learning progresses as the result of definitive models or principles that possess logical and numbered steps at the end of which may be expected the solution to a problem. This is not the case in art, nor is it in many intellectual areas. Very often the individual shapes a mental structure that penetrates to the core of a problem without necessarily relying upon objectively formulated systems or organized notations that have accrued in a sequential and logical manner. This is generally referred to as an insight. Even in the most logical systems such as mathematics, the student and later the adult practitioner utilizes this method of thinking. The individual instance of insight may appear to be imitative in nature, its images and concepts corresponding in its essentials to external structures that have relevant and similar features to the problem at hand, yet may be outside of accepted or predetermined procedures and models of logic. The imitation may be more a quality of fertile association and realization of congruent elements than an act of simple copying. In any instance, insights are quite prevalent during problem solving of any kind, intellectual, social or aesthetic, frequently being more rapid in arriving at solutions and more alertly penetrating in the realization of an explication than objectified approaches. There is a striking and immediate recognition and organization of pertinent elements which may then be acted upon, rejecting the peripheral factors and totally discarding the irrelevant—a natural artistic mode.

Bruner refers to intuitive thinking as implying "the act of grasping the meaning, significance or structure of a problem or a situation without explicit reliance on the analytic apparatus of one's craft." [7] It may be synonymous with insight for all practical purposes, though intuition appears to suggest a leap into knowledge that not only involved cognitive understanding but an inborn proclivity and "sixth sense." Its processes often lie outside of the rational progression or relationships of strict intellectual considerations. Though, as yet, no really fundamental explanations of intuitive phenomenon have been listed or confidently offered in any other way. The intuitive method of achieving understanding is one among the other learning considerations of inductive and deductive reasoning, of imitation and of reflex response. It probably cuts across any strict or isolating definitions of the other modes, but has to be recognized and encouraged as a legitimate thinking process as much as the others are. This does not claim that intuition is always of a positive nature, there are "bad" hunches and unsuccessful guesses as well as productive ones. However, what is important for education and should be reflected in the attitude of the teacher is that intuitive stabs or thrusts toward comprehension may be productive; teachers

[7] Jerome Bruner, *The Process of Education* (Cambridge: Harvard University Press, 1961), p. 60.

themselves should serve as exemplars of all the modes of thinking, insisting not upon one method unless it is indigenous to the problem at hand, and creatively guiding whatever mode is employed to productive ends.

The arts are more obviously bound up with insightful and intuitive schemes and means than most of the other subject areas. The learning or internal growth that is desirable and encouraged in the individual is less based on objective and verifiable conditions than on unique, subjective considerations, on felt interpretations of experience.

Learning Sets and Emotional Identification

This leads us to another notion that may have bearing upon the emergence and direction of cognitive behavior or a ripe, elaborated aesthetic expression. It stems from the internalized values that individuals have built into their personalities, probably referring back to infancy and early childhood experiences, as well as to the current willingness and desirability to learn particular things.

Frequently, the general tenor of early life experiences that revolve about security, satisfaction, love and other emotional considerations or in the lack of them sets up orientations in the individual which make him an apt pupil in specific subjects or an unsuccessful one, outside of inherent attributes. Some children simply find it difficult to learn to read, despite a normal or higher indication of intelligence as demonstrated empirically or through test scores. Others regard the workings of mathematics as an occult discipline that they cannot fathom. Still others are closed to the

A deliberate distortion of "correct" proportions may be utilized by an artist for expressive purposes. "The Reluctant Ploughshare," Jack Levine. [Collection, IBM]

Art
and
Education
in
Contemporary
Culture

·

246

Learning in art lies within the individual child rather than in any fixed surroundings, despite environmental influence. Kindergarten Class, Central African Republic. [UNESCO/ Louis Duré]

ideas and propositions of social studies while some few in their early school days reject the whole idea of art. This continues throughout the school career, the learning set operating in a positive or a negative way. These inclinations frequently assume long range activations, though they are prone to alteration and opposing influences. Again the example of the early enthusiasm for art that declines after adolescence may be presented. Its reversal but lost opportunity for many in later high school days and the wistful yearning for aesthetic experience among college students is yet another indication of the variability of learning sets. However, when the sets are deep seated and unconsciously operating they tend to remain influential throughout the life of the individual. Short range sets, though, may be manipulated in easier fashion, given strong enough motivation, and they are evident in student attitudes toward their art experiences.

These sets are operationally effective because the individual makes strong emotional identification with the conditions that have brought about the set in the first place. The ability to engage effectively in cognitive behavior and mature aesthetic understanding is, at least in this supposition, tied to the emotional characteristics that fulfill and impel an individual, either because of past associations related to childhood situations or more currently because of immediate identifications with particular heroes or social conditions. A young boy will reel off the batting averages of major league baseball players or a long list of important game scores because of an adulation of a particular player or team at the same time that his arithmetic or social studies is suffering from neglect and indifference. Concurrently, a junior high girl will reject an opportunity to engage in painting or ceramics, yet she will spend endless hours on clothing arrangement because of the admiration of an older girl or a movie star. These instances are too ordinary and trite though they do serve to point up the effects of emotional identification on cognitive behavior and the development of learning sets. The larger network of contemporary values as they orient thinking and develop "sets" has been explored in a previous chapter.

OPPOSING MODELS OF COGNITION

We can distinguish only in a crude way many variables and often indeterminate influences that seem to exist in learning theory and blur the precise understanding of cognition and artistic learning. Despite this, there are two broad schools of thought that Martin Mayer presents for our edification that oppose one another in setting up models of how students are to be taught.[8] On one end are those thinkers and educators who have been strongly influenced by contemporary science and its positivism while at the other pole are the provocative or cautious skeptics of codified scientific method who insist that there is a relative quality operating, not only in what constitutes knowledge, but in how it is understood and made to operate in individual and productive instances. Both extremes are literally fictions for the most part, the divergence in attitude resolved very frequently as a clustering of common ideas or a compromise locus somewhere in a large middle ground. Yet each extreme attitude does reflect valid beliefs that are based upon accepted assumptions.

Teaching Through Objective Models

The first group is somewhat a fusing of many of the basic ideas of experimental research's original concepts concerning education and the findings of science over the last half century. The advocates of this position develop the premise that a concrete, objective work is the indivisible referential of knowledge. That is, despite the many differences found among people, the individual variations must respond to the verifiable, physically existing, and objectively conglomerate world. The outlook is positivistic, and though it concedes there are large holes in scientific knowledge, it is only a matter of time before these will be filled in. Those that support this rigorous, precise, and meticulously objective outlook also assume that there is a regularity and a similarity of structure to all learning. They hold that the theoretical base of cognitive behavior has a definable core that all learning is subject to. This may be the principle that all learning seeks an intellectually tranquil equilibrium, a rounded out quality of meaning or the Gestalt factor of configuration, which sees knowledge as a process of closure based upon pattern.

The Woods Hole Conference that Bruner reported on,[9] identifies the act of learning as composed of three elements that are simultaneous and

[8] Martin Mayer, "Scientists in the Classroom," *Commentary*, April, 1963, Vol. 4, p. 35.
[9] Jerome Bruner, *The Process of Education* (Cambridge: Harvard University Press, 1961), p. 48.

Art
and
Education
in
Contemporary
Culture

.

248

episodic in nature: (1) *acquisition* of new information, which in the best sense is a gathering in of all the prior and present pertinent information bearing upon a problem, contradictory or otherwise, (2) *transformation*, the manipulation of the gathered data to fit the different or new endeavors so that the old knowledge is transcended, (3) and *evaluation*, the examination and testing of the new results to determine if it is adequate, fitting or operational in differing circumstances. Whatever the basic determining factor, the important consideration is that the person who is learning does so by a process of organization. The new and fresh material that an individual student experiences is structured in one or more of the above mentioned ways. This is accomplished in a regular manner, all students undergoing equivalent if not exactly similar procedures of organization.

Consequently, all the many and varied disciplines that reflect the human involvement with environment may be structured into important and fundamental components. Though not much has been said about the arts the assumption is that they too may be amenable to analysis for learning purposes, just as are the science, math and social studies. What follows is the necessity for pedagogical paradigms or teaching models. If the important structural elements of any given discipline can be analyzed and pertinent prototypes created that would embody these structural elements, then a regularized teaching method can result. This would merge with the basically similar learning processes that all students undergo in their confrontation with new, difficult or otherwise challenging material.

No doubt a teacher who utilized this approach including the models which, supposedly, the actual practitioners and theoreticians in a particular field would devise and then give over to the classroom would require a thorough understanding of the subject area to be taught. Though both the deductive (going from the general to the particular) and the inductive (going from the particular to the general) would be involved, the stress would be more with the probability and characteristically searching quality of the latter mode rather than with the anticipated and relatively "certain" conclusions of the deductive approach.

This structured approach to learning need not necessarily be a doctrinaire one for it would recognize the existence of intuition and the fact of individual differences. The less precise aspects of learning, however, would have to eventually return to the structured pattern to achieve validation and permanency. The individual differences would be considered merely surface idiosyncrasies that do not destroy the basic pattern but simply requires a psychological understanding so as to permit the teaching models to work properly. To this extent, Dewey is accepted as a guide. Thus both the child oriented and the subject oriented concepts would be carried through. There is no doubt though, that the stress falls upon the discipline itself, that whatever difficulty there is in learning is inherent in the material to be learned. Consequently, teaching is regarded as a means of structuring the raw experience that individuals have in such a way that the patterns of organization that are intrinsic in any discipline are then comprehended and made available for further use.

*Works of children's
art exist as concrete
products as well as
providing the process
for interpretive ex-
pression and response
to experience. [New
York Public Schools]*

Relevancies to Art Education

There is much to commend this approach, particularly in its emphasis on the material to be learned. If the assumptions are correct (and this has not been proven one way or another) then an effective and relatively standardized bridge between pupil and subject has been erected, requiring only an efficacy on the part of the teacher in empirically setting forth the working models. This has an obvious relationship to the hard core of the physical and natural sciences as well as mathematics. Its classification in reference to much of the remainder of the curriculum is still debatable, particularly in art, though the broad concept of structure remains valid.

There are certain relevancies to art education. Those art educators who insist that the teaching of art has a primary obligation in making a funded knowledge about art available would certainly tend to support the above thesis. They would insist that if education is to meet its responsibility to the student it would aim to develop an artistically literate student. This would require the acquisition of skills and broadly supported artistic concepts that may have already found their way into an academic outlook. There also would be the cataloguing aspect of art history, its archival characteristics as well as the appreciative ones that have deposited a particu-

Art
and
Education
in
Contemporary
Culture

·

250

lar philosophy of aesthetics. In short, the entire heritage of art, its many tried and respected attitudes, its history, its craft and sundry techniques and its relationship to the society that gave it birth would be taught. Out of the enormous wealth of material a structural base would be determined, organically growing from the accepted multiplicity of past theories, ideas and techniques of art and of current understanding.

This would certainly provide art education with a contained and disciplined body of knowledge that may gain for it the respect it so often does not command in the public school. More important, a stress could be put upon the "definable" values of art, the learning that stems from a structured version at least having the virtue of being intimately and organically identified with art, sensed within the confines of a characteristic structure rather than with some bastardized or otherwise spurious edition of the subject.

Subjective Approach

However, this approach may be anathema to some thinkers at the other end of the pedagogical spectrum. They, in their opposing concepts, can not accept the doctrine of an almost absolute criterion of reality being the concrete evidence of the external world. For them, like the poet who speaks of beauty as existing in the eyes of the beholder, reality is a shifting changing quality, determined subjectively. Some would say that it is culturally determined from within a group and differing from one group to another as do the anthropologists, sociologists, and other social scientists, or individually determined as do many philosophers and most artists. As for the need of similarity in learning procedures—the development of models so that the substance of a subject is grasped—the more loosely oriented group would question the effectiveness or importance of this condition. If the many variables that do enter into individual understanding and the wide diversity of prior learning persist in coloring learning as it is believed they do, then procedures have to vary. The immense reservoir of unconscious determinants or "learning sets" that may be traced back to the almost infinite number of individual living patterns are only exceeded by the unknown possibilities that could conceivably impinge upon a learning situation. As a result, there can be no logical or clearly analyzable structure inherent in any subject matter which would suffice for even a small majority of the students under the range of teaching conditions that may be practiced in a school despite the organized nature of a subject area. Therefore, the teacher is faced with the difficulty inherent in the individual student rather than the material to be learned. The only appropriate guide can be a knowledgeable aptitude and an intuitive awareness of the elements in play.

An Existentialist Position

We must briefly make note here of the existentialist position which denies the possibility that abstractly structured knowledge may be correct or even socially determined. They insist upon the individual as the sole arbiter of reality, and his subjective state as the real authority through which learning may take place. This learning is meaningful, never in the removed theoretical premises of an abstract structure but in the concrete manifestations of intuition and comprehension as they exist in the choices of action than an individual makes. For instance, John Paul Sartre comments about the image that enters consciousness, which may be construed to mean learning, in the following manner. "An image can only enter into consciousness if it is itself a synthesis, not an element. There are not, and never could be, images in consciousness. Rather an image is a *certain type of consciousness*. An image is an act, not something. An image is consciousness of something." [10] The existentialist position in education would then not see learning as divorced from the uniqueness and responsibility of individual consciousness, structured as an abstract series of conditions and attributes which can be manipulated as an external thing. Learning for them is actually the individual subjectively developing an awareness that corresponds to a condition of becoming, the immediate consciousness an act of choice, an affirmation that corresponds to being. This is intimately related to the expressive symbol making in art and to the intentional nature of an act of thought. Though these may appear to be esoteric considerations for the average teacher, they do have a very pertinent bearing on the current philosophical context in which learning occurs, the realization of its intrinsic values for the individual as well as the ends it will serve. At the very least, the creative areas such as art education may find some invaluable insights in the existentialist concepts since they consider the aesthetic processes central to the awareness of the individual and its stress fundamental in education.

EMPIRICAL JOINING OF OPPOSING CONCEPTS

In the more widely accepted attitudes that are prevalent in educational circles and those of the social sciences that deal with learning and its theoretical and practical implementation in the schools, neither one of the extremes of either position would be defended unequivocally. The positions would be regarded as oversimplified as they probably are in empirical terms. Yet the strong contentions and resulting pressures from the partisan viewpoints tend to enforce a more searching and profound examination of the middle ground. It may also be felt that both groups have grasped essential truths that refer not to one absolute act of learning that underlies all education, but to different aspects of its condition. Certain disciplines such as the sciences and mathematics lend themselves effortlessly to structured learning and the development of helpful pedagogic models with which to carry out that learning. Even subject areas such as typing and industrial arts can be systematized without too much violence being done to the intrinsic quality of the material. However, social studies, the humanities, and most particularly the arts, do not easily fit into a

[10] Jean Paul Sartre, *Imagination* (Ann Arbor: University of Michigan Press, 1962), p. 146.

Art
and
Education
in
Contemporary
Culture

.

252

highly abstracted series of analytical models that reflect a fairly stable organization. The pressures and variations from the culture outside, the vagaries, and the compulsions from the subjective nature of the human involvement, the imaginative expression itself, reject an easy or even careful analysis that can be relied upon to stand up in objectified versions. Both of the divergent theories have worth and are comprised of many basic elements, the most important of which is getting students to comprehend their nature and utilize this insight in positive and new ways leading to knowledge, productive thinking, aesthetic and creative understanding. The structured versus more intuitive approaches are not in a predetermined state of antagonism either, for each penetrates the other, neither one being the pure and precise condition it very often purports to be.

It may be that education requires the recognition and acceptance of either of the divergent modes, the structured model or the intuitive insights when each is a necessity and a blending of both whenever the context is feasible and natural to the learning situation. This, of course, essentially rejects the idea that structured learning is basically the only effective method, but it does not at all discard its very valuable possibilities in even such areas as art education where the emphasis is upon singular and specifically nonrepeatable learning experience.

For instance, in art education, Professor Hoyt Sherman of Ohio State University has developed a series of teaching models in drawing that have as their purpose the clarification of form concepts during the act of visual perception. He has devised a variety of instruments such as the one based upon the tachistoscope. This permits visual patterns to be flashed upon screens at very fast speeds. The assumption is that students repeatedly exposed to this process of having to fully perceive visual forms at very rapid rates develop an awareness of visual properties much sharper and more inclusive than those who are not exposed to the process.

The army successfully used this method in aircraft identification courses during the Second World War and a similar instrument is widely used in attempting to remedy reading difficulties in schools. The popular elementary flash cards are a manual form of the tachistoscope principle. The effectiveness of the instrument is not being considered here, simply its existence as an aid in teaching in the visual arts. Color wheels and framing devices for compositional understanding are additional simple examples of teaching models in art education though there are other rather complex examples of paraphernalia designed to assist the fledgling artist. There are, as well, numerous structural considerations of an intellectual nature concerning art that are also employed in art teaching. The various headings of art principles such as balance, dominance-subordination, rhythm and proportion are utilized in explanations of the artistically creative process in an appeal to structure. The teacher hopes this will assist in developing sensitivity to, and individual generation of, good artistic values and creative production. Similarly in the history of art, various styles or schools of painting or sculpture are grouped together as structural units based upon technique, subject matter or formal aesthetic

philosophy. Most of these devices and what may be thought of as structured attitudes have been neglected or viewed with suspicion for several decades, the emphasis being on individual expressive behavior that valued process well above product. Though this approach is genuine and in harmony with many of the needs of contemporary man, it frequently defeats its own purpose or only answers it in very partial ways. Even loosely structured learning would necessarily underscore the worth of the product of an artistic experience. As a philosophical gambit in the "game" of developing educated, mature, and sensitive individuals who are also creative, it may be disastrous to ignore the importance of product as a necessary move in the "game." The realization of the significance of a concrete art object and its evaluation in terms of good and bad may be an integral aspect of the creative process itself. This would lead to a more tolerant view of organized and sequential teaching in art, based upon a structured understanding. Even if this is a paradox on certain levels it deserves the attention and appraisal of all teachers who would be involved with teaching art, either as specialists or in the elementary schools, as classroom teachers.

It is vital, though, to the full artistic development of individuals, to have method in art education sufficiently supple in its implementation and freely pliable in its sources of understanding. The subject is much too intangible, the workings of its various parts not yet really ascertained. The firm core of individual and unique expressive procedures is a central consideration in art education that periodically shakes off the accumulated

Art education has to provide a range of sensory experiences, as in this sixth-grade art lesson, so that the art experience for the individual student is based upon a familiarity with the qualities of materials. [Detroit Public Schools]

Art
and
Education
in
Contemporary
Culture

·

254

theoretical structure surrounding it. Learning in art pursues its own ways and is not, except in the most generalized aesthetic sense beholden to any idea of a deliberately prescriptive or rigidly structured nature. The understanding and the making of art is basically resident in the thinking and feeling of the individual student as he or she becomes genuinely involved with the imagery and forms of art. The teacher's responsibility is to stimulate, enrich and guide the student toward an intensified encounter with aesthetic and expressive qualities of a high order, both as a process and a product.

The Creative Process

A sort of liberation . . . the mysterious becoming
external. Everything falls into place . . . I see.
PAUL CÉZANNE

THE creative process has been given rather broad, fresh and intense attention since the early nineteen fifties. Creativity has established a relationship to education that makes it a purpose of learning and a desirable quality for all to have. Numerous broadsides have been issued examining its qualities and attempting to define its characteristics. Psychologists have instituted serious and systematic studies and have developed concepts that, though enlightening in some respects, also frequently tend to be rather oversimplified, partially revealing, or limited to highly technical and complex abstractions. Creativity has almost been verbalized lately into meaninglessness while its vacillating image has been made to perform a variety of didactic services and others more suspect in nature. Though one can appreciate, for instance, the need of military establishments to produce creative solutions to problems that have a profound interest to everyone either directly concerned or the large mass indirectly involved, there is something almost ludicrous if not morally inexpedient in the picture of admirals and generals engaged in "brain storming" sessions or creativity seminars.

Though logically, creativity may have no moral imperatives, it is difficult to divorce its processes and symbols from the humanistic values they serve and the intimate personal purposes they are achieving. Consequently, there is a great deal of truth in John Dewey's thought in *Human Nature and Conduct*, that "The separation of warm emotion and cool intelligence is the great moral tragedy." Creativity sensed as a utilitarian value alone may produce results, but its greater consideration is in the synthesis of human values it is either furthering or rejecting.

THE BROAD SCOPE OF CREATIVITY

Creativity could, perhaps, also be sensed in a comparative relationship to its opposite condition, the lack of creativity. For education, it may be phrased in the following manner: how can creative behavior (or

Art
and
Education
in
Contemporary
Culture

.

256

independent thinking and acting) be developed in an individual and increasingly realized in a society where the stress is upon conforming modes of reaction and thought? The answer for the educator lies in examining the nature of the creative process, not only in terms of itself, but how it differs from the more orthodox and constrained manner of thought and action. Independent versus regularized, active versus passive, self-generated and self-evaluated versus the consensus of the group, outer directed versus inner directed, divergent versus convergent: there are many ways of naming the forces that have to be resolved through education or somehow brought into productive balance, hopefully achieving imaginative yet reasonable understanding and behavior. These broad concepts have a way of influentially filtering down to art education. Certainly, their resolution is fundamental to achieving a good art program.

Creativity is obviously to be recognized as something beyond proper thinking habits, beyond regularized, accepted and predictable processes and their products. Adjustment, maturity, normality, adequacy, soundness, intellectual, social, and emotional well roundedness, and any number of other accepted goals in education as in life cannot be the sole determining considerations in honestly examining creativity, for it has occurred outside of these conditions and often in spite of them. For some, creativity is involved with discovering or inventing novelty in the sciences or in the arts; for others, it is much more broadly based, like Erich Fromm's ability to see or be aware and to respond to the world, "the willingness to be born every day." [1]

This rather intense consciousness of the individual as he is confronted with the world and the symbolic transactions he conducts with it could become the slightly more elaborated creativity that Carl Rogers sees as, "the emergence of a novel relational product, growing out of the uniqueness of the individual on one hand, and the materials, events, people or circumstances of his life on the other." [2] Harold Anderson in his book [3] further elaborates on the perspectives of creativity listing such traits as "affection for an idea, absorption, concentration, intensity of encounter, peak experience, delight ecstasy . . . the totality of problem-solving and such elements as open versus closed, cognitive abilities, positive emotional involvement," and others. The list is continued in an array of "applicable" generalities: "desire to grow, capacity to be puzzled, awareness, spontaneity, spontaneous flexibility, adaptive flexibility, originality, divergent thinking, learning, openness to new, experience, no boundaries, permeability, yielding, readiness to yield, abandoning, letting go, . . . discarding the irrelevant, ability to toy with elements, change of activity, persistence, hard work, composition, decomposition, recomposition, differentiation, integration, being at peace with the world, harmony, honesty, humility, enthusiasm, integrity, inner maturity, self-actualizing, skepticism, boldness,

---

[1] Harold H. Anderson, *Creativity and its Cultivation* (New York: Harper and Brothers, 1959), p. 53.
[2] *Ibid.*, p. 41.
[3] *Ibid.*, p. 238.

The creative art process is a highly complex and an individually developed one. [PHOTO: © *Roy Stevens*]

faith, courage, willingness to be alone, *I see, I feel, I think,* just for temporary chaos, security in uncertainty and tolerance of ambiguity." This is an imposing list, somewhat disconcerting in its breadth and leading to a feeling of discouragement of ever recognizing, controlling and manipulating the variables through educational methods. Yet many of these qualities are actively operating during the creative experiences in an art class. Teachers are compelled to devote some attention to them in their philosophical development.

Art
and
Education
in
Contemporary
Culture

.

258

Creativity Possesses Differing Values

Perhaps the very concept that creativity can be cultivated is open to question. However, if teachers are to seek out those conditions, concepts and methods which hold out the greatest promise of potential development for students, they have a responsibility to continue a search for whatever possibilities of guidance that avail themselves. For many, the very word creative is synonymous in a mysteriously intrinsic manner with art, so that if art is to be taught or somehow presented there has to be an understanding of what creativity, at the very least, refers to.

Even this is open to a difference of opinion in its primary definition. Some observers insist that it is only possible to talk about the individual creative act, while others continue to list the traits of the individual creative person. The former concept suggests that creativity is an inherent condition and an actual or potential condition in all people; while the latter, though it does not discount the potential that may be latent in most people, stresses the greater amount of creativity that some people possess when compared to others particularly as it is demonstrated in a concrete form. It has been the responsibility of researchers to identify and isolate the characteristics of the varying groups and kinds of creativity. This may lead, after the findings are validated, not only to simple measurement but theoretically to a means of control and a guide to method. Though there is an element of unwarranted hubris in this approach, the behavioral sciences have engaged the problem.

Special Talent vs. Self-Actualization

Another approach to the idea of the dichotomy in the nature of creativity is expanded by Abraham Maslow [4] who distinguishes between "special talent" creativity and "self-actualizing" creativity. The "special talent" kind defines itself; it presents a complex of abilities and resolutions of problems in particular areas, recombining old elements or forming new ones in art, music, literature, philosophy or in the sciences. The painter or the physicist would be classic examples of "special talent" creators. The "self-actualizing" individual, on the other hand, may not give evidence of any singularly significant achievements in particular areas of endeavor, yet brings his own personality in his interactions or transactions with other people and the general environment to creative fruition. These people may not write a symphony or discover some new heavenly constellation, but theirs is usually a wholesome and rewarding mode of living, providing spontaneous opportunities for expression, as the result of a refreshingly candid and generally positive involvement with life's experience. There is a salutary measure of personal fulfillment in a variety of actions, an almost intuitive propriety of taste and elegance in a functioning self-actualizating personality.

[4] Abraham Maslow, "Self-Actualizing People: A Study of Psychological Health," in *The Self, Explorations in Personality Growth*, C. Moustakas, ed. (New York: Harper, 1956).

Children often dem-
onstrate creative
solutions to artistic
problems. "The
Ride," Third Grade
Drawing. [Ann Arbor
Public Schools;
PHOTO: Stuart
Klipper]

It is this personality pattern that many art educators adopted over the past three decades as an ideal one, as a developmental goal that the teaching of art could strive for. The teacher in this regard becomes a creative "companion," fostering a blend of process and personality. Creativity, in this viewpoint, is not necessarily manifest in any important way in the special products that an art lesson may elicit, but rather in the sincere and empathetic absorption with the problem solving and forming process. Art education, while it utilizes the forms of art, is not, in educational terms, the teaching of special skills primarily, or a development of artistic literacy with the particular purpose of aesthetic expression, though it is agreed these are important. Rather, the teaching of art is regarded as a practical educational instrument leading to a generalized quality of creativity. "Creativity" is thus a way of life with affirmative and rewarding connotations for all experience, not just the aesthetic. Correspondingly, personality development becomes a focal point for art education. Jerome Bruner states this in a more sophisticated way,

An act that produces *effective surprise*—this I shall take as the hallmark of a creative enterprise. The content of the surprise can be as various as the enterprises in which men are engaged. It may express itself in one's dealing with childen, in making love, in carrying on a business, in formulating a physical theory, in painting a picture. I could not care less about the person's intention, whether or not he intended to create. The road to banality is paved with creative intentions. Surprise is not easily defined. It is the unexpected that strikes one with wonder or astonishment. What is curious about effective surprise is that it need not be rare or infrequent or bizarre and is often none of these things. Effective surprises . . . seem rather to have the quality of obviousness about them when they occur producing a shock of recognition following which there is no astonishment.[5]

[5] Jerome Bruner, *On Knowing* (Cambridge: Harvard University Press, 1962), p. 18.

Art
and
Education
in
Contemporary
Culture

·

260

This condition succinctly communicates what many well intentioned art educators hope to infuse as a rewarding quality into their methods of teaching art. Though the quote begs the question of determining the distinctions between art and life, between natural occurrences and symbolized forms, the child in school is to be led to a vital appraisal of his experiences through his involvement with the conditions and problems in making art. It is hoped these would then be utilized as a means of continuously fresh or qualitative (and for the individual) original and productive encounters with the problems and tensions of existence. It is implied that the activities and insights of art have a transfer value that may be utilized in other areas of human experience, that the artistically creative process is a useful fundamental attribute of human behavior. Correspondingly, this behavior will help provide the effective surprises that are an accompanying and productive element in a creative interaction with any kind of experience. The student who has absorbed the lessons of art may then sally forth and favorably take on what life has to offer, finding a gratifying recognition of worth in the experiences encountered.

This attitude may possess a great deal of merit. It also does tend to downgrade the intrinsic values of art somewhat, making of them, as is pointed out elsewhere, instruments by which a whole host of foreign or extraneous values are confusingly projected into aesthetic creativity. For many, there would seem to be more solid educational possibilities in the approach to "special talent" teaching, insofar as art education is concerned. Whatever creative insights the student uncovers, whatever elements of the creative process he manages to develop in himself, whatever intensification of creative values and expansion of creative potentialities have reference to the visually symbolic act of artistic transformation. More important perhaps, as a guiding value, is the inherent and self sustaining morality and unique personal satisfactions of the artistically creative mode of knowing and doing. What is of primary concern in art education is the development in the student of the intrinsically creative values that are a part of the processes and the products of art and it is to this, a direction into primary involvement with art, that art teachers have to lead students. They cannot hope to convey the essential values of art by leading away from its sensory, aesthetic nature as the centers of their consideration. If any additional and transferable qualities do result from a participation in and an appreciation of artistic creativity, these will occur naturally. No doubt, the adjunctive values are considerable, but to stress them and teach with them exclusively through default of active aesthetic participation is to put the cart before the horse. The result may well be an educational impasse. It would seem art teachers have to concentrate on the direct artistic and creative processes, on the intrinsic elements of the act and properties of the product rather than deemphasizing them in favor of personality development. In doing so, they may be very well fostering those conditioning elements of education that produce self-actualizing personalities alert to the "effective surprises" of experience.

A freedom of be-
havior may have a
direct bearing upon
the creative produc-
tivity of students.
"Halloween Art."
[Detroit Public
Schools]

Task Satisfaction Against Ego Satisfaction

Obviously these elements of special talent as against self-actualizing considerations overlap and are interdependent at many points. A parallel consideration concerns the extrinsic motivations toward creativity as against the intrinsic ones. The intrinsic factors of creative motivation lie in the nature of the productive act, in the painting of a picture or solving of a problem. The extrinsic factors are those of self satisfaction which are related to the accomplishment of the creative act, but are not innately a part of it, such as the desire to be like someone else, to produce a democratic spirit, or to otherwise achieve status.

In art education, it would seem that it is not sufficient to concentrate strongly on the need of self expression, on the benign praise or ego contentment that may be utilized as motivating factors. This overvalues the outer shell of the creative act. Though these elements are present and indeed necessary, they are not the most vital or the real need for participation in the aesthetic experience. It is rather the "playfulness" of the situation, the challenge of the material, the inherent satisfaction of ordering the sensory data, the pleasure of achieving personal solutions,

Art
and
Education
in
Contemporary
Culture

.

262

the working with color, mass, texture and other artistic elements toward a symbolic unity of expression that constitute the lure and serve as the most exciting motivations for participation and appreciation.

The art teacher has to go beyond a simple though passionate desire to engender creativity. He or she has to treat the art activities and the creative processes that attend the experience as ends, as complete satisfactions in themselves, rather than as means to get other ends which only use rather than are inherently satisfied with the elements and conditions of art. If the creative experience is too premeditated in its motivational sources, utilized as an instrument and as a means, it appears to defeat its own purpose. It "sets" too many conscious and egocentered procedures when the necessity is for a fluid flow of preconscious and spontaneous imagery.

GENERAL DEFINITION OF CREATIVITY

There are currently a variety of other ways to approach creativity. It would be almost sheer nonsense to attempt to extend the discussion in that direction. Again, as in so many of the other considerations a teacher must actively and searchingly engage in, the individual understanding is likely to be a relative one, strongly dependent upon the value orientation of the questioner. The values that are operating in any encounter with the material of experience, even in an area such as creativity is likely to determine the larger aspects of acceptance or rejection of the material.

Creativity cannot have any but a loose definition though there are a variety of factors that it should not be difficult to find a common if not a completely generic agreement upon. Webster's dictionary is rather conservative in its definition, but it does stress two factors: "to bring into being or to cause to exist" and "the production of something new" in form or other character. The elements of being and newness may be generally agreed upon. A more complete summation is provided by June McFee: "Creativity is the ability to invent new symbols and ideas, to improvise on established symbols, to rearrange established organizations into new organizations, and to integrate new or borrowed ideas into previously organized systems or situations." [6] For the purposes of art education, in a narrow definition, creativity can mean the bringing into expressive being of a new artistic form or aesthetic idea, or a novel and fresh rearrangement of previous combinations of elements, expressively and aesthetically through active personal behavior interrelating with perception and experience.

An element of definition which is not given too much attention is the one that the creative act is basically a felt one. That is, the characteristic quality of personal creativeness involves the emotional, gestural and other internal and imaginative aspects of productivity. There is, in addition, the presence of tensions, of the need for their resolution, the recognition of the relative openness of creativity: its intermittent, off-balanced and

[6] June McFee, *Preparation for Art* (San Francisco: Wadsworth, 1961), p. 129.

incompleted nature, even when there is a configuration of forms and concepts. Any definition is a high level abstraction that is not all inclusive but the above may suffice generally in the present context.

CREATIVITY AND INTELLIGENCE

Since the schools see themselves primarily as the means of developing intelligence, some of the relationships between intellectual qualities and creative behavior may deserve added attention. Though there are many psychologists who are still uncertain about the components of intelligence, including those elements that make up intellectual activity, for many teachers the standard I.Q. tests serve as indicators of educational potential, frequently without any qualification. Correspondingly, though common sense has in the past unhesitatingly bracketed creativity and intellectual ability in a very close correlation, there has been no serious attempt to really study what the relationship may actually be, assuming that definite and reliable information may be garnered and evaluated.

In a rather germinal study of the relationship, Getzels and Jackson have provided us with some intriguing though not unsuspected ideas.[7] Using a large sampling of secondary students, the team compared the academic achievement of a group of highly intelligent but not highly original students with a group of highly creative but lower I.Q. metric students. An intensive creativity index was devised to score the creativity level (the upper 20% constituting the high) and the Stanford-Binet test determining the intelligence quotient (likewise the upper 20% constituting the high). They found, after the administering of the standardized achievement tests that there was almost no difference in the scoring, despite the rather large I.Q. difference. In fact, whatever difference there was in achievement was in favor of the creative group. Further testing, though, indicated the striking differences in the manner of thought that each group generally engaged in, in the quality of cognition, not only of the traditionally logical or associational variety, but those kinds involving fluidity, flexibility, metaphoric insights, freedom from limitations, intuitive leaps, divergency and those qualitative factors that are associated with unorthodox thinking. The creative student tended to be offbeat, occasionally nonconforming in his behavior and unruly in his thinking (in relationship to traditional ways). Independence and complexity characterized the creative student and yet this still reflected a negative relationship with school grades. What this may point up, and the findings have been independently "validated," is that education may have been stressing rather inappropriate values or at the very least, neglecting some that deserve a more positive and sympathetic acceptance. Certainly, those in the art class require some additional examination. In any instance, this kind of study is indicative of the direction that some investigations are taking. A brief theoretical summary underlying the Getzels-Jackson one as well as some other studies

[7] Jacob Getzels and Philip Jackson, *Creativity and Intelligence* (New York: J. Wiley and Sons, 1962).

Art
and
Education
in
Contemporary
Culture

•

264

of creativity and its relationship both to thinking and to personality may provide greater scope for understanding the research material.

A Theoretical Model of the Structure of the Intellect

J. P. Guilford is another and one of the most persistent of the psychologists engaged in studying creativity. His model of the "structure of intellect" [8] (below) has important theoretical implications for creativity

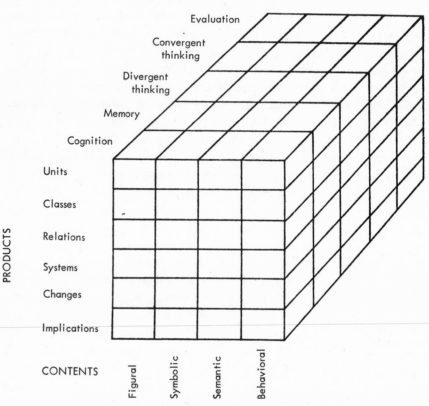

OPERATIONS

Evaluation
Convergent thinking
Divergent thinking
Memory
Cognition

Units
Classes
Relations
Systems
Changes
Implications

PRODUCTS

CONTENTS

Figural
Symbolic
Semantic
Behavioral

Theoretical model for the complete "structure of intellect."

studies if it can be accepted on face value. It is too complicated a theory to be fully explored here. Essentially though, the wide range of factors that constitute the intellect are broken down into four main classifications of properties. The figural are those that deal with concrete sense data, the perception and realization of visual qualities, and of auditory, kinesthetic and tactual as well. The semantic category includes meanings in verbalized form while the symbolic includes the structural relationships among words, numbers, syllables and various kinds of "code" materials. The fourth element, the behavorial is Guilford's belief in a social or empathetic category of intellectual material that may be recognized as a

[8] J. P. Guilford, *Creativity and Its Cultivation*, Harold A. Anderson (ed.), (New York: Harper and Bros., 1959), pp. 151 ff.

separate entity. These content categories of the intellect work in relation-ship to one another in actual practice. However, they have particular significances that are discovered through factor analysis: the little known figural and symbolic having to do with creative thought in the arts or in mathematics, the better known semantic related to general science and literature.

Divergent Versus Convergent Thinking

More pertinent though is the range of intellectual operations and aptitudes from the cognitive to the evaluative. The most important dis-tinction for the understanding of creative behavior is that between convergent and divergent thinking. Guilford illustrates the difference by citing the obvious and expected antonym of "high" as "low," of the answer to "what is four times five" as without alternative being "twenty." This is convergent thinking, a method of operation that "proceeds to a re-stricted answer or solution." Divergent thinking though would be likely to have a variety of responses as for instance to the question "What is the opposite of big?", the reply may include in addition to "small," such words as "insignificant," "bigoted," "inferior" or "diminutive."

Guilford identifies the divergent mode of thought as much more clearly related to creativity. The openness and ambiguity, the richness of imagery, the elaborate network of fantasy and other imaginative qualities, the excitement and even irritation, the general expansiveness of divergent thinking all seem to be inherent factors of that mode of intellectual operation and possessed in a marked degree by creative people.

The average kind of teaching that occurs in the schools is geared to convergent learning, knowing the "right" answers, categorizing and sys-tematizing what has been learned, producing acceptable imitations or spe-cific syntheses in some particularized form. This is even quite evident in many art lessons as, for instance, when making a papier mache globe or relief map, a lettered poster or concentrating on some craft technique in order to build a skill such as in pottery making or weaving. The expressive qualities that are involved, on the other hand, in drawing, in painting, or in sculpture are divergent in that they search out resolutions to problems and even cognitive tensions in unique ways that may take any number of forms, just as the creative designs that craft skills are directed to require divergent thinking in order to be realized. Divergent thinking is a more upsetting procedure, fraught with uncertainty, novelty and the disturbance of the unexpected. Many teachers tend to distrust its conditions and feel insecure if it is too frequently or intensely pursued. At the very least, the individual child will harbor an internal bewilderment when the natural and necessary divergent attitudes that are inherently a part of the creative process are, in many instances, superseded by the insistence upon convergent methods. Even when a classroom situation permits both kinds of thinking, unless there is an understanding guidance on the part of the teacher there is likely to be an aborting confusion. It is difficult for a child to move from an admonition of "stay within the

Art
and
Education
in
Contemporary
Culture

.

266

lines" when crayoning in the still widely used work books to a "paint whatever you like, dear!" during a "free" art lesson that may occur within the same morning.

Fluency and Flexibility

Fluency of thinking refers to the proliferation and ease with which ideas are generated and expressed, the fertility of symbols and the frequency with which they are manipulated. Guilford distinguishes four different types of fluency: word, associational, expressional, and ideational. Word fluency indicates the ability to provide the examiner with words of a specified length. For some mysterious reason the ability to do this correlates with ability in the arts and sciences. Associational fluency indicates the ease with which meaning is provided in congruent manner, how relationships of awareness are established. Expressional fluency is the rapidity with which words are juxtaposed or put into combinations with one another, while ideational fluency measures the quantitative occurrence of ideas within a limited time wherein a scanning process provides these idea responses to a given question.

Flexibility of thinking is a trait that deals with the ability of an individual "to roam around in his thinking" so as to meet new situations, adapt to changing pressures and the general ease with which different problem solving techniques are developed. Guilford identifies two categories of flexibility: (1) the "spontaneous" which demonstrates an ability to form a large variety of ideas, free from mental inertia, perhaps along a continuum, the opposite end of which is the narrow repetition of ideas in a fixed rigidity of thought, and (2) the "adaptive" which indicates the ability to sense out of the ordinary solutions and to successfully carry them out.

Finally, originality is a trait that makes use of responses that are not customary, that may be startling at first glance, being not of a common or expected nature but rather new, novel and "clever." Art possesses a great deal of originality and the making of it requires a more than average share in the possession of the doer.

The relationships these traits have to creative art experiences are rather obvious, though their analysis as individual factors purports to point up correlations and significant relationships that otherwise may not be discerned. However, an important consideration to recognize is that these factors never exist as independent agents but are very much dependent upon a larger combination of impinging elements, if not a total synthesis of behavior, that has a multitude of variables.

The average college student and frequently even the art major who is training for classroom teaching approaches the whole area of creativity with trepidation, and especially in the art education classes. Except for the minority, the shriveled up and long neglected qualities of expression, aesthetic playful behavior and manipulation of sensuous materials or the otherwise atrophied versions of what were once natural and enthusiastic desires and explorations in childhood are in late adolescence or early adulthood rigid and fearfully narrow limitations—the very opposite of fluency and flexibility. Though there may be genetically determining considerations, more important, in most instances, has been the influence of past experiences and cultural pressures. In the average instance, these have progressively degenerated from insouciant pleasure and relative creative ease of childhood, through the fumbling, limited or untutored and most unencouraged confrontations with art throughout most of the teens, to the hesitant or dismayed rigidities of the college years, meeting only with diverting trivia on the way.

The author has met literally hundreds of students training as classroom teachers who have travelled this path—in large part, due to the insensitive and indifferent teaching they themselves have experienced as well as to the prevailing values of an inartistic culture that insinuates its predilection for orthodoxy into the capacities of individuals. No wonder the requisites of fluency, flexibility and originality are in scant supply. It is not only the prospective grade school teacher who has fallen into this trap. There are large numbers of students who have somehow internally survived the negativism directed toward artistic behavior and secretly harbor genuine desires for a career in the arts. Many of them languish unhappily and fretfully in general courses of study when they would more appropriately bring their capacities to fruition in studio areas. This comment may be somewhat peripheral, but it does point up the effect that the environment may have upon learning and the possibilities of creative behavior blunting the innate characteristics of fluency and flexibility or intensifying them as the case may be. Though the aim in art education is not to produce great numbers of artists, genuine and productive behavior of artists in a creative context is as much to be considered a guide and a goal, particularly for teachers of art, as are the general concepts of creativity.

Teaching Implications

More specifically, some brief note of the immediate factors that affect the development of fluency, flexibility and originality can be made: A teacher who is cognizant of the conditions could better offer the kind of teaching that hopes to stimulate and activate the creative potential of each child, in art particularly, but actually throughout the entire curriculum.

One of the most important qualifications of any teaching method, even in the relatively free approaches usually suggested in art teaching, is the acceptance of a rather wide range of individual differences, of intrinsically varying abilities of response. Everyone is familiar with the concept of the "early starter" or the "late bloomer." In the more limited confines of the classroom there are students who can formulate what they have to say the moment the teacher presents an assignment or offers a suggestion, others require some time for reflection while still others have to ruminate and mull over the possibilities. Some, of course, are clever and quick while others may have the handicap of a dull or slow mind, an emotional "block" or some other impediment to rapid response. Consequently, time

Art
and
Education
in
Contemporary
Culture

·

268

and solicitous (but not patronizing) care has to be provided on a continuum dependent upon the nature of the child. Some resist new things, others find trouble even with familiar concepts and objects. Some can juggle a variety of ambiguous thoughts and creative stimulants that may even be at cross purposes with one another, others have difficulty with relatively simple and limited ideas. There are children who thrive on the nuances and subtleties of evanescent or complex concepts or involved forms. Others click in their minds, and in their productive behavior by collecting and collating formal conditions, confirming their findings in systematic manners. Still other students find an ease and completeness in operating on a symbolic level that is primarily verbal while their classmates may be more visually oriented.

Art teachers have to possess not only a scholarly awareness of individual differences, but more importantly perhaps, an intuitive insight of their presence in actual classroom situations. Though some of them may be amenable to classification, a hard and fast list tends to stereotype the attributes. This could have a contrary and rather limiting influence on teaching method and the development of a creative and artistic climate. The more open and liberal acceptance of individual differences necessary as a philosophical tenet of teaching may generate a greater intuitive sensitivity to the varieties that actually are encountered. The factors of flexibility, fluency and originality then take on themselves a philosophical orientation in the learning and creative process.

Another specific, outside of the one of individual differences, is the spread of procedures, skills and techniques that an average school provides. These may have unique values in special cases, but they may grate upon one another in the overall context of learning. Art education, for instance, incorporates a broad range of motor skills—of kinesthetic response, focused around the hand-eye coordination: the precise control of a pencil or pen for exact rendering, the loose, supple sweep of a brush for spontaneous painting, the nervously attenuated line manipuations in free drawing, the erratic pressures yet internally rhythmic motions of clay modelling, the unrestricted paper tearing for collage or the ordered conceptualization of form and manipulation required for lettering are only a few of the possible activities. These are subject to cognitive direction and purposeful ends just as are some of the more academic lessons: the stylistic restraints of penmanship, the neat divisions of space for arithmetic or similar assignments, the severely controlled (and unfortunate) aspects of copy book experience, the prescribed margins to be maintained in written composition and so on.

These different motor skills may have been internalized at some point existing as necessarily "correct" procedures, or a teacher may be inordinately insistent upon certain particulars he or she requires. A contradiction or confusion may result that puts the student at a disadvantage. The switch from one kind of activity to another may be too rapid or too arbitrary resulting in an inability of the students to effect a successful or complete changeover. These are pertinent factors that the sensibility of a teacher should take into consideration in presenting assignments and more generally be aware of in the overall learning and creative process.

Various Theoretical Relationships of Creativity and Intelligence

In addition to the factoral analysis and theoretical structure of the intellect provided by Guilford, there are many additional studies that have some interest for the art educator. They tend to confirm the fundamental understanding that though there is a correlation between intellectual ability and creativity, the two areas are by no means tied to one another. One of the difficulties that emerges is the inability to determine the real and inclusive nature of intelligence. Though there are a variety of factors that may be conceptually isolated, there is no guarantee that these are as actively influential in real life as they appear to be in clinical experimentation, nor are the almost infinite combinations of factors readily accountable for in experimental situations that necessarily isolate fragments of behavior.

Getzels and Jackson[9] refer to five different generalized conceptions of creative thinking in their study of the relationships of creativity and intelligence. Though they admit that these are not exhaustive of what is possible they treat them as theoretically significant. These are referred to in a variety of ways in other contexts throughout this text so that a modest mention of them now could offer at least the classifications that are pertinent to contemporary study in the field. They are (1) traditional logic, (2) classical associationism, (3) Gestalt formulations, (4) psychoanalytic, and (5) dynamic perceptual theory.

Traditional Logic

Traditional logic has perhaps the least amount of light to shed on artistic production. Its formulation of creative thought is based upon a systematized and piecemeal progression of steps leading to a final solution in a syllogistic manner. A rather simplified example from art history may be seen in the following logic: It is the prime function of the plastic arts (painting, sculpture and architecture) to create, simulate or enclose space and the techniques of aerial and linear perspective best achieve this. Consequently those artists who use perspective are most effectively or logically creating plastic art. The recording type of drawing and painting in this viewpoint may then be considered as an optimum learning experience in art, leading to logically deducible elements of structure that may confidently be utilized in the future. The full reasoning may be deductive or inductive in its approach but in each instance of creativity based on structural analysis the appropriateness of an idea or a supposition has to accord with the piecemeal laws of reason and logic. Inferences that are derived from general propositions or conversely broad assertions

[9] Jacob Getzels and Philip Jackson, *Creativity and Intelligence* (New York: J. Wiley and Sons, 1962), p. 77.

Art
and
Education
in
Contemporary
Culture
·
270

The development of creative expressiveness is a personal, open process. Preparatory sketches for a portrait of President Kennedy, Elaine de Kooning. [Courtesy of the artist, "Art News" and the Graham Gallery. New York]

that are formulated on the basis of specific evidence must both meet the condition of formal testing and evaluation. For instance, round forms and rectangular ones have specific patterns of light and shade distribution, or the further away an object is the smaller is its rendering. New ideas may be derived from the combination of older concepts that have been proved by the severe and accurate conditions of a reasoned syllogistic logic. Einstein's unified field theory which as yet has not been completely proven empirically was supposedly generated in this fashion. Many of the findings in the physical sciences make reference to this approach as do a host of ethical and religious suppositions. The thinking of St. Thomas Aquinas has this scholastic ring to it as much as the empirical and structural formulations of the positivistic scientists. The latter could even argue that art in its entirely doesn't exist as "real" knowledge requiring intelligence for its realization, because there can be no general abstractions or laws to rely upon in repeating a condition or positing an accurate solution to a problem in art—there are no logical syllogisms. The essential trouble

with this attitude is that it restricts the scope of knowledge to only that which can be formally tested and severely limits the possibilities of creativity to measurable dimensions only. Any intellectual and creative potency is subdued behind a facade of formalism, not only unsatisfactory in feeling but intolerable of the quirks, sidewise leaps and uniqueness of artistic creativity. It would be difficult to explain or stimulate creativity in art through traditional logic.

CLASSICAL ASSOCIATIONISM

Classical associationism is quite close to many of the ideas of conditioning. It holds that thinking is a series of ideas, or in more modern terms, of quasi-mechanical functions (stimulus-response or behavior elements). These chains of ideas exist in the individual as "remnants of perception" and it is in the interconnections that learning takes place. Reason is not of basic importance in this concept, but habits and ex-

Art
and
Education
in
Contemporary
Culture

·

272

periences from the past that have left their imprints are. Consequently, the number of associations and their intensity that an individual has accumulated may determine his learning as well as the richness of the links of connection that the associations stir up.

New learning or creative behavior in this view occurs in the course of trial and error, the individual being guided by the suggestiveness of his associations. In a very oversimplified way an example of this thinking in art education may be the efforts of young children to represent the human figure. At an early stage of their school career, the chain of perceptions is meagre as compared to a later date. Consequently, the youngster's schemes are rather inaccurate because the memory traces are not only relatively few in number, but the associations are crude and meagre. However, by trial and error, over a period of time, proportion and other elements of accurate representation make themselves known subject to the motor skills of the individual to portray them.

This stress on imitation, on mechanical procedures and on the oblique fortunes of chance appears to be a rather narrow and negative understanding of human functioning. It is actually contrary to the results in art, for as the individual accrues a series of perceptions and concrete experiences, the relatively free and spontaneous creativity gives way to a developmentally cramped and picayune concern with surface appearances that imitation emphasizes. There is, frequently, a banal and platitudinous result in the product if only conditioning and trial and error are relied upon as modes of teaching. The higher orders of man's capacities are summarily rejected because they do not appear to conform to a predetermined structure that insists upon the accuracy of its own theoretical formulation. Creativity, as a result, is reduced to a happenstance that arbitrarily flows from a mechanical conditioning and the undeveloped powers of intelligence.

GESTALT

Gestalt understanding rejects the compartmentalized thinking of logic and associationism. In its place is put a more complete structural emphasis on the totality of each thinking and creative experience, in its form and configural qualities. In the most common mode of thinking, there is first the problem situation, which is called S_1. It is here that the actual thinking process starts. After several steps of thought inherent in the process it ends in solution of the problem creating a second situation called S_2. The idea of closure, of "mending" the configuration that is structurally incomplete in S_1 is fundamental, as was seen in the chapter on perception. To use the example of artistic perspective again, a student desires to draw a human figure and a house on a flat two-dimensional piece of paper that he actually experiences in the space of three dimensions. That is the S_1 situation. The S_2 situation is the resolved expression as an illusion by means of graphic symbols (lines and values of light) of the desired representations, in two dimensions, as a drawing of "proper" relationships. The process of drawing, applying the "laws" of perspective and the skills of representation, becomes the intermediary step between the unfinished S_1 situation and the completed Gestalt of S_2. This theory of creative thinking has a number of attributes and Wertheimer lists them broadly:

(1) There is grouping, reorganization, structurization, operations of dividing into sub-wholes and still seeing these sub-wholes together, with clear reference to the whole figure and in view of the specific problem at issue. . . . (2) The process starts with the desire to get at the inner-relatedness of form and size. This is not a search for just any relation which would connect them, but for the nature of their intrinsic interdependence. . . . (3) Outstanding relations of this kind sensible with regard to the inner structural nature of the given situation . . . play a large role here. . . . (4) There is the feature of the functional meaning of parts. . . . (5) The entire process is one consistent line of thinking. It is not an and-sum of aggregated, piecemeal operations. No step is arbitrary, ununderstood in its function. On the contrary, each step is taken surveying the whole situation. . .[10]

There is a recognition, however, of the tensions inherent in thinking and in creative endeavor and the need for resolution. The theory is still vague in dealing with the initially formless promptings of emotion and tension that await the open envisagement of aesthetic structure. The transforming procedures and the forming qualities remain elusive despite the dynamic constructions the Gestalt investigators provide, these constituting only a partial uncovering of experience.

Thus, the theory stresses the idea of pattern and configural qualities of experience. This would seem to have a significant if not complete bearing on the whole area of creative visual symbolization. The idea that meanings, in addition to being created, occur in the inferential fragments of experience and are received as such by the perceiver permits on added understanding of how artists begin to particularize their form-making into specific directions. There is a controlling pattern that directs the nature of the perception or its symbolic mode. The control is established in terms of the innate universality of forces that inhere in particular states, or objects and then may be transferred into symbols. Psychologists know this as isomorphism. For instance, an artist can express joy by feeling that emotion internally as he begins to paint. The thought and feeling converge in the marks the brush makes, in the movements of the artist's hand, in the configuration of symbolic elements that are created on the canvas. The process is reversed for the onlooker. What is of importance in this idea is that the elements of perception are invariably patterned and that the patterns hold broad significance for humans. Obviously, this theory, if correct, can have many possibilities for art education. It can set up operational devices, "jumping off" points for creative exploration and symbolic forming which could guide a teacher along desired pedagogical paths. However, the translation of these ideas into structured models seems a long way off and perhaps fraught with pitfalls in its own development.

[10] M. Wertheimer, *Productive Thinking* (New York: Harper, 1954), p. 242.

Art
and
Education
in
Contemporary
Culture

·

274

PSYCHOANALYTIC THEORIES

The psychoanalytic interpretations may be summed up by noting that creativity can be linked to those mental and emotional processes that lie below the conscious threshold, or the ego, in Freudian terms. As was noted earlier, there is a strong element of determinism based upon childhood experiences and these tend to manifest themselves as irritants, excitations, and drives in many people through conflict between the restraints of reality and the freedom of desire. The creative individual is able to channel what for many is a resulting neuroticism into highly imaginative and productive acts, discharging the accumulation of tension resulting from the conflicts.

This classical Freudian formulation has been modified by later theoreticians in the area. Ernst Kris has shifted the location of the creative source from the unconscious to the preconscious mind, the latter being the internal condition that is "capable of becoming conscious easily and under conditions which frequently arise." [11] The importance of this new point is that the unconscious is lacking in pattern, is primarily interested in satisfying fundamental hungers and drives and is not subject to any restrictive or modifying influences. The preconscious, though it is still involved with primary process, permits the conscious state or the ego to utilize it without being astounded or horribly upset by its visions. Consequently, the creative individual is provoked and impelled by the fertile material from "down under" in a positive manner. Kris suggests that creative behavior shares this approach with sleeping states, with fantasy, with intoxication and with psychosis. The line between the genius and the madman is a thin one indeed, and the line between general creative behavior and neurotic dissatisfaction may also be rather slight. There is a resultant need for a great sensitivity and awareness on the part of teachers during the learning process and most particularly when creativity is being fostered and encouraged if a psychoanalytic base to creativity is accepted.

Preconscious Processes

The most recent psychoanalytic modification comes from L. S. Kubie and its structure is best defined in Kubie's own diagram and words,

In between (the conscious and the unconscious processes) come the preconscious functions with their automatic recall, their multiple analogic and overlapping linkages, and their direct connections to the autonomic processes which underlie affective states. The rich play of preconscious operations occurs freely in states of abstraction, in sleep, in dreams, and as we write, paint, or allow our thoughts to flow in the non-selected paths of free association.

Preconscious processes are assailed from both sides. From one side they are nagged and prodded into rigid and distorted symbols by unconscious drives which are oriented away from reality and which consist of rigid compromise formations, lacking in fluid inventiveness. From the other side they are driven

[11] E. Kris, "On Preconscious Mental Processes," *Psychoanalytic Quarterly*, 19, 1–542 (1950).

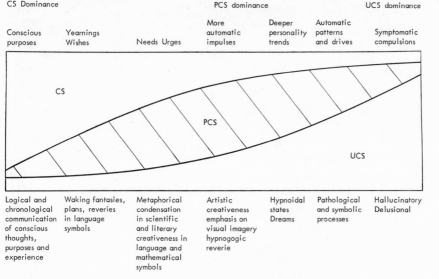

CS Dominance   PCS dominance   UCS dominance

| Conscious purposes | Yearnings Wishes | Needs Urges | More automatic impulses | Deeper personality trends | Automatic patterns and drives | Symptomatic compulsions |

CS

PCS

UCS

| Logical and chronological communication of conscious thoughts, purposes and experience | Waking fantasies, plans, reveries in language symbols | Metaphorical condensation in scientific and literary creativeness in language and mathematical symbols | Artistic creativeness emphasis on visual imagery hypnogogic reverie | Hypnoidal states Dreams | Pathological and symbolic processes | Hallucinatory Delusional |

[*From* Neurotic Distortion of the Creative Process. *by Lawrence S. Kubie* (*University of Kansas Press,* 1958), *reproduced by permission of the publisher.*]

by literal conscious purpose, checked and corrected by conscious retrospective critique. The uniqueness of creativity, i.e., its capacity to find and put together something new, depends on the extent to which preconscious functions can operate freely between these two ubiquitous concurrent and oppressive prison wardens.[12]

It is from this intense, abundant, imaginative and openly searching storehouse of preconscious material that the artist draws upon for his or her inspiration and understanding of creating symbolic forms. In a like manner, students on every level draw from this source to learn artistically and to create their own plastic images, developing an individual inventiveness and a fertile means of stimulating the discovery of forms and meanings all of which become the substance of a personally created world.

Examples of children's work (following) begin to suggest the source of preconscious activity in picture making. The coordination of hand-eye manipulation was dependent upon the selective decisions that welled up from the preconsciousness interplay of elements in the child in the first grader's painting of a lion's head (p. 277). In the limited store of past experience that clusters in the child's mind, he found the colors, shapes and plastic relationships which for him communicate the feline ferociousness and animal physiognomy. It has none of the subtlety, none of the profundity of a mature work, but its aesthetic and communicative effectiveness on its own level is forthright and spontaneous. The spontaneity, however, did not "just happen"; it was the result of the pushing and probing of various plastic images in the mind at a very rapid pace and the connection of various feelings and emotional states with the "feel" of a shape. Either of these operate as a brake on the vigorously associative tendencies of the preconscious, though the top picture, p. 276, is a rich, visual fantasy.

The creative process is thus viewed as originating in a subliminal manner.

[12] L. S. Kubie, *Neurotic Distortion of the Creative Process* (Lawrence, Kan.: University of Kansas Press, 1958), p. 44.

Art
and
Education
in
Contemporary
Culture

·

276

Preconscious imagery is often directly expressed in unrelated elements and doodling in children's art. Sixth Grade Drawing. [Ann Arbor Public Schools; PHOTO: Stuart Klipper]

The subliminal source, the preconscious, is capable of infinite possibility, great speed of transaction, and the establishment of fertile and significant relationships by associative and selective processes.

A sequel to the idea that creative sources are below the conscious threshold is that these elements are not directly accessible to the art teacher. The elements of intuition, hunches, compelling desires, "good notions," inspiration and imaginative fancies are fundamental and initial means of process probably in all creative work and certainly in the sensory-symbolic fields. The preconsciousness has not yet attained a status or necessity of reason, functioning primarily on impulse. This implies the need for sensitive and intuitive understanding "drawing out" of individual possibilities possessed by each student on the part of the teacher.

The metaphoric activity of the child's mind results in dramatic and expressive visual imagery. "The Fire," First Grade Painting. [Ann Arbor Public Schools; PHOTO: Stuart Klipper]

The impulse is excited by that rich cluster of possibilities that do exist in the preconsciousness. All of past experience, the range of personal inclination, the inner patterns of intelligence, of perception, of cognition, of subconscious imagery, of internalized values are the substantive elements that are brought into play. These are combined, related, fitted, and sorted in an intense and brilliantly rapid and selective manner which both the compulsive unconscious and the restrictive consciousness cannot transact as freely or as productively. The intuited image selections then form the central symbolic features that are subjected to the qualities of the sensuous material employed and the manner of its manipulation, in short, to the handling of the art media. Of course, various conscious and cognitive processes modify the final imagery as do the influences of the deeper unconsciousness, the density of a color, or the relativeness of size and position.

A spontaneous and effective symbolic transformation of preconscious imagery and emotional attitudes. "Lion's Head," First Grade Painting. [Ann Arbor Public Schools; PHOTO: Stuart Klipper]

These elements, central to art forming, give an aesthetic direction to the impulse that prompted the child to paint the animal head. They infuse imagination with a purpose and stimulate further rich fancies in the child's mind. In turn, the storehouse of thinking and feeling images in the preconscious is elaborated and expanded. The child, in searching his own mind, creates the indispensable conditions for symbolic understanding. The lion's mane, the whiskered area above the mouth denote the difference to the child between human and animal heads. Achieving this symbolically, even on a simplified diagrammatic level, leads to further learning of a more subtle nature and of greater sensory discrimination, all of which develop and operate internally.

The painting of a fire being extinguished (at left) has a similar set of visual symbols that are the result of preconscious scanning of feasible, ex-

Art
and
Education
in
Contemporary
Culture

.

278

pressive images. The contrasting play of dark and light is an effective visual metaphor that carries the dramatic quality of the fire. The sturdy, rectangular solidness of the fire engine is a bulwark against the writhing mass of flame behind it, while the firemen are the simplest delineations of direct human action against the awesome nature of fire. The latter has always been an impressive quality for humans and its sense of drama is one of the many feeling factors that the child has stored in his preconsciousness. The bulk of the engine, the conflict of the fire and water, the rising strands of smoke are also elements that the child spontaneously drew upon to create the metaphorically visual configuration. The stored elements of past experience, the wakening awareness of the range of variability in the environment, the imaginative play of form and feeling, the intensification of sensory reception and meaningful perception all combine in the preconscious to create the cluster of associations for the child. The bold hard handling of line around the engine denotes a mechanical quality, the impasto and thick surge of texture and the active manipulation of strokes gives us the fire, the wispy strands of light color the smoke that becomes the dense pall over the sky. The ground is relatively noncommital in its handling; it is a restful area against which the contrasts of the action are carried out. These are all visually metaphoric devices among other intelligible conceptions that are suggested by the seething mass of stored impressions that lie beneath the conscious façade of thought. The opportunity to concretely symbolize the experience (even if it is only an imaginative one) provides a basis for making choices. These choices are learning elements which enhance an emerging discrimination between relevant and irrelevant qualities. The nonrational feeling aspects of the experience are joined with the more consciously cognitive considerations so that a fully meaningful symbol is created. The objective cognitive examinations and judgments (proportioning the sizes, directing the positions of various elements, establishing the ground line, etc.) complement the more aesthetic factors of color, texture and intensity of expression. The total image, however, was dependent upon the generative and suggestive richness of imagery that the preconscious state initiated.

The clever and discerning portrait of man and wife painted by an upper elementary child is a much more acute transformation of experience. It makes use of more diverse experience and creates more subtle metaphoric images to communicate the student's particular conception. The man and the woman are no mere copies of stereotypes nor are they the visual clichés so evident in uninspired children's work.

The painting is actually a critical work, an interpretation of experience. The constrained, proper semblance of the pair is sensitively and knowingly evoked by the student who must possess a preconsciousness abounding in varied and vivid imagery. Obviously, there is thinking that is of a productive nature, fashioning purposeful relationships of a studied yet fresh intentness. The picture evidences a healthy blend of feeling, sensory impressions, objective thought and discriminating symbolic insight. The feeling stems from the student's own internalized value systems and emotional involvement.

A critical response
to experience through
visual symbols.
"Man and Wife,"
Sixth Grade Painting.
[Ann Arbor Public
Schools; PHOTO:
Stuart Klipper]

Something is being said about the pair because of how the child artist is feeling. There may be no simple or primary identification with the subject but the very manner of its style reveals some elements of emotional response. The sensory impressions indicate a sharp perceiving not only of detail, but of the configuration of related elements that make for a cogent perception. The frilly, lady-like hat perched on the woman's head and the very suitably worn lace collar provide an apt portrait of a type that is confirmed by the facial features and the hard edged expression. In a like manner, the respectable demeanor of the man is told by his proper hat, his stiff, bland features. Though in each instance, the figures exist not only as types but as individuals—that is, the expression in the eyes, the sense of particularity about the images. The thought is, for a youngster, subtly demonstrated by the degree of conscious control over the various parts and in the diversity of experience from which these discriminating symbols were decided upon. Finally, the symbolic insight is manifested in the comity of means, in the aesthetic composing of only the most pertinent and revealing characteristics. The handling of the art material and the painting technique are judiciously and sensibly executed, the whole procedure creating an expressive yet controlled imagery, stemming from fertile sources of imagery.

These various psychoanalytic systems of explaining creative behavior have an extremely controversial character; they remain intricate in their relationships and are not amenable to oversimplification. Yet the sensitively observed behavior of children and of creative adults appears to bear out some of the theoretic projections of psychoanalysis. There is an affinity between its broad interpretive schemes and those of the creative process as reflected in the attitudes and actions of artists, musicians, poets and others gifted in creatively expressive areas. There is no manner of objective testing that is

Art
and
Education
in
Contemporary
Culture

·

280

going to prove the case one way or another. For many, psychoanalysis is itself an art rather than a science and its "rules" are closer to the symbolic reality of painting or poetry than to the logical axioms of geometry or chemistry. As such the findings of this school of thought have to be accepted as insightful rather than clinically scientific.

DYNAMIC PERCEPTUAL THEORY

The last area, that of dynamic perceptual theory, is best expressed by E. G. Schachtel. He rejects the concept that the free and imaginative range of thinking, ideas, and creative stimulation found in the play of imagination, thought, and perception are always primarily in response to the necessity of discharging accumulated drive tension. Rather he assigns the creative process that grows from these sources and the freedom of its approach "to the openness of the individual to the world around him." The emphasis is upon the free, unobstructed perceptual processes that reject or rise above the limitations of common understanding.

Schachtel offers two basic modes of perception, means of relationship of communication between subject and object—the autocentric and allocentric. Schachtel describes the differences in perception as follows:

In the autocentric mode there is little or no objectification; the emphasis is on how and what the person feels; there is a close relation, amounting to a fusion, between sensory quality and pleasure or unpleasure feelings, and the perceiver reacts primarily to something impinging on him (although sometimes he may have brought about the impingement, for example by taking food into his mouth). In the allocentric mode there is objectification; the emphasis is on what the object is like; there is either no relation or a less pronounced or less direct relation between perceived sensory qualities and pleasure-unpleasure feelings—that is, such feelings are usually absent or less pronounced or of a different quality; the perceiver usually approaches or turns to the object actively and in doing so either opens himself toward it receptively or, figuratively or literally, takes hold of it, tries to "grasp" it.[13]

The growth of the individual is from a childhood autocentric condition to an expanding development of allocentric perceptions. However, as the change of process is occurring another element appears—that of secondary autocentricity. This is a necessary attribute of adulthood, but the manner and intensity of its unfolding determines whether the personality remains an open or a closed one in adult behavior. This secondary autocentricity orients the objects of an individual's perceptual environment in terms of need, utility and the avoidance of pain, discomfort and other negative conditions. The primary autocentricity that accepts security in a feeling of embeddedness in the familiar accepted pleasures and comforts that resist disturbance reappears in the late adolescent and adult as a "fear and avoidance of a full encounter and of everything new and strange that might disturb the secondary embeddedness in a closed pattern or routine." The

[13] E. G. Schachtel, *Metamorphosis: On the Development of Affect, Perception, Attention and Memory* (New York: Basic Books, 1959), p. 83.

latter is of course reflected in a status quo culture that has habitualized behaviors and associations in the friends, activities and other interests one becomes associated with.

Within this theoretical framework, creativity is seen by Schachtel as "the art of seeing the familiar fully in its inexhaustible being, without using it autocentrically for purposes of remaining embedded in it and reassured by it . . . [creativity is the] existential struggle between the two tendencies in man: to remain open toward the world . . . or to seek the security of a closed world," the former necessarily triumphing over the latter.

Getzels and Jackson point out that "this is no mean or easy victory, for to perceive things differently than the people we know—our parents, peers, teachers, leaders—can be one of the most frightening of experiences. To express these perceptions can be terrifying." [14] Creativity may be recognized as a relatively difficult undertaking in its social context, the learning processes that are inherent in its development subject to a variety of cultural mores that are internalized as individual restraints. The "convergent" versus "divergent" behavior of Guilford becomes the "closed" versus "open" behavior of this perceptual theory.

Schachtel emphasizes the value aspects in intelligence determination by noting that if the emphasis is upon being done with the new, then the quickly adaptive mind may be considered to have the greatest intelligence. However, if allocentric interest or a continuing openness to the world is regarded as desirable the contemplative, exploratory, curious (and eventually creative) mind possesses the greater intelligence.

The distinctive compelling properties of the creative mind are seen as

The main motivation at the root of creative experience is man's need to relate to the world around him . . . This need is apparent in the young child's interest in all the objects around him, and his ever renewed explorations of and play with them. It is equally apparent in the artist's lifelong effort to grasp and render something which he has envisaged in his encounter with the world, in the scientist's wonder about the nature of the object with which he is concerned, and in the interest in the objects around him of every person who has not succumbed to stagnation in a closed autocentric or sociocentric world. They all have in common the fact that they do not remain in a closed, familiar, labeled world but that they want to go beyond embeddedness in the familiar and in the routine, and to relate to another object, or to the same one more fully, or from another angle, anew, afresh . . . The quality of the encounter that leads to creative experience consists primarily in the openness during the encounter and in the repeated and varied approaches to the object, in the free and open play of attention, thought, feeling, perception, etc. In this free play the person experiences the object in its manifold relations to himself and also tentatively tries out, as it were, a great variety of relations between the object thus approached and other objects, ideas, experiences, feelings, objects of imagination, etc. In characterizing this activity as play I do not mean that it is playful rather than serious, but that it is not bound by rigorous rules or by conventional schemata of memory, thought, or perception. It may at times be playful, too; but

[14] Jacob Getzels and Philip Jackson, *Creativity and Intelligence* (New York: J. Wiley and Sons, 1962), p. 114.

Art
and
Education
in
Contemporary
Culture

·

282

that is not its main characteristic. It resembles the child's free play in his encounter with the world where playfulness, too, is not the main feature but the openness, the intensity of the interest, the repeated and varied approaches, which range all the way from the grave and serious, the absorbing and tantalizing, to the playful and the fleeting.[15]

This understanding would seem to suggest that passively adjusting behavior cannot lead to creativity. The need rather is for a quality of tension, immediate intellectual and perhaps emotional uneasiness—of a teetering, see-saw state of learning, of displeasure of a mind at rest, or the stability of a given answer or response, all of which lead to curiosity, exploration, active engagement, expression, and creative discovery. Many of these characteristics seem to parallel the observed behavior of artists and other creative individuals, and require development in the art lesson.

The theoretical development thus seems to have come full circle, from the primitive, unenclosed and unprotected exposure to a mysterious and wayward world—through a closed, reasoned and intellectually protected structure of facts and relationships in a contained sphere of existence—back out again into an open, perceptual and searching interrelatedness with a still mysterious but nonetheless, exciting and rewarding world. The creative process has permeated each of these conditions not only in pragmatic and materially rewarding ways but in artistic ones as well. Perhaps the creative process is some of each, or an inherent human quality that adapts to the exigencies of particular times and places. In any case, it manifests its theoretical structure—probably subject to change itself—in a variety of ways.

CREATIVE PERSONALITY TRAITS

Donald MacKinnon has made some fundamental studies into the nature of creativity and the traits of creative individuals. Though general in nature they tend to bear out the concept of openness. He refers to Jung's theory of psychological functions and types of personality as an aid in depicting the psychology of the creative person. According to this view it might be said that whenever a person uses his mind for any purpose he either perceives (becomes aware of something) or he judges (comes to a conclusion of something). Everyone perceives and judges, but the creative person tends to prefer perceiving to judging. Where a judging person emphasizes the control and regulation of experience the adjustment to status levels already determined, the perceptive creative person is inclined to be more interested and curious, more open and receptive, seeking to experience life to the full whatever the consequences. Indeed, the more perceptive a person is, the more creative he tends to be.

In his perceptions, both of the outer world and of inner experience, one may focus upon what is presented to his senses, upon the facts as they are, or he may seek to see, through intuition, their deeper meanings and possi-

[15] E. G. Schachtel, *Metamorphosis: On the Development of Affect, Perception, Attention and Memory* (New York: Basic Books, 1959), pp. 241–242.

*Creative visual
expression need not
be always
representational.
"Abstraction,"
Fourth Grade Crayon
Resist Painting. [Ann
Arbor Public Schools;
PHOTO: Stuart
Klipper]*

bilities. One would not expect creative persons in their perceptions to be bound to the presented stimulus or object but rather to be intuitively alert to that which is imaginatively capable of occurring, to that which is not yet realized; this capacity is, "in fact, especially characteristic of the creative person." [16]

Therefore if creative understanding and behavior are desired goals in education, it would seem necessary that the learning experiences be so structured or oriented that the perceptual processes are exposed to positive, provoking, and exciting stimulation. The resulting responses and classroom behavior should be encouraged in an expressive and open manner. This is a natural condition to foster in art, though it is often obscured or aborted by narrowly judgmental tastes or technically imposed canons of correctness. The learning process is *compelled* to be a relatively free and expansive one if the desired intent of creativity is to be individually fruitful. This calls for a rather difficult perceptual comprehension and sensitivity on the teacher's part, an allocentric personality pattern and all that it implies. It is even more particularly true in the light of the other traits of creativity that the investigators are compiling.

MacKinnon makes the following generalizations. They have not always been universally accepted as the keynotes or conditions of creativity.

Along with Getzels and Jackson, Torrance and others, though he finds creative people possess a relatively high order of intelligence, the latter is no absolute guarantee of creative behavior. The creative person is alert, fluent, flexible and discerning; he has a range of association and combinatory aptitudes, of seeking out the clever or unusual presentation of a problem and its effective yet aesthetic resolution. Creativity is involved with many of the conditions of intelligence, but there is no positive correlation, nevertheless, between the two in any ascending or progressive scale.

[16] Donald W MacKinnon, "What Makes a Person Creative," *Saturday Review* (Feb. 10, 1962)

Art
and
Education
in
Contemporary
Culture

·

284

The creative person is found to be comparatively divested of repression; he does not suppress the imagery and psychological provocations that the un-creative person does. In giving reign to his unconscious or preconscious mind the creative individual is able to operate in a symbolic manner that is more fundamental to expression and liberal understanding. Metaphor and other imaginative forms are handled with ease, permitting a more profound and eventually more meaningful involvement with the self. The realization of experience is not confined to judgmental and closed impressions, but is inventively and expressively formed by transforming the readily received perceptions of the outside world and the inner psyche.

This facility of intellectual and emotional movement in the creative individual is disclosed in a variety of ways. There is the revealing candor with which personal problems are discussed, the existence of psychological tur-moil and subjective agitation which is not necessarily a pathological quality but the reflection of complex, intricate and perhaps enigmatic personalities. Tension producing situations often seem to be invited by the creative individual like the child who will first throw his clay about almost in a fit of frenzy only to boldly and with ardor to shape it expressively not too long after. Sexual identification and similar interests also have not unusual but nevertheless unexpected attributes. Creative males for instance, manifest a tendency toward what are commonly regarded as feminine interests on a masculine-feminine scale. This does not refer necessarily to aberrations, attitude or behavior, but indicates the openness of the creative personality to all facets of experience.

Creative individuals are found to be more concerned with "meaning and implication" than with the rendition of fact or detail. They are conscious of their independence of mind and seem to shun the idea of imposition. They enjoy challenge and prefer to take on tasks that are incomplete. However, the simple solution to a problem is often not sufficient, the solution needs to be elegant also if it is to satisfy. MacKinnon sums up the characteristics generally of the creative individual as "a high level of effective intelligence, his openness to experience, his freedom from crippling restraints and im-poverishing inhibitions, his aesthetic sensitivity, his cognitive flexibility, his independence in thought and action, his high level of creative energy, his unquestioning commitment to creative endeavor and his unceasing striving for solutions to the ever more difficult problems that he constantly sets for himself."

CREATIVITY AND TEACHING

The implications for educational theory and for teaching methods are, if not clearly spelled out by these various psychological and sociological studies of creativity, at least suggestive of liberal approaches that may be employed in developing a creative classroom climate. There are probably no recognizably distinct factors that will invariably induce creativity. Edu-cation has to comfort itself with the understanding that the process is a relative one and is simply indigenous to man's thinking, behavior, and ex-

The artist creates new forms to express a personal vision. "The Outer Edge," Edith Dines. [Courtesy of the artist]

pression even if it is not too frequent a force or even accepted as a qualitative factor in ordinary learning. There are, however, certain general differentiations between creative behavior and that which is not creative. These may well be a desirable undercurrent of understanding teachers should possess. Their relationship to creative art education is more than a tenuous one. It is only when a teacher individually experiences the doing of art and the valued perception of its worth that the inherent creative qualities become apparent and understandable. It is at this point that teaching method can

Art
and
Education
in
Contemporary
Culture

.

286

then become the sensitive instrument, both in a searching and a guiding manner, with which to instruct and influence students.

These qualities are best recognized as distinctions between differing and sometimes opposing viewpoints and conditions. The most important perhaps, is one that is quite frequently alluded to in this text; the discrimination in teaching that has to be made between the mere transmittal of factual or procedural information as against the growth of wisdom and the need of "engagement" for the individual. Both ends obviously are required and if liberally developed capable of complementing one another rather than cancelling each other out. The "hard" facts that may be repeated and the singular discoveries of intuition are both essential to the art process at certain points, though the creative process is more characterized by the latter than by the former.

Art education, consequently, has to stress the exploratory conditions that lead to the making and appreciation of art. The teaching of art has to possess a straightforward awareness of the inherent conditions and consequent demands of creativity, assuming a responsibility that discards an effected or exaggerated sentimentality as much as it rejects an unfeeling, hard-nosed practicality.

As Bruner [17] suggests, the whole idea of creativity may be best understood as a metaphor which contains "paradox and antimony." He lists, for instance, detachment and commitment, passion and decorum, deferral and immediacy and the freedom to be dominated by the object as conditions which richly combine during creative periods. Others may be added such as recall and invention, imaginative perception and judgmental evaluation, ambiguity and decisiveness, gregariousness and solitude, interrelationship and isolation. All of these qualities are a part of the creative process and these are all, among others, inherent in the making of art. At one and the same time, an artist or a student who is involved in art activity must judge the forces that give shape to an object and invent new shapes or combinations of shapes; he must draw a spiritual sustenance from his kinship with other people and objective events, at the same time that he withdraws into the requisite solitude and concentration of creative behavior; he must be involved in his own internal, subjective and emotional drama at the same time that he objectively and concretely fashions the forms of his art and evaluates their worth.

This rather ambiguous and paradoxical procedure may seem confusing, yet it appears to be the most rewarding, the richest, indeed the inherent method of real artistic creativity. Its cultivation is problematical, though the recognition of its conditions, at least intuitively, are necessary to the teaching of art. The student has to be led to the adventure of discovery on his own.

[17] Jerome Bruner, *On Knowing* (Cambridge: Harvard University Press, 1962), p. 23.

The Symbolic Functions
of Art

Without poets, without artists, men would soon
weary of nature's monotony. The sublime idea men
have of the universe would collapse with dizzying
speed. The order which we find in nature, and which
is only an affect of art, would at once vanish. Everything would break up in chaos. There would be no
seasons, no civilization, no thought, no humanity;
even life would give way, and the impotent void
would reign everywhere.

GUILLAUME APOLLINAIRE

THE SYMBOLIZING ACT

WHAT occurs when a brush loaded with color is moved across a paper
surface and a child gleefully points to the forms created as trees, or
dogs, or houses? When a kindergartner guides his crayon in a circular movement, labelling the resultant oval form as a head, is special learning taking
shape? What is the quality and nature of the experience when an early
adolescent gazes at a painting in a visit to a museum? The overall answer
to these questions is that the student is engaged in some kind of symbolic
behavior. This kind of behavior is central to art education.

The processes of making art, the evaluation of one's own efforts and the
appreciation of some other artist's work are all rather complex happenings.
A number of elements went into the kindergarten drawing (p. 288) of the
balloon man for instance. The child was responding to the stimuli from the
environment, perhaps because he had actually seen the man carrying balloons, the teacher had read a story about such a character, or other imaginative internal associations occurred. The accumulation of memory traces in
addition were activated in the child's perceptual organization: how a
walking body looks, the shape of balloons, the delineation of grass and
flowers that had been previously seen. The child expressed the cultural
influences in regarding the scene and event as one that is generally approved
by his peers and his elder personal contacts, signifying fun, happiness and
play. The motivating guidance of the teacher was probably felt more indirectly as was the implementation of educational aims through creative

Art
and
Education
in
Contemporary
Culture

·

288

opportunities. But most important was the bringing together of perception, meaning, feeling and expression in one unified symbolic whole. The rubbery fullness, bright color, and soaring quality of the balloons, the smiling face and jaunty walk of the man, the animated grass field and the interested flowers, even the scribbled areas innately capture the sense of joy and excitement of the experience. The fundamental aspects of the experience are the spontaneously felt and the directly apprehended ones. The perceptions and the feelings of the occasion have been qualitatively transformed into sensuously visual symbols. The experience of the balloon man has been made vital and meaningful for the child, permitting an intensity of sentience and realization.

Any mature artist reflects a similar involvement with experience on a more sophisticated and profounder level. All art experiences provide the kind of opportunities through which imagination and awareness may operate, fulfilling a necessary human need. The process is intricate and complicated but the evidence that it produces, the actual symbols themselves are frequently organically unified in economical ways. The meaning, either implicit or explicit, has been integrated into the substance of symbols and it "comes across" to the alert and receptive creator or spectator.

This kind of activity is the usual one for the art class: the symbolic process synthesizing the component elements of creative and expressive experience. A realization of its workings and an appreciation of its pervasive influence is necessary to a personal understanding of productive and learning processes and may be considered a requisite to successful art teaching.

The Nonrational Attributes

Most education theorists stress the ordered, reasoned and intellectual aspects of education. As is pointed out elsewhere, our education is largely

Individual perception, meaning, feeling, and experience are expressed in unified visual symbols. "The Balloon Man," First Grade Drawing. [Ann Arbor Public Schools; PHOTO: Stuart Klipper]

a discursive one. The stress is on defining properties and on describing things and events. This is a recognized need, but not the only one man possesses. There are areas of culture and life which do not belong in the above categories, though they are common to all men. They are the uniquely human characteristics and activities that all too often have been ignored or blithely explained away in some sophistry of argument. There is the emotional and fantasy life of man, his "illogical" speculations that has led to magic, ritual, myth, a dream world, art and the like, all of which have only recently become the sources of serious study. The demonic, the incongruent, the imaginative and intuitive qualities have always characterized the sentience of man, perhaps even more than his logically reasoning attributes.

The experience of art is a direct symbolic means for children through which personal understanding of the self and the environment may be gained. University of Michigan Elementary Laboratory School [PHOTO: *University of Michigan News Service*]

> Any man deserving of the name
> Installed on the throne of his heart
> Has a yellow, querulous serpent
> He cannot still or tame.

As Baudelaire's poetry reveals, much as man may want to run from the supposedly primitive and oppressive aspects of these dark, hidden and disturbing factors, he cannot discount them and their motivations in the individual and their cumulative effects on culture. Emotion, either joyful or depressing, is central to the human condition and a part of its adventure with life. Sympathy, love, fear, hate, grief, ecstasy, anguish and eagerness are all of a piece with experience as are a host of other feelings.

It is these nonrational desires and acts of man that undo many of the

Art
and
Education
in
Contemporary
Culture

.

290

carefully plotted definitions that supposedly explain the logical reasons for his existence. Or at the very least, they do not permit an easily formulated philosophy; the answers are either deliberately limited, only partial in nature or are unknowingly thin and prejudiced. There are too many empty slots of meaning that, though ignored, have an insidious effect on a hard determinism derived from a blinkered and pragmatic scientism, a diversionary play of entertainment or concern with material qualities alone. Though there may be an emphasis on the logical propensities of man there is no successful hushing or taming of the emotional and imaginative "serpent" that all humans appear to harbor.

The child who painted the revealing, symbolic, happy-sad clown was engaged in expressing his immediate share of emotion, the melancholy as well as the delightful. He reinvented the visual configurations which are symbolically laden with the inner attributes of man and span a broad range from irrationality to deliberateness. The artistic symbol merges the thinking and feeling qualities. The elements of reason which attempt to order and evaluate the inconsistencies of human experience complementing the more hidden reservoirs of emotion and imagination during the process of transformation. Thus, the expressiveness and symbolic aspects of the artistic act are not just errant fancy, doodling or emotional outbursts. They develop and embody and finally synthesize in the art work the individual feelings and concepts that provide meaning for experience, permitting intrinsic satisfaction, further learning and profounder personal insight to occur.

The Inner Center

Certainly we cannot suppose that the most highly rational of animals, man, is that steeped in error and biologically irresponsible behavior that he acts counter to the categorized and adaptive needs of his species when he is emotionally involved or is moved by vague yet compelling inner forces. As Susanne Langer points out, "If a savage in his ignorance of physics tries to make a mountain open its caverns by dancing round it, we must admit that no rat in a psychologist's maze would try such patently ineffectual methods of opening a door." [1]

There are obviously other "reasons" for the seemingly strange and contradictory behavior. Nor is it the primitive and the so-called uncivilized societies, lower on the supposed ladder of progress, that alone are prey to irrational behavior. Those eccentric patterns of ritual and acts below the commonly agreed upon threshold of reason are a part of all of us. We all engage in errant daydreams, in inexplicable habits, and in foolish, yet compulsive conduct that appears to be knowingly ineffectual, if not outright contradictory in terms of rational survival.

Then too, the meaning of art, which possesses no obvious practical values, nevertheless, has been a constant action through all of man's history and a necessary one if we honestly examine archeology and history. In addition, there is a whole range of aberration from the rational such as dreams, blind and dangerous hostility, and childishly wishful thinking that belong to

[1] Susanne Langer, *Philosophy in a New Key* (New York: Pelican, 1948), p. 39.

The art work of children reflect emotional attitudes. "The Happy-Sad Clown," Second Grade Painting. [Ann Arbor Public Schools; PHOTO: David Churches]

man's nature and have not been exorcized through centuries of intellectual effort. A definition of man that disregards these factors cannot be considered a cornerstone in a mature philosophy, nor will there be a development of implication that can serve as a guide for secure and intelligent social action in any field, let alone education. The "total" child in an unsentimentalized and sophisticated version of this concept, his emotions and his aesthetic nature as well as his intellect, have to be considered in developing any creative teaching context. Successful art experiences are outgrowths of the full range of human qualities and of student attributes and potential, the nonrational as well as the rational.

The tremendous intellectual, aesthetic and social upheavals since the end of the eighteenth century and the accelerating rush of change so much a condition of contemporary living has set the mechanistic attitudes on end, proving to be like quicksand in swallowing the circumscribed theories that naively rest primarily on measurement. The hope of the Enlightenment, though noble and desirable, has not always extricated itself from the swampy, surrounding anti-intellectualism that confounded and twisted its rational humanism. The persistence and increasing intensities and barbarism of war, the clinically delving probes of science into mysterious and reason-disturbing areas, the testing ground image of political doctrine, the atom bomb and the almost desperate economic turmoil, the inhuman coldness of the machine and automation, the eroding influence of religion and institutionalized morality as well as the paradoxically ebullient surge of new and vital art expression in all media attest to the open-ended and symbolically bottomless collective human condition.

William Barrett, a contemporary philosopher notes,

. . . modern man seems even further from understanding himself than when he first began to question his own identity. Of documentation of external facts we have had enough and to spare; but of the inner facts, of what goes on at the

Art
and
Education
in
Contemporary
Culture

•

292

center where the forces of our fate first announce themselves, we are still pretty much in ignorance, and most of the contemporary world is caught up in an unconscious and gigantic conspiracy to run away from these facts.[2]

These facts include a concern beyond the practical achievements of a booming stock market, television, spaceships and suburban recreation rooms. The uneasy smugness of a self-satisfied materialism which sloughs off spiritual and aesthetic values and conscientiously sings hosannas of praise to the rational efficiency and technological superiority of modern man nevertheless lives on the edge of collapse. The "brink," both spiritually and actually is too often approached. It finds its counterpart in the educational programs which blandly half teach an almost arbitrary factual and sprawling curriculum in a defensive air of uncritical self justification. When reorientation in education appears, it too often either completely ignores or gives only passing acknowledgement to the center where the forces of our fate first announce themselves. That center is the nonrational core of man which also requires explication and expression.

An Inherent Gesture

Sigmund Freud in attempting a systematic formulation of human behavior and its philosophical import, took the irrational and the unconscious into consideration. Among his most important contributions was the recognition that human behavior was not only a response to adaptive needs, but "that every move is a gesture as well." This gesture of behavior is our personal image and expresses, not only the unconscious drives and ego demands, but exists for its own sake as well as an emblem of meaning. One of the prime conditions of behavior is the act of symbolizing, of providing meaning through the metaphoric tessera of which our personalities consist, which combine in individual patterns of understanding.

The insouciant and unconstrained figure on the ladder captures the carefree moment the child felt when he drew it. The sweep of the chalk, the bold lines, saucy look are symbolic gestures of behavior and personality. These characteristic elements of the experience operate well below the normal threshold at most times, making themselves felt when the opportunities for expression are afforded the individual and creative symbol making is encouraged. The art lesson is a natural educational means for this opportunity to be adequately developed, for the student to "act out" his feelings in a direct and approved way.

The great reservoirs of unconscious drive as well as the more precise stipulations of consciousness demonstrate in children as well as adults their compelling force in creating a resulting panoply of symbols. In order to more fully exploit the human potential this symbol making becomes, in a sense, a language. This language communicates, advises, enlightens, and gives form to the innate tensions that will probably always plague anyone who descended from the first audacious and bumptious pair who tasted the fruit of the tree of knowledge. The language is a rich and fertile one, not

[2] William Barrett, *Irrational Man* (New York: Doubleday Anchor Books, 1962), p. 23.

*Children's art work
serves as expressive
and aesthetic gestures
of behavior. "I'm
Climbing," Second
Grade Drawing. [Ann
Arbor Public Schools;
PHOTO: Stephen C.
Sumner]*

limited by its discursive elements: by words alone. Actually, it becomes the affective means through which an individual grasps and creates his own recognition of self as well as interpreting the surrounding environment; it lays the groundwork for the rational process as well as for the feeling ones. Man is a symbol-making animal and it is this characteristic that separates him from his cousins in the field, permitting him the intense awareness that stems from art. Properly guided, the student may then "invent" his own world, seemingly a necessary contemporary condition.

THE RANGE OF EDUCATIONAL RESPONSIBILITY TO THE STUDENT

Education has to take into consideration the nonrational and unconscious factors of human processes. For in not doing so the result is not only an imbalance of individual growth, but an impotent and insensitive interaction with the environment on the part of the student. The obvious stress on practicality and latent vocationalism in the average school reflects this one-sidedness while many of the mass conditions of contemporary living seem to abort or twist some of the inherent strivings of man in not providing genuine channels of other than materialistic expression. A pseudo art education or a superficial one cannot alleviate or modify this condition in any significant way and is as much a disaster as the complete absence of art teaching.

Art
and
Education
in
Contemporary
Culture

·

294

The emotional sources inherent in all persons, that which stimulates the imagination and gives rise to intuitive insights requires various and differing channels of authentic expression and personal commitment. This does not argue for the blundering or self-congratulating quality of "life adjustment." The answer similarly does not lies in downgrading the intellectual disciplines or in institutionalizing the oversimplified social conformity and practicality of mass values. It merely points to the additional and inescapable need in education of taking into consideration the emotional and nonrational human properties through vital, inclusive, and appropriate teaching contexts. Education may then be an even more complex procedure but it has to develop appropriate opportunities through which the imagination may be permitted to exercise its formative powers to symbolize experience directly as well as abstractly. In planning such curricular opportunities, educators are compelled to introduce and expand the humanities: art, music, literature and any of the other imaginative channels by which the nonrational propensities find expression. The student's attention and commitment are those of sharing rich imaginative constructions with those of the more intellectually logical and ordered structure. But both stem from the common base of being symbolic responses to the conditions of living.

More important, the implementation of these inclusive aims must rest with teachers who are themselves caught up in the invigorating and full span of intellectual and emotional symbolizing. Art education is fully dependent upon the direct relationship art teachers develop with students in their teaching dialogue and in the degree of intensity and understanding of the aesthetic and creative processes through which they instruct and influence students, based on personal involvement with the arts.

The average boy or girl will find their own way to expression and symbolically transforming experiences simply because of their human propensities. However, these are likely to be aimless, partial and narrow, or skewed to the cursory tinseled delights of mass cultural influence and subject to the constraints of a pervading conformity without a teacher's sympathetic and knowing guidance. The quality of the motivation, the pedagogical and aesthetic insight, the example that all teachers provide in their own personally developed ways are essential factors in providing legitimate, emotionally charged, aesthetically evaluated, and intelligently perceived experiences in art. In order to assist the indiivdual student to intensly explore the creative media and relate enthusiastically and sensitively to the art materials with which will be shaped the symbols of expression and the personally creative realization of the world, the teacher of art is required to search out his own meanings. In a position to influentially teach through them, he acts as the prism through which students may honestly experience aesthetic and humanistic values. To this end an enriched realization and natural partaking of the symbolic processes is an invaluable and necessary condition. These necessarily include an understanding of the pain, suffering and frustration which may be an integral condition of experience and expression as much as fun, discovery and manipulative success. Art teaching itself may be considered to take on a quality of gesture in a

*Art and play offer
enthusiastic oppor-
tunities for classroom
expressiveness.*
[PHOTO: *Pearl Green-
berg*]

fully developed implementation of the range of human emotional and intellectual potential.

THE SYMBOL AS MEANING

A symbol may be called an image or a design that has significance. The significance is determined by the uses, normally in a manner that goes much beyond what is superficially present in the image or design especially in artistic symbols and as Susanne Langer tentatively defines it, "any device whereby we make an abstraction is a symbolic element, and all abstraction involves symbolization." [3] In this sense abstraction is to be considered as any level of mental power to form ideas. This may further indicate that a symbol could be a concrete transformation of thought and feeling ranging from a single letter, a geometric figure, or an object such as a flag to a very complete pattern of parts such as a mathematical equation, a painting or a document of law. The object or pattern achieves its symbolic nature by acting upon the perceptual screen of the receiver, causing some manner of effect, no matter what the reason may be, that is beyond the mere literal recognition of the presented form in the case of the person creating the symbol. The perceptions, feelings and conceptions about particular personal experiences are brought together to form some concrete pattern: an image, a word structure, a combination of sounds or movements, and so on.

A particular significance emerges from this behavior of thinking and

[3] Susanne Langer, *Philosophical Sketches* (Baltimore: Johns Hopkins Press, 1962), p. 63.

Art
and
Education
in
Contemporary
Culture

·

296

doing. Any child in creating a drawing is accomplishing this. As a further example, a person may respond with patriotic emotion to a piece of cloth that has alternating red and white stripes with a blue rectangle in one corner overlaid with fifty white stars. However, the individual would have to possess particular cultural backgrounds in order be so affected patriotically; the culture would be American obviously, and the flag would have many connotations beyond the simple geometric pattern of shapes and colors. In fact, a symbol once removed so to speak, a photograph of the flag as it was draped around Kennedy's coffin, or flying half mast or proudly unfurled from the mast of a battleship have become almost holy images for many Americans. Yet there are other humans, citizens of foreign nations, who would not respond to the symbol of the American flag in a similar manner, so that symbolic meaning is very much open to interpretation.

We can take the example of two straight lines crossing one another perpendicularly. They may suggest that X marks the spot, or they may be part of a doodle drawn during an idle moment. As a young child's scribble the crossed lines may be representative of kinesthetic impulses and as any of these they have little symbolic value beyond what they seem to be. However, for the child the lines may also have some very specific internal conceptual value connoting a base of support or of psychological rejection. Conversely in mathematics the lines become a fixed quality with very precise denotations. A priest or a minister making the right angle configuration of a cross has yet another profound and diverse series of meanings, while the individual members of a congregation have their uniquely personal responses of an emotional, spiritual, and intellectual nature to the cross. In all of these examples the actual object of pattern of behavior may be perceived superficially as the surrogate for something else. Actually the symbol is charged with personal meaning directly embodying the conception and the feeling the individual has formed about an experience. The symbolic nature of individually human processes of perceptual response takes over, going beyond simple recognition or proxy understanding, complementing the presentational immediacy of sensory data.

A Prelude to Thought

This has tremendously important implications for educational theory. If the symbolic process is as fundamental and pervasive as it appears to be then much of learning and comprehension must stem from this process and center of human understanding. Langer, who has formulated a relatively new approach to philosophy based on symbolic values goes so far as to say, "As a matter of fact, it is not the essential act of thought that is symbolization, but an act *essential to thought*, and prior to it." [4] She goes on to say that symbolization is the essential act of mind, mind taking in more than mere discursive reasoning. In this view, the mind has a basic store of symbols (experience responses), and continuously engages in primary acts of symbolization even if there is no resultant use of the material. Yet this trans-

[4] Susanne Langer, *Philosophy in a New Key* (New York: Penguin Books, 1948), p. 33.

forming process is as necessary to reason as it is to aesthetic understanding, it seems to be the creative human matrix from which meaning emerges. All of our experiences are like grist for the mill, the mind performing its function of metamorphosis, not in any easy mechanical fashion but by some, as yet mysterious inner transforming capacity, so that the experience when it becomes a part of our personality has assumed symbolically oriented meaning. The process has a very natural development in artistic activity or appreciation.

Intrinsic Developmental Features

For the child, the process in art is at first a limited and loosely developmental one, then a fluid and changing one as the complexities of growing up occur and experience is broadened. The developmental making of art work may be likened to the emergence of coherent speech patterns that combine words to make some sort of communicative sense. As in speech, after the repertory of available sensory possibilities has been expanded and explored through practice, the pictorial images acquire a level of symbol communication. The energy reserves of the child and the store of preconscious imagery permit an immense expenditure of thought, feeling and deliberate action resulting in combinations of visual form. The resulting meaning incorporated in the art processes not only develops a sense of achievement but makes the thinking and feeling more intelligible in itself.

Once the dynamic and spontaneous form making is accomplished the child engages in symbolic experimentation that follows an uncertain spiral of refinement, elaboration and attention to detail. It is exuberant and highly inventive at points. At other times it is emotionally inhibited and intellectually constrained. Yet, if the teaching is positive, there could be a general progression towards a wide symbolic responsiveness in adolescence. This may be creative, involved with mature and authentic symbolic visions either in direct personal forming of materials or in active appreciation of the great works of art. The latter may be a vicarious symbolic experience, but it is a genuinely transforming one, nevertheless, when it is recreative.

At any level, it may be argued, and with any degree of responsiveness to experience, open or constrained, the student is symbolizing his experiences. This provides an innate channel of meaning as well as of learning and appears to be an inescapable relationship if that learning is to occur. Susanne Langer emphasizes this in, "The symbol-making function is one of man's primary activities, like eating, looking or moving about. It is the fundamental process of his mind and goes on all the time. Sometimes we are aware of it, sometimes we merely find its results, and realize that certain experiences have passed through our brains and have been digested there." [5]

A Ubiquitous Process

For example, if we consider the dimensional concepts of time and space, we can begin to sense the significance and the pervasiveness of the symbolic structure. Though in considering time there may be a nonserial order in the

[5] Susanne Langer, *ibid.*, p. 32.

Art
and
Education
in
Contemporary
Culture

·

298

universe that moves without sequence, disregarding human events, a constant stream of happening that is never ending, it is necessary for us to symbolically construct a past, a present, and a future if we are to assess our actions and not exist in some limbo of timelessness or constantly surging time. The memory of the past and the anticipation of the future become creative ideations that symbolically inform us of the quality of the particular event, place or object we are considering. We recreate the past, not simply through a collection of unrelated memories, but by means of synthesizing and relating pertinent elements of remembrance into a limited or focal order. The future is also conceived of as a condition that is symbolically antecedent of itself in the present, just as the past is also part of the here and now.

Similarly, space exists on a variety of levels for the human mind. In addition to the concrete and pragmatic space in which man acts, in which he walks or runs, flies a plane or shoots a rifle at a target there is the space of geometry. Man experiences the abstract structure of mathematics, symbolically containing an inherently human interpretive construction of the cosmos and its spatial elements. The artist, in a like manner, creates a variety of spatial orders ranging from the geometrically conceived laws of perspective, to the color and plane interrelationships that Cézanne pursued or to the "no space" of much of contemporary art. The child expresses the sense of space in art in a variety of ways: creating base lines, putting a line of sky on top of the picture plane, because sky is "up," "folding over" figures so that right and left or up and down are not in visual perspective, placing figures in 180 degree relationship to one another rather than, for instance, putting a figure at right angles to the ground he is resting on. The child's conception of space may stem more from internal "knowing" than from reasoning out the proper abstract perspective relationships.

So humans experience even something as basic as time and space through the symbolic patterns of experiential organization. The long happy day that is compressed into the fleeting feeling of a moment is as real as the actually short but psychologically anguished minutes before an unpleasantness that stretch on interminably. The navigational charts of an astronaut has the same spatial validity for us as the bull pen where a pitcher is throwing a ball. The stream of consciousness that Faulkner, Joyce, or Proust use in their novels creates its own time shuttling between today, yesterday and tomorrow while the historians conceive of an ordered progression of dates and events.

Some modern sculpture has denied volume as a measurement of space, utilizing interpenetrating planes and space itself, such as the holes in Henry Moore's sculpture to articulate the movement of the sculpted forms. The space of Dante's *Divine Comedy* with its nine levels of hell is no physically experienced space, nor is the Heaven of Christians, the Paradise of the Muslims, and the Nirvana of the Eastern mystics. They are artificially constructed domains which nevertheless have a sense of reality for the play of the imagination. Each experience exists not as a simple manifestation of a physical world but as a functional way of symbolizing human perception and realization, thus achieving a level of meaning. There is the perceptual space of physiological optics, the physical construction of the world; there is the abstract space of mathematical formula, the navigator's chart or the scientist's graph and there is organic space, which the mythical imagination, art and poetry appear to symbolically form, that of a painting's illusion or the locale of a myth. Time is, in a like manner, open to a variety of interpretive conceptualizations and it is only in a symbolic sense that we grasp the significance of any of these fundamental conditions.

The functional mechanism of behavior that makes this possible is worth a very brief comment. All animals other than man have a highly developed receptor system that triggers an almost instantaneous effector system. Animals react instinctively to a stimulus. Even when they do not as in laboratory experiments they evidence no more than the most rudimentary aspects of interpretive intelligence with no real qualities of imagination. There is a practical cast of mind in the animal that essentially responds to signs and signals but never really in a symbolic context.

The human mind, on the other hand, has developed an inhibiting arrangement between the receiving of sense material and a reaction to it as well as an imaginative, projecting quality. There is probably a neurophysiological base for this in the synaptic relay of messages in the brain. However, this is not our concern here. What is important though, is the recognition of this innately human power that may be called the symbolic system. Man does not, in a biological and cognitive sense, react instinctively to his environment and the stimuli found there. He stops, thinks, judges, weighs, and counterbalances the choices that become consciously apparent or that he unconsciously and symbolically devises. He is *instinctively symbolic*. His way of knowing is dependent upon the symbol-making powers he possesses. His picture of the world, his manner of reaction to it are determined by this inherent biological inhibition that activates the fluent symbolic screen in his mind. The screen has developed all of the varied strains of knowledge, each a prism through which man experiences a truth and a reality that is necessarily relative, or at least, of multiple dimensions.

History, science, language, religion, myth and art are all symbol systems that reflect the vast range of the human mind. In developing these areas man enlarges upon his imagination, upon his wholesome expectations and his anxiety ridden dread of the unknown, his illusions, fancies, dreams and his involvement with his own emotions. There is no easy and physically instinctual relationship with nature, not actual face to face confrontation without an in-between quality of interpreting the occasion in terms of human meaning.

No longer in a merely physical universe, man lives in a symbolic universe. . . . Physical reality seems to recede in proportion as man's symbolic activity advances. Instead of dealing with things themselves man is in a sense constantly conversing with himself. He has so enveloped himself in linguistic forms, in artistic images, in mythical symbols or religious rites that he cannot see or know

Art
and
Education
in
Contemporary
Culture

.

300

anything except by the interposition of this artificial meaning (symbolic trans-formation).[6]

This is a fundamental tenet in the philosophy of symbolic forms. If the preceding factors justify this attitude, then the symbolizing process does indeed pervade all of man's responses to existence.

THE TRANSFORMING EXPERIENCE IN ART EDUCATION

This concept has profound ramifications for all of education and is espe-cially pertinent in art education. To reiterate, symbolizing occurs with or without the teacher's cognizance and insight, though the latter are essential and a condition to forming student art experiences that are to develop to maturity. The art teacher has to be aware of and cater to the intricacies and nuances of symbolic processes. This could assist students not only to crea-tively order their experiences but also to keep in touch with the vitally sentient qualities that induce broader horizons and an intensity of per-sonally significant values. The symbolizing process has to be more than instrumental; it also has to be aesthetic and self sufficient in art education. The following joke may stress even further the innate human faculty of symbolic comprehension of experience, aesthetic or otherwise.

A man approached a young mother who had an infant in a carriage. He said, "What a lovely boy you have." The mother was pleased with the com-pliment, but added in a characteristic human fashion, "But you should see his picture!" In a peculiar way the picture, a symbolic image of the good looks of the child, had more significance and perhaps a greater reality (because it had been interpreted into symbolic form) than the actual flesh and blood boy in the carriage. This may be pushing the concept too much but it does communicate the strength of the symbolic drive in humans. Oscar Wilde's comment, "Life follows art" may also be considered in this regard as an insight into the primacy of the symbolic process.

In any case, the student who is producing symbols as art forms is in-volved in a fundamental and personally enlightening activity. The meaning or quality of awareness that is being created is based upon a number of mental and sensory functionings, as we have seen. These bring past mem-ories, present perception, varied stimuli, skill in material handling and various and sundry manipulative processes into play. Relationships have to be established. Fluency of thought and flexibility of imagery as well as internalized value orientations are tied together. They operate parallel to the ability to improvise, to make associations and to shape forms into necessary configurations of sensory units. The rich storehouse and dynamic activity of the preconscious mind is activated providing a many dimen-sioned approach to experience. The experience that is being transformed is further eliciting conceptions that will find their values symbolically vested in the imagery of the art work, adding to the student's sensibility, replenishing the store of images and intensifying that experience into a

[6] Ernst Cassirer, *An Essay on Man* (New Haven: Yale University Press, 1944), p. 25.

unique pattern that may become the basis of mature personality and productive development.

The process is essentially metaphoric as is the resulting form in that there is no direct transposition of experience to symbol. Though the artistic activity may be spontaneous, it is also one that sifts the elements through a blend of human functions: emotional feeling, intellectual ordering, enumerative combining, associative structuring, imaginative projection and finally, aesthetic composing. The latter is no mere arranging of colors, lines, textures, shapes and light values, but is an organic handling of the art elements. The aesthetic composing transcends mere placement and adjustment of parts in that it integrates the elements through the personal vision of the student. It takes on all the qualities of conception and, in fact, is one in visual form. Similarly, the other functions have a fluent organic base. These are involved with the imaginative elements of the mind and the feeling aspects of the personality, both of which reach out to the fantasy rich periphery of perception. The considerations of an experience thus have an expanded scope from which to create their measures, pushing and pulling the perceptions with new associations and suggestive possibilities that assume metaphoric insights and forms.

The picture of the train bumping along on its travels is an example of a child's natural visual conception. It brings together the experiences of the child with one of the popular objects of childhood—a "choo-choo" train. He has uncovered a mode of expression that can reveal his feelings and thoughts about railroading, trains and their way of travelling. Like the mother who referred to the picture of her child in order to vividly experience his good looks, the child in painting the train scene is interposing the symbolic act in order to more fully, and actually, realize the experience and feeling of trains. The individual images of trains, tracks, tree, telephone

A child's art work provides a means whereby the significance of experience— both of a thinking and feeling quality— may be combined in symbolic form. "Alan's Train," Second Grade Painting. [Courtesy of Alan Kaufman; PHOTO: Stuart Klipper]

Art
and
Education
in
Contemporary
Culture

·

302

pole, smoke, sky, sun and the scribbles of motion are symbolic resolutions of the child's intent, the actualized purpose of his activity. These have an aesthetic and sensuous connection with the art materials that are employed and the way they are handled. The scene is of a favorable disposition. The train with the artist sitting atop the first car merrily chugs its way across a childishly pleasant firmament against which the striking and vigorously symbolized countryside pattern of trees and poles are silhouetted while a benign sun shines down its approval. The brush motions, the fullness or leanness of the masses, the intensity of color are all bound up in the process.

What emerges is the symbolically visual image. It has caught the meaning of the child's thinking and feeling experience. Without the painting or the opportunity of concrete expression, the experience would probably have remained vague and formless, even in the excited mind of the child. The painting, however, provides a visual metaphor, concentrating a number of otherwise diverse qualities into a single intelligible unit. The symbolic processes have mediated between the physical world and the mind of the student.

DISTINCTIONS BETWEEN SIGN AND SYMBOLS

Meaning is, nevertheless, a complex and frequently an inexpressible quality in any too simple terms. The range of meaning seems to stretch like a gigantic rubber band. On one end is the literal and predetermined understanding that is so imbedded in our understanding that it is practically instinctual: crossing on a green light, stopping on red; on the other end, is the almost ineffable and profound interrelationship with a work of art, or the myriad satisfactions of love. Actually, the metaphor of a rubber band is not completely appropriate, for the distinctions between these end ranges of meaning is not one of degree but rather one of kind. It is the distinction that has to be made between signs and symbols.

A sign must have a physical or actual equivalent, while a symbol, though it may have particular denotations, is always a conceptual construction, as well that involves connotations of words and objects, metaphoric associations over and beyond their literal aspects. A sign is somewhat like an equation. On the left side is the sign itself: this equals the thing it stands for on the right side of the equation. A symbol has no such easy balance and cannot be reduced to such a simple formula. A patch of sunlight on the front porch is a sign that the sun is shining; a crocus coming through the snow is a sign of spring; an acrid odor is often a sign of something burning while a full stomach signifies that a meal has been eaten. These are natural signs and not much different from the artificial ones that man devises, such as a blazed tree being a sign for a Boy Scout that he is on the correct trail, a horn blaring that tells us to get out of the way of a car, of a traffic light turning red that is a sign to stop.

Pavlov in his famous experiment had dogs salivating in response to bells, conditioning the animals to respond to a sign denoting food that was not a natural sign associated with eating. In each of these instances the com-

mon factor is the one to one relationship between the sign and the existence of the thing, condition or event it signifies. This one to one relationship is not really an equal equation though; the sign and the object it
denotes, whether it be an idea or an act, are not simply interchangeable.
What is necessary is the interpreter: anyone acting as subject who jiggles
the equation on the basis of interest and availability.

Take, for instance, the red light: its availability at the proper time and
place is of interest, not in terms of itself, its shape, color and general appearance, but rather in terms of the action that will almost instinctually
or conditionally happen—stopping on the curb before being hit by a moving vehicle. The sign itself is easily available, more so than the object
which requires something to happen. The denoted object, too, is of more
interest—of greater importance than the sign itself, for the sign is merely
a neutral indication with no real intrinsic value. It has value primarily as
signification of something else which is of more immediate or necessary
concern.

This correlation of comparatively simple objects with more important
interests and their interpretation serves as the principal component of
animal intelligence. It is on this level that we share similar intellectual
behavior with the other animals. Our everyday activities are a countless
number of responses to signs and form the meaning of our common
purposes. However, just as Pavlov's dogs were conditioned to accept a
mistake in signs, so are humans liable to error. The conditioning, though,
may not be an outcome unless it is sufficiently and deliberately planned,
and this is always questionable in terms of human behavior. However,
error persists and is particularly evident when signs are artificial and a
multitude of meaning may be ascribed to them.

Like Langer we can use the example of the world gone mad with the
messages of bells. They can announce someone at the front or rear or side
door, the telephone rings its summons while a similar bell often informs
us of a period change in school. Bells toll us to church and wake us in the
morning, they warn us of fire and alert us of the end of a typed line. They
tinkle and toll, ring and boom; no wonder we are prone to error in the
cacophony! Yet we manage to disentangle the befuddling flood of signs
that society insidiously perpetrates or nature lavishly signals, to focus behavior into something that approximates purpose and order. When the
misinterpretation becomes too constant or serious in consequences, when
the margin of error is too pronounced, the mental institution, or other
disappointment and tragedy await. This is even more so true when a confusion exists between sign and symbol, when the latter is accepted too
easily for the former. Yet this margin of error is also the basis of the
ambiguity that permits us to respond to the illusions of representational art.

Connotative Awareness

It may be more appropriate to indicate that thinking is carried out on
two levels of symbolic transformation, one complementing the other. On
one level language is precise; it is as objective as it can be, translating ex-

Art
and
Education
in
Contemporary
Culture

•

304

perience and communicating it as a definite idea or as a signal, in specific terms from one mind to another. Phoning in an order for food, a teacher explaining a mathematical process, or an army drill sergeant giving directions for a physical exercise are examples of this thinking, while the formulas of science are even more precise means of denotation. However, there is another level of thinking that is not precise at all. This thinking is involved with impressions, images and associations that stem not only from words but from forms, movements, colors and other sensuous data. The manner in which a word is spoken, the kind of light that surrounds an object or the myriad tones and conditions that color a perception have an immediate significance, a personal set of connotations that provide a particular but not a precise meaning. Usually the connotations of this kind of thinking are unconscious, they are developed from an inner source. What is important is not the classifying of the experience but the realization that a good part of any individual's understanding derives from the latter area of rather inexact thinking and intuitive awareness. Most of the fundamental relationships that develop based on cognition are of a connotative kind, bathed in individual associations and suggestive symbolism. The scientifically specific and hard headed meanings are only a small portion of this human understanding, the thin skin that covers the less precise but still innately human ways of thinking. It is also important to sense that the latter is as much a way of thinking, of generating an idea as is the former, simply not doing it in verbally defined terms. It is toward this kind of thinking and of expressive gesture that art education addresses itself.

QUALITATIVE DIFFERENCES IN VISUAL IMAGES

Actually many of the artistic efforts of students may frequently be considered no more than signs, despite the symbolic activity that ostensibly went into their creation. The various stereotyped schemata that younger children develop are attempts for the moment, to fix a one to one relationship between the visual image and that which it is supposed to stand for: the rectangular box body, the oval egg head, the stick arms, the familiar house with smoking chimney and the sun with its everpresent rays. Still, these also evidence wide variety among children even if they share gross characteristics. When the various schemata are put into combinations, though, the simple equations of form and experience are surpassed and a viable fluent symbolism is seen. As the child imbibes of a greater variety of outside impressions and as the manual and associational dexterity increases, the constraining "picture sign" language is left behind. It is only in the emotionally disturbed and mentally retarded, in the neurotic and psychotic individuals, that rigid forms are repeatedly utilized in attempts at visual expression.

Signs and symbols are both necessary elements in human activity and both act as guides to the kind of responses the individual will make. Consequently, in the large scope of visual language, signs as well as symbols are utilized frequently, such as in architectural drawings, scientific diagrams,

The distinctions
between signs and
symbols are impor-
tant in education
and in art.

[TOP]
Alcoa Sign. [Alu-
minum Company of
America; PHOTO:
Newman Schmidt]

[CENTER]
"The Barber Shop."
[Collection, The Uni-
versity of Michigan
Museum of Art;
PHOTO: Stuart Davis]

[BOTTOM]
Ursine Park. [Collec-
tion, IBM; PHOTO:
Stuart Davis]

Art
and
Education
in
Contemporary
Culture

·

306

store placards and in much of advertising (lettering, corporation designations, brand emblems). Interpretation is of a narrow kind, even when advertising hopes to inculcate feelings that are only contrived rather than actual. The meanings are almost signalled to the observer and meant to do so by the creator. The images of art go much beyond this process, possessing innumerable connotations, inviting varied and particularly individual responses and interpretations. Though the art image may possess a commonly agreed upon concept, that concept is internalized by the observer with his own personal understanding. This operates for the creator as well, and begins to explain why it is accepted by critics that artists are frequently unaware of all the import and range of significance that their own symbols possess. The pictures on page 305 offer further clarification.

The Alcoa billboard is a visual sign that transmits its message direct and clear despite the abstract forms. In fact, they stand for the light tensile strength that aluminum is supposed to possess. There is little else that may be gleaned in the way of meaning from the sign, particularly after relating to the caption underneath.

The painting of Stuart Davis, "The Barbershop" despite the many signs it incorporates provides a symbolic experience. It possesses a wealth of possibilities as to how it may be interpreted. Its multileveled meaning is openly suggestive of many conditions and qualities; as such it is a symbolic image of an urban scene. Davis carries this range of visual interpretation onto a more abstract level in his work, "Ursine Park." The symbolism is even more fluid in its possibilities though it may be more intense and pointed in its use of artistic elements that find their sources in artificial landscape.

The Alcoa sign and the Davis paintings are all appropriate visualizations and serve their separate purposes well. However, the billboard is primarily a sign denoting information no matter how "arty" it is, the works by Davis are art and are interpretive creations. What is of importance is that the distinctions between them be understood and their differing purposes clearly accepted. This insight is essential in the art class. Teachers have to point it up to students during their expressive activities. They have to comprehend the different thinking and feeling involved in each of the cases, setting the stage for the appropriate kinds of student responses. Rather basic formations of value are involved.

The cultural extensions of this attitude lie in the distinctions that have to be made between the popular visual signs of advertising, cliché illustration, slick commercial design, eye catching novelties, spoon-fed or predigested art appreciation, and the genuine aesthetic symbols of art in painting, sculpture, architecture, and in those other visual areas that may excite us through their expressive forms such as photography, films, various crafts, and in the successful objects of industrial design. The proper province of art education lies with the unquestionable aesthetic grouping rather than the former with its spurious counterpart. Similarly, the activities in art classes should be guided into authentic symbolic directions rather than into cursory diversion with the signs of the times or their thin and tinsel-like, showy, pseudo pedagogical substitutes. The experience should be one of exploring the possibilities of individual interpretation, of discovering the uniquely personal meanings that experience possesses for the student. An apt transformation of this quality into concrete, felt and sensuous symbols rendering the openended meanings accessible to communicative form is the very stuff of art. It is quite distinguishable from the indifferent or derived forms that are contrived in shallow art teaching, where even the sense of plagiarism is somehow accepted as properly creative, an easy "in."

The examples of the horse drawings may point this up with greater clarity. The mimeographed horse is a bland, saccharine-pretty, conventionalized delineation of shape—more a vapid, adult imposed image, tediously and uninterestingly derived, without any of the animated, spirited qualities that drawings of horses should possess. The double horses of the child's drawing, on the other hand, are vital, awakening and maintaining a curiosity, animated in their expression and singularly experienced with a wealth of internal discovery of form and sensuous relationships, despite the improper proportion and the structural awkwardness. The mimeographed horses elicit a signal response, drastically narrowing the discovery potential of the student. When completed it is merely the confined image that doesn't even add up to a good sign. It actually may even confuse the child who colors in the shape because he is led deviously to believe that he created the image. The entire process is a dependent one.

The child who was encouraged to seek out his own expression may have had some difficult expressive hurdles but his independence was stressed. The impulses that lead to expressive activity require a free rein, the controls exercised by the searching aspects and the internal comprehension of the student involved, not by the predetermined and arbitrary correctness imposed from the outside. Though there are elements of the external stimuli that require a congruent rendering, these have to be achieved creatively by the child, the teacher guiding the process, not deliberately directing or constraining it. This has to remain in effect on all levels though the degree of sophistication of method and understanding increases in the higher grades and secondary levels. Art experiences may then aim for creation and appreciation of genuinely aesthetic symbols vitally expressive as well as communicative.

The Vitality of Myth

The symbolic area of myth may be used as an example that has a great deal to offer all educators, not only those that teach art. Ernst Cassirer did some of his most original thinking in his critique of mythical thinking. He demonstrates how its forms, its material and its own inner logic was a way in which primitive man explicated the world. Myth created an immense series of symbolic ideas and objects that developed a fundamental conceptualization which colored his actions and his understanding. However, it was not only primitive man who engaged in myth-making. It is a process which is still very much in evidence in the modern consciousness, and its forms are found in every human endeavor.

Art
and
Education
in
Contemporary
Culture

·

308

The distinctions
between the free and
independent forms of
the child's drawing
and the stereo-
typed adult image of
the mimeographed
drawing should be
obvious to everyone.
Picasso's work dem-
onstrates the search-
ing out process that
is followed by a
master.

[TOP]
"Mimeographed
Horse from Work-
book"

[CENTER]
"Knights on Horses,"
First Grade Drawing.
[Courtesy, Margo
Flower]

[BOTTOM]
"Horse," Pablo
Picasso. [Collection,
The University of
Michigan Museum of
Art]

The men who are often elevated to greatness in our political life are generally mythical figures, the restrictions and taboos that have been established around sexual and social behavior have a mythical quality, while many of the sports activities have developed the aura of mythical contests. Certainly, the thinking of young children and students in the primary grades has an affinity for mythmaking, while the social and emotional activities of many adolescents are reminiscent of mythopoeic behavior.

The important distinction to be recognized in mythical thinking is that it taps certain fundamental roots of awareness that are perhaps contrary to the currently overdeveloped emphasis on objectivity. Cassirer makes the point,

What is characteristic of primitive mentality is not its logic but its general sentiment of life. Primitive man does not look at nature with the eyes of a naturalist who wishes to classify things in order to satisfy an intellectual curiosity. He

Contemporary art has fertile associations with mythical viewpoints. "The She-Wolf," Jackson Pollock. [Collection, The Museum of Modern Art, New York; PHOTO: The Museum of Modern Art]

does not approach it with merely pragmatic or technical interest. It is for him neither a mere object of knowledge nor the field of his immediate practical needs. We are in the habit of dividing our life into the two spheres of practical and theoretical activity. In this division we are prone to forget that there is a lower stratum beneath them both. Primitive man is not liable to such forgetfulness. All his thoughts and his feelings are still embedded in this lower original stratum. His view of nature is neither merely the theoretical nor merely practical; it is *sympathetic*.[7]

Though the contemporary individual is not totally imbued with this sympathetic attitude like his forebears, he still retains a fundamental concern along these lines. The theoretical and pragmatic involvements that overwhelm this empathetic regard with one's environment are stressed in

[7] Ernst Cassirer, *Philosophy of Symbolic Forms* (New Haven: Yale University Press, 1953), p. 82.

Art
and
Education
in
Contemporary
Culture

•

310

Fraternity initiation rights are among the aspects of modern living that possess strong elements of myth. Psychologically, they share with art a symbolic means of expression. [PHOTO: *University of Michigan News Service*]

education and in the normal business of living. However, the sympathetic core manifests itself in a variety of guises when it is repressed; the examples mentioned earlier are some indications of this. The mythical perception in its primitive environment is one of emotion, responding to the actions, forces and conflicting powers of a world that is dramatic. "Whatever is seen or felt is surrounded by a special atmosphere—an atmosphere of joy or grief, of anguish, of excitement, of exaltation or depression" [8] Everything that exists, objects and happenings have a good or bad quality, they are either of positive value or they threaten existence. They are either familiar and friendly or foreign and hostile. Even today an individual who is under a strong emotional strain will tend to respond with a similar dramatic conception to the things that happen to be around during the experience. They take on the character of the particular passions that rule the individual at the moment.

Cassirer suggests that this response may be called a physiognomic one. That is, the mind that is mythically impregnated does not objectify the conditions of nature or of its environment seeking general laws; it "sees" things as specific, immediate, and in terms of their outward appearances. Yet, though the rise of science has generally superseded mythical perception, putting a statistical or empirical truth in its place, the quality of the experience, which antedates the scientific is still very much a part of a human orientation to experience, especially through art.

[8] Ernst Cassirer, *ibid.*, pp. 76–77.

Mythical Elements in Children's Art

Children give every evidence of engaging in such perceptions, particularly in their art work. In the drawing of the lion behind bars the young child has perceived all of the bulk and the essential form of the animal. It is a big shape and is placed properly within the picture's plane. However, the animal's presence is not a looming, ferocious or menacing one. In fact the facial features appear to be human. The young artist is extending his feelings toward the animal, perhaps even identifying with it on some mysterious level. But all of this is symbolically captured, probably, because the conceptual perception of the bars separating the lion from the child permits the latter to feel safe. The symbolic lines offer security from the otherwise frightening aspects of the caged king of beasts. The immediately real aspects of the perception and transforming experience are sensed in this instance, the particular atmosphere coloring the symbol forming. This does not necessarily express the limitations of the child's mind at the time of the drawing (he knows of the lion's ferociousness) rather, it mythically projects the extensions of the young mind into creative and alternative expressive possibilities. Here the kinship with the primitive is strongly felt.

The exquisite and charming work by a junior high girl (p. 213) is a more sophisticated example, evidencing some elements of mythical thinking. This sympathetic regard of perceptual stimuli permits the student to go beyond the confines of descriptive drawing. With cleverly organized patterns, pleasing repetitions and subtle improvisations of designed forms which have only large references to any "real" situations, the work of art offers an exceedingly expressive and poetic quality. It conjures up grace and rhythm, the hair suggestive of esoteric concerns that may have a ritualistic

Children's art work frequently reflect basic mythological qualities. "Lion Behind Bars," First Grade Painting. [Ann Arbor Public Schools; PHOTO: Stuart Klipper]

Art
and
Education
in
Contemporary
Culture

.

312

base in their shapes. Though the imagery goes beyond the immediate in suggesting a timeless context, despite the conventionalized relationships the action appears real and capable of happening, being arrested for the moment only. The entire work evokes a level of symbolic understanding that goes beyond ordinary experiences in order to better interpret them as well as to provide the creator with a felt expressive satisfaction. It is not only in the approach to symbolic activity, but in the content of school art that myth also finds ready avenues of expression.

Actually, all of art partakes of this sympathetic regard of things, no matter what level it is created on. Its initial and actual impetus is to be involved with physically concrete factors, the red of a cloth, the brilliance of the sun, the hairiness of an animal body, the softness of a brush or the fluid spread of paint. The thing to be symbolized possesses actual qualities as do the materials that will be utilized. Even when the work is abstract the artist cannot escape the sensuous nature of the materials he is using.

Consequently, it would seem that teachers can examine the relationships that do exist between expressive behavior and the symbolically mythic tendencies of humans. The insights gained may prove of more than passing interest to the teaching of art, but they have to be grounded in the sensuousness of each symbolic example in art as well as the result of abstract conceptualization. The child engaged in art work is almost by definition involved in the mythic and symbolic qualities of experience. Art education need not seek an imitation of primitive, sympathetic thinking though it may be enhanced if parallel contemporary insights were encouraged.

THE FURTHER NATURE OF THE VISUAL SYMBOL

The symbol, in contradistinction to the sign has many universal, variable and broadly conceptual characteristics while the latter is specific, unique and basically involved with practical information. As we have seen the essential difference that exists between the two and that divides them in kind is function. A symbol may have the surface properties of a sign and vice versa, the relationship determined between itself and object through the interpretive understanding of the subject; but a symbol has the added feature of conceptualization. The child who drew the horses was affording the onlooker a personal understanding of horses as well as intensifying his own experience of them. This is what makes the symbol a distinctly human attribute, or put the other way, the conceptual characteristics of symbolization create human meaning in an added dimension beyond that of simple information. Symbols function as the intrinsic arbiters of the mind. "Signs announce their objects," and all animals respond accordingly, but "symbols lead one to conceive of the object" and only man has that capacity. Though children may be led to conceptions about horses in the mimeographed example, it is of a rote quality, "announcing" its forms rather than instituting true conceptions.

Symbols may be developed in any manner, through words, discursive ideas, pictures, organized sounds or any other expressive form which would

The imaginative child
intensifies symbolic
expressiveness in art.
"Four Girls," Junior
High School Draw-
ing. [Courtesy, Robin
Wilt]

lead to conceptualized interpretation. A proper name, such as Alan is a simple symbol. Unlike the designation of a sign, a particular person need not be present for an image or a concept of Alan to emerge. There are numerous connotations which may be ascribed to Alan so that when the name is spoken or thought, there isn't only the signal recognition like smoke to fire, but a conception that is variable and differs markedly among the subjects thinking or speaking the name. Alan spoken by his mother may connote a very different image from Alan called by a crony, yet the proper noun signifies the same individual. In each instance there is not a carbon copy of an original Alan, but a symbol—a flexible, conceptualized image that has open-end possibilities of meaning.

A pictorial image may be understood symbolically in a similar manner, though the interpretive mechanism and the intrinsic aspects are much more complicated than a proper name. Cracks in a wall, peeling paint or cloud formations are excellent examples of deceptively simple sources for pictorial symbols. Whatever or whoever is being portrayed in the "mind's eye" is obviously not a specific object or individual, nor do the black whorls or ragged lines indicate in themselves any meaning. Yet a person does emerge or a series of objects, specifically a likeness to someone we know, the faceless mass physiognomy of modern man or a dramatic scene. The ordering of the parts induces a conceptualization that gives rise to many connotations. Before we know it we have supplied innumerable images of meaning: the accidental configurations may be experienced in all of its innumerable symbolic manifestations of meaning. The important point here is the fusing of perceptual images with an inner conception—with an anticipation of form that is bound up with feelings and

Art
and
Education
in
Contemporary
Culture

.

314

emotions. The latter elements are as important in supplying meaning as the physical form properties.

The amusing little drawing of the rabbit or duck head illustrates the flip of our mind as we vacillate between seeing a duck or a rabbit; in either instance, the meaning is dependent upon the concepts we have built up about the two creatures. In both instances, there are no real elements that are actually that of a man, a scene, a rabbit or a duck, but there are the patterned relationship of forms which are analogues, forms which correspond in certain vital manners to external things. The lines or mass that delineate a shape, the duck's bill for instance, are recalled or conceptualized as similar to earlier images that have been stored in our memory. The skill with which the forms are drawn, the sensuous interplay of texture and the other purely artistic devices belong to aesthetics and have nothing to do with the presentation of the content. This, incidentally, is one of the justifying reasons of modern art, in which the artist desires to free himself from the tyranny of the anecdotal, of the literally representative object and concentrate on the purely sensuous and intrinsically aesthetic elements. This also is unconsciously operating in most children's art work.

The Psychological Significance of Artistic Symbols

The visual symbol acts as a paradigm of feeling, depending often for its meaning on an anticipation of form and other unique interpretive perceptual aspects of each individual. [New York Public Schools]

Nevertheless, it would seem highly unlikely that any non-objective image is without psychological significance; every geometric or abstract design produces its own symbolic character. The artists have recognized this condition from the very beginning. The important non-objective painter Kandinsky, for instance, isolates the abstract condition of color and writes about its properties. His language may not be the precise denotative language of science. Yet the idea that the elements of art such as line, texture or color in themselves possess a significance that goes beyond their mere appearance is communicated.

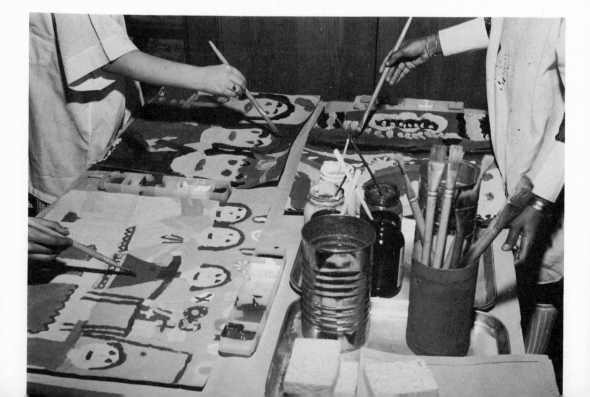

Rabbit or duck?

As . . . man develops, the circle of (his) experiences caused by different beings and objects grows ever wider. They acquire an inner meaning and eventually a spiritual harmony. It is the same with color, which makes only a momentary and superficial impression on a soul but slightly developed sensitiveness. But even this superficial impression varies in quality. The eye is strongly attracted by light, clear colors, and still more strongly attracted by those colors which are warm as well as clear; vermillion has the charm of flame, which has always attracted human beings. Keen lemon-yellow hurts the eye in time as a prolonged and shrill trumpet note the ear, and the gazer turns away to seek relief in blue or green.

But to a more sensitive soul the effect of colors is deeper and intensely moving. And so we come to the second main result of looking at colors: their psychic effect. They produce a corresponding spiritual vibration, and it is only as a step towards this spiritual vibration that the elementary physical impression is of importance.[9]

Generally speaking, color is a power which directly influences the soul. Color is the key-board, the eyes the hammers, the soul is the piano with many strings. The artist is the hand that plays, touching one key or another, to cause vibrations in the soul.[10]

The conceptualization of color as a separate entity is poetically expressed. In essence, Kandinsky indicates that color has intrinsic values that naturally produce symbolic responses. Psychology has developed several diagnostic techniques based on a similar assumption. The abstract ink blots of the Rorschach test is supposed to reveal facets of character when a subject tells an interviewer what the blots suggest to him. People seem to project their personalities or some significantly symbolic aspect into the blots. The accidental and literally meaningless forms are transformed into symbols. A skilled diagnostician supposedly is able to read the personality pattern that is thus revealed. Consequently, we may say that visual symbols may be considered to be paradigms of feeling.

The psychological projection of meaning thus is extended beyond the limitations of verbal language. Language or words are not the only means we have for experiencing intelligence or imbibing knowledge, though they are the most fully utilized and developed in the formal and logical sense. The discursive stringing out of ideas, thought, spoken or written image has always been the accepted method by which we reason, with

[9] Wassily Kandinsky, *The Art of Spiritual Harmony* (London: Constable and Company, Ltd., 1914), p. 48.
[10] *Ibid.*, p. 52.

Art
and
Education
in
Contemporary
Culture

.

316

mathematics as a pure extension. Yet, if the emotional, imaginative and intuitive inheritances are regarded as integral components of human organization and thinking, they must be assigned a place in the scheme of things. If meaning is as much dependent upon perception which is interwoven with our emotions as it is upon conception which is dependent upon logical construction as well as feelings, then we should accept the so-called nonrational tendencies, the total symbolic range as but additional channels and educational ways through which we apprehend the world and arrive at meaning and knowledge.

The Variability of Interpretation

This a fundamental insight that all teaching not only has to incorporate into its methods, it may be a state of mind that has to be cultivated, that goes beyond mere methodological procedures. It is, relatively, a free and permissive viewpoint that particularly through art teaching is ready to activate the imagination, utilize a selective eye, commit the self to symbolic decisions and to submit them to critical appraisal. To do this in the contemporary world is not only to invite the conditions of change, but to come to grips with the many faceted strands of contemporary existence, to be engaged in vital experiences. With modern science uncovering but not always explaining the contending actions of matter and anti matter, with the completely illogical nature of world politics and local social relationships, with the continuing depths that are found in the unconscious one can agree with Hamlet: There are more things in Heaven and earth, Horatio, than are dreamt of in your philosophy.

At least, the symbolic functions of art are not predicated upon a so-called material understanding. Their "reality" can run a gamut from the slightly altered reproductions of the objects of daily existence to the abstract forms of modern art. They include the mythical projections of forms and states of being that humans invest with meaning, the fairies, the totemic figures, the caricatures and the demonic semblances as well as the geometric combinations of stars, circles, crosses, arabesques and areas of pure color. The accidental splash and splatter of a brush on canvas may be as functionally artistic and symbolic as the most laboriously traced replica of an externally "beautiful" object. The passionate convolutions of Jackson Pollock have as much psychological quality, aesthetic potential and symbolic intention as the Sistine ceiling of Michelangelo.

This encompassing acceptance of variability is basic to art understanding and to a realization of its symbolic significance. The erratic splash or the carefully delineated form, the abstract shape or the representationally painted image are all psychologically significant and artistically symbolic because it is the individual mind that ascribes that kind of meaning to any image it confronts or creates. It is this merging of universality and particularity that provides art with its other than material qualities, infusing into the tabula rasa of the symbol image the thinking and feeling of the individual. This transformation is mysteriously fertile and enduring, probably because it is the source from which humans draw their basic relationships to the objects and conditions of existence. Consequently, the role of art education may be sensed as one that parallels the most fundamental human functions. Its teaching should follow the least impeded and most promising methods. These methods should not only have objective cognizance of the symbolic functionings of art, but are probably most efficaciously developed as a subjective state of mind.

THE SYMBOLIC MIND SET

The desirable state of mind for creative symbolism is probably evolved naturally with the continuing and exploratory activity in making and observing art. It is a spontaneous development that should relate emotionally and intelligently to the material of art and of the environment. The forms of art actually accentuate this intrinsic search for symbolic meaning that results when an individual confronts experience.

These forms may come from "out of the blue" for the artist and for the student. They may be fortuitous and inspired realizations, primary images that are "given" at the moment. The images may possess an aptness and an impact that sing out the symbolic intent like a clarion call. Everyone has hit upon such creative instances and children seem more creatively fortunate in this regard than most adults. However, this spontaneously derived symbolism is not as frequently available as teachers or students would like it to be, even amongst the gratuitous artlessness of the uninhibited young. More often than not the individual has to strive beyond the moment's inspiration; he has to struggle with the substance of transformation, before a symbol is created, that adequately embodies his thoughts and feelings.

The bridging of the gap between inner and outer components requires what amounts to a trial and error technique and the natural activation of the sympathetic viewpoint Cassirer writes about. There has to be a feeling out of the likely symbolic forms, a persistent manipulating of the inert media of art. The continuing handling of materials is not merely a physical skill, an arranging and externally patterned disposition of parts. It may appear that the art symbols emerge full blown from this activity almost as a direct result of the manipulatory sequences. Actually, what does occur is that in the give and take, the push and pull of confronting inner image with outer perception, the squiggles, lines, shapes, masses and colors precipitate an internal response. A line suddenly achieves meaning, a shape recalls an understanding, a color signifies a state of feeling. But because "of the perversity of inanimate objects" the art media often resist an immediate closing of experience, it does not too easily achieve a symbolic meaning. As the activity progresses there is improving possibility of hitting upon the proper, the "felt" relationships. When this point is achieved the child or the artist "knows" it not by a systematic analysis, but because he experiences the "extraordinary release" that the painter Dubuffet mentions. The release is not only a personal catharsis, it is the epitomatic crest of creative and aesthetic forming, the crucial symbolic

Art
and
Education
in
Contemporary
Culture

.

318

climax that distinguishes, each in its unique way, an artistic act. It is at this point that all of the personal attributes of the creator, the realized potential of the material and the imaginative conceptions merge into a unified network of meaning and form. Dubuffet is quoted as follows:

This much is sure, a picture interests me to the degree I succeed in kindling in it a kind of flame—the flame of *life*, of *presence*, or *existence*, or *reality*, depending on what we take these words to mean. To be sure, it often happens with me that my picture lacks this quality. I will have put certain figures in it, no matter what objects, people, places—they are recognizable but without being moving, they have no life . . . In any case, I go on working, I add and I take away, I change, I revise (notice that I work empirically, like a blind man, experimenting with every kind of means), until a certain extraordinary release occurs in the picture, and from then on it seems to me endowed with this very *life*—excuse me, *reality*. How can this be accounted for? I have no idea. I never know how I produced it, or how to repeat the same effect. It is a mysterious happening, and because of its very mysteriousness it drives me again and again to renew the experience each time I make a picture. Am I fooling myself? Is the impression my picture gives me of containing *reality* within it (as if by some magic I had evoked a warmth, a throbbing, a breathing, so compelling as to strike fear, as if I had hit on a dangerous mechanism for creating life, without knowing when or how), is this impression true only for me, or is it equally so for everyone who looks at the picture? [11]

It may also be proper to ask is this the way much of art is created? In a general sense, it probably would have to be answered, yes. The subconsciously compelling motivations, the mysterious store of images that reassert themselves again and again may change in format from previous activities or in different people but are of the same core of aesthetic experience nevertheless. The ineffable sense of understanding, of achieving the form that, for the moment at least, and perhaps in a universal sense for all time, if it is great enough, creates or contains some kernel of reality through art. It is the submission of experience and personality to the adventure of uniquely and freshly forming meanings, entranced with the imaginative, captured by the metaphoric, dependent upon the symbolic.

At this level, it is not a difference of degree but of kind between common sense responses to experience and those of art. The only thing they share is the intuitive root but the branches have become distinctly separated growths. Yet the root is significant for it indicates that the vast reservoir of thought and feeling, of inchoate imagery and the will towards symbol making lies beneath all attempts at learning and creating and is almost synonymous with the generating activities of art.

As a result, art education has to foster a consistent development of aesthetic activity. There is no external sequential pattern to this symbolic growth; there is rather the individual realization of form and the student's deepening understanding and heightened sensitivity in achieving his own idiosyncratic pattern of symbolizing.

[11] Jean Dubuffet, *XXe Siècle*, No. 9 (June, 1957).

The individual realization may be assisted in the open promoting of exploratory and experimental interactions of experience with materials and techniques and in the more loosely structured casting about for personal vision. The vision referred to is of the inner kind, not visual acuity. Since the art symbol has many roots, sunk into the soil of individual inclination and cultural influence, it cannot be induced as if it were an artificially produced entity, like a manufactured article. It is organic and viable, possessing a being of its own. This is perhaps the one main distinction between the high forms of art and those manufactured through popular culture. That difference is elaborated in the chapter on popular culture.

The art symbol possessing its own open growth potential can never really be considered as finished. It is itself insistently reaching out for ever more meaning, seeking perhaps a state of equilibrium it will never attain. The possibilities of its meaning remain unfixed because of the infinite number of minds that may come in contact with it. When the visual symbol becomes too defined, then it comes perilously close to the precision of a sign. At that point it forfeits its status and its power to set free a freely associative trend of thought and feeling. The cross is an old example of a fresh symbol that progressively has lost its aesthetic possibilities and circumscribes the nature of the symbolic response that a person can make to it. A much newer visual image is the vapidly pretty young female face of popular illustration that never has achieved symbol status, let alone the aesthetic attributes of art. Yet for the average person this level of "sign language" constitutes art. The mass, uncritical mind tends to lump all visual phenomena under one heading. This is a danger that art teachers have to recognize and plan to avoid.

HANDLING ART MATERIALS

The overall characteristics of the creative act occur within a context that extends beyond the immediate time and place, relating to culture, educational aims, teaching methodologies and the psychological background of the individual student. Yet the real essence of the art experience and a basic view of its workings lies in the sensuous manipulation of the art materials, and the actual transformation of perceptions into visual images as this activity occurs. It is this latter function of transformation, a symbolic one, that most profoundly offers an insight into the nature of artistic activity, suggesting teaching implications.

The child comes to working with art materials in a natural, eager and anticipatory way. This delight and relative confidence of involvement remains during the early years in grade school, permitting a direct and sympathetic degree of transformation of experience. It is when the literal-mindedness of descriptive drawing makes itself felt generally somewhere in the third grade that the easy symbolic and forming relationship with art is hindered by narrow or extraneous concerns, with difficult skills and the desire for culturally approved imagery. If the process of improvisational

Art
and
Education
in
Contemporary
Culture

•

320

forming is not arrested too sharply, the student may continue creatively into all the educational levels in spontaneous rapport with artistic activity with the support of a positive mind set. Creative or not, the continuing process, even outside of art, is a symbolic one. It is the art teacher's responsibility to see that students retain a fresh, imaginative and inventive attitude toward the whole process of responding to one's experience. They need to affirm a natural indication of these qualities and encourage them when they have been either inhibited or discarded by the student, for any number of reasons.

Just as the babble and gurgling of the infant mentioned earlier leads to language, so does the beginning manipulation of art materials by children lead to the shaping and forming of symbols in art. The early activity is rather pleasurable to the child, a form of play that permits a necessary kind of sensuous and kinaesthetic expression. All of the vague inner wondering, perceptual stimuli, bodily movement and compelling need to communicate find a ready outlet in the scribble, the motion of lines, the thick texture of paint spread over paper and in the intensity of color. For a while it seems the kinaesthetic and physically pleasing elements suffice. However, even from the very first scribble the child is relating his thinking, feeling and personal experiences to the sensuous and aesthetic attributes of the art materials. When the relationships achieve a focal point of intellectual readiness and physical dexterity, purpose becomes evident. This purpose moulds the conceptual and feeling approach to the making of forms so that the materials may be manipulated to create visual symbols. The simplest delineations suffice to establish meaning for the child. At the same time the inherent qualities of paint, crayon or clay and the characteristic working of these materials open up new horizons of sensuous possibility. These suggest many new direct symbolic interpretations of experience or elaborate the individual conceptions that are held about the child's own experiences. The naive and open beginnings are pleasant and natural opportunities for teachers to inculcate a positive and abiding interest in art expression. They can guide the children, unobtrusively or openly as the need may be, into the kind of motivating and working situations which would help develop aesthetic insight and felt personal expression.

The intriguing puddles of color, the drips of paint may excite an almost visceral feeling of texture and sensuous rhythm as a brush loaded with tempera is manipulated across the easel paper. The intense hues of a crayon line sharply etching a contour or softly covering an area imbue the child with a sense of mastery over his world. However, this mastery has to be channeled into some personal development of form, relating the sensuous attributes to the felt purposes of expression. This happens naturally to most children, though it is more structured and liable to progressive learning if a teacher orients and deepens the experience, tidying it up or expanding its possibilities, demonstrating relationships, suggesting possibilities. At first, the circular motion that makes spherical or lozenge shaped forms can be likened to physical shapes: heads, bodies, legs. Color can begin to contain not only local description of objects, but carry a psychological significance as well. The proportion and placement of shapes may be made to conform to symbolic purpose. Soon enough the schemata of form appear, the oval shaped heads, lollipop trees and multicolored flowers.

With the development of perception, the influences of the outside world, the accumulation of experience and the identification with particular groups, the art work progresses through a variety of forms and sophistications. The teacher is intimately involved with the aesthetic development of the child at this stage. Despite the easy transformation of vision, the child considers the teacher an authority from which source artistic understanding may be gained. As the child grows older, unless there is knowing teaching attuned to the finer sensibilities of current existence, the primary symbolic relationship and sensuously rewarding participation with art materials and aesthetic vision give way to "using" art rather than exploring its possibilities. The vital symbols are experienced more as signs, limited and set in range of meaning, parsimonious of the aesthetic and spiritual relationship with existence, assuming a more mechanical character. The need for expression remains nevertheless, if in a narrowed way. The individual seeks out the most convenient and accepted symbol channels and communicates through them, as popular relationship to the arts and bumbling inept instances of art education demonstrate.

DISCOVERY OF SYMBOLIC MEANING

The child who is engaged in art activity is involved in a very intense kind of symbol making. The transforming of personal experience into visual symbols provides an immediate, natural and penetrating mode of setting up meaning in that experience. For instance, the second grade average drawing of a girl standing within the close outside environment

Children's art work symbolically expresses the emerging awareness of environment. "Outside My House," Second Grade Drawing. [Ann Arbor Public Schools; PHOTO: Stuart Klipper]

Art
and
Education
in
Contemporary
Culture

·

322

of her home establishes for the youngster a number of important meanings. These all result from her familiar actions and surroundings. The familiarity of the experience is generally a base from which younger children evolve their symbol activity, expanding the scope as the experiences accumulate and as intellectual energy develops. There are various parts of symbolically visual organization of the drawing that are lacking in conventionalized order: the path trails off into nowhere, the flower pot on top of the forward construction seems incongruous, there is an inability to conceptually establish a horizon line. Yet the overall configuration is a sensible and significant one. The child has attempted to place herself and her home in some kind of proper spatial understanding. The relationships are extremely visual rather than emotional (as other more haptically oriented children may sense them).

In symbolically connecting the various elements of house, stone fence, trees, clothesline, sky, animal and self the child is sensing her more intimate relationships to the conditions, not only of her environment, but of a human being in the space of the world. There is an affirmation of the ego placed within safe, familiar surroundings, but there is also an expanding realization of the individual symbiotic relationships to nature. The mass solidity of the tree trunks and the emerging linear branches concretely confirm the conceptions the girl probably has developed about the phenomena of growth. The simple but well articulated shapes for head, hair, body and arms make concrete her own image of herself and of its functioning in time and space. Similarly, the slightly cruder circles and cones that symbolize the animal determine a personal connection. These symbols cause the inner realization of self and its transaction with commonplace living to exist on a more secure and vivid plane than if it remained just a vague and jumbled inner stirring. The dress and trousers that are on the clothesline may well symbolize the beneficent overlooking of the parents, a condition the child would be intently yet unconsciously reaching for. In all, each of the lines, squiggles, colors and shapes are invested with a personal meaning for the child. They make concrete the individual and unique encounter with existence as well as providing a channel of communication for the meaning that results from the experience. The various perceived elements are transformed into a symbolic whole. Each of the minor forms exist as a symbol in itself while the total pictorial image is to be considered as a symbolic configuration.

However, the art symbol also becomes the intrinsically expressive yet material mould for thinking and feeling that does not have a literal or practical cast. Its very lack of precision of meaning makes it capable of viable, individual insights. This paradox of embodying an imaginative order of experience in a concrete material way may be the source of the forceful surprise and shock of recognition that is referred to in gauging the creative effects of art. For the student in an art class as well as for the mature artist, the making of art symbols (and their appreciation as well) attests to the responsiveness that human awareness leads to. It becomes the focus for the inner life of images and a spur to further enrichment and intensity of additional imagery. The inner activity that precedes the actual symbol making is a swarming one of diverse impressions, of innumerable associations, of countless fancies, even in the child. This generative cauldron of thought and feeling is the human brewing of meaning. It establishes the individual person above brute instinct and provides qualities of import and consequence that bridge the gap between nothingness and purpose.

The process of symbol making in art is, however, not subject to the harness of material understanding, despite its final particular and observable form. It cannot be completely understood in the objective considerations of physical, physiological or abstractly logical construction. It possesses inherent qualities that are different from the reduction to external measurement or analysis.

In an oversimplified sense, modern art was inaugurated to escape from the stale, stereotyped image symbols that had progressively deteriorated over several centuries by becoming sentimental or simple minded. The artists over the past century have found that the symbols of art were amenable to a much greater range of form than had been heretofore believed. The art symbol can be correlated to the closely observed external world, but it may also be freely applied to any automatic shape or internal configuration. Since it is the mind that confers meaning upon the visual symbols rather than the other way round, the way was opened to a limitless exploration of the inner man as he found himself in concrete marks and aesthetic patterns. In the works of the traditional old masters, one finds that distortion, omission or deliberate detailed inclusion constitutes a relatively free symbol making process. Even more so the subtle techniques, the fine hatching, the passionate stroking, the accidents of glaze or impasto were themselves the hallmarks of symbolic process. It was the cultural veneer that imposed whatever formal reality that was demanded. In any case, the sensory handling of the media is as likely to produce significant symbolic form in the abstract as it is in the representational.

Students should not be confined to any narrowly defined progression of symbolic patterning. If there is to be any successful uncovering and aes-

Contemporary art ranges widely in its symbolic content and form, as is seen in the illustrations on the following pages.

"The Wall," Renzo Vespignani. [Collection, The Museum of Modern Art, New York; PHOTO: *The Museum of Modern Art]*

Art
and
Education
in
Contemporary
Culture

·

324

*"Sea Farer," Seymour
Lipton. [Collection,
The University of
Michigan Museum
of Art;* PHOTO: *Oliver
Baker Associates]*

*"Witches," Jan
Muller. Photograph
courtesy Staempfli
Gallery, New York]*

"Tahstvatt," David
Smith. [Collection,
The University of
Michigan Museum of
Art]

"Dinner Table,"
George Segal. [The
Green Gallery, New
York, Collection,
Seymour Schweber;
PHOTO: Eric
Pollitzer]

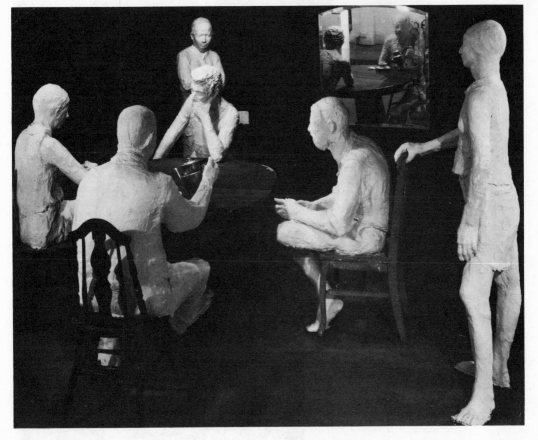

Art
and
Education
in
Contemporary
Culture

·

326

"Canto XX," Robert Rauschenberg. [Leo Castelli Gallery, New York; PHOTO: *Rudolph Burckhardt]*

"Begin the Beguine," Max Beckmann. [Collection, The University of Michigan Museum of Art]

"Number 3, 1954,"
Myron Stout. [Col-
lection, The Museum
of Modern Art, New
York. Philip C. John-
son Fund]

"I Saw the Figure
Five in Gold,"
Charles Henry De-
muth. [The Metro-
politan Museum of
Art, New York, The
Alfred Stieglitz Col-
lection, 1949]

Art
and
Education
in
Contemporary
Culture

·

328

thetic realization of those personally ineffable but vital stirrings of the inner self as well as the comprehension of the outer material world then the art class has to support a free and exploratory approach. This cannot rule out any style or mode of artistic understanding. The symbol is too vital an element and too indefinable a quality to be circumscribed within constraining limits. This would only make education an adverse agency rather than a spur to creative understanding. The art symbol in converting the mental and feeling impulses that exist in one order into another order of actual sensory substance is achieving the essence of creativity. This is an unfettered, exciting path of discovery at its best, and it is as such that teaching must accept and promote it. The child in the art class as the artist in his studio is pursuing a unique realization that forms its own reality when it is achieved. It cannot merely be either a camera eye image or an errant purposeless dab, though each has the potential of being art. This potential must be the discovery of the individual and art education to achieve genuine aesthetic validity has to stress this in its methods.

THE LANGUAGE OF VISION

Much of the thinking about symbolic forms implicitly refers to visual symbols as a language. Gyorgy Kepes has developed an elaborate set of ideas that are based on such an assumption. He suggests that visual forms constitute their own language and are necessary elements in the education of all individuals and in the adequate development of contemporary thought and in establishing currently appropriate meaning. He is quoted at length because of the significance of what he has to say:

The language of vision, optical communication, is one of the strongest potential means both to reunite man and his knowledge, and to re-form man into an integrated being. The visual language is capable of disseminating knowledge more effectively than almost any other vehicle of communication. With it, man can express and relay his experiences in object form. Visual communication is universal and international: it knows no limits of tongue, vocabulary, or grammar, and it can be perceived by the illiterate as well as by the literate. Visual language can convey facts and ideas in a wider and deeper range than almost any other means of communication. It can reinforce the static verbal concept with the sensory vitality of dynamic imagery. It can interpret the new understanding of the physical world and social events because dynamic interrelationships and interpenetration, which are significant of every advanced scientific understanding of today, are intrinsic idioms of the contemporary vehicles of visual communication: photography, motion pictures and television.

But the language of vision has a more subtle and, to a certain extent, an even more important contemporary task. To perceive a visual image implies the beholder's participation in a process of organization. The experience of an image is thus a creative act of integration. Its essential characteristic is that by plastic power an experience is formed into an organic whole. Here is a basic discipline of forming, that is, thinking in terms of structure, a discipline of utmost importance in the chaos of our formless world. Plastic arts, the optimum forms of the language of vision, are, therefore, an invaluable educational medium.

Visual language must be readjusted, however, to meet its historical challenge of educating man to a contemporary standard and of helping him to think in terms of forms. . . .

Today, creative artists have three tasks to accomplish if the language of vision is to be made a potent factor in reshaping our lives. They must learn and apply the laws of plastic organization needed for the re-establishing of the created image on a healthy basis. They must make terms with contemporary spatial experiences to learn to utilize the visual representation of contemporary space-time events. Finally, they must release the reserves of creative imagination and organize them into dynamic idioms, that is, develop a contemporary dynamic iconography.[12]

It may not be expected that art education seriously undertake the education of those artists that Kepes mentions, in a mass sense. Yet, in terms of what it may accomplish within its own set of aims, of developing artistically literate and creatively expressive students, the cues for art education have a parallel direction to head in. It is not only the primitive who innocently engages in visual and nonverbal symbolic language. This activity that does not have to resort to words is one in which all humans engage at all levels of society.

It is the young child and the artist who naturally utilize a symbolic language unselfconsciously. With a typical sense of fulfillment of experience they establish an expressive intensity of meaning without the need of exhortation. This realization of the nonverbal manner of thinking in a symbolic form through which meanings, that may not otherwise be shaped and communicated, find expression is an important element in the growing awareness of children and obviously the core of understanding in the arts or of art education experiences. In the case of the young child, the ability to achieve meaning without resorting to as yet an undeveloped verbal skill and abstract ability to conceptualize in a mature way permits meanings to be conveyed by symbolically nonverbal forms that otherwise would remain mute, inarticulated and perhaps frustrated feelings. Painting, sculpture, music, literature and the other arts, where the symbols are associations of words in connotation, sounds, forms, light values or colors, and where these elements become the symbols of balance, harmony, discord or other rhythms also become the containers of meaning, immediately wedding that meaning to form.

Yet simultaneously, the symbol forms consistently defeat any attempt to make the content verbally precise. The meaning that is directly experienced through a symbolic relationship with some nonintellectual form, but still an intelligible one, is a primary condition that cannot be further reduced. It touches the individual forcefully and without mediation while the logical conditions of explanation appear to be unnecessary to the quality of the meaning itself. Explanations are thus weak reconstructions of a more basic experience, extraneous and self defeating when the symbolic art forms are intense and free from deliberate intellectualization.

Actually then, to reiterate, most of the really significant human mean-

[12] Gyorgy Kepes, *Language of Vision* (Chicago: Paul Theobald, 1948), pp. 13–14.

Art
and
Education
in
Contemporary
Culture

.

330

ings, those that refer to emotions and values are communicated, not by logical analysis, but by the other symbolic modes that are connotative in character: art, drama, ritual and myth, by the poetry of words, the harmony of sounds and the transforming quality of visual forms. Certainly, a national flag embodies much more direct meaning of patriotism than does a score of Fourth of July speeches, unless the speaker has the strength and profundity of a Lincoln or a Roosevelt. Bach's monumental and sublime music is more expressive of the meaning of man's fate in its immediate harmonies than all the verbose tracts of moral philosophy, while the attenuated forms of Giacometti's sculpture forcefully shape the tragedy of existence on a fundamental plane without the intervening necessity of precise words. Kepes and many others stress as much, however, the need to create new artistic modes of relating to a rapidly changing and technological world and in establishing lines of appropriate communication. Though these are central to art education and to symbolic processes, the conditions of art should tend more to communion than to communication, in their most intense and characteristically aesthetic forms.

It is necessary to point up the need for change in art. At the same time, the forms in art must be recognized not as having a progressive development but a horizontal one. Each era characterizes its own understanding through a valid even if temporally limited symbolic insight and it is this factor that has to be stressed. It is not simply the replacement of outmoded shapes and styles that motivates art, it is the more positive search for adequate contemporary ways of expression. These are not always bound to the surface characteristics of the period, to its productive technology alone, but refer as much to the underlying spiritual quest. These may honestly coincide at times in a unified symbolic search, and such unity is desperately needed in contemporary culture. But it is not always a question of answering self evident questions but, as well, of finding the inner provocations and disturbances of the human adventure which lead to all worthwhile questions. This value approach has to orient the thinking in art education and has to be as firmly a part of the consciousness of the teacher actually operating in the classroom as it is in the mind of the most avant garde theorist and in the developing aspirations and experiences of students. Most important, though, is the underlying comprehension that must pervade not only the abstract notions of art education but the implementation of method based on the symbolic nature of individual response to experience.

Art and Culture

Art is the spearhead of every cultural advance, because it is the opening of the "inward eye," the
record of life from the deep unconscious drive to the
highest intensity of emotion and awareness.

SUSANNE LANGER

A STORY is told about Picasso that not only lends itself to the legend
that his life has become, but offers some symbolic insight into the
relationships between art work and the conditions of society, between
the artist and the larger culture that is the context within which he creates.
Picasso had painted a major canvas ("Guernica," p. 332), a stark and
powerful visual symbol of all the horror, guilt and destruction of war. This
was the artist's impassioned response after the wanton Nazi bombing and
obliteration of a small Spanish city bearing the same name as the painting.
When the Nazis occupied Paris during the Second World War Picasso
was visited in his studio by one of the German Gauleiters. The visitor
rhetorically or perhaps aggressively asked Picasso, "You are the painter
who made the picture, Guernica?" Picasso responded in his own inimitable
manner, "No! It was you who created it." Though the story may be
apocryphal it becomes a literary symbol itself trenchantly reflecting the
interweaving of individual and society, of artistic act and cultural impetus,
of experience and symbolic transformation.

CULTURE AND THE INDIVIDUAL

It may be said that an individual is "a product of his times" and what he
comprehends as meaning or produces in tangible form is a result of the
experiences in and the pressures of any particular culture. The conditions
of the culture provide some of the determining factors and become the
incubator of influence that will result in a characteristic organization of
beliefs and acts. The culture impinges upon the individual and shapes
his personality, just as in one of the components of that culture, education
consciously attempts to affect the development of each student. Not only
is there this individual relationship, but collectively, the various subcultures comprising a whole society will give shape and direction to the
larger societal entity.

331

Art
and
Education
in
Contemporary
Culture

•

332

However, at the same time there is the existential quality of each individual creating what may be regarded as a reverse feedback to culture. In each of the symbolically organized areas of culture there is likewise the autonomous attribute which offers a distinctive contribution, resisting the encumbrance and influence of outside factors. Art has its own internal structure that gives it unique creative impetus as does science or any other discipline. The child or adult engaged in the creative process is imposing his will on the material and shaping an image of the world in his own way. The great artist, in any case, appears often to transcend deterministic conditions that might limit his expression.

Obviously, neither one of these approaches is absolutely in operation; they are necessarily interrelated, engaged with one another in a natural dialectic stemming from a mutual need. For instance, the ultimate significance of a work of art may reside in its innate moral force and in its sensual forms which could be divorced from the surrounding conditions in which it was created. It is physically impossible, nor is it any longer a psychological requirement, to possess the personality or the outlook of a seventeenth century Dutch burgher, in order to appreciate a Rembrandt portrait. Yet it would be folly to deny the role of our own culture in influencing the kind of response we have to that work, or for that matter, the existing cultural pressures on an artist's creative process. The self and society, the work of art and its milieu, the unique artist and his actual culture, the individual student and the immediate fashions of his times are bound together in a mutual embrace.

Thus man is not only pushed blindly by an underlying and immutable determinism, by an inexorable march of history that he cannot control; he is not just a product of his times. He has that all important self awareness and a capacity to put history or his own time at a distance and evaluate it. Similarly, the student, teacher and artist can exercise a selectivity toward his environment and its events, adapting to parts of it, changing other aspects and generally providing a self chosen direction if

"Guernica," Pablo Picasso. [On extended loan to the Museum of Modern Art, New York, from the artist, M. Picasso; PHOTO: *The Museum of Modern Art]*

the impelling "climate" is an open one. However, this is accomplished within the matrix of the milieu. It is this very quality of transcending an immediate situation, bringing in both the heritage of time as well as the unique image of self to bear on a learning and creative situation that gives the overall human behavior its general freedom and its distinctive flexibility and range of form. Art education should provide the atmosphere and generate the appropriate experiences by which such creative attitudes and activities are engendered.

Educational Concerns of Balance

What is important for education is that the relationships between self and surroundings be on a balanced, sophisticated and individually vital level. This is not too frequently achieved, the necessary flexibility of balance being tipped to one side. More often than not, though, there is a rather vague and idealistic assumption of individual prerogatives and singular qualities residing in each person, there is in actual teaching practice today the results of mass attitudes, conforming ideas and an uncritical acceptance of strong cultural determinism. This is especially damaging in art education which intrinsically insists upon uniquely creative experiences. It is necessary to recognize the interactions between the individual and his society and to maintain sensitively the balance between the two, as well as to assess the qualitative aspects of the balance. What are some of the cultural conditions pertaining to art? Do these seep into the classroom affecting both the teacher and the student? Are there pressures, both subtle and potent, that direct or curtail a desired development of creative potential? Is taste a factor in art education?

These and other related inquiries may offer an art teacher some of the requisite insights in their search for personal understanding of values that have such a bearing on the teaching methods. The salubrious and stimulating climate that all teachers desire for their classrooms may, in part, be dependent upon the alertness to the cultural and social forces that do intrude in the school, whether one welcomes them or not. The depth of understanding that may be gained from a sincere appraisal of currently developing cultural conditions may help not only in explaining and alleviating some of the perplexing and inhibiting impasses in creative education, but might begin to suggest a philosophical position and ways of implementation that are more genuine to art, honestly fulfilling for the student, and perhaps, capable of raising the general level of taste.

ART AND SCIENCE

There is little doubt that science today is considered the most important component of knowledge and creates an influential context in the contemporary world. The arguments and the actions that support this idea go well beyond simple assumptions. Most of the energies of society seem to be directed into scientific or technological channels and many of the best minds tend to evidence an inclination towards material investiga-

Art
and
Education
in
Contemporary
Culture

·

334

tion. Even so eminent an art historian as Kenneth Clark [1] believes that the most creative and fertile minds are in science and that art has been, for the time, relegated to a less important level. This is, of course, open to argument. In any case, education has been fundamentally influenced by science. An art teacher, if he is not to feel superfluous, must examine the cultural and internal relationships that do exist between art and science. The dialogue between the two, the imaginative and the logical, cannot be escaped; the interplay becomes one of the basic aspects of educational content and method.

The Two Cultures

The two forms of thinking—the imaginative and the logical, have, however, in themselves, formed polarities in culture that are respectively reflected in the work of artists and writers as opposed to the work of scientists and various other technicians. Though each individual may possess the ability to think in either of the conceptual or imaginative modes, at least in the more simple forms, in practice there has been a rather divergent split between the two types, each reinforcing its own beliefs and methods of work.

C. P. Snow, the well known English novelist-scientist has emphasized this polarity in a terse, but pointed, even if controversial series of lectures: "Literary intellectuals at one pole—at the other scientists, and as the most representative, the physical scientists. Between the two a gulf of mutual incomprehension—sometimes . . . hostility and dislike, but most of all lack of understanding." [2] Snow too narrowly limits one pole to the literary intellectual and somewhat more broadly includes technicians along with pure scientists in the other. For our purposes the poles may be enlarged to include on one end the artists, writers, musicians, architects, dancers and all the other creative improvisers and interpreters who work with the basic ingredient of imagination—as against the other end of precise, supposedly objective individuals who conceptualize from a scientific structure of fact and observation.

What is disconcerting is that each remains, and often willfully, ignorant of the fundamentals of the other's attitudes for the main part. The technician and most scientists will rarely be literately conversant with the formal improvisations or basic philosophy of modern art or perhaps even aware of its significant examples while the average artist has not the foggiest notion of what are for him the esoteric concerns of the scientist. This lack of understanding more than superficially breeds a mistrust of one for the other in the most original and creative areas of artistic and scientific endeavor. Consequently, there can be little in the way of a synthesized realization of the hopes of liberal men for the kind of enlightened society man aspires to.

Snow indicates that education, on all levels, is one of the keys to healing

[1] Kenneth Clark, "The Blob and the Diagram," *Encounter* (January, 1963).
[2] C. P. Snow, *The Two Cultures and the Scientific Revolution* (New York: Cambridge University Press, 1963), p. 4.

*The art teacher,
deliberately or not,
introduces many
cultural values into
the classroom which
influence the creative
learning climate.
[Toledo Public
Schools;* PHOTO: *Tom
O'Reilly]*

the split, in bringing together the disparate aims and methods of the opposing groups. "Meanwhile, there are steps to be taken which aren't outside the powers of reflective people. Education isn't the total solution to this problem, but without education the West can't even begin to cope. All the arrows point the same way. Closing the gap between our cultures is a necessity in the most abstract intellectual sense, as well as in the most practical. When those two senses have grown apart, then no society is going to be able to think with wisdom . . . it is obligatory for us (the English) and the Americans and the whole West to look to our education with fresh eyes." [3] Snow suggests that we have a good deal to learn from the Russians and they from us in the educational sphere. But more pertinent is the need to bring together the opposing factions of art and science. For in the final analysis, the Industrial Revolution with its scientific and technological qualities is the only practical road to "the good life" for the greatest number. Yet, if purpose and meaning are to be infused into the clicks and grinds of machines and impersonal, institutional agencies as they affect the well being as well as the reason for being of the individual, then the arts and the humanities will have to be just as fundamentally considered. However, much of scientific understanding by lay people comes from a misreading of its continuously evolving premises. The fixed, mechanical ideas of nineteenth century science, the ordered and determined universe of Newton are still stubbornly frozen in most minds even when the scientists themselves have

[3] *Ibid.*, p. 41.

Art
and
Education
in
Contemporary
Culture

·

336

delved much beyond the optimistic but essentially undeveloped ideas of earlier investigators. Meanwhile, the magician's bag of tricks that technology seems to emulate is the cornerstone of much of popular attitude in the understanding of science.

Patterns of Similarity

All of these approaches have found their way into educational theory and current practices are good indicators of this. But even science is subject to change. Witness, for instance, the modifications that the phenomenon of electricity has undergone. From a mysterious and awesome force that the gods produced, it became the natural phenomenon that Benjamin Franklin unknowingly risked his life with when he performed his kite experiment. It then became a current, after that a wave, changed once more to a particle and may be considered all three in the future. Scientists have been able to discard one theory after another, not only on the basis of new objective information, but as responses to new image formations which particular cultures and times foist on them. Similarly, education has to feel free to modify its own image or invent a new one if need be. If the very philosophical position upon which science bases its own understanding is free to do so then education may have an obligation as well as an intellectual compulsion to follow suit. The arts have always felt themselves free enough in the hands of creative individuals to shape themselves as the various changing milieus and physical surroundings may have suggested.

Dore Ashton, in a sensitive chapter in her book *The Unknown Shore*,[4] a philosophical study of contemporary art, traces the parallel lines of thinking between many modern artists and scientists. She too points to the importance of the concept in science that separates the twentieth century scientist from his predecessors, that of the observer being a significant part of what he is studying. She indicates that this has happened in contemporary art beginning with Cézanne. This very factor of inherent subjectivity may account for some of the similarities that seem to exist between the modern forms of both science and art despite some superficial and formal differences. Ashton stresses this connecting link rather than the distinctions pointed up by Snow.

The factor of intuition may be the connecting link, its operation a fundamental process in aesthetic shaping and in the formulation of scientific comprehension. Certainly, there are many examples of artists who, in the broad encompassing of their imaginations, and even if superficially, were able to give body to their fantasies which later were to become scientific fact. In literature the popular example of Jules Verne is well known; in painting and sculpture we can point to some among innumerable others as an instance: Van Gogh's *Starry Sky*, Calder's mobiles or a Kepes painting. The intense emotional drive that compelled the artist to form his vision of spinning stars is quite close to the photographic

---

[4] Dore Ashton, *The Unknown Shore* (Boston: Little, Brown and Company, 1963), pp. 228–238.

plates of spiral nebula that were taken through telescopes at a later date. Calder's sculptural movements capture a sense of time and motion while Kepes gives us something of the microscopic mood. In a similar manner, the hypothetical formation of molecular structure that the scientists postulated several decades ago found their way into the consciousness of form that artists created.

Both art and science appear to be perched on the brink of a new epoch. The scientist is certainly forging ahead and uncovering a universe that is at once both ordered and contradictory. And as Ashton says, "Among the serious artists today the purpose is, as it always was, to discover and define the spaces in which human life transpires." [5] Education could hope to do no less than this and in order to achieve its goal of knowledge, wisdom and of sensitive awareness, it has to be alert to the contemporary attitudes in the very subjects it is endeavoring to teach. It has to recognize the increasing and changing fund of knowledge it has at its disposal, infusing that overwhelming spread with human meaning and purpose that go beyond efficiency and objective "truth."

J. Bronowski, an English mathematician, voices these sentiments in a passionate way, exemplifying the hopeful thinking of the concerned and cultured scientific mind. He voices the hope that science can exist alongside of art in harmony and mutual enhancement. Just as in the past "nations have not been great in science or art, but in art and science," so in the contemporary world there may be a salubrious interrelationship of the two. He continues, "The insight of science is not different from that of the arts. Science will create values, I believe, and discover virtues, when it looks into man; when it explores what makes him man and not animal, and what makes his societies human and not animal packs." [6]

Basic Distinctions

In a broad sense art and science do share a common insight in that both are symbolic constructions and both seek a truth and meaning for human existence. However, it is also important to recognize that the means each utilizes are essentially different in procedure, and often, even in purpose. Art is singular, given to the directness but also the grossness of the senses. It offers an infinite but subjective number of truths and generally stresses the individual character of the process, the product and the imaginative nature of the motivating experience. Science may also engage in imaginative constructions and elegant relationships, but it is primarily objective, insisting upon empirical validity whenever it can and on repeatable conditions. It seeks a reduction of knowledge to fundamental laws, gathering in the chaos of existence and experience, then imposing a logical and reasoned order. It is vital that education senses these distinctions, supporting both, but not confusing them. Otherwise, methods

[5] Dore Ashton, *ibid.*, p. 238.
[6] J. Bronowski, *The Common Sense of Science* (New York: Random House, Modern Library Paperbacks), pp. 147–49.

Art
and
Education
in
Contemporary
Culture

•

338

and aims are distorted and a basic philosophy suffers from a lack of solid footing. For this reason, art education has to be wary of any so called scientific method that is brought to bear on its development.

Future Considerations

An emerging culture, nevertheless, is unmistakably forming which is essentially scientific and technological. Cybernetics, automation, amazing speeds and distances for travel, remarkably sophisticated and fruitful experimentation and research in physics, biology, chemistry and the other physical and natural areas of objective study, as well as in the behavioral sciences, are all shaping a culture predicated upon universal physical and technological principles. These, in turn, will mean a drastic redirection of daily living that will affect everyone in profound terms in addition to affecting a revolutionary change in the environment. The art resulting from and expressing such change can only be different from what has already been created. The teaching of art has to reflect this open quality,

A culture that is not technological may provide a more cohesive base for visual and artistic symbols. "Painting by Young Balinese," Exhibition Circulated by the Smithsonian Institution. [Reproduced by Permission of the Smithsonian Institution]

anticipating its needs and character. It should shape the emerging culture where it can and generally provide each student with a personal aesthetic and expressive fulcrum from which point there may be an independent reaching out for the possibilities, adventures and insights of existence.

The hope is that culture may unify its many different strains and that education is best fit as the agency through which this may be accomplished for both the individual and society. However, no amount of theoretical conceptualization or generalized hopefulness will suffice. It is the teacher, at the head of the class, who in her daily contacts with students, in the specifics of her lessons and the manner of her teaching, whether in science, art or another area who serves as the direct and immensely influential channel for the thought, the awareness, the understanding and the values that students develop. Such a responsibility insists upon keen, sophisticated and knowing individuals who are engaged in a fruitful dialogue with culture and personal realization.

THE SOCIAL AESTHETIC BASES OF CULTURE

There are many ways of classifying the cultures that make up a society; the number of subcultures proliferate to a remarkable degree when they are examined. However, there are some broad guiding considerations that permit an interested investigator to develop and support the idea of large generalizations. Since our prime concern is the media of expression, aesthetic as well as a social criteria have the most value for art teachers.

Generally, this permits three categories to exist in determining the social-aesthetic organization of a civilization. These are known as folk, popular, and high cultures. (Some writers refer to them as folk art, mass or popular art, and high art.) Folk art and high art will be developed in this chapter. Popular art will have a full chapter following.

In one way or another, with changing emphasis, any country in the world possesses a pattern of the three classifications. Though there is no scientific validity with which to objectively support the existence of these categories, most observers who are intellectually concerned with the problem of group communication through various art media as manifestations of culture, would generally accept the existence of similar classifications. Though there may be individual modification as to make up or extent of influence, there is general agreement that something approximating the three cultures does in fact exist as cohesive and separate entities.

At the very least we may accept them as convenient intellectual or analytical pegs upon which to hang a necessary examination. Though they do provide the convenience they are also at the same time a danger that leads to an academic and sterile codification. This should be averted and can be, if only in the realization that what once belonged to a particular category in another time may well be assigned a different classification later on. Certain African sculpture was the obvious result of a folk art when it was first created. Though its origins are recognized, the same sculpture can now grace a museum and be regarded as part of

Art
and
Education
in
Contemporary
Culture

·

340

a high art form. What is of importance in the teacher's evolving understanding is the enrichment and dialectical experience that may result
from an active pursual of values. This requires some conceptual ordering
of educational insights and an additional intuited aesthetic response to
cultural conditions and products.

FOLK CULTURE

Folk culture is the oldest type of group expression. It is an indigenous
development arising from the daily involvements of the average individual
within a circumscribed environment. It threads its way into earlier
history through the innate heritage and accumulated traditions of the
tribe. Though folk culture is essentially a thing of the past in the
United States, some vestigial remnants remain in contemporary life.
Earlier the colonial period in America gave rise to a specific folk culture
as did the westering tendencies of the mobile pioneers. The large influx
of immigrant groups also brought differing folk ways and characteristic
folk art forms to the new country. All of these have left imprints on the
culture of America though the internal needs and external conditions
that shaped the folk culture have either disappeared or have been made
a part of the larger mass culture. The naive intensity, the excellent craftsmanship and the genuine though often crudely articulated artistry have
either evaporated because of the radical changes imposed on existence
through technology or have degenerated into vapid or vulgar forms empty
of real meaning and without the intrinsic integrity of the early versions.

We can illustrate some genuine and representative American folk
culture by pointing to such items as colonial furniture, the portraits of the
itinerant limners, the ballads of the pioneers, and the folk songs of
the southern mountaineers, the pottery and other craft work of the
aboriginal Indians, the spirituals of the slaves or the design motifs of
the Pennsylvania Dutch settlers. These and numerous other examples are
indications of spontaneous art forms that were developed by unified

*The painting ex-
presses some of the
enigmatic relation-
ship between the
mass of people and
the works of art.
"Workers and
Paintings," Honoré
Sharrer [Collection,
The Museum of
Modern Art, New
York. Gift of Lincoln
Kirstein;* PHOTO: *The
Museum of Modern
Art]*

groups living together. They were in specific and characteristic response to indigenous and particular conditions, the symbolic transformation of felt experiences into a concrete folk art shape that the individuals within the group had a need to express.

Though there were no conscious standards of a high order or a sophisticated aesthetic the art forms of folk culture often achieved a remarkable quality, possessing a sense of unity and an expressive intensity that made them actual works of art. The delineation of the folk art was usually intuitive and in direct association with the sensuous and psychological qualities of the surroundings. Though there were often utilitarian purposes for the forms, they were not intrusive. They derived their forms from a sympathetic rapport with active and mythical qualities innocently yet pragmatically weaving the conditions of art and life into sensuous symbolic relationships.

These relationships had a fairly tight compartmentalization. That is, though there may have been a parallel high culture existing at the same time, the two did not attempt to penetrate one another. Actually, each categorically respected the other's forms not only because of the political and social cleavage between classes, but because of the different immediate tensions each was resolving as well. In the industrialized nations of the west, the nineteenth century witnessed the uprooting of the folk cultures and the alienation of the high culture. It was only in the colonial areas and in those parts of the world where either one or both industrialization and political independence had not been achieved that folk art remained relatively pure. The tribal enclaves in Africa, the peon culture in Mexico or the peasant counterparts in Europe are a few instances of intensive folk cultures that have only recently been subjected to the changing influences of a new and different way of life. Consequently, the folk cultures are disappearing through a natural attrition or are slowly being diluted by the inroads of technological and political change.

The vestigial remnants of this kind of culture in the highly industrialized and urbanized countries such as the United States, Great Britain and other West European nations as well as the Soviet Union have become sentimentalized. They remain as charming anachronisms or they are exploited for their picturesque quality by the machinery of mass commercial interests and tourism.

Folk Culture in the Classroom

It is obvious that an art teacher has a rather difficult time disentangling the genuine aspects of folk culture from the embrace of adulterated understanding. Yet there is a tremendous amount of worthwhile material in folk culture that would be of great interest to students and it should be presented to them.

The presentation has to be free of any historical sense of superiority or aesthetic snobbery just as much as a trite mawkishness is to be avoided. Many artists, painters, musicians, dancers and writers have returned to the sources of folk art for inspiration, but never overlooking the gawky

Art
and
Education
in
Contemporary
Culture

·

342

"Indian Squaw,"
First Grade Painting.
[Ann Arbor
Public Schools;
PHOTO: *David*
Churches]

Folk art themes
require a sympathetic
but unsentimental
treatment in the
schools.

"Holland," Sixth
Grade Paper Mosaic.
[Ann Arbor Public
Schools; PHOTO:
David Churches]

quality if it is present or with any trace of condescension if there is innocence or a lack of polish. There has been the recognition of a symbolic directness and an unselfconscious freshness.

The development during an art lesson of a project of Indian beadwork, a ceramic piece fashioned after a Mexican design, an Eskimo totem pole made with cardboard, a papier-mâché mask utilizing an African form and similar units should not be arbitrary experiences or "cute" activities. These are all serious artistic manifestations of folk cultures and the integrity, the aesthetic appropriateness of their forms should be respected. This involves more than just superficial copying or relatively casual appreciation. Particularly when the lesson stems from a social studies concern it is important not to slight the art elements that underlie the folk cultures, though this happens more often than not. The folk objects then take on a thin illustrative value, their expressive qualities lost to the uninformed and insensitive stare of the curio hunter.

Just as important in art education theory is the recognition that though the folk art cultures have an immediate and genuine appeal for students and teachers alike, they are only a relatively small portion of the larger body of art. To limit art experiences, particularly on the elementary levels where the practice is widespread, to the admittedly appealing and rewarding folk arts is to deny students a necessary acquaintanceship with and participation in other art forms. "High art" may be more demanding at points yet it is as basic to the society that nurtured it as were the folk arts. Frequently, the sources of folk art such as holiday projects, social studies units and local group interests are provided with a maximum of ease. Teachers often restrict their art lessons to this material, cutting off the larger and more essential area of art experiences.

Many commercial and industrial artists such as those who are involved with advertising and comics, the composers of popular ditties or writers of widely disseminated magazine fiction, the makers of toys, consider themselves folk artists in the old tradition, in fancy if not in fact. Though there may be a superficial likeness, the relationship of these communicative products of the mass media to folk art is not only tenuous; it is essentially false. This will be examined further on. But it may be noted now that the conditions conducive to folk art are actually no longer in existence in the United States. Though there is a continuing interest in folk culture and some attenuated remains from an earlier day the impetus and the natural hierarchy of qualities that generate folk art are contrary to contemporary industrial and urbanized society.

HIGH CULTURE

Though high culture may not be as old as folk culture, it developed as soon as social organization became somewhat more sophisticated than simple communal living. It has paralleled the existence of each mature civilization and in fact reflects and expresses its highest achievements and aspirations. The priestly culture of Egypt, the philosophically based pat-

Creative activities possess inherent cultural values that orient student attitudes toward the arts as in this high school scenery painting for a school play. [*Pittsburgh Public Schools*; PHOTO: *Samuel A. Musgrave*]

terns of Greece or the politically inspired rule of Rome, the Mandarin dynasties of China, the churchly hegemony of the Middle Ages, the secular nobility of the Renaissance or the majestic courts of France and the Elizabethan reign in England—all created high art forms that may now be regarded as a continuum of pinnacles of cultural achievement. These cultures were sophisticated and intensely practiced ones, separated from the common run of endeavor, based upon the existence of a privileged or aristocratic class that had highly developed social backgrounds in addition to sensitive and aesthetically oriented educations, in short—cultivated tastes.

We can excerpt from de Tocqueville a concise explanation of the formation of these high cultures.

It commonly happens that, in the age of privilege, the practice of almost all the arts becomes a privilege, and that every profession is a separate domain into which it is not allowable for everyone to enter. Even when prdouctive industry is free, the fixed character which belongs to aristocratic nations gradually segregates all the persons who practice the same art till they form a distinct class, always composed of the same families, whose members are all known to each other, and among whom a public opinion of their own and a species of corporate pride soon spring up. In a class or guild of this kind each artisan has not only his fortune to make, but his reputation to preserve. He is not exclusively swayed by his own interest or even by that of his customer, but by that of the body to which he belongs; and the interest of that body is that each artisan should produce the best possible workmanship. In aristocratic ages the object of the arts is therefore to manufacture as well as possible, not with the greatest dispatch or at the lowest rate . . . The men of whom it is composed naturally derive from their superior and hereditary position a taste for what is extremely well made and lasting. This affects the general way of thinking of the nation in relation to the arts . . . In aristocracies, then, the handicraftsman work for only a limited number of fastidious customers; the profit they hope to make depends principally on the perfection of their workmanship.[7]

For thousands of years and in numerous societies the conditions that de Tocqueville describes prevailed and there was a consequent flowering of high art. The existence of knowledgeable, sensitive and obliging patrons provided the means whereby talented and inspired individuals were solicited and trained in the arts. This in turn created a closed group of cognoscenti or connoisseurs, an "elite," who succeeded in stimulating and enriching the artistic drives. Even when the patronage was dedicated to other ends in addition to the artistic, whether they were capricious, didactic, religious, or extolling the grandeur of a reigning group, the artistic values were rarely slighted. The high level of understanding permitted a profound quality of symbolic transformation. In this atmosphere, the ideal statuary of Greece, the religious frescoes of the Renaissance or the architecture of Baroque Europe was created, to name only a few examples. The relationship between a fastidious audience belonging to some institutionalized aristocracy or ruling group and the proud workmanship which was spurred by a profound and at times paradoxically permissive artistry based on vital standards gave birth to the magnificent quality and characteristic traditions of high art. An internal structure developed, infinitely variegated and unique but free from sheer utility, dedicated to an uncompromising excellence. The differing art forms became recognized disciplines with characteristic orders of expression that insisted upon aesthetic standards.

With the advent of industrialization and the collapse of privileged political classes, the commissions that provided sustenance to artists ceased. The "elite" group underwent a change as well. However, the aesthetic traditions that had shaped and succored a high art for long centuries remained. The artist became an independent creator, no longer working within an accepted social framework or under the benign patronage of a class that could knowingly and sensitively appreciate his creating. Though the intense traditions of integrity in such affairs, indigenous pride in craft and in symbolic worth of content remained as standards for the serious artist, the changing conditions have had a profound effect on the development of high culture for well over a century.

New Alternatives For High Culture

The creative artist cut off from a supporting and understanding audience had two broad alternatives within which to act. He could sell his skills

[7] Alexis de Tocqueville, *Democracy in America* (New York: Mentor, 1956), p. 171.

Art
and
Education
in
Contemporary
Culture

·

346

*The experimental
research of science
and its technology
creates its own and
new combinations of
forms and visual
arrangements as in
this sound chamber.*
[PHOTO: *University
of Michigan, Willow
Run Laboratories*]

and powers of expression to be utilized as a means of entertaining, enlightening, and generally communicating for profit with a steadily growing and increasingly literate mass public. Many artists have chosen this alternative, but because of the internal nature of their professional charge their art no longer adhered to the earlier traditions of an unencumbered excellence, internal integrity and high artistic standards. Different factors emerged, clustered around mass needs and the production of goods for profit. Though this may not have been a deliberate intent, the conditions that nurtured the commercial and popular alternative could not continue the earlier commitments; a new and popular art was created differing from both folk art and high art, based upon a radically new technology and subject to common denominators of mass attitudes. The popular artist, the illustrator, the advertising innovator, the designer and the general purveyor to commercial or popular appetites came into being. The new patrons, either as "nouveau riche" or as collective man, being less well educated and far less sophisticated, being much less influenced by traditional standards, wanted an art they could easily understand. The gulf widened between the serious artist who worked within the tradition of high standards and the immediate desires of a traditionless popular taste. Art became something esoteric and isolated from daily life.

Though the choice of alternatives may be not nearly as clear cut as the writing indicates, for all practical purposes the individual artist has been consistently faced with the dilemma of choice. The artist who elected to continue within the traditions that had given shape and substance to a serious art was thrown upon his own resources. This coincided with a very free and exploratory surge in the various art forms and probably caused it. Perhaps as the result of this lack of specific or defined attachment to patronage that the artist has existed with since the days of the French Revolution, a "continuing avant-garde" was established. This has been removed from popular involvement, though recent publicity given to "Pop" art and to the commercialization of "Op" art has confused even this issue.

The Avant-Garde

The avant-garde by its very nature is composed of those speculative and original individuals who are ahead of their fellow artists or citizens, searching out new ideas and new forms, provoking novel responses, teasing out the incipient characteristics of a culture, deliberately discarding the accepted solutions and generally transforming in fresh symbolic ways the conditions of life. High art retained an exacting and sophisticated quality, though a new audience of fellow artists, educated connoisseurs and critics supplanted the nobility or the church, forming a new "elite."

When there was an active and powerful aristocracy in the past to support a high culture, that culture did not suffer from a lack of recognition; an official stamp of approval was a matter of course. An avant-garde was not required. All the art that was produced was granted a ready audience. Even in the absence of honest understanding the implications

The modern artist probes into the psychological makeup of humans in his own subjective and sensual way. "Gripper of the Wand," J. E. L. Eldridge. [Courtesy of the artist]

Art
and
Education
in
Contemporary
Culture

·

348

of having a work commissioned by the high and mighty was sufficient to insure an eager or at least a receptive audience and the general acceptance and appreciation of the artistic endeavor ensued. When high art was cut loose from its social moorings this almost automatic recognition and acceptance was lost to a large extent. At least, it was lost when the art work initially appeared in public and the artist was maligned or ridiculed by the new audience of the popular mind as well as the official academics. However, the vital aspects of high art have always won eventual acceptance and acclaim. The story is well known of what first happened to the French Impressionists and Post Impressionists: the slander, the calumny, and the indignant rioting that was marked by umbrellas being poked through canvases. Yet within several decades the work of Monet, Van Gogh, Cézanne, Gauguin and many others of the avant-garde became the glory and pride of French culture. This has been enacted many times with other artists and in other countries.

In the United States, for instance, the shocked, mocking and quite violent reaction to the Armory Show of 1913 that introduced modern art to America may not have been completely reversed, but certainly among artists themselves the movement has had complete success while a growing part of the public at least is willing to be enlightened. Though the passive indifference and general apathy of the mass attitude is perhaps even more deadly than active hostility, there has been an obvious if naïve upturn of interest in the "high" arts. Similarly, with music, literature, the dance and drama. James Joyce no longer really shocks us other than in a proper artistic way, the twelve tone scale of Schoenberg is an accepted musical form while the fiftieth anniversary of Stravinsky's *Le Sacre du Printemps* has been greeted with standing ovations in the place of the initial angry rioting. Modern dance has an eager, enthusiastic following and even the experimental stage and the "theatre of the absurd" have made successful incursions into the public arena.

As a matter of fact, with the increasing attention the mass media has paid to some segments of a "so called" avant-garde since the 1950's there is a widespread publicity of the antics and aesthetic attempts at a good number of artists. However, one may genuinely question the merit of some of the work produced and the validity of some of the announced aesthetic aims. Nevertheless, no matter how much acceptance there is by an informed and critical historical overview or a popular peeping into the artist's psyche, high art travels its own narrow and precarious channel in the great average landscape of mass culture. It has need of those free thinking and committed people who, as John Ruskin defines them with wit, "should be fit for the best society but kept out of it." Their art seems to be created despite the suspicions of the man in the street and his lack of encouragement or in spite of a shallow, promoted popularity. Perhaps it is nurtured by a profound and natural rebelliousness against a complacent and materialistic attitude that is common in ordinary living, providing a necessary balance of values in the scheme of things.

In any case, the serious artist who is driven to his work, feeling compelled

*Experimental art
forms derived from
technological and
psychological sources
offer fresh approaches
to form. Student
"Op" art [George
Washington High
School, New York.*
PHOTO: *S. Martin
Friedman]*

to spurn the ease of what he believes to be the mediocrity and lack
of intensity that marks ordinary living, creates the potent individual
works which then enter into the stream of high art. The serious artist thus
presents a continuing psychological defiance of the commonplace in
insisting upon an engagement with the disturbing yet generative qualities
of his inner life and that of mankind in general. The result is an ongoing
creation of art works in the highest tradition ahead of the banalities of
the commonplace. The classroom perhaps is no place for the avant-garde
to be incorporated daily into a blackboard lesson, but its spirit is akin to
the young minds, the curious wonder, the restless search and the
imaginative probes of any alert student. There should be some meeting
ground that only the individual teacher may naturally provide through
the enthusiastic teaching of art.

The awakened national interest in "culture," prompted and partially
supported by government and private foundations, may have a salubrious
effect on both the expansion of education in the arts and the opportunities
for professional artists in all the varying fields of expression. However,
the entire area of government support of the arts, while deserving of
encouragement and reinforcement, should be approached with care and
continued questioning of values and standards. Otherwise, the avant-
garde, the freely exploratory artistic consciousness of society, may itself
become a mere propagandistic or popularly attuned showpiece.

Art
and
Education
in
Contemporary
Culture

·

350

CULTURAL AND EDUCATIONAL IMPLICATIONS

The implications may be that only in aristocratic societies were serious artists who were honestly committed to aesthetic values encouraged, their work recognized and appreciated. As Ortega, the Spanish philosopher argued, the mass, which has assumed political power, and insists upon its own commonplace values, has consequently lost respect for those values of the earlier elite that instigated and sustained a high culture. "The mass crushes beneath it everything that is different, everything that is excellent, individuals qualified and select." [8] This extreme position denies that a democratically organized society can foster a profound and excellent art. There are other critics who support this viewpoint, if not as strongly as Ortega. Yet at the same time, the arts in all of the democracies have proliferated to an extent that has never been matched previously. Though quantity is not the decisive or even a relative factor in art, the profusion of art over the last one hundred years in Western Europe and the United States has had a significant and lasting base of quality as well. No matter what the political base, many works that may be regarded as examples of high art are created. Perhaps the symbolic and humanistic attributes of art are too deeply buried in the human spirit to be more than superficially touched by the vagaries of most external conditions, harkening to a central core of creativity that cannot be more than temporarily overwhelmed by inhospitable forces. In this sense, the existential importance of the individual assumes the air of influence; good art is the result of the stress of a single person with vision who is acting upon his experience rather than apathetically succumbing to it. This realization should be a central point in any art education theory.

For instance, in the visual arts alone, painting, sculpture, architecture and serious film making have developed new forms and new schools that have a power of expression, a universal validity and are probably assured of a place in history. The great names of today's high art forms could match any of the past and their works do not fade on comparison. Picasso, Mondrian, Miro, Pollock, DeKooning in painting; Gropius, Wright, Van der Rohe, Saarinen in architecture; Moore, Calder, Smith in sculpture; Griffith and Fellini in film making—these are but a few among the scores of others that create a high culture—high, not because of any political aristocracy, but because of the innate and powerful urgency of expression through art based on integrity of purpose and purity of means.

It may not be primarily the continued existence of a high art that disturbs the critics who point to the welter of mediocrity that is a condition of modern living. Though they fear for a future serious art they stress the dwindling number of the "elite" who would sustain such an art. Dwight MacDonald, one of the most passionate and critical of the social observers, indicates that the changing cultural conditions fosters a pseudo-art that is inimical to the interests of "high" art; that the

[8] Jose Ortega y Gasset, *Revolt of the Masses* (New York: W. W. Norton, 1932), pp. 18-19.

audience for cultural products is now largely composed of "a large body of ignoramuses"; that "high" culture may indeed be in danger of extinction. The confusions that the decade of the sixties have ushered in between the forms of popular culture and their usages in supposely high art forms such as "Pop" art bear this out in many ways. This is the serious level of criticism that teachers of art have to address themselves to and resolve on the basis of a clarity of purpose, a profundity of educational understanding and a sensitivity to aesthetic values.

Ideal Aims

The existence of a high art in our contemporary culture obviously does not always insure its rightful recognition from critical sources or an appreciative mass audience with the necessarily fastidious and critical appreciation. It is here that art education has to sense its fundamental obligation, not only of "bringing art to the masses" but of developing a mass body of intense and informed opinion and appreciation through education. Then theory may point to high art as the fruition of a democratic way of life as well as of other political persuasions, for to reiterate, art cuts across the impositions of social doctrines. It is basic to man himself, not to the institutions he develops. As such, the ultimate responsibility for the future of serious art and the development of an honestly responsive mass audience lies with education. One of the most important social tasks of education is to define and enrich a democratic culture that will nourish a worthwhile and exuberant art. The art has to stem both from an experience that is neither trivial or absurd and an involvement with an excellence of an uncommon quality that has a cultivation and a morality. At the same time the common denominator should be raised to its highest point rather than to lowest, bolstering a direction away from mediocrity and toward an esteemed excellence of art.

Yet the confusions between the various levels of art cultures intrudes, the institutions of the times do have a profound influence on the cultural involvements of education and those of the average individual. "High" culture finds itself in a confounding situation, suffering, at times, from a self imposed "ivory towerism" in order to avert corruption and resorting to obscurity, at other times, in order to escape the deadly levelling aspects of popular attitudes that blandly improvise their own forms from "high" art sources. However, the characteristic quality of a work of high art is its unique power. It is an individual expression probing the depths of the human condition—of the creator and the audience as well. The latter must respond to it as individuals rather than as representative cogs in a larger order. "High" art is involved with feelings and ideas, with the peculiarities of taste and the intensities of visions and is committed to inescapable standards of morality and excellence. These standards may vary, but their integrity is mutually agreed upon by artist and audience. No doubt, there are many examples of supposed high art that do not measure up to even self imposed standards; there are countless instances of banal, pedestrian and otherwise unsuccessful works. Yet the attempt to

Art
and
Education
in
Contemporary
Culture

·

352

The contemporary
artist has profound
links with the
modern exploration
of the universe.

"Improvisation,"
Laszlo Moholy-Nagy.
[Collection, The
University of Michi-
gan Museum of Art]

"Trembling Veil,"
Gyorgy Kepes.
[Saidenberg Gallery,
New York]

[LEFT]
"Synthesis," Irving
Kaufman. [Rehn
Gallery, New York;
PHOTO: Geoffrey
Clements]

[BELOW]
"Ramapo Night,"
Richard Pousette-
Dart. [Betty Parsons
Gallery, New York;
PHOTO: Oliver Baker
Associates]

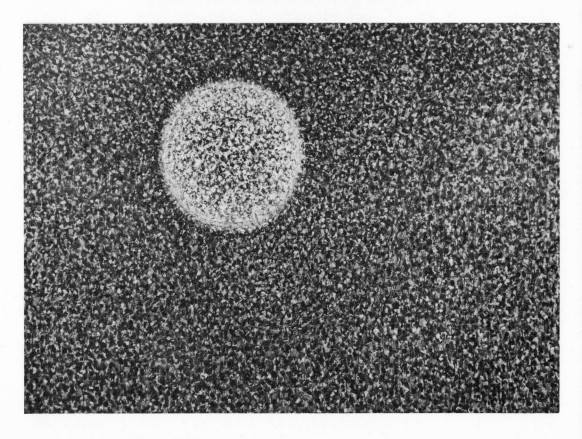

Art
and
Education
in
Contemporary
Culture

·

354

communicate the "human condition" on an individual and feeling level of integrity and worth is present, and the attempt to achieve a high standard is always an acknowledged purpose.

These are the qualities of high art that distinguish it from its more popular counterparts. And it is the recognition of these qualities that is encumbent upon an educational system that commits itself to the concept of excellence and worth in whatever it fosters. Art education must assume the responsibility of enlarging and enriching the base of aesthetic taste for the many as well as the "elite" so that the danger of its dwindling can not be a topic or concern. However, this can only be accomplished when there is no compromise with the qualities of art, no confusion between what is genuine and the pseudo-varieties of culture. There has to be a coherent and committed acceptance of purpose and responsibility that is activated by a passionate and sympathetic relationship to serious art and to the broadening and releasing role of democratic education.

Recognition of Barriers

It is not sufficient to point out the necessity of an art of value in providing a desirable vitality and intensity of cultural experience. Art education has to go beyond the listing of platitudes in the advocacy of creative activities. It has to make certain value judgments about some of the basic beliefs of the culture in which it exists, then courageously and with a mature conviction insist upon an adequately qualitative program of art in the school curriculum. This calls for an examination of many of the pedagogical and personal attitudes that are much too frequently taken for granted by art teachers, general educators and a good part of the lay public.

In examining and evaluating some of the influential and deterministic cultural factors, it is important that individual sensibility be brought to play in the process. It would be unfortunate to merely transfer gross values from one camp to another. Rather, in unearthing the broad tendencies of a surrounding culture it is hoped that the individual teacher may sense some of the symbolic play of human expression. But more basic, he may arrive at a personal assessment and maturity of insight that would sensitize and activate appropriate artistic and teaching qualities which would be felt by his students.

To achieve these goals, educators have to divest themselves of any easy or uncritical acceptance of popular or conforming sentiment simply because they are held by a majority. They have to reasonably assess attitudes that may be provoking and initially quite contrary to prevailing beliefs.

A viewpoint which has received almost no consideration in art education other than in an arbitrary fashion is the belief that the common level of contemporary living, including the scope of education, is impoverished to a large extent and concerned with trivialities. This kind of education may stem from the existence of a manufactured and commercially oriented popular culture that makes up the other part of the triad of cultures, our topic of the following chapter.

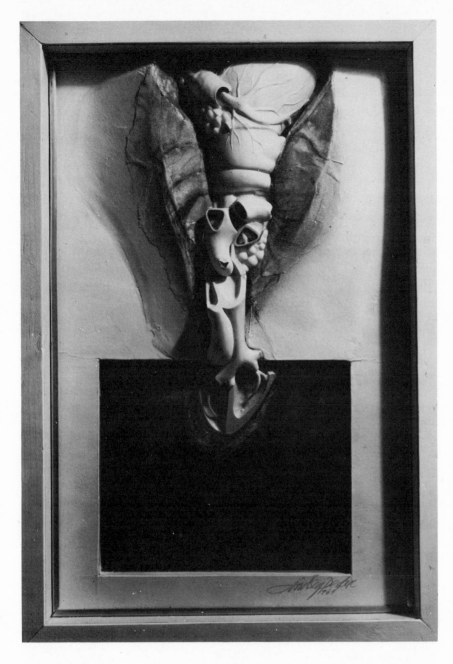

The images of
modern art have
expanded cultural
and aesthetic
sensibilities.
"Collage—Relief
III," Paper and
Plastic, Lindsey
Decker. [Courtesy of
the artist; PHOTO:
John D. Schiff]

In the well known vicious circle, some observers indicate an unconsciously insidious and pervasive influence emanating from the essentially artificial and contrived qualities of popular culture. Educators have to indicate a willingness to face up to the implied or even explicitly voiced criticisms of such understanding: the contaminating and corrupting influences of a depersonalized and industrialized society, the crass material values that sustain it, the moral quandary that often results, the dissatisfaction or more than vague dislike of most workers of what they do, the insensitive waste or relatively frantic use of "leisure" time that seeks relief from boredom and escape from effort rather than a fulfillment that requires commitment, an

Art
and
Education
in
Contemporary
Culture

.

356

atmosphere of consistent and largely accepted conformity that breeds its own debilitating ennui, the rejection or negligence of creative engagement that substitutes a thin and unsatisfying momentary diversion for the ardors and strong emotions of serious creative expression, the obligingly loose educational patterns that sometimes unwittingly provide a firmer foundation for values that are contrary to its expressed goals and on into a rather large number of casual factors and their consequences in inhibiting a desirable educational climate.

These negative cultural conditions have to be set against the more positive factors of contemporary living, particularly those of the American experience: the belief in the almost infinite potential of man, the abiding trust in the efficacy and uplift of education, the wistful but fundamentally sincere search for "beauty," the essential generosity that characterizes interpersonal relationships, the setting if not the achievement of an ideal of individuality and the hope that the riches of the land may be utilized in commendable and acceptable ways, and in the beginning support that the arts are receiving, no matter how small the percentage of the national budget. It is insufficient however, to voice these credit entries in the ledger. They are only a beginning for an education of merit and sensibility. The teaching of art has to go further in examining the full and constantly changing panorama of culture, the good with the bad, the spurious with the genuine in order to set the necessary conditions for honest and vital individual expression and cultural growth.

Popular Culture and Taste

We tend to perceive that which we have picked out
in the form stereotyped for us by the culture.
WALTER LIPPMANN

POPULAR culture has a pervasive influence in contemporary living. It insinuates itself into every nook and cranny of existence, in the classroom as well as in the mass media. Art education has been subject to its forms and the resultant confusion of aesthetic values has done much to inhibit the genuine development of aesthetic experiences for students. It is this confusion, this intermingling of real and pseudo values that should be of concern to any teacher of art, for the basic content of the subject area is involved. A broader examination of the properties of popular or mass culture would seem to be a necessary element in the theory of art education.

THE QUALITY OF POPULAR CULTURE

Dwight MacDonald characterizes "popular" culture, or as he prefers to call it "Masscult" as follows:

For about a century, Western culture has really been two cultures: [MacDonald also considers Folk culture finished as a strong force for all practical purposes with the advent of modern technology.] the traditional kind—let us call it "High culture"—that is chronicled in the text books, and a "Mass culture" manufactured for the market. In the older forms, its artisans have long been at work. In the novel the line stretches from the 18th century "servant girl" romances to Edna Ferber, Fannie Hurst and such current ephemera as Burdick . . . and Uris; in music, from Hearts and Flowers to Rock 'n Roll; in art, from the chromo to Norman Rockwell; in architecture from Victorian Gothic to ranch-house moderne. . . . It is not just unsuccessful art. It is non-art . . . Masscult offers its customers neither an emotional catharsis nor an aesthetic experience, for these demand effort. The production line grinds out a uniform product whose humble aim is not even entertainment for this too implies life and hence effort, but merely distraction. It may be stimulating or narcotic, but it must be easy to assimilate. It asks nothing of its audience for it is "totally subjected to the spectator," and it gives nothing.[1]

[1] Dwight MacDonald, *Against the American Grain* (New York: Random House, 1962), p. 3.

Art
and
Education
in
Contemporary
Culture

.

358

It is commercially self sufficient in that mass culture has developed new media of its own where the serious artist rarely ventures: radio, the movies, comic books, detective stories, science fiction, television, hobby interests such as "do-it-by-the-numbers" painting kits, and a host of related and similar leisure diversions.

Along with "Masscult" is the existence of a high body of work that is perhaps several notches above in pretended caliber. This MacDonald refers to as "Midcult," though it is still part of the popular culture. It is exemplified by the dollar reproductions of great paintings, the abridged versions of great classics, the community "pop" concerts, the Sears, Roebuck catalog that now sells original art work by mail order. "Midcult" boasts of large numbers of writers, performers, pseudothinkers and popular artists who give only the illusion of being involved with serious effort, with an expurgated and abridged version of a high order of intellectual search and a spuriously intense emotional expression. These are the interpreters and popularizers that are so much in evidence practicing various degrees of successful "communication," either in what they create as products or as speakers at local gatherings, at many adult education classes and at Chautauqualike forums.

The fundamental danger in the new cultural expansion is that it probably will be patterned within a "Midcult" setting. Much of this is to be expected, given the overall condition and level of involvement with the arts. Nevertheless, art educators, particularly, have a clearly recognizable function to initiate and persist in an insistence upon the most vital, pertinent, original and highest levels of art. They should stress that only standards of excellence be pursued in school art programs, pointing out wherever necessary the existence of adulterated or shallow qualities and practices.

The Development of Kitsch

Clement Greenberg, another critic borrows a German word *kitsch* to further describe the conditions of popular culture. He notes the large and newly urbanized masses that have developed and the effective spread of technology. Their consequent need for a culture different from the high traditional one and simpler in form, fit for mass, relatively untutored and unsophisticated consumption stimulates the development of a cultural product—*kitsch*—like a new commodity for a new market taking full advantage of new technology. However, Greenberg comments, "The precondition for kitsch, a condition without which kitsch would be impossible, is the availability close at hand of a full matured cultural tradition, whose discoveries, acquisitions, and perfected self-consciousness *kitsch* can take advantage of for its own ends. It borrows from it devices, tricks, stratagems, rules of thumb, themes, converts them into a system, and discards the rest . . . when enough time has elapsed the new is looted for new 'twists,' which are then watered down and served up as kitsch." [2]

[2] Clement Greenberg, "Avant Garde and Kitsch," *The Partisan Reader* (New York: Dial Press, 1946), p. 381.

*Popular culture
enjoys widespread
acceptance, particu-
larly among the
young.* [PHOTO:
Stephen C. Sumner]

In this manner high culture is adulterated, its impact becomes vicarious
and for the average comprehension the distinctions between popular and
high culture become vague if existent at all. The values between good
and bad all but disappear, aesthetic standards diminish, and there is a
resultant "homogenized" cultural atmosphere.

The criteria for experiencing art are established on the basis of populari-
zation and effortless enjoyment, "fun" and "easy" training of the mind.
The innately difficult aspect of art, the necessary engagement with emotionally exacting, intellectually challenging and sometimes subjectively painful
and time consuming, yet spiritually rewarding material bypassed, mini-
mized or corrupted. The older art forms derived from the high culture
traditions are abridged, condensed or otherwise simplified. This is especially
true in classic and serious literature, where "special" editions, including
many used in schools are practically rewritten. Those passages that are hard,
or involved with material that is not well known, are excised or reduced to
a low common denominator of understanding. The rendition of the classics
in flamboyant comics is perhaps the logical absurdity of this attitude.
Though it is difficult to radically alter the surface appearances of the visual
art forms, the poor reproductions, the loss of artistic nuance and exposure
out of a proper context accomplishes the same adulterating conditions.

MacDonald further points out the connection (between cultural traditions and popular culture) as not being that of the leaf and branch but
rather that of caterpillar and leaf. The popular manifestations of culture
figuratively devour the sources upon which they are feeding. The implied
criticism is that soon there will be little left of the course to "eat." This
may be an exaggerated forecast of gloom and doom—art is too fundamental a need and condition of human existence to disintegrate by

Art
and
Education
in
Contemporary
Culture

·

360

attrition alone. However, the rather negative position does underscore the distortions that lead perhaps to a pseudo culture in art, which like the emperor of legend wore no clothes, though no one noticed it.

On the other hand, it is only fair to note some of the more positive attributes of popular culture. Though the various mass media tend to reinforce an insensitive, if not brutal conformity, they also act as common cultural safety valves, expressing not only a popular sentiment but making as well an oftentimes artful comment on almost any subject. *Kitsch* tends to celebrate the homilies of daily rectitude, the virtues of the passing parade as well as the violence of destructive forces and the questionable venality of "making it." All of these elements of the human condition are marked, in symbolic fashion, with fantasy—a fantasy that possesses the liberating quality of humor and the catharsis of action even if experienced, paradoxically, through vicarious means. Some brief yet revealing inkling is provided that offers the common denominator of the reality of twentieth-century living and aspiration. It is immaterial in the long run whether this is as an overblown and hackneyed image of the impossible American beauty or in the more sophisticated lines of interior designers or car stylists.

The sad fact, nevertheless, is that the supposedly revealing glimpses, for the most part, are truncated and superficial experiences. They tend to become barriers to an authentic involvement with aesthetic qualities and a more profound artistic expression.

POPULAR INFLUENCES IN EDUCATION

An example from a bad practice in art teaching can illustrate the above criticism. In many drawing lessons the student, if not consciously urged not to copy some already existing drawing of a professional artist, will often use that kind of material as a model for his own work. Painstakingly, the student will ape the techniques and forms of a favorite cartoonist, an illustrator in popular magazines or even the work of a high level artist. There are countless pseudo creative attempts of this nature in the classrooms during art lessons and even more often at home. The likeness of movie stars, folk figures, Disney characters, "interesting" faces and scenes abound, limited only to the time the student is willing to give to the "artwork."

The essential fault does not even lie in the level of the work, the trite plagiarizing, the uninspired coyping. It is rather in the acceptance of someone else's solution to creative problems. If a student gives up the challenge of directly attempting to create a symbolic expression from the material of life (as most do), then the very essence of the art experience is denied him. In copying a head, for instance, from an art book or from a favorite magazine, the student is primarily involved with work in two dimensions, both with model and his own drawing. However, if he drew one from life, the need to transpose the existence of forms in three dimensions into the symbolic elements of line, color and mass in two dimensions provides one of the inherently creative conditions of the expressive experience an artistic problem solving situation. This requires a level of participation that values the creative process itself. It does not deny other art, but leaves that for the intellectual and emotional recreation of appreciation. Nor does this deny the appropriateness and the necessity of influence, but there is a strong distinction between valid influence and slavish, superficial copying.

The Implied Dangers to Art and Education

In any case, the integrity of serious art is put in question when only the simple appearances and surface characteristics of art are stressed. The effort required to create as a serious artist disintegrates and does not permit an unsophisticated and ill tutored crowd to become involved with art even if they would want to. This may not threaten serious art in the long run, but there are certainly short range ramifications that are adverse. Some serious artists, subjected to an insistent barrage of platitudes and who probably are not to be blamed for succumbing to the enticements of *kudos* and various material rewards will offer their services to *kitsch* choosing the completely commercial and popular alternative. The pressures and inspirations for serious art may turn it to aesthetically unrewarding and obtuse concerns while the whole of society may suffer artistic convulsions from the complex and entangled allegiances.

The results may be an anti-intellectualism and a distaste for art such as has generally inhibited the creative cultural strength of the United States. Or the negativism and philistine attitude in a more artistically productive

Broadway reflects the visual focus of popular culture. [PHOTO: *Stephen C. Sumner*]

Art
and
Education
in
Contemporary
Culture

·

362

state may arbitrarily identify serious art with antisocial tendencies that society suspiciously guards against and curtails if necessary. The book burning and antimodern art shows in Nazi Germany and the totalitarian imposition of stylistic fiat in Soviet Russia are extreme examples. The undercurrent of censorship in the United States is also an indication of this attitude as are some of the semiofficial but arbitrary critical pronouncements about modern art made by governmental administrators. The schools have felt this influence in the form of local vigilante committees which exercise a censorship in library purchases, class book discussions, the hanging of local art and in related ways.

Perhaps this critical level demonstrates the most pertinent and far reaching element of disturbance in the relationships of popular culture to society: its impact on education, and the consequent pressures not only from small outside groups but from larger forces at work as well. Though there are numerous and extremely effective teachers who work on excellent levels of instruction and inspire affirmative personal and cultural values there are still those whose presentation of material is open to criticism. They operate on a vacillating middle ground that disapproves of the obvious inferiority of the lowest denominator of mass understanding but is nevertheless only a form of the "borrowing" from "high art" sources that Greenberg mentions. The traditional culture is mined like a vein of ore and the result is treated not too infrequently as a glittering bauble. The surface appearance of serious art and culture is admired. Nonetheless, the difficult and demanding substance that could strike an even richer vein of personal response and aesthetic potential is bypassed. The discipline and necessary time, the intensity of focus and the involvement of one's own imagination which are all required of serious art and related culture are not emphasized. The contrary pressures are potent and the environment even in school often inhospitable for genuine commitment and intense experience in the arts. A consequent disenchantment with the intelligible as well as the imaginative aspects at the core of fine art is replaced by superficial and predigested considerations.

Art education has been more a prey to this level and method of popularly oriented subject presentation than most other curriculum areas; it is an undercurrent that is readily discernible in the art products that are normally seen in the schools, and in the level of appreciation or simple artistic and visual literacy that remains relatively undeveloped or puerile in understanding. Many of the experiences that children have during art lessons reflect the larger influences from the mass culture outside the school. Too often the teacher "sells" the ideas of art education by resorting to the signs and stratagems of the manufactured culture feeling that this may somehow reach the individual student's awareness and perhaps activate an interest and a participation in art. This may be done very deliberately. As such it deserves a chastising finger for utilizing teaching methods and concepts that are alien, for the most part, to the creative and responsive atmosphere that it is hoped will be engendered. But more likely than not, particularly when art on the elementary level is the responsibility of the classroom teacher, the

*An artist's response
to the visual
conglomeration of
popular culture.
"Broadway," Mark
Toby. [Willard
Gallery, New York;
PHOTO: Adolph
Studly]*

teacher himself or herself is likely to be ignorant of the forces helping to determine his or her own personal values and taste, and consequent teaching methods. Unfortunately, this operates frequently in the art area on higher levels where teachers generally accept the less vulgar manifestations of popular culture but still confuse it for a version of a refined and serious culture.

Another danger that is more than implied in the acute influence of popular culture in the activities of the classroom, in art education and also in other subject areas, is the figurative lulling to sleep of the individual intelligence and probing curiosity. The reflex and grossly conditioning factors that are an inherent part of mass art forms and most of mass communication, create deceptions and easily accepted illusions. These ask very little of an individual's intelligence and sensibilities, yet they are flattering, immediately

Art
and
Education
in
Contemporary
Culture

.

364

pleasing and sufficiently suggestive in sensory ways so that the psyche is gratified, despite the thinness of the art or communicative substance. The persistence of these superficial yet psychologically effective techniques invades the individual image the student may possess of his own personality, weakening the awareness of the self, narcotizing the play of sentient insights and generally providing a base for dependent thinking and aborted feeling. The shifting nuances, the welter of subtle and unique needs, the turmoil and richness of preconscious imagery, the vacillating but continuing searching probes, the direct apprehension of sensory activity, the almost infinite range of conceptual pattern, all of which comprise the personality—the self—of the particular student are either patronized, ignored or otherwise abused by the imposed and artfully contrived stimuli of popular culture. The necessity for speed, conformity of values, and the oversimplification of forms and ideas mitigate against the slower, the differentiating, and the complex nature of individual human nature.

THE TECHNOLOGICAL FORCES IN POPULAR CULTURE

The popular culture can be too easily traced to irrelevant sources, however. It is perhaps appropriate, at this point, to suggest that popular culture is not necessarily regarded by even the most vehement critic as the result of the national character of Americans, of political democracy or of any free institutions. The conditions of popular culture have spread over the world; in some instances they are deliberately manipulated as propaganda, in others they are the commodities, ideas, and forms most desired by a greater majority of the populace. But the diffusion of a vast machinery of "homogenized" culture cannot be denied: from the socialist realism of Russia to the controlled propaganda of China, from the twist, frug or latest discotheque craze danced on a Mediterranean shore to the comics read in London, from the mass circulation magazine covers of the United States to the floridy sentimental postcards south of the border. Obviously there are forces at work that stimulate and support the spread. The most prominent consideration is the parallel spread of the Industrial Revolution.

The radical innovations of an unbounded technology have inaugurated many economic and social changes that were bound to alter the groundwork and class considerations of the development of consequent culture no matter what classification they fell into. There was greater productivity, an increase in comfort and leisure, the raising of income on all levels but particularly on the lowest level. There has been a parallel commitment, in economic terms at first, and subsequently aesthetic ones, to an abundant but mass and standardized approach to production and consumption founded on efficiency and profit. Despite all the gains that technology can claim and they are tremendous as well as legitimate, there has been a parallel and related development, if not an arbitrary imposition of an inartistic and unintellectual mass culture. This threatens the very advances achieved by technology in value terms. The inherent confusions which congenitally seem to arise when the standard of excellence is allowed to be controlled by an insensitive and uninformed low common denominator finds its way into all of the nooks and crannies of living as well as into the large public areas. Education is as much affected as any other social institution.

Education being an integral element of the fabric of society, not only helps shape society in the best traditions, but reflects as well the moving forces, that are already present. Consequently, teaching often operates on the most representative level both quantitatively and qualitatively. Its broad results are a part of every classroom atmosphere. The technological revolution did not only change the superficial landscape, and the social and economic mores of modern man; it redirected basic philosophical thinking. It created new cultural patterns, reaching into the classroom as an important institution to find acceptance and support of its evolving premises. Popular culture, one of the most obvious of conditions of the spread of technology through the ubiquitousness of the new graphic process thus found itself reflected in many basic ways in American education, not the least of which are T.V. classrooms, teaching machines and "Laboratories" for learning.

The corollaries of an active, free technology influenced learning by producing the mass psychological and pedagogical conditions that in turn develop into popular culture: a rapidly growing literacy in the broadest sense of acquaintance with much of the world's thought and activity, past and present; an increasing wealth that provides for most, free time, and for some, leisure and opportunities for self realization encountered only by relatively few people in the past, a dedication to progress that though it esteems the dignity and traditional legacy of man still subjects him to the phenomena of the moment without really comprehending the radical nature of change and finally, an engineering implementation of scientific theory that creates those very material values that are oriented around things and their acquisition, rather than the more basic insights that provide meaning to existence.

"Technology," as Max Frisch in his novel *Homo Faber,* succinctly points out may be regarded as, ". . . the knack of so arranging the world that we don't have to experience it." Technology at once becomes a burden as well as an opportunity. The opportunities that can relieve the bulk of man in his unremitting struggle for daily bread (a rather basic purpose that is somehow looked down upon in an affluent society) creating opportunities for what could be an intense and creative self realization but is really only a redistribution of time, can at the same time burden society with unsuspected illusions and concepts which trap the average individual and keep him from a really vital engagement with experience. It is these latter illusions that confound not only the individual immersed in popular culture, but an educational environment that is perhaps unconsciously caught up in it.

The development of a language of vision that Gyorgy Kepes hopes for consonant with both art and technology becomes an important aesthetic and educational factor all the more, to offset a rampant mechanization.

Art
and
Education
in
Contemporary
Culture

·

366

THE FABRICATED IMAGE OF CULTURE

Though this may require an initial imaginative leap (illusion necessarily utilizing an underlying imagination), for too many educators there is a rapid deteriorization to unexamined habit which also has to be offset. Daniel J. Boorstin examines these illusions at length.

In nineteenth century America the most extreme modernism held that man was made by his environment. In twentieth century America, without abandoning belief that we are made by our environment, we also believe our environment can be made almost wholly by us. This is the appealing contradiction at the heart of our passion for pseudo-events: for made news, synthetic heroes, prefabricated tourist attractions, homogenized interchangeable forms of art and literature. . . . We believe we can fill our experience with new fangled content. Almost everything we see and hear and do persuades us that this power is ours . . . Life in America . . . is a spectator sport in which we ourselves make the props and are the sole performers.[3]

Material as well as philosophic illusions may distort the search creating a variety of "images" that blur the edges of knowledge. Though Boorstin may not accept an imaginative and intuitive base for knowledge existing parallel to a rational one quite as readily as an artist may, his use of the illusionistic connotations of image is distinct. It does not refer to the imaginative visions of "reality" as symbolically expressed by art but the actual lack of such visions that permits an "unreality" to exist as an article of belief, itself an antithesis and denial of art.

Boorstin can be clearly understood then when he says,

While all . . . uses of the image have become more important with each decade of the twentieth century, a more abstract image is the product of our age. Its tyranny is pervasive. An image in this sense is not a trademark, a design, a slogan, or an easily remembered picture. It is a studiously crafted personality profile of an individual, institution, corporation, product, or service. It is a value caricature, shaped in three dimensions, of synthetic materials. Such images in increasing numbers have been fabricated and re-enforced by the new techniques of the Graphic Revolution. . . . Tempted, like no generation before us, to believe we can fabricate our experience—our news, our celebrities, our adventures, and our art forms—we finally believe we can make the very yardstick by which all of these are to be measured. That we can make our very ideals. This is the climate of our extravagant expectations. It is expressed in a universal shift in our American way of speaking: from talk about "ideals" to talk about "images". . . . If the right "image" will elect a President or sell an automobile, a religion, a cigarette, or a suit of clothes, why not make it America herself—or the American way of life.[4]

Boorstin goes on to define the "image" as "synthetic, believable, passive, vivid, simplified, and ambiguous."[5] These six attributes may also be utilized

---

[3] From *The Image* by Daniel J. Boorstin, p. 182. Copyright © 1961 by Daniel J. Boorstin. Reprinted by permission of Atheneum Publishers.

[4] *Ibid.*, p. 186.

[5] *Ibid.*, discussed pp. 184–194.

Mass culture usually caters to the lowest common denominator of taste and commercial interests. [PHOTO: *Stephen C. Sumner*]

to help define the characteristics of popular culture. A brief expansion of each may sum up what has already been said and help provide some insight into those broad cultural factors that have an influence in art education. They may constitute a very broad rule of thumb against which a teacher may compare the notes of her own attitudes as well as the art work in her classroom.

Popular Culture Is Synthetic

Obviously all art is contrived in one sense; somebody deliberately sets about to create forms, to shape materials. There is a deliberate underlying purpose in the specific creative act, though it is not always capable of being reduced to words. In serious art there is a genuine involvement with the material, because of compelling expressive need. This, of course, need not result in a concrete work. Mozart could have hummed his sonatas to himself, Faulkner could have imagined his protagonists acting through his own literally unexpressed but nevertheless active mental processes and Cézanne could have played with colors and forms in his mind's eye; all of this could not have made them any the less artists in their own nature. However, in creating their tangible forms, they also were serving inherently expressive needs that require the authentication of their experience. This suggests social considerations of communication and shared expression that

Art
and
Education
in
Contemporary
Culture

.

368

may be beyond the purely personal, yet are developed primarily in subjective terms. Though Picasso may have had moral considerations as well as aesthetic ones in his work *Guernica* (p. 332) condemning the Fascists as well as relating sensuous and formal elements, the work was created primarily from the inner tensions and insights that prompted the expressive activity. It is a genuine expression that exists as a personal emotional and symbolic need in all people, but much more intense and compelling in artists. The purposes it may be put to may color the perception of the work of art, its cultural impact the result of its utilitarian or instrumental considerations. But the initial expressive qualities, those that exist in intrinsic terms, as visual distillations of emotion in symbolic form still are retained as a basic condition of fine art.

The art work in popular culture is contrived, however, generally in the strict terms of its short range purposes and rarely expresses the subjective nature of its maker. There is no genuine or felt involvement with living experience in order to shape it or in some way to symbolically master it. Rather the popular cultural forms are designed specifically to elicit predetermined understanding. They are created primarily to serve needs adjunctive or even hostile to art and not to act as vehicles of expression. They are deliberate in a sense that high art never is, manipulating artificial elements to produce conscious images beyond which the audience is not invited to probe. Though high art may have served very particular purposes in the past and consciously ordered the forms of expression, they invariably appealed to man's inner nature and to the more profound questions of the meaning of existence through religious or philosophical adjuncts. Popular culture in this sense plans all of its aspects to be on the surface, to be seen. There are no consciously lurking psychological indeterminancies or provocations, there are instead the carefully sorted and synthetically ordered elements which are expected to elicit particular responses. Though this may not always be successful the values cluster around titillation, success, abundance, business and entertainment, its forms are specifically designed with these factors in mind. These elements are determined as "good" in advance, not eliciting an opinion, but insisting upon one.

The prideful creation of a trademark of a large corporation, the happy ending American movies, the sentimental singing of Tin Pan Alley (not jazz), the sleek advertising renditions of manufacturers' products, the bright eyed, clear skinned, henna haired, wasp-waisted heroines and bronzed, muscular, square jawed, lean hipped men of popular illustration are a few of the more obvious popular culture visualizations that are synthetic in nature.

An example of an art lesson that has a platitudinous imposition of content and purpose is the banal illustrated letters that classes are prompted to send to sick playmates. In one way or another this reflects a commercially sponsored "greeting card" philosophy rather than a felt concern for experience. There is no real opportunity for a genuine expression of emotion or sympathetic relationship with the symbolic means at hand. There is a highly contrived and artificial situation that defeats, by its groupness and its

The unique expressive experiences of the art lesson offer one of the educational antidotes to the pressures of a conforming culture. [PHOTO: *S. Martin Friedman*]

intrinsically platitudinous purposes, the authentic personal and artistic involvement with real experience. In many more subtle ways this kind of emasculated and artificial experience is prevalent in art teaching situations that have an inescapable element of popular culture as a core value. One can point to the cartoon figures that children ape, the designs of musical notes that supposedly interpret music, the less than mediocre designs that are unconsciously influenced by mass produced decorative ware and a host of other synthetic and inartistic expressions.

Popular Culture Is Believable

In order to safeguard and further the purposes that prompt popular culture the realities of experience are often "doctored" so that a credible image may be created. There is conscious distortion, undue stress, rampant overstatement, bland understatement and considerable improvisation of methods in fashioning a desirable image. Though it may be "imaginative," this "doctoring" is quite different from the symbolic searching that serious artists are involved with. Modern artists consciously distort in order to arrive at a closer approximation of what they consider to be the truth; their aim is to more intensely reveal the essence rather than the surface appearances of their content. Too often in popular culture artistic license is used to excite the credulity of the mass mind rather than to uncover any nature of reality.

In art education, the desire of a teacher to have a child make something "pretty" or to make the art work "as you see it with your eyes" may fall into this category. The so called acceptable in mass terms becomes the believ-

Art
and
Education
in
Contemporary
Culture

·

370

able. In general educational terms it may be well to point out the need to guard against such a desire to present material that has as its impelling quality only the belief that it is believable. Since belief and reality are subjective conditions in art, in the final analysis, art education has a responsibility to make available every known consideration so that the *individual* development can be fully informed before it establishes its own meaning, and then it has to be ready to accept the unusual, the strange and the disturbing as well as the more conforming expressions, as valid works.

Popular Culture Is Passive

There are subtle, complex and indirect psychological parts to the passive nature of popular culture. A patent invitation to behave in accordance with the image model that is presented for public edification is presumed as well as the credibility of its audience. Popular culture, consequently, is not contrived to stimulate its viewers and listeners, so that they may act out of an inner and independent understanding, rather the contrary. It is hoped that the audience will respond to the forms of popular culture which are considered almost philosophically and artistically inviolate in a static way so that their self images produce actions toward the unquestioned correctness of the popular culture images. Both the popular artist producing his forms and the audience responding to them are expected to fit into the preconceived notions of the popular image.

For instance, the adolescently oriented world of the commercial song writer manufactures a form of love and romance, of "moon-June," "he-she," improbable and puerile apparitions of physiognomy and almost impossible ideals of behavior that have a bathos and a sentimentality. Yet, at least during the courtship days when these songs are most listened to, young men and women find themselves attempting, even if vaguely and intangibly, to fit into the patterns the content of the songs suggest. The actual musical forms are similarly on a simple rhythmic and melodic line that an individual may easily adapt to. This does not deny the authentic musical worth of good jazz which actually appeals, in its pure form, to more basic and genuine qualities of response.

There is also a wealth of striking, colorful and enticingly designed parts to popular visual culture. These become compelling devices that confidently insist upon attention, exerting an almost hypnotic appeal. With a mass response to be elicited, the overwhelming result is a species of conformity that is difficult to counteract. As others besides Boorstin imply, this may be one of the most characteristic qualities of popular culture, its invitation to conformity, suggesting psychologically that the mere existence of a vivid and tangible form should provide the basis for mass judgment and behavior.

The teacher of art has to be especially alert to this passive and conforming aspect of popular culture. It seeps into the classroom atmosphere, osmosis like, smoothly and insistently making itself felt. Art has to be presented in such a manner that it will awaken and enrich the responses of students, even on a passionately partisan level, yet this cannot be done without the dynamic aspects of creative involvement which are essentially opposed to the passive nature of mass art forms. In a genuine art experience there is a two way exchange, the symbol being an open, evocative quality that is like life itself. The creative process of the student in making his own art object or the recreation of experience through viewing another's has to be subject to change, to an active "dialogue" between the individual and the art work. The largely manufactured, rather than expressively created, forms of popular culture do not readily permit a necessary viable interchange. There is, on the contrary, an easy identification with values that have been settled beforehand.

For instance, the movie or television heroine becomes the prototype of many of the wishful drawings of young girls rather than an honest attempt to define character visually; the "pretty" and product exploiting layouts in popular interior design and homemaking magazines that are shown in "scrumptious" and heightened color become the visual pattern for the dream house, rather than permitting a development and expression of personal taste; the stereotyped delineation of popular comics and animated cartoons becomes the accepted measure of caricature, rather than an inventive and individual improvisation of forms. These all take for granted a ready and practically unquestioned acceptance of their forms and brook very little deviation from predetermined responses. This is the opposite response to genuine art forms.

Popular Culture Is Vivid and Simple

The forms of popular culture are bright and bold, saturated with an inescapable message that selectively captures the eye and the rest of the senses. Its prime motivation is getting across a simplified concept or image, discarding any elements that may complicate the expression. The serious forms of art, however, are dependent upon the profound, searching qualities that an artist deliberately probes for. As a result, fine art may be experienced on a variety of levels. Its intensity, though often vivid and simple, even narrowly focused, results from the natural and synthesized quality of its parts, from an economical expression of their innate characteristics as experienced through the transforming prism of the artist's vision. The vivid, colorful and striking impact of popular culture is more like the coarse, rouged, painted face of an old woman who wants to make an impression no matter what, rather than the ripe bloom of a young girl who makes an impression whether she wants to or not.

Similarly, the simple resolutions in good art are the result of a comity of means, of an insight and visionary capacity to reorder the chaos of unexamined nature or living in straightforward terms when it is possible to do so. However, fine art is often difficult and complex because its creative involvement with the material is on that level of profundity. Popular culture, on the other hand, is always simple, if not simple minded. Its simplicity is ostentatiously so. It makes its point, disregarding any qualifying aspects or the existence of nuances or overtones. Its simplicity is a mask for ignorance or the venal exploitation of unsophisticated tastes as much of it is so called "good design." More important, mass visual culture finds that it must be-

Art
and
Education
in
Contemporary
Culture

·

372

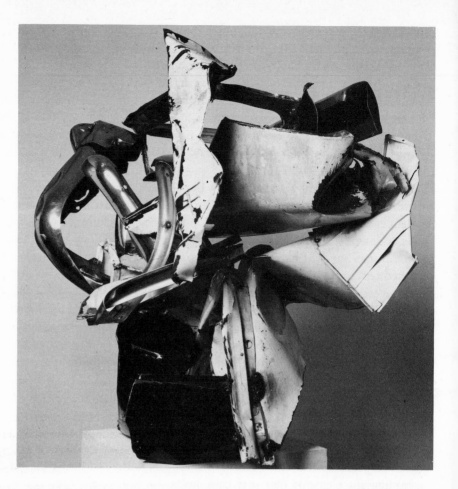

Some modern artists create new aesthetic forms from the cast-off junk paraphernalia of the technological society. "Mozo," John Chamberlain. [Leo Castelli Gallery, New York; PHOTO: Rudolph Burckhardt]

come progressively more shocking and boldly flamboyant in order to offset the jaded tastes of its overwhelming clientele. There is a sensory exhaustion which an overabundance of strong visual images produces and it must be overcome by images more glaring, striking and violent.

An overemphasized simplicity and vividness have made themselves felt in art education unfortunately. There is a plethora of projects and art ideas that comfortably and unelaborately provide a whole range of pseudo art experiences. They are relatively undemanding in understanding and execution; upon completion they have the striking though superficial and ordinary quality of popular culture images. The "how to do it" attitude and acceptance frequently falls into this category and their spread in the schools through countless "professional" magazine articles and books is readily observed.

It is not that relatively simple or conveniently presented projects are to be replaced by deliberately difficult undertakings. There are many invaluable though simple activities that could afford an honest experience with art. The danger is in consistently substituting a momentarily successful activity because of its availability and ease of handling rather than in planning for and initiating class art experiences. The latter may be difficult to structure and contain, may take unforeseen directions, and make time consuming and personal demands though they may possess desirable and challenging attributes that lead to art activities that do not suffer from affectation or pretense. The results may not always be as striking or uniformly "successful" but they will be honestly individual and more meaningful to both student and teacher in the long run.

Popular Culture Is Ambiguous

There may be some confusion in applying the term of ambiguity to popular culture. We have just finished saying that it was simple and vivid. However, the use of the term, in this instance, does not imply any profound quality or multiple level of understanding. In order to best meet the collective tastes of a mass clientele, the popular images utilize a bland, uncommitted, neutral approach so that no one would be offended if possible. For instance, advertising unhesitatingly accepts the varied prejudices, bigotries and unexamined habits that prevail in the mass culture: ethnic chauvinism, the social distinctions implied by wealth, the rather shallow values of materialism, the sometimes suspect ethics of sheer profit orientation to name but a few.

Yet, at the same time most manufacturers and their surrogate in the visual arts, the commercial designer, would like to appeal to as wide an audience as possible. This makes for more sales and greater popularity. The gap is largely bridged in creating forms that are psychologically vacillating and aesthetically extreme yet that are essentially uncommitted and vapid in content and orientation. They are made so the onlookers could readily mirror themselves in the image. There is no hint of any material that could be considered offensive to mass taste. Likewise, there is no controversial theme, for then there may be alienation of a large group and a consequent boycotting.

This approach is inimical to the searching and passionately committed character of serious art. In any genuine form of expression an artist reveals what he has discovered or invented, though this may be contrary to other viewpoints. There may be no readily appreciative audience or popular support, yet a serious artist pursues his own promptings. The result also may be an ambiguous work, but not because of a lack of any real content, rather because the content is real and challenging, existing on several levels at once, open to wide interpretation.

In relating this facet to art education, it is important for a teacher or administrator to know the intensity of involvement that is entailed in genuine art experiences. They have to question themselves consistently to determine, for instance one among many teaching attitudes, if the encouragement and direction they are providing for the art class is not an answer to their need to have adult oriented art in the show cases and corridors of the school building. The activities of any one student and the forms he produces may be deep responses to very individually felt needs. The finished work need not necessarily be pleasant or easily understood by everyone. There has to be that quality of encouragement and acceptance in the class so the individual student may create within the context of his

Art
and
Education
in
Contemporary
Culture

•

374

own motivations and values, permitting a variety of felt interpretations, the ambiguity of the work due to the mystery of art not to the desire to please everyone.

THE INARTISTIC QUALITY OF AMERICAN LIVING

If honest individual expression is to be fostered through school art experiences, the effects as well as the sources of mass culture require further explication for art teachers. They will have to be acquainted with some of the serious criticism of mass cultural expression in the areas that are socially and philosophically sensitive.

An outstanding poet and brilliant observer of American habits Randall Jarrell wrote, "Emerson, in his spare strong New England, a few miles from Walden, could write: 'Things are in the saddle/and ride mankind.' He could say more now: that they are in the theatre and studio, and entertain mankind; are in the pulpit and preach of mankind. The values of business, in a business society like our own, are reflected in every sphere: values which agree with them are reinforced, values which disagree are cancelled out or have lip service paid to them. In business what sells is good, and that is the end of it—that's what *good* means . . ." [6] Jarrell indicates that many of the values of the popular culture which he dubs the "Medium" are contrary to those of the arts, "where commercial and scientific progress do not exist; where the bones of Homer and Mozart and Donatello are there, always, under the mere blush of fashion; where the past—the remote past, even—is responsible for the way that we understand, value, and act in, the present."

Another damaging comment on the general level of cultural illiteracy comes from the controversial novelist and essayist, Henry Miller. He indicates that it is not only the manufactured visual vulgarity that covers the land or its arid commercialism, but the sticky, lost morass of spirit that is developed where only in the interstices of society can one sense an honestly open and fresh human purpose and an unencumbered and committed creative endeavor.

Miller may be quixotic and grandly indiscreet in his exaggerated despair but his indictment is as strong and direct, perhaps even overstated due to his basic concern for the artistic values so uncertain in his native country.

Nothing comes to function here (America) except utilitarian projects. You can ride for thousands of miles and be utterly unaware of the existence of the world of art. You will learn all about beer, condensed milk, rubber goods, canned foods, inflated mattresses, etc; but you will never see or hear anything concerning the masterpieces of art. To me it seems nothing less than miraculous that the young men of America ever hear of such names as Picasso, Céline, Gionno and such like. He has to fight like the devil to see their work, and how can he, when he comes face to face with the European masters, how can he know or understand what produced it? What relation has it to him? If he is a sensitive

[6] Randall Jarrell, *A Sad Heart at the Supermarket* (New York: Atheneum, 1962), p. 71.

An example of the imaginative production of which manufacturing is capable. "Solar Toy," Charles Eames. [Courtesy Aluminum Company of America]

being, by the time he comes in contact with the mature work of the Europeans, he is almost half crazed. Most of the young men of talent whom I have met in this country give one the impression of being somewhat demented. Why shouldn't they? They are living amidst spiritual gorillas, living with food and drink maniacs, success mongers, gadget innovators, publicity hounds. God, if I were a young man today, if I were faced with a world such as we have created, I would blow my brains out. Or perhaps, like Socrates, I would walk into the market place and spill my seed on the ground. I would certainly never think to write a book or paint a picture or compose a piece of music. For whom? Who beside a handful of desperate souls can recognize a work of art? What can you do with yourself if your life is dedicated to beauty? Do you want to face the prospect of spending the most of your life in a strait jacket? [7]

Though this was written during the forties, for some the urgency of its indictment is mitigated. However, to Henry Miller, some of the surface conditions may have changed, but the general stupor of the environment and its baleful influence still dog us. Art has become a commodity itself. Though the "museum without walls" has greatly expanded, there has been no important parallel upgrading of artistic values or personal commitment to aesthetic consideration. There is still a frenetic bemusement with the material conditions of existence, even when there is an overabundance. In 1962, Miller can still write, "No, things have not changed a bit . . . unless for the worse. *La vie en rose* is not for the artist. The artist—I employ the term only for the genuine ones—is still suspect, still regarded as a menace to society." [8]

[7] Henry Miller, *The Air Conditioned Nightmare* (New York: New Directions, 1945).
[8] Henry Miller, *Stand Still Like the Hummingbird* (New York: New Directions, 1962), p. *ix*.

Art
and
Education
in
Contemporary
Culture

·

376

This audacious and rebellious commentator goes on to say that only the conformists and the mediocre talents are pampered, petted and supported. This attitude, if it does in reality exist forebodes an almost impossible barrier between the so-called high arts and the popular mind in any significant or progressive way. The indictment is probably much too strong, the philistine qualities of American living much too exaggerated. Yet a teacher who is not acquainted with viewpoints such as Miller's may be short circuiting their own behavior in the classroom. His passion and extreme commitment to artistic values is an invaluable sounding board.

Considerations of Expediency

Perhaps it is, at least in America, that the workings of democracy and the fortunate abundance of a free and productive land have not yet succeeded in making of Americans an artistic people.

As is implied by the vernacular design sources mentioned by John Kouwenhoven, Americans are an adaptive and inventive people. Their major effort is not in wrestling with the stubborn material of living in order to creatively transform it, to make it expressive symbolically and actually where feasible, of national "goals," but rather to modify the environment, stamping it as practical, efficient, and conducive to "happiness," convenience, and ease of living. The spread of a popular culture is an admirable surface response to this pragmatic reality.

Louis Kronenberger cogently, yet with an essential humor, pinpoints this characteristic. Speaking of the American inability to really be an artistic people he informs us, "We are dedicated to improvement—to improving our minds and our mousetraps, our inventions and our diets." [9] No matter how successful a car design may be one year, generally next year's model will supplant it; no matter how proper and pleasing any designed object appears to be, it will have an added feeling of gadgetry about it and often a planned obsolescence. The sense of tradition that is so vital in any artistic process whether it is functional design, architecture or fine art, will exist as no more than a transient style, on its way out often before it is even broadly established. Similarly, quantity will become a measure of worth, the attractiveness of an object determined by how many others own it or desire it, not by any intrinsic attributes it may possess.

However, in a more general tone Kronenberger captures with clever, benign yet incisive insight some of the fundamental relationships that Americans have created between themselves and art. With a genuine sophistication which accepts art as a natural condition that is proper to the development of all individuals he seems to indicate that we have avoided art itself by the many artful blends that are otherwise contrived. He is quoted at length:

We have never as a people regarded art as something to live with, to freely delight in, to call by its first name. Perhaps this derives from something beyond an inventive streak that keeps us restless, or an awe that makes us uncomfortable:

[9] From *Company Manners* by Louis Kronenberger (New York: The Bobbs-Merrill Company, Inc.), p. 37.

perhaps had we had more opportunity to live with art, we might have acquired a more relaxed attitude toward it. It has never been on our doorstep; we have had to go in search of it, go doubly in search . . . as much to discover what it is as where it is. . . . The very "uselessness" of it . . . the fact that art, like virtue, is its own reward; again, the very magic of it . . . the fact that it cannot be reduced to a formula or equation; the utter arrogance of it . . . the fact that money cannot buy it nor American salesmanship or elbow grease achieve it: these are, at the very outset, reasons for mystification and distrust. *Its* kind of arrogance, of refusal to be won on intrinsic terms . . . as of a high-mettled, beautiful girl whom no suitor can win on the strength of his bank account, his family background, or his sober, industrious habits . . . seems improper, even unethical, to a people who can respect putting a high price on something, who can approve and even enjoy a hard tussle till things are won, but who can no more understand than they can approve that something is beyond negotiations, is just not to be bought. Art to their minds is not a high-mettled girl, but an extremely unreasonable woman. Art's kind of magic again . . . art's refusal to be achieved through laboratory methods, through getting up charts or symposiums or sales conferences, through looking at smears under the microscope . . . its magic seems behind the times, almost downright retarded, to a people with a genius for the synthetic. Art's kind of uselessness, finally . . . its non-vitamin-giving health, its non-pep-you-up modes of pleasure, its non-materialistic enrichment—quite genuinely confuses a people who have been educated to have something to show for their efforts, if only a title or a medal or a diploma. Art, for most Americans, is a very queer fish—it can't be reasoned with, it can't be bribed, it can't be doped out or duplicated; above all, it can't be cashed in on.[10]

This may be why art has had a most difficult time in honestly being integrated into any basic educational patterns. For despite the theoretical propriety of fostering art in the schools, the teachers, who after all, are direct influences in education and establishing social values are themselves frequently cast in the mould that Kronenberger so aptly conjures up for our understanding.

There is an implied need for an humanistic core to educational methods and content. This has to go beyond the mere lip service that it so often receives, infusing the curricula of the modern schools with a genuine and unadulterated content based on humanistic and aesthetic understanding. This would deliberately and conscientiously counteract the condition that Thoreau wrote of more than a century ago and one still prevalent if not increasing; that, "The mass of men lead lives of quiet desperation . . . A stereotyped but unconscious despair is concealed even under what are called the games and amusements of mankind."

These games and amusements have proliferated into the many faceted links of popular culture and the practical interests behind them.

The Economics of Taste

Ernest van den Haag[11] examines this problem in what he refers to as

[10] *Ibid.*, pp. 37–39. Copyright 1951, 1953, 1954 by Louis Kronenberger, reprinted by permission of the publishers, The Bobbs-Merrill Company, Inc.

[11] Ernest Van den Haag (with Ralph Ross), *The Fabric of Society* (New York: Harcourt, 1957), p. 70.

Art
and
Education
in
Contemporary
Culture

•

378

the "economics of taste." He points out that the material aspect, the goods and commodities which originally were only the possession of an elite small group now can be provided for the many, not because of quality or leisure time or any intrinsic values other than that they may be mass produced because of an efficient technology and done so quite cheaply. "However—only those things—good things and bad things—are cheap that are demanded by enough people to make mass production feasible." This puts culture, which is part of the productive aspects of society, on an economic basis. Though this may have provided mass groups with greater opportunities to experience "culture," it is only on the basis of shared popular tastes that this can be profitably and efficiently established. The lone person with unique, independent or developed taste that is outside the pale of popular acceptance is penalized in that he must either forego that which he prefers because it is either unavailable or exorbitantly expensive or he must pay the additional price, though the intrinsic material factors may even be lower in actual value than that of the popular item.

Van den Haag goes further in delineating the taste basis of popular culture relating it to the education picture,

People are prepared . . . throughout the educational process. Group acceptance, shared taste, takes the place of authority, and of individual moral and aesthetic judgment and standards. But . . . success is hindered by a discriminating personal taste which expresses or continues an individual personality, and success is fostered by an unselective appetite. Numerous precautions are taken, beginning in nursery school (itself hardly an individualized institution) to avoid elaboration of personal discernment and to instill fear of separation from the group. Group acceptance is stressed through formal and informal popularity

It is important that art activities derived from popular cultural sources go beyond the trite handling of materials and the stereotyped expression of form. [New York Public Schools]

*A provocative artist
who comments on
contemporary life
in an exciting way.
"West 48th Street,"
Richard Lindner.
[Cordier & Ekstrom
Gallery, New York;
PHOTO: Geoffrey
Clements]*

contests, teamwork, and polling. Education altogether stresses group instruction
. . . The student himself is so much treated as a part of a group that, except
in higher education (which is only partly immune), he may be automatically
promoted with his group regardless of individual achievement or variation.
Finally, the surviving individual talent is instructed not to cultivate, but to
share, itself.[12]

The cursory examination of education may be somewhat indiscriminate.
Despite this, the tenor of the paragraph reflects the pressures that education
is subject to and its effects in the overall cultural atmosphere. Education,
unless it is itself aggressively self conscious of its "evangelical" role and
strong in the belief of its essentially comprehensive but individually insur-
rectionary aims falls prey to those loose and questionable values that are
inimical to its best interests in the opinion of the severest critics. Then too,
unless educators in significant numbers are themselves the confident practitioners and honest exemplars of what they preach, the prevailing values
will remain of a doubtful nature. They will take a commanding direction
of school policy grounded in limited service concepts rather than ones of
creative exploration and preparation for change especially in the volatile
area of art education.

[12] Ernest Van den Haag (with Ralph Ross), *ibid.*, p. 173.

Art
and
Education
in
Contemporary
Culture

.

380

A Balance of Attitude

However, it would not be proper not to attempt a balance of attitude. David M. White says,

Mass culture in America . . . a hopeful picture of our future as we go into the era of extended leisure that Americans will share in the next decade or two. There has been a rehearsal of all that is ugly and pathetic in our popular arts by critics whose sincerity cannot be questioned that it is time that the other side of the coin be examined . . . If the "average" man is not quite ready to accept the best that art and literature have to offer him (and . . . I ask, in what period has?) these critics turn their anger on the media.

Yet it is just these mass media that hold out the greatest promise to the "average" man that a cultural richness no previous age could give him is at hand.[13]

The ideas of men such as Gilbert Seldes and Lewis Mumford, while they are sharply critical of many of the manifestations of daily cultural conditions and mass produced art and artifacts help in redressing the balance. Both these men have a sympathetic belief in the emergence of a new, broadly based, and necessarily popular culture. It would make no concessions to the banal or superficial, though it would attempt to integrate both the revolutionary factors of mass media and mass education. Alvin Toeffler in his book, "The Culture Consumers"[14] has collected a great deal of evidence supporting the concept that "culture" has become an important American pastime. He indicates an immense surge of interest in art, music, dance etc., though his argument is largely quantitative rather than qualitative. This becomes one of the inescapable problems of providing art for large groupings of people.

Eric Larrabee is another partisan of popular culture. As he says, "It is possible, on an old piano, to achieve art; but it is also possible, with an entire symphony orchestra and an audience in full evening dress, to achieve nothing but banality." In other words, it is not the media that is important.

If you really care about what is in books and paintings, there will be more than enough of them for you—and enough with them—to last at least this lifetime [earlier Larrabee pointed out the supposed availability and the relative cheapness of most cultural products in western society]. The only condition is that you confront your own need for art, and find it genuine. Abundance asks only that you choose. The twentieth century has no doubt more than enough in it that is worth ignoring, but it is the only century we are going to get. Time passes; eras have each their weaknesses and strengths; and the only divine purpose in history—as Robert Frost once said—is that it shall always be equally difficult for a man to save his soul.[15]

[13] David White (Rosenberg and White, eds.), "Mass Culture—Another View," *Mass Culture—The Popular Arts in America* (Glencoe, Ill.: The Free Press, 1957), p. 21.

[14] Alvin Toeffler, *The Culture Consumers* (New York: St. Martin's Press, 1964).

[15] Eric Larrabee, *The Self Conscious Society* (New York: Doubleday and Co., 1960), p. 60.

This, of course, poses the problem once again in individual terms. In the final analysis, it is the individual who creates his own existence, provided he senses the measure and quality of things and events in terms of sensitized awareness. The element of taste also becomes important as a guide to "cultural" opportunities.

LEVELS OF TASTE

It is one of the obvious cultural facets of education that teachers are concerned with the mass emergence of taste in a variety of ways. The example of their own likes and dislikes, the content of what they teach, the unconscious attitudes, fashions and beliefs that they unknowingly embody the pressures of society all have an influence in creating social taste in a broad sense as well as in directly acting upon individual students. Taste itself is a rather fundamental aspect of personality as well as a vehicle for social relationships despite the fact that it is difficult to contain or to define with any simple list of attributes.

As Russell Lynes says in his popular treatise on taste, "Taste is our personal delight, our private dilemma and our public façade." [16] This paradoxical delight and dilemma of taste is often thought of as a peculiarly inbred individual quality that somehow grows like Topsy. It is often regarded as an emblem of ourselves, as a mirrored reflection of internal projection by which we see ourselves. However, at the same time taste becomes a degree of commitment to particular values which we wear figuratively like an insignia on our sleeve for others to rate us by. At times we "read" the social class of people, sometimes arbitrarily by their tastes and frequently infer other and more potent aspects through the existence of that same factor of taste. Illogically, taste is regarded both as the product of many unconscious determinants, of long term sets of mind and habits as well as the spontaneous impulse responding to momentary fashions and fads on one level and to authentic individual understanding on another. Perhaps, because of the intricacy of qualities and the psychological confusion surrounding the subject we consign it to its own realm. As Rabelais informs us, "Everyone to his own taste, as the woman said when she kissed her cow."

Though we would like to think that everyone harkens to this ideal of democratic preference, that the entire affair is a personal matter, our actions belie this belief. Our private dilemma spreads into the public façade, or at least the problem of shaping our tastes to conform to what we envisage as the private image of ourselves vis à vis the stares and conjectures of the public attitude outside. Though we may insist that our tastes are our own, at the same time we permit them to be manipulated by what we regard as the important vox populi—the voice of the people. Our commercial society and its popular culture as we have seen has taken acute advantage of this situation. We are appealed to incessantly to buy this or consider that, to change our indiscriminate ways, to give vent to our secret

[16] Russell Lynes, *The Tastemakers* (New York: Doubleday Universal Library, 1954), p. 4.

Art
and
Education
in
Contemporary
Culture

.

382

desires and to generally capitulate to the mass imposition of values—all in the name of good taste.

The instinctive base then that underlies the popular assumptions of "each to his own taste" is essentially a fallacy. Though there may be some positive argument for this opinion on a sheer material base, it is quickly dissipated when the characteristically psychological and symbolic aspects of human growth is alluded to. As we have seen elsewhere, the perception of sensory data by the individual follows no simple equation of physical sensation and predictable response; there are complex reactions based upon the multitude of influences of an artificially created environment and the profoundly involved emotional relationships that human society engenders.

Influences in Taste

These attitudes of taste, to reiterate, are shaped by a variety of outside pressures. The most general, in addition, is the existence of change itself. Technical innovations and the discovery of new materials and processes are fundamental determinants of taste. They enlarge its possibilities offering new or an expanded range of choice. The introduction of metal into interior house furnishings, the development of cheap printing processes for reproducing pictures, the structural innovations in home construction that make use of a wide variety of different materials, among others, have created a refurbished and vastly different taste in the general physical appearances of homes over several decades. However, this is a normal development that probably has little to do with the quality of taste, but simply opens up the possibilities of choice. In a similar way, because of technical discoveries, sculpture which up to the end of the nineteenth century was largely confined to stone and bronze casting, to chipping and modelling, expanded its materials and processes to include iron, steel, plastics, and could be welded, cut, glued and otherwise worked in addition to the older academic means. The question of good or bad form still remains, though, no matter what the media employed.

However, the most important aspect of generalized taste development lies in the broad, encompassing and insinuating social pressures that an individual is subjected to. The value orientation of parents and peers, of the mass media and the many traditional sources of cultural inheritance are the compelling factors in shaping the collective taste of the individuals that make up various kinds of groups. These are in a complex relationship with one another, with the other identifiable determinants and with the growing self awareness that everyone experiences at one time or another.

EDUCATION AS A TASTEMAKER

We must accept the existence of educational institutions as transmitters and maintainers of the taste and teachers as influential "tastemakers" whether they want to acknowledge the role or not. Teachers are very potent cogs in the machinery. They either support or condemn general

The content and forms of popular culture have been utilized in a variety of ways by artists in the 1960's

"Elvis I & II," Andy Warhol. [Leo Castelli Gallery, New York; PHOTO: Rudolph Burkhardt]

"Brighter Than the Sun #1," James Rosenquist. [The Green Gallery, New York; PHOTO: Walter J. Russell]

Art
and
Education
in
Contemporary
Culture

·

384

ideas, setting up characteristic patterns of acceptance, rejection or indifference and in so doing create an atmosphere in which particular students'
tastes flower, become stagnant or atrophy. Yet, at the same time there is
also present the unique individual projections that students possess. These
may not be just as obvious. Both the teacher and the student become
embroiled in the pressures that make for the "low," "middle," and "high-
brow" level of taste that Lynes writes about. They become one of the
numberless digits that are mindlessly provoked by the large current
of economic pressure and fashion, unless they are "confronted with their
own need for art." If that occurs, then the labels and levels somehow
evaporate before the concern and involvement of the individual; and
taste emerges as the individual attitude that it genuinely could be and
that it culturally deserves to be.

Russell Lynes indicates three conditions that are common which make
for individual taste as against the conditions that pressure the direction
of generalized taste. "One is education, which includes not only formal
but informal education and environment. Another is sensibility, which
Webster defines as the 'ability to perceive or receive sensation.' And
the third is morality—the kinds of beliefs and principles which direct one's
behavior and set a pattern for judging the behavior of others." [17] These
are large and often intangible considerations which though present in
all learning situations are difficult if not inappropriate to instruct directly.
A specific syllabus would only make for dogmatic practices no matter
how positive they were considered originally, while a pious hope is a
rather ineffectual quality that merely perpetuates an indiscriminate status
quo. If taste is simply the symptomatic aspect of an individual's or group's
response to their environment, then perhaps it cannot be tampered with.
Lynes comments on this, "We are fortunate in America that we have so
many different ways of satisfying so many different kinds of tastes. We
produce hundreds of movies each year, some of them good by the most
discriminating standards, some of them bad by the least discriminating,
and the same may be said of paintings and of architecture and cookery
and probably of circus wagons. The point is that we have a tremendously
diversified basis of morality, education and sensibility and that the fric-
tions among them generate the kind of heat that gives light. It is these
conflicts of ideas and tastes that give the arts of our country vitality,
and that make the museum and the corner movie houses equally important
manifestations of our culture . . . Taste in itself is nothing. It is only
what taste leads to that makes any difference in our lives." [18]

Teachers assume an incumbent responsibility to assess the inherently
evocative aspects and the comparative worth of an environment and its
influence so that students may not only develop whatever creative potential
is theirs, but their taste as well. In the larger sense, there is the added
responsibility of attempting to affect the environment, so that the student
has the opportunity not only to develop within the ordinary confines

[17] *Ibid.*, p. 340.
[18] *Ibid.*, *pp.* 340–341.

of school studies, but is permitted to answer what are often regarded as indigenous needs, but most certainly are spiritual needs, for artistic creativity and genuine appreciation in day-to-day living. Art as one of the symbolic modes of meaning and communication requires open and sympathetic channels.

Educators have to evolve an understanding of the role, not only of the functionally visual, but of the inherently humanistic values of art as they may give added meaning to contemporary living. There should be an insight into the dichotomy that Lewis Mumford so aptly writes of as "those things of meaning with no use, and things of use with no other meaning." We have stressed the latter in our society providing an insidious societal stagnation which deepens the split between art and technics. In attempting to integrate the cold perfection of machine technology with our innately nonrational aesthetic yearnings, confounding confusions of false values frequently result, with all of the attendant dangers of a slick and shallow materialism and an impoverished aesthetic and spiritual life. This happens despite the intrinsic propriety of technology and perhaps because of a misunderstanding of its nature. Perhaps some new distinctions have to be made between the necessities of popular culture and the manufactured aspects of mass culture, creating that distinction where none now exists.

In any case, education has to specifically appraise the relationship, to examine the accepted patterns of taste to question the values and the socially approved responses of popular culture. The expounding of even sincere goals through abstract educational theory is an insufficient act. Each teacher has to face an individual responsibility in this regard, his own depth of education, sensibility to aesthetic and artistic values and general teaching morality are as much to be reflected upon, as are the conditions of the culture in which he lives.

14

The Visual World Today

> A work of art rises proudly above any interpretation
> we may see fit to give it; and, although it serves to
> illustrate history, man and the world itself, it goes
> further than this; it creates man, creates the world
> and sets up within history an immutable order.
> HENRI FOCILLON

ONE of the most distinctive conditions of twentieth century living has
been the popular emergence of the visual not only in art but as an
aspect of technology as well. Visual constructions have assumed an
importance that make their presence an essential condition of contemporary
living. The sensory images which we experience through varying degrees
of visual acuity and discernment have pre-empted the earlier channels
of discursive communication. Sights have tended to displace words, while
ideas are made into concrete forms. The old proverb that "one picture
is worth a thousand words" has literally come true. However, the picture
is no longer a simple illustration, but a vast visual spectacle that has been
imposed on the natural landscape, leading not only to a surface change
but a reorientation of man's image of himself as well. The resulting
influences on education are widespread, creating a continuing need for
curriculum examination and reassessment of teaching methods. Art education is particularly susceptible to this influence.

ART AS A CONDITION OF ENVIRONMENT

The importance of the visual and its growth developed gradually
throughout the rise of technology and of necessity, so that society could
keep pace with the tumultuous and demanding conditions of change
which are so characteristic of modern living. Man, in devising a newer,
differing set of symbolic systems, abetted by his genius for scientific and
mechanical application, provided not only a surer method of coping with
his surroundings, but in large measure created a dependency on his visual
responses. The elements of art have become modern tools, indispensable
for the highly complex civilization we live in, in addition to being the stuff
of beauty and expression. The visual in twentieth century society has an
extensive distribution and a pervasive influence. Art education has to

assume the role not only of transmitting this influence, but of guiding it and infusing its popular aspects with aesthetic value.

We are faced with dynamic and at times confusing concurrent images, not always synchronized to the limits of our ability to perceive them honestly. Nevertheless, the visual impressions we experience reflect a radical change in the external appearance of our environment and continue to be dramatically changing ones. Though art has never delineated the scope of the visual, until recently, the essential aspects of man-made visual images were chiefly confined to humanly dimensioned works of art, decorative crafts and comparatively modest alterations of natural landscape. Art possessed an intimate and particular appeal, never really being confused with the total scope of the visual. Even the grandiose scenes and monumentality of such artistically rich periods as the Egyptian dynasties, Periclean Athens and the Renaissance are experienced through a sense of human scale and understandable proportion. The awe inspired may have been lofty and far reaching but, in the final analysis, it could be contained within an individual span, whether it was physical, psychological or spiritual. The world outside may have been dangerous and vast, the scenes of majestic grandeur, of heart-rending challenge, yet they did not really impinge on the forms of art or confuse their scale.

Art, in addition to ritual and myth, provided a complement to the incomprehensible infinity and variety of nature. The forms it created captured some of its mystery and wonder as well. It magically hypostatized that mystery and transformed the wonder into an understandable dimension through visual symbols. These in turn created their own order, existing

The modern environment frequently emphasizes visual clutter. [UPI PHOTO]

Art
and
Education
in
Contemporary
Culture

·

388

as independent agents when they were not pressed into a "cause." Otherwise, earlier eyes saw nature as forest and mountain, as thick stands of trees in lavish foliage and as barren, hard and hostile crags, as laboriously cleared fields and the impinging green growth around villages, as the color delight of wild fields of flowers and the geometry of cultivated rows, as rivers running through the fertile abundance of nature and as oceans carrying the tiny dots of ships in vast stretches of dramatic and awsome passage, as the convoluted ridges of desert dunes and the table-top flatness of prairies, as the soft mists of morning and the enveloping darkness of evening. The huddled clusters of huts, boats or houses crowded in a village or city punctuated the grand rolling immensity of sea and land.

Man moved in a time set by the seemingly immutable rhythms of nature, rising and falling with the vagaries of weather, seeing the barrenness or the lushness controlled by the cycle of the seasons, conditioned by the constancy of a recurring day and night and oriented by the vistas of the everpresent hills, plains, forests and shorelines he lived in or near. The cultivation of fields, the hewing of timber, the mining and quarrying of rock and ore had but an insignificant effect on the environment. Only through the visions of art, the mass and space of architecture, and a continuing creative fervor did man devise new physical sights for his eyes to enjoy and act as a relief from the inherent chaos of nature. These were impelled from the springs of myth and religion as the store of concrete images enriched his sense of being and alleviated to a degree the fear and anxiety of a huge, brooding environment which would rarely be placated. The sense of power and mastery that a Parthenon or an heroic statue of David or a brilliant fresco on a Paduan church wall or the magnificent planning and bulk of a Versailles afforded man were essentially symbolic emblems rather than actual ones of a conquest of nature.

Today, the symbolic aspects, except within the relatively small enclave of the fine arts, give way to an actual change that is beginning to challenge nature in force and scope. With the advent of the Industrial Revolution, we seem to be engaged in a gigantic effort to transform the face of the land.

This not only startles our eyes, it impinges on our total visually symbolic consciousness. It rudely destroys some of the earlier relationships of art to its natural surroundings and creates a bewildering panorama of impressions. This is not detrimental in itself, but it requires new assessments and evaluations so that the role of art and that of the visual metamorphosis that is occurring can accommodate themselves to a newer and more appropriate philosophical "entente cordiale." Our acceptance of art is strongly influenced by the visual environment; and its impact on our individual understanding is profound. The environment itself acts in a variety of ways, ranging from one extreme when it spurred the imagination, inspiring new aesthetic concepts and forms as it did in 19th century France or during the Renaissance, for instance, or on the other end, acting as a detriment and inhibiting challenge, limiting or destroying aesthetic experience as it is suspected it did during the westward pushing frontier days of American history. The recognition of the environmental pressures is not complete, however, without a parallel evaluation of the specifically aesthetic and utilitarian qualities that result in society and that act as cultural arbiters in responding to artistic and symbolic forms. Teachers of art particularly have a need to be critically aware of these factors in their planning for pupils' art experiences and in setting a philosophical tone in the classroom.

THE CHANGING VISUAL PATTERNS

Today our landscape is basically artificial, and psychologically it is an incoherent one at times. It dwarfs our sense of individuality even as it expands our sense of power. The old fear of the implacable forces of nature has been largely tamed. We collect what is left of the virgin land and safeguard it in national parks much as we do the dwindling wildlife. We live more and more in a manufactured enclosure or in endless mass-produced technological fantasy that permits the introduction of nature only through a potted geranium.

Tremendous machines gouge out the side of mountains or like grotesque metallic beasts move countless acres of earth to make the measured mile

An artistic expression of the dynamism of the twentieth century's stress on movement. "Dynamic Hieroglyphic of the Bal Tabarin," Gino Severini. [Collection, The Museum of Modern Art, New York, Lillie P. Bliss Bequest. [PHOTO: *The Museum of Modern Art]*

Art
and
Education
in
Contemporary
Culture

·

390

that extends its network of concrete ribbon, bearing a harsh and relentless roar of traffic. Vertical pylons play a visual counterpoint against the ongoing miles of wire; extravagant forms and dizzyingly complicated machinery indicate the viscera of a factory while the complex components of a launching pad or an oil well are intricately silhouetted against a mute sky. A staggering mass of windows reflect an explosion of patterns of form in the city, the volumes of the buildings burgeon, their hard lines in endless repetition and improvisation providing a visual symphony of movement; the clicks and blinking lights of a computer mystify and intrigue the onlooker against a busy façade of dials and apertures. The conforming shapes of a builder's tract in the myriad subdivisions that sprawl over suburbia indifferently register on the collective vision while the disjointed image of color, mass and light marks the anchorless shopping centers that were onion fields just a while before or delineates the ravenous stretches of peripheral commercial roads dotted with their hot dog stands, "garden beautiful" emporiums and used car dealer lots. A warehouse packed with thousands of similar objects flicks across the retina like the broken record caught at one point, repeating an unchanging sameness, or a freight train loaded with hundreds of identical late model cars speeds by like a mechanical ballet choreographed by a metallic brain. The provocative play of interpenetrating planes, unusual shapes and almost sybaritic surfaces that are further intensified by the bubbling or humming lustre of an internal, intriguing and mysterious activity animates the visions of laboratories and the new places of scientific research.

Confusions of Visual Generalization

All of these sights are man made and the inherent image of an industrialized and urbanized culture. "There is an aesthetic of units and series, as well as the aesthetic of the unique and non-repeatable." Lewis Mumford has long been a keen observer who points to the need of recognizing these contemporary images and interpreting in a creative manner this new visual order "of machines and instruments, with their hard surfaces, their rigid volumes and their stark shapes." [1]

It is obvious that the new and constantly unfolding landscape has a fundamental influence on the development of visual forms and a forceful determination in the direction that art takes. As Gyorgy Kepes says, "The environment of man living today has a complexity which cannot be compared with any environment of any previous age. The skyscrapers, the street, with its kaleidoscopic vibration of colors, the window displays with their multiple mirroring images . . . the motor cars (all) produce a dynamic simultaneity of visual impression. . . ." [2] This exists both in the fine and the applied arts. The simultaneity, however, may bring about a confusion and a neutralized merging of aesthetic value as well as a vital dynamic quality which may well confound its own purposes. The visual signs of the

[1] Lewis Mumford, *Technics and Civilization* (New York: Harcourt, 1934), p. 334.
[2] Gyorgy Kepes, *The Language of Vision* (Chicago: Paul Theobald, 1944), p. 11.

environment and the symbols of art become interchangeable, vitiating many of the artistic values of a more universal nature. In this sense, though the overall visual creations may be the superficial or even the honest expression of an age, they are more the practical improvisations of technical and commercial needs as well as the idle entertainment of a moment. They then become the shared images of a mass consciousness requiring social approval and affirmation in order to be enjoyed. This is removed from the understanding of art that most critics indicate is the production of a work that has a life of its own rather than acting primarily as an instrument for other values. The aesthetic experience becomes attenuated like so many of the other daily encounters and activities of modern man, a thinning of the intensities that often exist when collective and practical concerns are generally the dominating ones. A limited invention becomes the philosophical order of the day rather than individual discovery and the procedural aspects of experience become more important than its substance. For instance, in discussing material for mass communication, the producer generally asks the question, "Is it O.K. for television or for magazine illustration?" and not "Is it good in itself?" The channel at the formative stage as a means of mass communication becomes more important than the dramatic material that it will present. Some critics go further in saying that the medium *is* the message.

In art there is a popular need to have taste, but little if any involvement with the actual forms of art as serious expressions of the human condition. The inferior artistic conditions and the stereotyped or questionable image that result have been amply demonstrated. As the popular arts spread, the superficial appearances and the underlying quest for mass success with mass audiences become the determinant of popular and artistic form. There is a blending of technics, commerce and art that makes the distinctions between good and bad art very vague, and unimportant in the final analysis. The fundamental influences of the environment have still not found their meaningful interpretation, except in ways foreign or merely adjunctive to the conditions of art. Art education suffers from this confusion of values and forms as much as the larger culture. Teachers, more frequently than not, accept the prevailing attitudes since they too are immersed in the culture and are usually unquestioning of its aesthetic character.

Popular and Technological Emphasis

However, it should be recognized that the new environmental conditions of vision are quite different from the older aspects of nature that determined the earlier interplay of perceptions and their consequences in artistic form. The traditional unordered world of nature with its subtleties and nuances, its tones, atmospheres of light values and delicate harmonics of colors and its preponderantly organic shapes has now been opposed by the complex geometry of man-made vistas. This has its consequences not in one large visual sense, but actually in a variety of ways. There are the technically determined symbols of industrial production such as in the concrete expanse of a dam or in the wired circuits of a radio; there are the forms of

Art
and
Education
in
Contemporary
Culture

•

392

a popular art that are mass produced and commercially oriented, prey to the dictates of market research, such as in advertisements, magazine illustration and consumer designed goods; and finally, there is either the rebellious rejection of the environment by some painters and sculptors such as the Surrealists and abstract expressionists or its spiritual but transformed acceptance by a Mondrian, a Gabo or the whole new school of modern architecture. The new "Pop" artist remains an intriguing but contradictory amalgam of qualities. Yet a general understanding of the current visual complexity tends to group all of these divergent visual trends under the one heading of "art," despite the obvious and mutually exclusive contradiction in psychological, philosophical and visually symbolic premises. What appears to be of prime importance to the contemporary but commonly uncritical mind is the ubiquitous visual imagery, making a jumbled and empirically argued pastiche of any underlying aesthetics. This response is not only an abstract condition of the larger sphere of environment, but is experienced in the more personal day-to-day encounters with visual elements that are subjected to the overriding qualities of utility, attention getting, diversion and a paradoxical production standardization. These values also seep into the classroom, as education mirrors cultural qualities and shapes them.

We cannot walk down a street without being accosted by an omnipresent intensity of visual experience. A changing configuration of posters, signs, marquees, window displays, electric lights and neon color makes the peremptory clamor of their presence felt through infinitely variegated patterns. Billboards blatantly blare their messages substituting dulcet semblances for the natural vision of landscape. Our movement is regulated by the periodic changing of color; otherwise we flirt with physical disaster. The enticements of commodities have been skillfully and cleverly designed to appeal to our eyes. Packaging has become a visual tintinabulation, crowding the colorfully packed shelves of stores and supermarkets. The manufactured article flaunts an allure and a design seduction that is difficult to resist. A vast and imposing array of optical excitement insinuates its indulgence of our senses at a continuous and tenacious pace, the cityscape becomes an inexorable presence.

Magazines and newspapers edify their readers by becoming pictorial compendiums and disseminate information through striking layout and visual blurbs. A riot of color, texture, line and mass projects the conspicuously consumed image of our advertising art. The camera reflects an omniscience akin to an earlier and pervasive iconography, in itself the source of an unending ability to make images. Motion pictures have expanded the scope of visual experience once limited to didactic illustration and the attendant need for elaboration in words. The ubiquitous television set has invaded the privacy of the home. It has captured the collective eye which has surrendered to a willing bondage.

Painting, sculpture, architecture and the various other fine arts have been spurred on to amazing quantities of works as well as to prodigious attempts at experimentation and the development of new forms. Though the

*Communication
through usual forms,
commercially and
culturally, as well as
aesthetically, is fre-
quently emphasized
in art education.
[New York Public
Schools]*

artist's studio is still a strange and rather esoteric place for the average individual, the works of the artist in reproduction are readily available. We have
what André Malraux refers to as "a museum without walls." We can enter
it at our leisure; in fact, we are constantly subjected to its abundancy, if
only in a superficial manner. Art, even when viewed skeptically by the
public, has become a standard, everyday experience at home, at work, at
school, for purposes of creation and recreation, exploitation and enlightenment, amusement and therapy, inspiration and a host of other reasons.

Unfortunately, the popular aspects of art are usually paced to a "do it by
the numbers" philosophy or an easily digested and cursory appreciation. The
overriding and indiscriminate theme today, with tongue-in-cheek, can
easily be summed up in: "Everything is art. You, too, can be an artist!" A
frequent result in art teaching sets rather arbitrary and superficial conditions for the classroom, blandly providing "art" experiences that have little
foundation in aesthetic or creative considerations.

MECHANISTIC CONSIDERATIONS

However, it is in the applied fields of art that we most often experience
the largesse of our manufacturing of the visual. The endless visual reservoir
has been steadily tapped to provide us with supposedly satisfying and functionally necessary images. Art is manufactured rather than discovered, its

Art,
and
Education
in
Contemporary
Culture

·

394

form is artfully contrived rather than symbolically created. It becomes a commodity to be exploited, to assist in production and sales, to decorate and enrich surroundings and entertain otherwise benumbed or unsophisticated sensibilities. Yet the resulting sight is frequently one of agitation and ferment as well as delight and appropriateness, of uneasiness as well as the desired satisfaction expected from an expensively supported media. Whichever way we respond, the ever-present visual image is a basic fact of current consciousness.

The importance of this dynamic visual environment, despite its bewildering multiplicity, has kept pace with the growing need for nonverbal communication. In an earlier era, during the preceding nineteenth century, when the tempo of living moved at a slower rate, when the means of production were not highly mechanized, when agrarian concerns were still heavy in the balance, the verbalized idea, the book as knowledge, the inhibited weighing of pros and cons prior to taking action was a proper manner of response. The seemingly clear and rational attributes of discursive behavior could be a fitting interaction between man and environment. However, this reliance on the discursive had to be modified, if not abandoned, with the headlong and radical change that accompanied scientific discoveries and technological innovations.

This change has occurred because twentieth century civilization has become a vast, intricate, interdependent and demanding agglomeration of industry, technological organization, mass mercantilism and packed urban living, the "changing century of the common man." The earlier and simpler relationships employing muscle or horsepower gave way to the present dependency upon machines, not only casually, but almost in terms of sheer existence. The earlier introspected behavior has changed into the modern spontaneous aptitude for surface appearances and reflex action. This stems from an economic reliance on mass production which in turn creates the psychological environment that values conformity, pragmatic functionalism and a shared "factual" quality in the nature of knowledge. The machine dominates the contemporary mind. This appears to be supported by the facts and attitudes of current living. Button pushing possesses particular prerogatives which have to be respected. We acquiesce, either with eager naivete, neutral understanding or imposed tolerance. We sub-consciously accept the preponderant sway of technology even while we consciously may reject or counteract many of its dehumanizing influences.

Erik H. Erikson points out in a perceptive comment in as basic a social area as child rearing the influences of the machine,

This idea of a self-made ego was in turn reinforced yet modified by industrialization. . . . Industrialization, for example, brought with it mechanical child training. It was as if this new man-made world of machines, which was to replace the segments of nature and the beasts of prey, offered its mastery only to those who would become like it, as the Sioux became "buffalo," the Yurok salmon. Thus, a movement in child training began which tended to adjust the human organism from the very start to clock-like punctuality in order to make it a standardized appendix of the industrial world. In pursuit of the adjustment to

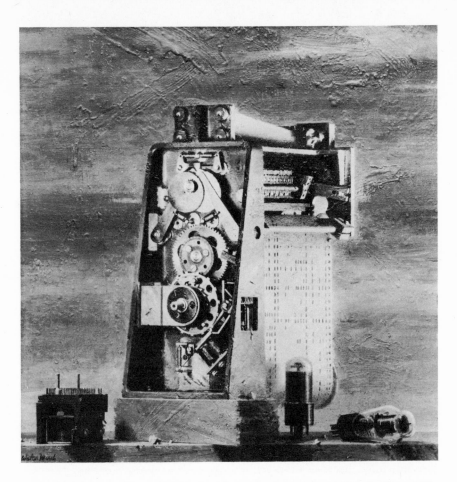

The mechanics of technology are central factors of modern living. "The Calculator," Walter Murch. [Collection, IBM]

and mastery over the machine, American mothers (especially of the middle class) found themselves standardizing and overadjusting children who later were expected to personify the very virile individuality which in the past had been one of the outstanding characteristics of the American. The resulting danger was that of creating, instead of an individualism, a mass-produced mask of individuality.[3]

Similar influences have subtlely invaded most aspects of American living, not least of which has been the educational establishment. The effects of a mechanical technology are obvious and close to being complete in the large areas of public living and the ramifications have strongly impressed our individual lives as well. The visual symbol, acting in the mass mind as the surrogate of art, if not its actual condition, merely becomes another tool in a socio-economic and programmed blueprint for adaptive action and the standardization of values. At the same time, to repeat what Marshall McLuhan points out, "Nobody yet knows the language inherent in the new technological culture, we are all deaf-blind mutes in terms of the new situation. Our most impressive words and thoughts betray us by referring to the previously existent, not to the present."[4] The visual apparatus

[3] Erik H. Erickson, *Childhood and Society* (New York: Norton, 1963), pp. 294–295.
[4] Marshall McLuhan and Carpenter, eds., "Five Sovereign Fingers Taxed the Breath," *Explorations in Communication* (Boston: Beacon Press, 1960), p. 208.

Art
and
Education
in
Contemporary
Culture

·

396

of the contemporary culture most often mines the traditional sources of art, without genuinely transforming them in any significant way or creating the base of a new potential geared to new conditions. It is against this loose value commitment that art education has to guard.

THE CURRENT UTILITY OF THE VISUAL

In any case, man has altered his relationship to his environment. He utilizes a mechanical complexity by which he can better control and manipulate the forces about him for his own end. This has required a concomitant alteration in human psychological (and physical as well) reaction which is necessary in mechanical operations. Speed, change, clarity and sureness of function are operating corollaries of a mechanical situation, resulting in the need for closely calibrated reactions and conditioned responses. A culture growing out of technics calls for instinctual and reflex action in order to insure smooth functioning. The visual image with its innate sensory qualities and educative functions is one of the most adaptable means through which this kind of behavior may be inculcated and developed.

In order to facilitate the growth and expansion of a dynamic technology and in order to integrate man into the cogs, gears, meshes and energies of the machine, society naturally evolved a firmer tropism toward the visual. Physiologically, the visual apparatus permits a diversified, yet highly intense intake of data. The configurations of vision are succint, clearly experienced and easily recognized on the surface. Though perception might differ with the individual because of psychological and physical variables, there is sufficient agreement in the manipulating aspects of today's social sciences so that a common denominator of understanding may generally be taken for granted. Normally, a person can learn quickly the intent of a color, an arrangement of geometric shapes or any other relationship of visual properties. It is possible to respond directly. If sufficient social conditioning has occurred, there may even be subliminal reactions in a classic stimulus—response manner. Of course, when there is a closer examination of the experience, tricky illusion and other varying individual perceptions run an entire gamut of unique connotations that may be uncovered, as the section on perception proves. Yet the average unsophisticated visual experience and reaction may be simply plotted and largely predicted within known statistical probability.

As a result, society could build its factories, lay out its cities, produce its produce its products, be distracted by entertaining forms, enjoy its decorative arts and mechanically travel the earth's surface and beyond without creating a chaos of bewildering contradictions, but rarely creating in the popular modes real works of art or an authentic lasting expression. Though today's visual objects are often created at the expense of the nonutilitarian values of art, they embody the sensual elements of art nonetheless, and are frequently presented full blown in this manner in the art class.

Paradoxically, there is at the same time a quickening of the aesthetic pulse. There is a recognition that many art forms stem from the visual sense: drawing and painting, sculpture, graphics, architecture and the numerous minor as well as the applied arts. These visual expressions possess, in a modern as well as traditional sense, not only intrinsic worth but a nearly universal significance which transverses spoken language, which surmounts political and social boundaries and has both a personally intimate yet socially wide appeal to all people. Not only do visual phenomena lend themselves to manipulative devices which may be broadly adapted or modified as utilitarian means in a technological environment. They are also a far-reaching channel of individual as well as mass communication, possessing in addition, the added quality of enhancement and decoration (even when it is of a trivial or picayune nature). This provides an aura of psychological acceptance of our times, or at least an alleviation from the crass and more dehumanized conditions. By means of art there is often a more conducive and attractive atmosphere in which the workers of machines, the consumers of its products and the inhabitants generally of our raucous, indiscriminate and optically splattered cities and highways can function. The visual in this sense has become the Esperanto language—a discourse with the felt and the visible which may transcend the limitations of ordinary communication and the shallowness of surface decoration, offering a more exalted and gratifying knowledge through aesthetic communion. However, this can generally occur only if the basic integrity of the expression has not been compromised by impinging commercial or other extraneous considerations. On a mass scale, only education can function to provide the necessary background and development for felt relationships to aesthetic experience.

The daily manufactured visual surroundings are primarily designed for business purposes. [PHOTO: *Stephen C. Sumner*]

Art
and
Education
in
Contemporary
Culture

•

398

TWO ASPECTS OF THE VISUAL SYMBOL

Much earlier in history, primitive man created a visual art of potent imagery. Art was inextricably interwoven into the very fabric of prehistoric and even later cultures; it served not only as an expressive channel but as the psychological means of a pristine involvement with nature. We have returned, in a manner of speaking, to this image making as a necessity of contemporary living, though with differing connotations, in part if not wholly. The return has been prompted by pragmatic values as well as separately symbolic ones. Public visual improvisation becomes an instrument of technical progress, built into the operations of industry more than in the psyche of the individual artist.

However, it was the virtual symbolic value that characterized the earlier visual images. They were symbols that portrayed a reality that was generally complete in itself. The bisons on the cave wall of Altamira possessed a magical reality for the creator and his audience that did not rely on any other agency for a confirmation of significance. In Egypt the statue of Pharaoh was the living embodiment of that divine figure; its mythical nature was accepted as a symbolic image of sympathetic magic. Though there was a relationship with certain canons of representation, the ancient art works did not clearly distinguish between reality and imitation; there was an abstraction from life and a direct, determinate relationship that permitted the work to possess its own sense of being. It was perhaps changed with the Greeks when their art symbols became abstract conceptions as well as concrete forms. The philosophical ideas removed the symbol from its role of prime and active meaning; it was no longer separate as a force, nor could it really be responded to as an independent agent. It had a necessary root in spiritual and intellectual awareness as well as being the actual symbol of recognition of a state of being. At this point ritual became religion, myth the beginnings of philosophy and science, while art developed as a dependent image of beauty.

The long history of art has subsequently regarded its works as both, a form of direct metaphysical truth that required a spiritual rather than an intellectual cause and effect, or as one of the many guises of a fundamentally logical order of rational ideas that delineated the quality of beauty and human emotion translated into sensuous terms. In both instances, art was divested of its immediate and direct properties as a means of apprehending and expressing reality without any intermediary forces. These same forces perhaps unwittingly took over as the basic conditions for understanding and utilizing the arts: a Byzantine fresco was beautiful because it was a reflection of Christian religious ardour, a Renaissance painting had significance because it was a sensuous extension of mathematical laws of perspective, an academic painting of the nineteenth century was highly regarded not because of its color or form but because these qualities somehow demonstrated a Victorian notion of propriety, sentiment and beauty.

In a similar manner, it is widely felt that a designed object in today's world has representative significance and consequently, current aesthetic worth because it captures the spirit and the function of its times. The sleek,

*Despite the visual
clutter, the sources
for interesting and
rewarding visual
design remain in
daily surroundings.*
[PHOTOS: © *Roy
Stevens; I. Kaufman*]

Art
and
Education
in
Contemporary
Culture

·

400

streamlining of an airplane fuselage bespeaks the speed and aerodynamic principles of flight while the lines, colors and textures of home furnishings, for instance, reflect the affluence and love of convenience of a society that engages in a production of abundance. The symbolic values of the visual objects particularly when they reflect functional qualities are rarely aesthetically independent. They have antecedent causes and can be comprehended only through adjunctive meanings supplied by industry, science or any of the other determining forces of a culture. Art has existed within the two contexts: being an instrument as well as an end in itself.

The Need for Distinctions

This factor should have a rather important bearing in the development of art education theory and its implementation in the classroom. The instrumental values that are part of the activities of art education may have valid cultural necessity. However, if art is to be more than a tool or a pedagogical means to somewhat limited and at times foreign considerations of its own nature, its role in education should be recognized as a more independent one. In reflecting the ideas and aesthetic commitments of the art that is being created, some distinctions have to be made between its double aspects. An emphasis on the singular and innately satisfying, expressive qualities of art activity has to be encouraged and developed alongside of the more functionally dependent ones. In this large sense, education could serve its role of creating new understanding of major human endeavor as well as transmitting older ideas.

It is the factor of art conceived as an instrumental value which prompted many of the leading artists of the modern period to reject some of the underlying philosophical structure and styles of earlier art periods. The technical developments in graphic representation during the nineteenth century, as an example, permitted the artist to divest himself of his didactic function. He no longer was the visual echo of the ideas of a church, a nobility or any government. He was free to create within the pure spaces of symbolic visions. These created their own substance of reality, not being subject to the prior philosophical ideas dictated by nonaesthetic concerns.

Cézanne sought a visual means that was not beholden to anything but visual structure. Similarly, Monet with the translation of light into color and atmospheric values, while Van Gogh reactivated an art that distilled the emotional essence of life directly into the sensuous medium of paint. This led to aesthetic exploration and visual experimentation that has flowered profusely in the twentieth century. The symbols of the visual arts once again became independent images, nonrational but valid configurations that indivisibly involved the personal understanding and commitment of the creator, who in turn was subject to the actual sensory qualities of the art elements. The fine arts have attempted to recreate an untrammeled perception of the forces that give substance to life, not necessarily denying the laws of logic of an intellectually pragmatic society, but suggesting that there are a multiplicity of ways for arriving at truth. Art education has a responsibility of presenting these ideas, at the very least.

TECHNOLOGY AS A NECESSARY CONDITION FOR
TWENTIETH-CENTURY LIFE

The
Visual
World
Today

.

401

However, though technology has engendered a fearsome mechanical imposition on our minds as well as on the landscape, it is not an inappropriate condition for our century. It also reflects our increasing ability to modify nature in a positive sense, permitting us better to answer our needs and provide the requisite design for an American environment that is a response to the aspirations of its citizens. Art education has a responsibility in this direction as well.

John Kouwenhoven provides us with a rather positive respect for the new processes and beliefs that emerge from a growing technologically oriented environment:

We hear a lot . . . of the notion that our system dehumanizes the worker, turning him into a machine and depriving him of the satisfactions of finishing anything, since he performs only some repetitive operation. It is true that the unit of work in mass production is not a product but an operation. But the development of the system, in contrast to Charlie Chaplin's wonderful but wild fantasy of the assembly line, has shown the intermediacy of the stage in which the worker is doomed to frustrating boredom. Merely repetitive work, in the logic of mass production, can and must be done by the machine. It is unskilled work that is doomed by it, not the worker. More and more skilled workers are needed to design products, analyze jobs, cut patterns, attend complicated machines, and coordinate the processes which comprise the productive system.

The skills required for these jobs are different, of course, from those required to make hand-made boots or to carve stone ornaments, but they are not in themselves less interesting or human. Operating a crane in a steel mill, or a turret lathe, is an infinitely more varied and stimulating job than shaping boots day after day by hand. . . .[5]

In arguing the appropriateness of a new relationship to the means of production, Kouwenhoven also presents us with a new kind of philosophical attitude that changes the base for the considerations of worth and artistic method. He seemingly substitutes efficacy, process and time resolution in the place of cultivated, aesthetically critical standards. This provides more for the common good and engenders its own aesthetic and other critical standards.

This strong belief in the technological processes as a progressive and openended means of achieving a democratic spread of the "good and the beautiful" has the characteristically hopeful note of the alert pragmatic mind. It reshapes man's image of himself, at least of those who live under the changing qualities of an expanding technology and an egalitarian social order. It points up the wide and necessary influence of the machine, accepting it as a positive condition in man's alleviation from the fears and labors of an earlier and undesirably savage time. For instance, the highly developed mechanical and industrial complex, the pressures of consumption of a technological economy, the continuing scientific discoveries and

[5] John Kouwenhoven, *The Beer Can by the Highway* (Garden City, N.Y.: Doubleday, 1961), p. 67.

commodity innovations of an energetic entrepreneurship during the twentieth century has led to a system of mass production. This influences the designer who can no longer really work in terms of individual craftsmanship, but must think of forms that will be reproduced in extremely large numbers. Therefore, the artist designer works on prototypes that accept the limitations of their mass methods of production, manipulating the elements of art in a new way and improvising on their forms in terms of innately present qualities.

Despite the visually clangorous sharpness of the industrial scene and the conglomerate kinetics of intricate machinery, there is that sense of power and what could be an intrinsically satisfying plan of achievement. The stress is on process and engineered efficiency, which develop a beauty of their own, besides being a source of our abundance. The attendant arts of advertising, of interior, and industrial design are probably necessary corollaries and intriguing challenges to bring together the aesthetic instincts of modern man with his trading, manufacturing and social propensities. Though there is much that is shallow and of a dehumanizing nature, there must also be a recognition of the characteristic and innate contemporary quality that is creating a new kind of culture. Technology is not only a source for products and wealth in general, it is also a fundamental and proper source of philosophical understanding as well as a generator of new creative visual form today.

As another practical example and one close to our area of interest, and despite the lag that frequently marks educational methods as they struggle to keep abreast of the changing character of society, educators use the metamorphosis of the visual image to its present position of importance as a means of instructional communication, as an aid in teaching. Not only method, but the very architecture of our schools has been revamped. The legacy of the nineteenth century, of the schoolhouse with the red brick façade and stilted fenestration, with the monotonous stretch of corridor and the coldly formal classroom has given way to the striking school building of today with its colorful use of exciting construction materials. The varying textured façades, halls and doors of glass, brick, tile, wood and metal offer attractive and inviting areas in which to learn.

The classroom itself has become a focal point of visual learning with large bulletin boards, display cases, dioramas and the parallel stress on pictorially effective teaching aids. Textbooks have long since been designed into visually animated tracts with handsome illustrations, eye catching color and provocative graphs. A wide range of the layout artist's craft has been knowingly integrated with the substance of the subject area to be studied. The rapid growth of audio-visual education has added another dimension to learning. We are at the beginning of a new mechanized era in education where knowledge is automatically presented to masses of students essentially in a visual way via television or other media of mass communication. Teaching machines have become important considerations in the teaching process; though the format is not wholly visual, the method has overtones similar to advertising gadgetry. No doubt, more educational methods will evolve and assume differing appearances, most likely visual. However, despite the very modern and efficient basis in outlook, the philosophical import is still open to question.

Though audio-visual education is regarded as a necessity today in our

The vernacular sources of current utilitarian design frequently give little attention to aesthetic considerations. [PHOTO: University of Michigan News Service]

Art
and
Education
in
Contemporary
Culture

.

404

schools, it would be extremely harmful to elevate this approach without carefully and incisively examining the probable consequences, both psychologically and aesthetically. There has to be a genuinely positive value orientation to the method and structure of the programmed learning that is being provided. What may at first appear as innocent and hopeful aids to education may well become mechanical and efficient conditioners of behavior taking the place of a more personally divergent education.

THE CONCEPT OF A DESIGNED ENVIRONMENT

This idea of a world that is measured and controlled, manipulated and made to produce through the imposition of forms molded along functional lines is a widely accepted one today. The recognition of needs, the description and force of their substance is calculated against the conditions in the environment and the social mood. These are then subjected to man's analytical and creative attributes, the result being a synthesized physical or intellectual product that at once answers certain individual needs and at the same time keeps the wheels of the spiritual and the economic complexes in the culture operating profitably, productively and in an ascending spiral.

The man who accomplishes this in the visual sphere is the designer. When successful, he becomes one of the key individuals in the contemporary world of technology and commerce, the shaper of its appearances. He not only reflects in his visual expressions a designed surface that has a sense of relationship with the moving forces of this culture, he tends to influence the internal concepts of that culture as well. He is not only the practical architect of the visually functional structure, he also becomes engaged in the cultural midwifery when the new forms are born and more often than not was probably present, in spirit if not in fact, at the actual conception of these forms. In his eagerly voiced belief of the wedding between the innate qualities of design and the sense of social commitment that he insists design functions perform, the designer creates one of the modern beliefs in the efficacy of planning. He adds his own symbolic twist to the modern social myths built around efficiency and the reciprocally productive understanding between man and his environment. In the final analysis the designer's vision presupposes a utopian concept of an ordered, beautiful world that responds automatically and in good taste to the needs of an individual as they arise. Though the various western cultures have not quite arrived at the automatic stage, the salubrious thinking of the designer is that this is simply a matter of planning and of time. There is a genuine and fundamental belief in the limitless possibilities of technology and in the ability to shape its products within an acceptable and pleasing aesthetic. The creative designer heeds the admonitions of Howard Mumford Jones and Gyorgy Kepes that there is a need for a new interpretation of the data of existence. Much of art teaching reflects this design concept, with associations of art to the home, to personal dress, to local surroundings, and to the products of industry as it responds to cultural influence.

It is necessary, however, to infuse this teaching, centered around design

*The urban environment with all of its visual excitement is becoming the predominant visual problem as well. New York City. [*PHOTO: *Eastman Kodak Company]*

considerations, with a quality of individuality that operates against the standardizing influences. Of even more significance is the need to envision the kind of harmonies and interrelationships that an insistent and growing automation may require. The future that lies ahead for most of the students in the schools is one of an ever broadening dependence upon technological means of production, and also of a computerized, data-laden living environment. This point cannot be repeated too often and the educational obligation of creatively preparing for it. There is the intense need to somehow mesh the currently disparate strands of individual identity, collectivized, mechanical procedures, and an immense store of knowledge that requires the warmth and worth of adequate human values. The spiritual and aesthetic considerations have to complement the depersonalized cybernetics and production logistics that are already a potent force in ordinary living. Art has to seek out blends of "the world that is too much with us" and the interior visions of men. This aspiration, symbolized in the sensuous and ideational forms that creative minds transform out of the experience of living, may serve as one of the generative aspects of a society that will provide a relevant quality of existence for the greatest number of its citizens.

THE BAUHAUS INFLUENCE

The ideas of the Bauhaus in Germany as they developed during the decade of the twenties are perhaps the most typical ideas of the new design outlook as well as the most developed conceptually. The Bauhaus saw the new technical age as a radical departure from the times that preceded it,

Art
and
Education
in
Contemporary
Culture

·

406

offering new stimulation, setting new challenges and demanding new solutions to problems and consequently new forms had to be created. They insisted upon a functional foundation for design, arguing that the best visual solutions, the most successful shapes were those developed along the lines of manifest needs of a product both internal and external. Given the conditions of the technology of the twentieth century, the designer had an encumbent responsibility to identify the functional aspects and their appearances in a designed manner through a contemporary viewpoint. The past was to be understood as a significant but finished condition that would offer no sanctuary for timid or conservative spirits.

Rather, it is the technical, social, economic and artistic trends of his own day as well as any other pertinent current information that the successful designer should utilize as source material for his own creations always bending to the spiritual concerns of the fine artist but shaping them within the confines of a necessary function. In turn, these creations would reflect an honestly workable yet highly aesthetic blend of materials and an innately appropriate development of form.

Interrelating the Arts

This synthesizing of the various and productive capacities of modern man in his technological landscape had its counterpart at the Bauhaus of bringing together the different visual art forms. The philosophy insisted that the distinctions between the fine and the applied arts were artificial, that the various arts of painting, architecture, typography, furniture design and photography, to name but a few, were really related efforts in visual form that had a base in rational design principles. If these were identified and utilized then a new sense of beauty could be developed: modern, functional and not merely decorative, but vital as an expression of man's most inner needs that were organically related to the burgeoning technology. They insisted that it was as significant to design a good toy or a successful turbine as it was to sculpt a portrait or to paint an odalisque. As a matter of fact, they suggested that it was probably more appropriate to design an

"Bauhaus," Walter Gropius. [Photograph, courtesy The Museum of Modern Art, New York. Reproduced by permission of the artist]

attractive, functional store front than it was to paint a spiritually thin or merely decorative picture, the commercial facade probably being more difficult to realize than the esoteric creations of solitary artists and more expressive of our times as an art form as well.

The Bauhaus was immensely influential, its ideas flooding the visual thinking of Europe and America. The influence was of an educational nature as well as an artistic and philosophical one, though its prime demonstration has been in a loosely defined and embracing visual style of a clean, uncluttered and functional nature. However, even before the advent of the Bauhaus and certainly since its inception the twentieth century means of production has attempted, in part, to bring to fruition the concepts that are characteristic of its structure and the Bauhaus so aptly crystallized.

This vision of a joining of technology and aesthetics had had its most potent expression in the buildings and designed panoramas of the architects and city planners. From the germinal ideas of Sullivan that "form follows function" to the latest engineered dymaxion hemisphere of Buckminster Fuller, the architects have proceeded to change literally the almost ageless styles of construction and to impose a radical yet appropriately new image on building. James Fitch,[6] the architectural historian at Columbia University characterizes this as "the first authentically original idiom since the twelfth century invention of the Gothic . . . its originality arose, not from any isolated theory of form or taste, but in response to new forces which, convulsing modern life at every level, demanded adequate aesthetic expression." This expression was and is being fostered by such creative architects as Frank Lloyd Wright, Walter Gropius, Mies van der Rohe, le Courbusier, Pier-Luigi Nervi and others.

The towering sixty story buildings of glass and steel, the exciting exhibition hall enclosures with their intricate and space defying structural engineering so satisfying to the technologically educated eye and the monumentally conceived yet strangely light and soaring edifices of reinforced concrete are really the synthesized versions of a contemporary designer's vision. They bring together not only the technological and aesluce a necessary sociological note being the inspired symbol orld that has taken into consideration all of the pertinent pects of contemporary living. The economy of the environthe political, social and aesthetic ideals find expression in

MODERN IMPLEMENTATION OF DESIGN CONCEPTS

However, while the mass, light and shadow, surface textural qualities and space experience of these modern builders affect us emotionally and intellectually, being the realization in dramatic and functioning symbols of the inner forces of modernism, they are as highly regarded (as they deserve to be) primarily because they are so conspicuously evident in their small

[6] James Fitch, *Architecture and the Aesthetics of Plenty* (New York: Columbia University Press, 1962), p. 5.

Art
and
Education
in
Contemporary
Culture

.

408

number. The greater majority of the man-made landscape is sympatheti-
cally observed as an eclectic clutter of outmoded, substandard, indifferent
or profit oriented shapes, which have no planned quality for social good
and aesthetic harmony. In fact, if the kindness is lifted, the scene may be
seen as one of essential ugliness and vulgarity that bespeaks not only a lack
of sophistication but in many instances, a venality of purpose. This is con-
temptuous of the designer's ethic which embraces social commitment and
planning stemming honestly from intrinsic values. This is even more evident in the almost total lack of community cooperation that city planners,
particularly in the United States, are faced with. There is little doubt that,
generally, business interests come before those of social welfare as expressed
in design concepts. The planning activities of architects and "environmental specialists," particularly when there are "useless" aesthetic considerations, are subject to the veto power and uninformed taste of many public
officials or profit minded executives.

The visual stress appears to be more widespread in the area of commercial
and product design. With the increased basis of wealth that is spread in
wider degrees and with a technology that feeds on mass production, the
need of attractive visual appearances becomes a necessity in economic as
well as in cultural terms. As a result, the designer in theory becomes an
integral element in production. As early as the latter part of the eighteenth
century, Josiah Wedgwood began to design objects for mass consumption.
Peter Cooper, in his visionary way added to this impetus by bringing into
America the controversial ideas that were generated in the industrial England of his day. However, it was not until the explosive advent of machine
production that dominates this present century that the designer came into
his own.

Until the Second World War much of the creative developments in this
area came from Europe, through the influence of the Bauhaus and the
designer-craftsmen of the Scandinavian countries. The works of Breuer,
Aalto, Petri and Copier are but a few that reflect the strong influences of
modern design in Europe.

However, since the war, the United States has been spurred into a native
design consciousness that is both resourceful and mature in its own way.
Eero Saarinen, Charles Eames, George Nelson and Raymond Loewy are
also but a few among the large host of designers who have worked or are
currently working in the United States. They have evolved visual styles
that are each differing, tending either toward a classic functionalism, plastic
organic quality or the sensitive merging of the two. The new production
processes that are the genius of American application of inventiveness and
the utilization of a startling number of new materials such as metal alloys,
plastics and artificial fibers that are the result of a chemical-technical
revolution have bred a freedom of form improvisation that is both refreshing
in scope and sound in design features. The materials, the tools, the processes
and purposes are given a satisfying aesthetic form without violating the
inherent integrity of each in their best instances.

In comparison to earlier times, the appearances and functional design of

*Technology produces
many new visual
images. "Single
Sideband Antenna."*
[PHOTO: *U.S. Dept.
of Defense*]

a product have been upgraded. As an example, the design in the automotive
field has had at points classically functional form though too often the
gadgetry, the status styling and the flamboyant lines have overwhelmed the
basic structural design of a car. There are many other instances of visual
planning: the crisp patterns of the airport or a grain elevator, the graceful
rhythms of a racing sailboat or a new bridge, the textural pleasantries of
contemporary fabrics or construction material for homes, the satisfying
suggestiveness of the biomorphic shapes of plastics and novel designs in
glass, the modular handsomeness of modern furniture or the sophisticated
improvisations in every manner of household fixture are all indications of a
new design consciousness that is not only visually appropriate but is more
international in scope today than ever before. Yet Garth Huxtable, a designer of over twenty-five years experience and a member of the American
Society of Industrial Designers, is moved to write, "of the vast number of
products mass produced in America today under the aegis of the industrial
designer, the general level of design is very poor indeed. The great emphasis
in industry is on yearly styling of products, rather than on the sincere effort
to create the best possible product. . . . Design is too greatly influenced by
outside pressures of advertising, market research, competition. The result
is overstyling and gadgetry, but seldom fine design." [7]

The designer, consequently, despite the secure philosophical position of
his place in a technological society finds that he is relatively insignificant in
the overall picture. Unfortunately, he is not even able to have that final
and necessarily unequivocal word in his own area. The only original quality
in so much of popular design remains in the original matrix that is created;
however, this becomes only a prototype with a peculiar lack of substance

[7] Garth Huxtable, "Industrial Design," *Art in America*, 2, 73 (1962).

Art
and
Education
in
Contemporary
Culture

·

410

when machine production creates very large quantities of imitations of the original.

Yet within this glut of overproduction and low mass levels of aesthetic appreciation, a particular ethic of design has grown.

VERNACULAR DESIGN

A germinal and influential viewpoint of the evolution of design and the arts in America returns us to John Kouwenhoven. He suggests that the essential characteristics of functional form and consequent design stem from the uses the average citizen has intrinsically employed from the material of his environment, a kind of grass roots designing. This has grown apace of the technological revolution, stimulating the inventive genius of a practical and democratic people.

"It was this tradition (of a natural and distinctively shaped vernacular) in which were developed, and kept universally available, certain elements of design and certain principles of structure which were a direct, uninhibited response to the new environment and which finally had decisive influence in the hands of men of skill and vision. This stream of art often failed to create beauty of its own. But its patterns at least reflected actuality, however ugly that actuality often was; and the forms evolved in it were firmly rooted in contemporary experience." [8]

These forms usually shared the characteristics of economy, simplicity and flexibility in response to the functional requirements that influenced their shaping. They were the empirical attempts of a people given to improvisation and improvement to most effectively utilize the opportunities provided by a changing and a challenging technological means of production. The intriguing element, in addition to the base of functional form, is the interjection of the democratic situation as a formative aspect of visual delineation, the designed object being not only the symbol of new physical forces, but of social and political ones as well. It is the unselfconscious and uninhibited novel responses of a democratic and technical mind that provide the creative insights for manipulating in a fresh manner the natural abundance of the environment and the processes of a technically oriented industrial growth. The restrictions and controlled attitudes that were contained in an earlier cultivated tradition could be overcome by individuals who were not bound by strict social and class distinctions that led to particular and committed artistic values.

This belief of vernacular sources creates the basis for advocating a strong tie between art and every day living. It provides the artist and designer with the inherently appropriate outlook for their creating within a meaningful contemporary context. It is not so much the planned and knowledgeable aesthetic of the designer sensitive to his milieu as much as it is an inherent state of process that is open-ended, characteristically American and inventively responsive to daily living demands. The suggestion is that the

[8] John Kouwenhoven, *Made in America* (Garden City, N.Y.: Doubleday, 1948), p. 19.

*City and regional
planning are implied
in the aims of art
education.* [PHOTO:
*University
of Michigan News
Service*]

American sense of form does not require a completeness, its psychological correctness is not the proportion of a fixed form but the ongoing quality that does not necessarily recognize a formal hierarchy of experience. The example of the skyscraper that may have twenty, forty or sixty-eight stories, yet not be altered essentially in design; the everchanging yet schematic skyline of a city, or its gridiron pattern of streets, and the improvisations of jazz are examples that are cited as the relatively free condition of American form that has its foundations in process rather than in a fixed, planned design.

Skyscrapers and music, ". . . are climactic achievements of the vernacular tradition in America. Neither implies anything resembling the cultivated tradition's negation of or contempt for the actualities of a civilization founded upon technology and shaped by democratic political and social institutions . . . The important thing about the vernacular is that it possesses inherent qualities of vitality and adaptability, of organic as opposed to static form, of energy rather than repose, that are particularly appropriate to the civilization which, during the brief life span of the United States, has transformed the world." This belief is further epitomized in, "America is process . . . it is not an artifact . . . a fixed and immutable ideal toward which citizens . . . strive. It has no order or proportion, but neither is it chaos except that it is chaotic whose components no single mind can comprehend or control." [9]

Though on the one hand Kouwenhoven indicates the essential factors of design to be based on contingency, on the need to invent always another element of process, and forms that are metaphysically unfinished in content

[9] John Kouwenhoven, *Made in America* (Garden City, N.Y.: Doubleday, 1948), p. 73.

Art
and
Education
in
Contemporary
Culture

.

412

as well as in shape, he appears to offset this very quality by suggesting that no single individual could ever really accomplish this at least with sensitive or absolute control. The designer, or the artist for that matter, is locked in the creative embrace of his time and place and is successful only insofar as he spins his creations for the strands of his active environment in some mysterious way, combining the ethic of democracy with the aesthetic of form. No doubt there is an unending American generosity of shaping and constructing, creating a vast store of images and processes, perhaps too overwhelming for any one individual to completely encompass. Yet the actual making of the art object or the imposition of any meaningful design is the creative and expressive leap that an individual takes. It is only after the form has been symbolically and concretely presented that the group, any group, is aware of its existence, touched by its quality and influenced in its creativity.

Kouwenhoven tends to blur the line between the expressively creative and the merely inventive, the individual endeavor and the social mixing pot, the aesthetic sense and the utilitarian product, the symbolic form and the shaping process. While there is a good measure of insight into the psychology of American visual forms, there are also confusions that distort otherwise basically helpful guidelines for either creative endeavor or the mature sensitive appreciation of not only the aesthetic but the larger symbolic values that are being expressed in the welter of visual forms that excites, enriches and confounds daily existence.

There is a representative democratic note in this approach, one incidentally that many designers and art teachers unconsciously hold. There is also an invitation for all and sundry to create, partaking of the open, rich and abundant spirit of American life. Yet the home workshop is not the same as an artist's studio, nor is the serious tinkering of even a talented handyman the same as that of a committed, trained designer. Though the vernacular process may operate, the ideas do not offer any solid understanding of why there is such a crippled ability in the mass to evaluate critically the designed forms of the environment, not only aesthetically but on native grounds of practical values. It actually might obfuscate the understanding, for despite the great swell of vernacular inventions and consequent forms of design the average individual still remains only an unsophisticated and essentially passive and ignorant consumer eschewing the necessary cultivation of sensitivity, despite the glamor of our window dressing of market research, advertising, and adaptive, not inventive design.

The Indiscriminate Spread of the Visual

Current attitudes continue to make the machine seem human. That is, in order to answer at least partially his creative and aesthetic needs, man adorns the machine, he decorates the landscape and attempts to instill symbolically a soul into the cold, hard unthinkingness that so smoothly performs his will. Now, this admixture of art and technics, of design and salesmanship, would have minor significance if the purely visual could be

*Designers offer
"blueprints" for the
planned
environment.
[*PHOTO: *University
of Michigan News
Service*]

separate and contained experiences, divorced from the more tangible aesthetic attributes, despite the practical sources they sometimes share. The utilized image could be regarded as much a mechanical necessity as a lever or a gear. Nevertheless, it is impossible to separate the utilization of visual qualities and their subsequent dominance from the aesthetically pure and psychologically symbolic aspects of art.

Visual experience has a broad and encompassing power. It evidences profound subjective elements that cannot be disintegrated or operationally categorized in fractions, serving particular ends without doing violence to the aesthetics of art. The experience takes hold of the mind in exercising a deeply rooted siren enticement and elicits an unconscious compliance. Our perceptions are not only screened by the anticipations we have built up in receiving them, but the outside object and scene in turn modify the psychological mechanism by which we achieve meaning. There is a dialectical interplay in the creation of our symbols and how we "see" them. The individual values are then formed, perhaps willy nilly, and become basic personality traits. Education serves as a basic transmittal line.

Because visual sensation is always and everywhere present today, there is little opportunity for choice, for a maturing discrimination; because the demand is for speed and efficiency, there is little chance that permits the development of honest individual taste (a time consuming situation and wasteful of images). The average response to art becomes inextricably bound up with the popular visual mode. There is a vague and blurry distinction between the common visual surroundings and the all too rare qualities of art; they are lumped together in a bland and generally unrewarding fusion of values. The unique reality of art becomes the esoteric possession of a relatively fortunate few, while the average person is frequently prey to the tyranny of a Pavlovian-like conditioning. Not only are our collective eyes subjected to a mass artistic inanity, but some of the basic values of society are shunted off onto a tangential track

Art
and
Education
in
Contemporary
Culture

.

414

with education becoming the focal point of some of the resulting confusions.

Modern man is thus the helpless victim of a fantastic array of sensory
experiences. The designer and the commercial artist are perhaps more the
victim of this visual jumble than is the consumer for they must create
within the crazy cacophony of the eye, the oversimplification and the
driving competition that lead to an ennervating unleashing of popular visual
material. It is simple enough for the sensitive individual to detach himself
from this optically fantastic menagerie or for the indifferent person to
ignore it, but for the commercial designer it is the very stuff with which
he communicates. As such, it presents an almost insurmountable obstacle
to honest creative endeavor and becomes a hard, insensitive tool of economic exploitation and competition as well as the insensitive and crude
visual backdrop of the average banal aesthetic understanding and the
aborted formative level of mass artistic appreciation.

We are asked to lend our eyes whenever and wherever we go.

Ours is an age of pictorialization. Wherever we go or stay, pictures surround
and besiege us. They stare at us from the pages of our tabloids and popular
weeklies, pass across the screen in a nonstop procession, and, with television
seeking new outlets, increasingly invade the last refuges of introspection, the
bars. There is no baseball game which cannot be vicariously attended by anybody everywhere; nor is there a remote work of art that would evade mass reproduction. Thus, a situation arises in which we are literally flooded with sights
and spectacles—a vehement and interminable deluge.[10]

Siegfried Kracauer was only noting the obvious when he wrote this
in the 1950's and it has greatly proliferated since then.

The visual image permeates our entire society, from our blatant city
streets to the bulletin boards of our schools, from the Sunday comics
to a television spectacular, from the consciousness of how we dress to
the abstract paintings on a museum wall, from the "designed" functionalism
of automated factories to the severely fenestrated facades of the new
glass skyscrapers—the image, popular or otherwise, has become a necessity
in our culture: not only as sculpture in our graceless shopping centers, as
gorgeous window dressing, as consumer products designed for a selling
eye appeal, as colorful record album and as lurid book jacket, as scrawled
obscenities on public walls or as the self-conscious canvases of a Sunday
painter, but as bedrock dream representations which color and complete
the American consciousness in a potpourri mixture of likeness and illusion, optical excitement, functionalism, commercial exploitation, emotional identification, desire, satisfaction and only rare moments of
transcendence.

THE DANGER OF SENSORY EXHAUSTION

We have become an eye-hungry people with an insatiable appetite for
more, for larger, or brighter, or more novel, or more lurid images. There is

[10] Siegfried Kracauer, "Pictorial Deluge," *Transformation* I, (1950), p. 53.

a confusing kaleidoscope that is fed by endless spectrums of color, by geometries of designed space, by undulating masses of sculptured surfaces. Or perhaps there is a positive and gratifying experience that lies within the visual clutter and bric-a-brac. Subtle and sensitive relationships may exist, a feeling for art. Yet this quality is drowned amidst the raucous and overwhelming quantity of the imagery. The aesthetic experience is vitiated against the massive and the insistent demands the environment makes upon the eyes and the consciousness. We are submerged by the visual and at the same time prevented from really perceiving it. Instead of leading us to inquire into the contents it often dulls the edges of understanding and stifles imagination. Oddly enough, the more we see, the less we are able or willing to practice the art of seeing, with all that it implies in personally spontaneous responses.

The very reason of efficiency and mass appeal that engendered the current development of the visual image comes into jeopardy, the entire manufactured paraphernalia of visualization teeters on a brink of satiety and soporific passiveness. There is a sensory exhaustion that often results in a lethargy of vital perception. The visual experience, with its interior and

The industrial designer creates a prototype to which production is later geared. [Courtesy, Ford Motor Company]

Art
and
Education
in
Contemporary
Culture

.

416

aesthetic insights bypassed, dangerously stresses a mechanical response. Man moves a notch closer to emulating the machine, the mass belt of reproduction conveying a surfeit of experience. Though the machine was created to perform functions which man himself either physically could not or culturally would not perform, there is the unhappy closing of the gap that separates sentient man from insensate machine. In order to further stimulate jaded looking and conditioned responses that benumb the twentieth century sense and truncate visual appreciation, the image becomes progressively bolder, cruder and more shocking. There is an assault on the eye which exacerbates the raw and battered sensibility of the artistically sensitive, which deepens the drowsiness of the average man, and grows into a cynical renunciation of mass culture with the parallel overtones of ivory towerism for the sophisticated. It is against this backdrop as well as that of an idealistically formulated philosophy that the teaching of art has to be developed.

There has to be an awareness of the context within which creativity is to be engendered or the delights and fulfillments of art is to be developed. Irwin Edman has eloquently commented on this point in a more general manner, throwing some light on the orientation of the artist.

Painters sometimes speak of dead spots in a painting: areas where the color is wan or uninteresting, or the forms inelevant or cold. Experience is full of dead spots. Art gives it life. A comprehensive art . . . would render the whole of left alive. The daily detail of doing or undergoing would be delightful, both in its immediate quality, and for the meaning it held . . . what we did would be stimulating as it is stimulating . . . to a painter to paint . . . all that we did would be an art. . . . living would be at once ordered and spontaneous, disciplined and free. There are a dozen reasons why that perfect functioning which would be an art of life, is the philosopher's blueprint and the poet's dream rather than a fact. In the life of the individual, a thousand factors of health and fatigue, of external circumstances, of poverty and responsibility, combine to defeat the deployment of resilient energies with exquisite wisdom. . . . The dead spots in experience are not avoidable. We work for leisure and we rush for peace . . . The ugliness of our streets, our houses, and our cities is a realistic interruption of what might, ideally speaking, be perpetual delight. That is one reason among a thousand others why the artist and the aesthete flee to the fine arts . . . For the artist they provide a realm where his intelligence can function freely over his tractable materials. . . . It is not to be wondered at that the world finds the artist often foolish in affairs, any more than that the artist should find the affairs of the world foolish.[11]

This is one of the polarities that art education has to take into account: the sometimes arbitrary and often narrow concerns of the average man and its reflection in the popular culture and education as against the deliberate and profound concern of the artist for what he regards as fundamental and significant spiritual and aesthetic qualities. The "average" man is too often left to trivial pastimes and stereotyped existence simply

[11] Irwin Edman, *Arts and the Man* (New York: Mentor, 1949), pp. 5-17.

Good design in utilitarian objects.

Furniture by Mies van der Rohe, sofa by Florence Knoll. [Courtesy, Knoll Associates, Inc.]

Table Silver "Caravel" No. 111, designed by Henning Koppel. [Georg Jensen Silversmith, Ltd., Copenhagen, Denmark]

because he is regarded as a standardized "product" of standardized environments. Superficially, this may seem true, but it is in direct opposition to the educational and philosophical belief of the uniqueness of each individual.

THE ALIENATION OF THE FINE ARTIST

Initially, in fear of the tangents of meaning and concern that the popular culture promised as an uncritical quality and gradually as a consequence of it actually happening, the western artist from the very beginnings of the industrial revolution until the present has accepted, if not actively sought, an alienation from his environment. This artist, who has been one of the creative vanguard, has tended to regard the masses of men as human barometers registering the forces and changes of society, shallowly reflecting these movements, but rarely transforming or expressing them in new and meaningful acts or works. That is, the average man is almost always acted upon, rarely generating his own expression which would then create its own significance as an act.

In order to safeguard his own individual insight and to nurture what is at best a tenuous and slippery creativity, the artist has been forced

Art
and
Education
in
Contemporary
Culture

•

418

into and has maintained his divorce from the body politic. This has permitted him a freedom to give vent to his own emotional and spiritual search. His art, in expressing and shaping his times, has become a forced departure from the narrow and static canons of an earlier period and the arbitrary rigor of current mass attitudes yet retains the vigorous aspects of older traditions. This has led to revolutionary changes in art, to a continuing avant-garde that has been involved with spontaneous and sometimes exotic experimentation. The experimentation has not always been an end in itself, nor has it always been aesthetically pertinent, but one of a number of means that serve as channels of exploratory symbolic insights that are then translated into fresh artistic forms. This has opened up new and exciting realms of art. The painters, sculptors and various other artists of integrity and talent of the past century have created on the edge of the unknown, exploring the rim of an endless abyss of unformed reality. Yet, even though most artists are distant from the everyday centers of society in a spiritual and creative sense, if their work is vital and imbued with intrinsic quality, that work becomes a part of the total visual lore. The very society which may have attacked an experimenting artist in the past and forced the conditions for his withdrawal most often accepts the artist's work later. The obvious examples of Van Gogh or Gaugin are quite well known and there are many others too numerous to mention. Yet this acceptance is rarely an open or truly comprehending one. Rather the overtones of trite sentimentality, the seeking of visual diversion rather than discovery, the gross swallowing of the image and the sly plagiarizing for commercial ends—all corrupt the art within the vacillating arms of a Philistine tolerance.

Perhaps the best of our creative people in most fields must exist somewhere ahead of the mass by the very nature of what they are seeking. Their insights may filter down to average understanding within time, yet it seems crudely profane to arbitrarily subject their accomplishments to the vulgarisms of an insensitive materialism when, as is the normal case, it does not deviate from its philosophical entanglement with utility or dilletantish titillation. Education, and particularly art teaching, has to develop aesthetic sensibilities which provide literate and perceptive backgrounds.

The Seduction of Popular Interest

This insensitivity to the genuine values of art is not readily countered in any really important manner by the growth of popular interest in art since the Second World War by the voluminous purchase of art books and the increased attendance at museums. As mentioned earlier, though the attempt has been made, the schools have not graduated a significant number of honestly informed and discriminating individuals. Paradoxically, at a time when the extensions of art proliferate in our society, the serious artist and his work suffer in a popular sense from a lingering spiritual isolation and an almost congenital lack of honest and fundamental understanding. The "finer" aspects of art are regarded with suspicion, disdain or with patronizing acceptance. When there is an uneasy tolerance, there is often an accompanying snicker that regards the artist as an irresponsible bohemian or foolish clown, his work the blobs and drippings of near derangement or some gigantic hoax. Not that the artist or his work is above criticism or that either is immune from a refreshing finger-pointing, but there is frequently in the vast recesses of the mass popular mind a blanket condemnation, a total laughter or an unremitting suspicion that derives from the abysmally polarized split in values mentioned earlier between "those things of meaning with no use, and things of use with no other meaning!" The social and intellectual psychology of the artist is illogically likened both to the hieratic, or conversely, to the culturally egalitarian premises that activate the experiences, perceptions and judgments of the larger groupings. Though his motivations and actions are often fundamentally different from that of the average individual, he and his work are subjected to the ostensibly democratic lens of the common and often culturally illiterate mind with the expected negative results.

In the middle 1960's, it became suddenly fashionable and correct to support a variety of artistically cultural efforts. Large industrial organizations began to exhibit their collections of art, for instance, and to increase them. Government began providing a number of subsidies and the national conscience was pricked a bit so that the artist could receive a measure of acceptance and respect. These are very positive steps that may yet have far reaching consequences in education and in the general cultural level of the American population. It may be premature and otherwise inappropriate to criticize these efforts. Yet, it is also necessary to do so if they are to assume inherently artistic directions. With this in mind, an art teacher may be asked to consider the comment of Paul Goodman, "In forwarding the fine arts, the government neglects the traditional, useful, and safe method of underwriting standard repertory and editions of the American classics, but it toys with the obnoxious official art of the Arts Councils, glamorous culture centers, and suppers for the famous. Meantime, free lances are bulldozed from their lofts and it is harder for creative people to be decently poor in their own way." [12]

Even when the so-called battle to make modern art an acceptable image is tentatively halted with a decrease of surface harassment for the artist, the latter is faced with unique problems in the American society. Widespread exhibition, popular publicity and a surprising material success (though still limited to relatively small numbers of artists) bring new and perhaps even more difficult problems to cope with. After the artist has won even a small admiring audience, as the critic Harold Rosenberg says, "The struggle of the modern artist is different from the campaign to make modern art prevail. In his struggle there can be no steady advance; the rising prestige of the tradition of the new merely confronts him with new problems, new obstacles. While an institutional buffer and a devoted audience now intervene between original works and the grosser forms of public contempt, ridicule, ignorance, and libel, the intellectual and psy-

[12] Paul Goodman, "The Great Society," *The New York Review of Books.* Vol. 5, No. 5 (Oct. 14, 1965), p. 8.

Art
and
Education
in
Contemporary
Culture

·

420

chological estrangement of the artist has not been materially reduced; it may even have grown deeper."

Rosenberg continues in a recent book, "Yet for all the attention lavished upon it and despite the circulation of art objects throughout the capitals of the world, art today is still sealed up in itself. The interest of today's vanguard public stimulates competition for its attention, but fails to supply a sense of intellectual community. The solitude of the artist has not been overcome, it has simply been contaminated . . . Lured out of his bohemian haven the painter now finds himself more completely cut off from his fellow men than ever, and the responses to his work compel him again and again to recognize that his conceptions still extend no farther than the canvas on which he inscribes them. He is gesturing in solitude after all." [13] This "devoted audience" proves a taskmaster in its own right in being facetiously "ahead" of the artist at times, suggesting an eternal merry-go-round for the ring of novelty and innovation, almost for its own sake not really understanding the shock of true originality.

This audience, however, even if it measures in the hundreds of thousands (and this is most doubtful) is no democratically significant dent in the monolithic attitudes of the hundreds of millions. Though a relatively small number of people do accept the forms of modern art, there is no hospitable ground of any significant size upon which the artist can confidently shape an intellectual, spiritual and psychological rapport beyond his own self and his immediate colleagues. There is no natural play with art for the average person and here the word "play" is used in its larger philosophical sense of expression and improvisation. There is a corresponding popular bewilderment concerning the plastic arts of the past century when they insist upon their integrity to "play" and a subsequent bastardization of the art experience that prevails in the marketplace where the expectedness of cliché or the simple-mindedness of an imposed or ill founded taste is most often employed. Only the surface qualities of art are lifted to do yeoman service in that marketplace while the mass and popular knowledge of art remains trivial and displaced, subduing or totally ignoring the latent capacities for profound and really satisfying experience. Layers of sentiment provide a sticky patina for art and it has been pointed out by Wallace Stevens that "sentimentality is a failure of feeling." Nor can education in the arts function on such a level.

The Emergence of Modern Art

Contemporary art exists on many levels, in many media and has a complexity that is impossible to encompass in any brief comment. It may be most appropriate to mention just an additional few of the more important philosophical and aesthetic factors that can help to provide the distinguishing characteristics.

There is no single date we can pinpoint and say, "Here is where modern

[13] Harold Rosenberg, *The Anxious Object: Art Today and Its Audience* (New York: Horizon, 1964), p. 261.

art started." However, it is generally agreed that it became a serious method of artistic outlook and stylistic involvement shortly after the middle of the nineteenth century. Politically, economically and socially, the western world had been in a ferment of change. The spate of revolutions, the rise of the common man and the consequent decline of the aristocracy, the push of nationalism, the seeking after mass markets and other dynamic forces all gave an impetus toward a breaking with tradition in most important public areas of living. Industrial development and technological progress led to urban centralization and radically new relationships between individuals and groups. Psychologically, both publicly and privately, the image man held of himself was further disturbed by radical discoveries in the physical sciences, by the Darwinian evolutionary idea, and the softened impact of religious doctrines. Western society was in the throes of change as it still is. It always seemed to be on the threshold of new understanding. The artist as well as anyone else was subject to these qualities that disturbed tradition. He reacted to them in his singularly open manner, rejecting or accepting elements in terms of his creative needs.

Changes in Artistic and Creative Values

Like the peasant who necessarily became the proletarian worker, the artist had to undergo alteration. The peasant gave up his closeness to the soil and likewise the artist was forced to forego his economic sources: the nobility, the church, and the ruling class that dispensed patronage. However, unlike the worker, the artist did not find a ready means of employment, so he was thrown upon his own resources. In the process, he recognized a freedom, a freedom to look, and more important, to "see," to inquire and to create without the confining limitations of a commission, no matter how advanced the patron who offered it. The artist became a speculator, philosophically and aesthetically, as well as economically. Whereas the worker merely changed figuratively from one form of almost literal "bondage" to another of psychological dimensions, the artist found that a whole new horizon of understanding was opening for him. Though his bread was not too easily or regularly buttered, somehow he managed to exist so that he could pursue those interests which he now found expanded the idea and the forms of art almost limitlessly.

A new series of values emerged for the creative individual that was shared by musicians and writers as well as those in the visual arts. Though tradition was never completely destroyed, in fact served as a firm base for formative ideas, there was a stress on the new, the original and the novel. Old ideas were not permitted to stand in the way of eager discovery, while fresh insights and provocative forms were consistently developed. This is as true now as it was with the Impressionists almost one hundred years ago. One of the continuing characteristics of modern art has been its constant search, its need to cast about for different ways to say something, its seemingly congenital inability to be satisfied with yesterday's solution. However, this has existed side by side with the

Art
and
Education
in
Contemporary
Culture

.

422

making of fine art, with providing visual solutions to innately artistic problems, so that despite the flux and flow of ideas and forms, there are the works which reflect not only their modernism but, when successful, create a universal image which transcends the particular time in which they came into being. In the latter sense modern art remains very much in the older tradition of producing intensely felt works of art. And if we examine the fabric of art history, we can also see that the need for discovery, the intent search for unique solutions has always prompted the really important artists of any time of change. Yet, we cannot honestly evaluate the art of our own time in any absolute way and claim any of it as being timeless masterpieces. This we must leave to the later decision of posterity. Our judgment may not be neutral, but we cannot support any extreme position without suffering from an officious or opinionated pride. Nevertheless, we do live with the contemporary art forms. Good or bad, they are ours. We owe them the respect of recognizing them as within the tradition of creative search; as such, they should serve as the vital basis of current art education experiences.

The insistence upon new and different approaches to the understanding of art and the making of its works obviously led to many innovations. Chief among these was the rejection of pictorial illusion, of representational images. The artist, in pursuing his unfettered search for more honest expression gave a great deal of attention to the actual properties of the materials he was working with: the painter rediscovered and affirmed the flatness of the surface he was painting on and insisted on a basic commitment to the obvious color and textural qualities of the pigments he worked with. The sculptor began to think in terms of mass and movement rather than a fleeting likeness and the architect designed to enclose and manipulate space in terms of the new functions and values of the new materials he had to work with rather than in the aping of a distant classicism. The actual depiction of objects was downgraded as an important artistic consideration: in fact, for some it came to be regarded as an obstacle. The camera had taken over this function in a manner by which the artist could never hope or want to complete.

As is observed by many critics today the new artist attempted to offer the elements behind appearances, the essence of experience. Allusion, innovation, quotation became the psychological bases from which developed abstraction and symbolization as the stylistic means while artists pushed the interminable sensual possibilities of their media to great lengths. Surprisingly enough, in this serious yet joyous exploration of artistic sensuality the artist looked for his inspiration and creative cues first in a return to nature herself, as with the Impressionists and their scientific seeing, but at the same time to the great body of art that had preceded the modern in time. However, in doing the latter the artist did not confine himself to one period or one master, but took the whole history and breadth of art as his province. Prehistoric art and the art of earlier societies as well as the art of children and the primitives have all been considered as valid sources of reference as were the venerable

The mobile has had a very strong influence on both serious and popular art forms. "Metal Sculpture," Alexander Calder. [Leo Castelli Gallery, New York; PHOTO: Rudolph Burckhardt]

old masters. All of man's artistic endeavor was used as a jumping off point for expression and experimentation and inspiration. Art then is experienced as a horizontal development rather than a vertical one. The modern artist does not consider one period or style "better than" another, though one may evolve from another. Each remains a reflection as well as an expression of its time. In this manner the artist has widened the public field of vision and has enriched its sense of art. Art education has one of its strongest cues in this attribute.

Subjective and Ideational Emphasis

The visual parodies and quotations that reflect this modern spirit are obviously seen in the work of Picasso, for instance, in the many "periods" he went through. However, this is not mere aesthetic cannibalism, for Picasso as well as any other serious modern artist does not simply plagiarize. In deliberately utilizing other styles, they transformed the sources into something personal and original, a statement of great force and validity, they used the older sources as "jumping off" points. Given this freedom to utilize the understanding of the whole range of artistic expression, artists developed the next obvious step. They turned their understanding inwards. The whole gamut of human emotion and psychological functioning became an endless source for creative ideas in art. The individual artist became his own model, his psyche the laboratory of his experiences, his personality the impelling condition of his style, his interior insights the guiding implement of the brush stroke or welding torch. The artist affirmed the ultimate worth of the single person and insisted upon the existential dignity inherent in all individuals. Philosophically he predicted or paralleled the individualized thinking of the pragmatists, the existentialists and the various shades of democratic reformers in many of their tenets though he rejected the common consensus as a means of artistic approval, insisting upon spiritual values or ideational aesthetic absolutes.

Art
and
Education
in
Contemporary
Culture

•

424

In stressing the idealistic viewpoint the artist created many new pictorial problems. Since one cannot drag out raw emotions and introspective notions and display them or actually make concrete an abstract consideration, the artists resorted to allusion, to aesthetic sequence, to sensory rhythm and distortion, to relatedness of abstract compositional qualities expressed by association. Through these ploys the essential meaning of experience was symbolically expressed. The meaning (though not as a simple equation) the artist revealed, oftentimes unconsciously, was conveyed in sensual terms of color, mass, texture, and visual movement. Subjective, intuited or ideational insights were transformed into art works that were basically symbolic of the artist's personality and his search for meaning and by extension the search and desire that mark all men. At the same time, the work created its own quality of reality, existing as a thing in itself, in a state of being which did not necessarily require other frameworks of reference.

Philosphically, the initial group of modern artists reflected the ideas of the German thinker, Kant. He held that reality existed in the mind, not in the phenomena of daily existence. In a similar vein, the modern artist sought his forms behind the visual appearances of things. The shapes, colors and lines created were not to be the graphic representation of the eye's image, but were to be symbolic of the greater reality of the mind's image.

The Structure of Cézanne and Cubism

Cézanne was one of the first of the moderns to consciously reject a traditional representation of literal appearances. He wanted to convey through his art an honest and "real" structure of form, without the illusion that even the revolutionary Impressionists had employed. His work achieves radical but ordered and imposed integration of design, form and color. His paintings reveal a basic and continuous relationship of artistic and philosophical elements that for some observers has its counterpart in the physical matter theories of science that reveal the unity of matter.

The problem became for Cézanne that of reconciling his physical "sensations" of depth, mass and color as they existed in nature and in his perception of them, with the inherent characteristics of a flat, two dimensional plane which constituted the given surface of the canvas. His personal solving of this problem led to a classically formal understanding of pictorial composition as "seen" by modern understanding. He created a style which, if it did not completely discard perspective, subjugated it to the more important internal vision of the artist and the "real" qualities of form and space. His system stressed two factors which were to influence much of the modern art to follow. Color modulation employed a series of dabs each of which existed as a plane in space, articulating the position and tactile relationships of objects as one. The other was reduction of shapes figuratively "to the cone, cylinder and sphere" creating an ordered and geometric basis for painting which served as an archetypal approach to art but not as a closed system.

This influence was followed by the artistic experiments of the cubists. They too sought a more fundamental reality behind surface appearances. However, they explored beyond Cézanne and created one of the most radical, intensely productive and influential of twentieth century styles. Their analytical approach and respect for formal structure coincided with the scientific inquiry which still is questioning the basic organization of the physical world, even at the risk of destroying the supporting assumptions of common sense and an earlier but simpler concept of cause and effect. This led to bold innovations which in turn produced dynamic pictorial relationships. If there was no absolute stability of structure, even though it appeared through the gross perception of the senses that there should be, then the artist was correct in searching out new methods of expression, pursuing an internal clarity and coherence. If change and the relative factors of period and place could alter a seemingly immutable concept of matter, creating in what appeared to be a solid and lasting rock the flux of an unsteady and transient play of energy, then the intellectual ordering of the art elements by painters and sculptors could attempt to express this change. Though the starting point of Cubist work is invariably a definite object, the artist could improvise and build upon its form by analyzing its structure, combining and rearranging the various aspects into a new and more unified order, establishing a visual design of significant quality beyond mere surface appearances accepting the multiple nature of the living, changing visual views that seemed to have more reality than the anachronism of static fixed views.

George Braque and Pablo Picasso were the foremost early innovators of cubism. The movement, however, developed in a variety of directions, the most important of which have been Futurism and Constructivism. The Futurists, working mainly in Italy, were stimulated by the modern qualities of speed, motion, and a philosophy of force. These were analyzed in terms of their visual properties, reducing them to complex and flickering compositions that expressed the contemporary feeling of kinetics and pressure. The constructivists transcended the obvious facets of motion and mechanization. In creating their precise and minutely balanced designs, they sought after a spiritual experience, hoping to influence the world through symbolic examples of harmony and equilibrium. Mondrian, Gabo and Pevsner advocated the discovery of new forms and visual relationships to more properly express the technological and scientific ideas and sophisticated emotions which some of them believed actually dominate the world today and to offer new visual organizations that embody man's aspirations as well as serving as a spiritual guide toward a more humane and integrated civilization. At the same time, nonobjective and abstract art entered the scene, the reasoning being that the nonrepresentational forms were a purer expression of artistic quality than the adulterated literal images of realism. Kandinsky and Arp were among the most influential of the early abstract artists.

Art
and
Education
in
Contemporary
Culture

.

426

EXPRESSIONISM AND SYMBOLIST TENDENCIES

There is a much greater diversity of styles and attitudes than those mentioned above. Parallel to the formalized and classical tendencies of Cézanne and the cubists has been the emergence of an emotionally intense art that has a fundamental abandon and distortion in its forms and colors. Van Gogh and Gaugin were the obvious progenitors of these provoking approaches. In the case of Van Gogh the searing, searching qualities and extreme self involvement led to a frenzied art where color, form and the very brush stroke were rapt expressions of the artist's emotional fervor. There was an implied questioning of man's nature, of his relationship to the universe and of his ultimate fate. Gaugin's work is of a similar vein, though his patterning and color took on a surface symbolism as well as an internal one. The flat, vivid color and marked outlines of forms were consciously tinged with a primitivism that sought a simple but visually exciting formula for the artist's feelings, images and ideas. One of his titles is indicative of the approach of these artists. Whence do we come? What are we? Whither are we going?

These questioning, convulsive and extreme spirits created the foundations from which developed such artists as Munch, Matisse, the entire German Expressionist School and had a strong influence on the non-objective painting of Kandinsky and the more recent school of American Abstract Expressionism. The impetus of this intuitive and relatively bizarre quality stimulated the inner fancies and compulsions of yet other artists. The wonderful, fairy-tale fantasy of Marc Chagall, the psychological probing of Paul Klee or the sometimes disturbing whimsy of Joan Miro are the most prominent individual examples of strong personal idioms in addition to the Surrealist school which employed the dream images suggested by Freudian concepts.

Modern art has ranged in philosophical viewpoints which for educational purposes may be reduced to several characteristic groupings. There are those, such as Mondrian, who prefer a personal anonymity in their work or those, such as Jack Levine, who relate to social groups. Others, such as Pollack, express a strong sense of sentient individual identity, as compared to Rosenquist, who possesses a kind of editorial detachment from society.

In all, there has been a very wide ranging expression of form, of varying and freely imagined artistic concepts, running a remarkable gamut of attitude. There has been a unifying feature though, in that almost all of the contemporary artists have felt that there is a disunity of external appearances. They have felt that a greater and more significant truth is behind the surface in the hidden or otherwise unseen characteristics of man and nature. These they have sought to express, the fragmented but sentient experience of the inner life and of the senses. Art had arrived at a point where it could be itself. It developed a directness and a force which spoke without any intervening considerations to the onlooker who was willing to divest himself of his own wall of exterior connotations to partake of the aesthetic communion. It achieved a direct and symbolic meaning that required no interpretive devices other than the integrity of individual human perception confronted by experience.

New Aesthetic Search

In achieving this directness and celebration of his own nature, the artist revolutionized the outlook as well as the surface of his art. Though he still sensed the greatness of earlier art he recognized its inability to express his own needs and the world today. Though he borrowed from many sources, he did not ape or copy them, but used them as potent sources for his own statements. He created a novel facet of contemporary reality that expressed his modern sentience. His art opened up a profound psychological awareness that not only mirrored the contemporary world but creatively gave it the open-ended variety of form that symbolically characterizes it. The intellectual freedom and daring speculation are as much a part of modern art as they are in the more accepted province of science.

Subject matter in its narrow connotations became relatively unimportant; for the realization of the artist, as it was with many others, rejected the implied morality in the sentimentally idealized or heroic versions of human nature or natural beauty. A greater moral truth was recognized in the actual creative process and in the innately sensual aspects of the various media that were handled with passion and integrity. Art then, that was freely conceived and freely practiced, was projected by the artist and his sympathizers as one of the basic moral truths. In a very deliberate manner, the artist returned to the earlier sources of his need for expression and his discovery of form, to those that characterized the pristine wonder of an unsophisticated and ingenious people. This, however, in modern times, paradoxically required an even greater level of sophistication so that creative process could transcend limitations of fashion and social pressure.

In addition to rejecting representation, the new artist changed the earlier considerations of pictorial composition, the idea that each work necessarily has a formal pattern—a logical or literary sequence rather than an aesthetic and sensuous one. The intricately devised schemes of space, movement, and rhythm were examined in the light of new concerns and the confining academic conceptions were discarded. Pictorial action became a thing closer to contemporary life, sometimes fractured and novelly distributed, sometimes a building up that conformed to its own laws of aesthetic order rather than any exterior canons of narrative or perspective correctness; object delineation was studied from a number of provocative viewpoints, figure-ground space relations assumed equal importance and the working structure was revealed rather than hidden by a painstaking craft. Surrealism appropriated the iconography of dreams, offering a displaced content to express the tangled labyrinth of psychological motivation. Expressionism opened up the emotional floodgates, directly transferring feeling into form. Cubism, we have seen, rearranged the pictorial universe of the canvas so that its construction followed the artist's sensibility of order, his feeling for aesthetic structure, and his intellectual awareness of

Art
and
Education
in
Contemporary
Culture
.

428

multiple viewpoints; it freed the artistic concept of space and time from an older, more mechanical serial order and created in its place a sensitive awareness of the paradoxically infinite variety of the artist's field of vision.

In a like manner, the earlier hieratic values in art stemming from an outmoded society which insisted upon an artificial order of concern ranging from what was considered banal to the supposedly sublime or heroic were discarded. Art dictated its own values, so that the apples in a Cézanne still life, the prostitute in a Rouault canvas or the newspaper in a Braque collage were as "right" and necessary in the artist's composition as supposedly were the nymphs sporting about in sylvan splendor in the shallow academic work of a century ago. The artist tapped his own sources of emotion and symbolic understanding so that the disintegrating public symbols of meaning that had earlier served as common property for both artist and layman no longer were valid. Like the priestly artist of ancient days, the artist created his own myths, transforming his experience and his environment in a new evocative manner.

The visual innovation in the new art did not simply concentrate on ridding itself of tired cliches and shallow sentiment. It was more interested in its own artistic concepts, in a genuine exploration of form and discovery of meaning than in any negative aesthetic vendetta. The inherent artistic problems and tensions of expression that were set in a reoriented outlook occupied the artist's attention rather than extraneous considerations. Though he often rejected the older and usually codified responses as well as the insensitive values of the materially powerful environment in which he worked, he could not divorce himself from many of the fundamental dictates of that environment. After all, drastic change had occurred not only to those conditions which shaped art, but to the basic organization of society. Science had become the controlling factor in the development of society. Its impersonal discoveries and its attendant technological applications had remarkably altered the landscape, afforded man more immediate control of his surroundings and as previously mentioned, drastically changed the image man had of himself. Darwin, Freud and Einstein inaugurated their own revolution, more potent than any in the political sphere. Ford, the Wright brothers and a powerful new class of entrepreneurs invested the findings of scientific research in mechanical application and mass production. The hard, sharpedged complex of industry imposed its calculated geometry of form on the softer nuances of natural landscape. Yet in going further, the electron microscope and the gigantic telescopes uncovered strange patterns and indeterminate sights which opened still other intricate and exotic visual perceptions. The probings of psychology and the vivid intellectual stabs of new philosophies distorted and refracted the earlier visions man created for himself. In all, the universe that man inhabited had undergone such drastic change that an earlier one, just one hundred years ago would appear not only as an anachronism but almost as an impossibility. These are considerations that any art teacher has to philosophically examine when contemplating teaching methods and substance, just as the artist has.

MODERN ART REFLECTS MODERN PHILOSOPHICAL ATTITUDES

The
Visual
World
Today

•

429

Artists have been and still are involved primarily in their own work, that is, in arriving at aesthetic solutions, in resolving artistic problems, in short, in making art. Their problems are those of the canvas, of space, of color and of the other pertinent visual elements and materials. They do not deliberately traffic with relativity, ideologies, psychoanalysis or other ideas "au courant" so that they may arrive at their forms though they do interpret them frequently; their concern is primarily that of their canvas, stone or metal and the elements of art. Picasso has indicated he is an artist first, interested essentially in visual and aesthetic problems. The American painter deKooning also insists that artists have a fundamental job to create works of art, not to "express ideas." Yet in developing a style, the larger human factors are always present; the style partakes of the temper of the times.

The artist is very much within the stream of history and draws his sustenance from the total human spirit. The complexities, contradictions and delineations of a very diverse civilization are mirrored in its art. On one hand contemporary art has as one of its compositional sinews the forms and patterns of science and technology. It integrates the sharp, ordered, yet cluttered and alternately crude and refined components of technology with the concerns of the canvas such as in Leger. Or the higher reaches of science, those of mathematical elegance may find an echo in the intricacies of Cubism or in the abstract harmonies of Mondrian, Brancusi or Pevsner. On the other hand, the turmoil and insecurity of much of today's ideologies and somber philosophies are reflected in the distortions and forceful, abandoned movement of a Pollack or deKooning. Earlier the emotional weariness of modern living was seen in Van Gogh or Munch. Psychology and its probing of human motives later found a ready visual ally in the Surrealist visions or of someone like Dubuffet or Giacometti. The subjectivity that prompts the man-centered researchers is already a highly developed avenue in art.

Though too much may be made of these parallels there is no doubt of a mutual interplay, of a cross fertilization of ideas and methods. Even more basic ideological understandings may be hypothesized. For instance, William Barrett [14] in comparing the outward three dimensionality of Renaissance art against the flat inwardness of today's art conceives each of the styles as indicators of the human spirit of its time. Giotto, in breaking from the patterned, flatness of the preceding Byzantine painters was in reality rejecting the introspection and inwardness of the Middle Ages. His art was the harbinger of the exultant extroversion and external exploration that characterized the Renaissance.

Much of the art of the fourteenth, fifteenth and sixteenth centuries was directed to a rediscovery of form in all its fullness; man looked out in art and in life, seeking to know the power of his environment. The art of the last century demonstrates an opposite quality. It has once again

[14] William Barrett, *Irrational Man* (Garden City, N.Y.: Doubleday Anchor, 1962).

Art
and
Education
in
Contemporary
Culture

·

430

Contemporary art
has a diverse range.

"Torres," Franz
Kline. [Leo Castelli
Gallery, New York;
PHOTO: Rudolph
Burckhardt]

"Untitled," Lee
Bontecou. [Leo
Castelli Gallery,
New York; PHOTO:
Rudolph Burckhardt]

"Boy," Ben Shahn.
[Collection, The
University of
Michigan Museum
of Art]

"Figures in a
Landscape," Morris
Kantor. [Collection,
The University of
Michigan Museum
of Art]

Art
and
Education
in
Contemporary
Culture

·

432

*"Seasons' End,"
Andrew Wyeth.
[Collection, IBM]*

*"To Miz–Pax
Vobiscum," Hans
Hofmann. [Kootz
Gallery, New York]*

"Sestina 1," Adja
Yunkers. [Courtesy:
André Emmerich
Gallery, New York;
PHOTO: John D.
Schiff]

become flat and subjective. The artist has turned inwards. Perhaps he
is once again being prophetic about the direction of society. The fantastic
external power and extroversion of attitude so much a part of the heritage
from the Renaissance may be denied or its importance modified. Despite
the material wealth, there may be a turning inwards of the human spirit
or some concern away from the overwhelming extroversion.

In any case, contemporary art has been primarily an interior art. Though
it is principally experienced through its visual elements and properly so,
it also communicates on a philosophical and psychological level. Despite
the great diversity of style and the richness of surface and the improvisations of techniques, the artist creates a relatively truthful image of modern
living. This image is unified in an intense empathy with contemporary conditions of life on the psychological plane that has been generated by the
artist's vision and it stresses the doubts, the emotional torments and the

Art
and
Education
in
Contemporary
Culture

.

434

anchorless existence of the twentieth century as well as its beauty, its geometry and its awesome power. The artist in the integrity of his search faces up to the existential factors that are the fundamental means of action and understanding in a rapidly changing and violent world. In addition to the grand technological innovations and scientific breakthrough, the progressive and humane legislation, this century has also experienced several gory world wars, the concentration camps of Germany, the viciousness of totalitarian systems, the mass religious and political killings in India and Africa as well as the prevailing condition of an unnecessary and senseless starvation and brutalization of spirit amidst the counter-vailing forces of an abundance of production and the recognition of a fraternal bond that encompasses all people. The works of art reflect the poverty of spirit of the era as well as its exalted aspirations even when they are lush in the sensual exposition of seeming trivia or of fundamental "beauty."

Aesthetic Attitudes Related to Art Education

The artist then, whether he is conscious of it or not, is thoroughly im-bued with the cultural aspects of his times, ideological as well as the tech-nical, the material as well as the aesthetic. He cannot escape some manner of choice which will affect his way of working and the tenor of his expres-sion. Consequently, the artist's works are living symbols of the social drama that is being enacted about him and, as such, primary sources for educa-tional purposes. However, the modern works of art cannot passively be absorbed. They require continuing educational and individual interaction. They have divested themselves (and the audience, hopefully) of formed habits and set skills, no matter how adroit these may have been. Many possibilities are preferred rather than a pat or enclosed traditional method. This attitude in the large body of art is no more than a transposition from the dynamic forces of society and an orientation toward the possibilities of the future. Such an awareness of choice is a natural condition for edu-cation and a necessary one for the teaching of art on all levels. Teachers individually have to interpret such emphasis upon an unascertained but beckoning future, creatively provoking the students in their charge.

Some part of this emphasis has to emanate from both the existing qual-ity of modern art and the manner in which various groups in society regard that art. All too often, given the contemporary overwhelming range of artistic reproduction and the trend toward predigested understanding, the response to the newer art has made arbitrary separations of meaning from symbol. Not that the response to modern art requires a set character—that would parallel the predigested comprehension. However, it should be rec-ognized that a slide or a magazine illustration is *not* the art object and may provide inaccurate or adulterated versions of the original. Nevertheless, the spread of mass communication creates its own philosophical attitudes and problems, which growing groups of serious artists are now addressing them-selves to. The diverting of original symbols into countless modified and repeated images may have produced still more novel and aesthetically arcane conditions which require a shifting direction for many artists. In any case, the teacher of art has to tread a wary and discriminating way in and around the swollen visual clutter, stressing the interpretive yet direct and individually developed encounter with the images of modern art that form the basis for a student's personal expression and appreciation.

The element of interpretation is fundamental to the mature artist as well. Philosophically, he no longer simply works within a closed tradition of imitation of either nature or master artists. Paradoxically, within a time and culture that move toward a spirit of conformity, the creatively expressive areas have underscored the uniqueness of each person and the singular elucidation of meaning. The latter may be no more than the instinctive reaction of an older tradition of personal distinctiveness or a rear-guard action of cultural rebels against an inexorable coming of 1984 and *Brave New World*. If so, the educators have a strengthened need to shore up the personal worth of each student, particularly through the liberating and rebellious influences of art.

However, the art not only mirrors the obvious qualities of its environment but draws from more profound sources in imaginatively expressing the inherently humanistic and universal attributes of mankind. The modern artist has rediscovered the internal sources of intuition and symbolic comprehension, recognizing the creative compulsions and formative understanding that are uniquely part of the human condition. The very junk and discarded bits of contemporary living that many of today's artists are motivated to employ affirms the limitless reservoirs of spirit that man actually does possess, paradoxically creating a "beauty" from ugliness, stressing a meaning rather than a senseless contingency, providing a symbolic understanding from the hesitancies and contradictions of superficial events. There is in the philosophical ramifications of modern art a recognition that in the supposed aesthetic irrelevancies and depleted spirituality of a machine controlled civilization that has discarded an outmoded morality, a new understanding and an exciting vision will develop possessing a redeeming grace and the possibility of broad social and spiritual as well as aesthetic salvation. Somehow, it is this vision that art education has to implement in the schools. It is this stay against cultural stagnation that an art teacher has to personally and enthusiastically, sensitively and directly translate into classroom method.

CULTURAL INCURSIONS INTO ART

Some of these philosophical understandings trickle down into the mass consciousness, but the greatest majority of the artist's insights are still utilized as devices that superficially alleviate the aesthetic quagmire and spiritual quandary modern man finds himself in; they are further pressed into service as practical means. There is a gross swallowing of the artist's vision, a sentimentalizing of the image through a sly plagiarizing, becoming artistic purloinings that have been foisted on the mass ability to perceive. Art, in the current experience of it, is only a small part of the total visual envi-

Art
and
Education
in
Contemporary
Culture

·

436

ronment, even though it may be regarded as a fertile fountainhead. For instance, the numberless building contractor façades and the ubiquitous kitchen linoleum that stem from the work of the Mondrian and De Styl group, the cozy interior color schemes that could not have been experienced without the color exploration of a Van Gogh, or the Fauves, the catchy posters and ads which derive from Cubism and Surrealism, the superficially tinkling mobiles appropriated from Calder and so on into the very large assortment of daily visual phenomena that evolved from the idioms of modern art. There is nothing intrinsically wrong in this. As a matter of fact, it always has been (sometimes too piously) the hope of reformers and educators that the art become a condition for democratic experience, that what was once reserved for the tastes of kings and noblemen become the property of John and Jane Doe. The hope is still a valid one; if an integrity of meaning and purpose is maintained.

Actually, one of the directions of modern art takes this very factor of anonymous popular form into consideration and exploits it in the development of its own forms. Allan Kaprow in creating the expedient and transitory conditions that are present in his Happenings is attempting to capture in another way—in a revolutionary artistic manner the direct qualities that are a part of everyday common living providing them with a new myth. However, he proves to be somewhat deeper than simple surface characteristics in investing the process with artistic ritual. Other artists of the "Pop Art" group have taken the actual forms of the visual glut that surrounds them and have utilized them as the base images of a trend in art that somehow attempts to bring together the new formal interests and discoveries of modern art with those of the "vernacular." The images of the popular arts: the comic strip, the bold advertisement, the visual bric-a-brac of daily production that is otherwise insignificant, both artistically and philosophically such as light bulbs, toilet accessories, beer cans, rulers and so on, find their way into the constructions of these "pop" artists. In a sense this may be considered as an anti-art, the topical and deliberately vulgar answer of artists who may have grown too weary of the lack of a broad congenial environment and intellectually honest understanding from a rather arbitrary and feckless audience. It may also reveal the undeniable insinuation and inexorable impingement of a monolithic "other directedness" in popular culture that has violated some of the conditions of art and has seeped into its mode of creation and symbolic content. But it is also in some ways a blurring of those distinctions that have supported art even in the recent past and a reflection, even if unwittingly on the artist's part, of the mass confusions that exist in the larger visual world. Even in satirizing the forms of popular culture it seems to approve of them almost defiantly at the same time setting up aesthetic contradictions. Critics quip about one artist as producing "advertising art advertising itself as art that hates advertising."

A parallel development has been the growth of "OP" art. This new variant of nonobjective art exploits the optical illusions and visual trickery that psychology has uncovered during the past fifty years. In its professed impersonality it appears to be developing tangentially or immune to the

The collective
creative act,
through which the
participating
audience may
make sense or
nonsense.

"Words" Environ-
ment Happening,
1962; Allan
Kaprow. [Courtesy
of the artist; PHOTO:
Robert McElroy]

main artistic currents of the past century. It may also be a harbinger of the automated and depersonalized world that cybernetics is breeding. In any instance, despite the confusions and contending aesthetic elements, both "Pop" and "OP" art are deserving of serious critical consideration; they have entered into the ongoing history of art and are enthusiastically championed by many artists. In the final analysis, it is the artist who makes art, not public opinion or private aesthetic allegiances. The only valid measures of worth remain in the symbolic level of artistry achieved and the genuine vitality of expression.

Once again there may be a new impetus in art away from more accepted or shared understanding. Just as there is a realignment in patterns of authority and loyalty in the nineteen sixties in many areas of existence with a crises mentality pervading the atmosphere almost as an accepted quality, so, in the arts, the balances are being reorganized. Energies are going off into new directions once again, leaving the timid or conservative commen-

Art
and
Education
in
Contemporary
Culture

•

438

tator behind, clutching a torn bag of outmoded rules. Perhaps it has bred its own undeserving *hubris* to posit even tentative equations, no matter how "modern." These merely limit the recognition of the infinite nature of man and only refer to what may be still regarded as the crudest comprehension of human qualities. Teachers, therefore, cannot make up any lasting rules in the teaching of art, much as the practicing artist, but they can point out the possibilities and enhance the need of students to pursue these possibilities as sources of original and viable insight.

However, more often than not the very attributes that make art great, its profoundness, its special level of understanding, its concern with the basic values and its uniqueness are extracted when it confronts popular demands: the marketplace and the medias of mass communication seem to stress the superficialities, the supposed simple mindedness (not simplicity), the recreational and the group conforming possibilities not the realization of individual vision. In the rush to feed beauty and art to as many as possible, in the unsophisticated grasping of the average individual for the tinseled delights of popularized art forms, there is a resultant confusion. Very little of the genuine emotion of art filters through; the ersatz, the substitute, the trivial, the cursory and the obvious are experienced instead. A similar result probably lies in store for art forms that are promoted primarily as business interests. Again, discriminating insights of teaching are required.

COMMUNICATION AND COMMUNION

Ours is an age in which the image has been re-established as an integral means of expression and communication, which may offer to those who knowingly desire it, communion as well. "The twentieth century has restored autonomy to the image. It knows that the image possesses powers that are its own and that need not be justified by the imitation of an object or the exposition of a subject." [15] Rene Huyghe presents an eloquent elaboration of this idea and we see its essence in the art of today. With this recognition of the power and the pervasiveness of the visual image, there is also the knowledge of the intangible but inherent and positive attributes of art that can beneficially touch the lives of people. The visual is not only the tool of society but its reflected conscience as well. There has been a tremendous creative verve in western art and a continuing ability to sustain this wide surge. There has also been a design revolution that has developed not only functional appropriateness but a contemporary beauty of new forms as well. There is no need really to confuse the two, for confusion merely breeds the tinseled hybrid to which we are daily subjected.

Actually, we have experienced the ending of Renaissance influence and the beginnings of art forms and concepts which are much more expressive of contemporary living. As material a civilization as the American has been able to give birth to a vital and very influential art. At the same time technology has provided us with a visual laboratory in which we may develop

[15] Rene Huyghe, *Ideas and Images In World Art* (New York: Harry Abrams, 1959), p. 62.

a blending of function, craft, and aesthetics. Some critics would like to see the division between the two almost arbitrarily abandoned. In fact, art education has generally assumed this belief though the results in the schools bear no evidence of any salubrious and justifying productions. Though a laudable aim in a democratic setting, it simply neglects too many facets of art and in attempting to impose a singleness of purpose on essentially diverse strains, it unfortunately misses the qualities and direction of both, frequently failing in its desired aims. Communication becomes standard and stultified while communion is almost completely neglected.

Hybrid Aesthetics

This failure has many sources, of course. The one of immediate concern is the enlarging of visual phenomena and the psychological training of perceptual responses to include all of art, commercial, industrial, as well as fine art with little or no reference to intrinsic distinctions. This destroys a hierarchy of values that formerly insisted that there was a major distinction between "creatively" pinching a piece of salt dough in the classroom and designing the Sistine chapel. Now, the designer of a successful packaging of bath salts may be considered almost on the level of a Picasso. The tight, highly disciplined and skillful manipulation of a tool and die maker is often regarded as significant, if not more so, than the work an artist like Henry Moore, the British sculptor.

In many other instances, the arbitrary mixing of simple sense data, craftsmanship, and materialistic mores even when they attempt to serve a high order of function and design blur the intuitions and aesthetically qualitative and differing aspects of fine art. This confusion is compounded into a tangle of sentiment, bewilderment, values at cross purposes with themselves and finally an unthinking reflex response, when it is too easily labelled as art, either in the school or in society at large. Even when there is a recognition of the distinctions between the popular image or its manufactured development and the pure aspects of fine art, the latter is generally relegated to some limbo of mystery. The persistent circumstances of our megalomaniac civilization (which unfortunately, may not really be deluded about its power) and its inbred mechanical and popular perquisites are difficult to deny.

It is important to stress the distinctions, however, particularly from the educational viewpoint if we honestly support the ideas of a free and meaningful education and wish to encourge the fullest development of each student's potentialities. This would indicate a needed emphasis on the fundamental and unadulterated qualities of art rather than on its appendages. This heightening of the aesthetic and the innately moral aspects of the visual experience may even serve as a positive element in heading off the cultural deterioration and stagnation which is so insidiously a part of twentieth century living. And this can be achieved through the teaching of art only when the student, like his exemplar the artist, is vouchsafed his innate and unviolated individual vision.

This could be best implemented in what Herbert Read calls a hybrid

Art
and
Education
in
Contemporary
Culture

•

440

civilization in which there is some division of human and social activities. The education in such an environment would stress the creative experiences of students, intensifying their sensibilities and enhancing their taste, it would

. . . accustom their hands and eyes, indeed all their instruments of sensation, to a creative communion with sounds and colors, textures and consistencies, a communion with nature in all its variety . . . They would carry within their minds, within their bodies, the natural antidote to objective rationality, a spontaneous overflow of creative energies into their hours of leisure. . . . then we need not fear the fate of those children in a wholly mechanized world. . . . The result would be a private art standing over against the public art of the factories. But that—in our painting and sculpture, our poetry and dancing, our artist-potters and artist-weavers—we already have. That is to say we have a tiny minority of people calling themselves artists. I am recommending that everyone be an artist. I am not recommending it in a spirit of dilettantism, but as the only preventative of a vast neurosis which will overcome a wholly mechanized and rationalized civilization.[16]

This may very well lead to a civilization where every visual object is a "beautiful one, where art and the machine, where symbolic expression and technology may merge." It is a desirable aim, yet it may also be very much in the future. Certainly, the confusion inherent in the contemporary blend of technics and aesthetics leads into some other direction that is not desirable; art, in the final analysis not only requires but insists upon a purity of vision and an unencumbered expression. It is only on this latter level that the spiritual concerns of art may be felt.

[16] Herbert Read, *The Grass Roots of Art* (New York: Wittenborn, 1947.), p. 91.

Redirection in Art Education

> I look forward to an America which will not be afraid of grace and beauty . . . an America which will reward achievement in the arts as we reward achievement in business and statecraft. I look forward to an America which will steadily raise the standards of artistic accomplishment and which will steadily enlarge cultural opportunities for all of our citizens.
>
> JOHN F. KENNEDY

A SERIOUS consideration of the role of art education in relationship to contemporary cultural and artistic conditions is basic to a successful teaching of art. The continuing dynamic force of twentieth century society coupled with the basic readjustments education is experiencing are felt in every curriculum area including the teaching of art. A sophisticated yet flexible understanding of the changes necessary in the substance and methods of art teaching appear to be encumbent responsibilities of each individual involved in art education: teacher, administrator, and theorist.

Fred Logan can write, for instance, of his insights as they enrich the concepts of art education, changing the emphasis somewhat in the middle nineteen sixties from that of an earlier time, retaining however an individual yet organic line of thinking.

Art education, practiced primarily to teach the arts, can no longer afford to rely on apologetic slogans to explain its own existence. The arts have engrossed man's attention and activities as long as history has left traces of his earthly existence. Certainly it is possible to teach art for the increase of skill among workmen, for the worthy use of leisure, for the stimulation of personal expression in a creative environment, for its correlative value in the teaching of "meaningful wholes," for the meeting the child's needs in the life of his home environment, for grasp of concepts of visual forms, for understanding of the creative attitudes and approaches to the work of the artist, for aiding the individual in achieving a 'self identification in the chaotic world, and finally for the nearest approach each individual can make to the quality we are currently labeling 'creativity.' Each art teacher, in varying degree, consciously or unconsciously, teaches art to accomplish these ends. . . . We will nevertheless be teaching the subject

Art
and
Education
in
Contemporary
Culture

·

442

of art. We teach art for art's sake and these associated values are inherent in the teaching and in art. Art teachers are essentially artists.[1]

The last three sentences sum up the emerging emphasis that are education will have in the coming decades. Prospective teachers should be supple enough in their thinking, sincere enough in their belief in art education, and intuitive enough as educators to recognize this stress. The emphasis on the intrinsic conditions of art primarily as the natural source of art education may modify many preceding attitudes and alter some current practices of art teaching, or one may say, they should do so. The various goals, purposes and presumptions that have attended art education are in the process of undergoing a serious of transformations.

CHANGE IN ART EDUCATION

Art education will concern itself more with a central cluster of values and experiences which stem directly from the art experience in its many forms whether it is of a doing or appreciative kind. The adjunctive factors of social and behavioral development will of course be present. Successful art teaching will always have to respond to the influences of the many peripheral pressures that touch art. The confusions, though, that entangle the art experience with foreign or unimportant factors require a continuous examination, the various parts necessarily assuming their appropriate and weighted places. The diffusion of "extracurricular" and otherwise damaging considerations in the art activities and classroom atmosphere afforded students will yield to a more aesthetic and genuinely creative set of experiences. In the early elementary years the "gimmicks," the educationally superficial "tricks," and the shallow "cute" projects wherever they are deserve to be discarded as is the philosophy supporting them. In its place an open-ended but serious foundation of aesthetic play, and expression of emerging form, of functionally creative mythopoesis, of imaginative and intuitive involvement with symbolic meanings, of critical and historical literateness based on perceptiveness naturally, adventurously related should assume the line of direction, without a strong instrumental emphasis.

The natural movement and characteristically intense gestures of the early primary grades have to be guided, through art, into channels of discovery and expressive form making for the developing child. A more aesthetically disciplined appreciation, product oriented and intrinsically artistic teaching of art in the upper elementary grades may ease the transition from childhood into adolescence. Personal development and growth are never simple undertakings nor will they be in art education. The professionally informed intuitions, the imaginative and sympathetic understanding of the art teacher and the level of commitment to genuinely artistic and creative classroom proceedings are primary determinants at this point. A naturally inspiring dialogue and direct interchange of qualities between teacher

[1] Frederick M. Logan, "Development of Art Education in Twentieth Century U.S.A." *Report of the Commission on Art Education*, Jerome J. Hausman ed. (Washington, D.C., National Art Education Association, 1965), p. 64–65.

and student may vitalize the tone for the experiences of the art lesson, carried on through all educational levels, including the development of critical faculties and motivating information about artists and art works.

For the junior high age, art may become a means of expressing all the pain and enthusiasm, the exploratory yet hesitant searching, the need for security and the opposite need for independence that occasionally becomes rebellion, the unfolding rapport with the conditions of existence and the awareness of the enlarging values of all experience but particularly the aesthetic and the symbolic. If the mass, commonplace influences have not been indelibly stamped upon the attitude and behavior of the individual student, the cruder forms offset by evocative teaching in the arts, there may be a sensible awakening to activities and a groundwork of intelligent analysis of visual forms that permits the student to go beyond the conforming mores of sex differentiation, social position, vocational narrowness and cultural inhibitions. The appreciation of and critical insight into art is important at this point, generally and specifically.

Art becomes even more intensive during the senior high school years where, hopefully, more students will be encouraged to elect at least one course or more in the subject. At this level, the student is on the brink of adult realization that can lead to mature understanding and expression. The natural romanticism of the period, its readiness for challenge, its quest for understanding and knowledge, its pride in accomplishment may find a positive channel in art classes. There can be no adulteration of content or lessening of profundity of experience; in fact, the art classes in high school should be closely and seriously allied to both the historical background of art and its current vitality of development outside the classroom. In all, the teaching of art should take on a more serious tone concentrating on intrinsic substance and critical evaluation at the same time that it enriches the symbolic development of aesthetic "play" and personal expression.

The curricular base of art education requires an expansion, on all levels, to include more of the substance and particular processes which help in producing the mind that is prepared to know or engage in an art experience. A change in the direction of including contextual information about works of art, of aiming for intensified analysis of art works would complement the creative aims in a very sound and fruitful manner.

Changing Aspects of Child Growth and Self-Expression

The concept of child growth and development through art may change in an important manner. Instead of art viewed as an instrument through which a goal of development is to be achieved, it will be sensed as an intrinsically humanizing factor that does not necessarily have to follow any narrowly temporal or other conceptualized and systematic pattern. Though growth and development does occur as the result of involvement with art, it will be seen as a fluid, continuing, and frequently inconsistent interrelationship between person, process, and product. These are dependent upon the qualitative factors of the immediate experience and its intrinsic worth, and upon erratically unique attendant factors that nonetheless infuse the individual's

Art
and
Education
in
Contemporary
Culture

.

444

existence with moments of "truth and beauty." There is no assurance of systematic development or continued growth in art. Characteristically, for the most part there is the sporadic and immediate revelation of individual truth and the spontaneous inculcation of new and qualitative values. These achieve symbolic significance where the experience has been genuine and may accumulate toward maturity.

In any general sense, education has built-in limitations and there are no practical guarantees of its efficacy for any period. Paralleling this, art education may be sensed as the uniquely and intrinsically human way of achieving a recognition of significance in living, by natural and aesthetic means, subject to the propensities of the individual and the demands of the symbolizing process. The unfolding of personality, though it may contain common points at particular times and in special circumstances, cannot be systematized or regularized no matter how positive or "progressive" the goal, without the danger of mass stereotyping and the eventual draining of worthwhile values. The process throughout has to be sensed as an open functioning, frequently inconsistent and discontinuous, but generally heading toward individual sensitivity, mature understanding, and expressive and aesthetic growth. It is to be recognized that the symbolizing activities of art provide the means of merging the inner compulsions with the outer realities and that this blending is a constant need and realization of all ages.

The emphasis on self expression will become involved with broader dimensions and greater aesthetic substance. Though the expression of the self is central to the creation of art, the factors of good and bad as value judgment in matters of taste, form making, and content will have to illuminate the actual quality of art expression as it is created in the class room. The process is insufficient if valued primarily as a means of catharsis, or "fun." It has to go further and become one of self realization that is based upon intensified observation, genuine aesthetic worth and expressive significance; there has to be real artistic purpose. The student will have to be stimulated not only in the broad sense "to express himself." In the doing he has also to be encouraged to assess the nature of his perceptions, to control the order of his aesthetic concepts in a manner that would result in sensitive use of materials and significant development of forms.

This does not only presuppose a deliberate and conscious manipulation of the elements and principles of art alone, but suggests that the deliberative and evaluative process of art should be organically interwoven with the underlying unconscious compulsions and determinations of the individual and by extension, the vital aspects of his culture. The symbolic emphasis of the art experience has to be reaffirmed as more than arbitrary accident or the presentational immediacy of sensory data and with wider meaning than the shallow or misunderstood attempts to undisciplined "self expression." There should be an exploitation in depth of particular materials and techniques. A balance has to be established for each individual based on qualitative artistic experience, between informed control and undisicplined feeling, leading to individual yet purposeful expressive acts. These would

also contribute to the continuing overall growth of the individual, provided the art experiences are authentic and the individual student ready at any given period to receive them.

Student growth and expression, in any change that occurs in the philosophy of art education, will be predicated on more substantial grounds than ephemeral development. A recognition will have to be made of the importance of the product created in the maturing of student capacities, of aesthetic or critical insight and in his competencies for creative expression and symbolic communication in establishing personal sensibilities.

It is toward the intensification of individual experience and the aesthetically significant shaping of the forms of that experience that art education is directed.
[New York Public Schools]

Art
and
Education
in
Contemporary
Culture

.

446

READINESS FOR ART EDUCATION

Some distinction can be made between systematized planning of child development in art and in the readiness of a student to engage in any particular art activity. Though the distinction may be fine, it is nevertheless a real one. Child development in art has normally been understood in a value sense. That is, certain activities were supposed to be "good" at certain ages, such as large brushes for first grades or detailed and mechanical visual planning for junior high students; others were considered "bad" such as the overly challenging techniques of water color for the primary grades on the limitation of the crayon for adolescents. There is probably a good deal of practical teaching truth in many similar empirical observations. However, it seems aesthetically and philosophically inappropriate to structure too stringently the developmental sequences, particularly if they are tied to what are often arbitrarily derived developmnetal values.

The arbitrary nature derives from the practice of assuming that child growth has a parallel line of development in aesthetic understanding and artistic manipulation. Though certain factors of kinesthesia, muscle dexterity, physical size, emotional identification and intellectual conceptualization do parallel the development of children's art at points, there is no support for a doctrinaire chart of do's and dont's. To insist upon one is to curtail the possibilities of teaching creatively. The conceptualized developmental sequences, such as J. Piaget's, are not to be utilized as bone dry and inhibiting directives for teachers, but rather as insightful realizations of the limits of children's understanding. These should inform and heighten the possibilities of teaching rather than limit them. Piaget himself calls for a stress on student auto-regulation, for an accent on the activity of the subject, for such self-directed teaching can influence human development. The underlying creative factors of most importance are the symbolizing process itself, the creative uses of the imagination, the exploratory handling of materials, the sensitive manipulation of technique to capture a vision, and above all the unique personality of the individual student. In these regards the kindergartner is ready to undertake art activity as is any adult.

The method of teaching particular levels of students should derive more from the intuited awareness and active creative participation on the part of the teacher, the result of concrete experience and immediate impressions as well as educational distance and theoretical supports. There are certain physiological, psychological, and physical factors that have a direct bearing upon the readiness of any student to engage in particular kinds of art experiences. These fall somewhat broadly into certain age groups. For even the beginning teacher the readiness factors are somewhat obvious.

For all practical purposes, when children are old enough to attend school, they are ready enough to engage in most art activities. They have attained a level of intellectual and sensory skill, of motor coordination and expressive need, to work with almost any medium. Admittedly, the younger children will have trouble with some techniques, conceptual and expressive, demanding somewhat developed skills of sensory manipulation, emotional balance, and intellectual comprehension. However, the educational skills and intuitive insights of a teacher should be able to sense these factors and plan for them accordingly without the recourse to detailed guides and without setting up any pedagogical fetishes. There may be some brief generalities that can serve as contextual rules of thumb in this respect.

The ineptness, apparent clumsiness and manipulatory limitations of the very young child are probably due to insignificant muscular development or the resistance and difficulty of certain tools and media. With some experience, any teacher easily determines the which and why of the problem, encouraging the type of activity that the young child may become creatively involved with. No experience, however, should be denied to students, if they indicate honest attempts to master a material or explore a technique, no matter what the level. The resulting frustration may be offset by a necessary exploratory bravado. When older children demonstrate limitations of use of materials or techniques, it is more likely to have psychological and cultural roots. There may be emotional disturbance, intellectual blocking, or external influences from friends, home and mass communication media —all potent factors that determine individual readiness and impinge upon art activities.

Individual differences are probably more a condition in art education than they are in any other area of learning. Some students simply have a greater intellectual capacity, a fuller creative range, a more imaginative preconscious and a finer motor coordination than others. As a result, some students will make easier and more fluent associations, have more flexible sources for relating elements, project more intense and evocative visions and handle the art materials with more originality, confidence and aptitude. These differences may be inborn, the result of "cultural deprivation" or simply due to differing rates of maturation. There may even be students who are congenitally incapable of experiences that have a visual and plastic base; they may translate their visions into sound, or movement or verbal symbols rather than in those of art. In any instance, the art teacher has to be aware of the singular attributes and capacities of each student and is obligated to teach with this in mind.

The most important element in understanding readiness in art education lies more in the teacher's determination of what can constitute the student's experience than in the abstracted and charted responsiveness of the student according to age level or objective testing. The basic need is to stimulate various experiences, to enrich the imaginative images that result, to expand the store of associations, to relate the experience and imagery to the visual symbolic forms of art. Such aims require an exploration of the transforming processes on many levels and in depth as well. This does not suggest exposure to a variety of materials and techniques for the simple sake of exposure, but rather suggests that art teachers have to acquaint students with the range of expressiveness that materials and techniques possess. If this is done sensitively and with general aesthetic understanding rather than with specific direction, students on all levels can intensify their own sensibilities and personally make the most artistic choices in converting their experiences into symbols.

Art
and
Education
in
Contemporary
Culture

.

448

Exciting and felt motivation would appear to be the basic key to inducing and meeting readiness or in challenging it. The art teacher has to plan and put into effect the stimulating, probing and vividly provoking experiences that create the "sets" for readiness. At first, this is of a direct nature. For the primary grade children experience is directly absorbed rather than vicariously accepted. The first or second grade child has not completely removed himself or herself from an immediate identification with the objects and events of the surrounding. This symbolic umbilical cord is gradually loosened and finally severed in the middle and upper grades. Then vicarious experiences may be employed, when growing children are capable of putting a "distance" between themselves and the stimuli that pressures or influences them. In the adolescent the full brunt of the rational process takes hold. Unless there is some knowing reversion to the earlier direct experiences, to open emotional presence, to spontaneous and felt sensory play and symbolic intensity, the art activity is likely to dissipate or to be channeled into rather confined directions.

Readiness on one level of thinking may be considered as much a symptom of the kind of teaching that a child is exposed to as it is the sequential or developmental progression of individual facility. This does not necessarily dispute the fact that students do undergo various stages of growth with characteristic patterns of capability in each. It suggests however in Bruner's words, "that any subject can be taught effectively in some intellectually honest form to any child at any stage of development." [2] If we change intellectual to either aesthetic or artistic, or better yet simply add them to the phrase, then the hypothesis holds as much for art education as it does for the discursive subject areas.

THE SPIRAL CURRICULUM AND GENERALIZED UNDERSTANDING

Bruner is only among the latest to advocate a kind of teaching that introduces the main ideas of a subject area right from the very beginning of a student's school career. The old traditional education was predicated on the assumption that the structural base is provided on the primary level and repeated in successive levels with increasing detail and subtlety of concept. Unfortunately, this was narrowly conceived in compartmentalized blocks. More pertinent, the earlier curriculum had far fewer subjects to teach, so that it could engage in this tightly arranged approach. With the expansion of the curriculum, it did not seem feasible to introduce the procedures of intermediate mathematics, most of the physical sciences or the "advanced" forms of literature and the arts until much later in a student's school career. A reaction to this was the unit or project study in a wide variety of subject areas in the elementary schools. These units, however, often distorted or adulterated the nature of the material presented for fear the young child was simply not ready to be exposed to "difficult" thematic concepts or into closely gearing learning to arbitrary levels of development or cultural levels of need and propriety.

[2] Jerome Bruner, *Process of Education* (Cambridge, Mass.: Harvard University Press, 1961), p. 3.

The active appreciation of art is one of the more important aims of art education. Class at the Metropolitan Museum of Art, New York. [Courtesy of The Metropolitan Museum of Art]

In hypothesizing the capacity of all children, of any age, to be introduced to any subject, provided the material is "translated" in honest terms and presented in an appropriately "challenging" manner, Bruner is merely updating an old doctrine. The updating is important because it is presented in open creative terms, built upon organic structural aspects of discipline rather than on arbitrarily arranged combinations of facts or isolated developmental charts. This teaching idea has special significance to art education because the main ideas of symbolic transformation are at one and the same time the essential "learning" substance of a serious work of art as well as of the schematic response to experience a first grader will create with crayons though they may differ in profundity and aesthetic value. The spiral curriculum supports the teaching conception of presenting the most fundamental understanding of a field rather than teaching specific skills and topics.

This approach is a natural one for art experience despite the unique factors of expression and form. Particularly in the individualized activity, in the stressing of exploratory techniques and the emphasis of learning and creating through discovery with which art education is involved, it is essential to acquaint all students from their very first encounter with art of the extensive range of generalized functions of the artistic and symbolic process. The unique adaptations to the conditions of art are reinforced through an awareness of these functions, setting the stage for increased observation, sharper critical analysis yet also stimulating imaginative and free associations.

This generalized understanding is developed in an organic manner: the student's emerging personality, his preconscious and more controlled understandings and range of imaginative possibilities interacting with a viable comprehension of the sensory materials of art, the various procedural tech-

Art
and
Education
in
Contemporary
Culture

·

450

niques, the underlying character of the classroom atmosphere and the intensity of the motivating impulses. Teachers have a good though varying measure of educational control over all these elements, which they exercise in their personal and professional ways.

For instance in drawing, a teacher on any level can talk about the hand-eye coordination. The teacher can suggest contour and gesture drawing, free exploratory means of achieving linear form. There may be a discussion of the importance of the sense of touch as well as the visual sense in drawing, the pointing up of relationships that may influence proportion and size. There could be open exercises of creating lines, with pens, pencils, wire, bits of wood or any other tool; in tempera, in ink, in wash, in crayon; making thick and thin lines, firm and nervous ones, continuous and broken ones, ad infinitum. There can be the study of various artists, from Ingres, through Daumier to Pollock and their different styles. There can be any number of open, generalized approaches to drawing.

What should not occur though, is a step by step procedure, a stereotyped routine, laying the groundwork for easy schemata and simple but artistically valueless formulas. If a student is dogmatically taught that a human figure is so and so number of heads tall, that only a certain instrument can perform a particular job of delineation, that one step of drawing must follow another, then the very spirit and creative nature of drawing is violated. Also important in an educational sense, the routine and particularized set of procedures do not lend themselves beyond the imposed solution of the time in which it is experienced. The student may come out with creditable, if stiff and unindividualized forms, but they probably would not be creatively utilized at some future time when a related but different drawing problem arises. Then too, formulas have a way of being forgotten, so that their educational utility is lost to the student. If they are deeply implanted by rote and repetition, the result is almost invariably stereotyped activity, a prejudiced viewpoint that inhibits the necessary avenues to continue aesthetic discovery. For drawing, like all learning and creativity in art is a route to discovery, the personal uncovering of sensory, aesthetic and psychological significance in visual forms.

The Loose Structure of Art Principles

In any art experience there is no categorically valid "how to" understanding, no reduction of observation or technique to a precise definition. This approach is too readily discernible in the stereotyped imagery of formula art. These are lacking in vitality and in the spirit of expressiveness that art naturally possesses if it is created spontaneously. It would seem teaching in art has to avoid the predetermined and narrow concerns, the arbitrary demonstrations, the mass topical lessons. No individual will ever really develop a sensitivity to artistic spatial characteristics through the dry imposed formulas of perspective. The color wheels, the theories of working from dark to light or vice versa, the compositional formulations such as the golden mean or any other of a vast number of supposedly objective principles free from personal bias or emotional prejudice are in a like fashion incapable of stimulating and maintaining creative relationships to art. They are not true generalities of artistic comprehension, but artificially constructed canons of correctness. They run counter to the inherent uniqueness of the artistic act and tend to stultify rather than motivate.

Students should, nevertheless, be acquainted with the various and sundry approaches to art functionally and liberally developed. However, they cannot be given to the impressionable and receptive minds of youngsters as the only correct way of arriving at successful art forms. It is the individual searching process that has to be stressed; personal discovery has to be underscored. With such personal procedure any approach to art may be provided as a choice to students.

The generalities of art lie in sensing the intrinsic characteristics of materials, the varying properties of sensuous elements, in grasping the aesthetically functioning aspects of technique and the relative attributes of aesthetic principles such as symmetry, dominance, color dynamics and so on, the interplay of form and content, all being guidelines rather than predetermined directions.

There probably is no objective sequential building of a learning structure in art education presented as abstract theory that can withstand the rigors of practice or the individual creative process. The art syllabus should make no specific or definitive determinations such as crayon drawing—first grade; or water color—fourth grade, but rather emphasize the subtle and expressive power of the processes of symbolic action and aesthetic forming. There is no firm longitudinal progress of systematized projects, of strictly graduated levels of difficulty of material, of an organized ladder of steps to competent skills, positive techniques, imaginative visions, aesthetic intuitions and mature symbolizing techniques. These latter are inherently individual qualities that may respond in a small way to sequential planning, but are much more uniquely attuned to arrive at value commitments and states of feeling encouraged within a conducive educational climate. As a result, the general ideas and understandings underlying art may be and should be presented on all levels, with perhaps an increasing sense of challenge and intensity as the student works his or her way through school but not strictly categorized by developmental grade level. The stress has to be on the overall refinement of taste and sensitivity as well as on an intensification of aes-thetic vision and the development of artistic values.

EXTENDING THE SCOPE OF ART EDUCATION

The actual scope of art education will have to be extended. For the past half century, the primary function of art teaching has been in the direction of student participation in the making of art. To this will have to be added once again the appreciation of art that others have created and the analysis and sensible study of great works of art in many forms and medias far more often than is the current practice. Obviously, the overwhelming number of students will not actively mature as professional artists, nor is there proof that early training in what is believed to be creative process has any real

Art
and
Education
in
Contemporary
Culture

.

452

transfer into the later pragmatic concerns of the average adult life, or that it will necessarily enrich the otherwise flattened aesthetic sensibilities of the mass citizen. Somehow the values become confused and distorted, the judgments narrow, gauche, or remain simply uninformed. Though it is still essential to provide for participating experiences, the real worth in art for most people will be in the development of an enriched, heightened and informed sensibility—an intensification of the responses to works of art. After all, throughout past history, art was produced by special and unusually endowed people. They possessed the extraordinary visions and the personal talents, creating on a level of energy and feeling that greatly transcended the commonplace, shaping the forms of art. The artist has always stood apart from daily concerns in one way or another and will do so probably forever. Perhaps this is why he can create on a high level, but in any case, it is an obligation of education to adequately present the work of serious artists, of this and of past times, providing a base of artistic literateness that may spread in the general culture as well as enrich the individual. Art appreciation should complement personal art production.

Defining the Range of Art Experiences

Art educators have an obligation to reexamine what is meant by art, both in the schools and in the popular extension of that concept as a verb— process (a "creative" making) and as a noun—object (a work of art). Earlier in history it was considered that art contained a rather extensive range of activities. There was no basis of distinction between, for instance, the crafts and picture making. Aesthetics and utilitarian functioning were considered as one. However, with the advent of the Renaissance, the work of art became an exceptional thing. Art and its creator were deemed to possess special qualities. A separation marked art from other craft activities, establishing distinctive hierarchies of prestige, social values and the need for refined tastes.

Subsequently, the development of art degenerated into the meretricious style of an official academy during the nineteenth century. But paralleling this, modern art was born, carrying on the inherited traditions of aesthetic excellence. In any case a sophisticated reaction to the hot-house tawdriness of academism set in and a popular one against the seemingly esoteric concerns of the avant-garde. Aided by the technological and social revolution, art once again was considered to include many "creative" activities and objects, as in earlier times, though the emphasis of religious and functional qualities changed greatly.

The twentieth century has witnessed a remarkable but indiscriminate spread of these so-called artistic works and procedures—of visual improvisation and craft activity. In the violence of the mass egalitarian reaction to the cultivated restrictiveness of high art, there has been a corruption of the essential nature of art and an adulteration of its values.

Art education, unwittingly or otherwise, has contributed to this unfortunate cultural hiatus of aesthetic worth by fostering a largely indiscriminate approach to the teaching of art. Personality development and a vague

creativity have been valued, frequently without the aesthetic base of substance that would lead to the professed aims. A more differentiating insight should point up the distinctions between the spiritual and aesthetically revitalizing qualities of serious and high level art as against the diverting, commonplace functioning, yet often thoroughly pleasing attributes, of recreational, household or commercial activities. The sympathetic regard for experience that characterized more primitive societies as naturally expressed in a full range of broadly encompassing but genuine art activities should again be cultivated. However, art education has to assess realistically the robotizing influence of a computerized, automated system, reorganizing in art an especially distinctive, unusual quality, no matter how passionately it is desired that it democratically pervade all of living. And this distinctiveness lies in the essential nature of art, in its spiritual mystery and moral commitment to a direct expression of integrity and intensity. These attributes enrich experience without an overriding regard for the accidental and extrinsic additions of transient or petty importance. They provide a level of meaning that is self-sufficient, that inheres in the very essence and form of the work of art.

Because only a relatively few remarkable individuals may achieve genuine art, the scope of art education should be extended by once again introducing the appreciation and trained perception of art. However, in a paradoxical way, the scope of what is actually presented has to be more firmly contained, focused upon authentic art experiences.

Art Appreciation

The term "art appreciation" may appear, at first, to be an unfortunate one as a description for an educational activity. It has many older connotations that are outmoded or inadequate in the study of art, such as the teaching of particular systems of artistic response, of predetermined critical yardsticks, of stereotyped selections for student viewing and of other in-

Art
and
Education
in
Contemporary
Culture

•

454

adequate teaching approaches. The unfortunate aspect to much of these past practices was the lack of direct perceptual stimulation and independent student analysis. Art appreciation classes usually illustrated a point in social studies or demonstrated more concretely an historical context. The art work assumed secondary importance and rarely was accepted for its own sensory and expressive qualities. Despite this, the term appreciation can still be utilized, for it aptly describes a range of educational activity within a particular subject area and is, in itself, a goal for art education.

However, appreciation has to be predicated on an individually active perceptual basis. The student must function in his own right and with his own growing capacities relating to the being of a work of art in a direct, unencumbered manner. Appreciation has to be developed through the actual works of art and not by seemingly logical yet arbitrary references to a particular history of art or system of aesthetics.

Though historical information may be of assistance, it is also extraneous and tangential sometimes. There is no absolute history of art in the sense that there are laws that govern physical properties, other than in a conventionally chronological way. There are many aesthetic and critical formulations that vie for teacher acceptance. These should only be utilized as guides and should not deflect the necessary freedom and teaching effectiveness with which to engender independent student perception.

It is the work of art itself that has to serve as the fundamental source for establishing an appreciative response. If the context within which it was created is considered important, then the supposed nature of the context has to be elicited from the sensory, aesthetic and expressive qualities that exist intrinsically in the work. Historical, critical, biographical and social contexts that are theoretically and abstractly presented before or after viewing the work of art, but independent of it, mitigate against a true appreciation of the artistic values. They teach something other than art.

Art teachers also have to consider that each work of art has another context, that which is created in a sensory and symbolic way by the immediate qualities of the work. This, too, may be a shifting context, in response to the personal qualities that each person brings to the experience. However, the context is a real one, one that may be experienced in an immediate and readily observed manner. The aesthetic and symbolic qualities are laid out, so to speak, for inspection, perception, and individual reconstruction. It is on this direct level of involvement with the sensory properties of art works that the most vital and genuine intensification and growth of art appreciation may occur, supported by a sophisticated, knowledgeable but challenging teaching method.

The student, during an art appreciation class, has to be made to shoulder the learning and perceiving responsibilities of the experience. He should not be permitted to respond to the experience through abstract concepts or another's viewpoint, accepting insights and judgments that are not personally developed, no matter how timid, faltering or puerile his own may be. Personal and independent responses should be encouraged, consistently stressing, however, that the response has to have some tie to the work of art. It may be difficult for the student to articulate a response, and it may not always be a necessity. But in some manner or another, perhaps through his own art creations that demonstrate a stimulating and inventive, rather than simply an imitative influence, the student should be guided to present his independent experience of works of art.

Appreciation may then be personally evolved through an elaboration of the perceptual and critical faculties, questioning the nature of what artistic meaning is, relating these elements back to the sensory attributes of works of art, leading hopefully to a singular realization of each work of art as one very natural kind of symbolic form that creates its own reality.

Art education, as a result, has an encumbent responsibility to present the heritage of art as well as a contemporary expression. It has to help devise individual channels that will adequately and with genuine feeling, not only study mature and representative works of art but achieve a critical, yet creative, vitally personal perception by the onlooker of artistic process that has become an object of art. This has to become more than a vicarious satisfaction, it has to become one of achieving self-realization by imaginatively aesthetic means of appreciation rather than stereotyped formal ones, of critically appraising works of art so as to recreate the passion, the insight and the symbolic meaning that moved the creating artist.

The implication is that art appreciation should not be strictly confined to traditional forms of visual art. Though many of the most intense statements in art continue to be made through the traditional means of painting, sculpture and architecture, the scope of visual expression has expanded greatly since the turn of the century.

There are, for instance, the various film techniques, still and motion, that some critics look upon as the only legitimately new art form of contemporary living. Certainly, these have created another facet of visual excitement and expression which deserves critical examination. It is not sufficient to permit the aesthetic concerns of film making to be left to the not so tender mercies of the commercial cinema, TV broadcasting and of locally insensitive snapshot faddists as means of exposure. The schools should offer some fundamental insights into appreciation of still and motion photography, providing opportunities to see older classic films and foreign ones as well. Similarly, the exploration of light dynamics, of kinetics, of assemblage and other constructions deserve classroom attention, both through participation and the study of current forms. There also should be a continuing study of the elements of popular culture, of commercial, industrial and interior design in an honest, discriminating manner. The natural antithesis between the high art forms and those of mass consumption require examination. Advertising, popular illustration, the comics, consumer products and home decoration are all appropriate areas of personal exploration. This may lead to more genuinely positive insights into their nature and their influence, good and bad, on individual taste. In a larger sense art education should be concerned as well with the elements of housing design, traffic routing, city planning and environmental construction that exert such potent determinations in modern visual terms.

Art
and
Education
in
Contemporary
Culture

·

456

Art education has to acknowledge its ties to the larger body of artistic expression. The interrelationships among the various forms of art, drama, dance, literature and music deserve attention. Particularly on the senior high school level, but on the lower levels too, a teaching focus of broad styles and philosophical currents of a certain time or place or of shared formal characteristics may enrich student literacy in the arts.

Obviously, there has to be a reevaluation of the curricular foundation of art education. It requires a good deal of attention to the sharpening and maturing of the powers of observation leading to the ability to analyze works of art, visual symbols, and the place of art in culture so that a creditable basis for appreciation may be established. There also has to be developed the knowledgeable historical and critical information about art that creates corollary contexts for significant relationships of the arts and cultural effort. This may suggest a humanities approach, wherein pertinent areas such as history, philosophy, sociology and the various arts other than the visual may be interrelated so as to provide extensive frames of reference and understanding in depth. However, care has to be taken against a strict academic approach. That would only clutter up the student's awareness of art already suffering from an overwhelming accrual of facts. The proper direction would seem to favor a general structure of underlying elements and principles with the methodological proviso that these are always based on individual interpretation of works of art. These general understandings indicate that the traditions of an art heritage have to be brought up to and into the concerns of contemporary culture. Art education theory of the recent past has tended to contain the experiences offered the student to those that were local and essentially a part of his own daily existence and within the vague culturally unanchored patterns of creativity. These are only partially valid and are limiting qualities if they are not continuously refreshed and given individual and aesthetic purpose. Whatever creative means are finally achieved by the individual are done so through his own sense perceptions, personal symbol constructions, and unique understanding. Existentially searching for meaning transcends the commonplace and provincial concerns of daily living and the "doodling" creativity stemming from standardized mass values. The rich spectrum of possibilities, the contending and vital forces of play in modern existence, the spread and scope of interrelating cultural, aesthetic, and spiritual elements are grist for the mind, body, and imagination of the individual. The teaching of art has to encompass them all if it will assist in the student's act of self identification and creative expression, if the "mind set," the "prepared" personality or if student readiness is to be successfully established in appreciating art.

THE NATURAL CORE OF ART VALUES

These overall considerations in art education are not always too easily grasped or efficiently implemented in the classroom. They frequently escape methodological structure and defy teaching organization. Yet teachers must attempt to give their insights and beliefs some foundation in rational

*The student has to
develop a core of
artistic and
communicative skills
so that his later
experience has an
adequate range of
understanding.
[New York Public
Schools]*

method as well as emotional enthusiasm so that their teaching may unfold
with valid meaning and an interacting value to the greatest number of
students. Nevertheless, the most important guiding factor in the development of an art teaching philosophy is that it has worth only as it reflects,
expresses and puts into practice the natural values of art, rather than any
artificial or deliberately limited or expanded considerations.

The qualities and values of art do not possess any absolute sense of organization. They are basically "of the moment," without any real systematic, cumulative fitting into pedagogical formulation other than that
each discovers in his own perceptions and evaluations of artistic process
and product over any given period of time a translation of understanding
and experience into teaching method. Yet paradoxically, there are general
if shifting symbolic and formal patterns mentioned above that underlie
art. These considerations are certainly central to any art education practices
that provide vital and satisfying sources of genuine artistic merit for
students. There are a number of additional basic characteristics that art
education has to be aware of that cut across any methods of teaching that
is practiced.

Art
and
Education
in
Contemporary
Culture

·

458

Manual Barken has referred to these as "subject matter in the field of art," [3] or as a core of common goals. Other leading art educators such as Jerome Hausman and Elliot Eisner have recently alluded to these elements in a variety of ways. These core characteristics have claimed the attention of many art educators in one way or another over the entire span of mass teaching of art in the schools without even becoming formally codified. This is probably impossible and unnecessary to do and also understandably so, given the fluid nature of art. It may be of assistance, however, to loosely outline a current listing of these essential factors. They would seem to be the necessary considerations upon which individual thinking can structure its own understanding of art and related teaching values that have a validity and purpose prevailing beyond the idiosyncrasies of fads. The intrinsic quality of these core factors goes beyond the limitations of doctrinaire attitudes and of the pious but relatively empty clichés of superficial beliefs. They are the ideas, constructions or even pedagogical metaphors that provide a teaching convenience yet stem from real experience. They are the generalities that may be confidently imparted to students in art without imposition of ideas or stultification of personal discovery, if sensitively presented through participation or appreciation.

These vital, though self forming "principles" of art education, subject as they are to variation, may still be categorized under verbal headings, though it must be understood that this is done primarily to achieve educational communication rather than to fix their nature. In actuality, there are no hard and fast divisions, but a flux and a flow among the various elements. The emphases are visual and creative, a blending of the rational, intuitive, and emotional elements of behavior. As such they are as changeable and transient as is life itself. Yet educators have a need of containing them in some form by which their substance may be transmitted if only in a generalized way.

Conceptual patterns underlie all education. A teacher has to accept rational bases of method primarily, if any teaching on any scale beyond the errant is to occur even if the activity to be motivated is nonrational. The idea has a pedagogical goal and a validity also for the individual child during his art activities, balancing off the emotional with the intellectual, refining intuitions and subjecting his expression and his work to analysis and evaluation, in other words, setting productive and critically appreciative purposes. Some scheme of teaching procedure has to be devised to incorporate these necessary elements without succumbing to their overly logical base and destroying the more spontaneous "feeling" of art. This is at once simple in format in that it reflects a total and organic dimension of concern characteristic of all aesthetic acts that have visual form, but complex as well, in that the process is made up of many varying, interdependent and essentially nonverbal parts that are integrally and delicately meshed with one another. It is probably much easier to write these ideas as balanced sentences than to face them in the practising arena of the classroom.

[3] Manuel Barkan, "Transition in Art Education," *Art Education, Journal of the National Art Education Association*, Vol. XV, No. 7 (October 7, 1963), pp. 12–18.

It is also easier to satisfy the core desire of even artistic impulses by particular and restricted responses. These may be direct but dry and unimaginative like the countless efforts to copy nature, what is "out there," or to ape the popular cartoon or illustration artists that dot the bulletin boards, or to study the "laws" of color through the color wheel and the supposedly "correct" methods of form delineation that are practiced in many classrooms. However, impulse is also fed by an abundant and lush stream of fantasy, of sudden and unexpected flashes of insight, of the whole range of unconscious association and evocative imagery that might lead a child to connect a surprising color and shape, or cause an expressive wiggle in a line or cover an area with an eye teasing texture. It is the ranging expansion of choice possibilities, of utilizing the peripheral but strongly imaginative and connotative elements that also provides for the generative substance of art and forms part of its core.

If the teaching of art promotes this many channeled activity, setting up the varieties of experience and stimulation that heighten and expand individual horizons, then the student is given the possibility of greater ranges of freedom and opportunities to make decisions. This is in keeping with the "becoming" quality that is an inherent human and artistic characteristic. The child who has to stay within the lines, or must exert only so much pressure on a crayon, or follow the prescribed canons of systematized approach is being directed into a one track kind of thinking. This limits the choice possibilities to the relatively meager store of approved approaches. This not only inhibits creative thinking, the exercise of the imagination, and vital personal symbol making, it constrains the individual search that is the adventurous condition of existence, making of it a dependent undertaking. The child who is abetted in following his impulses through a deep core of art experience with probing and associative flights of imagination, exploring the image laden sources of his inner existence as well as critically appraising the formal attributes of art is in a healthier position of achieving independent symbolic realization. This dichotomy is not as innocent and unelaborated as it is made to be above. Certainly, skills and techniques are channelized means to a greater freedom, while wild flights of fancy may be empty and purposeless. Again, the teacher is faced with the merging of various and contrasting conditions. The balance between thought and emotion must be struck in each instance.

THE SENSORY AND PERCEPTUAL CONSIDERATIONS

The considerations of sensory activity and perceptual understanding are central to art education. They form the physiological and interpretive base of symbolic activity, primarily in the visual area, but also incorporating all of the stimuli that play upon a student's senses. In turn the perceptual apparatus provides the basis of meaning, turning the raw sense data into conceptualized understanding or images that merge the twin human elements of feeling and thought in symbolic forms. They are the cues to comprehension of the environment as well as of the self.

Art
and
Education
in
Contemporary
Culture
·
460

Cézanne, Van Gogh,
and Gauguin
provided many of
the basic forms and
concepts that support
modern art
developments.

"The Starry Night,"
Vincent van Gogh.
[Collection, The
Museum of Modern
Art, New York.
Lillie P. Bliss
Bequest; PHOTO:
The Museum of
Modern Art]

"The Bathers," Paul
Cézanne. [Collection,
The University of
Michigan Museum of
Art; PHOTO: Graphic
Arts Corporation]

These elements include in their most basic pattern the actual sensory qualities of artistic symbols; the broad two and three dimensional qualities of differing and various art forms as well as the visual elements of color, tonal value, shape, mass, line, size, texture, and any other of the units of formal visual elements that the symbolizing process utilizes. The student has to develop an empathetic identification with these elements, the expressiveness of line, the tactile qualities of texture, the brightness and intensity of color and light as well as a sensory manipulation to translate these infinitely variegated feelings via brush, clay, pencil or crayon onto the surface that carry the visual symbols. Spatial understanding, the weight of masses, the spread of volume, the sense of color, the relative tensions of size, position and shape are also fundamental aspects of any art lesson as are any other sensory and perceptual factors of visual symbolizing.

The student has to become aware of the visually sensual elements by manipulating them in a personal exploration of form making and through a characteristic variety of creative techniques that provides a symbolic fusing of perception and sensory motor activity. In addition, students have to be sensibly exposed to other works of art, with a critical yet not a con-

Art
and
Education
in
Contemporary
Culture

·

462

fining analytical base of examination and appreciation that could develop aesthetically refined percepts—a cultivated insight and taste. Both of these experiences are required for a total sensory and perceptual development of the individual, the manipulatory and the reflective. In turn the complementing of the two sides of the art coin, participation and appreciation, is furthered by an increased finesse of sensory reception, critical evaluation, and a vitalization of perceptual realization. The Bauhaus in Germany has become famous for its art education that was developed along lines of direct involvement with materials. Moholy-Nagy, one of the most ardent advocates of this approach to art teaching, carried the ideas over to the United States. A sample paragraph of his writings on practising correlations may give an idea of this sensory emphasis in teaching art,

A number of exercises which confront the student are aimed toward self-discovery, that is, the awakening of his own creative abilities. The exercises are mostly built upon sensory experiences through work with various materials, with their technology, the skill of the fingers, the hands, the eye and the ear, and their coordination. This is accomplished through tactile charts composed of textures and hand sculptures carved out of wood, which are to be handled and felt; through machine-woodcuts which make lumber as elastic as rubber; though folding, rolling, cutting and other manipulations of flat paper sheets which lead to the understanding of basic three-dimensional structure; through plane, volume and space division and their further articulation. In addition there is work with sheet metal and wire, glass, mirrors, plastics, drawing and color, mechanical drawing, photography, group poetry, and music—a full range of potentialities.[4]

The teachers of young children or even secondary students in art will of course have to tailor whatever sensory exercises they devise to the level of the capacities and age groups they teach. However, the Bauhaus ideas if employed without dogmatic intensity, have an invaluable quality of exposing students in art directly to the materials they will use and of enhancing the sensory reactions to them providing an excellent base for symbolic correlation. There may be a bias toward the technological materials, but what is of significance at this point is the stress upon sensory experience. The alert art teacher should be able to incorporate productively into any kind of art experience in the classroom this play of sensuous and animated qualities.

Exploration and Depth

Students need to be aware of the spread of materials that artists employ obviously, enriching their sensory and perceptual base by being acquainted with the ranging possibilities of different media as well as inventing or discovering new ones. However, this has to be balanced with experiences in depth so that the school art experiences do not become a hodge podge of compulsive and arbitrary exposure to a confusing variety of material and techniques. It is not sufficient to just provide crayons, paints, clay, wire, styrofoam, wood, metal, paper, thread, brushes, pencils, inks, pipe cleaners,

4 L. Moholy-Nagy, *Vision in Motion* (Chicago: Paul Theobald, 1947), p. 68.

glazes, sand core castings, ad infinitum. If the art teacher is merely the dispenser of materials and the mechanical check to determine that exposure has been accomplished, then the whole educational affair smacks of mechanical gadgetry with little creative and purposeful learning occurring.

There has been an unfortunate tendency since the end of World War II adulterating the ideas of the Bauhaus to impress any and all materials into the services of art education, all of the junk paraphernalia and technological discard of the contemporary culture. This may expand the expressiveness of individuals at certain points but it also lessens a vital respect for the sensory materials that do carry on prime expressive functions. One does not necessarily teach more by simply providing more materials. More important, as a part of the exploratory doings, is the deepening of the sensory performance to enhance perception, so that discerning and adequate choices of material are made for the greatest expressive effectiveness. This may limit the range of exploration at some points, but in artistic expressiveness, quality is always more important than quantity.

Similarly, in art appreciation. It would be educationally aimless and personally unrewarding to simply survey the history of art, or to lightly skim the popular or best known examples, referring only to the Sunday supplement idea of art history, like taking the cream off the top of milk. What is required is a broad but intense coverage, giving not only the facts, figures and dates of simple exposure but recreating the artist's vision. This involves a refinement of observation, a heightening of aesthetic perception and a basis of critical appraisal. These develop with the direct experience of seeing art and of relating it to the contexts within which the symbols originated. More important is the immediate aesthetic context of the art as well as of the emerging value system of the student in the give and take of today's culture. The perceptual base has to undergo a continuing refinement and intensity that values the intrinsic, aesthetically sensory elements, but places them in felt relationship to the student's own experiences. The relationship between specific detail or instance and more generalized ideas or organization has to be taught, the former reflecting the latter in concrete symbolic constructions as well as the creative transformation of personal values. The total unity of expression required in any successful work of art has to be pointed out in creating it or appreciating it.

For instance, it is not sufficient when a student paints a figure to simply put in the proper number of physiological details; a nose, two ears, a mouth, hair, etc. It is the relationship (the rhythmic patterns, the thick and thin of line, the sensuous tensions of masses and colors) established between these elements that has to be creatively studied and aesthetically placed in order to achieve an artistic product, one that is expressive of some idea, of feeling as well as unconsciously reflective of the creator's personality. It is not sufficient to simply record the features or to meticulously copy in proportion, but through the sensory elements and perceptual understanding of art it is necessary to reflect on content, to express a sense of individual understanding, to interpret an inner vision. In appreciation the student has to be encouraged to see rather than just to look. It is not sufficient to

Art
and
Education
in
Contemporary
Culture

.

464

say "I like" or "I do not like"; there has to be genuine analysis, further examination and all the richer perceptions which induce aesthetic understanding.

Art education has to reinforce the differences that are felt naturally in the responses to a painting or handcrafted copper bowl, for instance. The latter may possess every facet of fine craftsmanship, of consummate skill, of creative verve, yet it promotes an experience that is on a different, and most often, on a less profound or broadly significant level than the painting. Obviously, a painting may be bad, possessing no positive or necessary artistry or expressive insight, offering no genuine experience for an onlooker or a spurious and shallow experience for the producer. This, however, raises the need for an intensified education in perceptual and aesthetic education. Students should be exposed to those experiences which, through perception in depth, would expand their consciousness of art and refine its frame of reference. Further, depth of teaching guidance should lead to more subtle, more refined, more nuanced responses, which would distinguish among the overwhelming cultural offerings of contemporary abundance. Then both the painting and the bowl could be honestly appreciated on the basis of qualities that are free from pretense and imputed, capricious or accidental characteristics.

In any case, the experience of art appreciation should grow, not primarily through abstract formulations, but through the honest involvement with genuine art and through perceptual intensification. An accumulation of these experiences added to adequate teaching sensibilities, should achieve a personally satisfying, perceptually enhanced, and otherwise functionally rewarding depth of appreciation for works of art and insight into the generic, but almost always cryptic qualities of the larger, humanistic aspects of art.

Touch and Movement

Art teaching is not limited to the visual sense alone, however. It is strongly involved with other human sensory reception, most particularly those of pressure, of kinesthetic quality, the tactile areas of touch and of movement. These have to be realized in an art program and planned for in classroom activities. There has to be a completeness of perception and a rich complementing of classroom sensory stimulation and activity involving hearing, tasting, smelling, touching and moving as well as seeing, if the full range of art possibilities are to be afforded the individual child. The sensitization of the various channels of "stimuli reception" would serve as part of the sensory core of experiences through art which could develop positive and rewarding skills as well as interrelating biological fundamentals and emotional responsiveness that feed artistic activity. To this extent it is important to offer a range of materials, with the understanding, however, that the basic media of art, the paper, paint, crayon, clay and pencil materials carry the bulk of the expressive needs. Though egg shells, beans, sea shells, toothpicks and machine leavings are exciting to handle sometimes, it would be rather a shallow art experience and a limited development of aesthetic sensitivity to make too much of them or give over a greater part of art activity to their arrangements.

Gesture

Gesture plays an important role in relating sensory experience and perception to expressive visual symbols. The movements of the body, head, arms, hand and face are themselves naturally expressive factors. They are frequently converted into the rhythm, movement, and manipulation of materials and shapes to make a vital and exciting visual imagery. The young child goes about this process in an unconscious and exuberant manner that many mature artists have envied. Those who do not possess any expressive restraints follow this childlike but not childish directness of movement into symbol. The slightly older school child, in responding to the awakening rational concerns and interest in literal objectivity cannot retain this sensory-symbolic fluency. Yet, the nature of gesture is so fundamental to artistic forming, that it remains a primary aspect of the visually symbolic attempts of the middle and upper grades as well as the junior and senior high student, despite its supposed inadequacy. However, its spontaneity is inhibited by the need of older children to order their experiences in some kind of logical and abstract manner, for the ever expanding learning context of experience keeps up a persistent tatoo of clamor and attention requirement focusing mostly on discursive forms or those created by more matured understanding. The child's mind surpasses his manual abilities, setting the pattern for adult reactions. These are intellectually accented or otherwise ordered by the mind rather than by direct expressions of the individual. Consequently, a symbolic intelligence is developed, making of gesture a kind of vicarious experience, stressing the qualities of mind.

Perception becomes more critically oriented as the sorting, selecting, and collating of sense data is pushed into further reaches than the primary identification of self with experience, into an emerging and insistent need to express the experience in some communicable form. This poses a problem of bringing together the emotional-feeling impulses that lead to gesture in the first place, the increasing scope of response to the environment that education and maturation provide and the necessary level of artistic skill and techniques required to symbolize the expanding world. The art program has to plan to exploit those elements of rational growth that would enrich the symbolic activities of students as they grow older. But what must be retained, if art is to mature in the individual, is immediate interaction with experience, a core of sensory and perceptual exploration that permits gesture to lead to imaginative and feeling discovery. The art program on all levels has to give attention to the sensori-motor apparatus and provide appropriate means for its creative exercise as it relates to the shaping of symbolic forms.

One of the means that opens up suggestive areas of sensory possibilities is known as synesthesia. This refers to a sensation produced upon one sense though the stimulation was to another sense. Poets make great use of this crossing over of sensory relationships as for instance Shelley's:

Art
and
Education
in
Contemporary
Culture

.

466

From rainbow clouds there flow not
Drops so bright to see
As from thy presence showers a rain of
Melody.

The art teacher should stimulate both a crossing over of sensory experiences as well as heightening the intensity of the visual and kinesthetic senses. An interrelationship between dance, music, poetry and sports activities plus other primary sources of sensory activity and art has to remain as an established pattern. This supplements and intensifies the visual sense in its perceptual adequacy and expressive desire to manipulate materials and project images with more feeling and facility and to appreciate its existence in another's work.

Motivating for Vital Response

Finally, the sensory and perceptual qualities in art are enhanced if a full and exciting array of motivating experience is provided. This is achieved, directly or indirectly, by the range and sensitivity of the teachers methods, the relatively intensive nature of the motivating presentation and as well the intrinsic, exciting nature of the actual art experience that is provoked or otherwise stimulated. The role of inspiration is an important one here; it is a quality that art teachers should engender, by their personality and their methods. Subsequently, the source of the experience may take on vitality that results in a more intense student involvement. Of course, there are no tangible means to suggest the development of this inspiring quality of teachers, while the quality itself is not of a concrete nature that can be demonstrated. However, it does mean that the art teacher has to guide, animate, impel, prod, arouse, and even exalt students in whatever way is natural to the personalities and the occasion. A rapport may be established that is either spontaneous, or slow and deliberate, but in either instance should involve the student fully.

This commitment to expression encompasses the stimuli that come from the external environment either as transmitted heritage, current culture, individualized excitation of experience or that range of internal force, compulsion, and propensity that makes for the unique individual personality and colors its manner of perception. Each of these large sources has to be appropriately drawn out by the art teacher, sometimes objectively, sometimes with pedagogical cunning through insinuation, inducement, provocation or even exasperation, and at other times with a practiced intuition. The method may call for individual analysis, straight art experience or correlated activities. Whatever the approach, the student's perceptual development is dependent in good part upon the sensitive awareness of the necessary and appropriate conditions that the teacher institutes, not in any theoretical correctness, but in the qualitative aspect of each immediate experience—the actual one at hand. The hardness of metal, the heat of fire, the intensity of color, the rhythms of play, the visit to the fire station, last night's social activity, the trip to a museum, the wonder of the human body, the stir of flowers in the wind, the evocative images of poetry, the reservoir of day dreaming and fantasy or the pride of craft and all the rich unending sources of individual, group and cultural experiences become the trigger for setting off a course of personal discovery and fulfillment. These are not only the necessary elements in perceptual activity. It is their sensitive observation and actual unfolding of felt quality when utilized through personal intensity and discovery that are central to art education. The pertinent creative elements are concurrently brought into play; knowledge, prior experience, personal values, critical insight, sensitivity, intensity, imagination, commitment, intuition and evaluation all concentrating upon the particulars of techniques and handling of materials, the total activity symbolically transforming the sense data and resulting perception into art forms that carry meaning. To achieve this, art teaching has to respect the inherent qualities of each student, "pulling out" the potential resident in the student, bringing him "to the threshold of his own mind and feeling" rather than regarding him as an empty vessel into which is poured the lore of the school.

THE AESTHETIC CONCERNS

The aesthetic concerns deal with the intrinsic qualities that a work of art possess and the inherently characteristic responses that the experience engenders. These a student becomes involved with in the creative process as unique and self completed end considerations, requiring no justification beyond their own existence. As such, an art teacher has to be aware of the constant distinctions between the various conceptions and formulations about art and the actual art object or the sensual process of its creation. The art teacher has a responsibility to develop a literate and knowledgeable individual student through the motivation of providing a background of adjunctive information: social, historical, physiological, and even through comparisons and demonstrations of actual differing techniques and styles of art. However, the adjunctive considerations do not serve as the direct and intensive experience of art itself, or as its pure aesthetic realization, either in experience or in other art work.

Perhaps DeWitt Parker's definition of art clarifies the ideal scope of the actual art experience or at the very least offers an insight into its particular and aesthetic nature. "Art is expression, not of mere things or ideas, but of concrete experience with its values, and for its own sake. It is experience held in a delightful, highly organized sensuous medium, and objectified there for communication and reflection. Its value is in the sympathetic mastery and preservation of life in the imagination." [5]

It is this aesthetic attribute of art education that we may consider as a central defining quality. Though it is related to factors such as intellectual usefulness, productive thinking, critical analysis, preconscious image formations, and comity of means, all of these factors are organically blended with the more sensory and intuitive ones to make each creative act or work a realization of imaginative qualities that finally exist for their own sake: a

[5] DeWitt Parker, *The Principles of Aesthetics* (New York: Appleton-Century-Crofts, 1946), p. 42.

Art
and
Education
in
Contemporary
Culture

.

468

unified expression, providing for each individual an innately human channel for qualtative interaction with experience. Though there may be valid attendant and instrumental considerations in making or appreciating a work of art, such as of the particular goals of personality growth or historical perspective, these are not to be confused with the indigenous and sensuous aesthetic qualities which metaphorically interpret, express, and preserve the "life in the imagination." No further justification is necessary for art activity. And it is through this primary aesthetic function, utilizing empathy, creative transformation, expressive skills and symbolic metaphor, that art education provides fundamental opportunities for educational experiences that possess inherent meaningfulness and make for sensitivity in living, acting hopefully against personal and social disintegration.

The aesthetic experience contained in art education offers not only the pleasurable contemplation of the "beautiful" and the satisfying expression of individual "reality" but a further incentive and continuing enthusiasm for experiences that, in the final analysis, become truly humanizing influences. In a world that is fraught with contending values, frequently unresolved as chaos, and in a culture that depersonalizes the individual, this is bedrock support for the ideal aims and goals of liberal education. However, there should be no moralizing on this point nor should there be a confusion over the uses of the terms beautiful and reality. These are meant in a metaphoric sense for they possess no generally agreed upon or collectively recognizable properties that differing personalities will accept, only those that the individual personality and experience invests them with. But the nature of reality and the conditions of beauty, the intrinsic morality of expression, whatever they may be, are revealed to the individual student only as they actually engage in art activities or appreciation, and as these activities have aesthetic base, and as they inform and enrich the bases for beauty and reality.

Cultivating Intrinsic Values

Stolnitz offers a reiteration yet also a further insight into the aesthetic experience in the following paragraph: "The aesthetic experience is preeminently one in which we accept and enjoy an object—and no questions asked. We do not use it as a sign, for practical purposes; we do not seek to extract knowledge from it; we are not concerned with its influence for good or evil. We meet the object on its own terms and we try to live its life. If our attitudes are truly sympathetic, we forego criticizing or challenging the object. In this, aesthetic experience is like love—at least until love becomes demanding and querulous." [6] But Stolnitz goes on to say that many questions are asked and that this may impinge upon the aesthetic values in their spontaneous and innocent state. Of course, the questions are asked in order for the questioner to be informed so that choices and values judgements may be made.

At this point, art education has to respect and plan for the distinctions

[6] Jerome Stolnitz, *Aesthetics and Philosophy of Art Criticism* (Boston: Houghton Mifflin, 1960), p. 369.

*The mature and
practicing artist is
the most valid source
for guidelines in art
education. [New
York University]*

between aesthetic experience and the critical examining of that experience. The first is a comparatively innocent and spontaneous activity with a willing submission on the part of the creator or onlooker to the object that has aesthetic significance. The critical appraisal of the experience is at the opposite pole, poking around, questioning, insisting upon demonstrable proof, comparing and relating various conditions and attributes. Both experiences need to be a part of education though the critical approach is often presumed the more advanced and desirable one even during creative periods. To this extent, it has to be offset by the primary, sensory, and perceptual elements of the aesthetic experience in their pure state. Fundamentally, art education should offer pristine, direct and immediate experiences, experiences that intensely and feelingly touch the creator and the percipient without the excessive mediation of analysis or other critical pressures. The student need not constantly question his experience or its symbolic transformation into visual means except to intensify the expression and to achieve visual literacy. This aesthetic experiencing should be the bulk of the stimuli presented to all levels of student; a direct, feeling awareness and responsiveness of values, a teaching by example, that provide their own reason for being. The intensity of color, its harmony or its clash; the fullness of mass, its weight or its density; the patterns of rhythms, their lyrical interplay or their tensioned dissonance; the feeling of light, its

Art
and
Education
in
Contemporary
Culture

·

470

geometric flatness or its atmospheric depth; the relationship of forms, their qualities expressive of human feeling or abstractly shaping a design—all of these elements among the infinite number possible serving as the virtual paradigms of life and as the concrete demonstration of the aesthetic experience, creating a symbolic unity.

These immediate aesthetic experiences are the core aspect of cultivating the ideal aims that a student should embody. They are among the few remaining natural experiences in a technological environment synthesizing a healthy direct intensity of experience, merging the poetic imagination, and feeling responsiveness with the more syntactic separateness of critical evaluation or the utilitarianism of practical concerns. Education, nevertheless, does get caught up in questions, in analysis, in formulation and in evaluation. These are important as well in art education, for they provide the basis for further value judgment and the development of taste. The actions, experiences and symbolic art forms of students should be subjected periodically to critical questioning and analysis beyond the direct aesthetic relationships. The only admonitions are that these rationalizing processes should not take precedence, that they should not occur too frequently, that they not turn art into utilitarian directions and finally and foremost, that they stem from pertinent and intrinsic sources of artistic understanding rather than primarily arbitrary or adjunctive considerations.

Metaphoric Prominence

Some observers indicate that the aesthetic experience may be stimulated by natural sources as well as artistic ones. To look at a lovely sunset, a well proportioned person, the light sparkling on the ocean or any other natural phenomenon may give rise to an aesthetic understanding, to intrinsic meaning for the observer. This kind of activity should be encouraged in art classes. However, the important concern in art education is the creation or realization of aesthetic experience through metaphoric understanding and symbolic expressiveness, through the need for works that embody experience rather than the experience itself.

Various writers continue to disagree as to the source of aesthetic quality. Some put it into a social or other contextual setting, others analyze it through objective factors, still others equate it with inborn human intuition. Whatever its genesis and development it nevertheless appears as an inherently self contained quality in the metaphors of various art forms. The lyrical poetry of a Poe, the musical joy of a Mozart, the stylistic tautness of a Hemingway, the graceful dance movement of a Nijinsky are each superb instances of aesthetic form symbolized in a metaphoric manner, as are the visual symbols of painters, sculptors and the art work of children. The role of art education is to foster this metaphoric and symbolic activity and to vigorously and honestly strengthen its place in the curriculum.

Empathy

The metaphoric quality of art sets up a relationship between the self-hood of the child and the nature of his experience. We may even say that for the moment of creation or appreciative realization it fixes that interchange as a concrete choice of meaning and provides it with form. If we accept the base of formative activity at this point as largely intuitive as it most probably is, despite the paradoxical need of critical evaluation, then the projection of feeling and thought onto an art object or in the making of it requires special insight. This is offered most cogently and feelingly through the process of empathy. Though not all observers would accept this base of what could be considered a form of mimicry, it provides the most natural understanding of how metaphoric projection occurs. There is a feeling of kinship with the qualities that stir up perceptual response and in their projection as metaphors. The self enters into the spirit of configural relationships. There is a satisfying flow and exchange of meaning, "stepping into anothers shoes" figuratively, feeling out the nature of the experience, "becoming one" with what is "out there."

Empathetic teaching and the encouragement of student empathy through teaching lead to felt meaningful symbolic processes and frequent encounters with aesthetic qualities. This quality combined with the comprehension of sensory involvement in the internal workings of artistic techniques, materials and processes leads to an effective utilization of metaphoric imagery and its projection as visual symbols—as art work by students or appreciation of another's art. There can be a continuing and natural base for aesthetic realization that is genuine in its beginnings and secure in its unfolding. Art teaching should provide opportunities to enter into the more intangible spirit of an aesthetic experience in addition to its concretely sensual and perceptual parts.

Form in Art

Art teaching if it is to have aesthetic content has to have a fundamental commitment to form: to understanding its nature, to shaping its various aspects, to realizing its meanings, to establishing the kind of classroom climate and teaching procedures that will bring the student into a fundamental and qualitative relationship with the many faceted attributes of form. The whole idea of form in art possessing an underlying pattern of intrinsic structural elements, of harmonies, rhythms, sensuous relationships and even of mathematical design and graceful balances follows a line of aesthetic reasoning. The elegance of the relationships in natural matter, the internal design logic of biological and of physical processes and of even happenstance forms would seem to indicate that the aesthetic aspect of forms is as much a part of the material world as it is of the symbolic one. (If the theories of the Gestalt thinkers in perceptual matters are accepted, the very way a human sees is through patterns that develop and coalesce as forms.) The emphasis on form in art education is touching upon what is probably a most universal condition. At the very least the underlying root of selection and synthesis operates in science as well as in art and they complement one another in creative work.

For the student it is the discovery of art as aesthetic form that should be induced. This would suggest that art activities stress an involvement

Art
and
Education
in
Contemporary
Culture

·

472

*The aesthetic
achievement of form
should be emphasized
in all art experiences.*
[PHOTO: *Stephen C.
Sumner*]

with rhythm, with pattern, with establishing sensory and refined conceptual relationships among the parts of their experience and its translation into symbols. The teaching of art should provide the stimulation and confidence, not only to study and understand form, but to unhesitatingly engage in formative activities. Despite the suggestion of underlying pattern, the concept of form does not exclude the improvisation, the invention or the discovery of new and novel forms. In this sense the process becomes the focus of a creative surge that eventually results in the metaphoric image. Henri Focillon, the great French art historian, comments on the ultimate point of free exploration of process—the accident, and finds that even in this seemingly chaotic sphere there is an ordering of parts and elements,

As accident defines its own shape in the chances of matter, and as the hand exploits this disaster, the mind in its own turn awakens. This reordering of a chaotic world achieves its most surprising efforts in media apparently unsuited to art, in improvised implements, debris, rubbish whose deterioration and breakage offer curious possibilties. The broken pen which spits out ink, the shredded stick, the rumpled paint brush, are all struggling in troubled world; the sponge sets free moist passages of light, and granulations of the wash sparkle where it is spread. Such an alchemy does not as is commonly supposed, merely develop the stereotyped form of an inner vision; it constructs the vision itself, giving it body and enlarges its perspective.[7]

The formative process and the apprehension of form may be seen as very much a free process that has a self generating and inherently potential aesthetic quality. The intrinsic patterns, proportions, balances,

[7] Henri Focillon, *The Life of Forms in Art* (New York: Wittenborn, Schultz, 1948), p. 76.

symmetries, and rhythms are subjectively created, the result of the perceptual ordering of the mind relating to the conditions of the material object or its sensory manipulation. This is not to suggest that accident or completely autonomous experiences preempt the art lesson. The unfortunate result would be simple diversion and relatively aimless and eventually uninteresting experiences. Just as form possesses an inherent pattern, even if it is accidental at times, so the teaching of art must develop its own personal harmonies and rhythms, even as its workings are also occasionally accidental or autonomously engendered through automatic or free association methods. Deliberately maintained chaos perhaps expressed in the continuously arbitrary choice and abundant variety of media and techniques that art education fosters in certain places can become formless in time if aesthetic purpose and symbolic intent are consistently bypassed. The freedom that is referred to, the positive exploitation of the accidental, is grounded on an already developed or prepared mind, or at least one which senses the need for aesthetic ordering at some point of the experience. The entire process of aesthetic forming, however, remains necessarily a free one. It is contingent in its unfolding upon a purposeful but immediate establishment of relationships. To impose ready made formal solutions or compositional formula in rigid ways is to abort the formative process before it actually starts to function. However, just as important in a functionally aesthetic sense is the need for creative patterns of metaphoric or symbolic relationships that "work together." This is known to artists as a search for unity. Unity is that state of relational stasis that is not a freezing or stagnation of elements in art, but their fitting in sensuously appropriate and pleasing terms of the expressive patterns conveying both aesthetic and symbolic meaning. Again

Personal growth and development through art activities should progress naturally within a broad but significant range of media. [Pittsburgh Public Schools; PHOTO: Martin Herrmann]

Art
and
Education
in
Contemporary
Culture

·

474

we strike a paradox if that unity or wholeness connotes a finished or stopped condition. Yet in art it serves only as the "jumping off" point for imaginative understanding and empathetic feelings. It is constantly a process of "becoming" even as it possesses a state of being.

The creation of forms in art is extremely viable, moving between value polarities. On the one hand, these forms are the elegantly composed sensory elements that strive for formal aesthetic unity, and depend on the intrinsic relationships among colors, lines, masses, and other intrinsic attributes. On the other hand, form in art is also the symbolic interpretation of human experience, providing unique psychological meanings, through unique or shared interpretation.

The Many Faces of Form

Art education has to recognize that form in art has many faces.[8] It may be representational, but it could also be abstract; it may be precisely geometric but it could also be erratically explosive; it may be classical but it could also be romantic. One critic setting a modern attitude goes so far as to say "The representative (subject matter) element in a work of art may or may not be harmful; always it is irrelevant." [9] He indicates that only the aesthetic aspects of form have any real artistic significance, that the colors, shapes, lines and their interrelationships directly provide us with meaning without the intermediary conceptions of literary or literal content. This obviously leads to an advocacy of abstract art, or at least indicates that the modern experiments are as much capable of aesthetic and artistic form and meaning as were the old masters. Paul Klee, the modern painter who was also something of a mystic says,

The artist is perhaps unintentionally, a philosopher, and if he does not, with the optimist hold this world to be the best of all possible worlds, nor to be so bad that it is unfit to serve as a model, yet he says:

"In its present shape it is not the only possible world."

Thus he surveys with penetrating eye the finished form that nature places before him.

The deeper he looks, the more readily he can extend his view from the present to the past, the more deeply he is impressed with the one essential image of creation itself, as Genesis, rather than by the image of nature, the finished product.[10]

The artist then is not primarily concerned with just visual representation, merely wanting to mirror nature, or copy the forms of the external world. The child in school starts out in a similar vein, but as has been repeatedly pointed out, this reflection of the material world becomes a basic concern of the child as he grows older. It remains one for most of the adults who have never outgrown their sixth grade ideas of art and live uncritically and indiscriminately within technological contexts. But for the individual who does grow in aesthetic sensitivity and creative sophistication,

[OPPOSITE]
Form is experienced both in the inherent workings of nature and in the symbolic creativity of art.

Shell photo. [*Courtesy, Eastman Kodak Company*]

"Under the Sea," *Third Grade Painting.* [*Ann Arbor Public Schools;* PHOTO: *Stuart Klipper*]

[8] With due recognition of paraphrasing, Katherine Kuh's excellent book and title, *Art Has Many Faces.*
[9] Clive Bell, *Art* (New York: Frederick A. Stokes, 1913), p. 25.
[10] Paul Klee, *Paul Klee on Modern Art* (London: Faber & Faber, 1948), p. 45.

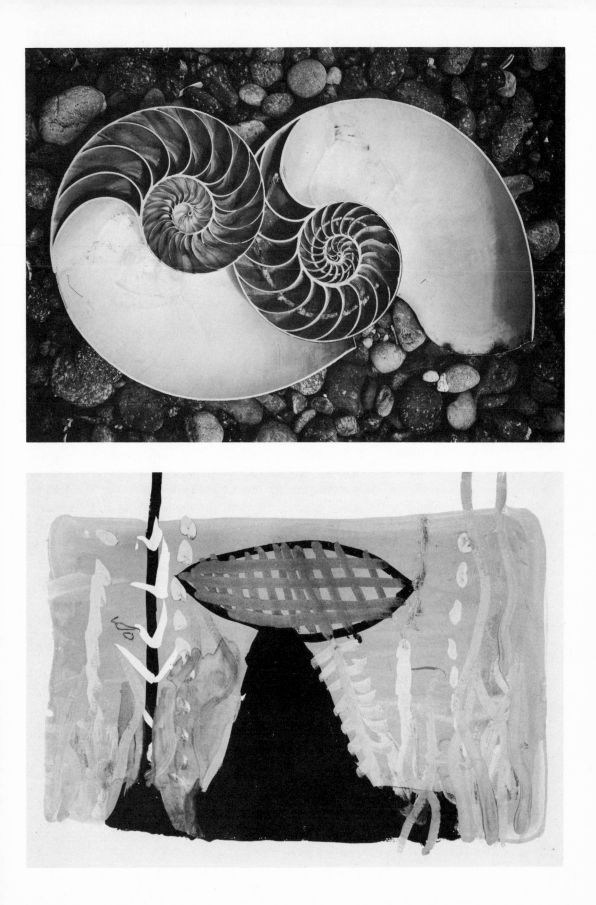

Art
and
Education
in
Contemporary
Culture

•

476

and of course for most of the artists, it is as Paul Klee so eloquently continues:

But our pounding heart drives us down, deep down to the source of all. What springs from this source, whatever it may be called, dream, idea or phantasy—must be taken seriously only if it unites with the proper means to form a work of art.

Then those curiosities become realities—realities of art which help to lift life out of its mediocrity.

For not only do they, to some extent, add more spirit to the seen, but they also make secret visions visible.[11]

Though there may be these mystical elements in shaping forms and in creating art, the average teacher unfortunately is in no position to completely trust to the happenstance and very free searchings of the mature artist. There is a need to organize lessons on a relatively rational basis, at least to provide the experiences that make for the "ready spirit" with which to fully explore the possibilities and forms of art. The art teacher has to attempt to broadly structure the learning, communication, and the personal exchange that will assist in motivating and informing (without imposition) the pupils in his or her care. The necessary climate of creativity has to be provided and this entails a measure of planning and knowledge as well as enthusiasm and sensibility. A bridge between the inner, spontaneous and mystical beginnings of art formation and the manipulative and critical skills of objective shaping or the teaching methods that lead to the refinement of "the secret vision" must be developed. As a result, the art teacher is required to invest the guiding insights gotten from mature artists and the immediacy of creative experience with personally discovered yet functional educational patterns. These should aim for adaptable and operating classroom art activities without, however, compromising the dreams, the images, the transforming creativity of art that does indeed have many faces.

Principles of Art

The aesthetic concerns of form have their own core properties that are sometimes summed up under the heading of principles of art. These so called principles are often referred to as rhythm, balance, dominance, proportion and by similar nomenclature, though different teachers and artists may add other factors or delete several of those mentioned. The actual list a teacher utilizes need not be a hard and fast one, though it is important for the student to be aware of the general principles if and when they are pertinent, as they encounter them in their work or in their appraisal of someone else's work.

Whatever the method of conceptual presentation of aesthetic principles, it is essential that it grow out of experience directly in contact with the concrete reality of works of art, either as a process or as a finished object. In this manner, the perceptual realization is not overly intellectualized but

[11] *Ibid.*, p. 6.

dependent also upon a sensory exchange. A genuine transaction of an aesthetic nature should occur for students if the sensory, perceptual, imaginative and expressive elements are fused in one experience properly guided by the art teacher. This is not to suggest the corollary of an equation of means that is abstractly formulated and may be utilized almost as an aesthetic theorem. To reiterate, it would be inappropriate to have abstractly formulated principles presented to young children or even secondary students in large amounts for the danger of a dry imposed concept may very well dissect, fracture and eventually reduce the enthusiastic vitality of aesthetic realization. Nevertheless, there are many so called principles that still are considered as core information if they are presented in a free and sophisticated manner without an insistence upon any doctrinaire systems or constancy or usage.

Person—Process—Product

Art teaching that is infused with an aesthetic quality requires an adherence to the relevant factors that operate in any single person-process-product combination. This is a complex and easily disturbed series of relationships that requires alert sensibilities leading to intuitive juggling of elements on the part of the instructor. It is the peculiar and open ended interdependence of these three parts, frequently in unconscious or accidental relationship that determines the depth or validity of the student's aesthetic experience. There are no absolutes, or definite rules of guidance, though teachers may believe they are encouraging aesthetic experience by stressing one or another part of the triad. For instance, the disciplined craft that is insisted upon in throwing a pot on the wheel after a traditional shape underscores the product; the cutting, tearing, matching, and pasting of an early elementary construction paper mural emphasizes the process; while the free wheeling dabbing and motion of a finger painting session gives vent to the personal expressive needs of a student.

In each instance, unless the teacher has effectively pointed up the other two parts, there is a lopsided experience that circumvents a fine aesthetic involvement. At certain points, one aspect may be required to be stressed in the overall unfolding of experience through art education. Yet a sensible joining of the three elements of the aesthetic experience is required for an authentic realization. The art teacher has to be intelligently aware equally of the person, the process and the product and the relationships among them.

The natural interrelationships that exist among the various forms of art merits teaching attention. The shared aesthetic concerns of literature, music, art, architecture, dance and so on, should be pointed out, the congruent principles of form and expression explored and the common philosophical and aesthetic qualities also examined. However, the distinctions are similarly important and each deserve separate attention. The understanding of symbolic variation in the needs of differing forms of expression builds an apt critical susceptibility to the nuances and structure of form. Even in the visual arts the differing viewpoints of two and three

Art
and
Education
in
Contemporary
Culture

.

478

dimensional work, or among painting, sculpture, architecture, graphics, film making, commercial art, and the crafts should be noted and explored and each studied as a particular form or process with inherent characteristics and unique potentials of expression. Not disregarding these innate patterns of differing art forms, art education can also present the congruent aspects and relationships of the arts.

Morality in Art

Though critical insights and broad cultural conditions may result from aesthetic involvement, it is necessary to repeat that their expression in sensory forms and their utilization as social, political or psychological means are separate from aesthetic realization. On the one hand, there may be truth, beauty, ugliness and tragedy in art but any narrowly "applied" moral, political or social consideration that may be drawn from them is perhaps distinct, yet it remains adjunctive to, but not intrinsically of, the aesthetic experience. The latter experience, if it is not to be vitiated and indiscriminately employed as an instrument for other than its own purposes has to be respected in educational practices, and specifically in art education, as a complete and rewarding experience in itself.

The moral qualities of art lie in the free and symbolic transformation and felt interpretation of experience. This should lead to the most expressively appropriate form, the unified composing of necessary elements which constitute the aesthetics of the occasion. The school child who searches out through the creative process the forms which will best convey his or her feelings and evaluations, at the same time that he or she is symbolically shaping "a thing of beauty," is engaged in a moral quest. The finished art work reflects the insights, value decisions and relationship of factors that fundamentally comprise any moral act. It possesses a relative degree of purity in aesthetic contexts that becomes a specific attainment of one of the profoundest aims of education—the realization of experience through the shaping of its meaning into the personal but sensuously communicative forms. The result is an inherently natural guide to value responses of understanding and action.

Aesthetic Distance

Finally, in the aesthetic concerns of art education the idea of aesthetic "distance" or "illusion" should be referred to. Art is not to be confused with actual living though it may provide a meaning or direction to the latter. The onlooker in the audience who will attempt to stop the action of a play he is watching because he has become totally involved in the narrative or the observer who will slash a painting because it offends him are both extreme examples of responses to art that supplant the validity of living action. A confusion between the two, art and life, clouds the values and insights of each and the interrelationships between the two. Children are particularly prone to the confusions because of their primary identification with the intense symbols of art without the developments of an intervening "distance" that is shaped with the maturing of personality. If art is to be intrinsically experienced, it has to be knowingly regarded as an "illusion." That is, the forms of art simply are not the same as the conditions of life. Though this "illusion" may have more meaning and truth than many living experiences, if it is to provide significance it must be experienced as an interpretation of life, as a guide to its understanding, but not as its displacement.

Art teachers should encourage a feeling of "distance" in students while they are making art or appreciating it, even while the students are paradoxically "living" the experience. The forms of aesthetic ordering and the symbolic metaphors characteristic of art should be recognized for their reflective, contemplative, speculative and interpretive roles even when they stand as end products possessed of an aesthetic self sufficiency. Art is to be presented to students as a parallel development to life and mutually interdependent. It should be emphasized as a transforming experience, with fundamental interchanges of meaning between itself and living. Yet there should be no real confusion of conditions and parts which may then obscure the development of either art or living. Art and life do not serve as simple catalysts for each other, being too enmeshed in one another's experience. They nevertheless do require this recognition of separateness for either to function effectively through education.

THE CREATIVE PROCESSES

Though the creative process may be the most mysterious factor in the making or appreciating of art it is one of the most evident. The process itself is a complicated and sometimes perplexing one that forms a caul like atmosphere within which each creative act unfolds but then joins with perceptual, psychological, cultural, spiritual and aesthetic factors. There are innumerable parts and conditions in the process—varying elements, which are only discursively isolated such as discovering, interest, improvisation, seeking, searching, probing, fitting, relating, objectivity, subjectivity, and the general transforming qualities. All of these lead to those defining yet seemingly paradoxical conditions of the creative act which Jerome Bruner [12] has listed as effective surprise, detachment and commitment, passion and decorum, and freedom to be dominated by the object. Though we may refer to any one of these elements separately, the creative process is a fusing of the parts that are distinguishable only through conceptual analysis. Creativity is a total organic undertaking when it occurs.

Arthur Koestler in his monumental book *The Act of Creation* [13] indicates a "bisociational" concept that provides a structural formulation for the creative act. This concept emphasizes the "matrix" present during any formative activity, "the habit or skill, any pattern of ordered behavior

[12] Jerome Bruner, *On Knowing* (Cambridge, Mass.: Harvard University Press, 1962), pp. 27–30.
[13] Arthur Koestler, *The Act of Creation* (London: Hutchinson, 1946), p. 38.

Art
and
Education
in
Contemporary
Culture

·

480

governed by 'code' of fixed rules." The "matrix," however, is subject not only to the acquired or innate code with its fixed requirement, but is dependent as well upon a flexible and dynamic strategy. The interaction between the two elements within the context of an occasion or a purpose stimulates a creative "leap" different from normal associations and constitutes the personal experience that leads to a creative act. Koestler suggests four criteria of creativity: originality, the improbability of the combination of the elements that are being considered, their constructive-destructive aspect, and lastly, the incidence of factors that are beyond or below ordinary consciousness. He also indicates that these factors apply to creativity in almost any area of genuine productive effort, and operate on multiple levels of complex rank and order. Consequently, art and science may be amenable to a daring new kind of investigation in their creative functions.

Hans Hofmann, a teacher and painter, puts it, "the process of creation is based upon two metaphysical factors: (1) upon the power to experience through the faculty of empathy, and (2) upon the spiritual interpretation of the expression—medium as a result of such powers. Concept and execution condition each other equally. . . . Every creative act requires elimination and simplification. Simplification results from a realization of what is essential." [14]

However, the simplicity of a work of art is not always echoed through its origins in the procedure of creativity; it frequently eludes the teacher who senses a confusing and paradoxical array of contending forces that are complicated and operate in peculiar and almost illogical ways at times. As a result, there is too often a compensating oversimplification and a parallel sentimentalizing of the process that offers only spurious and truncated experiences. Yet the creative process is one of the most significant in the teaching core of art education values. Not only is it necessary to recognize and respect this feature, but it is also important to respect the differing and intricate complexities of the process that each person may bring to it, or an act of metaphoric transformation may demand of it. The emphasis has to be on individual engagement and toward a free seeking.

As Camus says, "the only thought to liberate the mind is that which leaves it alone, certain of its limits and its impending end. No doctrine tempts it. It awaits the ripening of the work of life." [15] The teacher's responsibility in this sphere is to excite the student into the search for his own limits and to realize the productive and meaningful ends that hover impendingly in the nature of the individual's experience. These become the "work of life" and the parallel development of art, with all of the attendant skills, insights, techniques and created forms.

For each different student the creative process invites a panorama of new and novel explorations of which the teacher has not only to be

[14] Hans Hofmann, *Search for the Real* (Andover, Mass.: Addison Gallery of American Art, 1948), pp. 67–68.
[15] Albert Camus, *The Myth of Sisyphus and other Essays* (New York: Alfred Knopf, 1955), p. 116.

tolerant, but has to stimulate and affirm. Investigations purport to specify creative characteristics that are primary conditions in all creative activities. These may be rightly viewed with skepticism. At present they are little more than bland measuring devices or abstract examining procedures that remain as limited analytical means. They tend to oversimplify and subtract from the range of creativity, often serving only to support (and this is in an incomplete way) the obvious findings of actual experience. More important they may unwittingly orient values that tend to shape the creative act rather than explain it. Yet they also serve a purpose for educators in broadly identifying, at least, some of the creative factors that appear to operate a good part of the time during individual attempts to produce creative work. Generalized as core characteristics in art education they are broad attributes that teachers have to be aware of and involved with. Only in a liberal acceptance of these classifications as guides or tentative findings, rather than as structural directives, will research serve any positive purpose and act as other than compulsive moral adjutants or fashionable educational viewpoints.

Flexibility and Fluency

Personal flexibility and fluency of thinking are both characteristic creative elements that lead to individual discovery and to a symbolic invention of experience. Art teachers have to help provide the basic and fertile means whereby the student can dip into the rich ore of his own experiences and psyche as well as that which classroom learning has provided for him. In opening the educational channels that support a flexible attitude and engender a natural fluency of creative operation, art teachers are in direct communion with the highest ideals of liberal education. Free yet responsible, uncluttered yet personally structured, inspired and excited yet disciplined awareness are but a few of the multiple purposed paradoxes of engendering flexible attitudes and fluent activities through creative means.

Attitudes of Behavior

The student who demonstrates a greater share of creativity frequently manifests unconventional or even unruly behavior as well. The processes of creativity appear to feed upon a more freewheeling personal conduct than teachers have been generally ready to accept as daily routine. The facile and generative mind of the creatively gifted requires a provocative and exciting arena within which to act and a scope of behavior that chafes at the imposed restrictions of tightly ordered classroom codes.

Conversely, the conforming insistence upon muted or "disciplined" reactions may very well dampen or ennervate the creative potential of students. Obviously, this presents itself as a serious teaching problem in art and in other subjects. An uncontrolled classroom that permits an anarchy of behavior would also impede creative learning, if not making it impossible. Yet a classroom that operates under stringent strictures on behavior is likely to provide an uncreative brand of learning and activity.

Art
and
Education
in
Contemporary
Culture

.

482

Here again the level of student responsibility and teacher tolerance have to accommodate themselves to the needs of the process as it develops. Certainly, an art lesson is considerably poorer in creative verve if, for instance, a teacher imposes unnecessary silence. On the other hand, bedlam is not conducive to creative effort in art.

Art teaching should recognize the balance that has to be maintained. However, the most significant element is the uncluttered and subjectively uninhibited behavior that is required for creative activity. The teacher of art has to make every effort to promote the open, searching involvement with symbolic transformation, without placing even unintended restrictions upon the student's empathetic reaching for meaning through form except that discipline necessary in developing the "prepared" mind and the curious spirit. No ready list of dos and don'ts would suffice in creating the appropriate classroom climate, other than the internal gyrocope of sensitive awareness that each teacher must develop and refine for himself as it interacts with students and the immediacy of conditions.

Unconscious Sources

Related to the necessary freedom of activity for creative learning is the understanding that such learning stems in good part from preconscious and unconscious functionings. The rich store of associations, drives, inclination, desires, fears and imagery that lie below the threshold of conscious existence is a central source of raw creative shaping. Art teaching should seek to enrich this fertile source while it provides a series of connecting links—a pedagogical nexus, that encourages symbolic expression. In recognizing the importance of the preconscious origins of much artistic activity and understanding, art education has to foster those avenues of individual creativity which have ready access to the unconscious beginnings of form and appreciation. The mythopoeic element of response that characterize a student's felt reactions to experience should be encouraged and enhanced. The school child should be led into evocative encounters and stimulating confrontations with experience. The art teacher has to provoke the response to ordinary and daily happenings or objects with more than expected and routine recitals of nomenclature and procedure. He or she also has to invest the art experience with the exotic, the enigmatic, the dramatic, the foreign and even painful or disturbing elements. These then, through creative activities, take on a degree of familiarity or acceptance and become channels through which personal visions are formed and productive work is achieved. The consequences are an intensifying of the inner life of the student, a play upon his emotions, a spur to his imagination and a sharpening of his expressive need, all of which function in such compelling roles in creativity and lead to personal productivity.

Imaginative and Symbolic Attributes

The imagination, particularly, is a vital source for the creative process and its presence in art activities must not only be taken for granted; it must

*The art lesson should
be more than busy
work or a time filler.*
[PHOTO: *Stephen
C. Sumner*]

be consistently encouraged and reinvigorated in the student and in classroom atmosphere. This requires an enthusiastic teaching approach, one
with a sense of the dramatic, for the imagination does not conform to
any prescribed directive. It is free, surprising and spontaneous in its
operation, yet, it may be stimulated by the provocations of a perky, unusual nonconforming teaching methodology and one that genuinely admits
to the openendedness of art and creative endeavor. Otherwise, genuine
creativity is dependent on the resilient character of the individual student
who may perversely surmount the ineffectual or imposed pressures of the
more ordinary classroom climate. However, when the student succumbs
to the popular pressures, true creative insight is likely to atrophy. In any
instance, the imagination serves as the pump primer for art activity. It may
be intuitive and unconsciously hidden or concretely objective but it is
the *sine qua non* of creativity. It is intimately related to the preconscious
and the deliberately structuring activity of the individual and serves as a
rich source for symbolic understanding and creative shaping and is always
present during these processes.

The poet Wallace Stevens underscores this understanding when he says,

The imagination is the power that enables us to perceive the normal in the
abnormal, the opposite of chaos in chaos. It does this every day in arts and letters
. . . The truth seems to be that we live in concepts of the imagination before
the reason has established them. If this is true, then reason is simply the meth-
odizer of the imagination. It may be that the imagination is a miracle of logic
and that its exquisite divinations are calculations beyond analysis, as the conclusions of the reason are calculations wholly within analysis.[16]

[16] Wallace Stevens, *The Necessary Angel* (New York: Alfred A. Knopf, 1951),
p. 62.

Art
and
Education
in
Contemporary
Culture

·

484

The various definitions of creativity, though they span a wide gulf of function and attitude, usually agree that the creator exercises necessary degrees of analysis, evaluation, and subsequent control of procedure as well as drawing from preconscious and imaginative sources. After the initial surge of inspiration, after the spontaneous fervor and empathetic intensity that accompanies the early stages of creative doing, after the emotional involvement and the beginning intuitive stabs, there is also the necessity of instituting a calmer productive order. Discipline and the concrete formative structuring of the initial spontaneous forays into intuitive and freely imaginative resolutions of form take over. There is a more judicious study of relationships, analysis of parts, examination of content and evaluation of results that invite a colder but necessary sense of control. Feeling and thinking are brought into a proper balance so that the created metaphor may develop an effectiveness and an aesthetic quality that can escape the errant forms of pure cathartic self expression or personal resolution that is primarily an emotional therapy.

Consequently, the art program has to devise methods of engendering "thoughtful" control, but at the same time it must be sufficiently flexible in its procedures so as not to impose a narrow concept of skill or a limiting, abstract blanket of systematic and constraining logic that does not recognize the immediate needs of the creative act. The transforming means of achieving symbolic works becomes the inherent measure of creative activity in art education.

This symbolic attribute of the creative process has to be consistently underscored. Its individual nature has to be not only understood, but respected. Similarly, the generalities of form present also have to be appreciated. Art activities should encourage the search for meaning through metaphor that creatively transforms all levels of experience into concrete forms that then are responded to in personal and intense ways. The primary functional character of the creative process has to be accepted as one of the natural and desirable human channels of communication, beyond the simply factual or routinely practical. It has to be examined, studied, evaluated, not in a deliberately isolated manner, but as it operates in the vital intercourse between humans and experience, in the actual environment that is maturing it, providing its substance and setting the sense of its aesthetics. Therefore, the local and immediate conditions that the teacher and the students in an art class are affected by have a fundamental impact on the nature and extent of the creative processes that will (and in its extensions at later periods and places) occur within that environment.

Beyond the partially determining actuality of local conditions there is also the larger generality of symbolic meaning as a fundamentally creative and inherently human experience. This pervades the aesthetic and artistic act, permitting the meaning that a student searches out and reveals for himself to transcend the limitations of the immediate and the local. An act of self realization is involved, an extension of personal horizons, and a deepening of the vital sentience that makes for a growth toward productive maturity and feeds the lines of culture. The ever burgeoning area of symbol making and symbolic understanding becomes at one and the same time a creatively defined means of knowledge and an experience with meaning, a direct source of comprehension and one that mediates between the subjectivity of the self and the objectivity of the world.

The fullest creative realizations, however, appear to result not from any loose, ego centered desire to identify oneself as a creative being. The most productive and meaningful creative experiences seem to grow out of a pleasurable and direct involvement with the materials and processes of any particular creative form. There is an intrinsic quality of process or of material that intrigues the creative individual, rather than the extrinsic rewards of commendation or advancement. The symbolic transformations that occur are more usually the result of inner and personal satisfactions rather than a seeking for approbation. Art teaching, in order to induce expressive verve has to excite the student primarily through the sensuous media, through the pleasure of composition, through the aesthetic attributes and elements of art, and through the sheer joy of expression, all channeled through the powers of the imagination. These primary acts may be considered as intense engagements with living, as the genesis of productive and creative work. They stand not as mere surrogates for creativity, but as its essence, referring to the inherent human propensities that produce particular physical, mental and feeling tensions. The creative act involves a resolution of current tensions, a symbolic ordering that permits an ongoing development to mature, accrue images and retain understandings from the past. The tensions will always renew themselves; the need is for a searching personal vision and a vital sense of being amidst change, of catering to purpose and establishing an intensity of meaning.

There are the beckoning mysteries of the universe that invite speculation, the disturbing and exciting diversions from the routine forces of commonplace living, demanding a selectively different structuring. There is also the eager readiness (at least with normal students) to respond with feeling to the contingencies and unsuspected possibilities to which all existence is heir. All of these aspects have a distinctly profound bearing upon the creative attempts that both students and teachers engage in and should always underlie the art activities of the classroom. Thus, if the intrinsic qualities of the creative process become the focal point and inspiration for the student, then creative endeavor is more likely to result in productive symbols. The extrinsic elements would then follow as a matter of course, such as culturally higher levels of taste.

The significant appreciation of art through perceptual training is a personal re-creation of forms and values that works of art may stimulate. As such it is as much within the scope of creativity as is the making of art, except that it functions on a different level. The danger of art appreciation lies only in its being taught in a passive or popularized manner. Either of the latter approaches may well deflect the creative element in critical and appreciative response.

Art
and
Education
in
Contemporary
Culture

·

486

Whether the creative art involvement is in active participation or in real appreciation, the hallmark of the experience lies in the energies of change that have operated in the individual. The linking of thinking and feeling, the channeling of expressive urges and the symbolic transformation of form are creatively combined toward productive ends. Something new, different, intensified or revealed is given over to the individual student through the formative power of art and these discoveries constitute the creative qualities of the experience that each student must uncover for himself.

THE PSYCHOLOGICAL ELEMENTS

The psychological elements in relationship to art education could be overwhelming in their influence. As has been intimated, this is a widespread situation that has deflected many of the natural values of art education and has substituted others of questionable merit. However, the behavioral patterns of students do follow, at one level, certain statistical and regularized paths. The coding and presentation of this material could prove of help to art teachers. It is imperative though that the as yet, controversial statistics of behaviorism or experimental findings of newer psychological investigations not be utilized as formative pressures to influence or direct the classroom climate into statistically predetermined and perhaps inappropriate channels. More important, the main philosophical impetus for art education should directly emanate from the metaphors of art and the insights of artists rather than from the adjunctive or even hostile disciplines that purport to study the subject and its creators.

The psychological elements may be encouraged to study the perceptual relationships between the stimulus and experience, the cognitive process in the individual, the creative and learning processes of art, the behavioral responses in particular situations and the emotional makeup of teachers and students in groups as well as singly. But in relationship to the teaching of art the experimental research should be accepted only as general findings and not as the substitutes for those qualities that a teacher may develop as insight and intuition stemming from the nature of art, a real personal involvement with it and in the context of actual teaching.

Emotion and Feeling

Foremost among the psychological elements is the one of emotion. Art activity is almost always involved with the emotional state of the person whether it is in creative participation or in appreciative contemplation of another's work of art. The emotions are fundamental parts of expression in the student's art work. It would be almost impossible to isolate those factors in a work of art which could be considered as other than emotional from those that are patently so. In young children, the distinction probably never operates, while in older students, even up into secondary school or college, the unconscious emotional content more or less colors the manner and degree of control that a student exercises, so that the expression in many works of art is simply one step removed from the actual state that induces it in the first place. The step is of prime concern though, for it permits the transformation of amorphous and ineffable human conditions into symbolic and metaphoric constructions. These communicate to oneself and others, as well as serving a human need to make concrete the flux of feeling and to productively and aesthetically shape its content.

The emotions and derivative stimulations heighten the sensitivity with which students form their own images and intensify the response to the art that they are otherwise exposed to. They impel the movement and manipulatory features that are reflected in the delineation and rhythm of created forms. The vitality and energy with which a work is imbued is often the direct result of the play of emotions upon the imagination, the sensory receptors, and the handling of materials and technique. Simply inviting emotional catharsis or encouraging aimless feeling, however, will not guarantee productive or significant expression. There is the necessary parallel of a disciplined control and at least a generalized creative purpose that emerges during aesthetic play before the works of art can achieve an adequate and substantial basis of form.

Emotions are frequently involuntary and the result of internalized pressures derived from family, culture or other outside agencies. They operate during the art forming process whether they are invited to or not. While they may provide the expressive verve with which an art work is created, they may also interfere in the aesthetic composition of the symbols and in the critical evaluations that occur during the process. It is at this point that personal catharsis, which is a healthy activity for all humans for the most part, may hinder the artistically creative process. However, an effectively functioning art program and an alert art teacher are aware of the dangers of an ill restrained emotional irrationality that finds release but not productive transformation in art activities. Personal guidance, aesthetic direction, sympathetic concern and creative insights into the motivating factors can provide the opportunities for genuine and rewarding art experiences. These latter elements of successfully functioning art teaching require an understanding of some of the psychological sources that impel and color the emotions of students.

Perhaps a distinction should be made between emotions and feelings as well. The emotions are bodily excitements. Though they accompany human acts and the creative in particular, they do not set the tone of the act. It is the innately human characteristic of feelings, the body-muscular-movement tension that is the basic aesthetic response. Emotions have a relatively fixed quality while feelings may be as diverse as the innumerable situations that give rise to them.

The Changing Self Image

The amorphous but compelling image that each student has of himself or herself is basic. Art education has to provide opportunities for the healthy expression of this image, the feelings it engenders and the changes that

Art
and
Education
in
Contemporary
Culture

·

488

occur in it through growth. Drawing and painting afford the means whereby not only the self image, but the gestures of behavior and the kinesthetic responses to sensory experiences can be formed into expressive symbols. Further meaning is discovered as the image of the self relates to the environment, stimulating an unending source of feelings that are transformed into concrete and artistic symbols.

Obviously, art teachers should be acquainted with the emotional makeup of various age groups of students and the reflection of these emotional and feeling attitudes in art work. Both of these areas, child development and developmental characteristics in art work, have been grouped into tentative bodies of knowledge. The growth of the student from an inordinately ego centered child through the years of emerging youthful personality to the brink of an adaptive and hopefully healthy adulthood have been charted: the joys and pains of interacting with family and friends, the bothersome, mysterious and exciting concern with sex, the emerging sense of relationship to the world, the frustrations and satisfactions of learning, the impinging pressure of culture as it affects what was felt to be an inviolate sense of self, the slow accrual of information that leads to abstract reasoning as against the global responses of feelings and personal fantasies; and the change from a spontaneous and self centered making of art forms to either the refined sensitivity of a maturing involvement with creative forms or the self conscious, inhibited and inept handling of art materials and techniques that usually ends in a personal dismissal of art as a means of expression. Within the latter area of general art education knowledge, the particular features of student's art expression connote emotional and personal elements that psychology may identify. The size and proportion of figures and images may be referred directly to a student's feelings. Or the use of color, the rhythm of strokes and composition, the qualities of line may also be indicators of individual feelings.

All of the above are helpful and important guideposts in the teaching of art. They enrich the sensibilities of teachers and assist in achieving the aim of providing satisfactory art experiences for all children. However, they are insufficient in themselves to lay the groundwork that most intensely achieves the aim of satisfactory art experiences. For this it is necessary for art teachers to know their students in more than a cursory way and beyond the screen of developmental charts. Nor is it sufficient to be acquainted with developmental art characteristics; more important is an active insight into all levels of the creative process and the symbolic forming of art. These require a level of participation and a sense of commitment that are personal and authentic, felt directly or in close kinship through individual creative experience.

Though the frustrations and tensions of living enter into the psychology of art and frequently determine its outcome, there should be a parallel supposition of healthy expressiveness, of an attempt to reinforce the most positive elements of the self image. Frank Barron comments,

The image of the self is a complicated pattern, an artistic endeavor . . . to which we are committed whether we will or no. In psychological sickness our image of ourself blurs, the colors run, it is not integrated or beautiful. We become conscious of its existence momentarily, and hence awkwardness ensues. But in health there is no awkwardness, for the moment of health is the moment of unconscious creative synthesis, when without thinking about it we know that we make sense to ourselves and to others.[17]

In any case, the emotions and the feelings are vital sources for art experiences. The creation of symbolic forms in turn provide some of the psychological substance to emerging images of the self. The art experience permits a venting of feelings and the art symbol provides a congealing of meaning that adds desirable ingredients to the quality of the self image. Art work that is lacking in verve and aesthetic experiences that are narrow and stereotyped, can usually be traced to an unnecessary inhibiting or unhealthy bypassing of real emotional elements and attitudes toward the

[17] Frank Barron, *Creativity and Psychological Health* (Princeton, N.J.: D. Van Nostrand, 1963), p. 5.

Art should retain all of its mystery, wonder, and excitement—both as it is taught and as it is appreciated.
[PHOTO: © Roy Stevens]

Art
and
Education
in
Contemporary
Culture

·

490

self. When there is too heavy an insistence upon conscious control and an unresolved anxiety about form making, the results fail to express the image of the self with a vigor, a depth and an aesthetic suggestiveness that is necessary for a felt art symbol, free from pretense and personally valued.

Anxiety

Nevertheless, the contemporary world is an exceedingly complex one, comprised of multiple realities and a host of interpretations, most of which are riddled with some degree of anxiety. The intensity of these forces and the bewildering contexts that they create make it difficult to achieve and maintain what psychologists refer to as secure or stable identities. The image of the self too often dissolves in some crisis of anxiety, whether it is in the relationships among people, the shifting needs of vocational training, or in the peculiar and upsetting forms of modern art that invite disturbing responses. Many observers bear this out:

Evolving a personal style within a mass society can only be seen as a challenge. It is the kind of challenge which permits us to take little for granted, including our own motives. One must find his way into historical, interpersonal, and aesthetic worlds ordinarily inaccessible within the conventional limits of our sensibilities. To do this, we must be prepared to loosen the boundaries of our identities and to confront the anxiety that this exposure inevitably evokes without immediately foreclosing. This involves arranging life circumstances so that exposure to new materials and experiences becomes part of ongoing work and leisure routines. Regulating the circumstances of exposure to expand the boundaries of identity, without at the same time allowing them to become diffuse, is a most delicate task.[18]

Education shares in this delicacy and, particularly, the teaching of art. There are constantly forming anxieties centered around technique, subject matter, degree of talent, candidness of expression and of personal symbolic transformation. These, in a general way, reflect the larger anxieties and tensions of a culture that inevitably breeds such conditions. Art education has to demonstrate an awareness of these internal characteristics that are so potent an influence in its implementation of aims in the classroom. However, there must also be a conceptual comprehension that resolution does not occur unless there are tensions that require that resolution. Anxiety may be a terribly enervating constraint, but it may also be the impetus necessary to personal creativity. Certainly, the problems of self-identity, cultural pressures and personal anxiety are diffuse and vague, yet they do play important parts in education and require a mature attention in the teaching of art. The personal crisis of anxiety that usually accompanies the search for self-identity may be the very factor engendering exploration and the processes of creation, though its functionings are frequently well hidden in the preconscious or unconscious mind.

[18] Maurice R. Stein, *et al.*, in "Identity and History: An Overview" from *Identity and Anxiety* (New York: Free Press, 1960), p. 28.

Free Association

In order to constructively utilize the emotional strands of experience, meshing them with the heightened functioning of perception and the formative manipulation of materials, "feeling out" the expression of real personal vision, the art teacher has to sensitively balance the apparatus of method against the needs and personality of the student.

One of the most effective avenues to student response in art is through free association. Though uncontrolled free expression and simple catharsis were frowned upon above, it was only in those instances where the psychological devices become emotional enemas, the unrestricted escape hatch of errant neurotic imagings, aimless and shallow fancies or aberrant mental conditions without the necessary and proper guidance of a teacher's educational sensibilities. Otherwise, the fantasies and daydreams, the imaginative and fertile projections of an unfettered play with feelings, ideas, forms and sensuous materials, establish an important creative source for the making of art.

The art program should have no fundamental commitment to thera-peutic practices other than those which naturally are a part of creative endeavor and are derived functionally from aesthetic play. Serious therapy, the use of symbol associations and visually creative instruments and pro-cedures for diagnostic or curative purposes is the work of highly skilled and well trained personnel within controlled conditions. Art teachers, and especially the general elementary teacher, have no proper background to cope with special requirements of the field. More important, the basic aesthetic aim of art education is seriously deflected into inappropriate directions; the values of school art become skewed and narrowed at a time that they are required to be open and exploratory.

Though the average teacher may share some of the procedures with therapists, they are pursuing somewhat different goals: a sensitivity of feel-ing, a development of fertile imagination, confident involvement with creative symbols and expressive freedom. These personal attributes seem to be developed best when there is a stimulation of preconscious and subjective activity. The making of art is largely dependent upon this kind of activity for the qualitative material that serves as the raw substance of the forms that will be shaped or felt. The appreciation of art may lean more heavily on conscious evaluative techniques but still requires the imaginative base of inner intensities.

Ernest Kris, and especially Lawrence Kubie have done some interesting work in studying the role of the unconscious in creative action. They both point to the unmistakable function of subjective ferment that occurs below the threshold of conscious restraint, encouraging a necessary free associa-tion of perceptions, feelings, ideas and various other experiences that then become the basis of form and expression. The resulting metaphor is re-garded as the triumph of symbolic transformation. However, it had its beginning in the free associations of the artist's mind. The mature artist has always been aware of this. As Picasso puts it, "The artist is a receptacle

Art
and
Education
in
Contemporary
Culture

·

492

of emotions from no matter where: from the sky, the earth, a piece of paper, a passing figure, a cobweb."

Harold Rugg, in a remarkable book, *Imagination*,[18] attempted to formulate a theory of creativity before he died. He speaks of the "transliminal" mind as being in an "off conscious" state. This is a threshold situation, such as between sleeping and waking, between the unconscious and the conscious, a dynamic and formative state that is free, permissive, and full of associations, yet alert and magnetic. It is from this "transliminal" matrix that the visions for creative action are formed. And it is to this fertile source of personal feelings and aesthetic form that art education method should frequently address itself to. Enriching the store of images that could be made available to the student, widening the points of reference, intensifying the perceptual possibilities, increasing the "jumping off" points for speculation, encouraging fertile reveries and fantasies that lead to intuitions and what Rugg refers to as the necessary "flash of insight" are the fundamental psychological obligations of art education. Utilizing the most effective means of free association the art teacher, by example, gesture, anecdote, field trip, demonstration, sensory stimulation, et al., opens up the artistic and creative possibilities for each student.

The processes of free association have no strict categories. They cannot be predetermined by their very nature, though teachers can broadly plan for their happening, without predicting the outcome. Free associations are the immediate responses to the situation the student, or anyone for that matter, finds himself in, when the constraint of logical authority or strict conscious control is not in operation. They cannot be conditioned for then they are not free. They may operate in a priming and surging fashion forming rapid and intense response images and feelings or spill over into neurotic imaginings. There is always an element of distortion in the fantasies and imaginings of free association. Rather than be dismayed or repulsed by this characteristic the art teacher and the student have to jointly develop the images into metaphoric forms, into a symbolic effectiveness that results in a work of expressive art. The necessity to achieve this is one of the core qualities of art education while the means are almost as variable as the teachers who attempt to put them into practice. However, it must be understood that free association cannot be permitted to run rampant, that if it is to serve as the formative mold for artistic expression and valid appreciation it must be individually disciplined and guided with aesthetic and expressive purposes by the teacher. The free association cannot exist primarily as errant catharsis, but should be recognized as the unorganized core from which order and form emerge.

The classroom climate is obviously dependent upon many other psychological factors that influence the learning techniques, the quality of perception, the level of creativity and the actual technique and material as handling on the part of the student as expressions of behavior. The drives, forces, pressures, cues, sets, syndromes, conditions, and so on, are all partially determining characteristics. The teacher has to not only be con-

[18] Harold Rugg, *Imagination* (New York: Harper & Row, 1963). p. 40.

scious of their existence but has to gauge their impact on the learning and doing atmosphere and the feeling and thinking of the student. A sophisticated, sensitive approach with skillful and intuitive reining of the lines that shape the boldness and thrust of creative expression may be considered as a part of the basic equipment necessary to successful art teaching. In a like manner the student has to be encouraged to organically and expressively relate his emerging awareness and conceptualization of his self and his environment with the more unrestrained impulses of emotion, internal speculation and ardor of feeling in order to achieve an individual vision that may be productively transformed into art and established as personal meaning.

FIXING INTENTIONS IN ART TEACHING

The spread of concern in art education covers a rather wide range. This not only reflects the interrelatedness of art to culture and to life but it also indicates the broad scope with which any successful art teacher has to be intimately involved in areas that at times appear to be somewhat removed from the prime references of art. Perhaps it is that art itself invades the many different conditions of life. However, in the final analysis the cues for art education cannot be mirrored back from images that bend its shape to suit its own purposes. Whatever truth and meaning art possesses it does so in its own manner. The planning for art education and the implementation of these plans should derive from the intrinsic values of the art experience. The psychological, sensory-perceptual, aesthetic and creative elements form the core substance of the experience that art education may provide. Utilized with purpose they may serve to offset some of the drift in art education that encourages students to look and express but does not provide the basis for distinguishing or adequately valuing what is seen and felt. The personal discriminations and sensitivities required in the latter aim insist upon valid and pertinent experiences.

Any suggested guidelines should be accepted subject to the unique encounters and personal values that art teachers experience or evolve on their own. This joined to the insightful understanding of student needs, behavior and the felt conditions of art should make for honest and significant art teaching, an instructional elan that finds its worth in the intrinsic activities of the art lesson and in the consequent influences upon students.

One of the fundamental responsibilities of the art teacher is to lead the student, on any level, to establish sincere and authentic purposes for their art activities. This is obviously first felt through the example of the teacher's own aims during the art period. It is also personally and developmentally fixed for the student by subsequent educational exposure and method. Skills, techniques and artistic exposure aiming for visual literacy, a heightening of awareness and intensifying of sensibilities leading to aesthetic and creative yet individually expressive growth may be offered as basic intentions of art education programs.

Most educators would place skills and techniques at the head of their

Art
and
Education
in
Contemporary
Culture

.

494

list of purposes. This is probably a sound educational procedure. However, it is the substance of the skills and techniques that requires some examination. Another useful distinction may be made between, for instance, skills of representation and skills of expression. The former which most teachers would identify with in art are the particular ways of achieving recognizable forms and duplicating of visual forms. The laws of perspective, a sense of proportion, the recording of visual data and similar "sight" elements make up this skill. Without a doubt, these are important and necessary in the teaching of art. Yet, more fundamental to art education are the skills of expression. These include the elements of representation but go beyond in referring to a much larger sphere of symbolic transformation. Personal inventiveness, flexibility and fluency of imagery, imaginative projection, enriched associations, animated subjective inspirations and the "need of becoming" in an existential sense are the larger attributes that are the stuff of artistic expression involving the total and vital aspects of student personality.

These stress a basic ingredient in the experience of art, whether it is in the creative making or appreciative valuing of works of art. How an individual becomes informed of art processes and qualities is as important as what is being learned. The manner of learning in art is an actual part of the total experience; consequently, it is imperative that understanding that is imparted to students during art lessons be based on sensory, real and honest experiences. These should also be of an aesthetic nature leading to skills that are central to art expression.

These latter skills are similar to the expressive qualities mature artists have to develop. They are based upon insight and intuition more so than upon any systematic accrual of information. Yet, at the same time, they share with other school subjects and educational processes the fact of being learned. Simply because of the limited experience and a relatively meager store of preconscious and threshold images and associations, the methods and activities of the art lesson provide the basis of a first or second grader's understanding and proficiency in expressive skills. The later years build on these early experiences, becoming at one end of an expressive continuum the secure but stereotyped translation of feelings into approved forms or on the other end, the fertile, enthusiastic and individually felt forms that symbolically resolve the creative tensions that an expressive problem may pose. Though there is a natural ability in most students to initially approach their expressive needs in a creative and personal manner; the pressures of cultural conformity and diffident understanding that is not offset or changed by knowledgeable teaching become the basis of an unfortunately stereotyped and limited setting of expressive skills.

It is at this point that the lessons of the art produced over the past century may have educational relevance. The understanding that expressiveness need not be confined to visual acuity or representational imagery, that it may take on a great variety of form derived from an involvement with many senses and shaped in feeling rather than factual ways is an important one for art teachers to foster.

Similarly, any planning for art activities has to be cognizant that the student is to be guided into an act of personal discovery. There is no contained body of knowledge in art that has to be transmitted nor is there one correct method for shaping expressive forms and achieving aesthetic satisfaction. These desirable qualities are inherently a condition of the creative processes. The are best discovered, revealed, uncovered or otherwise made manifest by the students own questioning, probing, manipulating and imaginative handling of materials, concepts and experiences. The art teacher provides the inspiration that motivates, the stimulation that activates, and the pertinent creative insights and understanding when these are made necessary by individual or class needs.

The purposes of art education are best served through methods that induce creativity, introspective probing, and imaginative projection on the part of the student. Individual gesture, private experiences, significant personal happenings and a direct, perceptual exploration of materials and techniques as well as a sensitive awareness of aesthetic content in other art and in the larger environment provide the most desirable content for school art experiences. They direct the learning intentions into creative channels, possessing a natural kinship with intrinsic human aspirations and significant values.

Beyond the development of broad expressive skills that stress inventiveness and imaginative projection of personal states of being there is the growth of sensibility and an aesthetic awareness that would provide a minimum degree of artistic literacy as a necessary part of education. This involves social and cultural considerations that should be critically yet appreciatively studied by students.

The art teacher in serving as a mediating and initiating vehicle for these purposes is acting in a fundamental human capacity. The individual success of each effort will be determined by the intensity of commitment and passion of interpersonal exchange that each teacher permits to develop, just as their students are called upon to develop, in the final analysis, their own sensitivity and understanding. Art may then provide its fullest delights and richest insights.

16

Toward a Personal Teaching of Art

The sense of the miraculous, the sense of the infinite volume of life possibilities is essential to the depth dimension of personality. Life achieves a stereoscopic effect by combining views from various perspectives into a set of deeds and demeanors we call a personality. It would be strange if straightforward analysis of overt behavior succeeded in trapping all of the contrasts and nuances that give depth to the teacher and the teaching act. Perhaps that is why millions of dollars spent on isolating the traits of the successful teacher have turned up all sorts of interesting and valuable information about all sorts of things— indeed about everything except the object of the search itself.

HARRY S. BROUDY

FOR the prospective or actual art teacher who is to arrive at an individual and authentic method of teaching art there has to be the awareness of the changes that occur, not only in the happenings of the visual world outside, but of their reflection and active expression in educational attitudes and practices. These attitudes and practices rest not only upon the speculative explorations of the individual teacher's own mind and spirit as they are subjected to contemporary external pressures and cultural inclinations but are combined with compelling internal sources of individual psychology and feeling. As a result there can be a continuing development of insight into teaching methods and educational aims. New and differing assumptions emerge through personal philosophical discovery. The best minds in the area of art education move with the inherent impulse of the times, sensitively and intuitively attuned to the ever varying compulsions of life, complementing this relationship with the generally creative means of self realization that an intensively subjective search and insight provides. But at the same time they base their speculations and beliefs in the body of art itself and in its personal practice or in some intense kinship of self with art. This is necessary to a genuine commitment of the teaching values in art education that are aesthetically rewarding and personally significant to both student and teacher.

496

T. S. Eliot in his role as an essayist rather than as a poet has written, "So the critic to whom I am most grateful is the one who can make me look at something I have never looked at before, or looked at only with eyes clouded by prejudice, set me face to face with it and then leave me alone with it. From that point, I must rely upon my own sensibility, intelligence, and capacity for wisdom." [1] The teacher of course, acts not only as the critic in the classroom, but in many other roles. However, the critical faculties of teachers are rather basic to the educative process. If they are employed in the most appropriate manner, as T. S. Eliot suggests, then teaching does not only impart factual knowledge. Directly or indirectly it also instructs and sensitizes perception, encourages creative thought, intensifies innate feeling, and stimulates the imagination that lies at the bottom of personality like a shadow in a pool. The pupil is led to the subject, in this case art, knowingly and with sympathy. The individual can then "rely on his own sensibility" and perhaps achieve the creative and aesthetic insights, the realizations of imagination, the intensification of appreciation, the shaping of significant forms and a steadily maturing sensitivity and internally oriented personality growth which are the foremost aims in art education.

However, these responsibilities presuppose that teachers have "a sensibility, intelligence and a capacity for wisdom" which will permit them in their own way to be equal to the requisites of creative teaching. This implies a reliance upon personal attributes and an active pursuit of philosophical understanding.

The Differing Contexts of Meaning

As we have seen, our education generally is a discursive and reasonable one: the accumulation of much data and many resulting principles. Though appearances may sometimes be deceiving, on the whole we are taught to respect and accept that which we look at after reasonable examination. We pragmatically justify the mental and emotional responses we have as elements that must be fused with but superseded by an outer and logical reality.

An anecdote concerning the great French painter, Matisse, however, may illustrate the philosophical difficulty we often encounter in ordering our experiences. A lady, when visiting the artist in his studio, upon noticing one of his oils with an ostensibly representative though distorted figure, remarked, "Surely, the arm of this woman is much too long." Matisse answered politely, "But Madame, you are mistaken. This is not a woman, this is a picture."

This confusion of interpretation and probably resultant frustration of meaning reflects the larger confusions and frustrations we constantly face in the dynamic and complex organization not only of art but of knowledge in all of life as well. We are not only prone to confuse a painting with the

[1] T. S. Eliot, "The Frontiers of Criticism," *On Poetry and Poets* (London: Faber & Faber, 1957), p. 117.

Art
and
Education
in
Contemporary
Culture

.

498

real model that may have been used, we may also "misread" many other symbols of daily existence as well. When we look at a woman, there is an obvious physical relationship of proportions. Her arms surely conform to a physiological scheme where even a wild evolutionary mutation could never exceed more than the disproportion of several inches. To distort the parts of a body is to do violence to fact, to run counter to empirical observation, to offend human reason. No distinction is allowed for art as a form of knowing different from logical thinking.

Yet, many artists during the past century have felt compelled to distort the forms they create pushing beyond simple perceptual recognition of symbols. Actually, modern art has leaped over the ordinary and generally accepted pictorial boundaries in becoming involved with nonobjective and abstract forms. Are the artists mad in doing this; are they involved in some gigantic and adolescently mischievous creative prank or do they reflect the hallucinations of a chaotic world that has lost its time honored anchor of common sense? Or are human feelings being symbolically dealt with in a very profound way? On the other hand, even when we first look at the artistic efforts of children at the other end of the artistic scale, we may be charmed with the naivete of the effort but we often cannot accept the work as anything more than untutored doodling attempts. The sensitive awareness to the world, the genuine wonder, and the inherently compelling expressive quality escapes us. The aesthetic aspects, the art in the experience is frequently subjected to a level of understanding, to an exterior and imposed series of values that denies the intrinsic artistry and that we have categorically made a part of our understanding, no matter what the forms signify visually or emotionally.

As a result, art work, whether it is commonly academic, childishly simple or esoterically abstract, elicits a welter of contrary and confusing reactions that are determined largely by considerations other than aesthetic, though the latter is fundamental in its comprehension. There is little agreement on the tangled profusion of differing values and meanings that an undeveloped aesthetic response against a refined one may produce; each reacts within its own framework, claiming its own meaning.

The Distinction Between Looking and Seeing

Perhaps the unravelling answer may be in the distinctions between looking and seeing. This is not a mere semantic trifle; it actually calls attention to a rather basic factor in philosophy and by extension in education. Looking is merely the mindless act of our eyes in distinguishing color, size, light values, and other visual phenomena. Seeing entails the human context within which the visual phenomena acquire personal import, the tenor of individual understanding. The perceptual process is bound up with introspective qualities as well as sensory data. Actual or literal cognition and sensation may have no intrinsic meaning value; a fact by itself is a lost, lonely and meaningless digit, a sensation simply a mindless motor reflex action. Either assume genuine meaning only when it is introduced into a

context. And, of course, the context is produced by the human mind and central nervous system in response to characteristically human forces, needs, stimulants and emotions. The context is a variable one, since it is produced individually. The perceptual apparatus all humans possess, receives and filters whatever information and stimulus it encounters, but its manner of operation is strongly determined by the unique characteristics of each individual. If the source of meaning stems largely from this core, then the quality of meaning will obviously be of a relative and subjective nature. At the very least, in the area of creative endeavor and aesthetic appreciation, the individual who is involved in an expressive experience is compelled to develop a meaning that is intrinsically his own, if only by virtue of the uniqueness of the experience that confronts him. For instance, the reaction to the art materials themselves is a spontaneous and novel one when an individual is utilizing them for expressive purposes or when an onlooker is appreciatively experiencing an art object whether it is a painting, a symphony or a play. It is the student in his or her particular sentient attitude that establishes the essential meaning of the experience, despite any antecedent and unconscious determining factors which may be

Art teaching requires not only a sense of responsibility on the part of the teacher for the students under her guidance, but, in addition, an awareness of the many factors that influence the relationship, establishing a basis for a personal teaching philosophy. [New York Public Schools]

Art
and
Education
in
Contemporary
Culture

•

500

present. Actually the student has the inherent choice of bringing a particular kind of meaning into existence, the very combination of determining conditions being of a singular nature, if they are operative at all. In all instances, simply by taking a particular interpretive road, ascribing a specific meaning the student has made a relatively free decision, which could have ignored or denied any conscious attitudes and perhaps even deflected any unconscious compulsions that otherwise might have determined response.

A Basis for Philosophical Values

Though the everyday concerns of the classroom may seem somewhat removed from the lofty considerations of philosophy, this is not actually the case. The intellectual involvement and intuitive awareness that make philosophy a basic teaching guide that has to be respected has nevertheless suffered in this century. There has been the inherent anti-intellectualism and overwhelming social ideology of the doctrinaire progressivists, and those who have made only a shallow appropriation of Dewey's thought, over the past four decades, or from the tightly constrained emphasis on reading, writing and calculating of the critics of progressive education who authoritatively but narrowly and stentoriously define pedagogical philosophy. Art education cannot function naturally in either of these extreme positions. It requires a humanistically based outlook pluralistic in its sources yet one that depends upon individual awareness and the flowering of personal sensitivity. Both are the result of critical understanding, conscious but liberal value determination, and intense even passionate commitment to the feeling, existential quality of life.

One of the most important beliefs of an enlightened democracy is the fact of the uniqueness of each man and woman. Nevertheless, though we may know the world through the prism of our own senses, and knowledge may actually be a projection of our own interiorizing, the individual still exists within a group. Perhaps it is the innate dignity and equality of opportunity rather than the uniqueness that the concept and practice of democracy demonstrates. Education still has a primary responsibility, along with that of developing the individual, of meeting the demands for social conformity where objectivity and utility are often considered the necessary criterion and the group attitude the measure of the basic human unit of understanding. This actually presents itself as a crisis, for the intrinsically diversified nature of human beings may be in conflict with the cohesive tendencies of politically organized societies.

In educational terms, the individual may be only an extension of society, the subjects taught serving a social rather than an individual goal. Art may not always exist in harmony with these social factors or creativity with vocationalism or "learning the facts" of shared knowledge. The schools have allegiance to both ends of the educational tug-of-war and may find it difficult to come to any definitive stand on the questions: Just what is the role of the individual in relationship to society? What responsibilities does a singularly subjective personality have to the outside community and vice versa? Is the emotional factor of art too trenchant in its stress on uniqueness thus irritating the necessary rationality of shared responsibilities in democratic living? If not, where is the dividing line? Is it right to restrain the centrifugal aspects of individual freedom in order not to disturb the whirlpool swirl of typical centripetal group traits? Is education responsible to both ends; what policies do teachers have to reflect? Art education particularly must give attention to these problems. It purports to increase the level of individual consciousness while many other subjects maintain more or less a balance between the individual and society, or emphasize the latter. The teachings of art may also differ so radically at points from other methods applicable to other areas that it may be justifiably regarded with concern.

The Anomaly of Individuality

There are no easy answers or readily simple ones which an educator can freely accept. Yet this implication of individuality is central in any contemporary educational philosophy. Unfortunately, many teachers do not concern themselves with this question of conflicting interests in any meaningful way. They accept the bland propositions and tired clichés that are prevalent. Everyone believes in the individual; doesn't democracy teach us that? Yet, while the uncritical and superficial acceptance of the values of personal motives and preferences float vaguely in our consciousness, a thick blanket of conformity inimical to personal creativity is imposed on the mass. Education becomes a means of adaptation or adjustment as much if not more than a means of realization of the individual.

Conditions are too frequently presented as accomplished facts and the student is told he has to fit in. Knowledge becomes a projected image that has to be "captured" rather than created or recreated by the student. The contradictions of the position are either ignored or explained away by pointing to the necessities of the moment. Since World War II the "arsenal for democracy" has required a steady replenishment of predetermined percentages of skills. The larger needs of a cold war or a domestic social crisis begin to determine the content and direction of education rather than the inherent potential of the individual student.

Consequently, a curriculum that is technologically oriented or geared to supplying personnel on a numerical basis leaves little room for individual differences and almost none for the cultivation of a creativeness and a refinement of those human sensibilities that see in art a rewarding way of life and a source of mature values. The very condition that led to a free and individually oriented school system, the secularization and liberalization of man's thinking has been turned upon itself. The material and technological nature of our times, coupled with the relatively short range goals of crash programs for industrial, social or military purposes emphasizes a groupness and a collective attitude that tends to smother the individual in his attempt to control his own actions in the light of his own free will.

Art
and
Education
in
Contemporary
Culture

.

502

Consideration of The Ideal

The aesthetic and nonutilitarian values of art enjoy a precarious hold on the educational ladder, as is. The very real competition from popular and entertaining visual sources which are easily available and psychologically acceptable is difficult to meet; probably impossible when they are further supported by the external exigencies of a commercial and a mass oriented environment. The idealization of goals presented as desirable for American education and the affirmative cultural values that should filter down to the individual (including the rewards of the humanities), are thinly rationalized into some limbo of postponement or pseudo experience. What counts are the "necessities of the moment," the practical cares. Even the ideal values, expressed as positive aims, lose their intensity. The schools have been primary sources of establishing and crystallizing many of these American ideals. Because of the mimicry and parroting aspect of some of this contribution to commonly held values, the values have deteriorated as a vital motivation. They have either degenerated in a cynical dampening of aspiration or they have become transparently ornamental to be used at prescribed occasions. Like learning any catechism, the formality and rigidity of the presentation has tended to relegate the values learned to some high and lofty but immediately unworkable plane, to be utilized in a vague future.

The ubiquitous and unimaginatively framed, unfinished portrait by Gilbert Stuart of George Washington that hangs in many school corridors or classrooms is an apt illustration of this tendency to codify ideals as signs. The picture is not a true symbol which permits an open inquisitive and lively understanding of the man, it is rather an unquestioned and omnipresent image of a political catechism. Not that George Washington should not be appreciated for the great man that he was. Certainly, this is important and an obligatory transmittal of a piece of American history and a common, desirable heritage. However, the vital image of the first President and "The Founder of His Country" becomes almost a deified image that the average student secretly despairs of ever achieving an identity with. The picture itself is not seen as a work of art, nor is the man acknowledged as having lived other than as a semi-God. The very fact of its widespread but imposed influence drains the concept of a wise and virile founding father, leaving a rather bland vacuum that is easily but thoughtlessly filled with a reproduction.

Similarly, the aims and descriptions of democratic education are too readily voiced as ideals that charge our egos with what the historian Daniel Boorstin refers to as "pseudo-images." The actual workings in the classroom frequently bear little relationship to the ideal or are distorted and bent to conform to preconceived notions or the exigencies of the moment. This is as true of art education as it is of any other subject, particularly when the teaching of art is referred to, with high level verbal abstractions such as beauty, creativity and is stentoriously voiced as a birthright of every American child.

However, these ideals are necessary. When they are not unthinkingly

An example of the
visual clichés that
contemporary "pop"
artists utilize as
subject matter.
"George Washing-
ton," Roy
Lichtenstein. [Leo
Castelli Gallery,
New York; PHOTO:
Eric Pollitzer]

patronized they are the symbols of our aspirations and as such very fitting and inspiring goals in education. Their conscious, verbalized form creates a frame of reference. It is against this that we may check off our actual actions and at least partially assess their worth. The verbalized concept of freedom is what has largely stimulated the political democracy that Americans enjoy, even during the period of slavery moving always to a joining of real and ideal values. It is a living force in national development. The concept of education for all has provided the country with a truly phenomenal mass education. Yet, we should not permit the ideal to blind us to the fact that mass education means more than quantity. It means quality, which has not always been achieved in any real or abiding sense. The very fact that only a small percent of the population uses the facilities of the public libraries and that the greater majority of college graduates, after their graduation, do not read a worthwhile book a year despite the huckstering of paperbacks indicates that we are quite a distance from a truly literate (in the full sense) and mature culture.

Visual illiteracy is even more intensified than that surrounding the culture of words. The vulgarization of taste, the pell-mell disorder of so much of our environment and the relatively low level of mass involvements with genuine art experiences, all of these integral conditions of a popular and technological culture confront the art educator with or without ideals.

Art
and
Education
in
Contemporary
Culture

·

504

A Confusion of Values

Despite the earlier practical nature of much of American culture, the arts have played some small part in the realization of that culture, if only as grudging or unsophisticated responses to natural but generally repressed forces. However, the twentieth century has seen an immense proliferation of "artistic" elements in the American consciousness, which was reflected in the rise of art education, the development of an overwhelmingly popular and at times monstrous visual environment and in the utilization of art frequently in aesthetically arbitrary ways yet as an integral element in commerce and industry through mass communication media, free or inexpensive cultural institutions, distributive agencies and the many forms of applied design. These have often elicited ideal statements in education or have followed on the heels of broadly based art teaching in the schools. At least it has been hopefully felt that education in the arts has given rise to a growing awareness of aesthetic elements and a general rise in taste.

Though the following point was made by Alfred North Whitehead several decades ago, it fits the general appraisal of "culture" in any uncolored view of contemporary society reflecting a basic belief existing in art education. He says,

History shows us that efflorescence of art is the first activity of nations on the road to civilization. Yet, in the face of this plain fact, we practically shut out art from the masses of the population. Can we wonder that such an education, evoking and defeating cravings, leads to failure and discontent? The stupidity of the whole procedure is that art in simple popular forms is just what we can give to the nation without undue strain on our resources. . . . It would, however, require no very great effort to use our schools to produce a population with some love of music, some enjoyment of drama, and some joy in beauty of form and color. We could also provide means for the satisfaction of these emotions in the general life of the population.[2]

Whitehead is more than occasionally quoted by art educators, yet without any real evaluation of the essential correctness of what is being said. He is stating some ideals that have a connection with the teaching of art. Coming from so great a mind this is something that cannot be neglected. Whitehead was obviously in sympathy with the arts and had a great respect for individual worth. However, his evaluation of the role of art in education was from a somewhat Olympian height and he may have missed or confused the details. His statement seems to suggest the art education role as one of awakening in the student body a mass consciousness of art so that the popular craving for "beauty" may not be too disastrously frustrated. This does not really assert the realization of the individual through creative experiences. Though it implies the teaching of a fundamental grammar of the arts, it stops short of real personal growth through art. This is something less for art educators or classroom teachers to support than the full ideal

[2] Alfred North Whitehead, *The Aims of Education* (New York: Mentor Books, 1949), pp. 51–52.

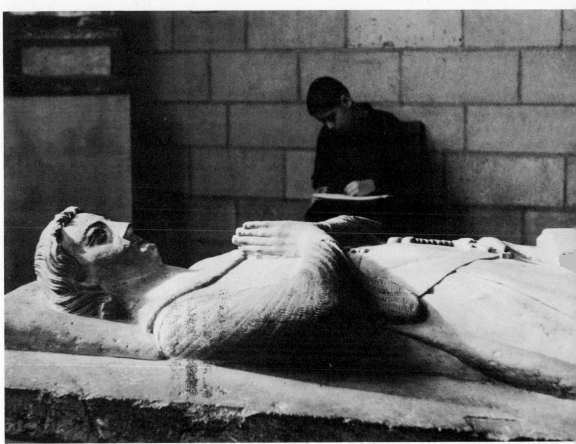

for instance, of, Herbert Read's concept of education through art, though it may be more practical.

Read says,

From our standpoint in the phenomenal realm in which we live and have our being, we can only *perceive* the values of the transcendental realm; and perception is the essential link between the two realms. We can only become increasingly and ever more accurately aware of these values by training or educating the faculty of perception to the end that it may have the quality of universal insight. . . . Every man is a special kind of artist, and in his originating activity, his play or work (and in a natural society, we have held, there should be no distinction between the psychology of work and play), he is doing more than express himself: he is manifesting the form which our common life should take, in its unfolding.[3]

The stress is on the individual attaining a level of perception so that the distinctions between real and ideal values can be mediated, the latter becoming more recognizable and capable of attainment through the natural, but necessarily educated and aesthetic propensities of personal vision. Read argues that this can be best realized in keeping with the organic and psychological human attributes through the medium of art. However, the art

The art experience should enhance the sentient qualities of all students. Youngster sketching at the Cloisters, New York. [PHOTO: *Pearl Greenberg*]

[3] Herbert Read, *Education Through Art* (New York: Pantheon, 1945), p. 300.

Art
and
Education
in
Contemporary
Culture

.

506

cannot be of a pseudo nature or limit itself at any arbitrarily popular accepted level, for then the common unfolding is statically determined well in advance of what each person can uniquely create and contribute. This concept is in keeping with the current emphasis on excellence. Yet, in order to be properly achieved, excellence cannot be collectively or arbitrarily standardized, but has to emerge as the individual response to a commonly held value. Art education in this sense cannot simply accept a statement of ideals, or its limited realization, it must seek a full implementation. Though the ideal be romantic and lofty it is more significant in influencing art education than the dry limited possibilities of "practical" consideration.

Freedom and Anxiety

The idea of individual freedom appears to have several inherent factors which education has only partially responded to, the stress or lack of it too often dependent upon the pragmatic considerations, rather than the actual individual involved. This is perhaps not as true of progressive education as it is of some of the more doctrinaire methodologies that have been suggested in its place, but the crude egalitarian variety is no less guilty of a lack of sensibility in regard to individual freedom. The effects and pressures that result in art education as well as the larger "development of the whole child" are as a consequence evident in the continuing crisis to which education has almost become innured.

Freedom appears to require of the individual that he act as a responsible being, making deliberate choices or enacting less conscious decisions in a spontaneous manner and responsive to the many different aspects of the "human condition." This insists that the configuration of one's being is involved in full education of the senses and the emotions as well as of the intellect, rather than in any fragmented application of parts. Art education in its ideal statement as a part of the humanities is dedicated to this end, though its implementation is frequently open to question. But the question or skeptical appraisal is even greater when the overriding influences in the larger body of education put an inordinate stress on fashionable or narrowly practical considerations. The contemporary emphasis is on extrinsive rewards, competitive grades for the academically talented, on rather inappropriate educational substances for the less intellectually gifted. The whole stress on a technologically centered and test oriented condition of learning breeds a constrained type of student.

Freedom requires a personal focus of activity and thought in addition to an involvement in all of the multiple facets of the human organization, emotional and unconscious as well as intellectual and rational. The ideal statement may never become an actuality, but its arbitrary realization only in part, is even less significant than its undeveloped potential and promise as a whole element. Correspondingly, only in the whole response of the individual based upon the synthesis of emotional, sensory, imaginative, objective and intellectual considerations is he even theoretically assured of meaningful freedom and the opportunity of self-realization and achievement of mature comprehension, if not wisdom. This ideal verbalized value may be regarded as a frame of reference against which the real operative values can be checked. The results may show, as intimated above, that the wants and desires of the individual may be in contradiction to the conditions of society.

This creates another factor mentioned earlier, that of anxiety. This is a normal and necessary quality if freedom is really to be achieved at any given time. Anxiety or tension appear always to be present if free and creative behavior is experienced. There can be no vital realization on the part of an individual without the worries, concerns, expectancies and unknowing anticipations—in short, the anxieties inherent in living conditions. To run away from this anxiety is to deny the approach to freedom and creativity. To neurotically encourage it is to distort or push onto a tangential track the inherently searching but productive quality of creative anxiety. The latter may develop too great a load for the individual to successfully utilize a necessary psychological aid to freedom and to creative doing and thinking. In a large middle ground there is a positive and generative displacement through educational means from a static equilibrium that induces change and creative behavior, setting the environment for the kind of alert experiences that Dewey speaks of in his most insightful writing. Consequently, in accepting anxiety as a necessary condition for creative involvements induces the appropriate "mind set" for extracting genuine meaning from experience and transforming it into vital learning and aesthetic form. The impulse toward experience that leads to art, as an example, in Dewey's words, "cannot lead to expression save when it is thrown into commotion, turmoil. Unless there is com-pression nothing is ex-pressed."

The Group and The Individual

Finally, in recognizing that the individual, like it or not, lives within the confines of a society, an inherent condition which may properly limit its expressions at times, true freedom recognizes its own limitations. In synthesizing the seemingly opposed factors of the individual versus society, education has to stress the relationship and exchange that should occur between the two. Freedom need not be anarchy, nor society repressive groupness. Nor is the pertinent factor operating in freedom or in social harmony when one acts upon the other in an arbitrary fashion, or unilaterally even in a controlled and beneficent manner. Actually, the essence of the realization of the individual and the welfare of the society lies in the continuing and dialectical relationships that are openly and for the most part tentatively established with one another. Education can achieve no greater end than to foster this viable interchange where the individual and the group interpenetrate each other. In this sense, a work of art and its process of realization, as well as a creative act of appreciation, are the unique offerings of individuals to society, while the total complex and quality of the environment is society's gift of necessity to the gregariousness and expressiveness of man. Art functions within both conditions. Robert Iglehart sheds some light in this area by suggesting that society's conception of what the child or the student is, influentially shapes the kind of education he will receive

Art
and
Education
in
Contemporary
Culture

·

508

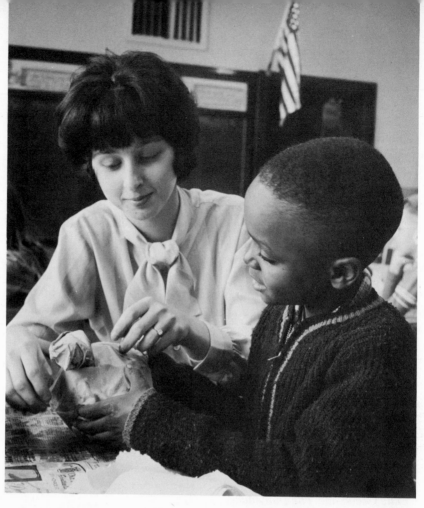

The art teacher
assists the child in
"creating his own
world." [Toledo
Public Schools;
PHOTO: Tom
O'Reilly]

and may determine the goals of education in very intense ways. In the past the child may have been no more than an extension of adult thinking, subject, consequently, to the strains and pressures of a particular adult viewpoint, whether it was Gothic or Romantic. Iglehart even goes so far to suggest that childhood is a contemporary "invention." Children as independent beings simply did not exist in past history except in a physical sense. The important educational cue in the past was that the child was expected to find the world, and education was organized to that end. But Iglehart says, "For the child of today there is no world which can merely be found . . . the modern world is a man made affair." Even for the adult the contemporary responsibility is the creation of the world, not only physically, but in terms of meanings, values, and relationships. Iglehart continues,

In these terms, it seems to me that the central task of the education of children . . . is to prepare them, not for a passive acceptance of the world, but for the creation of worlds . . . The real root goes down among the concepts and images cast up by the collective mind of the society. And in this image of a child who is himself the inventor, we have also the root of the new emphasis on the arts in education, and the source of a great many of our present troubles.[4]

[4] Robert Iglehart, "The Inconstant Child," *Aesthetic Form and Education*, M. F. Andrews, ed. (Syracuse, N.Y.: Syracuse University Press, 1958), p. 21.

The troubles are, of course, the still potent strains from traditional images and the development of teaching methods and substance that have no real relevance to today's student or cultural milieu.

EXISTENTIAL IDEAS

Another contemporary movement that may yet influence educational philosophy and that of art education particularly, is existentialism. The existentialist philosophy has made us aware of the many faceted image of man and the viable, subjective nature of his understanding of the world and himself. The presence of contradictory factors, of incongruent intellectual alliances merely indicates how the philosophy has cut across the standardized and academically sacred attitudes of past beliefs, posing new and provocative questions. Though the philosophy is very broad, encompassing a wide variety of different thinkers like Heidegger, Jaspers, Camus, Sartre, Tillich, Niebuhr, and Buber, atheists and religious men, radicals and conservatives, there is a central core of propositions that has important implications for education and the values it may engender in living. Existentialism, in addition, has influenced partially or totally many social thinkers and cultural observers of the contemporary scene as well as the creative doers. These all touch, in a basic theoretical way, upon the teaching of art.

Existentialism exists as a symbolic concept reflecting in its passionate avowal of the significance of the individual all of his weaknesses and strengths, his failures and his triumphs. The total range of the human condition is synthesized in the existential vision, its solitary being and its gregariousness, its faith in a transcendental truth and its lack of belief pointing to life as an "interlude between two great nothingnesses," its brutality, anxiety and absurdity as well as its joy, compassion and profundity. The strange paradox of life's "being" and its "nothingness" commits the existentialist outlook to primary concerns, to immediate and real problems rather

The realization of experience in an expressive art work goes beyond the simple recording of parts. "The Ship," Second Grade Drawing. [Ann Arbor Public Schools PHOTO: *Stuart Klipper*]

Art
and
Education
in
Contemporary
Culture

.

510

than to removed, timeless and abstract questioning. It does not provide an ideal scheme of perfection, but rather asks of the individual that he make his actions define the values that he is living as active choices instead of some verbalized or ideally constructed goal.

In order for men to achieve a reckoning with his own nature existentialism stresses certain attributes above others. It emphasizes intuitive understanding rather than formalized logic and reason, believing in the subjective quality of understanding. Knowledge is an equivocal aspect of interior comprehension, therefore, wisdom is preferred over the acquisition of facts. Man, in existential terms, is above everything else a passionate and emotional being, his intellect a procedural and relatively thin scaffolding that is only tenuously erected to explain the vital sense of being that has already occurred outside of the conscious manipulation of system and order. The individual is inescapably faced with his own uniqueness and the despair and anguish as well as the joy and happiness that often accompany that state. It is only in the honest recognition of these functions and qualities as they encounter the vast "nothingness" of existence that the individual can create his own intensities of meaning, searching out a personal realization of experience and directing his consequent actions. The existentialist places man above his environment and insist that any vital engagement with life can only proceed from this understanding.

The consequences of this attitude for education are far reaching. It presupposes that the student and the teacher have to be aware of the seriousness of the choices they make in responding to experience. It implicates the full range of the educational establishment as it is at the moment of learning, the experiences it provides or otherwise engenders, the real condition in which the individual finds himself. Any deliberate limiting of curriculum, any absolute or abstract ideals, goals and delayed procedures that deflect or defer the savor of the immediate and the vital, condition the student to think of himself as an object being acted upon, a cog in the machinery of society, necessarily leading to a conforming and conventionalized mode of thinking, feeling, and living. The existentialist condemns this approach, recognizing the inherent worth and distinctiveness of each individual who should explore the possibilities of the here and now and of the situation that intrudes upon his consciousness to the fullest. The implications for education indicate that formula or ritualized learning will have little vital significance in the burgeoning awareness of the student. Genuine involvement in education is a free engagement with experience in all of its multiplicity of suggestion and being. Consequently, it cannot be fitted into neatly arranged pigeon holes of understanding, nor can it impose an objective order without diminishing the ranging subjective nature of the people in its charge.

The emphasis in education cannot be primarily theoretical, abstracted and oriented toward supposedly objective goals which demand an intellectual rigor rejecting the intangibility of subjective understanding. Existentialism, if it has any insight to offer education, insists upon the unique individualized comprehension. This results from making deliberate value choices, recognizing that the consequences that flow from them are real and immediate, the choice made constituting a commitment of attitude and a response to inner motivation. The prime purpose involved may be an accounting that has to be made to oneself.

Central to this subjective stress and to the fulfilling quality that education can provide are the educational involvements with the arts. The existentialist recognizes that through the various arts there is a natural means of passionate and meaningful commitment. This leads to concrete choices of creative and cognitive form that serve as the symbolic realization of experience.

Educational Implications

This may point up the fragmentary nature of all experience, but it is at the same time involved with very real qualities. Education becomes more than an abstraction, the teacher's concern more than the simple transmittal of knowledge; the emphasis is put upon the individual engagement with a shifting, provoking experience of life and on the momentary and immediately expressive resolutions of artistic behavior or appreciation which are genuine insights into the self and the world that supposedly nurture the self. This creates moral conditions for vital acts of self-realization.

Existentialist education insists upon a continuing quality of self-examina-

Some contemporary artists stress an extremely impersonal quality of form, despite a cultural stress on individuality. "Luminous," Richard Anuszkiewicz. [Sidney Janis Gallery; PHOTO: Geoffrey Clements]

Art
and
Education
in
Contemporary
Culture

•

512

tion, of intuitive understanding complementing scientific objectivity, of an intimate interrelationship between teacher and student that liberates those inner and intangible powers that are the dynamic attributes of human nature.

The implications for education are written in rather obvious ways. The curriculum of any school has to include those subject areas such as art, music and the other humanities so as to provide students with opportunities for aesthetic expression and appreciation. However, these rather flexibly structured subjects cannot be subjected to any codified conditions; they have to be freely approached and genuinely experienced within the context of personal values. This does not suggest as some may be led to believe, a laissez faire attitude, but rather one in which the classroom climate and the teaching stimulus are enthusiastic, serious and "engaged." The latter condition not only insists upon a teacher's professionalism, but more important, heightens the recognition of the drama of learning, regarding knowledge and process as living and personally adventurous factors. Thus, a teacher has to possess an abiding sense of his vocation, and perhaps more important, a positive and salubrious regard for the actual and potential qualities of both the students and the area of knowledge that is being taught.

A further implication may be considered in the need to stress the creative possibilities of all learning situations. It is the problematic factor of any confrontation between student and experience that is basic to the unique and subjective learning that will take place. If only external classification and predetermined procedures are depended upon for correct method, the result will be apathetic and essentially disinterested students. They will look elsewhere for an opportunity to discover and shape what can be regarded as their authentic selves. Even in art education, and perhaps most especially there, if the teaching is doctrinaire, narrowly imposed from an authoritative height there is a natural withdrawal of creative involvement. This is just as true when the teacher provides no direction or defaults in offering stimulating guidance; there is in the aimless classroom a desultory or otherwise meaningless lesson. Some sensitive balance of forces is required, geared to the multiple qualities of the individual student and triggered by the innate sense of propriety that an enthusiastic and committed teacher develops with experience.

A Basis for Teaching Ideals

Education develops within the context of many patterns of understanding. Its forms and methods are oriented, either unknowingly and innocently or with deliberate dispatch, in accordance with the particular dictates of a basic philosophical position. Educators have to acknowledge these sources that impinge upon the way they teach, examining them and questioning them in the light of their own understanding and that of the aspirations of the society they live in. For instance, a position that recognizes the perfectability of man would certainly suggest a different curricular stress from one

The artist frequently interprets experience through provocative visual metaphors. "Painter with Model Knitting," Pablo Picasso. [Collection, The Museum of Modern Art, New York. Gift of Henry Church; PHOTO: The Museum of Modern Art]

that accepts either inherent human limitations or the existence of original sin. The point is not necessarily to deny any of these positions in the broad arena of philosophical and social thought, but to accept a fundamental commitment which would then infuse the teaching situation with a sense of purpose and passion.

The danger is that commitment may be to dogma and that a position once assumed would become a locked and categorical one. Yet this is no more a danger to the mature teacher than it is to foolishly ask for guarantees in living, knowing full well that any guarantee is impossible when the contingencies of existence are taken into consideration, when change is recognized to be the potent agent that it actually is. The teaching of art requires, at the very least, a tentative and open philosophical construction that would place its characteristic aesthetic and emotional experience within a framework that a teacher could support and from which he could draw educational sustenance and a personally impelling need for positive "engagement."

Jerome Hausman directly points up the need for an individual philosophy in saying, "Having reached as broadly as one could to encompass the scope of the arts and as deeply as is possible to grasp the significance of one's own actions as a teacher, every teacher of art is faced with the personal and social responsibility of dealing with problems from 'his point of view.' In their teaching, teachers are confronted with the task of making value judgements involving their conception of sound teaching in the arts. It is this conception that paradoxically must be held naively and rationally." [5]

[5] Jerome Hausman, "The Enrichment of Education Through the Arts," *Aesthetic Form and Education*, M. F. Andrews, ed. (Syracuse, N.Y.: Syracuse University Press, 1958), p. 54 f.

Art
and
Education
in
Contemporary
Culture

·

514

LEARNING AS DISCOVERY

At this point we may expand on the idea that learning which is achieved through a personal act of discovery, whether it is intuited or the result of the reasoned sum of a logically structured series of learning episodes, is perhaps the most effective both for art product and art process. It is not particularly a new idea; it has been implicit in much of progressive thought and liberal learnings in education. However, its restatement currently emphasizes a necessary focus in education. It points up the relatedness of learning materials, the need for personal organization to offset "information drift" and the pluralistic approaches to solving problems or achieving meaning and form in education. Discovery in learning provides for art education the necessary freedom of approach to create forms and understand another's expression in personal ways, yet it remains grounded in the core of art.

That is, if learning can proceed geared to the individual's own purposes yet within the context of a subject area, then the learning would be more effective, its essence more adequately digested. Of course, one of the prime responsibilities of education as a result would be to stimulate the kind of search in the individual that would seek out experience so that learning through discovery could occur. The pedagogical climate of a classroom becomes all important, the teacher functioning with critical detachment yet passionate commitment as a sensible guide and mentor by the more indirect methods of suggestion, dialogue and hypothetically presented ideas rather than the coldly determined ones of *a priori* exposition. This is a natural condition to develop in the teaching of art. The individual student may then engage in the fertile associations and suggestive combinations of preconscious imagery and generalized artistic understanding to "construct" his symbols.

However, it has to be understood that the stimulus provided by the teachers is not one that seeks its mirrored reflection in the student by influencing him to conform to what he supposes is correct in the teacher's estimation. Unimaginative teaching encourages the need for hints and signs of what is expected and tends to compliant, adaptive mirrored behavior and passive understanding. The teaching, in art or in any other subject, has to overcome this involvement on the part of the student with the bribery of extrinsic rewards, the need for continued reinforcement and dependent responses. The stress on personal discovery generated and enhanced by the sympathetic and knowledgeable gambits of the teacher who dares to transcend the finite world of rote exposition, may lead to learning appreciated for its own sake. The student, released from the closed imposition of extrinsic rewards which breeds imitation and the desire to conform, is encouraged to cope with the inherent possibilities of a problem situation, resolving the tensions that are present by demonstrating his own effective realization of the experience through adventurous associations and personal creativeness.

This is best achieved without a doubt in art education and perhaps as much so in most other areas, by stressing the symbolic nature of the learning experience, of the variable response that may be made by the individual, rather than by having him refer to predetermined and abstractly presented learning standards that have to be unquestioningly followed like danger signs. As a matter of fact, this is a definite state for successful encouragement of personal vision and the finding of suitable symbols of conversion of that vision and the experience that may have bred it. The so called objective verities of arithmetic, social studies and the few in art, such as multiplication tables, the preamble to the constitution and the mixing of color will not dissipate if the student is encouraged to engage in a personal dialogue with them. They remain the same in the structured approach no matter how they are learned, but

the effective uses the student makes of them, the quality of their transformation in learning, is very much subject to the nature of the learning relationship an individual has established with them. They have to be sensed only as one among many channels of realization that are available. And beyond the structured concepts lie the uncharted seas of creative endeavor and symbolic comprehension that have a disdain for extrinsic reward. Creative students care little if they have mastered a triadic color scheme; they care if the color expresses what they have to say—what they feel. Learning and creativity matures and intensifies only in response to the internalized and valued promptings of the individual. It is the intrinsic considerations of a learning situation —the delight and reward of coping with problems, the elegance of relationships, the sensory excitement of manipulation or the satisfaction of expressing inner states of experience that broadly constitute the discovery in learning and bring about the effective surprise of creativity. The psychologists themselves seem to support this idea as they analyze the developmental nature of learning. The more primitive and immature learning principles of conditioning and reinforcement are superseded when the individual engages in any truly

An artistic existential viewpoint. "Figure," Albert Giacometti. [Collection, The University of Michigan Museum of Art]

Art
and
Education
in
Contemporary
Culture

·

516

symbolic learning. The latter is a reflection of a more advanced development of mental processes and is involved in more complex and viable
procedures in establishing the knowledge that is part of intelligence, both
in intellectual and aeshetic terms.

Discovery, whether it is in the sciences, social studies or art involves
an open, flexible and relatively complex kind of learning, yet it appears
to be the most fertile in the adequacy and richness of what is learned.
The student's behavior during an art lesson is dependent upon his own
involvement with the material, no matter what its source, and to the
extent that painting, drawing and modelling are adventurous voyages of
discovery, rather than precise surveying trips, to that extent an honest,
intrinsically rewarding and lasting quality of aesthetic experience (as
learning) has occurred.

No one has yet structured the fundamentals of learning through discovery, though several loose assumptions may be made. One is that continued practice and effort will lead to a more successful manipulation: in the
art of inquiry, in the continuing expansion of aesthetic search, and in a
consistent rendering of expression. That is, the more a teacher encourages
students in the freer, dialectical involvement with the stuff of learning,
the more skillfully will the student's abilities to handle the material
develop. A child who is permitted an unencumbered approach to learning,
and personally guided in its intricacies, is likely to find ways of comprehension that are more exciting, more profound and more subject to
creative manipulatory handling.

Discovery Is an Individual Process

Another of the fundamental aspects of learning by discovery is that of
internally and characteristically developing personal and perhaps idiosyncratic ways of handling the material of the learning experience. These
are usually fluid in nature, almost like a loose hydraulic system, responses
balancing pressures, the whole procedure subject to the unavoidable and
mostly unpredictable bumps and barriers to hurdle of the individual learning ride. Hunches and speculation, that which "seems" right, hazarding
guesses and venturing conjectures, intuitive stabs and "smelling" out the
right from the wrong, the pertinent from the unnecessary, the "feeling
out" of the process are but a few of the unclassified means of achieving
learning outside of the formal means. These operate as "heuristics" of
discovery, the various and indigenous ways of knowing, that which has
not been known in any area of knowledge and understanding. They exist
in all the various disciplines, but they are firmly at home during the art
experience. Since art expression is as much itself an expression of emotion
and diverse search that has been transformed into symbolic concreteness,
the means of arriving at the form and the learning it implies can be
genuinely a felt one. It is dependent upon the economy of intuition and
the resolution of the tensions that the imagination devises and the
emotions generate rather than strictly adhering to the ordered and
measured system that logically rational thinking has structured.

*Personal discovery
is fundamental in
the art process for all
students. [New York
Public Schools]*

   This behavior is readily seen even in the superficial observation of a class of youngsters during an art lesson. Even in a "rote" art atmosphere, the singular quirks of personality will make themselves felt. In a creative classroom climate, each child approaches even an imposed art problem in a unique way, some enthusiastically plunging in, while others attempt a more prudent analysis of the elements. But the latter, once they are drawing or painting, apply varying "heuristics" or models of aesthetic form, individually "feeling out" what is to be expressed. If they have not been sealed off against failure or too much impressed with what should result in "correct" images imposed by the teacher, then the impulsive stabs of line or swipes of color may provide a rewarding means of achieving a satisfying art expression—a means of discovery of the self and the world. The constrained and almost tortured experiences that many students undergo in art lessons when a "by the numbers" and passively received method is employed is the opposite end. The weak, banal and thoroughly stereotyped images that result from insisting upon categorized copying or the accepting of narrowly schematic sequences, lacks any of the earmarks of discovery.

   It isn't that the more intuitive method is being pitted against the more rational one. It is simply that they work in conjunction with one another, each serving varying purposes, yet each requiring the other for the completion of knowledge and its effective use in terms of the needs of human beings. Both methods are a part of the learning process. They provide the student with the leeway to activity, and if need be, to independently engage in either or both as the necessity arises. This not only helps the student develop an internal identification with the material to be learned and transformed into some kind of knowledge symbol, it provides an encompassing organic approach to relate more fully to the environment.

Art
and
Education
in
Contemporary
Culture

.

518

Teaching insight also affirms the existence of individual differences and caters to them, but more important, establishes a natural base for the acquisition of meaningful learning and stimulates creative behavior as a result.

There seems to be no obvious or natural means of formalizing this process through education. Imaginative considerations have their own pitfalls and are not to be uncritically relied upon just as the reasonable qualities of learning may have stultifying and other negative results. Education has an unresolved challenge of engendering a discipline while it preserves the imagination.

Experience in Depth

If discovery is to grow as a learning method, it seems to insist upon the "well prepared" mind for continuing success. That is, the individuals who have a prior acquaintanceship with a particular area, a general familiarity with the intellectual or aesthetic terrain of the pertinent concepts of forms will more likely engage in successful learning by discovery than the individual who comes in ignorance.

It is essential that students be provided with more than cursory surveys of knowledge, though some variety of particular exposure evidently has its benefits. The need for this acquaintanceship with an area supports the ideas of those educators and psychologists who advocate a structural approach to learning. As we have seen earlier this may be difficult to integrate into the energies of creativity in art if not inimical to art education. However, the very processes themselves, of creative involvement with art materials for expressive purposes, lend themselves to a loose but enriched accumulation of experience. This occurs in the area that provides a necessary base for a continuing and progressively more apt and sensitive exploration of form and technique in arriving at the images of art.

Kenneth Beittel and Robert Burkhardt have been studying what they refer to as the dimensions of depth experience in art education, concentrating in their project on "The Effect of Self-Reflective Training in Art upon the Capacity for Creative Action." Their findings for older students, at least, indicate that it is necessary to provide a sufficient working experience limited to a single area in order to develop the necessary awareness and sensitivity for independent and genuine creative experiences. This depth of experience is developed through the concentration upon particular interests or assigned formal areas, not haphazardly or casually but over a period of time and progressively. This permits the kind of exploration and familiarity with process and product that may then be the base for further and perhaps more original discovery. The suggestion is that students perhaps learn in art through the internal establishment of sequential happenings and a growing ease of manipulation of the elements present. This stems from the opportunity to learn the "process strategies" or the inherent nature of the forms and modes of expression as well as the individual's changing realization of them—his own idiosyncratic understanding.

An experience in depth should support art activities on all levels. [PHOTO: ©️ *Roy Stevens*]

Experience in depth appears to provide this base of creative action. The depth dimensions include, among others, comparison of one's work with those of fellow students or the work of professional artists, the divesting of one's conventional viewpoints of perceptual behavior deliberately exposing the mind and the senses to new, provocative and changing attitudes and presentations, and the recognition of one's own working methods or "process strategies," as well as those inherent in materials and techniques. Finally, there is the ability to develop self evaluative techniques along with the manipulatory ones.

This concentration in depth of art experience obviously calls for, even in a loose interpretation, a relatively disciplined structure that presumes certain sequential happenings. These may vary for the individual, but a progressive learning seems fundamental. It is important, though, to stress the unique idiosyncratic nature of the disciplining and the personal rather than the objectified group progress. The sequence is guided by each student's own rate. Though the structure has not been identified or classified to anyone's real satisfaction, we have examined certain of the larger elements of the creative process that teachers have to be aware of.

Art
and
Education
in
Contemporary
Culture

·

520

These are the generalities mentioned earlier. If used in a knowing, educationally mature manner, yet with the intensity of existential engagement, these infuse a value quality that may happily lead to learning through discovery, or conversely, the satisfying discovery of one's own learning.

Uniqueness and Interdependence

Learning and creating in art may be seen as a very complex series of open processes. Much is dependent upon the orientation that is established for the individual student within the context of his classroom experiences. More is dependent upon the workings of his psyche in those hidden reaches of personality that are not objectively observable. The generalities of the external world also make their contributions, through their specific translation into individual works of art. The various ways of perception all have a "finger in the pie" though the intuitive mode of understanding and learning through personal discovery are the most natural and appropriate for artistic creativity. In all, the processes are far ranging and rather inclusive, resolving antagonisms, surmounting paradoxes, implementing an integration of values as well as fitting specific symbolic techniques to individual expressive needs. Rene Huyghe put it well in the following, "It is often supposed that the work of art reproduces natural appearance; but no matter how realistic the painter believes himself to be, we know that it is himself, his character, his very essence that he reveals; that he gives himself away in the manner in which he approaches reality in order to transcribe it, and in the choice he makes among its elements. If he attempts not realism, but the reverse, and seeks to express himself, to translate himself to others, though he essentially is unknowable to any but himself, he will have to find the elements of the language he needs in appearances borrowed or derived from the visible universe. Thus the artist cannot reproduce the outer world without by the same token revealing his inner world, and vice versa. In the work of art, each world lives only through the other, each can be conceived only with the help of the other, thus creating between them a third reality . . ." [6]

The Artist as Exemplar

Art education aims specifically for this third reality—the concrete artistic expression—but remains dependent upon the other two conditions. The symbolic transformation that brings this about would seem to come most intensely and truthfully through personal discovery. Thus learning in art must be guided as a finding out, a looking into, an internal probing and an external seeing, an intense and natural exploratory process that uniquely synthesizes the disparate elements of experience into a concrete shape, with the prize being two fold—a greater sense of self realization, and the creating of aesthetic forms that commune and communicate with people and conditions of a developing culture.

The most insightful source and model of expressive eloquence and authentic value to utilize in this aim is the artist himself. His creative

[OPPOSITE]
*The great artists
remain the best
examples and
influences in art
education. "Matisse
at Work."
[Courtesy, Pierre
Matisse]*

[6] Rene Huyghe, *Ideas and Images in World Art* (New York: Harry Abrams, 1959), p. 405.

Art
and
Education
in
Contemporary
Culture

·

522

restlessness, his passionate commitment, his continuing search, and his inherently aesthetic viewpoint are all elements in a working process that teachers and students alike may confidently be guided by. His open and exploratory activity, his singularly particular way of working, his intuitions and visions, his strong feelings, and fertile imagination in vital relationship with the sensuous materials of art and its transforming manipulatory techniques are the generalized substance of learning and creating in an artistic manner that teachers and students alike should examine for cues and clues to their own creative endeavors. Guided by a respect for an integrity of artistic expression, related through a personal commitment to both the aesthetic and educational values inherent in the genuine forms of art, and permitting the working habits and the productions of mature artists to serve as the exemplars of method and value, the teacher of art may be in a position to organize the procedures of the classroom so that discovery as learning becomes more than a fashionable cliché.

Any approach to art education has to be aware of the basic mystery of art, of its "magic." An individual teacher must himself or herself be artistic, inherently sympathetic and sensitive to the play of the senses and the symbolic character of visual forms. In addition, there has to be an insight into human development, particularly the attributes of students. This insight requires more than the supposedly valid research conclusions about creative behavior.

The highly structured approach or categorized understanding sometimes seem to unhinge the very quality they are attempting to define and control through pragmatic devices. Meaning, values and other infinitely variable and robustly viable human characteristics have not been too generally amenable to objective probing. Teaching wisdom may come more intuitively, not always having to rely on abstract and clinically or statistically oriented experimentation but on personal sensibility. Teachers may have to develop that extra "sixth sense," a vital intelligence to best cope with the above mentioned requisites of positive and creative teaching. They should perhaps intensify their own experiences rather than serve as the channel for someone else's experiences, unwittingly or otherwise. It is not necessary to arbitrarily deny the occasional and admittedly valuable findings of research, but it is not in the interests of good teaching in art and probably in other subjects to uncritically or with naive enthusiasm to rely too heavily on them. This does not propose an arbitrary disorderliness to which teachers have to submit. It simply suggests that each teacher's personality should be enriched by a personal sensitivity to certain operating intangibles that have a profound influence in art teaching.

It presupposes a committed dialogue between individuals that transcends objective theory and method. There is an understanding in genuine art teaching that goes beyond the mere accumulation of data or its conscientious implementation in the classroom. A felt communion on a poetic and a genuinely symbolic level is required, one that deals naturally and intentionally with the mystery and magic of art.

Index